PARROTS
THEIR CARE
AND BREEDING

PARROTS
THEIR CARE AND BREEDING
REVISED AND ENLARGED EDITION

ROSEMARY LOW

BLANDFORD PRESS
POOLE · NEW YORK · SYDNEY

First published in the UK 1980 by Blandford Press,
Link House, West Street, Poole, Dorset, BH15 1LL
Second Edition (revised) 1986

Distributed in the United States by
Sterling Publishing Co., Inc.,
2 Park Avenue, New York, N.Y. 10016

British Library Cataloguing in Publication Data

Low, Rosemary
  Parrots: their care and breeding.—2nd ed., rev.
  1. Parrots
  I. Title
  363.6'865   SF473.P3

ISBN 0 7137 1437 9

Typeset by August Filmsetting, Haydock, St. Helens
Printed in Yugoslavia

Contents

Text Credits

My grateful thanks are due to the following who so readily complied with my requests for information.

Australia: Fred Bohner, John Courtney, Fred Lewitzka, Michael Martin, Lex Salisbury, P.D. Shuttler, Lyn Williams.

Belgium: Johan Ingels.

Czechoslovakia: Vit Hylas, L. Sloboda.

Denmark: Jan Eriksen, Henning Jacobsen, Flemming Nielsen, Peter Them, Leif Rasmussen.

Germany: Thomas Arndt, Reinhard Blome, Wolfgang Burkart, Wolfgang Grummt.

Holland: Ronald van Dieten, J. Docters van Leuwen, Mr and Mrs J. Spenkelink, Herman Zomer.

Italy: Paolo Bertagnolio.

New Zealand: A. G. Caley, Dean Rallison.

South Africa: Neville Brickell, Peter Oderkerken.

Sweden: Thomas R. Brosset, Bengt Larsson, Sven Lennartsson, Birgitta Ullman.

Switzerland: Dr R. Burkard, Marie Louise Wenner.

UK: B. Aldred, David Alderton, Elizabeth Butterworth, M. Collett, John FitzGibbon, G. R. Greed, John Halford, Jim Hayward, Professor J. R. Hodges, Arthur Lamb, Mrs G. Narraway, Peter Olney, E. H. Peake, George A. Smith, Mr and Mrs A. A. J. Stoodley, Mrs and Mrs R. Wallwork, Rosemary Wiseman.

USA: R. J. Berry, Betty Byers, Dr J. M. Dolan, M. Fischer, Robbie Harris, Peter Jenny, Mrs E. Harwell, K. C. Lint, Bill De La Mere, Greg Moss, Mr and Mrs D. Mathews, Ramon Noegel, J. R. van Oosten, John P. O'Neill, Dr A. C. Risser, Wayne Schulenberg, Tony Silva, Paul Springman, Francis Wenke, William C. Wilson.

Zimbabwe: F. R. G. Townsend.

I am indebted to Joseph Forshaw for permission to quote from *Parrots of the World*, to Dr H. D. Groen for permission to quote from *Australian Parrakeets* and to George A. Smith for permission to quote from *Lovebirds and Related Parrots*.

Special thanks are due to R. H. Grantham for taking most of the black and white photographs; to Professor J. R. Hodges and R. J. Berry for reading the chapters on Australian Parrakeets and Macaws respectively and for making valuable observations on them; to George A. Smith for reading parts of the manuscript and making many helpful suggestions, also for his contribution on the subject of worming; and to Dr R. Burkard for making corrections and valuable additions to the second edition.

Thanks are due to the editors of *Avicultural Magazine, Foreign Birds and Magazine of the Parrot Society* for permission to quote from their journals.

I also wish to thank the German publishers, Ulmer, without whom the second edition (whose format and colour photographs followed the German edition) would have been far less attractive, and to Maggie O'Hanlon of Blandford Press for her invaluable work on the typescript of the second edition.

Photo Credits

Colour Photographs

Dennis Avon: p. 77.
H. & J. Beste (Ardea): pp. 81, 206.
H. Bielfeld: pp. 72, 224 (left), 245, 295.
T. Brosset: pp. 74 (twice), 84, 91, 92
 (left), 99, 102, 105, 109, 113
 (right), 118, 119, 122 (twice), 126,
 135, 136 (thrice), 138 (twice), 140,
 145, 148, 150, 152, 157 (twice), 158,
 163, 164, 167, 169 (twice), 177, 178,
 192, 201, 209, 214, 224 (right), 226
 227, 233, 236, 237 (twice), 240 (left),
 243 (bottom), 248, 250, 251 (twice),
 253, 257, 259, 260, (twice), 264, 266
 (twice), 270 (right), 274, 277 (left
 and centre), 278 (bottom), 282, 283,
 288, 289, 290 (thrice), 297, 300, 301
 (twice), 302, 305, 306, 307, 311, 313,
 314, 317, 320, 323, 326, 328 (twice),
 330, 331, 332, 335, 343, 347, 348, 350
 (twice), 364, 365.
G. Chapman (Ardea): p. 380.
John Courtney: pp. 194, 380.
K. H. Diefenbach: p. 23.
J.-P. Ferrero: p. 338.
K. W. Fink (Ardea): p. 353.
W. Frank: p. 62 (twice).
W. de Grahl: pp. 123, 127, 131, 139,
 234, 240 (right), 247, 255, 268, 270
 (left), 378.
A. Greensmith (Ardea): p. 371 (left).
D. Hoppe: pp. 144, 219, 223, 225 (top),
 241, 292.
K. Kolar: pp. 19, 38, 337 (six), 338
 (twice).
C. Laubscher (Bruce Coleman): p. 333.
L. C. Marigo (Bruce Coleman): p. 249.

J. L. Mason (Ardea): p. 204.
H. Müller p. 222.
H. Pinter: p. 358.
H. Reinhard: pp. 76, 78, 82, 83, 85
 (twice), 87, 89, 94, 95, 101, 104, 107,
 113 (left), 124, 134, 141, 160, 162,
 166, 173, 182, 183, 198, 210, 225
 (bottom), 228, 230, 231, 238, 239,
 243 (top), 246, 263, 272, 277 (right),
 278 (top), 285, 294, 319, 327, 363
 (Ardea), 366, 372.
P. Schauf: p. 115.
M. F. Soper (Bruce Coleman): pp. 369,
 371 (right).
P. Steyn (Ardea): p. 174.
A. D. Trounson & M. C. Clampett
 (Ardea): pp. 88, 98, 189, 191, 193,
 196, 202, 208, 215, 344.
R. Williams (Bruce Coleman): p. 205.

Black and White Photographs

J. & J. Arman: p. 191, 282.
Cage & Aviary Birds: p. 315.
R. H. Grantham: pp. 25, 48, 61, 143,
 144, 201, 211, 242, 261, 287, 291, 293
 (twice), 299, 343, 354 (twice).
Jim Hayward: pp. 41, 51.
Peter Jenny: p. 37.
Wolfgang Kessling: pp. 224 (twice).
Greg Moss: p. 300.
San Diego Zoo: p. 373.
U. S. Fish and Wildlife Service: p. 286.

Artwork

F. Weik

Preface to Second Edition

In the six years between the publication of the first and second editions of this book there have been many developments in parrot aviculture – so many that the text of the first edition rapidly became outdated. A very substantial revision has been made with additions and alterations for virtually every species. These take into account first breedings and other valuable information on rearing; the introduction of new species to aviculture – e.g. the Yellow-faced Parrotlet (*Forpus coelestis xanthops*); the Beautiful or Rose-faced Parrot (*Pionopsitta pulchra*) and the Marajo Island Amazon (*Amazona ochrocephala xantholaema*); and the impact of surgical sexing, which was not practised in Europe when the first edition was written.

The Fig Parrots were virtually new to aviculture and only one species had been bred in captivity. Although they remain rare, a little more information is available; four of the five species have been reared. Fig parrots are now accorded a chapter, as distinct from being included under Avicultural Rarities, although they remain such.

Since the first edition was published, trade in parrots has diminished (as predicted), although it is still substantial in many countries. Most South American countries have ceased, either temporarily or as a permanent measure, to export birds, resulting in greatly increased prices. In Britain, quarantine regulations and other legislation and the greater difficulty in obtaining import licences from the Department of the Environment has reduced trade. For these, and other reasons, the emphasis is increasingly on breeding, and more and more parrots offered for sale are aviary-bred, not imported.

The plight of parrots in the wild, many of which are threatened or endangered by habitat destruction, is attracting the attention of aviculturists, the more far-seeing of whom realise the importance of concentrating on vulnerable species. It is for this reason that, where possible, I have added recent information on the status of each species under the heading of Range/Habitat. (Robert Ridgely's 1981 paper on the distribution and status of mainland neotropical parrots, and Joseph Forshaw's *Australian Parrots* were invaluable sources of information which must be acknowledged here.)

An additional chapter demonstrates the significant role that aviculturists can play in conservation. I would urge everyone who keeps parrots to give some thought to this vital aspect of aviculture.

Importation of Parrots

Writing about parrots results in opposing and conflicting emotions. On the one hand is the desire to inform the parrot keeper, in the hope that his birds will be well cared for and that breeding successes will follow; on the other is the fact that for some people it creates an interest which did not previously exist in these birds and this will lead to increased importation of parrots.

Aviculturists who breed domestic species such as Cockatiels and a large number of species of Australian parrakeets and Lovebirds, produce their own supply but pet owners and keepers of other parrots rely mainly on imported birds. In some cases these imports are so numerous that wild populations have become severely depleted; an example is the Scarlet Macaw. At the time of writing, various factors have resulted in parrot export being much reduced, or curtailed entirely in some circumstances yet I feel that it is still too high. And there are too many losses between the time of capture and the retail bird-dealer.

Ideally, parrot export would be limited to a few numerous species with a wide distribution which are entirely suitable for captivity. (Too many species have been exported which require more careful management than is generally realised.)

If and when this comes about, the *breeding* of parrots will be even more important to the continuance of aviculture. My fervent hope is that this book will encourage aviculturists to think in terms of being self-sufficient. The era when fewer imports of wild-caught birds occur may be nearer than is realised. Many bird species throughout the world have had their numbers drastically reduced by deforestation, and the acreage of tropical rainforest dimishes daily at a horrifying rate. Wild bird populations have enough obstacles to overcome without being subjected to pressure from aviculturists of the western world. Let us look to the day when large-scale parrot exports cease entirely.

Introduction

The year 1504 is an auspicious one in the annals of the parrot enthusiast for it is recorded that it was then that the first parrot was seen in England. It is true that parrots were known to the Alexandrians, that they were considered articles of luxury, sometimes exchanged for slaves, by the Romans, and that to this day, by contrast, in many countries they are considered merely as items of food by native peoples. Perhaps it was not until they reached the countries of western Europe, however, that they were appreciated for their own attributes: their appealing personalities; endlessly fascinating behaviour; the beauty of their plumage or form; in many cases their affection for their human friends, and also that characteristic which has always intrigued man – their ability to mimic.

For several centuries it was enough just to keep parrots. It is only during the past century that aviculture as we know it has evolved slowly from the keeping of birds in which breeding successes played only an incidental part, if they occurred at all, towards the point where breeding birds for the pleasure and knowledge gained is the major motivation. It would be an exaggeration to say that this is entirely true, and perhaps it never will be the case. Nevertheless many books available to aviculturists have been outdated by the recent shift of emphasis which has occurred with the awareness that the mere keeping of birds is not enough.

Books giving comprehensive coverage of members of the parrot family in the English language start with Greene's three-volume classic *Parrots in Captivity*, published in the 1880s. It was followed by several others, the best known of which was written by the Marquess of Tavistock (the 12th Duke of Bedford) in 1928. Over half a century later the avicultural scene is a very different one, gradually beginning to use the knowledge and techniques of modern science. Increasing knowledge of the requirements of birds and improved dietary and veterinary aspects should ensure that today's aviculturists are more successful than their forebears and that those of tomorrow will bring to aviculture the techniques of a science. At the present time there is a tremendous amount of which we are ignorant and this applies especially to the diseases to which parrots are prone.

The emphasis in this book is on breeding parrots because that is the aim of the vast majority of those who keep them in aviaries, and because various factors which are rapidly changing this world will result in the export of few parrots from their countries of origin. The day may come when the aviculturist is the only source of supply because the importer no longer exists.

Parrot Topography

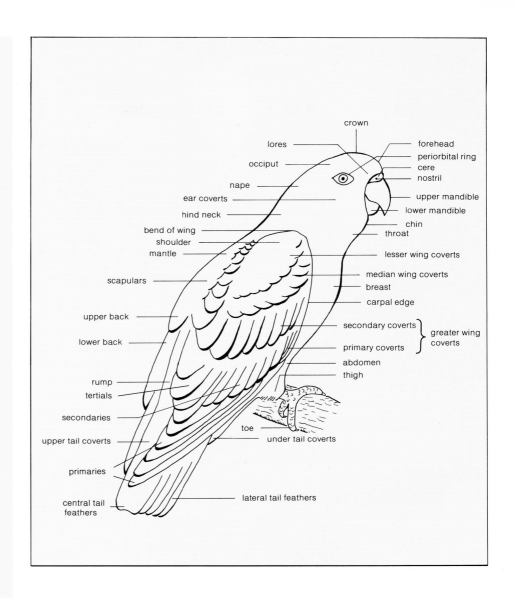

Notes to the Text

Descriptions: It should be borne in mind that colouration is extremely variable among birds of the same species and although I have given some of the more common variations it would be quite impossible to mention every variation for each species, even if these were known. Thus descriptions should not be taken too literally. I was once puzzled by the description given to me over the telephone of an Amazon Parrot with a white forehead and suggested that the owner should bring the bird for identification. It was a Blue-fronted Amazon with the feathers of the forehead creamy white instead of yellow. Minor variations such as this are common, especially in neotropical parrots.

In the text which follows, only those subspecies which are relevant to the aviculturist are described. For example, in the Golden-crowned Conure (*Aratinga aurea*), the only race, apart from the nominate one, is *major*, distinguished by its slightly larger size. This is deemed to be of no consequence to the aviculturist. In the White-eared Conure (*Pyrrhura leucotis*), at least five races are recognised but as this species has, for some years, been virtually unknown in aviculture, only the most distinctive races are mentioned. On the other hand, most of the subspecies of the Black-tailed Conure (*Pyrrhura melanura*) have been exported, albeit only rarely in some cases, and these are described to enable breeders to prevent interbreeding.

In descriptions, the colour of the legs and feet is usually omitted, except where these are unusual or useful for identification purposes. Often there is some variation among birds of the same species and, in many parrots, the legs are of a colour which is difficult to define accurately.

The plumage of immature birds differs little from that of adults in some cases, but usually has a softer appearance.

Length, from bill to tail tip, is approximate since there is wide variation among individuals.

Range/Habitat: Distribution details included under this heading may not always be accurate because, in many cases, much remains to be learned on this subject.

Because the emphasis in this book is on aviculture, only brief details pertaining to the wild life are given. Further information will be found in Forshaw (1973).

Aviculture: Mention is made of some captive breedings of each species where they have occurred, or of some of the first breeders in various countries. The intention was not to mention every known breeding or first breeding.

Numerous references will be found to a great aviculturist who had a profound influence in Britain and elsewhere, the 12th Duke of Bedford who died in 1953. As Lord Tavistock, he was the author of *Parrots and Parrot-like Birds in Aviculture*.

Frequent mention is made of Alan Lendon in connection with Australian parrots. A leading aviculturist and ornithologist, he made a useful revision of Neville Cayley's book *Australian Parrots in Field and Aviary*. Alan Lendon died in 1973.

I am indebted to both, for their books provided much useful information, as did Joseph Forshaw's *Parrots of the World* on natural history.

Weights: For many species, chicks and adult birds, weights have been added to the second edition. Hand-feeding of chicks has become a common practice and it is helpful to have an indication of weight in a wide variety of species. Weights of adult birds are useful for calculating medicinal doses. They also give an indication of the size and bulk of a species. It should be borne in mind, however, that there is often considerable variation among individuals of the same species.

Some of the weights recorded are taken from the data of field workers; others are for captive-bred birds. Where applicable, weights are given for male (M) and female (F).

Part One

Details of Care and Breeding Relevant to All Species of Parrot

1
Choice of Species

The choice of species for keeping or breeding must be based on knowledge of the various birds' characteristics, their voices, the cost of acquisition, their feeding and housing requirements, the attention required, whether or not breeding will be attempted and, indeed, whether the particular birds' personalities will be attractive to the keeper.

Aviculturists with neighbours must be especially careful in their choices as there are few members of the parrot family which are not noisy or whose voices would not be found irritating by those with no interest in them. Perhaps the only safe species in this respect are Grass Parrakeets, Hanging Parrots, and the small neotropical parrakeets of the genus *Bolborhynchus*. Certain small lorikeets also fall into this category but the only one generally available is Goldie's Lorikeet. Cockatiels in small numbers would prove acceptable to most people and yet even these birds have been the subject of a court order for nuisance to neighbours.

Another point which should be considered is that some birds require large aviaries; available space and cost of aviary construction are limiting factors for many breeders and they would not be able to consider birds which require an aviary of minimum length 4.5 m (14ft 6in); in this category are most cockatoos, *Psittacula* parrakeets of Ringneck size and larger, and all the Australian parrakeets, with the exception of *Neophema*. Many of the larger South American species do not exercise their wings very much, except in aviaries of very large proportions which few aviculturists can provide, and yet they can be bred satisfactorily in rather small aviaries. Aviaries only 2.5 m (8 ft) long or even slightly less and 75 cm (2 ft 6 in) wide are suitable for single pairs of Lovebirds, Grass Parrakeets and Cockatiels.

Those fanciers who are not in a position to provide outdoor accommodation need not despair. Many species of parrot will breed indoors and produce young of good quality. The main problems are soft-shelled eggs or egg-binding, due to lack of Vitamin D, which is obtained through exposure to sunlight. Without this vitamin, a bird cannot mobilise calcium in the body and the result is soft-shelled eggs or severe problems in egg-laying. My preferred method of supplying calcium and Vitamin D is to use the liquid preparation Collo-Cal D, obtainable from most veterinary surgeons. It can be added to foods such as bread and milk, or to water.

Many people want to own the spectacular cockatoos and macaws before experience has been gained with inexpensive and more easily bred species but for the sake of the birds they should not be too ambitious. An honest appraisal of the time and experience one has to offer the birds should be made before finally selecting the species to be kept. Mismanagement of macaws, for example, could be extremely expensive and prove so disappointing that interest in breeding birds is lost completely. It is common sense to learn the basics of bird breeding with Cockatiels, Lovebirds, Kakarikis and the less expensive Grass Parrakeets.

There was a time when practically everyone started off with Budgerigars or small seed-eating birds, such as finches, species which give an excellent grounding in knowledge of bird behaviour and requirements. Now, however, for various reasons, some people start with the expensive large parrots or the more sought-after of the Australian parrakeets. In the latter case, it may be imagined by some that quick and profitable returns are to be made with highly priced birds but it should be appreciated that if they were invariably prolific breeders they would not have such a high monetary value.

On this subject it might be noted that the more expensive birds are not necessarily the most desirable or the most suitable. There can be few more charming birds than the Cockatiel, which apart from the Budgerigar is the least expensive of all parrots. The highly priced cockatoos and macaws, which may owe their current popularity to being photographed as the pets of show business personalities, are truly suitable pets only for those who can devote at least a couple of hours a day to them. If tame, no bird requires more attention, if not tame, they are suitable only for a large aviary which is expensive to build and to maintain.

Breeding expensive birds poses many problems. If losses occur, suitable replacements, or even any replacement at all, can be very difficult to find. This is not merely unfortunate: to attempt to breed rare species or even those in danger of extinction when the necessary skill in bird husbandry is not possessed is most irresponsible. Most people will want to start with birds with which there is a good chance of breeding, so that sale of their young would help to offset the high cost of building aviaries and obtaining the initial stock. For this reason, Australian and New Zealand parrakeets and the freer breeding Lovebirds, such as the Peach-faced and Fischer's, will be a suitable choice.

Another factor which should be considered is hardiness. Most large parrots, with the possible exception of the Red-bellied Macaw, are hardy when acclimatised, although it should be realised that this can, in some cases, take three or four winters in a temperate climate. Some small species cannot tolerate prolonged periods of cold weather. If no fully enclosed accommodation is available and the aviaries are situated in an exposed locality, keeping Hanging Parrots and Grass Parrakeets should be avoided. Hardiness of the latter group is a question of

what the individual as opposed to the species can tolerate: if it harbours mycoplasma, under stress, such as can be caused by cold and damp, it will be subject to respiratory and eye infections.

The novice seeking to add another species to his collection will often ask which bird can be kept with the species already possessed and the short answer is that nothing can. Perhaps the one most important fact for the prospective keeper of psittacine birds to bear in mind is that, with very few exceptions, they must be housed one pair to an aviary for breeding purposes as few species mix satisfactorily.

Colony breeding, that is with a number of pairs of one species in the same enclosure, can usually be practised with success only in the case of Cockatiels. Possible exceptions are the Ringneck Parrakeet and other *Psittacula* species and members of the related Australian genus, *Polytelis*. Lovebirds are often bred on the colony system but if the aviary holds any unmated adult birds fighting is certain to occur.

The food consumption of various species, in terms of quantity and quality, must be considered before acquiring the bird. Generally speaking, although cockatoos are an exception, the larger parrots are more expensive to keep because their need for fresh fruits and vegetables is much greater; the lesser needs of parrakeets, except when they are breeding, can be satisfied by providing wild greenfoods or home-grown spinach beet.

The final factor to research is that of the individual's attraction to certain species. Before buying birds, the species should be studied in a zoo or private collection to discover whether it has the necessary appeal. It often happens that insufficient thought is put into buying birds because at the back of the buyer's mind is the knowledge that he or she can sell them again if they are found to be in any way unsatisfactory.

Consideration should however be given to the birds because change of environment can cause much stress. Indeed, a veterinary surgeon who autopsies large numbers of parrots has found that death within one or two days of purchase is extremely common. This is a point which is seldom made and which deserves more thought from those who consider themselves bird lovers.

2

Management

Four qualities are needed to care for birds well: a basic knowledge of their requirements, an observant eye to detect when something is wrong, a love of birds and imagination. Why the last? Anyone who can put themselves in the place of their birds and ask, 'What can be done to improve the circumstances under which they are kept?' is well on the way to keeping their birds well. The daily provision of a twig or a piece of wood for caged parrots or regularly renewed perches for aviary birds can make all the difference to their welfare and comfort.

Bird-keeping is largely routine punctuated unfortunately by mishaps, such as sick birds or breeding failures. There are many disappointments to be endured, but often these are brought about by neglect or ignorance on the part of the aviculturist. Circumstances resulting in death could be averted in a large proportion of aviary birds.

Caring for parrots is extremely time-consuming and many aviculturists make the mistake of owning more birds than they can properly look after. The temptation to buy more birds is often overwhelming – and is succumbed to at the expense of the other birds in the collection, who will suffer from hurried feeding sessions and possibly the failure to notice that a bird is unwell.

The parrot-keeper should realise how much he can influence the type of relationship which exists between him and the birds he keeps. There are sound reasons, other than sentimental ones, for talking to one's birds, especially those kept in aviaries. Birds look with suspicion on creatures which are silent and the voice of the person who cares for them should be as familiar a means of identification as that of other parrots.

It is accepted by many that plants respond favourably to the voice of the person tending them; if this is so, how much greater must be the reaction of some of the most intelligent and responsive of all birds? The calming effect of the constant presence of a sympathetic person can be very apparent. In one collection which I know, all the birds are tame and friendly, including the Australian parrakeets, because their owner, a retired man, spends long periods with them and talks to them

constantly.

Those who are unable to do this can adopt the habit of, for example, whistling in a certain way as soon as they approach the aviaries, so that the birds are immediately aware of their presence. Birds resting in the shelter may be startled by a sudden approach and some kind of 'contact call' prevents this.

Aviculturists should develop a routine for feeding their birds so that this is carried out at the same time daily and in the same order. In this way there is less likelihood of forgetting to feed any bird.

Before seed dishes are refilled, husks must be blown off or removed and containers cleaned when necessary. Dishes of small seeds such as millet or canary will contain fine particles of ground-up seed which form a powder. Rather than discard the entire contents of the container, this powder is easily removed by sieving the seed through a tea strainer.

Every few days it will be necessary to thoroughly clean the feeding shelves in outdoor aviaries as a layer of stale food can soon accumulate. In damp or humid conditions, this will become mouldy – and mould is a killer of birds as it can cause fungal infections such as aspergillosis. Aviary floors should be cleaned at least once a week in damp weather for the same reason; in dry weather, this is less important, although dusty seed and a dusty atmosphere might also be responsible for causing aspergillosis.

Every few weeks after the breeding season, concrete floors should be hosed down, scrubbed and disinfected. Aviaries should be inspected regularly for holes in wire mesh, or even in the floor, and for damage to woodwork.

Rodent Control
Rodents are a major bugbear in all aviaries where there is seed; it is almost impossible to prevent the entry of mice and a continuous battle is necessary to keep their numbers down. In covered passageways between or behind aviaries, to which no livestock has access, poison and traps can be placed. A small box with the front made of 1 in welded mesh, containing a mouse trap, can be placed inside parrot

aviaries, as only mice can gain access. The type of poison used should be changed after a few months as mice gain immunity to one type over a period of time. The most humane method is the use of 'catch-'em-alive' traps, advertised in avicultural publications. (The mice can be released in a suitable area, at least a kilometre from the aviaries, by those who do not wish to kill them.) It should be pointed out that mice will not enter these traps if other food is available. Therefore, food must be removed at night and the aviary or birdroom swept clean.

Rodents can carry disease, contaminate food and containers, create a huge increase in the seed bill and cause an unpleasant smell. They can also disturb smaller birds which are nesting and take over nest-boxes.

Rats can kill even quite large birds, and apparently sometimes kill for the sake of it but they are easier than mice to exclude. Young rats can gain entrance through 1 in welded mesh but adults cannot. I have also known rats to gnaw through the concrete base of an aviary and this emphasises the importance of laying welded mesh before concrete. Rats are easy to poison as they have well-marked 'runs', tunnels leading to the aviaries, in which poison can be placed.

Contrary to popular belief rats and mice may use the same aviary.

There are many other kinds of vermin which can gain access to an aviary if 1 in welded mesh is used, including stoats, weasels, snakes and mink. Cats, foxes, racoons and birds of prey can injure or kill birds through this size mesh, which is why $1 \times \frac{1}{2}$ in or $\frac{1}{2} \times \frac{1}{2}$ in is recommended for all birds. The ideal welded mesh is $\frac{3}{8} \times \frac{3}{8}$ in but it is not easily obtainable and is expensive. It excludes all vermin.

Winter Management

In a temperate climate during the winter months, birds in outdoor aviaries have to survive from 4p.m. to 7 or 8a.m. without feeding. In cold weather, food is the principal form of producing body heat yet many fanciers expect birds to exist for 15 or 16 out of 24 hours without food. While large parrots can tolerate these conditions, it is more difficult for small species to do

so. There is thus a great advantage in constructing aviaries with enclosed shelters and installing electric light in the shelter, allowing the occupants to feed until about 10p.m., an extra six hours during the shortest days. This is almost the equivalent of heating the shelter at night, for food will be converted into body heat. If it is not possible to provide electric light, provision should be made to house small birds indoors during severe weather.

When water freezes, it must be renewed so that parrots can drink at least once daily. Fruit, such as grapes, will help to quench their thirst but water must never be neglected.

When the weather is so cold that parrots tend to be inactive, one should try to give favourite tit-bits two or three times daily; this will encourage them to feed. One should ensure that all food offered is of good quality and provide bread and milk to those that like it, in addition to the usual foods; this is more nourishing than seed and greenfood may be difficult to obtain.

Ensure that the roosting perch is a wide one so that the breast feathers partly cover the feet of the roosting bird. Look carefully at the feet; any birds suffering from frost-bite will need to be taken indoors at once if serious disfigurement is not to result.

Covering the sides, or roof and sides, of aviaries with polythene during severe weather can make an enormous difference to the comfort of the occupants. It will protect them from wind, cold, rain and, to some degree, from frost.

It is very important to check that nest-boxes of those birds which roost in them are waterproof at the start of the winter. I once neglected to do this for a pair of Yellow-backed Lories which were at least 20 years old with near fatal consequences for one of them. One morning, during a period over which the temperature had been below zero for several days and nights, one of the lories was found on the floor stiff and apparently lifeless. A flicker of life was seen from one eye so the lory was placed in the warmth of an infra-red lamp. After several hours of lying on its side, it revived sufficiently to rise to its feet, after being given a teaspoonful of warm nectar. Next day, to the delight of both birds,

it was re-united with its companion, who had been brought indoors to ensure it did not suffer a similar fate, and they were soon returned to the aviary after inspection of the nest-box. This was found to have been leaking which was why the lories had roosted in the open-fronted shelter. The box was repaired and placed in the shelter and, in fact, the lories spent all the cold days as well as the nights inside.

Escaped Birds

Birds kept indoors are subject to fewer hazards, especially when permanently confined to their cages. Those let out for exercise should not have access to such dangers as aquaria, which should be covered, fireplaces, which should be shielded, and, of course, open doors or windows. A tame bird may make no attempt to leave a room, but if it is frightened by a loud noise or sudden movement it may instinctively take to the wing and disappear at speed through a window.

Birds which escape, whether from house or aviary, without having time to take stock of their surroundings, seldom return. Those which fly to a nearby tree and leisurely survey the area, even though they then fly off, usually return without too much trouble. Certain species have a natural homing instinct and seldom go far and, if they do, they are capable of finding their way back. This applies to some parrakeets, conures, lories and macaws for example, while others, such as Cockatiels, seldom show much homing instinct and quickly become hopelessly lost.

If a bird escapes and stays in the area, the best procedure, if possible, is to catch up its mate and place it in a cage near the roof of the aviary. A corner of the wire-netting roof should be unstapled and turned back and a perch placed prominently below. Food is positioned further inside. If this is not possible, or where pet birds are more likely to return to their own cage, the bird's cage, or one roughly constructed from wire mesh with a door which drops down and is released by a long string, can be placed in a prominent position.

Sometimes the larger parrots fly into a high tree and are too frightened to descend, although they have no intention of flying off. It is best to coax such birds down. Unless they are very tame, climbing the tree is likely to make it fly off. Presenting food or its mate in a cage may have the desired effect of persuading it to climb down. For species which normally roost in a nest-box, one can even try placing their nest-box in the tree. As a last resort the bird can be hosed so that it is unable to fly off.

Catching and Transferring

A vital piece of equipment in any bird-room or aviary is a catching net, obtainable from aviary suppliers. Those made of dark-coloured materials are preferable. The rim should be padded to prevent injury. The sight of the net invariably causes the birds in my collection to scream or to fly about wildly so I always conceal it until reaching the aviary containing the bird to be caught.

When catching the larger birds, a small parrot cage (the smallest size obtainable, not fit for permanent residence) is taken into the aviary and the bird is transferred from the net. A box can be used for a very small parrot which is to be transferred to another aviary. The temptation to transport birds in the net must be resisted as accidents can very easily happen and one can easily let go of the top of the net, allowing the bird to escape.

In most collections, one large and one small net will be found useful. When releasing a bird into an aviary from a cage, the door should be opened and the bird allowed to find its own way out. If it shows no signs of doing so, the perch should be removed and the bird should be gently coaxed. Turning the cage on its side, so that the door is uppermost, often encourages the occupant to climb out.

If a bird refuses to be coaxed, it will have to be handled. Large parrots should be picked up in a folded towel, small ones in a hand protected by a lightweight glove. A thick glove is useless for the purpose as it does not allow one to grip the bird properly. When holding a parrot in a towel, this should be wrapped around the body so that the legs and wings are firmly enclosed and its eyes are not covered.

However, it must be held in a grip which does not allow it to use its beak! The thumb and finger, or two fingers, should be placed on each side of the beak so that the bird is unable to turn its head.

Parrots of all sizes can inflict a painful bite and care must be taken to prevent the bird gripping the hand or any other part of the body. Remember, too, that parrots can bite very effectively through a catching net. Most bites received by parrot-keepers arise through sheer carelessness. The cause is almost always fear or provocation, with the exception of some individuals among the larger parrots which take a malicious delight in catching their owner unaware. A parrot's beak is an extremely powerful instrument and the large species are capable of inflicting serious injury, although, as if in awareness of this fact, the two with perhaps the most powerful beaks, the Hyacinthine Macaw and the Palm Cockatoo, are usually extremely gentle.

Catching must be carried out as quickly as possible and with a minimum of disturbance. It is sometimes easier to catch a bird which is confined to the aviary shelter; this has the advantage of not upsetting birds in adjoining aviaries. It should always be remembered that parrots, especially small species, are most susceptible to shock and this alone can cause death.

Transferring a bird from one cage to another can often be accomplished without handling it, by placing the doors of both cages together and persuading the bird to enter. Removal of the perches will aid this process.

I prefer to place a parrot in a new aviary at mid-day. Many will not feed at first and, if moved early in the morning, may not eat at all that day. This will not harm a large parrot which is healthy but could adversely affect a small one, especially in cold weather.

A parrot should never be introduced into an aviary containing another bird which has been in residence some time. The established occupant will regard the aviary as its own territory and the newcomer as an intruder. Failure to realise this on the part of inexperienced aviculturists must have resulted in the death of many birds. Existing occu-

pants should therefore be removed from the aviary for a few days to allow the newcomer to become confident in its new surroundings before being introduced to its potential mate. It may even be necessary to adopt this procedure after removing a sick bird for several days or weeks. This is especially true if the one remaining in the aviary is the dominant member of a pair, for it may attempt to reassert its dominance on the return of its partner.

Many birds die shortly after going to a new home because they suffer stress at a change of this kind and need careful attention. It is not always advisable to place a new bird immediately in an outdoor aviary. Some will benefit from a few days in a cage, during which time they can get used to new management and feeding methods. They are more likely to feed in a cage, finding the food more easily than in an aviary. It is an excellent idea to catch up the bird's prospective mate during this period and to cage the birds side by side. The possibility of a violent reaction when they are eventually introduced is thereby lessened.

On introducing birds to an aviary, the food should be hung at perch level as a nervous bird may not descend to the feeding shelf. A millet spray hung at the end of the perch will induce many birds to feed. After a couple of days, the food containers can be removed towards the feeding shelf, then placed on it. Such precautions are not always necessary but are worth bearing in mind.

Growth of the Beak

The beak is made of a substance called keratin; like the nails of a human being, which are similar, the beak grows continuously. New parrot-owners are sometimes worried about the fact that their bird's beak is 'flaking off'. This is a perfectly natural process and is the manner in which the beak is renewed. The outer portion is shed as the beak grows. In some old birds, the growth rate of beak and nails is abnormally rapid, making trimming a necessity. If the owner is not confident enough to carry out this task, the bird should be taken to a veterinary surgeon.

Using a pair of nail clippers, it is a

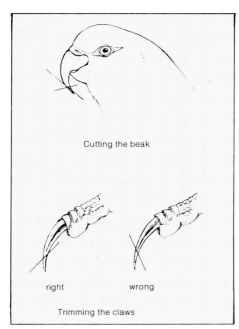

Cutting the beak

right   wrong

Trimming the claws

Trimming beak and claws.

simple matter to trim the nails; in most cases it will be necessary to remove only the tip of the nail. If the nail is cut too far back, bleeding will occur when the vein is cut. Often the vein can be seen if the foot is held up to the light and this should be done before trimming. The same applies when cutting the upper mandible, which is not difficult in a small bird; care must be taken that the bird's tongue does not get in the way. Because of its thickness, it can be difficult to trim the upper mandible of a large parrot and cutting the lower mandible of any parrot is not an easy task. With the larger birds, filing may be a better alternative.

In some small parrots, such as caiques and Fig Parrots, the upper mandible grows very quickly but need never be trimmed if they have an ample supply of wood on which to gnaw. Indeed, cutting the beak should be avoided. The natural shape and length of the beak will be restored if the birds are never without wood. As an example, a male Salvadori's Fig Parrot, obtained four months after importation, had an overgrown upper mandible which, after only a few weeks in my possession – and much damage to the aviary woodwork – was of normal length and shape. Some species and not necessarily the large ones,

have a greater need to gnaw than others: this is true of the Iris Lorikeet. A pair of mine, which are housed indoors and for which it is not always possible to keep up a supply of fresh twigs, are given a regular supply of wooden clothes pegs which keep them occupied and their beaks in good trim.

A parrot's beak can become overgrown almost imperceptibly and for this reason it is most important to look regularly at the upper mandibles of all birds. If this is done, trimming with nail clippers will be a last resort only.

Feather Plucking
It was long believed that feather plucking was caused by dietary problems but there is no evidence to support this; it is almost always psychological in origin, especially in birds kept as pets. Over the years I have received numerous requests for advice from the owners of pet parrots which have suddenly started to pluck themselves, after perhaps years during which the habit did not develop. As an example, I was asked for advice by the owner of a Blue-fronted Amazon which, after ten years, had suddenly started to pluck

A feather-plucking Blue and Yellow Macaw. Parrots should not be chained to a stand.

itself. He told me that he had recently married and moved from his former home, leaving the Amazon in his mother's care. The reason for the bird's behaviour was immediately apparent: it did not enjoy the attention it had formerly received and was missing its owner. Feathers were being removed out of frustration and boredom.

Feather plucking is comparatively rare in Amazon Parrots but is common in Grey Parrots. These birds are extremely intelligent and if they have nothing with which to occupy their beaks and minds they will almost certainly resort to plucking themselves. It is also common in macaws and cockatoos, two other groups of birds far above average intelligence. It is the height of cruelty to keep such birds under conditions which are so unsatisfactory in regard to their mental well-being that they resort to plucking.

A major cause of feather plucking in parrots is a frustrated desire to nest, especially in pet birds which are permanently denied the opportunity. Even those kept in aviaries will occasionally denude the abdomen of feathers but, after the moult, they usually stop until the breeding season returns. Such cases are not serious and require no attention.

Occasionally a bird will severely pluck its mate. There is then no alternative but to separate the two birds because, if the situation is allowed to continue, the damage could be irrevocable, with the feathers never growing again. The pair should be reunited at the time of year when they are most likely to nest, in the hope that this activity will divert their attention from feather plucking.

The single bird which plucks itself severely is the greatest problem.

Feather plucking can be difficult or impossible to cure once it has taken a firm hold, thus a remedy must be sought immediately the habit is acquired.

Most parrots in which the habit is fairly recent will cease to pluck themselves if they are placed in an aviary with a bird of their own species and of the opposite sex, in the hope that they will breed, and this is the most likely cure. Achieving this will be out of the question in cases of certain birds. If the problem is psychological in origin and cannot be rectified, due to, for example, the death of the owner, the bird should pass into the care of someone who can do their utmost to help it. When such birds are paired successfully and it has subsequently been necessary to remove the mate of the reformed bird the plucking recommenced. In happier cases, such as that of a Citron-crested Cockatoo which was severely plucked, the provision of a mate was recommended, and two years later the owners reported that the pair had successfully reared young and the bird was completely cured.

For the bird which, for some reason, cannot be provided with a mate, yeast should be added to the diet in the form of brewer's yeast or a proprietary yeast mixture for birds, available from most pet shops. Crushed tablets of Vitamin B, which help to promote good feather growth, can also be given. The yeast or tablet should be offered in an item of soft food of which the bird is particularly fond rather than sprinkling it on seed. It should be given daily for some months or as long as necessary.

The bird should also have every possible device to occupy its beak and mind. If it is necessary to leave the bird alone for long periods a radio should be left on to provide diversion. The parrot should be given as much attention as possible, provided that this can be maintained. A supply of fresh twigs for gnawing must always be available. I can recall the case of a feather-plucking cockatoo which was regularly supplied with twigs, resulting in an improvement in its condition, and on the first day on which twigs were not provided it started to remove its feathers again.

Nuts are excellent objects for occupying a parrot's attention. A bird will try for hours to crack a walnut. Some pet birds will enjoy playing with a bell on a chain (all metal – plastic toys will be broken) and for the larger birds a bone or a piece of hide on which the bird can chew will provide hours of diversion. Care needs to be taken when they are introduced because some parrots will be extremely suspicious or even afraid of them and it is best to provide twigs and toys from the outset. Great care must be taken that they are entirely safe and cannot crack when bitten, perhaps trapping a bird's foot in the crack. Suspended toys must never be hung by material such as string which could result in the bird strangling itself.

The diet of a plucking parrot should be as varied as possible and include fresh vegetables. If these are refused a multivitamin and mineral additive should be placed on the food.

Finally, it is important that the bird's plumage, or what is left of it, receives as much moisture as possible. If the bird cannot be encouraged to bathe, it should be sprayed at least two or three times a week with warm water. This should be carried out in a warm room so that there is no danger of the bird becoming chilled.

3
Aviaries

Parrots are among the most difficult and expensive birds to house, both because generally speaking each pair requires an aviary to itself and because strong materials have to be used since parrots are so destructive.

The beginner to parrot-keeping who may have kept birds before and already have an aviary may be able to adapt it for, say, a colony of Cockatiels. It will, however, rarely be of a really suitable design or constructed of materials which would have been selected if the aviary had been purpose-built for parrots. For most species, in any case, a row of flights, rather than a large aviary, will be needed and the foundations of an existing aviary will probably be the only part which can be utilised.

Those who have not kept birds previously should not start too ambitiously: one range comprising three to six flights is recommended, and a few pairs of parrakeets or lovebirds would be suitable. If this advice is not heeded, problems may arise. Indeed there was a case where a friend of a large-scale breeder of Australian parrakeets became increasingly interested in the birds and decided, after joining a bird club and visiting other aviculturists, to take up Australian parrakeets. No expense was spared in constructing twelve well-made aviaries. A dozen pairs of parrakeets, including some of the more expensive species, were obtained several months later when young birds were available. They resided in their new aviaries for three days precisely. He was dismayed to find that, in his own words, he had 'an aversion' to them. The moral is obvious: start on a modest scale. Three to six flights are recommended for the beginner. There is much to learn and it is better to make one's discoveries on hardy and inexpensive birds such as Cockatiels rather than with Princess of Wales' Parrakeets and Crimson-wings.

From the outset it should be realised that, although some individuals of the smaller species will mix with finches and other birds, most will not and an aviary should be provided for each pair. One sometimes sees large aviaries, usually in zoos, where a number of species of parrots live together in apparent harmony; however, there is a high degree of risk in mixing different species. Some will be compatible until they come into breeding condition, when their temperament really can change overnight. Countless sad stories have been told by aviculturists of birds of different species which lived together for years before, suddenly, one turned on another and killed it. I believe that aviculturists have a moral responsibility to avoid needless deaths of this nature. Some of them arise from that fault of which nearly all bird keepers are guilty – keeping more birds than they have the time or the space for.

Range of aviaries.

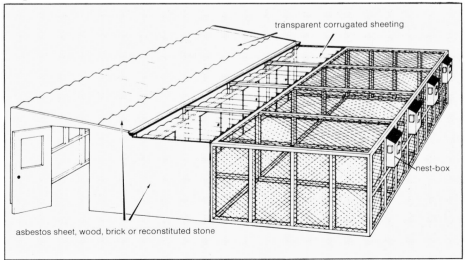

transparent corrugated sheeting

nest-box

asbestos sheet, wood, brick or reconstituted stone

Having decided which species is to be kept, and having found out its requirements, the first task is to prepare the site. This should be in a position where the birds will give least offence to neighbours who may not like their voices. Thefts from aviaries are common and, for this reason, aviaries should, if possible, be sited within view of the owner's house.

Often there will be little or no choice regarding the site of aviaries. Where there is, it should be borne in mind that birds from open, semi-desert areas, such as Cockatiels and some Australian parrakeets, thrive in bare, open aviaries, which are situated away from trees. Indeed, it has been suggested that the very presence of overhanging branches could make them uneasy. In the wild, such sites would be susceptible to attacks from snakes, for example. On the other hand, birds from dense tropical forest, and this applies to the majority of species from South and Central America, Indonesia and New Guinea, much prefer a situation which is well shaded by trees. They will certainly breed in dark, secluded aviaries and it is well worth moving a pair which has failed to breed in a more open situation to this type of environment.

A range of aviaries can be a most attractive focal point of any garden – or it can spoil the appearance completely. With a little thought, it is a simple matter to make aviaries smart and neat and a worthy frame for their occupants which will look even more eye-catching when well housed.

Shelters which are constructed of a reconstituted stone, for example, are most pleasing in appearance. And the shelter roofs can be neatly covered with felt tiles. Aviary woodwork, which should always be on the outside of the wire, to lessen the damage from destructive beaks, can be painted with a coloured wood preservative which is preferable to paint.

Flower-pot holders containing gaily-coloured geraniums or other plants can be hung on the shelters, and vines such as honeysuckle, Russian vine and clematis can be trained to grow between aviaries. If they grow over the top and the birds are able to nibble them, this will not matter; they will provide natural and attractive cover

and are strong enough to withstand some damage.

It must be remembered that the aviary floor could be a means of escape. Some of the larger parrots, especially cockatoos, have a tendency to burrow and could escape with ease through an earth floor. Concrete laid over wire mesh is the safest floor covering. Breeders of Grass Parrakeets often prefer to leave part of the aviary floor as turf; here again, wire netting must be laid on the floor to keep out vermin. It should be sunk to a depth of several inches around the perimeter of the aviary.

Although grass floors do provide ground-feeding birds with hours of enjoyment, as they eat the grass seeds and search for minerals, they are also a health hazard. Most Australian parrakeets, also other species, harbour *Ascaridia* worms; the worm eggs will be ingested by birds feeding from the ground and the chain of infection will start all over again. On shingle floors, worm eggs are likely to work their way through the shingle and out of reach of the birds. On concrete, which should be regularly hosed or washed down, the eggs should be washed away. In suspended aviaries with wire floors, the birds will never have access to the worm eggs.

Concrete is the most hygienic floor surface, especially if it is laid on a slope with small drainage holes at the lower end, for it will be a simple matter to hose it down.

When the site has been selected and the ground prepared, it should be covered with $\frac{1}{2}$ in wire netting. This will exclude most vermin with the exception of mice. The concrete base is then laid on top of the netting.

Welded mesh and wire netting are available in a range of sizes and gauges. Welded mesh is stronger, firmer and neater in appearance and is favoured by most parrot keepers. For Lovebirds and the smaller parrakeets, $1 \times \frac{1}{2}$ in welded mesh or the more expensive $\frac{1}{2}$ in can be used.

Although 1 in welded mesh is much used for the larger parrots, it does allow the entry of vermin such as young rats, stoats and weasels. It is really not at all suitable, as I found by bitter experience: one night a fox or some other predator frightened one of

my parrots which fell to the aviary floor. As the parrot climbed up the wire to its perch, the predator caught hold of its leg, pulled it through the wire and bit it off at the top of the thigh. This could not have happened if $1 \times \frac{1}{2}$ in mesh had been used and this, the strongest material available, is the best although there are some species among the largest parrots which even chain link cannot be guaranteed to hold.

Mesh as large as 2 in square is sometimes used in the construction of aviaries for macaws and cockatoos. In addition to allowing the entry of a wider range of vermin, access will be allowed to sparrows and other birds causing seed expenses to escalate. If it is essential to use a large mesh or chain link because a lighter gauge would not contain parrots with powerful bills, smaller mesh can be placed in front of the heavy gauge wire. This is unsightly, but appearance is less important than the welfare of the birds.

Most large parrots will be safely contained within 10 gauge (1 in square) welded mesh (obtainable in sheets not rolls). The gauge used for most large species is 12 and for small birds, such as Grass Parrakeets, 16.

Whichever kind of wire is used, it should be rust-proofed with non-toxic black bitumen paint before use. This makes the occupants of the aviary easier to observe and gives a neater appearance.

All wood used in aviary construction should be treated with a preservative. In aviaries for very destructive birds, the use of wood should be avoided: metal piping or angle iron is a more practical alternative.

Wire mesh or netting should be stretched tightly across the aviary framework as sagging wire is most unsightly.

Building with the future in mind, aviaries should be constructed in sections, otherwise it will be impossible to move them and material which could have been re-used will have to be scrapped, involving much expense, inconvenience and loss of time. The sections are screwed together and can, if necessary, be dismantled in a matter of minutes.

It is essential that partitions between aviaries should be double-wired for all

Range of aviaries belonging to a German breeder. Attractive planting in the vicinity does much to enhance their appearance.

except Grass Parrakeets and Kakarikis. Even if aviaries are built for Grass Parrakeets, in later years they may be utilised for other birds, so it is wisest to bear this in mind when they are built. Serious injuries, such as the removal of a mandible, can be inflicted through wire. Young birds will be especially vulnerable because, on leaving the nest, they usually spend some time clinging to the wire and are not capable of defending themselves from attack by birds in adjoining aviaries.

The design of aviary shelters will depend on the climate where the birds are kept. In temperate climates, fully enclosed shelters are preferable. Many parrots can tolerate cold but have poor resistance to cold with damp. If it is possible to shut them inside a fairly spacious shelter during damp or foggy winter weather, they will fare much better.

If it is necessary to provide heat, perhaps for birds which have never previously wintered outdoors, placing a small heater with a ceramic infra-red element in the shelter is a much more satisfactory alternative to caging a bird indoors for several months. Paraffin heaters should not be considered for, although they might be safe if meticulously maintained, on countless occasions they have been responsible for the deaths of entire collections of birds. A suitable appliance is an electric wall heater which must be covered by welded mesh.

In some areas, a fully enclosed shelter will be of real use for perhaps only four or five weeks of inclement weather each winter but it is vital to have one for it is during this period that losses are most likely to occur if birds are not able to roost out of the wind and damp. Most parrots have an intense dislike of wind; this is true even of birds kept in subtropical climates where the wind is warm.

The entrance from the flight to the shelter can be by means of a square access hole, or preferably by a hinged flap of wood which can be let down as a landing flap and shut with a bolt or button at night. This will prevent draughts and will quickly confine the birds to shelter or flight when necessary. As an alternative in individual aviaries rather than in ranges of flights, a sliding cover to the entrance can be operated from outside the aviary by means of a metal rod.

Some birds are susceptible to frost-bite, resulting in deformed or missing toes; this will not occur if they roost in a fully enclosed shelter. It is often stated that a male bird with frost-bitten toes will be rendered useless for breeding purposes, because it has difficulty in keeping its balance during copulation, and though this may be true of some birds, I know of a male Ringneck Parrakeet with mere stumps for toes as a result of frost-bite who fertilised eggs for many years.

A further advantage of fully enclosed shelters is that if complaints are received about noise during the early hours of the morning, it will be possible to confine the birds to their shelters at night, thus reducing the sound to some degree.

The winter climate of Britain, most of Europe and much of the USA is not ideally suited for parrots; the loss of stamina which many suffer during winter and long, cold springs results in their taking longer to come into breeding condition. One successful British breeder of parrots has overcome this problem by totally enclosing his aviaries in glass, with windows at the front which can be let down during warm weather. A sprinkler system is installed to compensate for the lack of rain on his birds' plumage. The shelter of every aviary is equipped with electric lighting which switches on automatically during the early hours of winter mornings, thus reducing the hours of darkness during which parrots do not normally feed. This has resulted in fewer winter deaths and in the parrots coming into breeding condition much earlier in the year.

Enclosing aviaries in glass is too costly for most aviculturists but polythene panels, which can be buttoned into position during the cooler months of the year, keeping out wind and frost, are nearly as effective and much less expensive.

The shelter should be constructed slightly higher than the flight. A perch placed at the highest point of the shelter will be out of draughts and will provide a cosy roosting place for birds which do not use their nest-box at night. For those that do, fully enclosed shelters are not essential, although they can be an advantage especially for the less hardy species. Birds which roost in their boxes are not exposed to wind or to frost, and the close proximity of another bird will assist in maintaining its body temperature.

In tropical and subtropical climates aviaries can be less substantial and more open in their construction. A design which impressed me for its simplicity and usefulness in Florida was that of the aviaries of Ramon Noegel, housing species which varied in size from Sun Conures to Scarlet Macaws. They were individual units, made entirely of welded mesh and were raised 90 cm (3 ft) off the ground. The height was approximately 90 cm (3 ft) and the width was about the same. Length varied up to about 3.5 m (12 ft). Nest-boxes were attached to the outside along with food and water containers which were inserted into slots. Cover in the form of a plastic sheet was placed over one perch. The aviaries are situated beneath trees, a setting which provides shade and protection from the wind.

These suspended aviaries have become so popular in the USA that they are now more widely used than the traditional type. They have the great advantage that droppings, seed husks and discarded food fall through the wire bottom: a most hygienic arrangement. A net on a stick is used to catch birds in these aviaries.

An alternative design for warm climates is a range of all-wire open aviaries, with covered back or central passageway. The flights extend the full depth to the ground but the small feeding areas under the covered passageway do not. To facilitate catching the occupants, a wire slide can be made which can be inserted while they are feeding.

Also in Florida, I have seen aviaries which are designed to be hurricane-proof and which would provide excellent protection against prolonged or extreme cold. Built of breezeblocks and concrete on each side of a central passageway, only the ends and a small section at one end of each flight were constructed of chain link. Traditional aviaries used in Europe could be much improved on and in many areas it would be more realistic to consider this design. While aesthetically they would be less pleasing, they would afford far more protection for the occupants.

Before deciding on the size of the aviary, it should be borne in mind that all sizes of welded mesh are available in widths of 90 cm (3 ft), and some sizes are also obtainable in 1.2 m (4 ft) and 1.8 m (6 ft). In heavier gauge wire 1.8 m (6 ft) widths can represent a considerable saving in wire and in labour time but it should be pointed out that more wood will be needed to support thinner gauge wire.

There are two methods of joining together two lengths of welded mesh where a batten is not required, as on a roof, for example. Threading the two sections with wire can be neat and satisfactory, provided that the wire is pulled tightly. The special clips sold for the purpose of joining lengths of welded mesh have two disadvantages: they rust quickly and they are easily removed by some of the larger parrots. Regular inspection of joins made with these clips is therefore essential. It should also be noted that some birds can remove wire staples with the utmost ease and could quite easily dismantle the aviary within a few hours. This is especially true of some cockatoos.

The normal height of aviaries is 1.8 m (6 ft), provided that this suits the height of the owner. Minimum width should be about 75 cm (2 ft 6 in) for small species such as Lovebirds. Cockatiels and small parrakeets, and 1.2 m (4 ft) or 1.8 m (6 ft) for large parrots, cockatoos and macaws. The length will depend on the space available and the species kept. Flights only 2.4 m (8 ft) long are suitable for Lovebirds, Cockatiels and Grass Parrakeets. Most other parrakeets and most lorikeets require flights about 3.6 m (13 ft) long and the larger parrakeets, such as the larger Rosellas and Alexandrines, will benefit from flights which are up to 6 m (20 ft) long, although this is not essential. In most cases, the length of the flight is the most important dimension; the width is relatively unimportant for birds which spend much time flying. The depth will matter where aviaries are positioned lengthways along a path and the occupants cannot move away from observers by flying the length of the aviary; nervous birds will require extra depth.

To avoid disturbing birds unnecessarily, access to each aviary should be direct and not via the adjoining flights. If a safety passage or corridor is incorporated in the design, the doors should open on to this passage, as should feeding hatches. The latter are an essential part of aviary design as it would otherwise be necessary to enter each aviary to feed the occupants and this can be very time consuming. Also, when in breeding condition, some parrots are extremely aggressive and will, if allowed the opportunity, attack any-

Half-depth shelters in a range of parrakeet aviaries: the lower half lifts up to provide access for cleaning and feeding. A safety passage of welded mesh prevents birds escaping.

one who enters their territory. The hatch can open on to a shelf on which the food and water containers are placed or the containers can be slotted into a hinged piece of wood.

I have found it necessary to use specially designed safety hatches for fast-moving birds which are also fearless and aggressive. Lories, in particular, can move with such speed and are so inquisitive that they could be out of the hatch before the food containers can be removed. The food containers on the feeding shelf are covered with welded mesh and holes are cut above the containers to allow the birds to put their heads through.

Also with safety in mind, doors should not reach to the full height of the aviary; they should be just large enough to admit the owner in comfort. Feeding hatches should also be as small as possible and hinged at the top so that they automatically drop down.

An additional safety measure is to padlock all aviaries. It is true that this will not prevent entry by a determined thief but it will guard against mischievous children and constitute a deterrent to thieves.

Where possible, nearby ranges of aviaries without covered corridors behind them should be linked by roofing the connecting pathway with wire netting and having a door at either end, which will act as a giant safety porch and prevent the escape of a bird which gets out of its aviary. Individual aviaries which are not part of a range should be fitted with a safety porch of double doors enclosed within a porch. If a number of individual aviaries are in use which do not have to be entered often, a portable safety porch could be used, which could be hooked in a matter of seconds onto the aviary to be entered. It is worth exercising some forethought to prevent birds escaping, something which, alas, is very common and entirely unnecessary.

Aviaries for indoor use will be similar in design except that there will be no need for a shelter. They can be constructed either entirely of wire mesh, reaching to about 60 cm (2 ft) above the floor, or of the more usual type reaching the full depth. If the former design is used, newspaper can be placed on the floor below the cages, enabling rapid cleaning with no disturbance of the occupants.

Indoor aviaries have much to recommend them for small species and those who do not have a garden need not give up the idea of keeping and indeed breeding parrots. The larger species will also breed indoors, but the noise factor often becomes a problem. If this is not the case, it should be remembered that many large parrots, from Hyacinthine Macaws to Grey, Eclectus and Amazon Parrots, have reared young indoors, many of them in circumstances which might be thought far from ideal.

Basements and attics have successfully been adapted into breeding rooms. The most important factors are light and ventilation. The use of the excellent natural daylight fluorescent tubes is recommended. If the atmosphere is too dry for successful hatching, a humidifier can be installed. However, in my limited experience of indoor breeding (confined to small lories and Eclectus Parrots), dead-in-shell has been non-existent, suggesting that many cases are the result of low air temperatures rather than low humidity.

For ease of cleaning, plastic or ceramic tiles can be laid on the floor. The initial expense is worthwhile, especially as tiles greatly improve the appearance of the room. Wallboard or tiles can be used on the walls and will prove easy to wash down. Hardboard treated with a gloss paint is an alternative. Emulsion paint gives an attractive appearance at first but will prove more difficult to keep clean and will need to be repainted frequently.

Windows must be covered with wire netting on a removable frame; this can be buttoned into position. Unless this precaution is taken, there is a danger of a bird severely injuring itself if it hits its head against the glass, or of escaping if the window is left open. This applies whether or not the birds are permanently caged in the room. It will rarely prove practicable to have the occupants loose together, although this could be satisfactory in rare cases, such as a colony of Cockatiels.

The best accommodation for an indoor breeding room is a range of flights, each one made individually. The temptation to make a range as a single unit should be resisted as the flights would be very difficult to clean. About 1.8 m (6 ft) should be left at the end of the range so that each flight can be moved along, allowing thorough cleaning of the sides and floor. If suspended aviaries are used, this will not be necessary.

There are a number of advantages to housing small species, such as Grass Parrakeets, other small parrakeets, Lovebirds and small lorikeets in this way. They are not subjected to interference from predators or other disturbances which may deter or prevent successful breeding, and frost and severe weather conditions do not affect them. This will prevent losses of young which are just starting to feather in unfavourable weather conditions, and losses from egg-binding in species which insist on nesting at an unseasonable time.

The main disadvantage to indoor flights is that the birds are denied access to sun and rain. Bathing facilities and regular spraying can replace the latter – but spraying birds indoors creates much work. Nothing can entirely replace sunlight as a source of Vitamin D but a multivitamin additive in the food or water will usually result in the birds' keeping in good health. Provided that the young are fed well, they should be of a quality which is equal to those bred in outdoor aviaries.

In recent years, thefts of parrots, especially from outdoor aviaries, have become increasingly common. It is not only the expensive species which are the target for thieves and therefore all those with outdoor aviaries are advised to install an alarm system. A simple system can be installed quite inexpensively by the do-it-yourself enthusiast with a knowledge of electronics. Others are advised to consult a security company. Great strides have been made in recent years in the development of security systems involving, for example, the use of infra-red beams. These provide protection for aviaries – but where cats or foxes are likely to set off the alarm, it is advisable to have a double set of beams at different heights.

An alarm system can be linked with floodlighting so that, when the alarm goes off, the aviaries are automatically lit by floodlights. However, a manual system of operating the floodlights is preferable if the alarm is likely to be triggered by animals. Likewise, the alarm can ring inside the house only, so that neighbours are not disturbed.

Even where an alarm system is in operation, it is advisable to secure all aviaries with good quality padlocks, preferably the close-fitting type which are expensive and recommended by crime prevention officers. I have no sympathy with the viewpoint that padlocks are useless because a thief can cut through wire. While this is so, cutting welded mesh is time-consuming and noisy and any action that will delay a thief is worth taking.

One of the distressing factors associated with theft is that of identification by the rightful owner. The birds may be recovered – but the owner is unable to prove that they are his property. Valuable birds can be tattooed under the wing with the owner's initials or even marked with invisible dye which shows up under ultra-violet light. In addition, a file should be kept with a photograph of each bird and notes of identification, such as missing or deformed toes or nails.

4
Feeding

A varied diet is vitally important as all the thought, time and expense that has gone into obtaining suitable birds and providing the best possible accommodation for them will otherwise be wasted.

Feeding a collection of parrots can be a costly undertaking and this is partly why the majority of breeders of parrots concentrate on those species which are likely to produce enough young to offset food bills. Whether or not the species kept are free-breeding, it should be borne in mind that it is much easier to provide a varied diet for a small collection of parrots. In urban areas it may be difficult or impossible to provide sufficient wild greenfood, for example, to offer to all pairs during the breeding season and it may be equally difficult to find the space to grow spinach beet or other cultivated greenfood. Although such foods are not essential all year round, while chicks are being reared, they may well make all the difference between mediocre and superior young birds, especially if the parents refuse bread and milk. Similarly, of the birds which require plenty of fruit, only as many should be kept as one can afford to feed generously with this.

The cost and type of food necessary will play an important part in determining the maximum number of birds in a collection. It is far better to keep a few pairs which receive a varied and nutritious diet than a large collection that has to subsist mainly on seed with the occasional addition of apple.

The time available for feeding is another aspect which must be taken into consideration: it is not the refilling of seed vessels which is the most time-consuming task but rather the preparation of numerous small extras, especially during the breeding season. As mentioned in Chapter 2, a strict routine should be adopted in feeding a collection because it is less likely that an enclosure will be overlooked if the aviaries are attended to in the same order daily.

The actual process of feeding is a more enjoyable task with parrots than with most birds since many demonstrate so clearly their approval, or otherwise, of the food offered. Some species become very tame and wait on the feeding shelf to see which extras are on that day's menu. The evident enjoyment of a favourite tit-bit makes feeding a most rewarding task and the provision of such delicacies as a piece of cheese can be an important factor in taming and steadying some parrots. Among the larger birds in my collection, there are very few which will not take choice food items from my fingers, even though they are not tame in the usual sense of the word. This does not apply in most collections of smaller birds, such as Grass Parrakeets and Lovebirds, which rarely develop any rapport at all with their owner.

Storage and Containers

In planning to keep parrots, seed storage arrangements will have to be made and thought given to the types of food and water containers which will be necessary.

Seed bought in quantity is packed in strong paper or hessian sacks, which mice have little trouble in entering. Unless stored in an area which is free from vermin, it is advisable to empty seed into large plastic dustbins or large purpose-built metal containers. Smaller quantities can be stored in tins or any suitable airtight containers of glass or plastic. It is essential that the storage area is dry. Damp conditions cause seed to become mouldy and such seed can cause serious, even fatal, disease in birds. Peanuts and pine nuts are especially susceptible and any not in first class condition should be rejected.

The type of food container provided will depend to a great extent on the size of parrot. Many of the larger species will treat unsuitable containers as playthings. For macaws, cockatoos and other large parrots, heavy metal hook-on containers are essential. In addition to the built-in ones in cages they are also useful for birds in aviaries but usually because of their small size they are not adequate for a day's supply of one type of seed. Metal containers are unbreakable, although species with powerful beaks can bend the hooks.

Plastic hook-on containers are ideal for less destructive birds as they are easier to keep clean than metal containers and they hold more. Unfortunately, some of those available have metal hooks which many parrots delight in breaking off. For small birds, glass, earthenware or plastic dishes which stand on a feeding shelf can be used.

The size and type of water container used will depend on the species and whether or not it bathes. For large birds which do not bathe in a container, earthenware dog bowls are most suitable as they are heavy enough to prevent most birds from turning them over. For small birds, plastic hook-on drinkers can be used. Birds which do bathe will require large, shallow containers of enamel, glass or stainless steel. Any kind is suitable if it is easy to keep clean.

For several reasons, I am not in favour of the use of seed hoppers for parrots: they are suitable only for small seeds, such as canary and millet and, in any case, require constant attention to remove the fine powder which results from birds shelling seed and to ensure that nothing impedes the flow of the seed. They also make it too easy for owners to give too little attention to their birds; no one should keep birds if they do not have the necessary time to devote to daily feeding. In any case, it is essential to spend some time each day with one's birds because a sick bird or one that is being harassed by others will otherwise be overlooked. Should it be necessary for seedeaters to be unattended for a couple of days, open dishes are to be preferred to hoppers because of the danger of the flow of seed becoming blocked in a hopper.

At some time or another, most aviculturists will have to leave their birds in another person's care. Precise written instructions should always be left even, indeed especially, when the person entrusted with their care is another aviculturist. For a non-fancier, all seeds and foods should be clearly labelled and feeding instructions should be attached to each cage or aviary.

Nutritional Requirements

Proteins are vitally essential in the diet of all creatures because they are the flesh-forming components of foods and the only means of repairing wear and tear. They also provide energy and warmth. All the soft parts of a bird's body contain protein. Without it a chick cannot develop and neither can a bird moult successfully or lay eggs. Parrots differ widely in their protein needs; ground-feeders appear to need less high quality protein.

General health will be affected if the diet is deficient in protein – and this is not uncommon in captive birds which eat only seed. It has been estimated that chicks and breeding hens need at least 18 per cent protein in their diet.

Major sources of carbohydrates are sugars, starches and fibres. They are used for heat and energy, although some energy may be obtained from protein.

Fats and oils are a more efficient source of energy than carbohydrates: half the quantity of fats and oils give the same amount of heat and energy as carbohydrates. Some are also sources of Vitamins A and D which are important for birds which do not have access to sunlight, without which they cannot manufacture those vitamins.

Vitamin A is used to keep in good condition the membranes lining the moist surfaces of a bird's body, such as the eyes and mouth. It is synthesised from the colouring agents, the carotenes, in plant material. Many seeds, including sunflower and millet, are deficient in carotene. Some parrots, especially Eclectus and some of the South American species, have a great need for Vitamin A. In Eclectus and lorikeets a deficiency results in moniliasis or candidiasis which manifests itself in the form of a swelling in the mouth, often just under the lower mandible. This is especially common in newly imported birds. Any parrot which suddenly ceases to eat hard seed should be examined for a swelling in the area of the lower jaw. A single injection of chloramphenicol suspension directly into or adjacent to the swelling frequently effects a cure. Birds which have suffered from a deficiency must subsequently be given plenty of greenfood or fresh vegetables, especially carrot and corn; fortunately Eclectus and most large parrots are fond of these foods.

Vitamins of the B complex are the ones most likely to be deficient in parrots. One of the most important is Vitamin B_2 (riboflavin). It is necessary for the enzyme system that enables the body cells to utilise food energy.

Brewer's yeast is the richest source of riboflavin. A yeast mixture specially prepared for birds can be obtained at any pet shop; its regular use, sprinkled on seed, will prove highly beneficial. Riboflavin is found in much smaller quantities in meat, cheese, eggs, green vegetables, milk, whole grain and fortified cereals. Yeast is also the richest source of thiamin (Vitamin B_1) and pyridoxine (Vitamin B_6). Many birds obtain vitamins of the B complex by eating old faeces.

There are numerous vitamin and vitamin/mineral preparations which can be added to a bird's diet. They can be obtained in liquid or powder form, and thus there is no excuse for birds dying or even ailing due to a deficiency of a vital vitamin. Cod liver oil is widely used by Budgerigar fanciers and has been blamed for the high incidence of French moult in many aviaries. It is mixed with the seed and the oil goes rancid in quite a short time, which results in the Vitamin A and D being destroyed. It is therefore desirable to feed these vitamins in another way – preferably on food which will be consumed the same day. Some liquid vitamin additives are unpleasantly flavoured so it is advisable to give them in nectar or to use a fruit-flavoured additive, which most birds will drink.

Seeds

Feeding each kind of seed in a separate container, rather than a mixture, is advocated. Less wastage occurs because the birds are more likely to have before them the seeds they eat. Many parrots will steadfastly refuse certain foods and there is usually little point in persevering beyond a reasonable trial period. If mixtures containing unwanted seeds are offered, and it is rare for all seeds to be liked, it may appear to the owner not familiar with a bird's preferences that the bird has plenty of food before it when, in fact, it may be almost starving. In addition it is impracticable to offer mixtures containing seeds of widely varying sizes such as sunflower and canary seed, as the smaller seeds tend to get lost. Each kind of seed should initially be offered in a separate container so that the owner knows exactly which kind each bird eats and can see at a glance how much food has been consumed.

To discover the food preferences of a newly acquired pet parrot which is eating hard seed, the owner should buy a packet of parrot mixture and carefully note which seeds are eaten. Most parrot mixtures contain 90–95 per cent sunflower seed, the remainder being made up with peanut kernels, peanuts in the shell, pine nuts, chillis, hard maize and, in some mixtures, oats and canary seed. Having noted the preferences, the favoured items can be bought separately and sunflower, pine nuts and peanuts, once found to be acceptable, can be mixed or offered separately. Small seeds and fruit and vegetables should be provided in separate containers.

Birds must *always* have food available. There should be no thought of rationing. Considerably more non-perishable food than the bird or birds can eat in a day should be provided. Of perishable foods, quantities small enough to be consumed immediately should be given so that none is left on the feeding shelf to decay or to be dropped in the water container.

For most parrots, seed will form the basis of the diet. All large parrots should be offered sunflower, pine nuts and peanuts; small seeds, such as canary, white millet, buckwheat and hemp, should also be offered. Smaller species will make their choice from sunflower or safflower, canary seed, white millet, hemp, linseed and niger. Some will also eat peanuts. Pine nuts are usually too hard. Millet sprays are relished by most parrots, large and small; they derive great enjoyment from removing the seeds from the spray and this can be the means of tempting a sick bird to feed.

Of the small seeds, millet and canary are the best known and the most widely used. Millet seeds are round and of several types, the largest of which is white millet; panicum is the smallest and is yellowish brown in colour; red millet is not normally used as a bird food and Japanese millet is offered mainly to finches. Millet will form a fair proportion of the diet for small species, such as Lovebirds and Grass Parrakeets and to a lesser degree for Cockatiels and some Hanging Parrots.

Many large parrots ignore it but some, especially Eclectus, will eat large amounts and should always have it available.

Panicum millet is the most useful for breeding birds as it is believed to break down more easily in the crop to a creamy consistency and is therefore of value to pairs with very young chicks. Millet grows wild in the Far East and Africa. It can thrive in conditions where soil would be too dry and poor for the successful culture of wheat or maize and it requires little water or cultivation.

Canary seed will usually be eaten by the same species which eat millet. It is a shiny, pointed, oval seed, yellowish brown in colour. It is grown in many countries, including Britain, and there is no reason why the aviculturist with sufficient land should not grow his own crop. If this is done, it is not necessary to thresh it. The birds obtain great enjoyment from removing the seeds, just as they do from spray millet.

Both millet and canary seed are deficient in fats and oils and should not be fed without the addition of oily seeds, such as niger or sunflower. For small species, niger is an excellent food but large parrots can seldom be persuaded to eat this small, long, shiny black seed. It has a high oil content and a danger to watch out for is that if the seed coat is broken and the oil exposed, a chemical change could take place causing the seed to become rancid. Birds which will eat niger usually become addicted to it without any harmful result and, as its price has increased enormously in recent years, it is not likely to be fed in excess. Birds in my collection which relish this seed include such varied species as Cockatiels, small lorikeets and Red-capped Parrots (*Pionopsitta*).

Maw or poppy is more often fed to finches than parrots but it is worth trying with the smaller parrots.

Hemp is an excellent food, a favourite of most parrots. It is very expensive to purchase but its food value is high and it is economical to use because it has a thin husk. The dangers of this seed used to be greatly exaggerated and one was often recommended the number of grains to give daily; the main point to remember is that it does have a high fat content

and larger parrots should not be given it in quantities which could cause obesity.

Oats and groats (oats without the husk) will be enjoyed by many birds. They can be fed dry or soaked; in either condition they break down easily in the crop and are therefore useful for birds rearing young.

Few of the other small seeds available are likely to appeal to parrots. I have tried radish seed, for example, after reading that it was enjoyed by Cockatiels, but *all* my birds, regardless of species, refused to sample it. Sesame, however, will be enjoyed by small birds but it is expensive and not easily available.

While the quality of small seeds obtained from reputable merchants does not vary greatly, there is, in my experience, considerable variation in the quality of sunflower seed, especially since the mid 1970s, when the best sunflower seed started to be used for human consumption. Occasionally the seeds are so slim that the birds will make no attempt to husk them but will drop them uneaten. If fed such seed, the health of a parrot which relies mainly on sunflower will suffer. It is therefore most important to buy good quality seed which is plump and full in appearance.

Most parrots prefer white to striped sunflower and show least enthusiasm for black sunflower which, when fed in a mixture of sunflower seeds is often wasted, probably because the birds are influenced by appearance rather than taste. Unfortunately, white sunflower is more expensive than striped and has become more difficult to obtain. Striped sunflower is sold in two sizes by some seed merchants: the small grade is usually used for finches and very small parrots only.

A seed which looks something like small white sunflower, and is much less expensive, is safflower. I have not been able to persuade parrots to eat it when sunflower is available. Pine nuts which are nutritionally superior to sunflower seeds, are a relatively new addition to the choice of parrot foods available. Many of the larger species consume them with frantic enthusiasm, even to the exclusion of sunflower seed, if allowed to do so. The danger here is that the supply of pine nuts has proved erratic, with supplies failing for long periods. In appearance they are dark brown. Two types are available in the UK: Russian (large) and Chinese (small). If there is any sign of exterior mould they should be returned to the supplier or washed well before feeding. No more than can be eaten in one day should be fed to birds in outdoor aviaries in wet weather as if left un-eaten for a few days they could become mouldy.

Peanuts, fed either in the shell or as kernels, preferably should be those sold for human consumption. According to an eminent aviculturist and veterinary surgeon, those sold for birds have sometimes been discarded for human consumption because they are infected with the poisonous mould, *Aspergillus flavus*. He found that liver damage by chronic poisoning was common in captive parrots and concluded that, in many cases, peanuts were to blame.

Soaked seed is of great value for birds rearing young and for newly fledged young as it is easier to digest than hard seed and it is essential for those which do not receive greenfood. Seed should be soaked for 24 to 48 hours. It is important that the water in which seed is soaked is changed after about 24 hours and that the soaked seed is thoroughly washed before being offered. Some breeders provide only soaked seed while young are being reared or ensure that some soaked seed is always available. For soaking and sprouting, sunflower, canary seed and oats are most often used. Sprouted seed is even more beneficial. After being soaked it should be washed and placed on trays or blotting paper in a warm place and left for at least 24 hours until small shoots are seen.

Those fortunate enough to be able to obtain wheat in the ear will find that it is a favourite with many birds. Some cockatoos which will not eat loose grain will eat various foods in the ear, whether it is corn-on-the-cob or spray millet.

Corn-on-the-cob is one of the most valuable foods it is possible to offer to parrots rearing young. Some would rear on nothing else if given the opportunity. In northern temperate climates, the season for fresh corn is a short one in autumn but frozen corn cob which

has been thawed is equally acceptable. Unfortunately, it is expensive to purchase but, even so, the quantity needed to rear a nest of the larger parrots will cost only a fraction of their value.

An inexpensive alternative, which may be less eagerly eaten, is whole maize which has been boiled for about two hours and until soft, then washed and drained.

Food Values

It would be very wrong to allow any bird to exist on only one kind of seed as most seeds are deficient in some respect. Their food values are given below. It should be remembered that protein is a very important item of the diet and that different seeds have varying amino acid constituents. Those of peanuts are superior and those of millets are especially poor.

Vitamin Sources

Fresh vegetables and green leaves are the major source of required vitamins. At any greengrocer, one can purchase a number of items which will be relished by a wide range of members of the parrot family and which will supply the necessary vitamins. Carrot, for example, is inexpensive and a great favourite of many birds, including the true parrots, parrakeets and certain small lorikeets. Many large parrots are fond of celery and it is offered to mine daily. Carrot and celery can be cut into pieces or grated and added to rearing foods.

Raw onion has a reputation as a health food and a pair of Palm Cockatoos which were known to me consumed it avidly, but I have never been able to persuade my parrots to sample it. Some parrots will eat the stalks of cabbage and leaves from Brussels sprouts and cauliflower, but not with the enthusiasm that they show for most greenfood.

The most popular cultivated food is, without doubt, spinach beet or perpetual spinach. It can be grown with ease in any fancier's garden or even in a window box. Its great asset is that it grows throughout the year; thus a few rows will provide even a large collection with a constant supply of fresh greenfood. The owner of only two or three birds will find it worthwhile to plant a row. Spinach beet is an excellent rearing food.

The owner of a small number of birds who is not able to obtain other forms of greenfood will find that a bunch of watercress, with the stems in water, will keep fresh for several days.

Wild greenfood is becoming increasingly difficult for many fanciers to gather, but those who are able to obtain chickweed, dandelion, sowthistle and seeding grasses from uncontaminated areas should take full advantage of this source of supply. One must, of course, be certain that no crop spraying has been carried out in the area as greenfood so treated can prove fatal to birds.

The only greenfood I know which is relished by all parrots is chickweed and it is of great value for birds which are

Seed Food Values (in percentages)			
	Carbohydrate	Protein	Oil
sunflower	20	24	47
pine nuts	12	31	47
peanuts	19	26	47

	Carbohydrate	Protein	Fats and oils	Mineral	Water
canary seed	52	14	5	2	14
millet	61	15	5	2	13
hemp	16	16	32	4	12
niger	15	17	33	7	8
maw	12	17	40	6	15
linseed	18	—	40	—	—

rearing young. However, it should not be offered to the latter in large quantities unless a supply can be located which will last throughout the rearing period. Following wet weather from early spring until early summer and during the autumn, chickweed can be found growing in immense quantities on some areas of waste ground. The whole plant can be used. Enough can be gathered to last for a week, provided that it is stored in a sack in a fairly damp place. To ensure a supply of chickweed during the winter, some fanciers even go to the lengths of growing it in a greenhouse.

Many kinds of grasses, too, can be offered, but annual meadow grass (*Poa annua*) is generally the most favoured. It is also the easiest to collect, as some other grasses have very strong stems.

When greenfood is fed, no more than can be eaten the same day should be provided. Warnings are often given about the dangers of stale greenfood but it is unusual for parrots to show any interest in it when it becomes limp. Feeding small amounts of greenfood several times daily when birds – especially parrakeets – have young, stimulates the male into feeding the female and young more often than he might otherwise.

Some parrots, especially cockatoos, are reluctant to sample fruit but this fact should not give cause for concern if the birds will eat greenfood. Non-starchy vegetables are generally richer in protein than fruits, although banana is an exception. Fruits, however, like vegetables, contain a wide range of mineral elements and, of course, they help to add variety to a bird's diet.

Apple is the most widely used fruit for parrots and most species will eat it. To avoid wastage it should be cut into narrow slices or chopped into pieces. For small, non-destructive birds, like Hanging Parrots, half an apple can be impaled on a nail on a branch and the birds will derive enjoyment from eating it in this manner. Contrary to popular opinion, apple does not have to be sweet. A pair of cockatoos in my collection refuse to sample the best shop-bought apples but green apples which fall from the tree above their aviary are relished.

Grapes or cherries are attractive to most large parrots and can be the means of inducing stubborn birds to sample fruit. I once persuaded a parrot to start eating fruit by attaching grapes to the branches of a small tree growing in its aviary. Example, however, is the best teacher and parrots are quick to copy other birds housed with them or those they can watch nearby. Oranges and tangerines too are relished by most of the larger parrots and oranges can be cut into slices.

Many newly imported birds will eat banana but lose interest in it after a while. It is sometimes stated that it is not advisable to give banana to birds but I had a pair of Yellow-backed Lories which consumed a whole banana every morning and evening, in addition to half an apple daily and nectar. In 15 years they never had a day's illness.

Soft, but not over-ripe, pear is eaten in preference to apple by some lories. A favourite fruit with many species is pomegranate, an excellent source of iron. Birds love extracting the seeds but unfortunately this fruit is expensive and has a short season. Those who grow soft fruits can experiment with almost any in season, such as redcurrants.

Dried fruits, such as dates, soaked sultanas and dried figs, will be relished by some parrots. Dried or soaked figs are the favourite item of diet of my Fig Parrots, but they eat only the seeds.

In the autumn, berries provide a superb and favoured natural food. The purple-black berries of elder and the deep red ones of hawthorn provide a valuable supplement to the diet and one which is free for the gathering. Some birds I know would eat hawthorn berries in preference to all other foods. A real effort should be made to introduce these berries into the diet of all parrots. Berries of ornamental shrubs, such as pyracantha and rowan berries, will also be eaten. Rosehips can also be offered. If accepted they can be dried well and kept in a refrigerator in good condition for several weeks.

An item whose value as a food few fanciers have discovered is pussy willow or sallow. A breeder of Lovebirds discovered its use by accident when offering it as nesting material. The Lovebirds consumed the buds, bark, leaf, stalks and even the catkins and made the various forms the major part of their diet, out of preference. It was found that Australian parrakeets would eat it but in much smaller quantities.

One often reads of the dangers of feeding leftovers from the table to parrots but provided a little common sense is used and no foods are given in excess, little harm will result from this practice. Tinned fruit, cooked vegetables, biscuit, cake and bread can be offered. Crusts from toast are enjoyed almost more than any other item of food. A good use for stale bread which would otherwise be wasted is to lightly bake it in the oven for the larger parrots. It should be remembered that during World War II, when seed was unobtainable, many parrots survived almost entirely on food from the table. I am not recommending this but merely pointing out that, in moderation, it adds variety and is not harmful.

Some aviculturists tend to forget that seed is not the natural food of all parrots. It *is* the natural food of the species most widely kept and bred, all from Australia: parrakeets, including the Budgerigar, Cockatiels, also Zebra Finches and grass finches. The reason why they have adapted so well to captivity is that they originate from arid areas and for a large part of the year survive mainly on seeds.

Unfortunately, the recipe for success with these birds has, over the years, gradually been applied to most other members of the parrot family. In many cases, their requirements are totally different and, under natural conditions, seeds would form only a small part of their diet.

Many parrots in confinement, especially the large species, are destined to spend their whole lives on a diet consisting mainly of seed. The tradition grew up partly out of ignorance as to what the birds' natural habitat was but also because of convenience and cost. Seed prices have now risen to such a degree, however, that there can hardly be a more expensive method of feeding parrots. It is an ill wind which blows no good however and aviculturists may, in spite of themselves, be encouraged to introduce more variety into their birds' diets. Parrots will certainly appreciate this for it has been found that they have a better sense of taste than most birds, thus it is not surprising that they show decided food preferences. It is believed that domestic fowl have no taste buds in the tongue and that pigeons have about 30. Parrots, on the other hand, are said to have as many as 300 or 400.

Many collections of parrots comprise widely differing species, yet the food offered to them tends to become standardised. The birds would benefit if a little less routine and rather more thought was introduced into their diets.

At San Diego, one of the most important and progressive of the world's zoos, medical staff examine diets of various species from several aspects, including reported food preferences in the wild, occupational therapy of food items (not necessarily related to nutritional value) and practical considerations of foodstuff availability, perishability and economy.

The subject of occupational therapy is especially important in the case of caged parrots which seldom have enough with which to occupy their minds and beaks. Such foods as spray millet and corn-on-the-cob, wheat or grasses in the ear, will provide great enjoyment and occupation. And a suitable bone will provide hours and even days of activity.

Similarly, it is of value to provide, in a separate container, such seeds as canary and white millet, which some large parrots like, for it takes them longer to eat the same weight in these seeds than in sunflower because of the time spent husking them. Parrots enjoy peanuts in the shell because of the attraction of crunching up the shell. However, if the peanuts are then discarded, as sometimes happens, this becomes an expensive item.

San Diego's list of considerations for feeding is useful only up to a point with parrots. Most, such as Pesquet's Parrot, are known to take large quantities of fruits and that species will not eat seed at all in captivity but only fruits and various soft foods. The diet of most parrots, however, is quite varied in the wild, consisting of fruits, buds, leaves, seeds, insects, nectar and nuts. While seed forms only a small part of their diet, or may never be encountered, many parrots could exist

on little else in captivity. They are extremely adaptable in the matter of diet and, in the wild, parrots often raid cultivated crops; however, this adaptability must not be abused and every effort should be made to provide a varied diet.

This will result in healthier birds and will also add interest to their lives; bored parrots and those which are incorrectly fed all too often acquire the habit of feather plucking which is usually only curable if the diet and conditions under which they are kept are altered.

Diet also influences the desire and ability of birds to breed and it is of vital importance in the case of laying females. The egg must contain all the nutrients required by the embryo before hatching and, if its contents are deficient, the embryo or the chick will die in the shell. Even a minor deficiency of a certain vitamin or mineral could result in the death of the chick, before or after hatching. As it is almost impossible to know in which area the diet is deficient, a balanced diet is essential.

The most likely deficiencies are of the amino acid lysine, Vitamins A and D and B_2 (riboflavin), calcium and certain trace minerals, especially manganese. Lysine is found in the oily seeds – niger, hemp and maw – and deficiency is likely – indeed common – in birds fed mainly on millet and sunflower. It can manifest itself as patches of yellow in the plumage of a predominantly green bird. Breeders sometimes become excited at the appearance of such a bird, believing that it may lead to a pied mutation, but this is not the case and if the diet is corrected the plumage will become normal at the next moult. Cuttlefish bone, which is taken readily by all parrots, is the main source of calcium. Old mortar rubble is equally valuable.

Trace elements will be obtained from a mineral grit specially formulated for birds. All seed-eating parrots need grit, which is used in the gizzard to grind up food. This is best sprinkled on the ground for birds which use the aviary floor, or sprinkled on the feeding shelf for others. Many parrots will ignore grit if it is placed in a small container, yet pick it up from the floor.

Softfoods prepared by the breeder

must be offered to birds with young, those which are newly imported (especially young birds which have yet to learn to eat hard seed) or sick birds which suddenly refuse to eat hard seed. The most widely used food is bread and milk. Milk contains amino acids and calcium and is therefore important for feather and bone growth of young birds. It is important to persevere with bread and milk for there are few parrots which will not eventually come to accept some form of softfood. Its value can be enhanced, especially as a rearing food, with the addition of bone meal which has a very high calcium content and is invaluable for growing chicks. Its use will prevent rickets.

All kinds of items can be used but the emphasis should be on protein, without which no chick can develop. It has been found that, where parrots of the same species are reared in the same collection, those pairs which are offered bread and milk or some other nutritious softfood, produce larger young than those which feed their chicks mainly on seed.

Some birds prefer sweet foods, while others show a positive dislike of them. Finding an acceptable food is therefore a question of trial and error, especially for those species which are not regularly bred in captivity.

Among foods which can be offered are brown or white bread or trifle sponge soaked in honey and water or in nectar as made up for lories, sweetened baby cereal, many kinds of breakfast cereals, tinned strained meals prepared for human babies, soaked bread mixed with hard-boiled egg, boiled rice sweetened with honey, and bread and butter pudding made with eggs and milk. Proprietary canary rearing food will be eaten by many parrots.

Foods prepared for livestock, such as lucerne nuts, which have a high protein content, are also suitable. These should be soaked for two or three hours and added to a rearing food. In the USA, the various chows for livestock, such as trout chow and dog chow, are widely used by breeders of parrots and other birds.

A condition which, regrettably, is common in the larger aviary-bred parrots is rickets, caused by calcium deficiency. Milk and cheese are the best sources of calcium. Many of the larger parrots are extremely fond of cheese, but because of the expense it will be possible to offer it only to some breeding birds; a single pet bird can be given a small cube daily.

If birds rearing young refuse to take bread and milk or cheese, calcium should be introduced into the diet by means of the liquid preparation Collo-Cal D, which also contains Vitamin D.

Calcium, in the form of cuttlefish bone, must always be available for laying hens as calcium is required to form eggshells. If it is not provided, the bird has to draw on the resources of its own body and calcium will be taken in excess from the bones, sometimes resulting in paralysis. Every breeder is aware of the hugely increased intake of cuttlefish bone by a hen which is laying, and by those which are rearing young.

Protein can also be offered in the form of meat and livefood. Contrary to the popular opinion of some years ago, meat is not harmful to parrots. The greatest treat which one can offer most Amazon Parrots and macaws is a chop bone or part of a chicken carcase with some meat remaining.

Maggots have proved to be of high value in the rearing of young cockatoos, Hanging Parrots, Australian parrakeets and some lories. However, the maggots must be thoroughly cleaned before used and should not be fed until the black line visible down the centre of the body has disappeared. Failure to do this may well result in the death of parents and young from botulism. Some cockatoos will take immense quantities of maggots while rearing chicks, almost to the exclusion of other foods, and in some cases this has been responsible for breeding successes. But, if the birds will take it, meat or bread and milk is a better source of protein.

Relatively few parrots will eat mealworms, which are in any case an uneconomical method of supplying protein. Many are required to make a significant contribution to the diet and they are extremely expensive to purchase.

Mention must also be made of nuts, which have a high protein content. For parrots other than macaws, brazils and walnuts must be cracked. Incidentally, the larger nuts make excellent and safe playthings for pet parrots.

Newly Imported Birds

Feeding newly imported parrots is not as straightforward as feeding those which are established. Now that quarantine is compulsory in most countries, it will normally be the importer who has the sometimes difficult task of weaning young parrots from soft foods such as boiled maize. This should be mixed with soaked sunflower seed and eventually with hard sunflower and other seeds. Occasionally, the same procedure will have to be adopted with adult birds which are not eating seed.

Some newly imported birds need constant attention. It will be necessary actually to push soft foods down the throat of some extremely young birds which, in actual fact, are too young to have left their parents and should never have been exported. Occasionally very young cockatoos, whose beaks are still soft and pink, are received by importers. These birds require heat and hand-feeding at regular intervals. The same treatment will be necessary for some birds, including adults, which are suffering from stress and seem to lose the will to live. Eclectus often fall into this category. No one should even consider importing parrots unless they have the time or the staff to ensure that throughout the quarantine period the birds are under constant supervision.

A most important point to be borne in mind by American aviculturists obtaining birds from USDA quarantine stations is that the birds may have been fed only on turkey starter mash or game bird chow with medication. They may be completely unfamiliar with seed and must therefore be gradually weaned on to it. At first soft foods such as boiled maize, wheat bread and fruit must be given.

Experiments have been carried out with a pelleted food for parrots; however, this has not proved a suitable form. Parrots grind up pellets – if they will eat them – wasting much in the process. Even soaked, they are unpalatable to most birds.

5
Breeding

The captive breeding of parrots is important firstly because the species which are in greatest demand, Australian parrakeets and Lovebirds, are, respectively, not exported, or exported less often than formerly from their countries of origin so that the breeder is the most important source of supply. Another reason why experienced keepers will become breeders is because keeping parrots can be a fairly expensive hobby and the sale of young helps to offset expenses.

There is still a large trade in wild-caught parrots of species which are not consistently bred in captivity; trade in birds inevitably involves some degree of suffering and can sadly result in the deaths of many newly caught birds. Although conditions have improved in recent years, there is room for a great deal more improvement, especially in the form of new legislation in exporting countries. Many countries have of late ceased to export birds and, if the trend continues, a smaller number of species will be available to aviculturists unless a huge effort is made to breed some of the many species which cannot yet be considered domesticated.

A large percentage of imported parrots are destined for the pet trade and, were these imports to cease, a much greater effort would be made to breed them because their monetary value would be far higher. This has happened to some degree in the USA where many breeders hand-rear young parrots hatched in their own aviaries. The resulting young are tame and affectionate birds, sold at well-deserved high prices and are inestimably superior to their wild-caught counterparts which are often nervous, or adult, or otherwise entirely unsuitable for the pet trade. Breeders who supply the pet market can be proud of the fact that they are, to some extent, reducing the demand for imported birds.

A breeder will find that birds reared in his own aviaries are usually the best birds with which to breed. From their early days they can be accustomed to the breeder's foods and methods.

The enjoyment and satisfaction gained from breeding birds far surpasses the mere keeping of them. There is so much to learn on the subject, the study of which can pleasurably fill a lifetime.

Finally, there is conservation (see Chapter 10). While it is not suggested that birds captive-bred for generations could be returned to the wild (they would probably be too tame), at least the species would continue to exist.

The very first requirement for breeding is a true pair of birds. Sexing is one of the major problems of breeding parrots in which the plumage is alike in male and female.

The following methods of sexing are possible.
1. A method which has become more widespread since the late 1970s is the use of the laparoscope or endoscope. It enables a bird to be sexed quickly and, in most cases, conclusively. The bird is first anaesthetised; I believe that the best method is the use of a face mask, administering a small amount of gas which enables the bird to regain consciousness after about two minutes. Behind the last rib, a tiny incision is made into which the laparoscope is inserted. The instrument normally used is 2–2.7 mm wide, depending on the size of the bird. Using a light source, it is possible to see whether the bird has testes or ovaries. These are easily distinguished in adult birds in good condition. In young birds, sexing may be impossible or even incorrectly carried out. It may also be impossible in overweight birds.

The laparoscope can be used to obtain basic data regarding the reproductive physiology of a bird – whether its sexual organs are active or inactive and therefore whether it is likely to breed in the near future.

The chances of laparoscopy having a harmful result are extremely small when carried out by an experienced veterinary surgeon. Indeed, many birds have nested within days of being sexed surgically.

The laparoscope can also be used as a diagnostic tool. It can reveal, for example, whether a bird is suffering from air sacculitis, avian tuberculosis or aspergillosis as it provides a good view of other organs, including the liver and kidneys, and also the air sacs.
2. At San Diego Zoo, and it will probably become a service at other zoos, aviculturists can submit droppings of their birds; these are subjected to steroid analysis. The sex of the bird is determined by the oestrogen/ testos-

terone ratio in its faeces, although these can vary in composition according to whether or not the bird is in breeding condition. This method is in its infancy and results are not 100 per cent accurate but provide a good indication. Equipment to carry out these tests is again extremely expensive and thus few organisations have it available.

3. A similar method to (2) above using the pulp of feathers, has been used.

4. Observation. There are many factors which the experienced aviculturist takes into account when assessing the sex of his birds, but none is conclusive. Head and bill shape is a good indication where other birds are available for comparison: the male usually has more height above the eye and the head and upper mandible are larger.

The male's demeanour is bolder; females have a tendency to crouch rather than stand on the perch.

In some species, males are noisier than females. And females often bite harder than males.

Of birds kept in cages, those which spend much time scratching on the floor or chewing up newspaper are almost invariably females.

Copulation and display are not reliable indications of sex as sometimes, where two birds of the same sex are housed together, one will assume the role of the other sex. Of Lovebirds which carry nesting material this can be an indication of sex; although males are sometimes seen to carry it, they rarely take it into the nest-box.

5. Allowing birds to chose their own partners by housing several in an aviary is by far the best method of finding true pairs. It is rarely possible with the larger parrots because of the cost but incompatibility can be the cause of breeding failure in some pairs of large parrots.

6. Experienced breeders often find it relatively easy to sex parrots before they emerge from the nest, or during a short period after. Those who specialise in a certain species often notice differences which are not generally known. For example, a Florida breeder, who has reared more than 50 Grey Parrots, told me that males could be distinguished in the nest by their darker colour. The males of many species are often brighter in nest

feather although, in adult plumage, male and female could not be described as sexually dimorphic or the difference is so slight as to be hardly perceptible.

7. The pelvic bone test can be applied. In adult female parrots *in breeding condition*, the pelvic bones, the two small bones just in front of the vent, are further apart than they are in adult males. This is not a reliable guide although if the pelvic bones of large parrots are so far apart that one can place a finger between them the bird is unlikely to be a male.

After years of living in close association with parrots, which are among the most intelligent of all birds, I know that to attribute anthropomorphic (human) characteristics to them aids greatly in understanding their needs and their psychology. The more intelligent birds – and perhaps also the smaller ones whose actions may be more difficult to interpret – know the whole range of emotions from joy, sorrow and jealousy to love and intense dislike.

In the larger species, it is most noticeable that different kinds of relationships exist between pairs, just as they do in human beings. There are couples who squabble a lot yet are generally compatible, others who are indifferent to each other and some (especially in cockatoos) who are so totally devoted to each other that it is no exaggeration to describe them as being in love.

The pair bond, although differing in pairs of the same species, is very close in lories and cockatoos and almost non-existent in Eclectus and most *Psittacula* Parrots, in which the female is usually the dominant member of the pair. It varies in conures and Amazons for example. Some pairs of the same species are very close, others not. But this can also be true of cockatoos. The strength of the pair bond does vary in individual pairs.

Having obtained a true pair of parrots, they should be placed in an aviary suitable for breeding purposes (see Part Two for the requirements of particular species). They should not be housed in an aviary adjoining one containing another pair of the same species, except in the case of certain sociable birds such as Cockatiels. With

aggressive birds, including the larger Australian parrakeets, this could result in infertile eggs, as the male will spend most of his time making war on the neighbouring male instead of courting his female.

With very few exceptions, such as Cockatiels and some Lovebirds which can be bred on the colony system, each breeding pair should be the sole occupants of an aviary.

The birds must be provided with a suitable nest-box or nesting log. Species which have bred for generations in captivity seldom need the stimulus of an attractive log to induce them to nest. They will accept most nest-boxes with little hesitation.

The construction of the nest-box is important because, unless the nest is free from draughts and reasonably free from damp, the welfare of chicks and adult birds could suffer. The nest-box will be used for roosting by some species and, if it is built well, it will make a secure and cosy place for them to retire to at night.

The base should not be too large or chicks could become chilled when very young; indeed females will usually choose smaller boxes if a choice is available. If the base is square, each side should be approximately the length of the body (that is, excluding the tail) of the species, or slightly larger. Height should be generous because chicks could leave the nest prematurely if the nest-box is too shallow. About three times the width of the base is a suitable dimension.

Wood used should be 19–25 mm ($\frac{3}{4}$–1 in) thick to insulate the interior and prevent the gnawing hen from reducing the box to splinters. The bottom of the box should be fixed inside the sides rather than nailed on the bottom and the top of the box should be sloping; both these features will help to prevent rain entering.

The entrance hole should be just large enough to admit the bird for which it is designed. For large species with powerful bills, it can be a little too small as the activity of enlarging the entrance could be just the stimulus necessary for breeding. A perch should be provided on the outside of the box just below the entrance hole and, inside, a few pieces of wood should be nailed. This allows the birds to climb

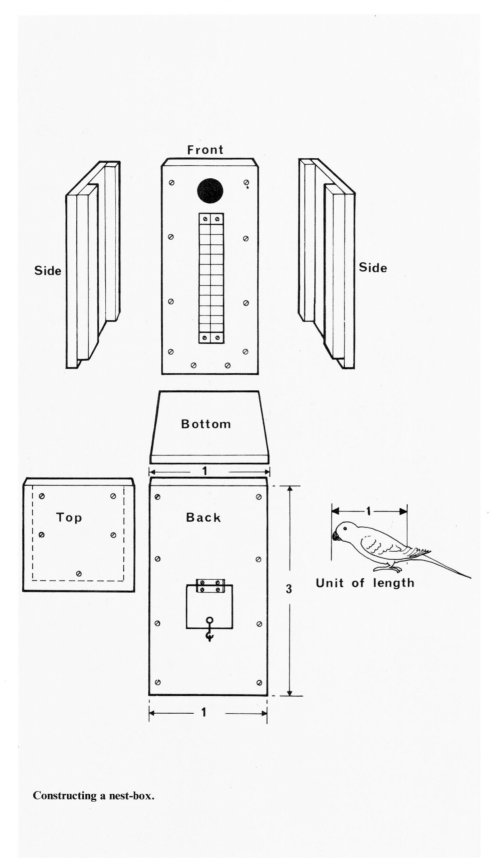

Constructing a nest-box.

in and out easily without catching their claws. Because of this danger, wire netting or welded mesh should never be used. It can have fatal results to an adult and to the young, which could starve to death.

It is most important that a securely fixed perch is positioned within easy reach of the entrance hole. The young of many parrots, conures and lories may want to leave the nest on numerous occasions for short periods before finally spending most of the day in the aviary so they must be able to return to the nest as easily as they left it.

An inspection door is essential. A removable lid is a convenient means of inspecting a small nest-box, but some birds will panic if inspection takes place from above so an inspection door in one or two sides of the box, a few inches above the level of the nest (which, allowing for nesting material, will be raised above the base of the box) is preferable. The door should be large enough to admit a hand, should a young bird or adult need to be removed in an emergency. In a tall box, an inspection door just above nest level is essential because it will not otherwise be possible to reach the nest proper without taking the box down.

Nest-boxes facing north (south in the southern hemisphere) will admit less light than those in other positions, and a dark box is preferred to one which admits much light. Most fanciers construct nest-boxes with round entrance holes in the middle of the box near the top. A quicker and easier method, and one which is just as acceptable to the birds, is to cut a square out of one corner of the box before it is assembled. The interior of the box will then be unevenly lit, so that the occupants can use the corner which is most to their liking.

Nesting material to a depth of at least 5 cm (2 in) should be placed in the base. This can consist of peat which is pressed well down, or a mixture of peat, soil and wood. The pet litter obtainable in compressed packs from pet shops is excellent for this purpose. There is the danger with sawdust that it has been produced from wood which has been treated with harmful chemicals. Some females will throw out any nesting material provided and manufacture their own by gnawing tiny slivers of wood from the inside of the nest-box. It is for this reason that pieces of wood should be nailed to the inside of the nest-box at the start of each breeding season.

In order to keep the nest clean and dry while it contains young, the female may gnaw throughout the period that the young are in the nest so that the droppings are buried among the slivers of wood, resulting, at the end of the season, in several inches of gnawed wood. On one occasion, because of the parents' ferociousness, I was unable to renew the peat in the nest of a pair of lories which contained two young. The nest would have become very wet and insanitary if the birds had not gnawed the roof of the box – indeed to the extent that the roof caved in and had to be repaired.

Large nest-boxes or barrels can stand on the ground. Smaller boxes must be securely fixed to the side of the aviary by means of a large screw attached to it. The head of the screw fits into a small hole in the back of the box. Alternatively, two large metal picture hooks can be attached to the back of the nest-box and hooked over a wooden bar attached to the aviary framework. Nest-boxes should not be screwed directly to the side of the aviary because of the difficulty of removing them in an emergency.

Nest-boxes are usually placed in the flight but in certain cases, where for example very nervous birds are concerned, it can be better to place the box in the shelter. This situation will also provide greater protection from the elements. It is a good idea to provide two boxes, one in the shelter and one in the flight, so that the birds can decide which is most suitable. For birds which are double-brooded, two boxes should be provided as a matter of course as the female will often start to lay before the young of the first round have left the nest.

For birds which are reluctant to nest, boxes of more than one design can be provided. The addition of a wooden spout to the nest entrance, for example, will make it more private and perhaps more desirable. This can consist of a short wooden tunnel, the same diameter as the nest entrance.

Natural logs are undoubtedly very attractive to many birds, especially the

L-shaped nest-box used here by Lilacine Amazons.

larger parrots and cockatoos, but they are difficult to hang and to inspect and, in the case of the whole tree trunks, very difficult to manoeuvre into position. However, for rare and rarely bred birds (such species as Pesquet's Parrots and Palm Cockatoos have nested in tree-trunks), they are worth every effort.

Nest inspection is important in order to check the progress of the young, so nest-boxes must be placed in an accessible position. Because some parrots are so aggressive that it is impossible to enter their aviary without being attacked while they are rearing young, the nest-box should be hung in a position where inspection can take place

Nesting log hung at an angle.

from outside the aviary, a hole being cut in the wire to coincide with the nest entrance. This has disadvantages where space is at a premium. It is wise to fit a padlock to such nest-boxes.

It is often difficult to know when to place the nest-box, barrel or log in position. For birds which roost in their boxes, the box is left in position throughout the year and, in practice, those who keep large parrots such as cockatoos and macaws rarely go to the trouble of removing the nest out of the breeding season, even though the birds do not roost inside. This point therefore applies mainly to parrakeet breeders. *Psittacula* parrakeets are early breeders and their nests should be in position by early February. For Australian parrakeets, March or early April is the best time to start breeding.

The nest-box can be an important factor in stimulating parrots to breed, but there are other factors.

Birds from tropical climates know little variation in day length so increased hours of daylight do not act as a stimulus to breeding activity as they do for birds from temperate regions. In some tropical areas, where there is abundant food throughout the year, birds can and do breed at any time and, in captivity, this habit persists, for example in Lovebirds, lories and Eclectus Parrots.

For parrots from arid regions, heavy rainfall is the main stimulus. They cannot breed until the rains come to produce a plentiful supply of food. These would be seeding grasses in the case of many species of Australian parrakeets which originate from arid areas. Aviculturists in dry areas could therefore use sprinklers to induce certain species to nest, limiting their use to just prior to the desired season.

As they come into breeding condition most parrots become more noisy and active than usual and will be seen displaying and mating. In neotropical parrots the male usually keeps one foot on the perch during copulation; in other species, the male mounts the female.

Before the female lays she will spend increasingly long periods in the nest-box. Shortly before she starts to lay, her vent will appear swollen and her droppings will become loose. Immediately before egg-laying she will spend most of the day in the nest-box.

A female known to be on the point of laying which emerges from the nest and spends a long period sitting on a perch looking fluffed-up and dejected, is almost certainly egg-bound. It is imperative that immediate action is taken. Extreme care must be exercised in catching an egg-bound hen; the use of a thick towel rather than an ordinary catching net is usually to be preferred. If a hen on the point of

laying was handled roughly, the egg could be broken inside her, causing her death.

The egg-bound bird must be placed in a small cage in the heat of an infra-red lamp. No other treatment is necessary. Infra-red is the best kind of heat under the circumstances as it seems to have a relaxing effect on the bird; if an infra-red lamp is not available, a hospital cage could be used or a small room in which the temperature can be raised to 33°C (90°F).

Sometimes an egg-bound bird is temporarily paralysed in the legs, perhaps as the result of pressure on a certain nerve. This is rectified after egg-laying. After the egg has been laid the temperature must be slowly reduced. How quickly the female can be returned to the outdoor aviary will depend on her condition and the temperature outside. If it cold, it is wise to keep the bird inside for a few days to prevent a recurrence of the problem.

Another serious problem, but a rare one, is prolapse of the oviduct. The patient can usually be saved if immediate action is taken. Delay in treatment will result in death. Usually the distal portion of the oviduct is prolapsed through the vent, often together with the cloaca and possibly even with the rectum. The condition is due to excessive straining in an attempt to pass a partially impacted egg or to continued straining after the egg has been laid.

A bird with a prolapse should be taken immediately to a veterinary surgeon who is used to treating birds. If immediate treatment is not possible, the prolapsed oviduct should be sprayed with a solution of saline to keep it moist. If the organ dries out it will prove impossible to put it back into position.

Treatment is quite straightforward. The prolapsed organ is sprayed with an antibiotic powder and replaced simply by pushing it with the middle finger. A purse-string suture ensures that it will remain in position; without stitches the prolapse may recur. The stitches can be removed four days later.

Hasholt (1966) recorded that, of 38 cases of prolapse of the oviduct, shell abnormalities existed in 28, five of which were soft-shelled. This underlines the importance of adequate calcium for females prior to laying. If Collo-Cal D (C-Vet Ltd, Bury St Edmunds) is added to the drinking water or bread and milk, soft-shelled or thin-shelled eggs will not occur. A prolapsed oviduct can be the direct result of calcium deficiency but it can also be due to flaccidity of cloacal muscles. Overweight birds, especially those that have been caged for long periods, are the most susceptible, hence the warning not to breed from overweight birds.

Eggs will usually be laid on alternate days. In large species, such as cockatoos, the interval between eggs is sometimes three, or even four, days. All parrots' eggs are white. The number of eggs laid varies not only with the species but with their geographical distribution; birds inhabiting areas near the Equator usually lay small clutches and breed more than once during the year, for food is continually abundant. Those which lay large clutches may be taking advantage of a seasonal food supply, such as seeding grasses. Small clutch size is usually related to a longer incubation period in the species and vice versa. Except in the case of most cockatoos and certain small lorikeets which are rare in aviculture, incubation is carried out by the female only. In some species incubation commences with the laying of the first egg, so that the chicks hatch on alternate days; in others, incubation does not commence until the second or third egg has been laid, so that the first two or three chicks may hatch on the same day.

A very large percentage of parrots' eggs laid in captivity fail to hatch. They may be infertile possibly because mating has not occurred, either because the female has spent too much time in the nest-box or, in species in which the pair bond is poorly developed, because the male is not in sufficiently high breeding condition to overcome his fear of the female. If mating has occurred, the eggs may still be infertile because of the poor condition or immaturity of one or both birds. It sometimes happens that the first clutch of the year is infertile but the eggs are fertile thereafter. It is unusual for eggs to be infertile consistently when mating has occurred. An-

other possible reason for infertility is that mating is attempted but is not successful due to the presence of a lipoma (fatty growth) in one of the birds (the most common site is on the abdomen, near the vent) thus impeding copulation.

A reason often mooted for infertile eggs is that insecure perches have been used for mating: it is my experience, however, that parrots will usually seek out a secure surface and some will mate on the ground or even in the nest-box. Nevertheless, one experienced breeder of the larger parrots found that infertility was reduced when a rough, flat board was provided for mating purposes.

Very many eggs are fertile but fail to hatch. There are several reasons, not all of which are well understood. If the female leaves the nest for a long period, the eggs will of course become chilled and the embryo will die. This is rare unless the nest is actually deserted as it has often happened that a female has left her eggs for several hours, yet they have hatched. It is less likely to affect the embryo if the hen leaves the egg towards the end of the incubation period. George A. Smith, who has studied hundreds of parrot eggs, maintains that hatching failure is usually directly attributable to insufficient loss of moisture during the incubation period.

Embryos die early in the incubation period for other reasons including weakness in the parent birds or, more often, a dietary deficiency which results in the lack of some vital component. One breeder stated that he had increased the percentage of eggs which hatched by feeding certain minerals.

According to George Smith (1979):

The two periods of incubation when mortality of the embryo chick is greatest are during the first three to five days when 25 per cent of all embryonic deaths take place and especially during the last three or four days when about 50 per cent of the non-hatching chicks die.

The losses in the first few days are from poor hygiene (bacteria migrating into the egg from a dirty or cracked shell), overheating, chilling or jarring of the eggs. But the 'late deaths', the ones known as dead-in-shell, arise just as much from poor maintenance of the correct incubation temperature (cold, damp nest-boxes), as from too dry an

atmosphere. An embryo may die because insufficient water has evaporated from its egg during the incubation. From weighing eggs that contain the dead-in-shell chicks and knowing the weight of the fresh egg, it has been found that desiccation of parrot eggs is less frequently a cause of dead-in-shell than the opposite – too great humidity.

The correct humidity can be difficult to maintain, as many breeders of Lovebirds, for example, know; when kept indoors many young die in the shell, despite attempts to increase the humidity just prior to hatching. The problem is also found in birds breeding in outdoor aviaries, but to a lesser degree.

Other losses can be caused by the eggs being cracked, broken or eaten during incubation. Some females will insist on throwing out of the box all nesting material and this can result in the eggs being cracked. If the damage is slight and is discovered at once it is possible to repair the egg using sticking plaster.

Some birds are habitual egg-breakers or egg-eaters. A cure worth attempting is to blow an infertile egg of the same size, retained for the purpose, and fill it with plaster of paris. Alternatively, plastic eggs can be purchased from some avicultural suppliers. As the eggs are laid they are replaced by the dummy eggs: if necessary, the nest can have a concave bottom with a hole in the centre. The box has a false bottom containing peat or sawdust and the egg will fall through on this. If the false eggs cure the habit, the female can be allowed to incubate her own eggs: alternatively, they will have to be transferred to another nest or placed in an incubator.

There should be no qualms about examining the nests of species which have been captive-bred for generations; it is the rarer and larger birds which can present difficulties, unless the nest-box is placed on the outside of the aviary.

In this case, the nest can be inspected on one of the rare occasions on which the incubating bird leaves and it will be none the wiser that inspection has occurred. The nest should not be inspected when a bird is still inside, unless it is known that the bird can gently be persuaded to move – but such birds are rare.

Nest inspection in the case of aggressive birds where the box is not placed on the outside of the aviary may be quite impossible; or, if carried out, may cause so much disturbance that the birds desert. Many breeders state that they have never known a bird to desert their eggs or even to kill their young as a result of nest inspection – and this may well be the case with parrakeets and lovebirds. The larger parrots, however, are a different proposition entirely and, on occasion, in the case of nervous birds, nest inspection has proved disastrous. It is very much a question of knowing the birds concerned. Tame ones are usually very tolerant of nest inspection, in which case it should be carried out regularly so that one is immediately aware if something has gone wrong and eggs and young which would otherwise have been lost are saved.

Regular nest inspection has another advantage in the case of the larger parrots in that when their young leave the nest they will have much less fear of people than those reared in a nest where inspection was never carried out. As an example, the first Eclectus Parrot which I bred was so nervous when it fledged that it was in danger of severely injuring itself in the aviary before it was independent and could be removed. In subsequent nests, it was found that the female did not resent nest inspection, thus the nest was inspected often after the young hatched. By the time they left the nest they were thoroughly used to the sight of people and consequently did not fly about wildly in fear.

Many breeders remove the eggs to test for fertility, but there is little point unless it is intended to move eggs to other nests. If, for example, it was found that only one egg in the clutch of a Cockatiel or Grass Parrakeet was fertile, it would not be worth the pair spending several weeks in rearing one youngster if the eggs could be removed, the fertile egg being placed in another nest. The pair would then nest again with the possibility that the next clutch would contain a higher proportion of fertile eggs.

If this kind of fostering is not to be carried out, I feel that the female should be allowed to incubate for the full incubation period as there would

appear to be a definite breeding cycle in most species and to remove the eggs may break the rhythm of the cycle. In any case, this act must cause stress to the birds and to do it unnecessarily is cruel. However, many breeders will not agree on this point.

After the eggs have been incubated for four or five days it is quite easy to ascertain whether they are fertile. A 'clear' egg, one which has not been fertilised, looks and feels light and often retains the shiny appearance of a freshly laid egg. A fertile egg looks duller and darker. On holding eggs up to the light, strong natural light or electric light, an infertile egg will appear clear, exactly as it was when laid, while a fertile one looks more solid, darkened by the developing embryo and blood vessels. (If a fertile egg is accidentally dropped and cracked it will ooze blood.)

There is one golden rule which should never, under any circumstances, be broken. If the hatching date is overdue and the eggs are fertile but, it is feared, either addled or containing chicks which have died in the shell, do not open an egg to discover whether the embryo is still living. If it is, this action will kill the chick it contains. On countless occasions one hears of fanciers testing a clutch of eggs which they were about to discard only to find a living chick, perhaps on the point of hatching. . .

Never interfere with eggs until a week beyond the estimated hatching date of the last egg laid unless, of course, a chick can be heard which is apparently unable to hatch without assistance. Opening an egg that has not hatched will reveal at what stage the embryo died. If, early during the incubation period, the egg-shell assumes a dark, blotchy appearance, it has become addled.

Some hens will continue to incubate long overdue eggs while others appear to have some instinctive knowledge of when hatching was due and will break up the eggs if this does not occur at the right time. A female Eclectus in my possession will normally incubate for only a day longer than the correct period. On one occasion her two eggs were laid with a four or five day gap and thus she was in error in breaking up an egg which contained a chick

near to hatching; possibly it had died in the shell and she was aware of this.

The correct incubation temperature for a parrot's egg is about 37°C (99°F). If, due to cold weather, the incubation temperature is slightly lower, the eggs could take slightly longer to hatch than under normal conditions. It must be pointed out that the incubation periods for eggs incubated naturally can vary by two or three days (or even more); thus incubation periods given in this book should be considered as approximate.

Behaviour of the male is often a good indication as to when the first chick has hatched. While there are some male parrots which have little interest in their young, there are many others which are just as interested, even fascinated, as the breeder.

Such birds will spend all day inside the nest for the first two or three days after hatching or, if belonging to species where the male feeds the female at the nest entrance, will spend hours on the nest-box perch and will peer inside as soon as the female leaves.

The 12th Duke of Bedford (1932) had a Barraband's Parrakeet which was typical of this kind of bird. He wrote of it:

> When the eggs were due and overdue (not before) the cock, whenever his mate came off, would go up to the entrance hole, put his head inside and look and listen long and anxiously, then he would go away and do something else, but about a minute later he would hurry back and make another careful examination in the hope that a happy event might have taken place in the interval.

It is not only the father who is interested in the newly hatched young; often birds in adjoining aviaries, even those which have never reared young themselves, can be seen climbing on the wire near to their neighbour's nest-box if it is on the floor, having been attracted by the sound of chicks.

I once kept an aged male Ringneck Parrakeet which had reared many chicks in his younger days in the same aviary as several conures. When one pair hatched young he was to be seen on the nest-box perch peering inside.

There must be something very compelling in the voice of a newly hatched chick which stimulates not only the parents into wanting to feed it. This is an essential quality; otherwise, in a nest of several young, where there could be 10 to 14 days difference in the ages of the first and last hatched, the youngest would never be fed. In some cases, this is what happens, or it is fed so seldom that its growth rate lags behind and it dies.

During the incubation period, the male feeds the female at the nest entrance or inside the nest-box. He will continue to feed her for about two weeks after hatching in most cases and may then enter the box to feed the young. Some males never enter the box and therefore do not feed the young until they are old enough to climb up to the nest entrance. I have seen other males feeding the young from the time they are two or three days old but this is unusual. It is very much a matter of individual behaviour, rather than something which applies to certain species.

In those males which show little interest in their offspring, increased food consumption will be a guide to the chicks' presence. And, of course, one can hear the chicks squeaking to be fed.

If only one chick hatches, one egg should be left in the nest to help support it and to keep it warm when the incubating bird leaves the nest. The owner of a tame pair of Grey Parrots, who was able to examine the nest frequently, described how the single chick wrapped its wings around the egg for warmth when the female left the nest. When the chick became too large to need the egg, the female destroyed it.

Females will sometimes fail to feed their young; this is more likely to happen with the first nest and with a pair in which neither male nor female have bred previously. If a slightly older chick of the same or a very closely related species can be placed in her nest, its stronger pleas for food may stimulate her into feeding it and then her own young. This ruse is worth trying.

If hand-rearing (see Chapter 6) and fostering are out of the question, the chicks can be kept alive by feeding them with a syringe full of baby cereal, wheatgerm and bone meal four times daily. It is to be hoped that in a few days the female will start to feed them.

Fostering of young to other nests is often successful. Much will depend on the temperament of the female, and the species fostered. While it is preferable to move young to the nest of the same species, or the same genus, some hens will rear the young of unrelated and even much larger species. In the case of a size discrepancy, the fostered chicks may not be fed when they become larger than the foster-parents. As an example, three Princess of Wales' chicks aged about two weeks were fostered to a pair of Bourke's Parrakeets who fed them well. Supplementary feeds were also given to assist the Bourke's but after a few days, the Bourke's left them and the chicks were then removed for hand-rearing.

It is impossible to predict whether a hen will accept the young of other species; for high among the factors which can affect this is individual temperament. Some hens are very accommodating and it is well worth retaining them for this reason alone. Others will kill chicks which are not their own. The most important factors for success are that the age discrepancy between the chicks in the nest and those fostered should be as small as possible and that their appearance and voice if of different species, should not be vastly different.

As an example, where chicks of conures which remain in the nest for eight weeks are fostered to the nest of Redrumps which remain in the nest for only 30 days, the hen may cease to feed the young after about one month, in which case it may be necessary to hand-rear them.

Newly hatched chicks have been fostered to a female which had been incubating for only two weeks, and the young were reared. To make such a drastic alteration to a female's breeding cycle must, however, lessen the chances of success.

On hatching, some parrot species have a few wisps of down which are just visible on close observation; others are sparsely covered in down and others more densely. In some species, the down is abraded off to leave them quite naked. Other species acquire a second down; unlike the first, which is white, pink or pale grey, this is dark grey and more dense. Down is poor protection against the cold in a temperate climate, however, especially for the young of the females of the many species which cease to brood during the day when the young are about two weeks old. This is the age at which deaths of chicks in the nest are most likely to occur and such fatalities are regrettably common. Some hens brood the young for a longer period than others, so a knowledge of the habits of individual hens is valuable. In the winter, losses can be averted by removing

Derbyan Parrakeet approximately 1 month old.

the young for hand-rearing where necessary.

The three main causes of death in young chicks are failure of the parents to feed the young, chilling when the female ceases to brood them and malnutrition. Either the food given is deficient in some respect or the parents fail to feed the young often enough. Those who have nest-boxes on the outside of aviaries or can inspect the nest daily will be at an advantage. Where necessary, supplementary feeds can be given once or twice daily, using a syringe for speed.

If bonemeal or Collo-Cal D is added to supplementary feeds, one can be certain that the young will not suffer from rickets. This is not uncommon in the larger parrots whose need for calcium appears to be greater in proportion to their body size than that of the small species. The young of parrots which eat bread and milk will seldom suffer from this problems as milk has a high calcium content. Nest inspection will reveal whether any young have feet with grossly swollen joints which is an indication of rickets. If so, some way must be found to give them bonemeal or other food with a high calcium content. Most hens eat large amounts of cuttlefish bone while rearing young but this alone may not be enough to prevent the problem.

It is very disheartening to have watched eagerly over a nest of young, perhaps of a rarely bred species, only for them to emerge from the nest with soft, rubbery bones as a result of rickets. Sometimes the breeder has made every attempt to prevent this by offering foods rich in calcium but these have been ignored by the parents. In such cases, supplementary feeding or hand-rearing must be resorted to in future nests.

George Smith (1979) is an advocate of weighing chicks because:

> If the chicks are regularly weighed and these measurements plotted on a graph, then the estimated weight for days ahead can be reasonably accurately forecast. The advantage of weighing chicks, and it takes but a few seconds using an accurate spring-balance (Pesola) and a paper envelope, is that when the weights do not correspond with the estimate from the graph then a foreknowledge that something serious is happening to

the chicks, is obtained. In most cases all that is needed is to give the chicks a few supplementary feeds of say Farex and milk. Or they can be fostered or taken in for hand-feeding.

The observant breeder will watch for another sign which indicates problems ahead: diminishing intake of food by the adults or lack of interest when favourite rearing foods are offered.

Parrot chicks spend between 4 and 13 weeks in the nest, according to species. Brief details of the development of various species are given in Part Two. These can be taken only as an approximate guide because the development of birds of the same species can vary according to their circumstances. Shortly before leaving the nest they will be as heavy, or nearly as heavy as an adult, but much of this weight will be lost immediately after fledging when they are learning to feed themselves.

A problem which sometimes occurs when the young start to feather is that of plucking by one of the parents. Some birds pluck a few feathers from the head or back of the young; this is not severe and the feathers will be replaced as soon as the birds are separated from their parents, but others pluck their young so severely that they are unable to fly on leaving the nest or are liable to die of exposure.

There are several possible solutions. If the young are rare species or especially valuable for some other reason, hand-rearing can be considered, but the problem here is that by the time the chicks are well feathered they can be more difficult to hand-feed than very young chicks, as they have the disadvantage of having to overcome their fear of human beings.

An alternative to hand-rearing is fostering to another nest. Another is that, if the male parent is the culprit, the female can be left to rear the young on her own. If the female is to blame, the remedy is sometimes found in letting light into the nest-box: the lid of the nest is removed and the nest will therefore have to be placed in the shelter to prevent the young being exposed to the weather. This solution has been effective with some hens who then continue to feed their young but not to pluck them. Other remedies include

smearing the young with cold cream – but never with an oily substance.

Occasionally chicks emerge from the nest with a nail or part of a toe or toes missing, the result of injury by the parents. It is difficult to suggest reasons for this. Parrots which defend their nest very aggressively from human intrusion may possibly mutilate or kill their chicks as a kind of displacement activity. The male of a pair of Dusky Lories in my possession is extremely ferocious while rearing young and will attack anyone who tries to touch the nest; this is occasionally necessary to renew the peat. During the fourth year in which the pair reared young, one was attacked and bitten on the beak and had most of one toe bitten off (and was therefore hand-reared).

Fractures of the leg, known as greenstick fractures when they occur in very young chicks in which the bones are still soft, can occur but appear to be rare. There is no need to destroy a chick thus afflicted; although the leg may set itself at an abnormal angle, the condition can improve. A lory chick which I removed from the nest for hand-rearing was found on X-ray to have a greenstick fracture of the left leg, which was held at a right angle to the body. There seemed little hope that it would ever be normal, yet by keeping it on welded mesh, it was forced to use its legs at a very early age. By the time it was old enough to perch, it could perch normally, its oddly-set leg being apparent only when it ran on a flat surface.

In other cases, foot deformities are due to rickets, as already mentioned, or possibly due to a deficiency of manganese or some other mineral.

Another problem which can become evident before the young fledge is French moult. This condition is well known to breeders of Budgerigars but is less often encountered by breeders of other parrots. Flight and tail feathers of affected young fall out at about the time they leave the nest; the feathers are poorly formed, usually with blood in the quills.

The precise cause or causes of French moult are not yet known. Numerous theories exist. In birds which are not badly affected, the feathers will grow and it will be difficult to distinguish them from normal birds. Those which are badly affected may never recover completely.

If chicks die at a very early age, they dry up and disappear without trace in the nest litter. It is sometimes thought that the parents have killed and eaten the young, but this is not the case. Dead chicks which have been mutilated are found in the nest, but it must not be assumed that the mutilation has invariably occurred before death. Chicks could be chewed up after death by the female when she is preparing the nest for the next clutch of eggs; just as she will destroy eggs which have not hatched. Some hens do leave such eggs intact.

Nervous birds are more likely to kill their young for they may be continually under stress when rearing birds so close to man. It is for this reason that tame birds are generally so much more useful for breeding, although it must be born in mind that, for the simple reason that they have no fear of people, some tend to be very aggressive and will not hesitate to attack anyone who enters the aviary.

I doubt very much that chicks die from being brooded too closely though they may die from natural causes and then be flattened as the female broods the other chicks.

Most chicks will leave the nest as perfect but usually smaller and duller replicas of the adults; the problems described above, with the exception of French moult, are not commonly encountered in the free-breeding species.

Some young parrots are extremely nervous on fledging and others are composed and unafraid. Those in the latter category may have spent several days, or even weeks, looking out of the nest before they actually leave it and this seems to have a steadying effect on them. Most will start to feed themselves soon after leaving the nest but one of the parents will continue to feed them for at least two weeks afterwards. Some newly fledged parrots husk seed with such ease that I wonder whether the parents have taken whole seeds into the nest before they fledge. Certainly there are some cases of this being found in the nest-box. It is of interest that hand-reared parrots will attempt to husk seed long before they would have left the nest. A Goffin's

Cockatoo which I reared could shell sunflower when eight weeks old.

It is desirable to leave young birds with their parents for at least one month. Certain cockatoos and parrakeets are so murderous towards their young, usually the male towards his male offspring, that it is wise to remove them as soon as they are independent. Alternatively, if the female is not incubating a second clutch, the male can be removed and the female will feed the young.

At all times the reactions of the parents to their offspring should be watched closely to see if any bullying occurs. The young of small species can be removed to large flight cages or small aviaries where they should be retained for a while, to ensure that they are feeding well, before they go to a new home. The purchaser should be advised exactly how they have been fed.

Identification

In free-breeding species which have been aviary-bred for generations, the young can be fitted with closed or split rings for identification purposes. This is especially important in breeding mutations when it is necessary to know the genetical make-up of each individual; and in all other birds to prevent close in-breeding. Rings for the smaller species can be obtained from ring-makers who advertise in the fancy press. Split rings, of various colours and numbered if required, can be fitted at a very early age, at about six days, or later in some species. The ring is passed over two toes and the third and fourth toes are gently eased through the ring, using a matchstick pointed by burning.

If large parrots are close-ringed, special steel bands must be used, such as those made in Switzerland closed by means of a pin. There is also the risk, with all parrots, of the ring catching on a piece of wire or welded mesh in the aviary. Unfortunately, many birds have lost a leg or died as a result of an injury received due to the presence of a ring. A ring (band) is not permanent proof of identification as it can be removed and certainly would be if the bird was stolen. A method in its infancy is tattooing an identification

mark under the wing; in the future this method could well gain in popularity.

If it is necessary to distinguished the members of a pair, a mark can be painted on the bill of one.

Young birds mature quickly and, if left with their parents, may be indistinguishable within a few months. If it is intended to leave the young in the aviary for some while, and the species is one which loses its signs of immaturity at an early age, a distinguishing mark of some kind must be made early on. One breeder of Nanday Conures, in which the young quickly assume the appearance of the adults, made sure he could distinguish the young by cutting an inch or so off their tail feathers.

Specialisation

Because shortage of aviary space is a perennial problem of most breeders, they may be tempted to part with all of their young. This so often results in months spent searching for a suitable replacement when one of a breeding pair dies. With the rarer species, every effort should be made to retain the young, initially at least, even if it means having to dispose of more common species.

The breeder who specialises has a number of advantages over those who keep just one pair of many species. Only those who specialise are likely to make a lasting contribution to aviculture and most breeders are guilty of keeping far too many species. If they had the wisdom to specialise, their breeding results would improve for several reasons: unrelated young are available to pair together if more than one breeding pair is kept; foster parents of the same species are more likely to be available; when more than one pair is producing young, the standard of the species is more easily upgraded, the choice of young to retain being larger; a deep knowledge of one species is more valuable in that it is more likely to lead to breeding successes than a superficial knowledge of several species.

Sustained captive breeding of the rarer parrots is only likely to be successful by those who keep several pairs. There is too much that can go wrong and less chance of obtaining true pairs if fewer than three pairs are obtained to start with. It is almost impossible to build up an aviary-bred strain of any species using fewer than this.

Indiscriminate 'collecting' of species is a fault of many aviculturists. Those who aim to make a worthwhile contribution to aviculture will eventually either concentrate on several species with which they do well or choose the members of one or perhaps two closely related genera. The aim of most breeders is just to enjoy their hobby but how much more satisfying is it if they can gain valuable experience in the process; they can make their knowledge available to other aviculturists by publishing it in one of the journals pertaining to the subject.

There are other ways in which breeders can make a small contribution to science. Many of the larger museums welcome discarded eggs or bodies of chicks or adult birds which have died. Veterinary surgeons who specialise in avian problems could benefit from more material for autopsy.

Breeders are urged to maintain records however modest their activities may be. These will be invaluable for tracing back lineage, to avoid pairing closely related birds together and to record laying and hatching dates along with details of development. They will result after a few years in a source of much valuable information. The practice of using numbered closed rings on all chicks will be a valuable aid to record keeping. Details relating to often-bred species can be more difficult to obtain than those relating to rarely bred birds for which informative breeding accounts are usually published. In many instances, published information on commonly bred birds is sadly lacking even in basic details.

Artificial Incubation

Artificial incubation of the eggs of parrots and other birds has become increasingly common during the past few years. Sometimes the whole clutch is taken to induce the female to lay again or, where no foster-parent is available, to save eggs of a sick female or one which has died: artificial incubation may also be employed because eggs have been deserted.

Many aviculturists have realised the benefit of an incubator for emergency use. If only one or two chicks are saved each year, this will in many cases recover the cost of the incubator and more. Economics aside, it is more important that, with the rarely bred species, no egg or chick is lost which could have been saved. Every means possible must be employed to improve breeding results.

A suitable incubator to commence with is a small model, such as the Marsh Farm's Turn-X or Roll-X. It must be realised, however, that all incubators are manufactured with poultry in mind. Because the eggs of poultry have been incubator-hatched for many generations, they have a greater tolerance of fluctuating conditions than those of exotic birds. Nevertheless, consistently good results can be obtained if careful attention is paid to detail, particularly the following points:

1. Thermometers. Two should be used as a safeguard against a faulty model. They should have increments of 1°F. It is impossible to obtain accuracy with a thermometer showing increments of 2°F. The thermometer bulb should be placed in close proximity to the eggs; if necessary drill a hole in the side or top of the incubator to allow this. Note that, in incubators where the thermometer is mounted behind a glass window, it may register a temperature which is different to the temperature of the air surrounding the eggs.

2. Incubation temperature. Temperatures between 36.9° and 37.5°C (98.5° and 99.5°F) are generally used for parrot eggs in forced air incubators. For most species not enough work has been done to determine the optimum temperature. A number of factors affect this, such as egg size, shell thickness, environment and clutch size. How much variation in temperature can occur before hatching is significantly affected is not known for parrot eggs but it is imperative that the temperature is constant throughout the incubation period. The temperature should be checked daily as it can be affected by environment (the incubator is best placed in a room where the temperature varies as little as possible)

and by other factors; for example, if a clutch of unincubated eggs was placed with an egg which had been incubated for some while, they could cause the temperature within the incubator to drop. Eggs should be warmed to room temperature before being placed inside the incubator. (They may be placed inside a brooder for several hours.)

3. Humidity. Quite a lot has been written on the subject but the fact is that, for most species of parrots, the optimum humidity for eggs is not known. It is probably in the region of 50 per cent relative humidity (84 degrees dry bulb reading). Just prior to hatching, eggs require a much greater degree of humidity. They can either be transferred to another incubator or to a hatcher or, if all the eggs are due to hatch at the same time, the humidity within the incubator can be increased.

It is difficult to read the humidity gauge on some incubators. I use a combined hygrometer and thermometer (made by Casella, London) which measures only 7 cm (3½ in) in diameter, placed on the incubator grid. It is very easy to read.

4. Turning of eggs. Manual turning of eggs is not recommended because it is time-consuming, subject to human error (the task could be forgotten) and because the regular opening of the incubator allows heat to escape. Most incubators are equipped with an automatic turning device and a grid on which the eggs are placed. Unless the grid is the correct size an egg will not be turned. The standard ring in the Turn-X, for example, is too large for most parrot eggs, being made for Chicken and Pheasant eggs. The smaller size, for Quail eggs, should therefore be obtained.

5. Handling eggs during incubation. Some experienced breeders weigh eggs to ascertain that the correct weight loss is occurring and adjust the humidity accordingly if it is not. (An egg normally loses 16 per cent of its weight during incubation.) I doubt, however, that they achieve a hatch rate which is very much higher than the breeder who leaves the eggs alone for the duration of the incubation period. Generally it is not necessary to open the incubator to ascertain whether an egg is fertile. The beginner is advised not to handle eggs unnecessarily.

6

Hand-rearing

The greater part of this chapter is based on a paper read by the author at the First Ecological Conservation Foundation Symposium in Seattle in 1978.

Every season, every breeder of parrots is likely to lose some young in the nest; it would be very surprising if none were lost for there is so much that can go wrong. Aviculturists with the time and inclination can substantially increase the percentage of young reared to maturity by hand-rearing. This is, of course, not always successful but losses in hand-rearing are more often due to mechanical faults in incubators and faulty thermometers (and these will be rare), rather than to inherent difficulties in the actual rearing procedure. I refer to results of experienced aviculturists. Newcomers to hand-rearing are almost certain to experience some losses. Sometimes, for no apparent reason, a chick will prove more difficult to rear than others of its species but once a little experience has been gained, or even from the outset if common sense is applied, the percentage of young hand-reared will be much higher than the percentage reared by the parents.

Hand-rearing, until the 1970s, was usually resorted to only in an emergency. San Diego Zoo has undoubtedly done more than any other establishment to open the eyes of bird breeders to the potential of hand-rearing birds, especially parrots. As one example of what has been achieved there, between 1929 and 1960 one pair of Bare-eyed Cockatoos produced 63 young, all of which were hand-reared. A supreme example of the success of a private aviculturist in hand-rearing an endangered species of Amazon Parrot is that demonstrated by Ramon Noegel of Florida since 1974 with *Amazona leucocephala*. Few breeders can hope to emulate these successes but, on a smaller scale, they can make an extremely useful contribution to aviculture if they make the fullest use of their breeding pairs.

A major reason for removing chicks from the nest in a temperate climate, especially when birds insist on nesting in winter, is the fact that many parrots cease to brood their young during the day when they are two to three weeks old. This fact must be responsible for the death of more chicks in the nest than any other single reason, except possibly inadequate feeding. As it is totally predictable in most species, losses from this cause can be averted

by those prepared to hand-feed the chicks which should be removed before the critical period is reached.

There are a number of other reasons for taking chicks out of the nest, not least of which is the satisfaction gained from watching a chick mature. The tremendous insight into its development which follows is sufficient reason for attempting the experiment at least once. The knowledge gained cannot but help make the aviculturist more aware of the needs of his birds and their young.

It is now more important than ever that aviculturists should regard themselves as producers rather than consumers. Few collections make the best use of their breeding pairs, especially of those species which are difficult to breed or not easy to obtain.

Where hand-rearing can be undertaken, it is wasteful to allow a pair of parrots to spend up to half a year rearing a nest of young, even if they are successful, when removal of the clutch to an incubator or removal of the chicks will usually cause the pair to nest again.

A few species of parrots are continuous nesters: when one brood is reared the female will lay again, regardless of the time of the year. Eclectus Parrots are an excellent example of this category: the young spend about 11 weeks in the nest and the clutch consists of only two eggs; two nests of two young is the maximum that a pair could rear in a year. However, if the young are removed at a week old, as many as five nests of two could be reared, including two young reared by the parents.

If successful in hand-rearing, the breeder must keep a sense of proportion and should allow the female to attempt to rear her young to fledging on occasions. The removal of her eggs or chicks constitutes a considerable physiological shock and, especially to the larger or more intelligent parrots, a severe emotional shock also.

An important reason for hand-rearing cockatoo chicks is that, when two hatch, the younger is often neglected and dies when only a few days old.

Hand-fed cockatoos are not subjected to two dangers which result in the death of many parent-reared birds. First, male cockatoos are likely to attack their sons. Young birds are most vulnerable between the time they leave the nest and when they become self-supporting. This also applies to some Australian parrakeets. Another hazard avoided by hand-feeding is feather plucking which can be the indirect cause of death of the young. This problem is very common in cockatoos and lories and is known in most parrots. An extremely important reason for hand-rearing is that the bird will suffer no stress at being in captivity. As birds in a state of stress are more prone to disease and are far less likely to breed, the significance of this is huge. And when hand-reared birds have young, fewer problems are likely to arise simply because such birds are not upset by the presence of people.

It should be mentioned here that the belief that hand-reared birds will not breed is sheer myth and has been disproved on countless occasions. Indeed, I know one breeder of the rarer Australian parrakeets who hand-rears young specifically to retain for breeding purposes because he finds such birds are steadier and therefore preferable to parent-reared ones. They are also preferred because unlike others of their kind they do not remain aloof towards him.

A hand-reared parrot which is subsequently kept in close association with man is a joyful, exuberant creature which has no fear of man or any other animal. As a pet it is, of course, extremely rewarding.

The final reason for hand-rearing is that, if correctly fed, the young will often be superior to those reared by their parents. This is especially true in the case of conservative feeders which refuse the nutritious extras essential for the rearing of healthy young of some species. Often one can compare the young from the same pair and find those which are hand-reared bigger, bolder and with brighter plumage than those which are parent-reared.

A heated cage measuring 46 × 31 cm (18 × 12 in) × 41 cm (16 in) high allows ample room for small species to run about as they develop. The size would need to be increased for large birds such as macaws. A simple wooden structure with the front made of Perspex provides hours of fascinating viewing. Two 60W light bulbs can be used to heat it and these are controlled by a thermostat. The bulbs are placed in the roof.

Young chicks of small species can be kept in an incubator for a few days but care must be exercised with certain types of small, inexpensive incubator to see that chicks do not climb into the wiring.

Where no electrical equipment is available, young birds can be placed in an open-topped box in a warm airing cupboard, in a box over which an electric light bulb is suspended, or in a box with a hot water bottle covered with a cloth. A polystyrene box is most suitable because of its heat-retaining properties. Alternatively, a cardboard box can be lined with polystyrene tiles.

Until chicks are feathered, a temperature of 32–33°C (90–92°F) is essential. In my experience chicks show signs of discomfort if the temperature rises above 35°C (95°F); they lie down, pant and call restlessly and they seem almost as uncomfortable if the temperature falls below 29°C (85°F) before they are feathered. However, reaction to a high temperature seems to be very much a matter of individual tolerance. Two British aviculturists who have hand-reared Hawk-headed Parrots both kept the chicks, when young, in a temperature of 38°C (99–100°F). Harry Sissen told me that, on one occasion, when the chicks were a few days old, he reduced the temperature to 35°C (95°F); the result was that the chicks appeared so lethargic he increased the heat to the previous temperature. What is important is to find the temperature which suits individual chicks.

If they are not warm enough they will not feed with any enthusiasm; if the temperature is far too cool, digestion will not occur and the chicks will die or their growth rate will be affected.

As the feathers break through, the temperature can be gradually reduced. By the time the chick is weaned the temperature should be the equivalent to that of the room in which it is kept.

An accurate thermometer is of the utmost importance. A friend once lost two macaw chicks when the temperature rose too high. He then placed three thermometers in the incubator and, to his dismay, each one gave a different reading. As a precaution, two thermometers can be used in each incubator or brooder.

I place very young chicks on a bed of paper towelling in a small cardboard box inside the heated cage. The paper is changed at each feed. An extra piece of paper can be tucked into each side of the box, or some sawdust placed there, so that the chick is in a hollow and able to support itself on its legs: a smooth surface could cause splayed legs. When removed for feeding, the chick should be placed on a surface which offers a good grip, such as a towel.

The cardboard box can be discarded when the chick is old enough to move about. The bottom of the heated cage is then lined with newspaper and a layer of wood shavings is placed on top. Shavings have the advantage of keeping the chick's feet cleaner, they will need changing less frequently than newspaper and have greater absorbency.

A container of water, with the top protected or holes punched in the lid, supplies the correct humidity. It also provides an object against which single chicks like to huddle and will therefore be of some psychological value.

While being fed, very young chicks which have little or no down must be kept warm as the room temperature could be 11°C (20°F) below the brooder temperature. Also the feeder's hand could feel very cold to the chick and, for this reason, I wrap young chicks in a paper handkerchief while they are being fed.

It is important that whatever implement is used for feeding is warmed first. One breeder found that chicks would take cold food from a warm syringe but not warm food from a cold syringe. Where spoon-feeding is carried out, the spoon should be used to stir the food when it is heated. Unless the spoon is warm throughout the feeding period the food may be refused. The temperature of food and spoon should be tested by sampling. Where more than one chick is being fed, the food must be kept warm during feeding. One way is to place it in a small fireproof dish which fits into the top of a half-pint fireproof jug containing very hot water. The water has a dual purpose for it can be added to the food if it is too thick. If a large number of chicks is to be fed, a micro-wave oven will prove invaluable for heating the food. This idea was suggested to me by Pat and Don Mathews of Allison Park, Pennsylvania; they heat a 124 g (about 4½ oz) baby food jar full of food for one minute at a medium setting and can then feed up to 20 Cockatiels and other parrots at one feed.

It is advisable to give the very first feed after removal from the nest when the chick's crop is empty. Very young chicks should be fed every two hours during the day; observation of the crop content will reveal how often to feed a chick and how much food to give it. Feeds should be given shortly after the crop is empty, except during the night. As they grow, some chicks will need to be fed only every three or four hours.

Young chicks rarely cease to beg for food even though the crop is bulging, so care must be taken not to over-feed. While feeding a chick, the feeder must watch the chick's crop as this is the only way to determine when enough food has been given.

On the day following removal of a young chick from the nest, I give a feed at 3 a.m. The 3 a.m. feed, gradually delayed until 6 a.m., is offered to chicks of very small species up to the age of 10 or 12 days. Otherwise the chick is not fed between 11 p.m. and 6 a.m. and, under normal circumstances, the crop will be empty well before the first feed. If it is not, one knows that all is not well and that some means of emptying the crop must be tried as described below.

Food should be mixed daily and any surplus discarded after 24 hours.

After each feed, the chick's beak and, if necessary, the plumage should be wiped. Cotton swabs should be moistened with warm water to wipe out the mouth and lower mandible of large parrots after each feed, removing excess food from under the tongue. It may also prove necessary to clean the feet with damp cotton wool to remove excreta which has hardened. This should first be soaked with water to prevent a nail being removed with the hardened matter.

The actual process of removing the chick from the nest can be difficult in the case of some of the larger parrots, because the female so rarely leaves the nest and is so quick to return when she does. The problem can be overcome by situating the nest-box on the outside of the aviary and dropping a piece of tin over the entrance as soon as the female vacates the nest, if necessary attaching string to the tin and operating it from a distance. This device is also useful in the case of aggressive parrots which will attack anyone who enters their aviary while they have young.

If a chick is removed from the nest due to an emergency, one has to do the best one can whatever its age, but for planned hand-rearing, the best age for removal is usually between five and ten days, when the chick's eyes are still closed.

It is possible to incubate the egg artificially and to rear the chick from the egg. In this case, on the first day, the young bird should be fed food of a very liquid consistency. Some breeders use an eye-dropper for the first day but I have never used anything but a spoon.

At the outset one has to decide whether a syringe or a spoon is to be used for feeding. Those who have experience of both methods almost invariably use a spoon because it can cause no possible harm to a chick; also, this method is more natural because the chick feeds from the spoon almost as it would take food from its parent's mandible. Sudden death of syringe-fed chicks can occur probably caused by food entering the windpipe. Symptoms displayed in such cases are loss of colour and extending the wings as though hot, sometimes accompanied by cries of pain. Death is usually rapid. It is true, nevertheless, that probably more breeders use a syringe than a spoon, partly because it is a quicker method.

The only occasion on which syringe or eye-dropper feeding may be necessary is in the case of a chick which is in an extremely weak condition, although I have had success in spoon-feeding chicks which, on removal from the nest, were so weak they could scarcely hold up their heads. Warmth and food resulted in a very rapid improvement in their condition. However, a syringe will be necessary initially to force-feed feathered chicks which have been abandoned and are old enough to reject spoon-feeding due to fear.

Some breeders go to unnecessary lengths to prepare foods, grinding up canary and millet seed after removing the husks. There are many excellent cereal preparations for feeding human babies which are based on ground vegetable grains and which are further supplemented with minerals, protein and vitamins. These foods are compounded to give a complete diet and may be fed to young chicks after being mixed with water. Many Australian parrakeets and other parrots are reared only on baby cereal but this food does not suit all species and, in any case, most parrots will do better on a more varied diet when they are a few weeks old. Manufacturers of dried and tinned foods will be happy to provide an analysis of their products so that their suitability for various species can be judged.

At San Diego Zoo, the food used for hand-rearing parrots consists of wheat heart cereal, Gevral Protein, trout chow, shelled sunflower seeds, finely chopped lettuce, corn syrup, fresh egg yolks, plus small amounts of Vionate vitamin powder, iodized salt, L-cystine and calcium lactate.

A blender can be used to make a fine meal from sunflower seed and peanuts which have been hulled and washed in water. For rearing Amazons and macaws, a smooth mixture of sunflower and peanuts blended with water, raw pumpkin seed, raw wheatgerm, soya bean flour, calcium powder and wheatgerm oil has proved very successful for Ramon Noegel. Soya bean flour has a very high protein content and can even be used to replace milk. A drop of a liquid vitamin/mineral preparation is added to the food once daily.

Whatever formula is used – and hardly any two aviculturists will employ the same one – it is essential to include calcium for the larger parrots to prevent rickets. The fine powder produced from scraping cuttlefish bone is a convenient form to use. Alternatively, calcium lactate tablets can be crushed using a rolling pin.

Other items which can be used in the diet include soya flour (high in protein), turkey crumbs, Canary rearing food and fresh fruits and vegetables, such as carrot, spinach, apple and banana which have been processed in a blender.

Ramon Noegel uses mashed ripe banana or apple for at least one third of each feed as he has found that this prevents food remaining in the crop. The latter can be a major problem and is one of the most common causes of death in hand-fed chicks. It is for this reason that it is extremely important to check the condition of a chick's crop before each feed. If food remains after a period of time when the crop would normally be empty, no more food should be given and immediate action must be taken. The first step is to mix hot water with molasses (obtainable from health food shops) and to give a few drops, if necessary massaging the crop to break up the solid mass. Alternatively, the crop can be emptied by means of a length of soft tubing through which the crop contents are sucked up. This will probably be more traumatic for the breeder than the chick. Unless the crop can be emptied by some means, however, the chick will die.

Food is less likely to remain in the crop if it is of a runny consistency. The food which a newly hatched chick receives from its mother is of a very thin consistency. As the chick matures, thicker food is given. In this respect we should copy nature. If in doubt regarding the correct consistency, it is better to add too much water. This means only that the food will pass through the crop more quickly and that more frequent feeds will be necessary.

Cleanliness is of the utmost importance in hand-rearing. The chick itself must be kept spotlessly clean, also all the equipment involved in its rearing, from the spoon or syringe to the brooder or cage. Infectious diseases can spread with ease and rapidity among chicks. At the first sign of any illness, a chick should be isolated and its food and feeding utensils kept separate. Veterinary assistance should be sought. It is important to act quickly because veterinary treatment usually includes sensitivity tests, the results of which take several days to obtain.

Perhaps the most common problem with chicks is candidiasis. The mouth of every chick should be examined daily. If white spots or lesions become apparent, veterinary help should be sought at once. Candidiasis can also affect the crop, causing vomiting. There are a number of excellent antibiotics available which are safe to use on chicks: specific ones to cure candidiasis, for example, and broad spectrum antibiotics, such as Clamoxyl, which I have found to be safe and effective.

Never hesitate to consult a veterinary surgeon if a chick is ill. Although most will not have experience of treating parrot chicks, they can use laboratory facilities to isolate the cause of its illness and to prescribe the appropriate treatment. Many chicks die because professional expertise is not used.

It should also be borne in mind that the more veterinary surgeons who are involved in work of this kind, the greater will be the knowledge and interest of the veterinary profession.

When feeding a number of chicks with success, it is easy to become blasé about the process and to miss the signs of impending problems. The main indications that a chick is thriving must never be overlooked. They are as follows:

1. Emptying of the crop at normal intervals. The first thing to do on picking up a chick is to look at its crop. If it contains food when normally it would be empty, do not feed the chick. Check the temperature in the brooder and note whether the chick feels warm. Failure to digest food could be caused by a low temperature but is usually a sign of a problem which is less easily rectified. If a chick's crop has not emptied overnight immediate action must be taken. If the food remains from the feed given two to three hours previously, observe the chick closely. Place it in a separate container with a clean lining so that it is possible to ascertain if food is passing through it.

2. Skin colour. Note any abnormality. If this has changed significantly and the chick appears lethargic it may be too late to do anything. If the skin colour is normal and the chick is active, there is less cause for concern. In most species the normal skin colour is reddish pink.

3. Weight gains. Chicks should be weighed at regular intervals, preferably daily or every other day. Information gained from rearing other chicks of the same species and/or the pattern of growth for the individual chick will provide an early warning system if the chick is not thriving. Chicks generally cease to gain weight a little while before they leave the nest.

4. Feeding response. If a chick does not respond to the spoon or syringe in its usual manner, it is either dying or cold.

Chicks which die should not be discarded. If a post mortem examination can be carried out by a reliable source, valuable knowledge may be gained that could prevent further losses. Dead chicks in good condition will be welcomed by some museums, especially the Bird Section of the British Museum (Natural History), Tring, Hert-

Grey Parrots, aged ten weeks, hand-reared from the day of hatching.

fordshire. They should be packed in a crush-proof container and sent without delay, or kept in a refrigerator until dispatch is possible. No chick of any but the most common species need have lived in vain. It can contribute to scientific knowledge in some way.

The most difficult part of rearing chicks is usually weaning. This should start not later than a week before the chick would have left the nest had it been left with its parents, or as soon as it shows reluctance to take food from the spoon or syringe. Lory chicks, however, will start to feed themselves several weeks before weaning would occur naturally. If the chick has been weighed daily, it will be noticeable that weight loss starts to occur at about this time and continues until just after the age at which it would have left the nest. Daily weighing is advisable because it will reveal at an early stage any abnormality in the growth rate.

If a chick proves difficult to feed, shaking its head when offered food and eating little, it is ready to be weaned and should be offered different foods. Seed-eating parrots should be introduced to hulled sunflower seed which has been soaked for at least 24 hours to make it easier to digest; the kernels can be chopped into pieces for small birds. This should be scattered on the floor of the brooder or cage a few days before the chick is thought old enough to start to eat on its own. It should also be offered soft fruits and vegetables such as corn-on-the-cob, apple, pear and banana.

The age at which chicks are weaned obviously varies according to how old the young of each species is on leaving the nest. In Australian parrakeets, this occurs when they are between five and six weeks old; thus hand-fed birds will start to pick up soaked sunflower seed when aged 30–40 days and will be completely independent at seven to eight weeks. Lories are the easiest birds to wean. If a dish of nectar is placed on the floor of the cage they will usually drink with little hesitation; some will sample soft banana or pear. When chicks are feeding well from a dish they need be fed only early in the morning and late at night. To complete the transition, only an evening feed is given and finally this is dispensed with.

No one should lightly undertake the task of feeding the large black *Calyptorhynchus* cockatoos which can take up to ten months to become fully independent. The white cockatoos spend up to three months in the nest if left with their parents and if hand-fed may make no attempt to feed themselves before about 11 or 12 weeks old. On the other hand they may attempt to eat seed and other items when only two months old.

If the death of one or both parents, or some other reason, makes it necessary to remove a fully feathered youngster, difficulty could be experienced at first in feeding the chick because it will react with fear to human beings. However, at that age chicks are very adaptable and soon adjust to their new circumstances. A Dusky Lory which I had to remove from the nest at nine weeks because it had a fungus infection was completely tame within three days, as was a Goffin's Cockatoo, taken out of the nest at ten weeks because the parents stopped feeding it.

Where it is possible to handle chicks in the nest almost daily and to pick them up and talk to them, no problems should arise if they are removed shortly before they would have left the nest. However, this is possible only when the parents are tame enough not to resent human interference. Attempting to handle chicks whose parents are not tame or tolerant could result in the chicks being killed or mutilated.

If more than one species is to be hand-reared at the same time, it is worth bearing in mind that some species behave aggressively towards others. A friend who was hand-rearing four *Pyrrhura* conures of a rare species found it necessary to remove from the nest a Red-capped Parrot (*Pionopsitta*) aged 12 days, a species of slightly larger body size than the conures. The latter are well-known for their spiteful tendencies but the breeder did not expect these to become evident at the early age of five weeks. He was horrified to find that they had turned on the Red-capped Parrot and injured it so badly that it subsequently died.

If, through necessity, a single nestling which is to be used for breeding is hand-reared, it is vitally important to introduce it to others of its own kind as soon as it is independent. I hasten to add that these should not be its parents who would regard it as an intruder. If required for breeding, it must not be allowed to become too dependent on the person who reared it or too used to human company. The temptation to make a pet of it must be resisted. Its dependency must be cut off gradually yet fairly rapidly because the longer it remains with people the more it will identify with them.

One point which should be borne in mind when rearing chicks is the tremendous variation in the reaction of individuals of the same species. One should therefore rely less on a pattern of behaviour than on one's own common sense and observation. A lament from one breeder who was hand-rearing for the first time was that books don't tell you how often a chick should be fed. Ultimately this factor and others must be governed by the requirements of the individual chick.

7

Mutations

Mutations in some species of parrot have become so numerous that a knowledge of genetics will be useful and even essential to some breeders. New Cockatiel and Lovebird mutations arise frequently and the mutations of Ringneck and other *Psittacula* parrakeets are being reared in larger numbers than ever before. Sooner or later a mutation, perhaps a White Cockatiel or a Blue Lovebird, will find its place in most collections and to pair it sensibly a basic knowledge of genetics is necessary.

Unless colour breeding is the main aim, a few basic rules are all that need be learned and, to those who have bred Budgerigars, these will be familiar.

There are three basic types of mutation: dominant, autosomal recessive and sex-linked. The only dominant mutations found in parrots so far are in Lovebirds and Budgerigars, also the Grey mutation of the Ringneck Parrakeet and possibly the Silver Cockatiel. All that needs to be determined in respect of most mutations therefore is whether they are autosomal recessive or sex-linked. As a general rule, mutations in which the eye colour is changed are sex-linked, and this occurs in Lutino, Albino and Cinnamon mutations. There are exceptions: of the many known Lutino mutations those in the Nyasa Lovebird and Elegant Grass Parrakeet are not sex-linked but autosomal recessive.

If a bird of a dominant mutation is paired to a recessive mutation, the young produced will be of the dominant mutation or variety, but are said to be split for the recessive colour, that is, under certain circumstances they have the ability to produce young of the recessive colour. This will not be apparent from their visual make up and one has to refer to tables of theoretical expectations when pairing these birds.

A male Cockatiel of Normal appearance, for example, has the ability to pass on the gene for Albino (in the Cockatiel known also as White or Lutino): it is thus described as Normal/Albino (Normal split for Albino). This applies only to males, for no female of any species can be split for a sex-linked colour. A female can be split for an autosomal recessive colour, however.

Sex-linked Mutations

In any sex-linked mutation, there can be sex-linked males (e.g. Albino Cockatiel), Normal/sex-linked males (e.g. Normal/Albino Cockatiel) and sex-linked females (e.g. Albino Cockatiel).

It should be borne in mind that the expectations from various matings given in this chapter are theoretical ones and apply over a large number of results, with more uneven results being likely in a single nest or over a small number of pairings.

In the matings using a sex-linked mutation given below, the White Cockatiel is used as an example but the same results will apply with any sex-linked variety in any species.
1. Sex-linked male × Normal female (Lutino male Cockatiel × Normal female Cockatiel) = 50% Normal/sex-linked males (50% Normal/Lutino) *and* 50% sex-linked females (50% Lutino).
2. Normal/sex-linked male × sex-linked female (Normal/Albino male × Albino female) = 25% sex-linked and 25% Normal/sex-linked males (25% Albino and 25% Normal/Albino) *and* 25% sex-linked and 25% Normal females (25% Albino and 25% Normal).
3. Normal male × sex-linked female = 50% Normal/sex-linked males *and* 50% Normal females.
4. Normal/sex-linked male × Normal female = 25% Normal/sex-linked and 25% Normal males *and* 25% sex-linked and 25% Normal females.
5. Sex-linked male × Sex-linked female = 50% sex-linked males *and* 50% sex-linked females.
6. When two different sex-linked mutations are paired together the following results (using Albino and Cinnamon as examples – but any two sex-linked mutations can be substituted) are obtained: Albino male × Cinnamon female = 50% Normal/Albino/Cinnamon/White-faced males *and* 50% Lutino/White-faced females.
7. (In Ringneck Parrakeets, for example, which have Albino and Lutino mutations, the following could be paired but with little point, for the Albino would be 'wasted'.) Lutino male × Albino female = 50% Lutino/Blue males *and* 50% Lutino/Blue females.
8. Lutino/Blue male × Albino

Lutino Ringnecks aged 5 weeks.

female = 25% Lutino/Blue and 25% Albino males *and* 25% Lutino/Blue and 25% Albino females.

The following pairings show what happens when, using the Ringneck Parrakeet as an example, an autosomal recessive mutation is paired to a sex-linked one.

1. Lutino male Ringneck × Blue female Ringneck = 50% Normal/Lutino/Blue males *and* 50% Lutino/Blue females.

2. Blue male × Lutino female = 50% Normal/Blue/Lutino males *and* 50% Normal/Blue females.

3. Normal/Blue/Lutino male × Blue female = 12½% Normal/Blue, 12½% Normal/Blue/Lutino, 12½% Blue and 12½% Blue/Albino males *and* 12½% Normal/Blue, 12½% Lutino/Blue, 12½% Blue and 12½% Albino females. (The problem with this pairing is that the Blue males would have to be test-mated to discover which were split for Albino.)

4. Normal/Lutino/Blue male × Lutino/Blue female = 6¼% Normal/Lutino, 12½% Normal/Lutino/Blue, 6¼% Lutino, 12½% Lutino/Blue, 6¼% Blue/Albino and 6¼% Albino males *and* 6¼% Normal, 12½% Normal/Blue, 6¼% Lutino, 12½% Lutino/Blue, 6¼% Blue and 6¼% Albino females.

5. Normal/Blue/Lutino male × Normal/Blue female = 12½% Normal/Blue, 12½% Normal/Blue/Lutino, 6¼% Normal, 6¼% Normal/Lutino, 6¼% Blue and 6¼% Blue/Lutino males *and* 12½% Normal/Blue, 12½ Lutino/Blue, 6¼% Normal, 6¼% Lutino, 6¼% Blue and 6¼% Albino females.

6. Blue/Lutino male × Lutino/Blue female = 12½% Normal/Blue/Lutino, 12½% Lutino/Blue, 12½% Blue/Lutino and 12½% Albino males *and* 12½% Normal/Blue, 12½% Lutino/Blue, 12½% Blue and 12½% Albino females.

7. Blue male × Lutino/Blue female = 25% Normal/Blue/Lutino and 25% Blue/Lutino males *and* 25% Normal/Blue and 25% Blue females.

8. Blue/Lutino male × Lutino female = 25% Normal/Blue/Lutino and 25% Lutino/Blue males *and* 25% Normal/Blue and 25% Lutino/Blue females. (This is a good pairing

because the genetical make-up of the young is known without test matings.)
9. Lutino/Blue male × Lutino/Blue female = 12½% Lutino, 25% Lutino/Blue and 12½% Albino males *and* 12½% Lutino, 25% Lutino/Blue and 12½% Albino females. (This is not such a useful mating because all the Lutinos would have to be test-mated to discover which were split for Blue.)
10. Blue male × Albino female = Blue/Albino males *and* Blue females.

How Mutations Occur

Some colours are the result of mutations which prevent the production of a certain pigment; thus, in a bird which is normally green, such as the Ringneck Parrakeet, inability to produce yellow pigment results in a bird which is blue, the shade of blue depending on the shade of green of that species. In the Blue Ringneck Parrakeet, for example, this mutation is an especially pleasing shade of powder blue because the normal Ringneck is a soft green. Similar mutations are well known in the Budgerigar, Fischer's Lovebird and Masked Lovebird, and it has also been established in the Quaker Parrakeet.

Blue mutations of this type are autosomal recessive in their manner of inheritance.

When a mutation occurs in a green bird which prevents it from producing melanin the result is a Lutino, an all-yellow bird with pink or red eyes. Melanin is a pigment which takes the form of black oval granules in the feather barb. The granules absorb light and prevent it from being reflected. Thus a bird with an excess of melanin in its feathers appears black, and one which lacks melanin totally is either Albino (pure white) or Lutino.

When a mutation occurs which causes the melanin granules to be reduced in size, only partial light reflection occurs and the result in a bird which is normally green is an insipid shade of greenish yellow. If it has blue in its plumage, this colour becomes very pale blue and any other colours are reduced in intensity. Examples are the Yellow Masked and Yellow Fischer's Lovebirds which would more accurately be called Dilutes. These mutations are given the name of Par-Yellow by George Smith (1979). They

are autosomal recessives in their manner of inheritance.

In a corresponding blue mutation (Par-Blue) the shade of blue is greenish blue, or sea-green. An example is the Blue Peach-faced Lovebird, which would be more accurately named Dilute Blue to prevent confusion when a true blue mutation occurs.

Pied birds occur when scattered areas of the epidermis are unable to produce melanin. Birds which are normally green will be pied with areas of yellow and those which are normally blue will be marked with areas of white.

Due to a defect in the feather barb, less blue light than normal is reflected from a feather, resulting in an olive-green mutation, of a dull dark green. It is dominant in its manner of inheritance. Examples are found in the Budgerigar and in various Lovebirds.

Autosomal Recessive Mutations

The manner of inheritance of autosomal recessive mutations is different from that of sex-linked mutations. And as already mentioned, it is possible for a female to be split for a recessive mutation. The most common recessive mutation is the Blue which will be used in the examples below, but any recessive mutation paired to a normal will produce the same results. It should be noted that the results are the same regardless of the sex used, that is, Green male × Blue female produces the same results as Blue male × Green female.
1. Blue × Normal = 100% Normal/Blue.
2. Normal/Blue × Normal = 50% Normal and 50% Normal/Blue.
3. Normal/Blue × Normal/Blue = 50% Normal/Blue, 25% Blue and 25% Normal.
4. Normal/Blue × Blue = 50% Normal/Blue and 50% Blue.
5. Blue × Blue = 100% Blue.

Acquired Colours

A bird's plumage colouration can change as a result of a dietary deficiency or an alteration in the bird's metabolism. The most common change is the acquisition of areas of yellow feathers in a green bird or of white

feathers in one which is blue or black. Parrakeets and Amazon Parrots which are pied with yellow are not uncommon. It is, in almost all cases, useless to retain such birds for breeding in the hope of founding a pied mutation; often the colouration reverts to normal after a moult. A common cause is a deficiency of the amino acid lysine.

Where an alteration occurs in a bird's metabolism the result can be dramatic and beautiful. An interesting example is that of a Moustache Parrakeet which, after five years, moulted to become a Lutino; even the eye colour changed. P. Done of Ellesmere Port described what happened: 'At the beginning of the moult, I noticed that each moulted feather was replaced by a yellow one. The lilac feathers are now pinky orange and the moustache has slowly disappeared. It has taken him longer than usual to moult' (Done, pers. comm. 1973).

A coloured photograph showed the bird at the beginning of the moult when it was almost normal except for yellow secondaries and yellow feathers on the shoulders. In the second photograph it was depicted as almost pure Lutino, except for the blue crown and green nape feathers. A few black feathers remained on the 'moustache'. Eventually these, too, were lost and the bird was pure yellow except for a few green feathers on the head. The pupil of the eye became reddish brown.

'Forced' Colours

Certain native people have long been aware of methods of changing the colouration of a bird's plumage. One method is to take it from the nest when very young and to hand-feed it, including fish oil in the diet. In Colombia, in the Amazon area, I saw a Festive Amazon Parrot which had been fed in this way, resulting in large areas of red in its plumage. It was over a year old and its owner told me that the areas of red had increased at the first moult. Through an interpreter, I spoke to the Ticuna Indian woman who had reared it. She said that it was necessary to give the fish oil only once or twice while the chick was being reared but, to be certain of its effectiveness, to give it two or three times.

Natives carry out this practice in

order to increase the value of the hand-reared birds, for the result is a more colourful and beautiful bird.

Presumably certain types of fish oil are more effective than others – but it may be that all are likely to have some effect. In 1978, I saw a Hawk-headed Parrot which had been hand-reared by Ramon Noegel in Florida which had some almost totally red tail feathers. It may be significant that, while being hand-fed, cod liver oil was regularly included in its diet.

Amazon Indians have another method of altering plumage colouration, according to Wallace (1972):

> They pluck out those feathers they wish to paint, and in the fresh wound inoculate with the milky secretion from the skin of a small frog or toad. When the feathers grow again they are of a brilliant yellow or orange colour, without any mixture of blue or green, as in the natural state of the bird; and on the new plumage being plucked out, it is said always to come of the same colour without any fresh operation.

Breeding Mutations

Before taking up the breeding of a mutation, the aviculturist should consider whether he has the necessary aviary space. When breeding mutations, it is often necessary or desirable to retain whole nests of young, partly because in some cases only test-mating will reveal which birds are split for a certain colour and partly because one needs to be selective and to breed only from the best coloured birds. Their colour cannot be assessed until after they have moulted into adult plumage. With a rare mutation, it will often be advisable to retain every bird bred from a certain pair.

For this reason, with the possible exception of Cockatiels (in which some mutations are well established and which can be kept and bred on the colony system), it will be advisable to specialise in one mutation or perhaps in two 'compatible' mutations, such as Lutino and Blue in the Ringneck Parrakeet. These two mutations can be paired together and the resulting young used to breed Lutinos and Blues, and indeed the splits used to breed Albinos, whereas if for example only Blue and Isabelle Ringnecks were kept, the two strains would have to be kept separate as no useful purpose would be served by pairing them together.

Building up a strain of one of the rarer mutations can be a long process, fraught with disappointments, and should be undertaken only by those with the necessary enthusiasm and staying power. Breeders of the rarer mutations should carefully select the breeders to whom they sell their surplus stock for, in inexperienced hands, a mutation can easily be lost or spoiled.

Where possible, the breeder should be highly selective in the birds he retains, keeping only the strongest and the best coloured for breeding purposes. Debility or a hereditary fault (such as poor eyesight in pink-eyed or red-eyed birds) could so easily be bred into a mutation if care is not taken initially. With rare mutations, inbreeding is often inevitable and this will fix undesirable characteristics just as surely as it will fix the desirable ones.

Ringing of birds is essential for identification purposes. Split rings, that is, rings that are not closed and can be put on a bird at any age, will suffice for many species – but not for Lovebirds which are able to remove rings. Closed rings can be put on a chick only when it is a few days old and can be removed only by cutting, whereas a split ring can be removed easily. Careful records should be kept from the outset and these will prove invaluable in later years.

8
Parrots as Pets

It cannot be too strongly emphasised that anyone considering owning a parrot must be capable of giving a good deal of time and affection to it. A tame parrot is a great responsibility: it simply does not fall into the same category as a tortoise or a goldfish, or even some cats, and its requirements can be as time-consuming to fulfil as those of a dog. It should also be borne in mind that parrots are very long-lived and will be more permanent residents of the family than children.

A young bird in captivity which is tamed and becomes part of the family will gain all the companionship it needs but few adult birds will ever lose their fear and only in a large aviary will they be able to a lead a life free from stress. Thus it is essential that a parrot which is kept as a pet is either young or tame.

Parrots are extremely sociable and in the wild would spend their entire adult lives with their mate or as part of a flock. It is needlessly cruel and can indeed prove fatal to confine them closely and to deny them company and amusement.

More than a little thought needs to be given to how the parrot can be kept contented. Most parrots, particularly the larger birds, have a very strong need to gnaw and if this is not possible they will resort to removing their own feathers out of boredom. Plucking can, of course, be caused by other, notably psychological, factors. It is notoriously difficult to cure except in the very early stages and prevention should be the aim. Many sympathetic owners leave a radio on in their absence; this is an excellent idea, especially when parrots have to be left during the day while their owners are at work. Because of the damage parrots can cause, and the hazards they could meet, it is seldom practicable to leave a bird out of its cage while the house is empty, although there are some which will sit for hours on the top of their cage and never make any attempt to leave it. Such birds will usually flap their wings vigorously from time to time and the exercise they gain in this way is almost equal to that of flight.

All the larger parrots will occupy themselves for long periods if adequately supplied with wood, twigs or pieces of branches. Smaller species can be given various toys, such as mirrors, bells, balls, cotton reels and nuts. Some parrots, especially conures and lories, are very playful and love to lie on their back in play, juggling with a nut or grape. And larger birds, especially females, like to scratch on the cage floor; for this reason the removal of the wire grid above the tray which is found in some parrot cages is advisable.

It is thoughtless and unkind to confine a parrot permanently to a cage, although it will need one as a place to retire to, and it is a simple matter for someone who is even moderately skilled to construct a cage which is far more suitable and spacious than those commercially manufactured, and which will cost very much less. The materials required are simply heavy gauge 25 mm (1 in) welded mesh and either a metal base, which can be constructed by a local metal-working company, or a wooden base. The frame is made by simply wiring sections of mesh together and it can then be stood in the base. Newspaper used on the cage floor is renewed daily and once a week the cage can be lifted off the frame, if necessary with the birds still inside, for a more thorough cleaning. Alternatively, the cage floor can be made of welded mesh, below which is the floor proper, made from wood or metal. The space between should be generous, so that a brush can be used to clear out the seed and droppings.

Such cages are invaluable for the large macaws and cockatoos; in fact they have advantages for nearly all parrots. Using this method, anyone could afford to house a pet Amazon Parrot, for example, in a 1.2 m (4 ft) cage – an impossible luxury otherwise.

The traditional parrot cage is quite unsuitable because its single perch and restricted area condemn the occupant to a life of inactivity. It is true that many of the larger parrots are not particularly active when caged but they would have more freedom of movement if the cage was large enough to allow two facing perches at the same height and a higher perch for roosting. All parrots will roost on the highest perch and a cage which does not have enough space for a perch at an angle above the main perch, with headroom to spare, is not large enough. A length of branch from an apple tree will be ideal for this purpose but will need to be renewed occasionally. It can be wedged into position or fixed with a wire staple.

Many cages are fitted with only two containers, one for food and one for water, which are in any case inadequate for most parrots and would need to be refilled at least twice daily. It is therefore advisable to buy strong metal hook-on containers so that fruit, sunflower seed and the small seeds can be separated. For the larger parrots who will treat these as playthings and unhook them, scattering the contents, a heavy earthenware dish can be placed on the floor instead. Some birds resent the intrusion of a hand inside the cage, so one which has several containers incorporated in the design is most useful.

When buying or making a cage, attention should be paid to the door fastening. Virtually the only escape-proof type is the screw; an intelligent parrot will soon learn how to operate most others and some of the larger parrots can even undo padlocks. I know of two cases, incredible though it may seem, where parrots have learned to undo padlocks with numbered combinations.

The cage should be positioned out of draughts and direct sunlight; thus placing a cage in a window can adversely affect a bird's health. Parrots do, however, enjoy seeing what is going on outside, so a view out of a window, without being too close to it, will be appreciated. One side of the cage should be against a solid wall if possible to provide some sense of security. The best level is table-height; above eye-level is unsuitable as a tame bird will want to be in the centre of things. For this reason, the most lived-in room in the house is the only place for a parrot. It is extremely cruel to banish it to an unused room because it is noisy. This problem can usually be overcome by covering the cage with a blanket. It is not necessary to cover the cage at night unless the bird could be disturbed by, for example, car headlights.

Newspaper is the best floor covering; it is quick and easy to renew and inexpensive but some birds will chew it or carry it about; as an alternative, pet litter or a sand and soil mixture can be tried. The floor covering should be changed daily and the cage cleaned thoroughly once a week.

It is not recommended to keep pet cockatoos and macaws on stands; the use of a chain for this purpose is deplored. The bird receives no exercise and a chain can be a danger. A large cage, such as that described above, is always more suitable, although it might be inadvisable to make a change for a bird which has long used a stand. Parrots are very much creatures of habit and often seem most unhappy when moved to a new cage, although it may be larger and apparently more suitable. Thus the best accommodation possible should be obtained from the start. If a stand is used temporarily it should never be positioned in the centre of a room where people can pass on all sides. A corner is the best position; the bird will feel more secure and people will pass only in front of it.

One problem in keeping a parrot in the house is that the fluctuating temperature can cause the bird to moult continually. There is nothing that can be done to prevent this but a multi-vitamin preparation containing a high proportion of Vitamin B should be included in the diet to keep it otherwise in good health.

Parrots normally moult once a year. In established birds, or those bred in captivity in the northern hemisphere, the moult usually, but not invariably, occurs between July and September. Some birds have a fairly rapid moult during which they present a sorry sight in contrast to their usual faultless plumage, although others have a very gradual moult which is scarcely noticeable. During the moult, moisture on the plumage is even more important than during the rest of the year; spraying a bird encourages it to preen, thus removing loose feathers and particles of skin and feather sheaths.

A parrot which is sprayed regularly, allowed to bathe or put outside in its cage during a shower of rain, will acquire the most beautiful bloom to its plumage. A pet Yellow-fronted Amazon of mine is invariably admired for this reason. The plumage of many captive parrots is quickly saturated by rain but I can stand this Amazon outside in her cage during a heavy shower and the water runs off her plumage,

only the feathers of the forehead remaining wet. Obviously one cannot do this during cold weather when the bird comes from a heated room, but during warmer weather there is no greater treat that one can provide for an Amazon and many other parrots. If this is not possible, a parrot kept indoors should be sprayed at least twice a week. If the bird is not tame enough to be removed from the cage the base and tray can be removed and the cage stood over a sink. A really tame pet can be taken into a shower with its owner. Most parrots will attempt to bathe in the entirely inadequate water containers incorporated in the cage. What a pity that an enterprising cage designer has not included a really large water container! So often it is difficult to persuade parrots to accept dishes placed on the cage floor as baths or to prevent them tipping them over. Earthenware dog bowls are most suitable for this purpose and, as many parrots in the wild bathe on foliage, a wet lettuce leaf or other greenfood will induce many of the smaller species to roll in it ecstatically.

Many parrots come from tropical areas of very high humidity and moisture on their plumage is absolutely essential to keep it in good condition and to provide the waxy sheen which is characteristic. The combination of correct diet and water should keep a parrot in really gleaming feather condition, in contrast to the dull and lifeless plumage of the unfortunate birds which never have access to water.

Spraying also helps to keep down the dust produced by a parrot's plumage which can aggravate conditions such as asthma in its owner. The dust is produced from a type of feather known as powder-down which is found only in certain groups of birds, notably in cockatoos and in some other species such as Amazon Parrots. The barbs of powder-down feathers continually disintegrate to produce a powder which is used to clean the feathers and is responsible for the bloom on the plumage.

Newly imported parrots are often in very poor feather condition but, except in the case of cockatoos (more likely than other species to be suffering from a feather disease), this need not deter the buyer. At the first moult, most feathers will be replaced by perfect ones. It may be two or three years before all the flight feathers are replaced but a parrot is capable of flight with only two primaries in each wing, so this is not a major drawback if the bird is to be a pet. Many imported parrots, even small species, have the flight feathers cut because they are kept in a compound before export. Such a bird would have to be caged until it can fly as in an aviary it would be at a serious disadvantage if it was nervous. To introduce such a bird to another which can fly would be especially foolish as, if the newcomer was attacked, it would stand no chance of escape.

Some people feel that very tame birds should have their flight feathers clipped as they will be safer, should they find themselves outside by mistake, since they cannot fly off; also, initially, it is easier to tame a bird which cannot fly. If a parrot's wings are clipped, growth of the feathers must be watched carefully at moulting time. Neglecting to do this has probably been responsible for the loss of as many birds as those which might have flown off had they been full-winged anyway. A parrot needs only two primaries on each wing to enable it to fly. Personally, I do not like to see pet birds with clipped wings as they will gain so much more enjoyment from their outings in the room if they can fly. At one time I had three Amazon Parrots which spent much time out of their cages and had the complete freedom of the house. It was a joy to encounter one suddenly swooping down the stairs! I suppose there are not many people who will allow their pet this kind of freedom – but anyone who does will be rewarded by the extra enjoyment it brings.

Patience and kindness are the main qualities needed for taming parrots. I have occasionally received letters from people who ask whether they should use gloves and a stick to try to tame their parrot. That anyone who keeps a parrot has so little understanding of it as to ask such a question fills me with sadness.

The first requirement is a young bird. All young parrots are tameable whereas all the kindness and patience in the world will make little impression on most adult birds. Before actually buying a parrot which appeals to you, it is worth finding out what the young of the species looks like. This should not take too long and the chances are that the bird will still be there on returning to buy it. It is worth the trouble of checking that the bird under consideration is young enough to be tamed. The larger parrots are long-lived and can be a companion for life so this is not a partnership to be rushed into. It is very distressing for a bird to frequently change homes so no one should ever buy a parrot with the thought in their mind that they can sell it if it proves unsatisfactory. Birds are not merchandise to be bought and sold at the whim of the owner. This applies especially to adult birds which have been years in one place and are likely to take a long time to settle down in a new home.

Unless a parrot is so tame on arrival that it wants nothing more than to be handled, the first steps towards taming it are to leave it alone and make no attempt to handle it. The bird should be placed in the busiest room in the house; it will become used to people and will soon realise that they are not causing it any harm. After a couple of days, when it will have recovered from its journey and started to feel at home, it should be spoken to often and softly.

If, after two or three weeks it shows interest in its surroundings and seems to have lost most of its initial nervousness, the cage door can be opened to allow it to climb on top of the cage. Under these circumstances, few of the larger parrots will try to fly off at first, unless frightened. No attempt should be made to approach it closely, let alone handle it, when on the top of its cage.

It is not easy to tame a bird which is confined to a cage, partly because even very tame birds look on their cage as their own territory which is to be defended. The golden rule when taming a parrot is: let it come to you. This method of taming may take longer than some which are used but it is far more satisfying because it is based totally on trust.

When the parrot finally does go to its owner of its own accord, it is best to pretend the bird is not there; sudden movements such as putting out a hand to it or trying to stroke it may cause it to lose its confidence. Once it knows that you mean it no harm and are actually taking very little notice of it, its tameness will increase very rapidly. Then is the time to gently stroke its head, perhaps with a small twig at first, as many birds are nervous of hands.

Of course there are birds which are so tame that they simply will not leave their owner alone, in which case the slow progress outlined above is quite unnecessary.

Before letting a bird out of its cage, all possible hazards, such as uncovered aquariums, possibly poisonous house plants and unfriendly cats and dogs, should be removed, all doors and windows should be closed and access to a kitchen where cooking is in progress should be denied. It must be noted that the fumes given off by Teflon-coated pans which are allowed to burn are poisonous to birds.

If the bird samples some substance which is poisonous, immediate veterinary attention is imperative. The bird should be taken to a vet, together with samples of the suspected poison, any vomit and the most recent droppings. If no veterinary surgeon is available and it is known that a poisonous substance has been consumed, the bird should be given raw egg white mixed with kaopectate or Pepto-Bismol; alternatively, give activated charcoal mixed with a few drops of a mineral oil and enough water to give a pasty consistency. The dose for a Budgerigar or Canary is 0.15 to 0.3 ml (3 to 6 drops), for a Cockatiel 1 to 2 ml ($\frac{1}{5}$ to $\frac{2}{5}$ of a teaspoonful) and for a large parrot 3 to 6 ml ($\frac{3}{5}$ to $1\frac{1}{5}$ teaspoonful). If lead poisoning is suspected, an X-ray should be taken as lead can be seen in the digestive tract. Calcium disodium versenate should be given by injection and repeated for a few days. There is no antidote for the fumes from Teflon-coated pans but oxygen therapy may help (Gallerstein, 1983).

The length of time it takes to tame a bird – or to teach one to talk – varies greatly with the individual. It is a strange fact that some birds make no progress over a period of several months then suddenly become tame almost overnight; with others, the process is a very gradual one, usually with confidence increasing in leaps and bounds after a certain stage has been passed.

There is great joy in a tame and affectionate parrot and teaching it to talk is in my opinion of no importance whatever. Many parrots will learn to repeat a few words whether or not the owner makes a conscious effort to teach them; the vocabulary acquired by some birds is quite phenomenal but the number of birds capable of this is very small and few parrots learn more than a dozen phrases.

Many people will, however, want their parrots to learn to talk and so long as this is not the only reason they are acquired – and thus not a source of regret if they fail – there is no harm in attempting to teach them a few phrases.

To avoid confusion, only one person should teach a bird to talk, preferably a woman whose voice is usually easier for it to copy than a man's. A simple phrase such as 'Hello' or 'Come on' should be chosen to start with and another should not be taught until the first has been mastered. The phrase should be repeated at every possible opportunity.

Because it is not under stress, a tame bird is more likely to learn to talk than one which is nervous of people. One cannot predict how long it will take for a bird to learn its first phrase: some take months to learn the first phrase while others can repeat it after a matter of days, especially if obtained when very young.

Many prospective parrot owners want to know which species make the best talkers. A good Greater Hill Mynah is far superior to almost all parrots in the accuracy of its mimicry and the extent of its vocabulary. A mynah will talk any time and anywhere, while many parrots, especially Greys, will not talk in strange surroundings or among strange people; in short, it will not mimic unless totally relaxed. However, it is probably true that a parrot can add to its vocabulary throughout its life while a mynah learns all or most of its sayings while young.

The Grey Parrot is undoubtedly the next best with several species of Amazons, notably Yellow-naped, Yellow-fronted and Blue-fronted, close behind. Some cockatoos are also quite talented but macaws and most cockatoos seldom learn more than a few words. Some small birds are excellent talkers, the most notable being the Cockatiel. However, the voice is quiet and rather thin in quality. Conures, lories and many species of parrakeets also learn to talk; in fact, if obtained when very young, almost any species can be taught.

Parrots can also be taught by other parrots in nearby cages and young birds bred in aviaries from parents who talk can quickly learn their sayings. Some former pets retain their talking ability in an aviary; others do not. The male of my pair of Greys completely ceased to talk after a couple of years in an aviary, although the presence of another parrot in itself does not prevent a trained bird from talking.

Many parrots mimic the sounds around them and even the calls of other parrots. A Black Lory which I bred and brought into the house before it was three months old learned to imitate to perfection the calls of the Cockatiels housed near it, and its father, in an outdoor aviary, does a muffled imitation of a human conversation.

It has often been said that, in the wild, parrots do not mimic other birds but this statement is impossible to prove or disprove.

Amazon Parrots are particularly adept at mimicking laughter and the sounds made by small children. One in my possession grows wildly excited at the sight of a small child, talking and shrieking in a high-pitched voice. At some time, she obviously belonged to a family with a young baby as she can imitate the cry to perfection. She is now a breeding bird and to hear the sounds of a human baby issuing from her nest-box is most incongruous.

Teaching a parrot to talk has amusement value only but there are two useful exercises which a parrot can be taught. The first is to step onto a stick so that it can be carried about. Many parrots are nervous of hands and will never allow themselves to be carried on their owner's hand; others, though not tame enough to permit this, have no objections to climbing on to a stick. In this way a bird can be transferred to its cage or to another cage without the need to catch it. At first, the stick used should be long enough to enable a great distance between bird and trainer. The stick is slowly and gently placed in front of the breast, just above the bird's legs; the action it induces, to step on to the stick, is almost automatic in most of the larger parrots.

Similarly, the smaller species can be finger-tamed with the method used for Budgerigars. When the bird has settled down sufficiently not to panic when its owner places a hand in the cage, the hand is slowly moved towards the breast, then gently pressed against the breast just above the legs. Short, frequent lessons are necessary until the bird steps on to the offered finger. Once it becomes used to this it can be lifted out of its cage.

If a bird is let out before it is trained to return to its cage on stick or finger, and proves difficult to return; it should not be chased about the room. The room should be darkened by closing the curtains or turning the light out after having ascertained exactly where it is, then it can be picked up quickly in a towel. Alternatively, if its cage has a removable base, the tray and base should be withdrawn and the frame of the cage quickly placed over the bird. When the light is turned on it will simply climb back up to its perch.

The pleasure gained from caring for a pet bird is a subject alone worthy of a book. One of the most fascinating aspects of the parrot as a pet is, to me, not that it can talk or that it is beautiful, but that each bird is different with a personality which, especially in the larger parrots, is just as individual as that of a human being.

The potential lifespan of the larger parrots is very long – approximately equal to that of a human being. It is usually very difficult to prove longevity because so often the bird has not remained with the same family. Ages of 97 and 98 years were claimed for Blue-fronted Amazons, in separate instances, which had been with several families. However, there are instances of Amazon Parrots which had been with one owner for between 47 and 56 years – and these are almost certainly not exceptional.

Perhaps the most famous cockatoo living today is 'King Tut', the Moluccan who arrived at San Diego

Zoo in California in 1925 and was adult when received. At the time of writing he is thus at least 62 years old. He still whistles, sings and dances, mimics cats and chickens and speaks a few words. This cockatoo, which has worked in cinema and theatre, has a gentle and affectionate disposition.

Another famous long-lived cockatoo was the Greater Sulphur-crested which resided at London Zoo from 1925 until 1982. The family who presented him to the zoo had kept him as a pet since the beginning of the century.

Lifespan of the smaller species is much shorter. However, I have a male Cockatiel which is 32 years old, whose female died when she was 29 years old. The potential lifespan of the larger Australian parrakeets is probably well into the twenties and, although it is exceptional, Budgerigars have also lived to this age. Parrotlets have reached at least eighteen years of age.

9
Sick Birds: Causes and Care

The section on parasites is kindly contributed by George A. Smith MRCVS.

Most of the diseases suffered by parrots which are well established in captivity or aviary-bred (as opposed to recently imported) birds can be avoided by good management. If the following points are observed, disease will be rare.
1. Stressful situations (such as overcrowding or persecution by a dominant bird) must be avoided.
2 Enclosures should be made mouse-proof (difficult – but to this end it is worth investing in $\frac{3}{8}$ in wire mesh).
3. Birds should not be exposed to harsh weather conditions.
4. A vitamin and mineral supplement should be provided regularly, on fruit, softfood or a favourite item of food. It is not very effective on seed or in water.
5. Maintain a good standard of cleanliness regarding aviaries and food and water containers.
6. Do not try to economise by buying poor quality (and usually dirty) seed and other foods.
7. Check birds carefully twice daily, especially at first light. In the winter, it is imperative to check all aviaries immediately there is sufficient light. Handle each bird for a thorough examination two or three months before it is expected to breed. If it appears overweight provide a less fattening diet. Clip nails and beak (not normally necessary except perhaps in aged birds).
8. Worm species known to be susceptible to parasitic worms before and after the breeding season.

It is a regrettable fact that many captive birds die because of their owner's failure to act swiftly enough. In birds the course of most illnesses is extremely swift and so the moment one is seen to look even slightly unwell it should be caught up for close observation and treatment.

Anyone who does not have time to observe their birds closely twice daily should not be keeping birds. A sick bird deteriorates so rapidly that, in many cases, one which becomes ill and is not attended to is beyond help 24 hours later.

To recognise a sick bird, four basic points should be looked for. Firstly, it will shut its eyes frequently in the early stage of an illness before it has deteriorated to the stage where it is sleeping with the head tucked into the feathers of the mantle with both feet on the perch. Secondly, the eyes will look dull and, in some cases, sunken. Thirdly, the feathers, especially those of the head, will appear ruffled. Fourthly, the droppings will usually be abnormal in colour and consistency. To gauge this it is, of course, necessary to know the normal condition, which varies greatly from bird to bird. It is a common fallacy that green droppings denote a sick bird and although this may be true of some species, it does not apply to the larger parrots in which the droppings are green more often than not. The droppings of seed-eating parrots consist of two parts: the white part is urine, and the lack of it denotes that something is wrong with the kidneys, while the other part varies from black or brown to green in colour. The consistency of the droppings depends mainly on how the bird has been fed. In those lories which feed entirely on nectar in captivity, the droppings are liquid or almost so, and in parrots which are fed mainly on seed they will be fairly solid. A parrot used to a mainly seed diet which is suddenly given fruit will have looser droppings than normal and this is no cause for concern.

In many sick birds the droppings are very watery, which is a different effect to that caused by fruit. The colour, too, may be different.

If the only symptom of those listed above is resting on two feet when the head is tucked into the feathers of the back, the bird is not ill. A sick bird *always* has dull eyes; young birds and certain individuals often rest on two feet when they are asleep.

The only condition which can be confused with illness by the observant owner is that of a hen which is about to lay and which may show some or all of the symptoms described above. Knowing the bird in question is a great help because some hens always look ill before laying and yet pass the egg without any problems. In the case of a bird which has not laid before while in the owner's collection, it can be very difficult to decide whether or not she needs help. Normally a hen which is about to lay will be in the nest-box and thus the criterion for judging if she is ill is how long she spends out of the box. If she does not return, and her condition seems to be deteriorating, she needs heat and must be caught. Extreme care and gentleness must be used in handling such a bird: if the egg inside her was broken during catching she would die a very painful death.

The first and most vital requirement of a sick bird is heat. This cannot be over-emphasised. Heat alone will often be enough to save an ailing bird.

I am not in favour of the use of hospital cages for sick parrots as the dry atmosphere affects many birds adversely and, in any case, most hospital cages are too small for the larger parrots. The best source of heat is an infra-red lamp. Every owner of even a single parrot should invest in one. It will cost only a small proportion of the price of the bird and could well be the means of saving its life. The lamp should be positioned to one side of the bird's cage, so that it can move out of the heat if it so desires, and should not be directed at the bird's food which can be spoilt by the heat of the lamp. The lamp should be placed approximately 20 cm (8 in) away from the cage. If an infra-red lamp is not available, the bird should be placed near a fire or radiator and the cage covered with a towel to retain as much heat as possible.

The next step is to give a broad-spectrum antibiotic in the water or on a favourite item of food. It is recommended at this stage as it is seldom possible to diagnose illness in a bird; in cases where it is, a more specific antibiotic can be given.

The first two steps to take, then, in the case of a sick bird are to provide heat and antibiotics. If the bird is injured or suffering from shock, heat alone is all that is recommended.

The next step is to consult a veterinary surgeon. A bird which has been in a high temperature and requires 29–32°C (85–90°F) should not be taken to a veterinary surgeon's surgery as the journey and change of temperature will affect it adversely. A bird which is suffering from an injury such as a broken leg, can be moved providing it is not acutely nervous.

It should be borne in mind that, except where poultry are concerned, very little indeed is known about the diseases from which birds suffer and many veterinary surgeons have little experience with birds. Even if the complaint can be identified, there is usually little more that one can do apart from giving heat, antibiotics and, where appropriate, vitamins.

Antibiotics can be given in powder or suspension (liquid) or, in the case of large birds which are less likely to suffer the effects of shock, as injections, but the shock of an injection can result in death in nervous birds.

If the antibiotic is to be placed in the bird's drinking water, then fruit or other foods on which it could quench its thirst should be withheld. Alternatively, the antibiotic can be placed on a favourite item of food or inside a grape.

Some sick birds cease to feed, in which case it may be necessary for a veterinary surgeon to dose the bird, using a syringe with a tube on the end. The tube is placed in the bird's mouth and gently pushed down the throat so that the liquid is directed into the bird's crop. If necessary, food can be given in the same way.

Diagnosis

Because the symptoms hardly vary, especially in bacterial and viral infections, it is extremely difficult to diagnose a disease in a living bird. If the bird dies, an autopsy should be carried out by someone with experience of bird autopsy; this is the only method of determining the cause of death and, in many cases, even a post-mortem examination fails to reveal this. For the best results, the body should be as fresh as possible and should therefore be stored in a refrigerator (not in the freezer section) until the autopsy can be performed.

It should be emphasised that a description of the bird's symptoms alone, without the body, are meaningless in trying to establish cause of death.

While viral infections and the like are difficult to treat because of the lack of knowledge of what is wrong, such conditions as eye disease or tumours may be satisfactorily treated. Tumours are not uncommon in ageing parrots (and especially in Budgerigars) and may or may not be cancerous. Removal of non-cancerous growths is not a complicated procedure. It is best to find a veterinary surgeon who has some experience of this kind of work. Fatty growths or lipomas are particularly common in Roseate Cockatoos (see p. 215).

Moniliasis

Ill health may cause a bird to lose its appetite, but if a bird which otherwise appears to be in good health ceases to eat, it is wise to examine the inside of its mouth. If a swelling is found in the lower jaw, possibly under the tongue, immediate veterinary treatment is necessary. The reason will probably be moniliasis caused by a deficiency of Vitamin A. It is very common in newly imported birds, and is often reported in Eclectus Parrots and in Amazon Parrots and cockatoos but could affect any species. An injection of chloramphenicol into the swelling often cures the problem.

Moniliasis is also known as candidiasis; it is caused by the yeast-like mould *Monilia (Candida)*. It is extremely common in lories. Before buying newly imported lories the inside of the mouth, also the skin surrounding the lower mandible, should be examined for the fungus *Candida albicans*. It will appear as a soft yellowish white growth if it is still growing; an attempt to remove it at this stage will cause bleeding, possibly severe loss of blood. The best course of procedure is to obtain a prescription for Ketoconozole (Crown Chemicals). About $\frac{1}{10}$th of a 5 mg tablet for a bird as small as a Meyer's Lorikeet (50 g/1$\frac{3}{4}$ oz body weight) is crushed and placed in the nectar until the infection has gone. The great advantage of this method (compared with the use of Nystatin for example) is that the bird being treated never has to be handled. *Candida* can grow extremely quickly and can spread to the air sacs of the body, so immediate action must be taken when it is seen.

A bird which has suffered from candidiasis must be given large amounts of Vitamin A and a high level must thereafter be maintained in its diet to prevent a recurrence. This is best given using one of the multivitamin preparations for human use which can be obtained at any chemist. The label should be examined to ensure that Vitamin A is the main component.

Vitamin Deficiency

Many birds, especially those which refuse fresh fruits and vegetables, will benefit from the regular addition of multivitamins to the diet. After a course of antibiotics, there is a greater need for vitamins than usual. George A. Smith, the author of *Encyclopedia of Cockatiels*, who is a veterinary surgeon, writes, 'In my experience many cage birds, whether the symptoms be "fits", "loss of feathers", "crusty eyes", or "vague unwellness", are in actuality suffering from a vitamin deficiency'.

Stress

The same writer states:

> All diseases, even though they are usually attributed to a specific microorganism or deficiency of some food item, are aggravated or precipitated by stress of some kind. Stress includes all those circumstances and conditions which create disturbance or an unease in what would otherwise be a normal mental or physiological state. Any animal of any kind that is perfectly well fed and housed but is unable to relax because of overcrowding will fall ill. If disease organisms are present, these will introduce a specific disease. The disease process or organism causing the stress may be treated specifically, but without also reducing stress this disease or another will again make the bird ill. Even otherwise harmless bacteria, molds or viruses can create a disease if the stress is great enough.

This should help all aviculturists to a better understanding of their birds. Stress is the greatest killer of birds in captivity. A pair of my lories, for example, suddenly started to vomit after they had been in my possession for about four years and had kept in perfect health. Nothing, to my great regret, could be done to stop them vomiting; on autopsy, death was found to be due to the protozoan, *Trichomonas* in the crop. This had doubtless been present for years and had been aggravated by stress. The birds, which were very nervous for lories, had recently been removed to a different aviary and would not use the nest-box

for roosting. It would seem that, in this case, the move created the stress which resulted in their deaths. The only death which, to date, I have ever had among my fairly extensive collection of Amazon Parrots, concerned one which was placed with a bird of which it was frightened. The other bird never caused it any harm but the stress of the situation was enough to kill it.

One reason why I am an advocate of hand-rearing is that hand-fed birds usually have little fear of anything or anyone and are therefore far less likely to suffer from stress.

Another aspect of stress is that a sick bird can suffer equally from being parted from its mate as from the illness itself. Therefore, unless the sick one appears to be suffering from something which is infectious, the two birds should be housed together. Another advantage of using an infra-red lamp instead of a hospital cage can be seen here, for the bird which does not need heat will simply move out of range of the lamp (and a pet bird need not be moved out of its cage which, in itself, is an experience which causes stress). Birds in which the pair bond is very strong, i.e. cockatoos. Cockatiels, lories and most South American parrots, should not be separated during sickness.

Eye Disease

This used to be a major problem in newly imported Australian parrakeets and is occasionally seen today in birds which have been imported under conditions which leave much to be desired. A bird with any form of eye disease should be isolated in case it is infectious; the perches in the cage should be frequently washed or changed because irritation will cause the bird to rub its eye on the perch.

Eye diseases have a variety of causes and some respond to antibiotics. Among those which have been successful in treating eye conditions are Aureomycin (Cyanamid) and chloromycetin eye drops and ointment and vibramycin given directly into the crop. Eye disease can be caused by a deficiency of Vitamin A, in which case tablets made for pigeons with 'one eye cold' will often effect a cure.

Birds, especially ageing ones, can be

affected by cataracts. Unfortunately, there is nothing which can be done in such cases.

On a few occasions, successful eye operations have been carried out on parrots. One of these occurred as long ago as 1896. A two year old Grey Parrot had what was described as a 'travelling tumour upon the under-lid of the right eye' removed by a surgeon at the Royal Westminster Ophthalmic Hospital. She recovered from an operation very quickly and 'talked and whistled better than ever'.

Feather Disease

A particularly distressing problem, this seems to be most common in cockatoos (especially in the Lesser Sulphur-crested). Birds affected have generally been imported and the condition becomes apparent at the first or second moult in captivity. The replaced feathers are of such poor quality and so brittle that they break off when the

Young Lesser Sulphur-crested Cockatoo suffering from a feather condition.

bird attempts to preen them. This eventually results in the pathetic spectacle of a bird unable to fly and almost completely devoid of feathers. It can survive in this condition for a number of years. In some affected birds, the beak grows abnormally long, is soft and requires frequent cutting. This condition sometimes affects the nails as well. The cause has yet to be established; possibly a virus is to blame. Very few cases of a complete cure have been recorded, despite prolonged feeding of various additives. The usual multivitamin preparations have no effect.

Psittacosis

This is the name given to the disease ornithosis, which affects very many species of birds, when it is found in parrots. It is common in pigeons and poultry and, although the disease can be transmitted to man, poultry workers are far more likely to be affected than parrot keepers. In human beings, the symptoms are such that the affected person will probably believe that he has influenza although there is no cold or cough. He will have a high temperature and be feverish, alternatively shivering and hot, and will perspire heavily during the night. The body will ache and, after a few days without treatment, the lungs will be affected, making breathing difficult after any exertion, such as walking upstairs. Fortunately, psittacosis responds rapidly to the tetracycline drugs, thus there is no cause for alarm if the disease is suspected. A doctor must be consulted immediately and informed of the probable nature of the illness.

It was formerly believed that psittacosis was caused by a virus, but it is now known to be due to an intracellular parasite, *Chlamydia*. The incidence and severity of the clinical infection in birds varies widely with the susceptibility of the host and the virulence of the particular strain. Confirmation is difficult in live birds since symptoms resemble those of other avian diseases.

Infected birds shed large quantities of aerosols containing the parasite in nasal discharge and in the droppings. The route of infection is primarily through inhalation of the aerosols; thus good hygiene and ventilation are important factors in preventing its spread. It has been advised that those who work with a large number of birds, such as on the premises of an importer, should wear facial masks.

Symptoms in birds include nasal discharge, conjunctivitis, loss of appetite and diarrhoea (sometimes blood-tinged) – all common symptoms of other infections; diagnosis can be made only by laboratory tests using tissue extracts from dead birds or cloacal washings or blood samples of live ones.

Parasites

Parasitic Worms

These are a major problem in certain species of parrots, notably the Australian parrakeets.

***Ascaridia columbae*, the Roundworm:** This is the most common parasitic worm. It has quite a large body and can easily be seen, when adult, as a string-thick, dirty-white, 4 cm (1½ in) long filament with tapered ends. It lives in the bowel. The natural hosts were probably members of the Columbiformes – pigeons and doves. When they began to parasitise captive parrots is not known; it may have been quite recently. It is only since the 1950s that they have been known to be pestilential in parrots. Before that time, as in the case of *Capillaria* (see p. 63), they were never recorded. Whether or not this assumption of recent infest-ation is correct, once they have infected parrots, they are very contagious in their spread and have affected almost every captive species; ground-feeding birds are particularly susceptible.

Each female *Ascaridia columbae* can lay about a million eggs per year and, as most infestations are multiple, a parrot containing less than ten worms will be voiding at least 10,000 eggs each day in its faeces. When passed by the bird, intermingled with the faeces, they are not infectious but need to 'mature' over several days for the embryo to develop. In warm weather, they could mature in less than a fortnight, whereas, in cold weather, fresh-laid eggs could remain unembryonated.

The embryo *Ascaridia* worm, inside its egg-shell, is very tenacious of life and, although drought and direct sunlight are fatal, it can otherwise remain viable for months and perhaps even for a year or two. In the wild, the astronomical number of eggs laid by the worms is essential to increase the otherwise almost negligible chance of another bird eating an embryonated egg. In an aviary, however, the chance of infection by other parrots' faeces is a certainty. This is because faeces are splashed with rain, or can be carried on utensils, or by feet or insects feeding on faeces, or by earthworms eating old faeces and then entering previously uninfected aviaries and depositing the worm eggs in their casts.

It is not generally known that parrots eat stale faeces, but in fact it is

Worm eggs under a microscope – left, *Capillaria*, right *Ascaridia*.

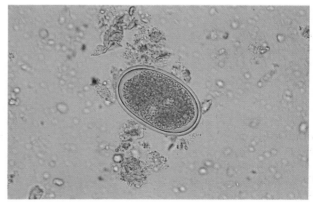

essential behaviour for, unless they practised this *refection*, as it is called, they might be short of vitamins of the B group, particularly biotin and cyano-cobalamin (Vitamin B_{12}), which are deficient in a diet of seed. In consequence, it is not uncommon for chicks to be heavily infested while in the nest and may in fact be harbouring hundreds of worms.

When mature worm eggs are eaten, they hatch and the microscopic larvae bore into the thickness of the bowel wall, creating an inflammation. They are said to reach maturity at six weeks although examination of infected chicks suggests that it is more commonly eight weeks before the worms begin to lay eggs. They are found in heaviest concentration in the lower duodenum and the first part of the small bowel. Their presence causes the bowel wall to dilate and huge knots of worms may accumulate. In one 30 g (1 oz) Parrotlet, the worms which killed it weighed 3.5 g, more than one tenth of its weight.

Treatment of worm infestation ought to be routine and frequent. The most certain method involves catching each bird and administering the medicament by individual dosing. Some aviculturists rely on dripping portions of the vermifuge into the open bill; this could administer the correct dose but more frequently probably does not do so. Other breeders use a crop-tube, attached to a hypodermic syringe, and squirt the contents directly into the crop; another method is to use a hypo-dermic needle and inject it through the crop wall, into the crop. The problem is that all birds resent handling and the catching and administration, no matter how carefully performed, includes the risk that a bird may die during the handling, or after, due to shock or complications. In any case, these methods are not likely to be used during the actual breeding season and are not performed often enough to keep potential infection at low level.

Worming ought to take place through administration in the drinking water or food. The perfect substance would be tasteless, harmless if over-dosed and soluble in water. No such substance is presently available. Piperazine salts are slightly bitter and may be somewhat toxic, as death has

often been the result of slight over-dosing. Antipar (Burroughs Wellcome), the form most often used, is not particularly effective against larval or immature worms and it does not affect *Capillaria*. Levamisole (ICI's Nilverm and Nemicide) is bitter, although seemingly fairly safe in over-dosage. When made particularly thirsty, by depriving them of water for a day beforehand, some parrots will drink a solution diluted 1:10, but many will not.

Treatment ought to be prophylactic and take place at monthly intervals. As one can never be sure that treated water will be taken, it is probably pref-erable to place one drop of the neat solution on a piece of fruit or on a small portion of bread or milk or some other favourite food item. All captive parrots in outside aviaries ought to be wormed even when worms have never been suspected or diagnosed, otherwise infestation will inevitably occur.

Capillariasis: The *Capillaria* worm usually found is *C. obsignata* (of pigeons); it is possible that several other species might occur for lesions of *Capillaria* affecting the gizzard have been shown on autopsy, even though the worms were not identified and *C. obsignata* inhabits the small intestine.

Capillaria are almost as prevalent as *Ascaridia* and their effect is at least as damaging. However, because of their translucence and tenuous shape, and the fact that they live partly embedded in slime, they are not readily observed in the bowels of dead parrots, unless special attention is paid to identifying them. They are probably more de-bilitating than *Ascaridia* with smaller infestations and birds affected are frequently 'unthrifty' in general ap-pearance. They can be eliminated with routine worming, using a broad-spectrum vermicide.

Tapeworm infestation: Because tape-worms require an intermediate host to carry their larval forms, it is extremely improbable that they could ever prove to be of consequence in aviary-bred birds. However, many nectar-feeding parrots are found to carry some when they are first brought into captivity and infestations can be alarmingly high. Mebendazole fed in the nectar, at the appropriate strength for ten days or so, will be very effective and not

harm the birds in any way whatsoever. A well-tried and successful cure is Yomesan (Bayer; Leverkusen, Germany) in tablets which must be crushed in the nectar (one tablet per 14 g/5 oz body weight or, for a large lory, about half a tablet per bird).

Akibiasis
This is infestation with a parasite of the genus *Akiba*. Some parasites are microscopically small and live within the bloodstream of the host. All such blood-inhabiting parasites depend upon blood-sucking arthropods, such as insects, ticks and mites, for their dissemination. The arthropod spreads the disease by transferring the organ-isms, on its mouth-parts or in its saliva, from an infected host to an-other in its search for blood upon which to feed. As there are numerous biting insects in the tropics, it is not surprising that a careful analysis of blood from practically every imported parrot will show parasites in the serum, the red blood cells or the white blood cells. It is fortunate that the vectors, those biting arthropods neces-sary for their spread, are absent from most temperate climates. However, there is a parasite, normally endemic in temperate birds, which is spread by 'biting midges' and can fatally infect parrots. The parasite is a leuco-cytozoon ('animal inhabiting white blood cells') and unfortunately, during its life cycle, builds up to large num-bers by forming cysts in the muscle. When these are formed in quantity in the muscles of the heart and gizzard, they can kill parrots. There is no known cure. To avoid deaths from this cause, those who keep parrots should either fill in ornamental ponds or stock them with fish to eat the larval midges.

Scaly-face
This condition is caused by infestation with the mite *Knemidocoptes pilae*. It lives in the thickness of crusts, raised by its presence, on the exposed skin of birds. It can sometimes be found on wild finches. It is just large enough to be visible to the naked eye and norm-ally lives at the bottom of tiny pits or encrustations. These holes can fairly easily be made out on visual examin-ation. In the Budgerigar, heavy infest-ations may affect all parts of the face,

including the surrounds of the eyes, the lids, the angle of the gape, the face, the cere and the legs, especially the junction of the scaly part of the leg with the feathered part. It has been seen in several other parrots and, in Kakarikis, natural resistance appears minimal and the untreated disease frequently becomes rampant. Invasion of the whole skin can take place. The affected bird loses its feathers and becomes noticeably itchy.

It has been suggested that, although many of these cases must stem from contact with scaly-faced Budgerigars, many must be contracted from the perches cut from twigs upon which infected wild finches have wiped their feet and bills. In the past, treatment was by topical application of benzyl-benzoate or slightly dilute Dettol (Reckitt & Colman). However, it is better to avoid catching the birds to treat them, except initially to house them in a building in which a dichlorvos strip (Vapona, ICI) is suspended. Although theoretically very poisonous to birds, dichlorvos does not prove so in practice. Breeders of Budgerigars and Canaries, as well as those of parrots, who do not avail themselves of the benefit of one or more of these vaporising insecticides in their birdrooms, are perhaps more negligent than wise. Dichlorvos kills all arthropods, including red, northern and airsac mites, feather lice, fodder mites (which can cause bronchitis in the bird-keeper), biting flies, houseflies and, for those who feed nectar, wasps.

Red Mite and Northern Mite

Dermanyssus gallinae, the well-known red mite of poultry, can be a terrible pest of birdrooms and nest-boxes. As this full-stop-sized mite generally hides in crevices away from the host during the day, a breeder might be unaware that his birds suffered from an infestation. However, when he paints his birdroom or cages, he might find that the freshly painted surface becomes dotted with the myriad corpses of red mite on the following morning. In nest-boxes, red mite can wreak havoc causing anaemia among chicks. Treatment is by dusting nest-boxes and their contents with a vegetable-derived insecticide, such as pybuthrin or pyrethrum. Where birds are bred indoors, dichlorvos entirely prevents the mite.

The northern mite, *Ornithonyssus syliarum*, is far less common, yet, as with red mite, can be found on New Zealand parrakeets. It differs from the red mite in that it lives permanently on the host and uses crevices only to lay its eggs.

It should be stated that under good conditions parrots are extremely healthy, with a potentially much longer life span than other families of birds of comparable size. Unfortunately, the cause of death of many, perhaps most, parrots in captivity is attributable to incorrect management and often to a small detail which could easily have been rectified. Incorrect feeding or some detail of management which may appear trivial to the inexperienced keeper often results in severe stress, which is a killer of parrots, and failure to worm parrots or rid them of other parasites also accounts for the unnecessary deaths of many birds. A little more thought given to the welfare of parrots in collections is needed in order to prevent disease, for the cure is seldom easy.

10
Conservation and the Aviculturist

In 1904, *The Avicultural Magazine* contained two paragraphs referring to:

> . . . unsuccessful nesting of a pair of Carolina Conures *(Conuropsis carolinensis)*, a species which, unfortunately, appears to be fast approaching extinction. In going round his aviaries one morning, Captain Nicholl discovered an egg in a corner behind a dead stump of a tree, which he describes as about the size and colour of a pigeon's. The following morning there was a second and on the next two mornings a third and a fourth. [Clearly this is incorrect as conures lay on alternate days.]
>
> During the time the eggs were being laid, the cock Carolina did not go near the nest but, from the fifth day, he, together with the hen, sat continuously. The two birds never left the nest, except to feed, for three weeks, not even moving when their food was brought to them in the morning; so I fully expected to see, some day, young birds instead of eggs, but I was disappointed and, on examining the eggs, found they were all addled.

By 1904, it was known that this conure was virtually extinct in the wild. In 1907, a Dr Eimbeck, who toured European zoos, had found only one Carolina Conure alive – in Hamburg Zoo. Despite the fact that zoological collections in Europe and in its native USA contained a few specimens, some of which had laid eggs, little interest had been shown in breeding this species. Indeed, it would appear that the pair mentioned above had not even been provided with a nest-box.

Thousands of Carolina Conures had been imported to Europe and thousands more had been kept in captivity in the USA. According to Dr Hopkinson, noted for his compilation of avicultural records, the species never reared young in Britain. As the Marquess of Tavistock wrote in 1929, it could have been saved if 'aviculturists had not been too lazy and unenterprising to make the effort'. The same could be said for those in charge of the specimens housed in zoological collections.

The last two Carolina Conures known to exist died in Cincinnati Zoo, one in the summer of 1917 and the last one on earth in February 1918.

The tragedy is that the Carolina Parrakeet (called *Conuropsis*, though clearly an *Aratinga* conure) belonged to a genus of extremely free-breeding birds. The closely related Golden-capped Conure from Brazil, now endangered by deforestation, became available to aviculturists only in the 1970s. It is being bred in large numbers in the USA and its captive future is secure.

So times have changed in that it would be unthinkable today that a species known to be approaching extinction should not be the subject of a careful breeding programme. Captive breeding as a means of conservation has been accepted. But many conservationists have been slow to take it up, and a few still oppose captive breeding.

However, the Marquess of Tavistock's remarks about aviculturists being 'lazy and unenterprising' still apply today, even if to a lesser degree. Aviculturists could do much more to win the respect of conservationists. Generally speaking, however, their record in establishing rare and endangered species of parrots is better than that of zoos.

In recent years, attention has been focused on the plight of many birds which inhabit rainforest, as clearing and fragmentation of this type of habitat have been severe. Except in Australia, the majority of parrots are primarily rainforest dwellers, thus man's destruction of their environment has had a serious impact on many species.

Island-dwellers are, of course, the most vulnerable. As their range – never large in the case of species which occur on small islands – contracts, their numbers dwindle to danger level. The most notable examples are the Amazon Parrots of the Caribbean islands. Hazards which they have to face include dramatic natural ones – destruction of habitat, food and nest trees by hurricanes and volcano eruptions. The magnificent St Vincent Parrot *(Amazona guildingii)*, for example, now confined to the centre of this small island, has had to contend with both since 1979. Population estimates are difficult to make in the mountainous terrain it inhabits, but the general consensus is that about 400 birds survive. That is not a small population in comparison with that of most parrots of the Caribbean Antilles.

There are few birds outside St Vincent. Legal export has occurred only in exceptional cases but, as with most rare and beautiful parrots, attempts have been made to smuggle them from the island.

In 1980, a consortium was formed by zoos and the two private aviculturists in possession of this species, in order that the best use should be made of the few birds in captivity. The result has been the movement of unpaired birds and the setting up of potential breeding pairs.

One member of the consortium who has been successful in breeding the St Vincent Parrot is Ramon Noegel in Florida. He has an unparalleled record for breeding endangered *Amazona*, unmatched by any zoo or private aviculturist. He presents an encouraging example of what can be achieved by one man who works relentlessly for the future of the rarer parrots in aviculture. Since 1974, the world first breedings of Grand Cayman, Cayman Brac and Isle of Pines Amazons (all endangered subspecies of the Cuban Amazon (*Amazona leucocephala*), Black-billed, Tucuman and Yellow-shouldered (*A. barbadensis*) Amazons have occurred in his aviaries.

Until he concentrated his efforts on breeding *A. leucocephala*, including the nominate race from Cuba, and wrote articles publicising their plight in the wild, this species had received little attention.

Some threatened species are not rare in aviculture at the present time. In some cases (for example the Queen of Bavaria's Conure and Cruentata Conure), only aviary-bred birds are available, whereas others, the trade in which is fairly recent, have never been properly studied in the wild and imported birds are the main source of supply. That source may be depleted within the next few decades.

This applies especially to those species found in the only remaining areas of extensive rainforest – in Indonesia and New Guinea, and in South and Central America. In these areas, burgeoning human populations and the cutting of forests which have stood for millennia, as a quick source of wealth for impoverished nations, have resulted in the catastrophic decline of some rainforest species.

In many cases, the scale of the decline is impossible to quantify. Few studies have been carried out, except on the most highly endangered species (such as the Puerto Rican Amazon) which, of course, receive priority. However, parrots confined to a relatively small group of islands whose timber concessions have been sold in recent years must be declining very rapidly as their habitat is destroyed. Goffin's Cockatoo is an example. It has been exported in large numbers since the early 1970s when the Tenimber Islands, its only habitat, were opened up. So extensive has the trade in this species become that Goffin's has, for some years, been the least expensive cockatoo available. The market has been flooded with this delightful little cockatoo.

It is supply and demand which fixes the price. Ironically, cockatoos which are so common in their native habitat, Australia, that they are treated as vermin (shot and poisoned), such as the Roseate and the Greater Sulphur-crested, command extremely high prices outside that country because their export on a commercial basis is forbidden. Their high prices lend them the status of worthwhile investments as there is a ready sale for the young. Those who wish to make some contribution towards conservation will gain more satisfaction from breeding Goffin's or the more expensive Citron-crested which is similarly threatened.

Goffin's are currently so common that many people might deride the idea that they could ever disappear from our collections. I am sure the same belief was held of the extinct Carolina Parrakeet. Considering the large number of Goffin's which have been exported, breeding successes have not been numerous. Greater effort must be made on behalf of this very attractive cockatoo.

The breeding of the larger parrots has made gigantic strides forward since the 1970s. Many species which were bred only occasionally or rarely in that decade are now reared on a large scale. One reason for this great progress is surgical sexing. Other veterinary advances and increased distribution of information by successful breeders, have helped to increase successes.

A further reason is the shift in emphasis from keeping the larger parrots as pets to maintaining them under conditions which permit breeding. Yet another factor is the realisation that very large aviaries are not necessary in order to breed the large parrots. The danger here is that, when aviculturists are successful with birds in very small enclosures, they are tempted to reduce the size of the aviary even further.

The large macaws, for example, breed very readily in small enclosures. These magnificent birds have suffered a very serious decline in the wild and are now mainly restricted to remote and sparsely settled areas. This is partly due to lack of habitat but also, regrettably, due to the large demand from the trade. Most of the macaws have extensive ranges in the wild; nevertheless, in Central America, the decline of the Scarlet Macaw (*Ara macao*) for example, has been severe. It is now extinct in El Salvador and is in danger of extinction in Costa Rica within the next few years.

My own opinion is that it is irresponsible to keep such birds as pets, that the only possible justification for maintaining them in captivity is to breed from them. In any case, the large macaws and cockatoos are totally unsuitable as pets for the average household. Many suffer extreme boredom from close confinement and stress (often resulting in feather plucking) from being denied the opportunity to breed. Fortunately, surgical sexing has removed what was previously the principal barrier in breeding macaws. Once they have been sexed and paired, they usually nest readily and it is imperative that more people should allow them to do so. Those who own single pet birds should consider either obtaining mates for them or placing them with a breeder.

Aviculturists should attempt to keep up with current literature concerning the status of parrots, rather than depend on books or papers published some years previously. The widely held view that once prevailed was that certain Grass Parrakeets (*Neophema*), notably the Splendid and Bourke's, were nearly extinct in the wild. Not only are they now bred in aviaries by the thousand, it is recognised that they are not endangered. This, unfortunately, is not so in the case of the Orange-bellied Parrakeet (*N. chrysogaster*), not to be confused with the orange-breasted colour phase of the Turquoisine. Its population is currently estimated at well below 200.

Intensive studies have been made into its habits since ICI announced its decision to build a major petro-chemical plant on the site of this parrakeet's main wintering area in Victoria. For reasons unconnected with the parrakeet, it was eventually decided not to proceed but attention had been focused on the plight of this small parrot and since then much has been discovered about this species and its biology. A decision may be made to undertake a captive breeding programme. Initially, a pilot breeding project will be carried out using the closely related Blue-winged and Rock Grass Parrakeets.

Conservationists were (and some still are) traditionally against captive breeding as a means of conservation, even declaring they would rather a species became extinct than survived only in captivity. Fortunately, a more enlightened view is gradually becoming apparent. Unfortunately, however, it will be too late for some species. For example, in 1981, the International Council for Bird Preservation recommended that a captive breeding programme should be undertaken as one of the desperate measures to attempt to save the Imperial Parrot (*Amazona imperialis*) from extinction. Its perilously small population, already depleted by shooting, had not recovered from the damage to its habitat which Hurricane David did in 1979. In 1981, it was believed that 40 to 60 birds survived. Since then it has been further imperilled by habitat destruction and it has not been possible to attempt a captive breeding programme. Had this been instigated ten years previously, there would probably have been some hope for the survival of this magnificent bird.

As each year passes, more progress occurs in breeding the rarer parrots – and, indeed, the more common ones – in private and zoological collections. Many more species are being bred to several generations, thus laying down the foundation of aviary-bred strains which will be of vital importance when wild-caught birds cease to be available. This applies equally to species which are at present common in the wild – for they will become avicultural rarities unless a solid foundation of aviary-bred stock is established while the birds are available to do this.

The story of the Carolina Parrakeet is a cautionary one. It could happen again. The status of some species of parrots which are well known in captivity is unknown in the wild. Many have not been studied in their natural habitat, especially those from New Guinea and Indonesia. Aviculturists could be harbouring stocks of species for which captive breeding will be the last hope. The status of a species, particularly those from islands or with a limited range, can change suddenly and dramatically for the worse when man interferes with their habitat.

It is vitally important for all available parrot species to be established in captivity. It is multi-generation breedings of captive-bred parrots which must be the aim of all aviculturists. Specialisation is therefore the key to success.

Part Two

The Species of Parrot

11
Australian Parrakeets

The birds discussed in this chapter are the most widely kept group in Europe, accounting for perhaps as many as 60 per cent of the parrots in aviculture. In the USA, there tends to be greater diversity within each collection and the percentage of Australian parrakeets kept is very much smaller. In Europe, there are many collections consisting only of these birds. As a group, they are often referred to as the Broadtails, excluding *Neophema* and the Swift Parrakeet.

Australian parrakeets have three major advantages: the ease with which many reproduce themselves in captivity, often resulting in a self-financing hobby; the fact that all the birds available have been aviary-bred for generations, thus there are none of the problems experienced with wild-caught birds; and their colour and beauty. In addition their voices are not loud or harsh and they are not destructive. The last factor results in aviary interiors remaining neat and needing little maintenance.

They have a disadvantage which is considered by some aviculturists as being of no consequence but is quite important enough for others to by-pass the whole group: it is their lack of response (with a few exceptions) to their keeper. While some become tame and confiding, most remain indifferent. There is not often the rapport which exists between many other kinds of parrots and their owner.

Feeding: These parrakeets require a varied assortment of seeds, with sunflower and peanuts in larger proportions for the larger species. Seeding grasses are an important item of diet of all species in the wild so these, and other greenfood, should be offered throughout the year. Greatly increased quantities should be provided when young are in the nest, together with a rearing food such as bread and milk; and soaked or sprouted sunflower seed in preference to dry sunflower. Sprouted mung beans may also be accepted. Most species will eat apple – but greenfood is far more important than fruit for these birds.

A particular note should be made that prophylactic worming is probably more necessary than for any other group of parrots. Being ground-feeders, Australian parrakeets are especially prone to harbour intestinal worms. This is something which all breeders of these birds, especially the larger species, must be prepared to cope with. Probably these worms are the most common cause of death, even though most breeders treat their birds with a preparation to kill the worms and eggs of *Ascaridia*. This needs to be carried out at least twice annually. (See also Chapter 9.)

Accommodation: These parrakeets are essentially aviary birds and should never be considered by those who require a colourful pet bird. Close confinement is cruel; they will not thrive in a cage. And hand-reared birds tend to be aggressive rather than affectionate.

In Europe, change in the size of aviaries for these birds has occurred over the years. In the 1930s, the Duke of Bedford advocated housing pairs in flights 9–12 m (30–40 ft) long whereas previously they were often housed in very large mixed aviaries where they must have been responsible for the deaths of many small birds. Few aviculturists had the resources of the Duke of Bedford but, until the 1960s, it was usual to house these birds in aviaries 6–9 m (20–30 ft) long. By the 1970s, the cost of wood was so high that aviaries exceeding 6 m (20 ft) in length were rare.

In Australia, the native parrakeets have seldom been spaciously housed except when included in mixed aviaries containing, for example, finches and doves. Indeed, an Australian aviculturist visiting Europe for the first time in 1978 expressed his amazement at the length of the flights for Australian parrakeets. By the same year, a number of breeders of some years' standing had revised their ideas and no longer believed that long flights were necessary for the larger species. Lest the fashion should swing too far in the other direction, it should be pointed out that flights measuring at least 4.5–6 m (15–20 ft) are a desirable minimum for the larger parrakeets. The exercise they allow can only be beneficial and, in smaller aviaries, the occupants could become lethargic. Perches should be placed within a few inches of each end – and none in between – so that the maximum flight area is used.

Australian parrakeets are hardy, with the exception of two species of *Neophema*, the Splendid and the Turquoisine, which have little tolerance for damp conditions and will therefore benefit from aviaries which can be enclosed with panels of polythene or glass during inclement weather. In cold climates, a type of aviary described by Groen (1962) can be used for these species. A small range would be completely boarded in, except for a window in the back and the sloping front. This front has glass panels which fit over the wire netting and are removed during the winter to admit direct sunlight only. The downward sloping front has two advantages: it admits some rain and it prevents parrakeets from roosting on the wire at night. These aviaries are particularly suitable for rare and valuable winter-breeding species such as Hooded and Golden-shouldered Parrakeets. It is possible to heat them without any heat-loss and to provide artificial light if necessary.

In contrast to that type of aviary, most Australian parrakeets will do best in entirely open aviaries, that is, those situated away from trees. Groen had an interesting theory on this point. A tree-climbing lizard, the goanna, is a major hazard to the eggs and young of parrakeets in Australia. The incubating bird, hearing the goanna progress up the bark of the tree, will leave her nest. But if it has progressed by means of an overhanging branch from another tree, she will not be aware of its proximity, thus sites with such branches are avoided. As an example which would appear to confirm that this factor can prevent some pairs from breeding in captivity, different pairs had occupied an aviary of an aviculturist, the last in a range, above which were numerous branches from a near-by tree. No young were ever reared there, yet the pairs in the other aviaries in the range were successful.

Breeding: More Australian parrakeets are reared in captivity than any other group of parrots. Western European countries, especially the Netherlands and Germany, could be described as a hot-bed of parrakeet breeders. Species which are rare in other European countries and in the USA, for example, are relatively common. In the Nether-

lands alone, there are estimated to be over one hundred actual breeding pairs of Hooded Parrakeets whereas, at the time of writing, there are few pairs in Britain which are producing young. The falling prices of a number of species formerly considered as rare indicate that greatly increased numbers are being reared, and it is to be hoped that the trend will continue.

Grass Parrakeets
Neophema

Few parrots have achieved such huge popularity among aviculturists as the members of this genus. The combined total reared every year in European aviaries is greater than that of any other genus of parrots, with the possible exception of the Cockatiel. Five of seven of these diminutive Grass Parrakeets are well known aviary birds and three are immensely popular. Sexual dimorphism varies from the extreme to the slight.

Bourke's Parrakeet differs from the other members of the genus in being mainly brown, pink and buff in colour, whereas the others are predominantly green with blue frontal band or forehead and other areas of bright colour. It has been placed in the monospecific genus *Neopsephotus* by de Grahl (1973) and other taxonomists. It is of interest that while the green *Neophema* hybridise readily among themselves, Bourke's has never hybridised with any other species.

Feeding: No problems are encountered in feeding these small parrakeets. They should be offered canary seed, white millet and hemp, also niger, small sunflower seed, linseed and groats. Millet sprays will be relished. Soaked seed and plenty of seeding grasses, chickweed and spinach beet should be offered when there are young in the nest. Greenfood of some kind should be included in the diet all the year round. A nutritious rearing food is essential for the production of first class young; one leading breeder offers wholemeal bread and milk with honey; another gives bread and milk as well as digestive biscuit. Proprietary Canary rearing foods will be eagerly eaten by many parrakeets. These foods should be

offered in advance of the breeding season and form a valuable tonic during the long, cold days of winter.

Accommodation: In these days of small gardens and close neighbours, *Neophema* prove ideal aviary occupants: their voices are inoffensive and they actually do better in small aviaries than in large ones. An enclosure 2.4–3 m (8–10 ft) long, 76 cm ($2\frac{1}{2}$ ft) wide and 1.8 m (6 ft) high is ample for a breeding pair. Larger enclosures have the great disadvantage of the nervous, newly fledged young gathering enough speed on the wing to injure themselves against the welded mesh or wire netting. This can also happen to adult birds if disturbed at night. The aviary must include an enclosed shelter in which the birds can be shut during severe weather. These birds are not in the least destructive and their aviaries will always remain neat in appearance. They have even been kept in planted aviaries.

Neophema will bathe in standing water and on wet foliage but do not usually rain-bathe. Some will also sunbathe, puffing out the body feathers, drooping the wings and flaring the tail.

They derive great enjoyment from nibbling at the grass in turf-floored aviaries; indeed, anyone with a large expanse of lawn might consider constructing portable aviaries so that a fresh supply of grass was readily available. It is difficult to keep turf in good condition in aviaries which are permanently sited.

Breeding: Most species are readily available so breeders should take care to pair together only healthy, unrelated birds, retaining the young which show the best colour.

Most *Neophema* are fertile at one year old. Some females may lay only one clutch during their second year but are usually double-brooded thereafter. The nest-box should be introduced by the end of March. The measurements are not of great importance although the box should be deep enough for the young not to emerge prematurely. The suggested size is 31 cm (12 in) deep and 15 cm (6 in) square with an entrance hole which is just large enough to admit the birds. A couple of inches of damp peat or a peat and soil mixture should be pressed down on the bottom of the box.

Bourke's Parrakeet (*Neophema bourkii*).

strips of material on to the wire or placing a screen of PVC in position.

The young should be removed when they are independent, that is, about three weeks after emerging from the nest. In immature birds, females tend to have more white spots, also larger spots on the under side of the wings.

Bourke's Parrakeet
N. bourkii

This is, without a doubt, one of the most delightful of all parrakeets. It has no vice and possesses every possible virtue, being a free breeder, hardy, gentle and confiding by nature and having an attractive warbling song with no loud or harsh notes. It can be kept with finches and small soft-billed birds and, out of the breeding season, with other Bourke's. However, pairs must be given separate accommodation during the breeding season.

They are most active at twilight; their large dark eyes provide a clue to their crepuscular habits. Quiet and often seeking shade during the day, the strange whistling sound made by their wings can often be heard at night, also their gentle twittering call notes. Even in an aviary, their plumage provides a good camouflage, seeming to merge into the branch on which they are sitting.

This species can be whole-heartedly recommended both to the beginner and to the more experienced parrot keeper. It is certain to provide great enjoyment.

Description: This is the most distinctive of the Grass Parrakeets, being the only one which has no green in its plumage. Upper parts are brownish, with light buff margins to the wing coverts. The abdomen is pink and this colour margins the brownish feathers of the face and breast. Wing margins are violet; under tail coverts and sides of the rump are pale blue. The male has the forehead blue; in the female the face is more strongly tinged with white. There is less pink on the female's breast feathers which are marked with buff. The wing stripe is present in the female. The bill is greyish horn-coloured and the iris is brown. Length: 20 cm (8 in).

Immature birds resemble the female but have less pink on the abdomen.

When the nest-box is placed in position, the male may drive the female about and she may lose a few feathers in the process but, unlike the larger parrakeets, serious damage almost never occurs.

The clutch usually consists of four to six eggs, although as many as ten are not rare. As the female will not be able to incubate more than seven eggs properly, additional ones should be removed. The incubation period is 18 or 19 days and often does not commence until the second or third egg has been laid. The young are covered with long white down on hatching. They are brooded closely for about ten days, by which time they have a good covering of pin feathers and their eyes are starting to open. They usually leave the nest when aged between 28 and 30 days, exceptionally as early as 24 or even 21 days when it may be necessary to return them to the nest.

When the young of the first nest fledge, the female may already be incubating the second clutch. It is advisable to provide two nest-boxes as the second clutch is then likely to be laid in a different box. If this happens, the male will invariably finish feeding the young of the first clutch. Some males will persecute certain youngsters. Some young are independent as soon as five days after leaving the nest, when it is preferable to remove them if persecution occurs rather than risk them being killed by the male.

Precautions to prevent them injuring themselves when they leave the nest should be made in advance of the anticipated date. Because they appear not to see wire netting or mesh, that at the end of the aviary must be rendered obvious or screened in some way. Suggestions include placing twiggy branches at the end of the aviary, growing convolvulus over it, tying

Some males have a trace of blue on the forehead; their heads are larger and flatter. Adult plumage is acquired at the first moult which occurs at the age of four or five months.

Colour is variable in this species. Breeders should select for the best coloured birds, retaining those which have the deepest coloured pink and blue areas as these are most attractive. The extent of blue on the male's forehead also varies, this area being small in some birds.

It is not uncommon for birds with pink or red in the plumage to breed young with an increased amount of this colour; this has happened on many occasions in the Bourke's Parrakeet. In at least one instance, this was due to a mutation which must have been sex-linked, for only the females were affected. Dutch aviculturist, Herr Goosens, paired a Normal male with a female bred from an Isabelle male. The first seven young reared were four Normal males and three females with rose-tinted backs. After moulting the rose colour intensified. In 1973 the pair reared two more rose-backed females.

One aviculturist who bred a Bourke's which was almost entirely pink was dismayed to find that the male attacked it when it left the nest, presumably looking on such a brightly coloured bird as a rival. The male was removed and the female finished rearing it. It was less pink after the first moult.

To date, three mutations are firmly established, but several others have occurred and been lost. In the early 1960s, W. R. Partridge of Evesham bred a Fallow – a Dilute bird with black eyes.

In Belgium, a partly white bird was bred with a rosy tinge to the breast and head and a bluish sheen on the flanks; there were dark scaly markings on the head and neck.

Birds pied with light yellow on the back and wings have also been bred.

The three established mutations are the Isabelle (Cinnamon), the Yellow and the Pink (Rosa). All are expensive at the time of writing.

The Yellow has the upper parts yellow, the head and breast pale pink, the cheeks white and blue areas paler than in the Normal bird. One breeder described the young of this mutation

as naked until ten days when a 'tight cotton-wool' down appeared, while two other breeders of this mutation stated that the down was no different to that of the Normal.

The Yellow mutation is recessive and therefore takes a long time to establish. Because it is necessary for breeders to keep so many of the normally coloured young, each one ringed for identification, it is doubtful whether it will ever gain the popularity of a sex-linked Lutino mutation, for example.

As yet most specimens of this mutation are under-sized.

The Isabelle mutation is lighter yellow on the upper parts. A good specimen is strikingly coloured with little barring on the breast. Like the Yellow, it has red eyes, and pink feet. Those being bred in Britain at the time of writing are recessive in their manner of inheritance; in Europe, a sex-linked Isabelle mutation had occurred.

The Rosa (Rosy, Rose or Pink) mutation first appeared in young bred by Herr Goosens of the Netherlands in 1970 or 1971. The colouration is variable, described by Erhart (1982) as follows:

> . . . soft rosy reds which cover almost the entire body. Only the tail, the primaries and a few of the secondary wing feathers remain dark. Some blue remains on the rump and on the secondaries, but the blue frontal band on males as well as the intense blue on the underside of the wings are missing.

This mutation is sex-linked in its manner of inheritance. Chicks are dark-eyed. When they are about nine days old, the feet of Normal Bourke's turn dark; those of this mutation remain flesh-coloured. At 16 days the first rosy feathers are visible on the back.

Range/Habitat: Bourke's Parrakeets inhabit the interior of southern and central Australia and prefer the dry scrubland associated with acacia. They spend much time feeding on the ground, where their brown upper parts provide superb camouflage. Semi-crepuscular in their habits, they drink before dawn and after sunset. Seeds are the main constituent of their diet.

Decline in populations of this species was thought to be so severe

that, in 1958, Bourke's Parrakeet was included in a list of extinct and disappearing birds. It is now known to be common throughout much of its extensive range and it may well be increasing.

Aviculture: This species was first exhibited at London Zoo in 1867. When importations were received in the late 1870s, Gedney noted that Bourke's were readily sold at 'prices equal to £2 per oz weight'. However, in 1884, Greene described them as being 'as rare as a Phoenix'. The pair obtained by W. Fasey in 1904 were probably the only living specimens seen in Britain for 15 or 20 years. They reared two nests, of two and five, in 1906, and gained for Mr Fasey the Avicultural Society's medal for the first breeding of this species. From that year until the start of World War I, Bourke's were reared on many occasions. Keston Foreign Bird Farm was the first to breed them after the war and was mainly responsible for making them available.

The earliest breeding record in Europe dates back to 1877 when Belgian breeder H. Kessels reared 19 in five nests! In Germany, Russ was successful in 1880.

In Australia and the USA, this species has been bred since the early 1930s. The Duke of Bedford, then Lord Tavistock, supplied Californian breeders with birds when they were feared to be near extinction in the wild. The climate in California proved ideal for them and they were reared in large numbers.

Bourke's are now bred in every country where aviculture is pursued and have become one of the most popular of all parrakeets. They are quite often used to foster the young of other *Neophema* and, they are also reputed to have reared Many-coloured Parrakeets.

The clutch usually consists of four or five eggs. When the chicks hatch, after an incubation period of 18 or 19 days, they are covered with white down. They leave the nest when aged between four and four and a half weeks old.

In Switzerland, Dr Burkard has bred this species on the colony system; five pairs in an aviary measuring 2 × 8 m (7 × 24 ft).

Splendid Grass Parrakeet (*Neophema splendida*) – male left, female right.

Splendid Grass Parrakeet (or Scarlet-chested Parrot)

N. splendida

Description: This is undoubtedly one of the most beautiful of all parrakeets, the male having exceptionally lustrous plumage. The male's head is blue, of a deeper shade on the throat and cheeks with an almost luminous quality. The wings are broadly edged with pale blue; under wing coverts and outer edges of the flight feathers are dark blue; the rest of the under parts are yellow. The breast is scarlet. Upper parts are green and the tail is green, the lateral feathers being blue tipped with yellow. The bill is greyish black and the iris is brown. Length: 19 cm (8 in). Weight: M 40–44 g (about 1½ oz); F 36–37 g (1 3/10 oz).

The female lacks the red on the breast, this area being green. The blue on the head is duller and more re-stricted than in the male; the lores are blue (not white as in the female Tur-quoisine). The wing is broadly edged with blue, of a lighter shade than in the female Turquoisine.

Immature birds resemble the female but are slightly duller. Young males usually show more blue on the face than females. About two or three months after leaving the nest, red feathers begin to appear on the breast; exceptionally, these may be apparent on fledging. Adult plumage is assumed at about five or six months.

An especially detailed description of immature plumage made by F. C. Barnicoat (1982) is worth quoting:

> The young cocks tend to be bigger es-pecially with regard to the head and feet . . . . Furthermore, colour is the main distinguishing feature. In the males, the blue on the wings is wider and brighter, especially the dark blue on the primaries, and the blue on the face is more ex-tensive and of a darker, cobalt shade in contrast to the female's turquoise shade. Males also have a brighter yellow on the belly, which extends higher up than in a female, and far brighter under tail coverts. Females are generally more olive green and males more of a grass green especially on the rump.

A number of colour variations are known but, to date, only the blue mut-ation is firmly established. Others bred in captivity are Yellow; birds pied with yellow; Cinnamon; and, in Australia, a Fawn mutation.

The Blue mutation (autosomal re-cessive) was established in Australia by D. Ikin in Melbourne. In Britain, it was established by Professor J. R. Hodges (1975) of Pinner who stated:

> In general the green of the normal is replaced by blue, the yellow by creamy-white and the red of the cock by a pinkish-apricot. The blue can vary from almost violet to a greenish-blue, the

chest colour from a pale pink flush to orange and the underparts from cream to white. In some cocks the blue of the back and face is particularly intense and the underparts are snow-white with hardly a trace of pink on the chest. Others are greenish-blue on the back, orange on the chest with the abdomen and under tail coverts very pale yellow. The hens exhibit a similar variation and some have blue chests, bluish-green backs and cream underparts whereas others are deep blue on the chest and back and white on the abdomen and under the tail. When the young leave the nest they are a lovely powder-blue rather like that of the blue Ring-necked Parrakeet. Splendids have a feather texture which appears to be different from that of the other species of their genus and the green feathers of the back and wings have some degree of iridescence. This is particularly noticeable in those mutants in which the blue pigmentation is less intense and they appear blue in dull light and shining blue-green in the sun. I have heard these described as 'poor coloured blues' but, with their orange chests, they are quite as attractive as the deeper coloured specimens. There is usually an inverse correlation between the intensity of the blue and the depth of the pinkish-apricot on the chest, but, last year a cock was reared from a pair consisting of a deep blue cock and split blue hen, which has a dark green back and yellow underparts and an almost completely yellow chest.

Professor Hodges found that Blue Splendids are as large and as hardy as their normal counterparts. At first, Blues were paired together but the resulting chicks invariably died within 24 hours of hatching. The Australian breeder reported that mating two Blues together appeared to introduce a lethal factor which caused the death of the embryo or the newly hatched young. Subsequently, Blues were paired to Normals and the split Blue young were paired to unrelated Blues, producing Blue and split Blue young in approximately equal numbers.

A pair of Blue young produced three nests of Blues (four, five and five young) for George Smith, contradicting the 'lethal gene' theory.

Professor Hodges found that fertility was good among the Blues but they seldom reared more than two or three young and, furthermore, usually proved single-brooded, moulting in July. The mutation is only slowly being established in Britain. In Germany, Winfried Krause has established a variety in which the entire breast and abdomen are red.

Range/Habitat: The Splendid Grass Parrakeet inhabits the interior of southern Australia. It is an irregular and scarce visitor to some areas, locally common in others. Usually in small groups, it is sometimes seen in quite large flocks. Sightings of this unobtrusive little parrakeet have never been common; indeed, in the early years of the twentieth century it was feared to be extinct. Great was the excitement of ornithologists when it re-appeared in 1932 in the vicinity of Adelaide.

Aviculture: The Splendid has an interesting avicultural history. A pair were received in 1871 by London Zoo – the first seen in Europe. (That young were reared a short time after was recorded in error.) It was not seen in Europe again until 1933 when a pair was presented to King George V; shortly after, another pair was obtained by the Duke of Bedford. He sent them to Keston Foreign Bird Farm where they reared young in the following year. The male of the breeding pair was an exceptional bird with the entire under parts scarlet. No wonder that Boosey described his first sight of the pair as 'one of the most thrilling moments of my avicultural career'.

In the 1940s, Splendids became available to European aviculturists and to those in the USA; the first breeding there occurred in 1947 in the aviaries of David West in California. In Australia, S. Harvey of Adelaide was the first breeder in 1932.

Many of the Splendids received from Australia at this time were not good specimens or were suffering from mycoplasma. Thus the Splendid acquired a reputation for being difficult to breed or delicate. This is partly justified, for many breeders of *Neophema* have found this species more susceptible to sudden death when apparently in perfect health than are other members of the genus. It seems to dislike damp conditions; indeed, it was the opinion of Dr H. D. Groen that 'in Holland they have never prospered as well as in other European countries and I have the impression that in our country their numbers increase but little and that this is due to the wet climate'.

That aviary-bred Splendids developed some kind of resistance to the European climate became very clear when the figures collated for the 1977 Breeding Register of the Parrot Society were examined. Much to everyone's surprise it was found that, next to the Cockatiel, more Splendids had been bred than any other species, the total being 1,400 – an increase of just over 50 per cent on the previous year.

Whatever the fate of this species in its natural habitat, it is certain to survive in European aviaries while its popularity is maintained at this level. It has every conceivable virtue, being tame and confiding, exceptionally beautiful, the possessor of a quiet almost finch-like voice and, of course, being very ready to breed in aviaries.

The Splendid has hybridised with all the commonly kept *Neophema*. It would appear that most, if not all, of the hybrids with the Turquoisine Parrakeet are infertile.

Turquoisine Grass Parrakeet
N. pulchella

Description: The male is distinguished from the Splendid by the dark red bar down the wing (formed by the inner wing coverts) and by the uniformly yellow under parts. The face and the upper wing coverts are turquoise-blue. The entire upper parts, from the crown, are green. Under wing coverts and outer edge of flight feathers are dark blue. The under side of the tail is yellow. The bill is greyish black and the iris is brown. Length is 20 cm (8 in). Weight: M 37–44 g ($1\frac{3}{10}$–$1\frac{1}{2}$ oz); F 38 g ($1\frac{3}{10}$ oz).

The female is duller throughout and lacks the dark red patch on the wing. There is less blue on the face and the breast is dull greenish.

Female Turquoisines can be distinguished from female Splendids by the slightly lighter shade of green, smaller amount of blue on the head and face which is confined to the top of the head and small areas above and below the eyes. The blue is a slightly deeper colour as it is on the wings.

Immature birds resemble the female; males have more blue on the face and usually show at least an indication of the red wing bar. Individuals vary in this respect: some show red on the wings while still in the nest, others appear to develop it after several weeks out of the nest and, more rarely, the red is not apparent until after the first moult at about five months.

A well-known colour phase is the Orange-bellied in which males and females have a large patch of orange on the abdomen. This phase occurs in the wild and is not the result of captive breeding. John Courtney informed me:

I have observed Turquoise Parrots in the wild for many years. Plain yellow-bellied and orange-bellied occur together in the same area. Yellow-bellied are numerically more common than rich orange. In nests of young examined by me, the young are usually all plain yellow or are all orange. However, Sandy Hunt of Delungra examined a nest in the first week of December 1984, in a tree stump on his farm, in which two of the young were plain yellow on the breast and the other two rich orange.

A mutation which, at the time of writing, is bred only in small numbers is the Yellow. It is extremely attractive, being clear buttercup yellow with the red shoulder stripe and the blue areas retained; at least one strain has combined the Orange-bellied characteristic. This black-eyed mutation is recessive in its manner of inheritance. It originated in Australia.

The Pied mutation, as yet not well known, was developed in the Netherlands in about 1970 by Bob Fregeres of Den Dolder. Heavily marked birds are difficult to sex; the wing patch is orange-red in both sexes. Males have a small band of white on the forehead which is usually lacking in females. This mutation is sex-linked in its manner of inheritance.

Range/Habitat: This parrakeet inhabits south-eastern Australia, in scattered locations from south-eastern Queensland to northern Victoria. It declined dramatically during the early years of the century but its numbers have recovered in some areas, probably due to the discontinuation of grazing. It is seen in pairs or small groups, in timbered grasslands and open forests.

Aviculture: The Turquoisine's history parallels that of the Splendid in that, during the early years of the century, it

Turquoisine Grass Parrakeets (*Neophema pulchella*) – male left, female right.

was believed to be extinct and 70 years later, its numbers in captivity had increased to such a degree that they may well exceed those in the wild.

During the nineteenth century, it was bred in Europe on many occasions. One of the earliest successes occurred in Paris in 1855; at London Zoo it reared young on many occasions between 1860 and 1882 and, in Belgium, young were reared at Antwerp Zoo in 1861. During this era it was said to be so abundant in its natural habitat that it was a common ingredient of 'parrot pie'.

The widespread introduction of sheep resulted in the destruction of the grasses on which it fed and this factor contributed to its decline.

During the late 1920s it was reintroduced to European aviculture, after an absence of 40 years. In the USA, F. H. Rudkin's rearing of four young in 1933 was a first success. By this time, Australian aviculturists had established it to several generations, finding it both hardy and prolific.

In 1960, when export of Australian

birds ceased, Turquoisines were expensive although fairly well established in Europe. At that time many breeders on the Continent reared them in indoor cages and the resulting young were hardly able to survive in outdoor aviaries, as British owners of these imported birds discovered. However, this time, faced with no new source of supply, aviculturists made a good job of building up aviary-bred stocks so that today the Turquoisine is one of the least expensive and most prolific of all parrakeets, and is invariably recommended to the beginner.

More aggressive than some of the *Neophema*, adult pairs must be housed on their own and preferably not next to other Turquoisines or Splendids. The male's display is slight: he draws his plumage tightly together, slightly spreads and expands his wing from the shoulder and walks with a swaggering gait. Some males are rather quarrelsome and continually chase the female, especially when they come into breeding condition in advance of their mates. Because of their aggressiveness, they sometimes prove more difficult to pair up than other *Neophema*. When excited, the male will fly about wildly, spreading his tail to show the striking yellow feathers.

Turquoisines are almost invariably double-brooded. Some pairs would be ready to rear a third nest, but this should not be allowed if their stamina is not to be impaired. Also, they may moult before the young are reared and thus neglect them.

When the young fledge they should be removed fairly soon after they are independent as some males will attack their male offspring. The young tend to be extremely wild on leaving the nest.

One breeder found that they were so prone to scalping themselves on the aviary roof that he fixed a panel of clear plastic on a frame on the under side of the roof, thus preventing injury to their heads when they flew upwards.

In 1970, the *Magazine of the Parrot Society* published a survey of the results (or lack of) of 28 pairs, two of which made no attempt to breed. The 26 pairs produced 242 eggs in 46 clutches, giving an average clutch size of 5.2. Just over half the eggs (126), hatched out and, of these, 108 young lived to leave the nest, which, at 85 per cent, gave a higher rearing average than Bourke's (72 per cent) or Cockatiels (79 per cent). However, 15 (14 per cent) of the fledged young did not reach independence and one can assume that some of these losses were due to injuries. Sixteen of the 26 pairs were double-brooded and four females laid third clutches.

The Turquoisine has hybridised with the Elegant, Blue-winged and Splendid Grass Parrakeets and probably with other members of the genus.

Elegant Grass Parrakeet
N. elegans
Description: Whether perched or in flight, this bird well deserves its name. A slim, graceful bird, the male has the crown and upper parts rich golden olive with a conspicuous frontal band of dark blue, behind which is a narrower line of light blue extending to the eye. The under parts are yellow, with a greenish tinge on the breast and a small orange patch on the abdomen in some birds; wing coverts are blue and pale greenish blue and the under wing coverts are dark blue. The tail is blue above and yellow on the under side. The bill is greyish black and the iris is brown. Length: 23 cm (9 in). Weight: M 42–51 g (1½–1⅘ oz); F 42–45 g (1½–1⅗ oz).

The female is a duller shade of olive without the golden hue, and without the orange patch on the abdomen. The wing stripe, invariably absent in the male, is occasionally indicated in the female.

Immature birds resemble the female or are duller, but lack the frontal band. Adult plumage is assumed at about four months.

The only mutation established so far is the Lutino. In 1972 T. Slagmolen, a Belgian breeder, produced a Lutino from a pair which were of Normal appearance; it died at the first moult. When a male Lutino was bred from Normal parents in 1974 it was realised that the mutation was not a sex-linked one, but recessive. When split birds were paired together, the result was 25% Lutinos, 50% Normals split for Lutino and 25% Normals.

The Lutinos were weak and if they succeeded in getting out of the shell, they usually died at the first moult.

Elegant Grass Parrakeet (*Neophema elegans*).

Progress was slow because it was necessary to test mate all the young, to discover whether they were split. By the beginning of 1978 Mr Slagmolen had seven Lutinos and seven known splits. Slagmolen (1978) described the Lutinos as being:

> . . . extremely beautiful, buttercup yellow with a clear white stripe on the forehead and white wing feathers.
>
> The orange spot between the legs remains on the males, a feature which looks extremely good against the yellow plumage. Although its inheritance is recessive, the hen has the brown legs and red eyes of a sex-linked Lutino.

Range/Habitat: The Elegant Grass Parrakeet has a wider distribution than most *Neophema*, having increased its numbers and range during recent years. It is found in the extreme west of Western Australia, over much of South Australia and western Victoria. Immelmann (1968) thought that it was one of the most abundant of the genus. One reason he gave for its increase was the cultivation of clover – its principal food in some areas.

It spends much time quietly searching for food on the ground. Seeds, of marsh and other grasses, and wild and cultivated fruits are the main items of its diet. Immelmann remarked on their excellent camouflage and how often they would 'fly up only a few yards in front of the observer's feet without the least indication of their presence beforehand . . .'.

During the breeding season, they are seen in pairs or small groups; at other times large flocks are encountered.
Aviculture: This parrakeet was first imported into Britain in 1859 and the first breeding took place at London Zoo in the following year. In Belgium it was first bred by Mascré in 1880 and in France by Decoux in 1935. In the USA, J. H. Arnold of California was the first to be successful, in 1930. He obtained three pairs from the Duke of Bedford and, three years later, had 54 Elegants. The species did so well there that in 1951 David West stated that it was the only *Neophema* which was 'commonly available'.

Although they often prove to be prolific, they did not become readily available and low-priced in Europe until the early 1960s. Dr H. D. Groen (1962) wrote:

> . . . until 5 or 6 years ago they were rarely seen in our aviaries, the majority apparently were sold abroad by the dealers. Only recently people have started to discern their charm and many good qualities as aviary birds and they are now widely kept and bred and highly in demand. I have been keeping three pairs for many years and they have proved to be very reliable in producing their offspring every season. As a rule they are double-brooded, in fact I do not remember any of them ever omitting a second brood, and the clutches contain from three to five youngsters. The birds are kept here in spacious flights, overgrown with grass, and the young are exclusively fed with the seeds of these grasses, the tray with the usual seed-mixture practically being left alone.

In a survey carried out by the Parrot Society of breeding results in 1969, it was found that six pairs produced 14 young which left the nest; however, only six of these lived. In the 1976 breeding register of the Parrot Society, 27 members reported breeding 271 young, while the following year 70 members produced 409; allowing for increased participation in the register, this still indicates the growing popularity of this parrakeet. If it has a fault, it is that it is less active than many parrakeets.

Among the other members of the genus with which the Elegant has hybridised are the Blue-winged, Turquoisine and Splendid.

Blue-winged Grass Parrakeet
N. chrysostoma

Description: This species has a similar colour scheme to the Elegant but it is much greener below and less slender in build. The male is olive-green on the head, mantle, breast and rump, except on the crown and face which are yellow. The rich blue frontal band is edged with paler blue and does not extend quite as far as the eye. The abdomen is yellow; some males have

an irregular patch of orange in the centre. All the wing coverts are blue (deeper in colour and more extensive than in the Elegant) and the tail is bluish grey. The bill is greyish black and the iris is brown. Length: 22 cm (8½ in). Weight: M 48–61 g ($1\frac{7}{10}$–$2\frac{1}{5}$ oz); F 44–49 g ($1\frac{3}{5}$–$1\frac{3}{4}$ oz).

The female is usually duller in colour. According to Professor J. R. Hodges, the only reliable guide to sex is the colour of the primaries – jet black in the male and brownish black in the female.

Immature birds are duller than the female. They lack the frontal band and have the wings dull slaty-blue. The wing stripe is present in females, absent in some males. The bill is horn-coloured. Adult plumage is acquired at the age of eight or nine months.

One ornithologist noted that in the wild, colouration varies according to the season. Before breeding, the orange

spot on the abdomen is particularly bright; later it fades and finally it almost disappears.

Range/Habitat: The Blue-winged Grass Parrakeet is found over an extensive area of south-eastern Australia, also in Tasmania and the islands of the Bass Straits. Found in a wide variety of habitats, it is the least specialised *Neophema* in this respect. In south-western Queensland and New South Wales, it is a summer and autumn visitor only. It is common in many parts of its range and its numbers have increased during recent years. Unlike other *Neophema*, it is closely associated with man, especially in Tasmania. However, in late autumn when the temperature there drops almost to freezing, it departs to the warmer climes of the Australian mainland. Its diet is similar to that of the Elegant. Highly social, it associates in flocks even during the breeding season. It is

Blue-winged Grass Parrakeet (*Neophema chrysostoma*).

common throughout much of its breeding range, especially in Tasmania.
Aviculture: First imported into Europe during the 1870s, this species has never been common in captivity. It was first bred in France in 1879 by Bigeau and in Germany in 1886 by W. Harres. In Britain, the Avicultural Society's medal for the first breeding was awarded to W. A. Fasey in 1909. In the USA, the first successes were gained in 1930 by Dr L. Patrick and at San Diego Zoo. S. Harvey was the first to breed it in South Australia in 1935.

The most consistent breeder of this species in Britain is Professor J. R. Hodges who has kept it since 1964. After breeding most of the *Neophema*, he reached the conclusion that this species was the most robust. At first, breeding results were disappointing but their breeding performance gradually improved to give an average of more than 20 young annually from three or four pairs. To date he has reared more than 200 birds of excellent quality, using only the best young to form unrelated pairs.

Professor Hodges (1970) has found that, unlike Splendid and Turquoisine Parrakeets, which may commence to lay a week or so after the boxes are placed in position, the Blue-wing rarely lays before the end of April. Perhaps as a result, he has not had one case of egg-binding. Females brood young closely during the day until they are about ten days old and at night until they are at least three weeks old. He has found this species almost invariably double-brooded.

It is a curious fact that, despite its prolificacy in the hands of some breeders, this parrakeet has not become well established in captivity. An extremely hardy bird on fledging, the young are not prone to injuring themselves by flying into wire, as so often happens with other *Neophema*. This makes its scarcity all the more puzzling. In 1976 and 1977, members of the Parrot Society reported breeding only 18 and 39 young respectively (by five and six members). One of these pairs, in the possession of Professor J. R. Hodges, must have set an all-time productivity record for this species by rearing 68 young in nine years. 'Retired' on loan to a friend in 1976, they reared two more.

Clutch size is usually four to six, but nine or ten eggs have been recorded. In display, the male Blue-wing draws himself up to his full height, depresses his shoulders to show the blue on the wings and makes a two-syllable call.

Inoffensive in character, Blue-wings are best housed on their own. They have been found not to damage growing plants, thus experiments could be made in keeping them in a planted aviary. In every respect they make ideal aviary birds, being quiet and gentle.

Rock Grass Parrakeet
N. petrophila

Description: This is the dullest coloured member of the genus, being brownish olive above, also on the breast; the abdomen and under tail coverts are dull yellow. The frontal band is dark blue, with an inconspicuous line of pale blue behind it. The lores and the area around the eye are pale blue, less extensive in the female. The carpal edge of the wing is light blue; under wing coverts and outer webs of flight feathers are blue. The tail is dull blue tinged with olive. The bill is greyish and the iris dark brown. Length: 22 cm (9 in). Weight: M 47–52 g ($1\frac{7}{10}$–$1\frac{4}{5}$ oz); F 54 g ($1\frac{9}{10}$ oz).

This species is not easy to sex. Females are usually duller with a narrower frontal band. Some males have a small orange patch on the abdomen. Because of its heavy build, where no comparison can be made a single bird is likely to be judged a male.

Immature birds are slightly duller than adults and lack the blue frontal band and the blue on the face, which is olive. The wing stripe is present. Adult plumage is assumed at about five months.
Range/Habitat: As its name suggests, this species inhabits rocky islets up to 20 km (12 miles) offshore and along the coastal sand dunes of southern and south-western Australia. It is common throughout its range. It forages for the seeds and fruits of grasses and shrubs and nests in rocks above high water.
Aviculture: This species is now unknown in aviculture outside Australia. It was imported into Europe as long ago as the 1870s but in small numbers, presumably because its dull colour-

ation, especially in comparison with the other *Neophema*, and its tendency to obesity, resulted in there being little interest in it. Alan Lendon described it as fat and sluggish and tending to die suddenly when apparently in good health, and Edward Boosey thought it 'quite the dullest and least interesting member of the family, both in temperament and colour'. Shortly after the export of Australian fauna ceased in 1960, Dr H. D. Groen (1962) wrote that there were 'odd pairs in Germany, Denmark and Switzerland, but I have not heard of any of them nesting'.

Dr Russ is reputed to have reared one young bird in Germany in 1879; if so, this was the only European success. With the exception of Dr Polak in the Netherlands before World War II, probably few breeders made persistent efforts to breed this species, being discouraged by infertile eggs. Presumably obesity was the cause.

The Rock Parrakeet has seldom reached Britain. In 1938, N. H. Dixon obtained a pair, the female of which probably laid at least one egg that year. In the following year, another pair was obtained. They co-existed peacefully in an aviary measuring 3 × 0.9 m (10 × 3 ft) × 2 m ($6\frac{1}{2}$ ft) high. One female laid in a cavity in half a ton of rockery which was built up to resemble a miniature cliff, with rocks and sand. A chick hatched which probably died soon after.

Later, three birds were obtained by Professor J. R. Hodges. Far from being dull birds, they were active and tame and the possessors of 'great personality'.

In Australia, this species has been bred on a number of occasions. In South Australia, the first breeder was G. Pearce of Port Augusta in 1936. Later, W. K. Penney of Plympton was also successful; in both cases they nested among rocks but this species will accept an ordinary nest-box quite readily. Mr Penney noticed that the birds' nails and upper mandible grew quickly before he placed large rocks in their aviary. A problem of trying to breed them in a 'rock warren' was that it became overrun with mice. It was therefore rebuilt 23 cm (9 in) higher, on a mouseproof foundation.

Other successful breeders in South Australia were Alan Lendon, in 1941 and 1947 and, more recently, Eric Baxter. He found that females were not fully developed until two years old but that well-developed males could be used for breeding at one year.

This species was bred in Adelaide Zoo in 1941. F. Lewitzka, former Superintendent of Birds, provided me with the following notes on the Rock Parrakeets there:

> The average clutch size is four or five eggs. The male does not feed the young until they are well advanced and climb up to the entrance of the nest-box. They are not as active as other *Neophema*s and have a tendency to become fat, resulting in low fertility; for example, in clutches of five and four eggs, two eggs in each clutch were fertile. Their food consists of canary seed, panicum, white and Japanese millet and, when breeding, groats. Seeding grass heads are provided all the year round.
>
> Breeding aviaries are 4.3 m (13 ft) long and 1.05 m (4 ft) wide. Nest-boxes used are 37 cm (14 in) long × 13 cm (5 in) × 15 cm (6 in), hung at an angle of 45°. Similar sized natural logs are also used.

In Western Australia, Hartley King of St James bred the Rock Grass Parrakeet in 1962. For four years he had kept two pairs without result, for some of the time in a very large aviary with finches and other parrakeets. It was here that a female nested in a log behind a lemon tree which was sprayed for 1½ hours daily. Mr King was quite unaware that the pair were breeding until he took the log down and found four young inside. They were successfully reared and he attributed the result partly to the humid site chosen.

Orange-bellied Grass Parrakeet
N. chrysogaster

Description: This species is distinguished by its rich, dark shade of green on the head, back and rump. Breast and face are of a more yellow shade of green; the abdomen is greenish yellow marked with a large patch of reddish orange. The frontal band is of a bright mid-blue with an inconspicuous pale blue band behind it; the wing is narrowly edged in the same shades of blue and the median wing coverts are pale blue. Bill is greyish brown and the iris dark brown. Length: 20 cm (8 in). Weight: 48–51 g ($1\frac{7}{10}$–$1\frac{4}{5}$ oz).

The female is duller throughout; the frontal band is paler and of one colour only. According to Hamilton (1938), the yellow tinge on the inside of the thigh is missing in the female.

Immature birds are duller than the female; the orange patch on the abdomen is smaller. The wing stripe is present.

Range/Habitat: The Orange-bellied Parrakeet inhabits Tasmania, especially the western areas, islands in Bass Strait and the coastal regions of south-eastern South Australia and western Victoria. It has been found up to 60 km (37 miles) inland but is mainly a coastal species, being found in sand dunes, tidal flats, swamps, open grasslands and light scrub. This species is migratory, leaving the mainland to breed in Tasmania. Seeds, fruits and berries comprise the diet. The extent of the decline of this species was not realised until studies commenced in 1978. The population numbers only between 150 and 200 individuals. In recent years, positive steps have been taken by the National Parks and Wildlife Service to preserve the population.

Aviculture: This parrakeet is almost unknown in aviculture outside of Australia, and few have been kept there. The birds trapped by Dr Hamilton of Adelaide, said to be the first ever in captivity, hatched young which were not reared. In 1950 he informed Alan Lendon that he believed that a young bird was reared in his aviaries during World War II when they received 'minimal attention and practically no observation'. If so, that was a first success anywhere in the world.

In the early 1970s several pairs reached Europe. According to de Grahl (1973) the first European success was that of van Brummelen in the Netherlands in 1971. Three young were reared from five eggs. In the following year J. Postema of Gieterreen, the Netherlands, hatched five young, only one of which was reared. This species has not been established in aviculture.

It has reached Britain on very rare occasions only. There are vague references to its having been exhibited at London Zoo many years ago; otherwise the pair at Keston Foreign Bird Farm may have been the first. Later this species was included in the collections of Alfredo Marques in Bed-

fordshire and Lady Baillie in Kent. At the research centre of the National Parks and Wildlife Service in Hobart, wild-caught Rock Parrakeets and Blue-wings are being kept and their diets carefully monitored in case a captive breeding programme for the Orange-bellied Parrakeet is deemed necessary.

Budgerigar
Melopsittacus

The single member of this genus, the Budgerigar, which is closely related to *Neophema*, has become the best known and most ubiquitous member of the parrot family. No other bird, with the exception of the Canary, has given so much pleasure as a house pet. Care of this species is identical to that recommended for *Neophema* except, of course, it will breed readily in a cage. This should measure not less than 76 cm (2½ ft) long.

Description: The Budgerigar, *M. undulatus*, has been bred in captivity in a far wider range of colours than any other species of bird or animal. The wild Budgerigar has the upper parts and part of the head barred with yellow and black; the forehead and face is yellow, the mask being decorated with three small black spots on either side of a blue mark, known to fanciers as the cheek patch. Under parts are bright green and the tail is greenish blue. The bill is greenish grey and the iris white. The cere is blue in the male and brown in the female (whitish brown in a female not in breeding condition). Length: 18 cm (7 in). Domesticated Budgerigars are much larger and less graceful in shape than their wild counterpart.

Immature birds have the bars on the head extended down to the cere and the throat spots replaced by flecking. Their colouring is duller throughout and the iris is dark.

Range/Habitat: The Budgerigar has a very extensive range over the entire inland areas of Australia, being absent from coastal areas, Cape York Peninsula and Tasmania.

Inhabitants of grasslands, scrublands and open plains, they are found in immense flocks and must surely be the most numerous of all Australian

Budgerigar (*Melopsittacus undulatus*) female.

parrots. They are nomadic, moving around in search of the seeding grasses which form the main item of their diet, and water.

Aviculture: Because it is able to exist in arid, unfavourable conditions, it could be said to be pre-adapted to captivity, thus it is not surprising that the Budgerigar was the first species of parrot to become domesticated and is still kept and bred in far, far greater numbers than any other. No other small bird makes such an attractive pet if obtained when young, or so readily becomes tame or learns to mimic. When John Gould brought the first Budgerigars to England in 1840 he could hardly have foreseen this species' unparalleled popularity.

Budgerigars lay four to eight eggs which are incubated by the female for 18 days. Young birds spend about 30 days in the nest.

There are many excellent books devoted to the Budgerigar, for pet owner and breeder, thus its manage-ment will not be covered here.

In an emergency, Budgerigars can make useful foster-parents for species of *Neophema*.

Rosellas
Platycercus

The members of this genus are among the best known of all parrots in captiv-ity, probably because most species are positively gaudy and their bright colours and readiness to breed have long made them favourites with avicul-turists. Their plumage pattern is most distinctive: in all species the feathers of the mantle have the centre black and the edges coloured. There is a promi-nent patch of colour on the cheeks, extending to the throat. The under side of the tail is blue and the bill is horn-coloured. As Lendon pointed out (Lendon & Cayley, 1973), the Rosellas can be divided into three groups by

plumage colouration: Pennant's, Adelaide, Yellow and Green Rosellas; Brown's, Mealy and Red (Golden-mantled) in which group there is no distinct immature plumage, young birds being duller versions of adults; and a third group containing only the Stanley Parrakeet, the only Rosella which can be sexed readily and with yellow instead of blue or blue and white cheek patches.

Feeding: A varied diet is necessary; sunflower, canary seed, hemp, wheat, oats and spray millet should be off-ered, with as much greenfood as pos-sible, especially when young are being reared. Large quantities of wild and cultivated greenfood should, if pos-sible, be fed several times daily.

In a census carried out by the Parrot Society in 1970, it was found that of 51 pairs of Rosellas owned by members, 25 pairs fed on seed and other foods reared 70 chicks. The 26 pairs fed only on seed reared only 31 young. J. T. Walton (1973) described a nutritious rearing food offered to his Rosellas just prior to hatching and while the young were being reared. It consisted of brown and white bread, milk, honey, egg, biscuit and a proprietary rearing food mixed into a soft paste. This was taken enthusiastically by most pairs until about the 26th day after hatching, when small seeds began to form a larger part of the chicks' diet.

Apple is the fruit most likely to be eaten by Rosellas; pear and grapes can also be offered. Berries, such as those of hawthorn and pyracantha – natural items of diet – will be relished, also those of elder. *Platycercus* and *Barn-ardius* species in aviaries have been known to feed earthworms to their young; their need for animal protein can be satisfied by the provision of chop bones.

Accommodation: Rosellas are extreme-ly aggressive birds and on no account should they be housed with any other species of parrot. If possible, housing them within sight of other Rosellas should be avoided and placing pairs in adjoining aviaries is usually a serious mistake, for the male will spend most of the breeding season attempting either to murder his male neighbour or to woo his female one. Whichever species is housed next to Rosellas, it is imperative that the aviary is double-wired as Rosellas can inflict serious or fatal injuries to other birds through wire netting or mesh.

They are enthusiastic bathers and must always have available a large, shallow water container.

While few people would attempt to keep Rosellas at liberty, it should be mentioned that, as liberty birds, pairs are not a success. They are likely to take off and never be seen again. It is of interest that a hand-reared Pennant's Parrakeet which escaped when just over one year old, lived wild in the Lake District for 20 months, probably mainly on wild berries during its first winter – but during the second winter few berries were to be found. The bird belonged to J. Strutt of Kirkby Stephen.

Breeding: Immature Rosellas have a row of white spots on seven or eight feathers on the under side of the wing, which form a stripe when the wing is extended. These are lost by the male in the first or second year when the primary wing feathers are moulted. In the females of *flaveolus*, *eximius*, *adscitus* and *icterotis*, the wing stripe is present in adult birds.

In all Rosellas, it is usual for the male to have a broader head and larger bill, with a noticeably broader upper mandible. Often the male is more brightly coloured, but this is not a reliable indication of sex. In immature birds, the surest guide is the shape of the head and young can be sexed fairly accurately in the nest when there are a number of birds for comparison. Except in the Mealy Rosella, the male has more height above the eye; the head and bill are larger.

When male and female are introduced, they need to be watched carefully for the male may be extremely rough, even murderous, and will not necessarily accept the female provided. In some cases, the female must be removed for her own safety. Occasionally, the problem can be overcome by placing male and female in adjoining aviaries until the male is seen attempting to feed the female (if the aviary is not double-wired) or the female solicits copulation. The male should be introduced to the female's aviary – not vice versa. An alternative solution to an over-aggressive male is to cut part of the flight feathers on one wing so that the female is easily able to escape from him.

In display, which is most pronounced in the male, the tail is spread and moved from side to side, the shoulders are squared and the head is sometimes jerked up and down.

The breeding life of Rosellas can be long, starting at one or two years and extending into their twenties. They lay large clutches and may prove double-brooded, thus a good pair can be responsible for producing a very large number of offspring. The Red (Golden-mantled) Rosella is especially prolific – and this is the species with which beginners usually make a start. Other species, too, quite often rear broods of eight or nine young. Some pairs are exceptionally good foster-parents and will rear young of diverse and quite unrelated parrot species. Groen (1962) mentions a pair of Mealy Rosellas which reared three species of parrakeet in one nest! He also states that ten is the maximum number of eggs a Rosella can cover.

Chicks have long, fluffy white down. The male feeds the female for about two weeks after the chicks hatch; he then feeds the chicks directly and continues to do so until two to three weeks after they have left the nest. Sometimes the female will lay again before all the young have left the nest; for this reason it is advisable to place two nest-boxes in position at the start of the breeding season, so that the female can lay the second clutch in another nest, if she so desires. If a second nest is not available, she may pluck the young which remain in the nest while she is incubating.

Nest-boxes for Rosellas should be from 60–120 cm (2–4 ft) high and 23 cm (9 in) square, with a 6 cm (2½ in) diameter entrance hole, or slightly larger for the larger Rosellas.

The female usually broods the young for about two weeks during the day. A case is on record of a female which ceased to brood the young at night after all six had hatched – yet all were reared. Such behaviour is exceptional, however.

Young birds assume adult plumage at the age of about 15 months, in most cases. The Duke of Bedford (1928b) noted how the red in the plumage of Rosellas 'fades suddenly to a brickish hue' at the onset of the moult. 'The change is as quick and remarkable as the change in the foliage when the autumn frosts begin.'

Pennant's Parrakeet
P. elegans elegans

Description: This bird is known in its native country as the Crimson Rosella. It is one of the most handsome and striking of all parrakeets, with its colour scheme of crimson and blue. Entire under parts are crimson, also the head except the violet patch from the lores to the cheeks. Feathers of the nape, back and wings are black, edged with crimson; median wing coverts are black; bend of the wing, under wing coverts and outer webs of the flight feathers are blue. The tail is blue, tipped with white. The bill is greyish white and the iris is brown.

Length: 36 cm (14 in). Weight: M 123–169 g ($4\frac{3}{10}$–6 oz); F 112–146 g (4–$5\frac{1}{10}$ oz); newly fledged young 138 g ($4\frac{9}{10}$ oz).

Females usually have the head and

Pennant's Parrakeet or Rosella (*Platycercus elegans elegans*).

bill smaller – but in some birds sex is difficult to determine. Males seem to predominate and many 'pairs' are eventually found to be two males.

Immature plumage is variable. More typically, young birds are mainly green with the crown, throat, upper breast, thighs and under tail coverts red and the cheek patch violet. Such birds assume adult plumage with the first complete moult in the second year. Alternatively, immature birds may be more red than green, with green in the areas which will become black. Lendon (Lendon & Cayley 1973) states: '. . . it seems certain that immature *nigrescens* are not green and that a dull red juvenile plumage occurs in the northern part of the range of the typical bird'.

Range/Habitat: The range of Pennant's Parrakeet is eastern and south-eastern Australia. It has been introduced to New Zealand and Norfolk Island. A plentiful bird of coastal areas and adjacent mountain forest, it is even found on the outskirts of large towns. Immature birds are seen in flocks, while adults form small groups.

P. e. nigrescens
Description: This race is altogether darker with narrow red edges to the feathers of the back. It is slightly smaller, 112–120 g (4–4¼ oz).
Range/Habitat: North-eastern Queensland.

Aviculture: This species is extremely hardy. In the days when it was exported, losses among newly imported birds were apparently few. In addition to its beauty and hardiness, its voice is pleasant. Groen (1962) states: 'Their call note is rather melodious, not very loud and no neighbour will take offence at it'.

A number of aviculturists have reported feather biting or feather plucking in this species – a vice which is not common in Australian parrakeets. Varying degrees of the problem are experienced, from chewing off the tail feathers to denuding the body so that only the grey down is apparent. Why this problem should afflict Pennant's Parrakeet is uncertain. However, it does not affect the breeding performance of some birds, which rear young despite their feather condition.

For long a favourite bird with aviculturists, this parrakeet was bred in France as long ago as 1874 and reputedly by Gedney (1880) in Britain in 1876. Gedney made the curious statement that the nestling down is 'a bright fawn colour'. In the USA, the first breeding was probably that by J. C. Edwards of Los Angeles in 1927.

It does not have a reputation as the most reliable breeding species. Hens which eat their eggs or fail to incubate are not uncommon; on the other hand, some pairs are extremely prolific and annually rear clutches of seven – or more. Even year-old pairs have been known to rear seven in one nest. Five to eight eggs are laid.

Adelaide Rosella
P. e. adelaidae
This bird is sometimes given the scientific name of *P. adelaidae*. Forshaw (1973) states:

> In my opinion the Adelaide Rosella is a hybrid population so I use the name *P. adelaidae* merely for convenience not as an indication of specific status. It is generally considered to be a hybrid between the Pennant's and Yellow rosellas for both these birds are found within its range. When paired together they produce a Rosella which is identical to the Adelaide and the young, when mated together, breed true.

Description: Plumage of this Rosella is variable. Breast and crown are brick red and the nape and sides of the head are yellow. The remainder of the plumage is not easily defined. There is usually a black patch on the shoulders; the edge of the wing, the cheeks and tail are blue, or greenish blue in the case of the tail. Mantle feathers are black, edged with

Adelaide Parrakeet (*Platycercus elegans adelaidae*).

yellow, reddish yellow or buff. Rump and upper tail coverts are a mixture of red and yellow. The bill is greyish white and the iris of the eye is dark brown. Length: 36 cm (14 in).

The female is usually slightly smaller and duller.

Immature birds are dull red on the crown, throat, upper breast, thighs and under tail coverts; the violet-blue patch from the lores to the cheeks is present. Breast and abdomen are dull greyish green and the upper parts are olive green. The 12th Duke of Bedford described the young as 'decidedly smaller than young Pennants of the same age and of a more golden-olive colour'. By the age of 12 months 'they are almost as red on the breast as they will ever become and the pattern on the back is very marked, though not yet perfect'.

Range/Habitat: The range of this parrakeet is small and is divided into two areas by a 70 km (about 45 miles) strip. It inhabits southern South Australia from the southern Flinders Range to the Fleurien Peninsula south of Adelaide. It is abundant in its habitats – timbered country and parks and gardens in Adelaide.

A Lutino mutation has been bred in Australia. The red colouration is retained on the forehead, breast and wings; cheeks, wings and tail are white. It is recessive – not sex-linked – in its manner of inheritance.

Aviculture: From the avicultural viewpoint, this Rosella does not differ from the Pennant's. It, too, has a long history and was exhibited at London Zoo in 1863 and first bred in Britain by W. R. Fasey. The 12th Duke of Bedford, one of the few consistent breeders of this bird, found that Adelaides were single-brooded and began to moult soon after the young flew. In France, Madame Lécallier was the first breeder in 1927.

A unique alliance in the Duke of Bedford's collection was that of a male Adelaide and a female Cuban Amazon. The latter laid eggs at liberty in an oak tree but she was either killed or died while incubating them.

Green Rosella (*Platycercus caledonicus*).

Yellow-bellied (Green or Tasmanian) Rosella
P. caledonicus

Description: It has the under parts rich yellow with an orange tinge in some birds and a red frontal band. Cheek patches are deep blue and the feathers of the nape, back and wings are black edged with dark green, the coloured margins being less prominent than in other Rosellas. Median wing coverts are greenish black; under wing coverts and outer webs of flight feathers are green marked with blue, the lateral feathers being pale blue tipped with white; under side of the tail is blue. This is the largest of the Rosellas, measuring 36 cm (14 in) and having a bolder build than the other members of the genus. Weight: M 105–165 g ($3\frac{7}{10}$–$5\frac{4}{5}$oz); F 90–130 g ($3\frac{1}{5}$–$4\frac{3}{5}$ oz).

There is local variation in colour, the birds from the eastern part of Tasmania being brighter than those from the colder western part.

The female is slightly smaller and the throat is usually tinged with orange. Sexing is easier than in some other broadtails.

Immature birds are greenish yellow below and on the head, and dull green above – the origin of the alternative name Green Rosella. The blue cheek patch is present, also the wing stripe. Adult plumage is acquired with the first complete moult at about 14–15 months.

Range/Habitat: The Yellow-bellied Rosella inhabits Tasmania and the larger islands in Bass Strait. It is a common species in Tasmania, seen in flocks out of the breeding season, even in urban areas. Hawthorn berries are a favourite food and one which is easily provided in captivity during the appropriate season. In addition to holes in hollow tree limbs, this Rosella sometimes nests in crevices in derelict buildings.

Aviculture: This species has never been well known, even in Australia. It was uncommon in European aviculture until the mid-1960s when breeding successes occurred in Belgium, the Netherlands, Germany and Switzerland. It has been regularly bred since then but perhaps because it is not brilliantly coloured, the demand for it is not large.

In 1934 the Duke of Bedford wrote that the Yellow-bellied Rosella had been imported not infrequently during the last 20 years: 'but ... few people in England, I fancy, have been very successful in preserving it for any length of time'. He commented on its:

> ... great fondness for green food. No Broadtail needs or appreciates a larger amount or a greater variety, and fresh branches should be supplied regularly throughout the year. Most individuals acquire a taste for mealworms and the staple diet should consist of canary, millet, oats, sunflower, and peanuts, together with apple.

Yellow (or Yellow-rumped) Rosella
P. flaveolus

Description: This bird is often considered as a subspecies of *caledonicus*. It can briefly be described as resembling the Yellow-bellied Rosella except for the upper parts: the feathers of the nape, back and wings are black, broadly edged with pale yellow; rump and upper tail coverts are dull yellow. Some adult males have red on the

Yellow Rosella (*Platycercus flaveolus*).

Red Rosellas (*Platycercus eximius*).

upper breast and Cayley (1973) found that, 'Some males improve with age, the older they are the brighter the plumage; others remain quite plain in comparison'. The bill is horn-coloured and the iris is brown. Length: 33 cm (13 in). Weight: M 110–135 g ($3\frac{9}{10}$–$4\frac{3}{4}$ oz); F 105–117 g ($3\frac{3}{4}$–$4\frac{1}{10}$ oz).

Females have the head and bill smaller; the red frontal band is less clearly defined and the feathers of the throat and upper breast are tinged with orange-red in many individuals.

Immature birds differ from adults in the dull greenish yellow on the head and under parts and the dull green on the back and wings. They can be distinguished from young Adelaide Parrakeets by the yellower under parts.

Range/Habitat: The Yellow Rosella is a species closely associated with rivers. It is found in the interior of south-eastern Australia, in southern New South Wales, northern Victoria and eastern South Australia. It frequents eucalyptus along the Murray River and its tributaries, and the Lachlan and Murrumbidgee Rivers. Forshaw

(1973) states that it is common in its restricted range but that it was more numerous prior to the development of large-scale irrigation along the rivers, also that this Rosella is more arboreal than others. Cayley (1973) states that it spends much of its time on the ground, feeding on seeds and other plants, also on fruits and grain.

Aviculture: The Yellow Rosella has never been a common aviary bird, even in Australia. When Australian birds were exported, the supply of this species was erratic and never numerous.

The first breeder in Britain was W. R. Fasey (1904); two young left the nest but one died. The single bird at London Zoo was the only other one known to Fasey at the time. Four eggs were laid. He noted that 'the black spots on the yellow ground of the old ones are only just discernible on the young, and instead of the bright yellow ground colour a greenish hue exists'.

The Duke of Bedford owned a pair which first bred in 1926, which he described (1932) as:

. . . a model couple, very gentle and devoted to each other and extremely prolific . . . . Like many good breeding pairs they were, for many years, abnormally wild and nervous. It has taken them nearly nine seasons to acquire a taste for peanuts!

In his possession they had hatched nearly 60 eggs. On occasions, this pair was double-brooded.

In South Australia the Yellow Rosella was bred for the first time in 1946 by H. J. Packer. In that year, and in 1947, they were double-brooded, as they were in 1948 in Alan Lendon's possession. This species has also been bred in Adelaide Zoo in recent years. In the USA, San Diego reared four young in 1975. A private bird park in Germany, Tropicana in Neuweid, has had consistent success with this species in recent years.

Golden-mantled Rosella
P. eximius
This bird has become synonymous with the Red Rosella; regardless of the

subspecies, aviculturists – or certainly those in Britain – tend to refer to *P. eximius* as Golden-mantled. Correctly speaking, the latter name should refer only to *cecilae* which has the feathers of the mantle and part of the wings edged with yellow. The rump colour is another distinguishing feature: bluish green in *cecilae* and pale green in the nominate race. However, in captivity, so much cross-breeding has occurred that specimens which are intermediate in appearance are common.

Red (or Eastern) Rosella
P. e. eximius

Description: This bird has the head and breast red, cheek patches white and the feathers of the mantle and wings black, broadly edged with greenish yellow. The median wing coverts are black and the under wing coverts blue. Central tail feathers are green, tinged with blue, the lateral feathers being tipped with white. The bill is greyish white and the iris dark brown. Length: 30 cm (12 in). Weight: M 120 g ($4\frac{1}{4}$ oz); F 90 g ($3\frac{1}{5}$ oz).

The female has the red areas on the head and breast duller and less extensive. The wing stripe is present. Regarding sexual differences, Groen (1962) states:

> The cheek patches are snow-white in the male and in the female often grey-white, but this difference is very faint and only conspicuous when both birds are seen next to each other. Some hens are just as brightly coloured as males and then the brown-grey feathers round the eyes may give a decisive answer, as these are not present in the cock. Also the green feathers from the back of the neck running up to the crown are typical of the hen.

Immature birds differ from the female in having the nape and hind-crown green.

In Victoria, Australia, the Catt brothers attempted to establish a stud of Lutinos and T. L. Stally (1978) mentions breeding a very pale Dilute hen, probably a Cinnamon, in 1977. In 1978, four young were reared, three of which were Cinnamons. They were described as pale lime green, whitish cream instead of yellow, orange-pink instead of red and pale cinnamon where the Normal bird is black. The eyes were plum-coloured. In Belgium, a Pastel mutation was established by a well-known aviculturist, the late Dr Swaenepoec. He obtained some Pastels in the late 1960s which gave poor breeding results initially. He outcrossed them to split birds and to the best Normals available, gradually producing a good strain. In this mutation, the black markings on wings and tail are replaced by light grey in the female and an even lighter shade in the male. The yellow on the under parts is as vivid as in Normals.

Range/Habitat: The Red Rosella inhabits south-eastern Australia and Tasmania. It has been introduced to New Zealand in the vicinity of Auckland and there is a smaller population near Dunedin. Professor Hodges informed me that it is numerous in the Mount Bruce area. The race from Tasmania, *diemenensis*, which has larger white cheek patches and the red on the head darker and more extensive, is not numerous there. On the Australian mainland, the Red Rosella is extremely common. Food consists of various seeds (including Scotch thistle, *Onopordan scanthium* – a serious weed pest), berries, including two which can be provided by the aviculturist – hawthorn and pyracantha – also cultivated crops, wheat and fruits. Red Rosellas can be seen in the suburbs of Melbourne, Sydney and Canberra, feeding on weeds and berries.

Aviculture: The Red Rosella was one of the first Australian parrakeets to be named, being figured and named by Shaw in 1792 in his *Naturalist's Miscellany*. One of the best known of all parrakeets, it was freely exported until 1960 and has been regularly bred in Europe since the 1870s. It is now the most firmly established of all the larger Australian parrakeets. In Britain alone, well over 1,000 are reared annually at the time of writing. It is the most free-breeding and therefore the least expensive of the Rosellas; these two facts make it ideal for the beginner with the larger parrakeets. It is usu-

ally double-brooded and may rear as many as eight or nine in a nest, and many females will readily act as foster-mother to other species, even to parrots which are not even distantly related.

Average clutch size is six or seven. As an example of prolificacy, and one which is not exceptional, two females (mother and daughter) reared 54 young in 11 nests; they were single-brooded. Another pair reared ten chicks from ten eggs. A second nest-box was provided when the young were three weeks old and the male finished rearing the young while the female laid a second clutch of seven eggs.

Growth of young is rapid: the eyes are open by two weeks, and soon afterwards grey down has replaced the white down and pin feathers are starting to appear – first on the wings, then on the under parts.

Some Golden-mantled Rosellas will rear young when one year old; indeed, one pair was successful in rearing eight young in their first nest at that age.

Stanley Parrakeet (Yellow-cheeked or Western Rosella)
P. icterotis icterotis

Description: This is the only member of the genus which is sexually dimorphic. The male has the cheeks yellow, the rest of the head and under parts being red. Feathers of the back and wings are black, broadly edged with dark green with scattered red feathers in some birds. Median wing coverts are black; under wing coverts and the outer webs of the flight feathers are blue. The central tail feathers are green tinged with blue, the lateral feathers being pale blue tipped with white. The bill is grey and the iris dark brown. Length: 25 cm (10 in). Weight: M 59–80 g (2–$2\frac{4}{5}$ oz); F 52–71 g ($1\frac{4}{5}$–$2\frac{1}{2}$ oz).

The female has the cheek patch a duller shade of yellow and the head and upper breast green, faintly marked with red and yellow. Frontal band is red; under parts are suffused with green. The wing stripe is present.

Immature birds are mainly green with some reddish feathers on the forehead. After the first partial moult in

Stanley Parrakeets or Rosellas (*Platycercus icterotis icterotis*).

the autumn the sexes are more readily distinguished. A year later full adult plumage is assumed.

Range/Habitat: This Rosella favours open country; it is found in grasslands and cultivated areas, clearings and trees bordering water courses. Forshaw (1973) states, 'It is common, though not plentiful, and seems to be benefiting from increased cultivation of cereal crops'. The nominate race is found only in the coastal areas of south-western Australia.

P. i. xanthogenys
Description: It has the cheek patches very pale yellow; the feathers of the back and wings are margined with greyish buff in the male and buff in the female. Rump is greyish olive and the central tail feathers lack the green tinge.
Range/Habitat: Found in the drier interior of south-western Australia.

Aviculture: The Stanley Parrakeet has several advantages over other Rosellas: its small size (the smallest of the genus) makes it ideal for those who cannot provide long aviaries, it is friendly and confiding, and adult birds are readily sexed. All these assets add up to a totally delightful aviary bird which nests readily in aviaries.

Strangely enough, there are no records of nineteenth-century breedings for this species. First successes were recorded by the following: in England in 1908 by H. D. Astley, W. T. Fasey and Perkins; in the Netherlands in 1915 by Blaauw; in France by Madame Lécallier in 1919; in Germany by H. Hampe in 1937 and in the USA by I. D. Putnam in 1938.

In an analysis of breeding results carried out by the Parrot Society in 1970, the results of 22 pairs of Stanleys were examined. Six pairs did not lay and the remainder reared only 28

young between them. The interesting aspect of this enquiry was that it showed that not one pair was double-brooded. The success rate was highest in pairs which had nest-boxes measuring 25 cm (10 in) square × 47 cm (18 in) high – but that was almost certainly an incidental factor. It should be borne in mind that while this size is suitable for this small Rosella, a nest which is twice that height is recommended for the larger Rosellas. Stanleys usually lay between five and eight eggs.

A box of this size should be filled to a depth of 15 cm (6 in) with decayed wood. The number of eggs laid is usually between five and eight.

When young hatch, large quantities of spinach beet should be offered. Basic diet should consist of canary seed, sunflower, hemp, peanuts, millet spray and apple.

Stanley's have hybridised with all the Rosellas, also with the Redrump Parrakeet.

Brown's Parrakeet (Northern or Smutty Rosella)
P. venustus
Description: This is one of the most unusual and pleasing in its plumage and colouration, also one of the smallest of the Rosellas. Regrettably, it is the rarest in captivity. The head is black and the cheeks white with a small patch of blue beneath the cheeks. The feathers of the upper parts are black, broadly edged with yellow; a black patch decorates the shoulder and the remainder of the under parts are yellow with narrow black edges to the feathers. A most pleasing contrast is provided by the red under tail coverts. Central tail feathers are blue, tinged with green, the lateral feathers being pale blue tipped with white. Bill is greyish white and the iris dark brown. Length: 28 cm (11 in). Weight: M 92–112 g ($3\frac{1}{4}$–4 oz); F 88–92 ($3\frac{1}{10}$–$3\frac{1}{4}$ oz).

Immature birds are duller than adults.

Plumage is variable in adults; some have scattered red feathers on the head and abdomen; others have some blue-tinged cheek patches. According to Dr Burkard, who has bred this species to the fourth generation, the sexes can be

Brown's Parrakeet or Rosella (*Platycercus venustus*).

distinguished – more easily in young birds. The cheek patch of the male is purer white and slightly larger, extending nearly to the eye. The male's head is slightly larger and the black deeper.
Range/Habitat: Brown's Parrakeet inhabits north-western and northern Australia, from the Kimberleys, Western Australia, east to the Northern Territory and the Queensland border. Locally common, sedentary and never encountered in large numbers, it is believed to be declining. An inhabitant of open eucalypt savannah and fringe woods along water courses and rivers, on the east coast it is even found in mangroves. It usually nests near water and the clutch contains only two or three eggs which are laid during the rainy season – December to February.
Aviculture: Brown's Parrakeet was one of the last Australian parrakeets to be exported: a pair reached London in 1899.

This species is notorious for its habit of breeding during the winter, resulting in its having been bred less frequently in captivity than any other Rosella, and in almost having died out in collections. Very few females remain and, under the circumstances, pairing an unmated male to a female Mealy Rosella could be the best use for such a bird. In the early 1960s, I saw a hybrid in the collection of Reg Partridge of Evesham which was almost indistinguishable from a pure Brown's – although it had one eighth Mealy blood in its veins.
E. J. Boosey (1956) hybridised with the Brown's for a different reason – an attempt to produce a spring-breeding race of this species. He bred a hybrid which was three-quarters Brown's and one-quarter Red Rosella which he described as:

> ...the most beautiful Broadtail cross I know, though the first cross Brown ×

Rosella runs it very close.... It might be called the Crimson-headed Brown's Parrakeet, for it is exactly like a Brown's, but instead of being black, each of the head feathers is deep crimson with a wide black border, those feathers in the first cross having, as one would expect, only a very narrow border of black.

In Britain, the first successful breeding occurred in 1928 in the collection of the Duke of Bedford. He found this species exceptionally difficult to pair up. In most cases, the male would attack the female immediately they were introduced and had to be removed at once. Other males showed no interest in the female provided.
Of the male which was the first to breed for him, the Duke of Bedford wrote:

> I decided I would subject the unreasonable cock to the discipline reserved for impossible bullies and cut his wing sufficiently to render it out of the question for him to overtake and injure his companion. The plan was successful beyond my wildest hopes, for not only was he as meek as Moses on his first meeting with the lady, but he soon began to feed her and from that day to this has been a model husband and father.

E. J. Boosey successfully reared many Brown's Parrakeets at Keston Foreign Bird Farm but the young showed the same preference for moulting during the summer and nesting in the autumn. This species is normally double-brooded – and one pair produced nine young in two nests in one year, contributing towards the total of 30 bred by them while at Keston.
Boosey (1953) wrote:

> Of all the Broadtails I have kept I have found Brown's Parrakeets by far the most difficult to re-mate, and one of the most deadly aggressors if they happen to disapprove of the partner you offer them.

Referring to the prolific pair mentioned above:

> When eventually the hen died, the cock was very pathetic and quite inconsolable and indeed did not long survive his wife. Any hope of re-mating him was quite out of the question as he savagely attacked any hen that was put with him.

Another successful breeder, T. R. Holmes Watkins (1958) believed that:

If you are lucky enough to maintain the necessary high condition throughout the winter months a nest should be introduced in the aviary flight early in February, and, if the gods are on your side, and late March is mild, and without severe night frosts, there is every chance of success.

In the USA, Brown's have reared young on a number of occasions, especially in California where the mild winters suit them well and they can nest as early as January or February. David West (1956) wrote of his female:

> The most interesting thing, and also the oddest when one compares it with other members of the Rosella family, is the fact that the female Browns brooded the chicks constantly until about the twenty first day. Usually a female Rosella will quit brooding at night after about the tenth day, and sometimes this is productive of fatal results if the nights are cool. I am quite sure that if the Brown's had quit brooding the solitary chick would have died as the nights were still very cool. I could not help but wonder if she instinctively realised that this was the case?

Also, the female brooded throughout the entire day for the first three weeks.

According to Dr Burkard (pers. comm.), Brown's should be paired up when young, because older birds do not readily accept a mate. He believes this species to be the most aggressive in defence of its territory of any *Platycercus*.

Blue-cheeked Rosella
P. adscitus adscitus
Description: It has the feathers of the back and wings margined with creamy yellow, suffused with blue, and the rump yellowish blue. It has more blue and less white on the cheeks, the blue extending to the neck; there is some yellow on the breast and sides of the neck. It otherwise resembles the Mealy Rosella except for its slightly smaller size. Adult plumage is acquired at the age of about 15 months. Weight: M 131 g (4⅗ oz); F 112 g (4 oz).
Range/Habitat: The nominate race is found in the Cape York Peninsula and in northern Queensland as far south as Cairns. It is an inhabitant of timbered lowland country. It feeds on seeds,

including those of injurious weeds, on blossoms and on cultivated grain and food crops. Unevenly distributed, it is common in some areas.
Aviculture: The Blue-cheeked Rosella is less common and much more expensive than the Mealy. In Australia, the first breeder was Sir Edward Hallstrom, followed by Alan Lendon in 1966 when one was reared from a clutch of five eggs. In immature plumage it was described as being a considerably duller version of the adult. This race has now become quite common in Australian aviculture and has been bred at Adelaide Zoo on several occasions. The first breeder in Britain was probably D. G. Washington in 1968.

In Germany, it was first bred in 1969 by A. Preussiger.

Mealy (Pale-headed) Rosella
P. a. palliceps
Description: This subspecies is unmistakable, with its yellow-tinged white head and white cheek patches. The feathers of the mantle have black centres and broad golden-yellow margins and the rump and back are greenish blue. Median wing coverts are black; under wing coverts and outer webs of the flight feathers are blue. The upper breast is yellow with a blue tinge and the rest of the under parts are light blue or ashy-grey tinged with blue. The area of the vent and the under tail coverts are scarlet (sometimes lighter in the female). Central tail feathers are dark green at the base, shading into dark blue, or blue, the lateral tail feathers being light blue tipped with white. The bill is horn-coloured and the iris is dark brown. Length: 30 cm (12 in).

This subspecies is not easy to sex until taken in the hand: the female has a wing stripe.

Immature birds are duller than females; the wing stripe is present. Red or grey markings on the head are common.
Range/Habitat: Found in north-eastern Australia, from northern Queensland, south of Cairns, to north-eastern New South Wales.

Mealy Rosellas (*Platycercus adscitus palliceps*) – female left, male right.

Aviculture: The Mealy Rosella was exported to Europe at least as early as 1863 when a pair was exhibited at London Zoo. A number of breeding successes were recorded in the nineteenth century, the earliest being in Belgium in 1872. In the USA, W. J. Sheffler was the first breeder in 1931. Twenty years later Alan Lendon (1949c) wrote: 'In the United States this species appears to be practically domesticated; at any rate, it is said to be the commonest of all the Broadtails in that country'. If that was so, it fared better there than in Europe where it has never been among the most numerous of the Rosellas.

The Parrot Society Breeding Registers for 1976 and 1977 showed that 38 and 37 members reported breeding 149 and 153 Mealies respectively – or less than one sixth as many as Red (Golden-mantled) Rosellas.

The ease with which they are bred varies. Dr Groen (1962) found the Mealy Rosella to be particularly free-breeding, while some breeders to whom he sold young achieved no results and pronounced them useless on account of their viciousness. On checking the circumstances of those which had failed to breed, he found that they were in the hands of breeders who had little space at their disposal and owned many Rosellas. Thus it would seem that it is especially important to house Mealy Rosellas well away from other Rosellas.

T. Bolton (Anon., 1977) had a female in his possession which habitually laid so many eggs she was unable to cover them all. However, on one occasion she was successful in rearing eight young from nine eggs.

Once, when she showed no sign of incubating, her first five eggs were placed under a pair of Cockatiels. Four hatched and the Cockatiels fed the young Mealies with 'exceptional zest' on more greenfood than they normally consumed when rearing their own young, also on hemp and soaked oats.

The Mealy had commenced laying in May but did not go broody until July – by which time she had laid at least 25 eggs. She then incubated seven or eight eggs and reared five young.

A female with a preference for winter breeding was described by R. Taylor (1978). She laid during January and hatched two chicks; two others died in the shell. When the young were half grown the male was found dead – but the female completed the rearing of her young unaided. A second male was acquired and the female went to nest – in December.

This species is usually single-brooded.

An aviculturist with extensive experience of *adscitus*, W. Howarth (1977) pointed out that 'the nucleus of our European stock did not always fall clearly into either the Pale-headed or the Blue-cheeked variety and therefore European breeders could not easily maintain two distinctive races'. He urged that those who own 'either of the two distinct varieties should be encouraged not to cross-breed the varieties into obscurity'.

Barnardius
Barnardius

The two members of this genus are included with *Platycercus* by some taxonomists although they have very distinctive plumage colouration. Also, there are trivial anatomical and behavioural differences. Unlike Rosellas, they never form large flocks. They are, however, equally quarrelsome but more difficult to sex and not as free-breeding. None is very common in confinement and all are expensive.

Barnard's Parrakeet (Mallee Ringneck Parrot or Bulla-bulla or Buln-Buln)
B. barnardi barnardi
Description: The male is dark green with a broad frontal band of dark red. Cheeks, shoulders and margins of the wings are light blue. A yellow band decorates the lower breast. The mantle is dark blue and the rest of the body plumage is greenish blue. Central tail

Barnard's Parrakeet (*Barnardius barnardi barnardi*).

feathers are green, darker and bluer at the tip; outer tail feathers and under surface of the tail are blue. Bill is greyish white and the iris is dark brown. Length: 33 cm (13 in). Weight: M 114–143 g (4–5 oz); F 105–138 g ($3\frac{3}{4}$–$4\frac{9}{10}$ oz).

The female usually has duller colouration on the back and less red (or yellow) on the abdomen.

Immature birds have the crown and nape brownish and the back and mantle greyish green. The wing stripe is usually present. Adult plumage is assumed at just over one year.
Range/Habitat: This race inhabits the interior of south-eastern Australia.

Eucalypt scrub – mallee – is the preferred habitat. According to Forshaw (1973), this parrakeet:

...does not seem able to withstand encroaching settlement. As the mallee and open woodland are cleared for grazing or cultivation the parrots gradually retreat. They are still considered to be common but in some areas numbers do appear to be declining.

The diet of this species consists of seeds (especially those of paddy melon and wild bitter melon), berries, fruits, blossoms, leaf buds and insects.

A wild mutation, a Lutino, was recorded by Lang (1927), who:

...saw a pair of young albinos of this species which a woodcutter had taken from the nest; they were of a pale yellow colour, with pink feet and red eyes.

B. b. whitei
Description: Male and female have the mantle dark greyish green and the crown and occiput brownish.
Range/Habitat: This race is found in south-western Queensland and north-eastern South Australia south through westernmost New South Wales and the Flinders Range, South Australia.

B. b. crommelinae
Alan Lendon (1949b) mentions this variety – 'a bluish variant with the yellow areas considerably restricted' which could not be regarded as valid.

Aviculture: Barnard's Parrakeet was first exhibited at London Zoo in 1853. In France, Baron Cornely bred this species in 1884; from seven eggs, six young were reared. In the USA, I. D. Putnam was probably the first breeder in 1944.

The first breeder in Britain was Mrs Johnstone in 1902; two young were reared and three more in 1903. London Zoo bred this species in 1912 and the Duke of Bedford bred it on a number of occasions between 1913 and 1950.

From four to six eggs, constitute the normal clutch. The incubation period is 19 days. In display, the male Barnard's chatters continuously, spreads his tail and moves it rapidly from side to side, and squares his shoulders.

This species is well established in the aviaries of German and Dutch breeders but is nowhere common.

An interesting account of a successful breeding was published in 1932 by Dr Evelyn Sprawson. The pair's nest-box was:

... of 2 in wood, about 4 ft high, partly filled with earth, and with a layer of peat moss on top. Although all three nests were in the flight, the hen had no doubts as to what she wanted: she did not look at either of her old nests, but made straight for the new one and used it with hardly a preliminary inspection...

The young were comparatively easy to sex as they left the nest, not only on account of the lesser size of the heads and beaks of the hens (there were two), but also on account of the markedly duller colouring, particularly of the green patches over the ears. What seemed remarkable to us was the difference in colouring of individual young: both the parents are of the ordinary, rather pale green (on the upper breast and abdomen) type of Barnard, but some of the young are quite of the darker type called by Matthews in his big work *B. b. whitei* – indeed, no two young are identical in colouring, and the crown of the head (for instance) varies from almost yellow in one to dark green in others.

We have never seen the parents less concerned and worried over the feeding of their family before leaving the nest; indeed, except for the occasional disappearance of one or both of the parents, we would hardly have known that they had a family.

Rearing foods consisted of hemp, canary seed and wheat (all soaked), groundsel and an occasional chop bone; the last was preferred to all other foods. The author noted the liking of

Barnard's, also Pennant's Parrakeets, for worms taken from the grass floor of their flight.

Several writers have commented on the aggressiveness of this species towards humans and the Duke of Bedford noted that:

In captivity, or indeed at liberty in this country, individual cock Barnards are apt to display the most curious and at times irritating peculiarities of disposition. One very beautiful male in my possession was tame, that is to say he had no fear of humanity. He took but little interest in the society of females of his own race, but devoted his life to the persecution of mankind. For this purpose he stationed himself at the lodge gates and, swooping down upon passers-by, endeavoured to seize them by the nose!

Cloncurry Parrakeet
B. b. macgillivrayi
Description: It is pale green with the cheeks and lower ear coverts pale blue, merging into bluish green on the sides of the head. The abdomen and a ring round the nape are yellow. Weight: M 120–128 g ($4\frac{1}{4}$ – $4\frac{1}{2}$ oz); F 99–106 g ($3\frac{1}{2}$–$3\frac{3}{4}$ oz).

Immature birds are generally duller except for the red frontal band; this is lacking in the adult.

Range/Habitat: Range of the Cloncurry Parrakeet is isolated by a large, almost treeless, expanse from that of *barnardi* and *whitei*. It is north-western Queensland and eastern Northern Territory.

Aviculture: This parrakeet was not described until 1900. Even in Australia it was almost unknown in aviculture prior to the 1940s. A pair imported by the Duke of Bedford in 1939 may have been the first to reach Britain; possibly no more were imported until 1963 when a collection of birds was sent to London Zoo by Sir Edward Hallstrom. It included a pair which raised one youngster in 1967 – probably a first British breeding.

The first captive breeding occurred in the aviaries of Alan Lendon in Adelaide in 1939; one youngster was reared. In 1940, 1941 and 1942, his paired reared two nests of three. The

Cloncurry Parrakeet (*Barnardius barnardi macgillivray*).

female raised three young with a different male in 1943 and nests of three and two in 1944. In 1945, she reared two and in 1947 one. Sir Edward Hallstrom also achieved good results from one pair: for three years they reared one nest of four each year and in the fourth year nine young in two nests.

In recent years Cloncurry Parrakeets have been bred in many collections in the Netherlands, Germany and Switzerland; in Britain it remains rare but has been bred.

Port Lincoln (or Bauer's) Parrakeet

B. zonarius zonarius

Description: This handsome bird, with its solid, dark colouring and large size, is unmistakable. The head is entirely black except for some blue feathers on the cheeks and the sides of the neck and, in some birds, a red frontal band. The abdomen and nuchal collar are yellow; the breast is dark green. Feathers of the thighs, ventral area and under tail coverts are yellowish green. Central tail feathers are dark green marked with blue, the lateral feathers being pale blue tipped with white. The bill is light horn-coloured and the iris is brown. Length: 38 cm (15 in). Weight: M 142–170 g (5–6 oz); F 121–136 g ($4\frac{1}{4}$–$4\frac{4}{5}$ oz).

Sexing is difficult; in some females the head is brownish black. The wing stripe is present in females, usually absent in males.

The Duke of Bedford (1928b) mentions a blue Port Lincoln Parrakeet, a captive bird which never produced young.

Range/Habitat: Central and south-western Australia, west from Eyre Peninsula, South Australia and Tennant Creek, Northern Territory to the central region of Western Australia is the home of the Port Lincoln Parrakeet. Common and widespread, it is found in varied habitats, including the arid interior, semi-arid wheatbelt where eucalypts predominate, gardens and parks, and in dense coastal forests.

According to Immelmann (1968) they are 'by far the most abundant Parrots in the west and south-west of Australia'. A noisy ground- and tree-feeding bird, its diet includes seeds, fruits, nectar, larvae, the corms of onion grass and cultivated fruits and cereal crops.

Aviculture: This parrakeet was not common in European aviaries but its numbers have increased since the late 1970s. In Germany it was bred as long ago as 1879 by Herr Kohler in Weissenfels; four young were reared from four eggs. In France, Rousse bred it in 1884 and, in Belgium, Count Celle de Sprimont was successful in 1880. In Britain, the first success occurred at London Zoo in 1934.

In 1938, E. N. T. Vane reared young from his pair which were catholic in their choice of food: sunflower, hemp and oats were the favoured seeds; canary and millet were also offered. During the breeding season, they consumed a wide variety of wild and cultivated greenfood, potato, carrot and even tomato. It is of interest that they collected earthworms from the damp earth around the water bowl, broke them up and apparently fed them to their young. Mealworms were ignored, however. The two young had lighter bills and were slightly duller and smaller. The male started to moult in June, thus a second nest did not materialise.

George Smith (1975) commented on how terrestrial the Port Lincoln Parrakeet is, seen on the ground as often as on the perches. He noted that:

> . . . they cut off pieces of plant stalk, such as grass, and run these through a munching bill to extract the juices. This is so evident that even when chickweed is fed they soon leave off searching for the seed capsules and start eating the stalk as well. Plant juices are rich in protein and a source of water which might explain how these birds survive in hostile environments. An oddity of my birds is that they prefer canary to almost any other seed and eat very little sunflower, will take bread and milk, eat all kinds of fruit and appear to prefer the kernel of hawthorn *Crataegus monogyna* drupes to any form of food.

George Smith recorded the incubation period as 19 days and that young fledge at about 35 days. The male of his pair was an egg-eater and was

Port Lincoln Parrakeet (*Barnardius zonarius zonarius*).

Twenty-eight Parrakeet (*Barnardius zonarius semitorquatus*).

placed in an adjoining aviary while the female incubated her eggs (usually seven) and was returned when the young hatched.

Twenty-eight (Yellow-collared or Yellow-naped) Parrakeet

B. z. semitorquatus

Description: This race differs from the nominate race in its green abdomen, prominent red frontal band and larger size. Males, adult and immature, usually have a larger head and broader upper mandible. This is the largest of the Australian parrakeets and has a powerful bill. According to Alan Lendon, the male has a flatter head, the female's head being smaller and rounder. M 142–191 g (5–6¾ oz); F 134–199 g (4¾–7 oz).

This bird is named after its three-syllable call note, with upward inflection, which is said to resemble the words 'Twenty-eight'.

Range/Habitat: This race is found only in south-western Australia, south of Perth and east to Albany. Its population intergrades with that of the nominate race, thus birds intermediate between the two forms are found where hybridisation occurs.

Aviculture: As uncommon in captivity as the Port Lincoln Parrakeet, it was first exhibited at London Zoo in 1862. The first breeder was probably Count Celle de Sprimont in Belgium in 1881; and in France it was bred by the Marquis de Brisay in the same year. In Britain, the first success occurred at London Zoo in 1912 and, in Australia, Alan Lendon bred it in 1945 and Adelaide Zoo in 1946.

In Australia, A. Budden reared a yellow Twenty-eight in 1974 – the first bird of that species he had reared. In 1926, Perth Zoo, exhibited a blue Twenty-eight.

Psephotus
Psephotus

Of the five medium-sized, long-tailed parrakeets which comprise this genus, one – the Red-rumped Parrakeet – is very well known; three are met with more rarely in aviculture and the Paradise Parrakeet is now unknown, for it may be extinct. Sexual dimorphism is pronounced in all but the Blue-bonnet, which is an aberrant member of the genus and is sometimes classified in a genus of which it is the sole member.

It should be noted that the pair bond is stronger in *Psephotus* species than in other Australian parrakeets. Mutual preening occurs in the Red-rumped, Many-coloured and Blue-bonnet Parrakeets.

With the exception of the Redrump, they are even less suited to close confinement than other Australian parrakeets. On no account should they be caged. The Duke of Bedford wrote of the Hooded:

> No Parrakeet suffers more quickly from the effects of close confinement and even six months in a cage on hard perches will produce overgrown and deformed bill and toenails, wry tail feathers and a general sad disfigurement.

A pair of Hooded Parrakeets in a certain zoo in the 1960s unfortunately bore testimony to the truth of that statement.

Broadtailed parrakeets in general are not safe companions for other birds and *Psephotus* species are notoriously aggressive. Members of a pair will work together to outwit and even to kill other birds with which they are housed. Redrumps and Blue-bonnets are undoubtedly among the most pugnacious of all parrakeets.

The experiences of Charles P. Guy (1945) are typical:

> Youngsters can be safely kept together until they start to feel grown up, and then the trouble starts. Unmated hens appear to be fairly mild with each other, but introduce cocks *that are in good condition* and the male birds will fight it out to a finish.
>
> I once picked up two adult cocks that still went on fighting in my hands.

Psephotus parrakeets will sometimes breed with success in their first year. Four to six, rarely as many as eight, eggs are laid. Incubation period is usually 19 days. Young emerge from the nest when between four and five weeks old. Occasionally pairs are double-brooded and this is more likely in the Redrump.

Red-rumped Parrakeet

P. haematonotus haematonotus

Description: The Redrump is among the best known of all Australian parrakeets. The male is distinguished from other members of the genus by the bright red rump. It is mainly green, brightest on the head and breast, bluish green on the mantle and dull green on the wings. The outer webs of the primaries are blue and the median wing coverts are yellow, as is the abdomen. Vent and under tail coverts are white. Central tail feathers are green, tinged with blue, the lateral feathers being blue tipped with white. The wing stripe is absent. The bill is black and the iris is dark brown. Length: 27 cm (10½ in). Weight: M 68–70 g (2⅖–2½ oz); F 54–65 g (1⁹⁄₁₀–2³⁄₁₀ oz).

The female is drably attired in greyish olive and is lighter and more yellowish olive below. The median wing coverts are pale blue and the rump is green. Abdomen, vent and under tail coverts are white. The wing stripe is present. The bill is grey.

Immature birds are duller versions of the adults; males have less red on the rump. Adult plumage is acquired by a moult of the body plumage at the age of about four months; the wing stripe is retained until the second moult. The bill is grey. Immature females resemble adults but for the yellow bill.

The Yellow Redrump is, in effect, a Dilute mutation not a bright Yellow.

Females are a pale creamy buff.

Immature Yellows are a purer shade of yellow in the nest. When adult, the feathers of the upper parts are suffused with greenish grey, brightest on the head.

The Redrump has a pleasant call which is not likely to annoy neighbours. Indeed, the German name for this species is *Singsittich*.

Range/Habitat: The Red-rumped

Parrakeet inhabits the interior of south-eastern Australia. The Redrump is one of the most abundant parrots of eastern Australia. It is found near water, being replaced in arid areas by the Many-colour and the Blue-bonnet. It prefers open plains, lightly timbered grasslands and cultivated areas, including city parks, below about 1,250 m (4,000 ft). It is said to be extending its range, having benefited from agricultural activities. Immelmann (1968) states that Redrumps have become more numerous in fields and gardens than in their natural habitat and that they 'often come into the homesteaders' poultry yards and eat from the food pots with the fowls, or look for thresher waste and scattered grain inside sheds and barns'. However, Immelmann also states that they have to compete for nesting sites with European Starlings and House Sparrows. In some areas people hang up nest-boxes for the Redrumps which are popular birds.

They are opportunists, like the species which seek to usurp them, and will breed in abandoned House Sparrows' nests in the thatched roofs of sheds or barns, in fence posts or even in tunnels in banks dug by nesting Bee-eaters.

The Redrump is terrestrial in its feeding habits. Forshaw (1973) describes flocks which 'move over the ground like sandpipers on a tidal flat, the birds scurrying here and there to pick up seeds and fluttering from the shade of one tree to that of another'. Their flight is high, strong and rapid with some undulations. Food consists of various seeds and vegetable matter, especially leaves of thistles, also chickweed.

Red-rumped Parrakeets (*Psephotus haematonotus*) – female left, male right.

P. h. caeruleus
Description: Both sexes are paler throughout, the male being bluer in shade; the central tail feathers are more strongly tinged with blue. The female has the nape and mantle more greyish green.
Range/Habitat: This race is found in the Innamincka area of South Australia, north to Coongié Lakes, north-eastern South Australia.

Aviculture: The first recorded breeding of this species dates back to 1857 in London Zoo. In Germany, Dr Bodinus of Cologne reared young in 1863; in 1865, Baron Cornely was successful in the Netherlands and Touchard in France in 1869. The first breeding in the USA did not occur until W. H. Browning reared young in 1929 while the first breeding of the Yellow there occurred in 1955 in the aviaries of David West.

The Redrump has long been one of the most popular and free-breeding of all Australian parrakeets and is invariably recommended for the beginner. Figures published in the Parrot Society Breeding Register show that, in 1977, only Splendid and Turquoisine Parrakeets were reared in greater numbers. The Redrump is therefore one of the least expensive of the Australian parrakeets. It is probably used to foster young more than any other species, with the possible exception of the Golden-mantled Rosella. One Australian breeder used Redrumps to foster the young of Pennant's and Mealy Rosellas, Barrabands, Princess of Wales' and Twenty-eight Parrakeets. In some species, the chicks are three times the size of Redrump chicks.

They will rear the young not only of Australian parrakeets but of quite different species. One successful breeder of *Pyrrhura* conures habitually uses Redrumps as foster-parents but has found that not all Redrumps will accept the young of these birds. Young *Pyrrhura* spend three or four weeks longer in the nest than the young of Redrumps, thus one should be alert to the fact that the foster parents could cease to feed them before they are due to fledge.

Redrumps lay four to six eggs. Incubation usually commences with the laying of the second egg and lasts for 18 or 19 days. In a nest which was closely monitored in the wild, the first chick emerged 17 days after incubation commenced (the day after the second egg was laid). The chicks are covered in creamy white down. Pin feathers start to appear at about eight days; they can be sexed at just over two weeks old. Young leave the nest after about 30 days. Many pairs are double-brooded.

When the young emerge, a close watch must be kept on the male who is likely to persecute his male young soon after they fledge. If necessary, the male must be removed from the aviary.

In captivity, all Redrumps will readily try a wide range of seeds and should therefore be offered as many kinds as possible. Greenfood, apple, corn-on-the-cob and bread and milk should also be included in the diet of this species.

Redrumps have hybridised with Many-coloured, Hooded and Blue-bonnet Parrakeets, with various Rosellas, also with Barnard's and Pileated Parrakeets.

The first Yellow to be seen in Europe, a female, was imported from Australia in 1935 by the Duke of Bedford. He passed it on to Edward Boosey who paired it with a male Redrump chosen for its outstanding colour. All expectations were exceeded when the Yellow reared ten young in

Many-coloured Parrakeets (*Psephotus varius*) – male left, female right.

two nests – five males and five females. The original Yellow was mated with one of her sons to produce the first Yellow male ever seen.

The Yellow is the most widely bred mutation of any Australian Parrakeet. Indeed, if the figures indicated in the Parrot Society Breeding Registers are typical of breeders' results, Yellows accounted for a large proportion of the Redrumps kept in Britain in 1976 and 1977. The numbers bred by members were 265 and 370 respectively, while the Normals bred totalled 320 and 671. Occasionally female Yellows are bred which have some red feathers on the rump. One such bird, bred by Edward Boosey at Keston Foreign Bird Farm, became spotted all over with red after a moult.

In 1968 Russ Rowlands bred a blue specimen in South Australia.

The Duke of Bedford kept Redrumps at liberty but recommended

they should be shut up in the autumn when the bare trees made them susceptible to attacks from owls. He found them to be good stayers as long as male and female were together; if one died, the other immediately strayed.

Many-coloured Parrakeet (Mulga Parrot)
P. varius

Description: In size and shape, it resembles the Redrump but is more colourful with a different arrangement of colours. The yellow forehead and red patch on the crown distinguish the male and the orange frontal band the female. The male is green, paler on the lower breast; abdomen and thighs are yellow, variably marked with orange; the under tail coverts are yellow. There is a yellow patch on the shoulder, sometimes marked with orange feathers. Two transverse bands mark the light green rump: the upper is dark green, the lower is brown. The under wing coverts and outer webs of the primaries are blue. The wing stripe is absent. Tail is dark blue, tinged with green, the lateral feathers being tipped with white. The bill is dark grey and the iris brown. Length: 27 cm ($10\frac{1}{2}$ in). Weight: M 56–65 g ($2–2\frac{3}{10}$ oz); F 53–70 g ($1\frac{9}{10}–2\frac{1}{2}$ oz).

Colour varies considerably in males, both in the wild and in captivity. Selection for the most highly coloured birds is desirable for these are very beautiful indeed.

The female is mainly brownish green with the forehead dull orange-yellow and a dull red patch on the crown and on the median wing coverts. The wing stripe is present. The bill is brownish grey.

Immature birds are duller than adults; they show the wing stripe. Males have some red on the abdomen. Full adult plumage is assumed at 12–14 months; after moulting at about six months old, the red on the male's abdomen is more obvious. Young males can be distinguished in the nest after the second week when the feathers appear on the wings.

Range/Habitat: The Many-coloured Parrakeet has a wide distribution over the interior of southern Australia and is a common bird in many parts of its range but rare in the south where it has declined due to clearance of mallee. Arid scrublands, sparsely-timbered grassland and the grass of mulga (*Acacia aneura*) are its favourite habitats. Found in pairs or small family parties, Forshaw says they are: 'unobtrusive birds lacking the bustling activities so characteristic of *P. haematonotus*'.

Seeds of mulga and other acacia, grasses, fruit, berries and other vegetable matter comprise the diet.

Aviculture: Its quiet voice and its beauty recommend the Many-coloured Parrakeet as an aviary bird. It was first exhibited at London Zoo in 1861.

Early breeding successes with this species were those of Verviers in France in 1876 and Count Celle de Sprimont in Belgium in 1882. In Britain, the first breeder was the Reverend C. D. Farrar in 1902. In the USA, David West was the first breeder

– in 1953. He had two pairs, both of which started to nest on March 10. One pair deserted their young at about two weeks; the other pair reared six young – on large amounts of bread and seeding grasses.

These parrakeets have a tendency to nest early in the year, as early as February. Some pairs are double-brooded and third nests have been known. Four to six or seven eggs are laid.

Many-coloured Parrakeets have never been common in British collections; George Smith (1975) estimated there were probably not more than 150 breeding pairs in Britain in that year. That estimate may have been overgenerous for, in 1976, nine Parrot Society members reported breeding a total of 27 young and in 1977 nine members reared 34. Successes in European aviaries would appear to be much more numerous.

George Smith thought that the poor breeding rate was due to the fact that:

> . . . many hens become indifferent to the need to brood their chicks once they are more than a day or so old. This would be all right if the weather was favourable. Secondly they seem more susceptible to worm infestation, pseudo-tuberculosis and other diseases than are Redrumps. This sensibility to disease is certainly aggravated because most people seemingly expect their birds to subsist entirely on seed. Mine, just like the rest of my collection, have a small amount of bread and milk daily, often supplemented with greenfood and fruit when available.

A successful German breeder of this species, Dr Overlander (1971), offered a mixture of grated carrot, biscuit, calcium mixture and a vitamin preparation soon after the young hatched. Food containing egg was discontinued as the chicks' droppings became sticky. Basic diet consisted of sunflower seed, loose and spray millet, and hemp out of the breeding season, carrot and various greenfood and, in autumn, apple. Turf and sawdust mixture was used as nesting material because it helped to keep the nest warm and retained moisture in dry weather. Dr Overlander found that some one year old males were not fertile while one pair, both birds of which were under one year old, reared two young.

He related how he attempted to change the mates of two pairs and that:

> Since the birds could see and hear each other, although across the wire of several cages, the cocks called continuously to their old mates, without paying the slightest attention to the new wives with whom I had provided them. After a fortnight of this, I had to reunite the old pairs, and promptly everybody was satisfied. The old pairs immediately sat preening each other, which proved that they had always been very much attached to each other. It was most probably my error that I placed these birds where they could both see and hear their old mates.

E. N. T. Vane advised of this species (1952):

> . . . if it is ever necessary to change their quarters, always try to keep the same box for their use. The old hen which used to pluck herself always *would* use a rotten log which was patched up and filled with old nails and wire to hold it together, yet she had the choice of three lovely solid boxes. When one year the log was removed she refused to go to nest at all until it was returned, when she was inside within a few seconds of my getting out of the flight.

Many-coloureds have hybridised with Red-rumped, Golden-shouldered, Hooded and Blue-bonnet Parrakeets.

Paradise (or Beautiful) Parrakeet
P. pulcherrimus

Description: The male has the forehead red and the crown and nape brownish black. The upper parts are brown and the under parts and rump turquoise; lower abdomen, thighs and under tail coverts are scarlet. The median wing coverts are red and the under wing coverts and the outer webs of the flight feathers are blue. Tail is bronzy-green with a blue tinge, the lateral tail feathers being tipped with white. The wing stripe is absent. The bill is greyish and the iris brown. Length: 27 cm ($10\frac{1}{2}$ in).

The female has the forehead yellowish white, the feathers being faintly tipped with red; crown and nape are dark brown. The face and breast are buff yellow marked with brownish orange and the under parts are very pale blue with a few red feathers. The wing stripe is present; there is very little red on the wing coverts.

Immature males have some green or blue on the face and breast and darker crown and wing coverts. The wing stripe is present in both sexes.

Range/Habitat: The Paradise Parrakeet inhabited central and southern Queensland and northern New South Wales; it may also have been found in northern Queensland. Forshaw (1973) states: 'Small populations probably survive in some remote areas, but until there is some tangible proof of this the species must be regarded as being extremely rare, if not already extinct'.

Aviculture: The Paradise Parrakeet was discovered by John Gilbert, Gould's assistant, in 1844. Enraptured with its beauty, Gilbert asked Gould to name it after him – but Gould was not in favour of naming birds after people. Gilbert was killed by aborigines in the following year, before he knew of Gould's decision.

Next to nothing was known or published about the Paradise Parrakeet although, in a work published in 1868, Diggles mentioned that it nested in termitaria. Extraordinary as it may seem, at this period and until about 1880, the Paradise Parrakeet was quite well known in European aviculture and reared young on a number of occasions in the aviaries of wealthy enthusiasts. Some European successes include those achieved by Count Celle de Sprimont of Belgium (1878), Princess Gustavus of Cröy in 1882; Prince Ferdinand of Saxe-Coburg-Gotha (later ex-king Ferdinand of Bulgaria) in 1880. Princess Gustavus also reared hybrids between a Paradise Parrakeet and a Redrump, probably in 1880 or 1881.

Nineteenth-century writers extolled the beauty of the Paradise Parrakeet and Reverend (later Canon) Dutton called it 'surely the most beautiful Paroquet that exists'. Nevertheless, he disposed of his pair to London Zoo because of their annoying habit of trying to burrow into the wall of the room in which they were housed! As the Duke of Bedford commented, the ardent aviculturist would 'gladly sacrifice every wall in his house if a nest of young were likely to be reared!'

It is an extraordinary fact that Dutton had kept four species of *Psephotus* – Redrump, Blue-bonnet, Many-colour and Paradise, and stated that the Many-colour was 'the rarest, and, according to my experience, is quite as delicate, if not more so than Pulcherrimus. My bird was shy, too, like Pulcherrimus'.

The Paradise Parrakeet also had a reputation for delicacy. Gedney knew 'of no other variety of the parrakeet tribe that will die upon such short notice and insufficient grounds' – due, he believed, to incorrect feeding. He thought it 'undoubtedly the loveliest of the parrakeet tribe, combining the most vivid and varied colouring of plumage with an extremely graceful outline, and a temperament remarkable for great gentleness of disposition and attachment'.

Lendon (Lendon & Cayley, 1973) examined the possible reasons for the sudden and irrevocable loss of this species to aviculture. Firstly, the source of supply to the export trade may have ceased with the death or movement of the trapper, although Paradise Parrakeets could often be obtained in Brisbane bird shops for 5*s* per pair until the turn of the century. Secondly, its choice of nesting site rendered it susceptible to attacks from predators, feral animals and man. Thirdly, it declined because of the destruction of its feeding grounds by grazing animals which aided the spread of prickly pear (*Opuntia*). Fourthly, the combination of these environmental alterations was exacerbated by the continuous years of severe drought in the 1890s. In 1917 Mathews stated in *Birds of Australia* (Volume 6) that it appeared to be extinct.

As a result of conversations with old settlers, in 1918, A. H. Chisholm initiated an inquiry into the continuing existence of the Paradise Parrakeet. In 1921, he received a letter from O. H. H. Jerrard whose photographs and observations confirmed its survival. In 1926, Miss Florence Irby saw five Paradise Parrakeets. (Her uncle had found nests in river banks, as had another observer.) That year, Chisholm advocated captive breeding and a motion was passed by the Royal Australian Ornithological Union urging State governments to encourage its

breeding in approved aviaries with a view to re-establishment by liberation in suitable sanctuaries. The resolution was never acted upon.

Lendon concluded his account by mentioning a colour slide he had seen of a male Paradise Parrakeet; the owner of the slide 'steadfastly refuses, probably wisely, to disclose the source of the photograph but it would appear to be convincing evidence that the species is not extinct'. That slide and Jerrard's photographs (one of which can be seen in the *Reader's Digest Complete Book of Australian Birds*), together with a colour photograph of a mounted specimen, are the only photographs known.

There are Australians who, to this day, remain convinced that the Paradise Parrakeet is not yet extinct.

The claims of one well-known aviculturist to have kept this species at an isolated location for many years are quite widely believed.

Sir Edward Hallstrom produced hybrids between Hooded and Many-coloured Parrakeets. Lendon (1955) saw them and stated:

> . . . the adult cocks are quite close to Paradise Parrakeets (although having a yellow instead of a red frontal band), the adult hens are not a bit like Paradise hens, but are intermediate between Hooded and Redrump hens, without even as much colour as a Many-coloured hen.

Golden-shouldered Parrakeet (Antbed Parrot)

P. chrysopterygius chrysopterygius

Description: The Golden-shoulder male has the forehead pale yellow and the crown and nape black. The rest of the head and the under parts and rump are turquoise and the upper parts are greyish brown. Median wing coverts are golden-yellow; under wing coverts and outer webs of flights are blue. There is no wing stripe. The feathers of the thighs and under tail coverts (also the abdomen) are scarlet, tipped with white. The tail is greenish blue, the lateral feathers being tipped with white. The bill is greyish and the iris is dark brown. Length: 26 cm (10 in).

The female has the forehead buffish yellow and the cheeks, neck, throat

Golden-shouldered Parrakeets (*Psephotus chrysopterygius chrysopterygius*) – male left, female right.

and upper breast dull grass-green, shading to turquoise on the lower breast. Crown and nape are greenish brown and the back and wings are dull yellowish olive. Rump and upper tail coverts are pale turquoise and greyish brown. Abdomen and under tail coverts are greyish green, with some pale red feathers on the lower abdomen. The wing stripe is present. Weight: M 56 g (2 oz); F 54 g ($1\frac{9}{10}$ oz).

Immature birds resemble females. Young males have blue cheek patches and darker colouring on the crown. Some males show pinkish red feathers on the abdomen. Adult plumage is assumed at between 12 and 14 months.

Range/Habitat: The Golden-shouldered Parrakeet inhabits the southern part of Cape York Peninsula, mainly the interior in semi-arid savannah and open forest where termitaria are numerous. According to Forshaw

(1973), it is absent from areas in which it was previously found and is now quite rare. He states:

> On Cape York Peninsula illegal trapping of adults and removal of young birds from nests have endangered *chrysopterygius* and rigid enforcement of protection laws is urgently needed to save it from extinction.

Mattinson (1976) did not agree regarding the cause of its decline, attributing this to a number of natural occurrences; such as increase of their predators and of introduced cane toads in plague proportions.

Seeds are a principal item of the diet of this ground-feeding species; nectar, pollen, blossoms and leaf buds are also eaten. They are found in pairs or small flocks and are not shy.

Joseph Mattinson (1976) had studied the Golden-shouldered Par-

rakeet in the wild for ten seasons when he wrote:

> The actual breeding area is normally associated with a river or creek running through an area of from two to fifty acres which forms a black flat, so called because of the black soil, and it is in this that the special termite builds its mound. Other termites build in the hillier country, in the red earth, but the Golden-shoulder breeds only in the termitaria on the black flats. The black flats are normally covered in water in the wet season thus the parrot has a supply of seeding grasses growing right outside the nesting hole – a sort of millet, and the parents feed this extremely green feed, and in fact I have never observed the nesting Golden-shoulder to eat dry seed.

Mr Mattinson believed that the Golden-shoulder will not breed in a late or dry season because much rain is needed to soften the ant beds. In the dry season, the termitaria become so hard that a pick is needed to penetrate the outer layers. Both parents enter the nesting chamber; the male, therefore, does not feed the female at the entrance. During incubation, the female spends the majority of the time off the nest in the vicinity, except during the first week when she stays inside. An instance was related of a nest which had been deserted three days previously yet the three eggs inside contained living embryos – for a termite mound forms a natural incubator.

The range of the Golden-shouldered Parrakeet has contracted. Forshaw (1981) states:

> Local extinction is a real danger because there appears to be no immigration into areas from which birds have disappeared and this highlights the vulnerability of each breeding population.

Aviculture: The Golden-shouldered Parrakeet first reached Britain in 1897, when eight birds (seven of which were females) were imported.

Sir Edward Hallstrom was a most successful breeder of this species. In 1953, he obtained two males which produced 16 young when mated with Hooded Parrakeets. He described the hybrids as being prettier than either parent; the breast and neck was turquoise and the wing patches were larger than those of the Golden-shouldered and slightly smaller than those of the Hooded. In 1957, he proved that the hybrids were fertile. At that time he had 15 pairs of Golden-shoulders. It was his experience that birds only just one year old would rear young.

He found, as have others who have attempted to breed this species, that the main problem was the female's failure to brood the young; she would sit alongside them but not cover them. In 1961, the aviaries were covered with plastic and radiators were installed; thereafter there were few losses.

In Australia, the next breeder was Alan Lendon in 1961 (1962). The first of five eggs was laid on August 29. Three chicks had hatched by September 23 and all five by the following day. The first left the nest on October 28 and two more on the 29th. The breeding took place in a box supplied by Sir Edward Hallstrom. It measured 15 cm (6 in) square and 25 cm (10 in) high and was fitted with a funnel entrance 10 cm (4 in) long and 5 cm (2 in) square.

By 1968, Joseph Mattinson had reared 38 young. By 1976, he had constructed a range of 15 aviaries, each 18 m (60 ft) long, clad in a small ripple iron with only the front of wire netting. The near presence of pairs coming into breeding condition stimulated less forward pairs. The divisions between aviaries were solid ones to prevent males fighting the neighbouring males instead of mating with the females. Breeding results improved when 15 cm (6 in) natural spouts were added to the entrance of nest-boxes; some birds were reluctant to enter nests without these.

One female tunnelled under the seed hopper and made a chamber in which she laid eight eggs, hatched five and reared three. The incubation period was given as 21 days. Some females incubated continuously while others left their eggs for up to three hours. Most young spent five weeks in the nest; some fledged as early as four weeks. Ten to 11 days, between the nestling down and pin feather stage, was found to be the most critical period; later losses were prevented by using heated nest-boxes. Three to nine eggs had been found in clutches laid in the wild and eight young were the most seen in one nest.

Mattinson's birds were fed on millet, canary, sunflower seed, spinach and biscuit. Apple was not eaten. Washed coarse sand covered the aviary floors. During the breeding season, the quantity of spinach and biscuit was increased. Millet and other seeds were fed at the milky stage.

In Europe early breeding successes occurred: in Germany in 1966 by W. Etterich of Essen and in Switzerland by Dr R. Burkard about 1968. Dr Burkard believes that animal protein is vital for successful rearing and provides ant pupae and hard-boiled eggs, as well as soaked seed, including spray millet. Golden-shouldered Parrakeets are more difficult to breed than Hoodeds. Dr Burkard has found the incubation period to be longer, at 23 to 24 days (rather than 21 or 22) because females incubate less tightly. This species appears weaker genetically, resulting in the loss of young and poor fertility in males.

Hooded Parrakeet (*Psephotus chrysopterygius dissimilis*) – male.

Hooded Parrakeet
P. c. dissimilis

Description: This bird is distinguished by its black forehead, brighter and more extensive yellow on the wing coverts and by its lack of scarlet on the abdomen. Under tail coverts are salmon-pink. The female has the crown and the sides of the face pale greyish green and the vent and the under tail coverts salmon-coloured. Length: 28 cm (11 in). Weight: M 50–60 g ($1\frac{3}{4}$–$2\frac{1}{10}$ oz); F 54–59 g ($1\frac{9}{10}$–2 oz).

Immature birds have the bill yellowish. Males usually have brighter blue cheeks. The body feathers are moulted at three or four months; adult plumage is assumed at 15 months or later.

Range/Habitat: The Hooded Parrakeet inhabits the north-eastern region of the Northern Territory from the Arnhemland Plateau east to the MacArthur River. Its habits are similar to those of the Golden-shouldered. It, too, has declined, the probable reason being interference with ground cover, especially seeding grasses.

Aviculture: One of the most beautiful of all parrakeets, it was rare in captivity until the late 1970s. It is now being reared in large numbers in Europe. Some are spring-breeders.

Hubert Astley was the first breeder of this species in Britain. In October 1911, his pair produced five young which died of cold in the nest; in the following year they reared four. Astley forced the young birds from the nest on November 16 and placed them, with their parents, in a warmer aviary. The young ones were feeding by themselves by December 8. They were reared on fresh gentles, biscuit sop, chickweed and shepherd's purse. In 1913 the pair nested during the spring and reared two young.

E. J. Boosey (1956) hit on an ingenious idea for persuading Hooded Parrakeets to nest in the spring. One February he replaced the male Hooded with a Redrump who had an urgent 'desire to raise a family as soon as he felt spring in the air'. Instead of moulting, as she would normally have done, the Hooded was chased into the nest by the Redrump. She laid four eggs and reared three hybrids. The following spring the Redrump was removed after he had driven the Hooded into the nesting log but before mating had occurred. The male Hooded was then introduced and three fine young Hooded Parrakeets were the result.

The 12th Duke of Bedford bred this species on several occasions but it was his experience that healthy young were not produced in heated aviaries. This, however, was not the experience of an extremely successful Scottish breeder, Dr Mitchell Benvie who, during the late 1950s and 1960s, reared numerous young in rooms heated at 16°C (60°F) during the winter. Artificial light was not provided.

In Australia, Alan Lendon was very successful with this species which he first bred in 1936. One pair reared 33 young. It was his experience that, whether wild-caught or aviary-bred, after several years in captivity, their habit of winter breeding was lost, although they were, nevertheless, very early breeders and moulted particularly early in the year.

Lendon (1950b) wrote:

> The display of the Hooded is very pleasing and consists of the cock alighting with great ceremony on the perch near the hen or following her along the ground in a series of exaggerated hops, the shoulders being simultaneously depressed and the crest feathers on the head being erected in the form of a tiny crest. Hens also have the power of erecting the feathers but seldom do so unless very excited.

A remarkable pair of Hooded Parrakeets was owned by A. H. Gardner of Sydney. By 1950, they had reared over 60 young to maturity during the previous 16 years. In 1959, the male was still alive, aged 29 or 30 years, and two 15 year old females were still breeding. In Switzerland, Dr R. Burkard has bred this species since 1965. By 1984, he had reared young to the tenth generation and made more than 150 pairs available to other aviculturists. One male and three females produced 83 young between them in the years 1965 to 1978. He lived for over 20 years. In the Netherlands, Germany and Switzerland, the Hooded Parrakeet is kept in many collections.

Blue-bonnet Parrakeet (Bull-oak Parrot)

P. haematogaster haematogaster
Description: This parrakeet was formerly placed in a separate genus, *Northiella*, because the outer five primaries are attenuated into spatulate tips; however, a genus based on a single unimportant morphologic feature is untenable. The Blue-bonnet also differs in its larger and heavier bill.

The pale brown body colour distinguishes the Blue-bonnet from all other parrakeets. It has the forehead, forepart of the crown and lores mauve-blue; the breast is pale brown marked with pale yellow. The abdomen is yellow with a large ventral patch of red and the vent and under tail coverts are yellow. Wing coverts are bright olive and the under wing coverts and outer webs of the flight feathers are blue. The tail feathers are blue, tipped with white, the central feathers being bronze-green tinged with blue. The wing stripe is present in the female only. The bill is greyish horn and the iris is grey-brown. Length: 28 cm (11 in). Weight: M 88–105 g ($3\frac{1}{10}$–$3\frac{7}{10}$ oz); F 74–84 g ($2\frac{3}{5}$–3 oz).

Males can usually be distinguished by the larger bill and by the richer blue face of the male and brighter red on the bend of the wing.

Immature birds are duller than adults with less red on the abdomen. The wing stripe is present. The first moult occurs at about four months.

Broadtails are noted for their aggressive tendency – and the Blue-bonnet is perhaps the most quarrelsome of all. I once watched a pair housed with Pheasants make the latters' life miserable by driving them about. Housing Blue-bonnets with other parrots would be a fatal mistake.

Blue-bonnets are also notable for their playfulness, a characteristic almost unknown in other broadtails: they will roll together on the ground or play and swing on anything provided to indulge their playfulness and active ways. The Duke of Bedford (1928b) described the Blue-bonnet as a 'curious little avian monkey' which 'differs as much from its relatives in manner as it does in colour'. To him it was the liveliest of all parrakeets, running and leaping with great activity.

When excited, it erects the feathers of the forehead and raises the wings in a folded position and, as described by Groen (1962), makes 'fast nodding motions, by which the head is moved to almost between the legs'.
Range/Habitat: The nominate race inhabits western and southern New South Wales, north-western Victoria and south-eastern South Australia.

Blue-bonnets inhabit open plains, arid scrublands and lightly timbered grasslands, and cultivated areas around farms and water troughs. In railway sidings, they feed on spilled corn. Seen in pairs and small parties, they are fairly common, spending much time feeding on the ground; they fly close to the ground. A curious habit is to run quickly, adopting an unusually upright stance for a parrakeet. Various seeds, fruits, blossoms, nectar and berries form the diet. Grit and charcoal are also eaten.

It is fairly common except on the periphery of its range.

P. h. haematorrhous
Description: Known as the Red-vented Blue-bonnet, the red on the abdomen extends to the vent and under tail coverts; the wing coverts are brownish red, not olive, and the shoulder is pale green not blue.
Range/Habitat: This race is found in southern Queensland and northern New South Wales.

P. h. pallescens
Description: The colouration is paler than that of the nominate race.
Range/Habitat: It inhabits the desert area of the Lake Eyre Basin, South Australia.

P. h. narethae
Description: *P. h. narethae* is known as the Little or Naretha Blue-bonnet. It has the forehead and lores turquoise and the cheeks rich purplish blue. Head and breast are pale brown, mottled with pale buff. The upper parts are more greyish in tone than in the nominate race. Rump is olive-yellow tinged with orange. The under tail coverts are red and the median wing coverts are scarlet. This is the smallest subspecies and the easiest to sex. The female has the turquoise on the head duller and no

indeed they were by Lendon (Cayley & Lendon, 1973). He believed that *narethae* should be separated on account of its behaviour and the fact that 250 km (400 miles) of desert separated it from the eastern form.

Aviculture: Blue-bonnets are not among the easiest parrakeets to breed; but they became more common in European collections during the 1970s.

The earliest success was that recorded by Count Celle de Sprimont in Belgium in 1878 and the next by Baron Cornely in France in 1882. The first British breeding was probably that by Duncan Parker in 1910. The female had prepared the nest in the previous year – but did not lay. In March 1910, she laid in a hollow tree stump and young birds left the nest on May 14 and 19; they had been completely silent while in the nest. In addition to seed, they were fed on plain cake. Little interest was shown in greenfood. In the Netherlands Dr Polak of Amersfoort bred this species in 1938.

In Australia, Alan Lendon was the first breeder. In 1939, his Red-vented Blue-bonnets hatched six chicks from six eggs; two were reared. A male and a female, both had well-marked shoulder patches and the male had yellow under tail coverts, the female's being red. They left the nest in October and moulted in December when the male's coverts were replaced by bright red feathers.

Lendon (1950a) wrote of this species:

> Blue Bonnets are not very easy to mate up, frequently disapproving of mates provided for them. Once mated they are extremely devoted and indulge in a good deal of mutual preening, an unusual trait amongst Broadtails. They also play, rather in the manner of lorikeets with sticks and stones or occasionally with one another.

He noted that hand-reared birds usually lose all fear of human beings, being extremely aggressive and savage.

English breeder J. H. Wrenn (1981) noted of his pair that the female laid the first of five eggs on March 5. She commenced incubation when the fifth egg was laid, on March 13. The first three eggs were infertile, the fourth egg hatched on March 31 (18 days) and the fifth egg on March 30 (17 days); the

Blue-bonnet Parrakeets – Yellow-vented (*Psephotus haematogaster haematogaster*) left, Red-vented (*P.h. haematorrhous*) right.

orange tinge to the yellow abdomen.
Range/Habitat: The Naretha Blue-bonnet is found in the area of Ceduna, South Australia, east to Kalgoorlie and in Rawlinna, Western Australia. Records from Ceduna could have related to illegally trapped birds which have been released there; if not, and *narethae* was found to be sympatric with *pallescens*, the two forms would have to be treated as separate species, as

last egg contained a chick which died in the shell. If the eggs were correctly identified, the incubation period was shorter than previously recorded for this species. Mr Wrenn recorded that the chicks were covered in thick white down on hatching. Eyes opened at 10 days; at 13 days, the second slate-grey down was apparent with the down on the crown being white. The female ceased to brood the chicks after they reached nine or ten days old. They left the nest at 37 days.

The first breeding of the Naretha Blue-bonnet occurred at Adelaide Zoo in 1941 when three young were hatched. They resembled the female except for the bill which was white, not horn-coloured. In the same year, Mr Catt of Sydney was also successful. In Germany, three aviculturists bred the Naretha Blue-bonnet in 1971: K. H. Stegeweit of Ahaus and H. J. Niessen and H. Pferdmenges, both of whom came from Rheydt.

Blue-bonnets have hybridised with Red-rumped and Many-coloured Parrakeets and with Red and Mealy Rosellas.

Polytelis
Polytelis

Members of this genus are quite different from the other Australian parrakeets in behaviour and appearance; indeed, they show similarities to the *Psittacula* parrakeets. This is especially true from the behavioural aspect, for females are dominant over males, the courtship includes bowing and head-swirling and they are the only Australian parrakeets which can be bred on the colony system. Visual points of resemblance to *Psittacula* are the red bill, sexual dimorphism, the fact that immature birds resemble females and the long tail, elegant outline and softer, muted colours.

Forshaw (1973) states that:

This genus is transitional between the *Prosopeia-Alisterus-Aprosmictus* group and the *Platycercus* group, although general external appearances are markedly different from either. Despite superficial similarities to *Psittacula* I do not

think that it is closely allied to the Afro-Asian genus.

G. A. Smith (1978c) disagrees:

True the skull and the skeleton do show a resemblance to the broadtails: indeed it would be strange if they did not; for they are subject to the same evolutionary pressures: living as they do on the same continent and eating much the same foods...

Smith believes that the resemblance of the polytelids to the broad-tailed parrots is due to convergence and their resemblance to the *Psittacula* parrakeets is due to kinship.

Polytelis species make attractive aviary birds: they are beautiful and, unlike most Australian parrakeets, become tame and friendly. This is especially true of the Princess of Wales' Parrakeet.

Some pairs prove prolific but others are poor breeders and *Polytelis* species remain expensive. They are, however, well known and popular with breeders. A disadvantage is their susceptibility to mycoplasma – especially in the Rock Pebbler, although this can often be cured with chloramphenicol ointment.

A problem which sometimes occurs is paralysis of the legs. Ron Hastings, a well-known Australian aviculturist, believed that paralysis often occurred after night disturbance resulting in injury to the head. He stated that paralysis could also be caused by a form of arthritis and that injury and stress are predisposing factors (Hibbert, 1980).

These birds are fond of rain-bathing and seldom bathe in standing water. They are not as active as Broadtails and spend much time sleeping during the day.

Feeding: The basic diet should consist of sunflower, pine nuts, hemp, canary seed, millet, oats and wheat. Peanuts can also be offered. Usually the larger seeds are preferred. Fruit should be provided; sweet apple is most likely to be accepted and they will also take orange and pomegranates. Spinach beet and the usual wild foods, especially the heads of dandelion and thistle, should be provided as often as possible. Mountain ash berries are relished, also the berries of hawthorn and elder. G. A. Smith (1978c) found that they are not destructive to turf floors, even

though they like other forms of greenfood.

Barraband's Parrakeet (Superb or Green Leek Parrot)
P. swainsonii

Description: Few would disagree that this male is among the most elegant of all parrots. Its colouration is grass green, darker above, with the forepart of the head, throat and cheeks yellow. The crescent of red which borders the yellow on the throat and cheeks is an extremely effective contrast. There is a bluish green wash on the nape, the outer webs of the primaries are blue and the under side of the tail is black. The bill is red, the feet brown and the iris is orange.

Most males are more slender and weigh slightly less than females. Length: 41 cm (16 in). Weight: 122–157 g ($4\frac{3}{10}$–$5\frac{1}{2}$ oz).

The female is a duller shade of green but she is readily distinguished by the absence of yellow in her plumage. There are a few red feathers on the thighs and the inner webs of the tail feathers are pink, except the central

Barraband's Parrakeet (*Polytelis swainsonii*) – male.

pair, but there is no red on the throat. Face and ear coverts are greenish grey washed with blue. The iris is yellow.

Immature birds resemble the female although it is usual for males to be a slightly brighter shade of green, often with a hint of red and yellow on the throat. Immature plumage in males is variable, at least in captivity, for occasionally they leave the nest with colouration almost as bright as the adult's.

The first moult usually occurs at the age of three or four months when males will usually have slightly more colour than previously; however, full adult plumage is not attained until about 18 months – and not necessarily then. I know of a bird which misled its owner for two years and moulted into male plumage in the third.

Another indication of sex is vocalisation. Young males usually start to chuckle and warble when a few months old. Hens never do this.

Range/Habitat: Barraband's Parrakeet inhabits two small areas in northern Victoria and the interior of New South Wales, nearly always in the vicinity of a river except near the eastern edge of their range where they are found in open forest. They are partly nomadic, moving on in search of flowering eucalypts of which they eat the blossoms and nectar. Seeds, fruits, wheat, nuts and berries are also taken by this ground- and tree-feeding species. It is seen in small flocks which stay together even while breeding.

Some years ago, fears were expressed regarding the survival of this parrakeet. However, it remains common within its range, which is an area used for agricultural purposes – thus there is unlikely to be much alteration to its habitat. In fact, cultivation of subtropical crops such as rice, which require abundant water, is said to have resulted in an increase in its range.

Immelmann (1968) states that, for nesting purposes, they use eucalypts and 'favour holes in large side branches, immediately above water. Their holes are almost completely inaccessible to man, and therefore their breeding biology is almost completely unknown'. Of particular interest is the fact that: 'In contrast to other parrakeets, the males form small groups even in the breeding season, leaving

the group several times through the day when the sitting hen requires feeding'.

Aviculture: This species has never been as numerous in captivity as at the time of writing and is now more common in aviaries than when it was exported. However, it was never exported in large numbers and, until after World War II, was rare in aviculture.

One of the virtues of this lovely parrakeet is its gentle nature. In a large aviary, several pairs have been known to breed successfully. It would not be advisable to attempt such an experiment unless the aviary was very large. Because Barraband's Parrakeet is naturally sociable, breeding results might be improved by having several pairs in close proximity. Some aviculturists never have any success with this species, perhaps because their single pairs need the stimulus provided by the presence of other members of their kind.

In display, the male Barraband's:

will fly in a very slow and laboured fashion around the hen, bowing as he alights with contracting pupils and uttering a great variety of calls. When very excited he will puff his head feathers, draw his body plumage tight, partly spread his wings and race to and fro round the hen in a series of rapid hops, 'scroogling' at the top of his voice. If the object of this attention is favourably impressed she crouches motionless with puffed head feathers and partly spread wings. It is noteworthy that the full courtship display is not in any sense a preliminary to actual pairing. It takes place months before the birds are in full breeding condition and is not repeated later; hens in breeding condition invite their mates to feed them with monotonous calls and up and down movements of the head (Bedford, 1928b).

Barraband's lay four to six eggs; they generally prefer a natural log to a nest-box and a log about 1.8 m (6 ft) tall should be offered to a female which shows no interest in nesting, or a box 1.2 m (4 ft) deep. Incubation lasts for 19 days. Two or three years is the age at which they usually start to breed; occasionally attempts are made when a year old but success at this age is most unlikely.

On hatching, chicks are covered in white down. They leave the nest when about five weeks old. A careful watch

should be kept on the male parent who may attempt to kill his sons, especially if they are brightly coloured on emerging from the nest, as occasionally happens.

This species has been bred in Europe for the past century. The first recorded breeding took place in France in 1881; the breeder was Duval. In Britain, in 1900, the Reverend C. D. Farrar was awarded the Avicultural Society medal for the first breeding. The young were reared entirely on hemp and canary seed and flowering grass. The male slept in the nest at night after the young were about ten days old. In the USA, the first breeding apparently did not occur until 1940 when I. D. Putnam was successful in California.

De Grahl (1974) mentions a pair which reared four to five young every year for 20 years. While many pairs must be consistently successful, it is doubtful whether many are equally prolific. In Britain, demand always exceeded supply (suggesting that many pairs failed to breed) until 1978 when the price dropped drastically and surplus stock was easy to obtain. Some indication of the increase in breeders and breeding pairs can be gauged from the Parrot Society Breeding Registers. That for 1976 indicates that 33 young were reported as reared by 18 members, while in the following year 119 were reared by 62 breeders.

Some female Barraband's will show a desire to nest when only a year old, although it is doubtful that a male would do so. N. D. Cooper (1977) records an interesting case of how the problem of a male too young to breed with a sexually mature female was overcome. A breeder with three pairs of Barraband's had one pair consisting of a fully adult hen and a young male. When the female of a regular breeding pair was incubating, the male was transferred to the aviary which had contained the young male, the latter being moved to the aviary of the sitting hen. The old male copulated with the hen which had been housed with the young male and after a few days was returned to his proper mate, in time for the hatching of his young. The eggs of the third pair were found to be infertile and the male was again removed to pair with the third hen – after his young had hatched – and was then returned. Thus he fertilised the eggs of three females in the space of a few weeks! The pairs proved very tolerant under the circumstances – such an experiment might not always end in success.

Barraband's Parrakeet has hybridised with Princess of Wales', Rock Pebbler, Crimson-winged and Australian King Parrakeets. A plate published in *Avicultural Magazine* in 1924 depicted a hybrid between a male Barraband's and a female Princess of Wales'. The hybrid was a slim, elegant bird, mainly green above with a wide patch of yellow on the wing. Forehead and entire under parts were scarlet. The breeder, Hubert Astley, was curious as to whether the large area of scarlet on the breast and under parts of the hybrid meant that it had reverted to the colouring, or part colouring, of some remote ancestor.

Rock Pebbler (or Peplar) Parrakeet (Regent, Smoker, Black-tailed or Mountain Parrot)

P. anthopeplus

Description: In body size and weight, this is the largest member of the genus and its proportions are slightly less elegant. The male is bright yellow on the head, breast, abdomen, rump and part of the wings. The mantle is olive with the scapulars olive in the centre, otherwise blackish. Primaries and secondaries are black, dark blue on the outer web. There is a broad band of red across the inner wing coverts and the greater coverts are black. The long central tail feathers are black above, the others being dark green; the under side of the tail is black. The bill is coral-red and the iris orange-brown. Length: 41 cm (16 in). Weight: 140 g ($4\frac{9}{10}$ oz).

The female is almost entirely olive-green, brighter on the rump, breast and abdomen. The colour of the tail is a guide to sex for in the female the lateral feathers are margined and tipped with pink on the underside. Females are duller throughout. The iris is brown. Weight: 130–170 g ($4\frac{3}{5}$–6 oz).

In captivity and in the wild, there is variation in the shade of yellow, some birds being particularly bright.

Rock Pebbler Parrakeets (*Polytelis anthopeplus*) – female left, male right.

Forshaw (1973) stated that birds from south-western Australia tend to be duller but that this was not a constant geographical feature.

Immature birds resemble the female; however, males are usually a yellower shade of green, especially on the head and breast. Full adult plumage is normally acquired by the age of 15 months. One breeder found that he could sex immature birds by the colour of the culmen, which was lighter and more lustrous in the male and duller and less shiny in the female. Newly hatched chicks weight about 6.75–7 g (about $\frac{1}{4}$ oz).

Range/Habitat: The Rock Pebbler inhabits two locations of southern Australia which are several hundred kilometres apart: south-western Australia and a smaller area in the interior of South Australia from south-western New South Wales and north-western Victoria to eastern South Australia. In south-eastern Australia,

it replaces Barraband's Parrakeet. According to Lendon (Cayley & Lendon, 1973), the western population has increased in abundance and range since the settlement of the wheat belt; now, however, the species is declining throughout the wheat belt. The eastern population has also declined. It is interesting that the two populations are found in different types of habitat: the eastern in mallee (eucalyptus bushes) and along the banks of the Murray River, in tall eucalyptus trees, avoiding areas settled by man and, in marked contrast, the western population, in the wheat belt, which has even spread to the neighbourhood of Perth.

Rock Pebblers feed mainly on the ground, especially on wheat, and also take nectar from the trees. According to Immelmann (1968):

In contrast to Barraband's Parrakeets, they prefer holes in the vertical main trunk of the tree. The breeding holes chosen are often amazingly deep, sometimes the floor of the nest chamber is more than 16 feet below the entrance hole, and the birds have to climb this great distance vertically up and down. Rock Peplar Parrakeets occasionally also breed in holes in the ground in vertical river banks.

Immelmann comments also on their strong, high flight, stating: 'They are by far the best fliers of all Australian Parrakeets and thus need the longest flights possible, at least 20 to 26 feet long'. Groen had reached the same conclusion on this point, writing: 'Being large birds and keen fliers, Rock Pebblers should be housed in a spacious aviary'.

Aviculture: This species was exhibited at London Zoo as long ago as 1864 and has been regularly bred in Europe since 1880; however, it was rare in collections until after World War II. It remains one of the more expensive of the Australian parrakeets. However; Groen (1962) states: 'Rock Pebblers are free breeders, and require only little encouragement with regard to their nesting site, many hens being quite content with an artificial nest box of the hanging type . . .'.

In Britain, it would appear that this species has recently become more prolific; the Parrot Society Breeding Register figures for 1976 and 1977 respectively were 17 (7 breeders) and 28 (17 breeders). The 1984 Register recorded 107 birds bred by 21 members. In the Netherlands and Germany, it is reared in large numbers.

Courtship display in this species is less pronounced than in the Barraband's. The male bows low and stretches his head high, sometimes regurgitating seed with a semi-circular movement of the head. He will also fly up and down, uttering a call which sounds something like 'Cank, cank, cank' which does not have the irritating quality of the call of the Princess of Wales'. The red in his wing coverts is seen when he rapidly shivers the wings.

When in breeding condition, the hen will lower her body and make a plaintive squeaking sound. Females lay readily and breeding failure is most often attributable to the male. Females usually prepare the nest by scratching out all the debris, often gnawing slivers of wood from the inside, on which the four to six white eggs are laid. Incu-

bation period is 19 days and newly hatched chicks are covered in white down. When the young are about three weeks old, the female ceases to brood them during most of the day. Some females are very tolerant and not only accept nest inspection but allow themselves to be gently removed from the eggs and young. The latter usually leave the nest when about six weeks old.

One Australian aviculturist found that his Rock Pebblers preferred nesting sites on the ground, invariably nesting among elephant grass or under tin shelters.

There is a record of one pair which bred when only 11 months old but many birds will not attempt to nest until they have reached two years.

The first recorded captive breeding occurred in Australia in 1865, when three were reared by a Mr White. In Britain, Mrs Johnstone was successful in 1903.

This species has hybridised with both the other members of the genus, also with the Crimson-winged Parrakeet.

Princess of Wales' (Princess Alexandra's or Rose-throated) Parrakeet (Princess or Spinifex Parrot)

P. alexandrae

Description: The male is one of the most graceful in outline of any parrot: indeed, in proportion to its body size, few or no parrots have a longer tail, surpassing in this respect other long-tailed birds such as the Ringneck Parrakeet and the Papuan Lorikeet.

The male's colour scheme is most pleasing, being a combination of attractive pastel shades. The crown and forehead are bright blue, throat and foreneck a delicate shade of pink and underparts soft bluish grey. Upper parts are soft olive green, wing coverts a bright shade of light green, secondaries and primaries dull pale blue and the rump violet-blue. Thighs and lower flanks are rose pink, the rest of the flanks being bluish. Tail is olive-green, tinged with blue at the tip, the lateral feathers being blue-grey edged with

Princess of Wales' Parrakeet (*Polytelis alexandrae*) – male.

pink. The two central tail feathers are very long, accounting for half the total length of about 45 cm (18 in).

A unique feature is the spatule tip to one primary feather in each wing; in captivity this often breaks off. The bill is coral red and the iris orange. Weight: 92–100 g ($3\frac{1}{4}$–$3\frac{1}{2}$ oz).

The female is readily distinguished by her shorter tail, mauvish grey crown and greyish blue rump. She lacks the spatule on the primary. The bill is paler red. Weight: 105 g ($3\frac{7}{10}$ oz).

Colouration of adults is variable – as it is said to be in the wild.

Immature birds resemble the female, with duller plumage and shorter tail. The shape of the head is an indication of sex; it is usually larger and flatter in the male, with the crown colour slightly brighter. When a few months old, males make a chuckling call and erect the small feathers of the crown. Full adult plumage is acquired at the second moult.

The first mutation recorded in a *Polytelis* was the Blue Princess of Wales': it is an autosomal recessive mutation. The pink areas, the throat, under tail coverts and the pink-edged tail feathers, are white; wing coverts are sky blue and the body is blue-grey.

In the Lutino mutation, the pink areas of the plumage are retained, making a beautiful contrast to the yellow areas. The mutation known in Europe is recessive, not sex-linked.

Range/Habitat: Because of its nomadic habits and secretive ways, little is known of the wild life of this parrakeet and its status is difficult to assess. It is generally considered to be rare. It inhabits the semi-desert area of the centre of the western part of Australia. Seeds, especially those of grass, form the main item of diet. Tall eucalypts on the banks of creeks are the favoured nesting sites. Like most birds of the desert area, the breeding season depends on the rainfall, which ripens the grass to provide food for the young. When breeding, several pairs apparently form a colony.

One of the greatest charms of this parrakeet is its fearlessness, an inherent feature, apparently found in wild populations, presumably because they inhabit remote areas and have had little contact with man.

Aviculture: This species was discovered in 1862, first reached Europe in 1895 (London Zoo) and was first bred in Britain by H. D. Astley in 1912 on the colony system. It has hybridised with *anthopeplus* and *swainsonii* and the Crimson-winged Parrakeet.

The Duke of Bedford (1928b) summed up the characteristic trait of this bird with his usual sympathy:

No Parrakeet is naturally so fearless of mankind nor so easily tamed and, while it dislikes being touched and handled, as do all species which have not the habit of caressing their mates, none is more delighted by being spoken to and noticed by its owner and none will give him a devotion more free of cupboard love. Almost any Princess of Wales will come up and display if you cluck and chirrup to him for a few minutes and tell him he is a pretty bird. Aviary-bred young, instead of being desperately timid, will be sitting on your arm and feeding from your hand before other young Parrakeets will be even reasonably steady....

The persistent, ringing and far-reaching call note is unfortunately a feature of the display – and this may be carried out almost throughout the year. This factor should be given careful consideration by those with near neighbours for it is quite as annoying as the harsh shrieks of a macaw, for example – and more persistent. Many have been the complaints from neighbours about this species in built-up areas.

In display, the male will repeatedly fly the length of the aviary, with pupil dilated and tail flared on landing. In the words of George Smith (1979), he will then jump:

. . . once or twice up and down or he may, instead of bouncing, simply walk towards his hen with his feathers sleek and his head held so that his beak points slightly upwards with his red eyes blazing like rubies. Then may come the most curious feature, for it may be shared only with some Rock Pebblers, which can best be described as a rapid 'running-on-the-spot'. This produces a slight drumming noise and is followed immediately by several bowings and upward stretching and perhaps further running-on-the-spot.

The head is then swung from side to side and a curious ticking noise made in the throat. The jumping display sometimes carried out on the ground is very reminiscent of that of a male *Psittacula*.

The fluctuation in price of this species during the early 1980s was typical of – but more extreme than – that which has occurred for many Australian parrakeets. Jim Hayward (1984) described how this occurred. During the late 1960s, Princess of Wales' Parrakeets cost about £80 to £100 per pair. The females were high priced due to scarcity and breeding vices such as egg-eating. Prices were pushed up by Continental breeders purchasing British-bred birds and the lifting of the South African parrot import ban. Most early breeders had great difficulty in obtaining youngsters, being dogged by all the classic problems – infertility, egg-eating, laying from the perch and French moult. Although some of today's breeders struggle to raise a few young, others have excellent results. Double-brooded hens, young pairs of the previous

season breeding and even productive attempts in winter are becoming far more numerous. Greater prolificacy invariably resulted in lowered prices. By the early 1980s, these had reached rock bottom in Europe – £15 per pair. Within two or three years they had increased again to a much higher value.

An unusual example of prolificacy was a pair which reared 20 young in four clutches for a British breeder in 1984. An experienced Australian breeder of this species, Charles Hibbert, recommended that the nest-box should be hung at an angle of 45° and that it should measure 18 cm (7 in) square and 65 cm (26 in) deep, with an entrance 65 mm ($2\frac{1}{2}$ in) in diameter.

Californian aviculturist Betty Byers, experienced in hand-rearing many species of parrot chicks, described the young of Princess of Wales' as the noisiest she had ever fed:

Their constant chatter does not cease (even after they are fed) until I am out of their sight. They are a thin bird, sometimes looking like a featherless flamingo with their long thin legs and necks and their thin bodies.

She recorded weights of 7 g ($\frac{1}{4}$ oz) at three days and 104 g ($3\frac{7}{10}$ oz) at fledging (Byers, 1984).

This is one of the few parrakeets in which colony breeding proves successful. It should be stressed that, if colony breeding is to be attempted, the pairs must be introduced to the aviary at the same time.

This species will sometimes attempt to breed when a year old – although two years is more usual. The clutch consists of four to six eggs. They tend to have glossy shells which should not be confused with those of infertile eggs. Incubation period is 19 days. Chicks have white down on hatching, which becomes fairly long. Their eyes open at about ten days and they leave the nest when five weeks old.

Nevertheless, this species is firmly established in captivity and the breeding life of some pairs is long. E. N. T. Vane had a pair which reared three young when 23 years old; in the following year the female did not sit on her eggs and the year after that she did not lay.

The Blue mutation first occurred in

Australia in a colony aviary belonging to George Ruddle in 1951. Californian aviculturist David West bought the first Blue from him and in 1953 produced two split Blue birds. In 1962, the mutation cropped up again in Australia, in the aviaries of a Mr McMillan, and it first appeared in Europe in the Netherlands in the late 1950s. The mutation is fairly well established in Australia but remains rare and expensive in Europe and unknown in Britain.

In 1975, the Lutino mutation occurred in the aviary of an East German breeder, D. Meyer of Halle. Two females were bred. Birds with pink markings on wings and breast are occasionally bred and usually moult out these feathers which are replaced by normal ones.

Purpureicephalus
Purpureicephalus

Pileated Parrakeet (Red-capped Parrot)
Purpureicephalus spurius

Description: This single species of its genus is recognised by the distinctive plumage colouration and the unique bill shape. There is a space between the upper and lower mandibles, the upper one being elongated and less rounded than in most other parrakeets and the tip of the lower mandible rests in a notch of the upper. Quite different in character from the Rosellas, the Pileated Parrakeet is shy yet noisy – the male with a continuous chattering call – and extremely active.

It is among the most beautifully and unusually coloured of all parrakeets, immediately recognised by the mauve breast and abdomen. The male has the crown and nape red, also the thighs and under tail coverts; the small feathers in front of and over the eyes are green with blackish bases. The rest of the head is a most unusual shade of lime green, also the rump and upper tail coverts. The rest of the upper parts, including the tail, is dark green. The tail feathers are marked with blue and tipped with whitish and are light blue on the under surface. The bill is

Pileated Parrakeets (*Purpureicephalus spurius*) – male left, female right.

dark bluish horn colour and the eyes are brown. Length: 36 cm (14 in). This species is slim. Weight: 105–156 g ($3\frac{7}{10}$–$5\frac{1}{2}$ oz).

Females are variable; some have the red areas on the head replaced with green-tinged red; in others they are green. All the colours are duller, especially the under parts which are greyish mauve. The female's head is considerably narrower. Weight: 98–135 g ($3\frac{1}{2}$–$4\frac{3}{4}$ oz).

Immature birds are duller than females, being mainly green with the under parts greyish mauve and a few red feathers on the frontal band and under tail coverts. The first complete moult occurs at 12–16 months. E. J. Boosey, a consistent breeder of the Pileated Parrakeet, stated that he knew of no parrakeet in which the young left the nest so small and then gradually grew to the size of their parents.

Range/Habitat: The principal food of

this species in the wild is the seeds of the fruits of eucalyptus marri (*Eucalyptus calophyllo*). Its bill shape has evolved to enable it to deal easily with these seeds. Cultivated fruits form part of the diet, in addition to various seeds, including those of grasses; blossoms, buds, insects and their larvae are also eaten. This parrakeet is apparently still fairly common, despite persecution by farmers whose crops they raid.

The Pileated Parrakeet is found only in the south-western corner of Australia, south of the Moore River near Perth, in marri forest and surrounding areas, including parks and orchards in the vicinity of Perth. It is generally common, except at the eastern limits of its range.

Aviculture: The Pileated Parrakeet has a special appeal for most aviculturists fortunate enough to keep it but one disadvantage is the damage to woodwork rendered by its powerful bill. Boosey found it necessary to cover the exposed woodwork with sheet zinc or wire netting and another breeder nailed pieces of wood to the framework so that the birds could gnaw them.

Boosey (1956) summed up their attributes by describing them as: 'very lively, intelligent, and inquisitive birds, always on the move, and although they are classed as Broadtails, which they undoubtedly are, they remind me in some ways of lorikeets'. When making the latter analogy, Boosey probably had in mind the active, restless nature of these birds. However, unlike many lorikeets, they tend to be shy.

In Britain, the first breeders of the Pileated Parrakeet, in 1909, were the Reverend H. D. Astley and W. R. Fasey; each reared four. Probably it was not bred again in Britain until 1949 when Keston Foreign Bird Farm was successful. The pair proved to be consistent breeders, the parents of nearly all the aviary-bred Pileateds in Britain by the end of the 1950s. During the first three seasons, they reared 17 young and even proved double-brooded during one year. While rearing young, they consumed large amounts of sweetened bread and milk, preferred hemp and lost interest in sunflower and peanuts. Flowering ryegrass and seakale beet were provided daily.

These birds were enthusiastic bathers and the female would bathe during incubation and return to the nest still very wet. The young birds commenced to bathe a few days after leaving the nest. Boosey commented on this because young parrakeets do not usually commence to bathe at such an early age – usually starting about two weeks after independence.

Other consistent British breeders were the late Len Knowles and G. A. Smith. The latter's pair was invariably single-brooded:

> When they hatch, the chicks are typical broadtails with long, white, rather thin down eventually replaced by a darker, grey down that comes with the feather pins and there is the invariable white nape-spot of broadtailed parrots. Their bills, as far as I can detect, look rather as other broadtails; but the parents with their elongated bills appear to have some inefficiency in feeding them as the chicks, from the earliest age, always have much food smeared over their heads . . . . (Smith, 1975).

George Smith noted that the shortest incubation period was 19 days, that incubation commenced as the clutch neared completion and that the young stayed in the nest for 33 days. He mentioned that this species has been known to breed at one year old, when still in immature plumage.

In the 1950s, T. R. Holmes Watkins in Wales reared young from a pair of Keston-bred birds. He noted (1958):

> Pileateds have the reputation of deserting their eggs and even young on the slightest interference. The female is certainly very alert during the early days of incubation, and will leave her nest on the slightest suspicion of danger. Once the embryos are developing, however, I have found them sit as closely as other Parrakeets. A clutch can vary from three to seven eggs, and incubation appears to take twenty days. The young are remarkably silent for the first couple of weeks.

At the time of writing, there are comparatively few breeding pairs in Britain; the Pileated is probably better established in Germany and the Netherlands. In the USA, where it was first bred by Dr L. Patrick in 1928, it is rare. In Australia, Adelaide Zoo bred the Pileated Parrakeet in 1938 and on many subsequent occasions. In South

Australia, Alan Lendon was the first breeder in 1948. After six years of failure, the female laid six eggs and four young were reared.

This species has hybridised with the Red-rumped, Red Rosella, Stanley, Mealy and Pennant's Parrakeets.

Lathamus
Lathamus

Swift (Red-shouldered or Clink) Parrakeet
Lathamus discolor

The single member of this genus is related to the platycercine parrakeets. It has some superficial points of resemblance: red under tail coverts and the presence, in most birds, of the wing stripe; it also has certain anatomical features in common with them. Any similarity with lorikeets is due to convergent evolution: Swift Parrakeets feed on pollen and nectar and thus have a fine bill and the tongue is said to be adapted for this method of feeding, but not developed to the degree of that of the lorikeets.

Alan Lendon (Cayley & Lendon, 1973) put forward the interesting theory that it:

> . . . may be an aberrant southernmost representative of the Opopsittidae. There is a striking resemblance in the red tipping of the inner webs of the innermost secondaries which occurs also in all the Australian fig-parrots.

Comparing this species with lorikeets, Lendon said:

> It is predominantly a nectar-feeding bird and it clambers about amongst foliage in very much the same way. However, it has not the typical, jerky movements of the lorikeets, mated pairs do not preen each other nor do they rest close together as do lorikeets, and it is said that the tongue is not extensively brushed as are those of the typical lorikeets.

It might be mentioned however that Fig Parrots do move jerkily and indulge in mutual preening.

Description: It is dark green above, yellowish green below. Forehead and forepart of the cheeks is scarlet, the lores are yellow and the crown is blue. The throat is crimson bordered with yellow. Outer webs of the flight

Swift Parrakeet (*Lathamus discolor*).

feathers are blue; under and lesser wing coverts are dark red and the wing stripe is present in some birds. The narrow, pointed tail is dull brownish red; feathers of the under tail coverts are dull crimson, margined with yellow, some with green centres. The bill is horn-coloured and the iris is yellow or brownish yellow. Length: 25 cm (10 in). Weight: 50–74 g (1¾–2⅗ oz).

Females are usually described as being duller. P. D. Shuttler informed me that:

> ... careful observation with known-sex birds has shown that in season the hen bird is a more yellowish-green than the male who, in most cases – but not always – has larger patches of red. A male ready for breeding has distinct red flecks in the breast and underparts which the female does not have. The males have slightly thicker legs of a slatey-grey colour while the hen's legs are tan to grey.

Immature birds are duller throughout

and have less red on the throat and under tail coverts; the wing stripe is present. The iris is brown. John Yealland thought young birds were decidedly prettier than adults, with their 'smoother and fresher green with the facial markings more delicately tinted'.

A Yellow mutation was described by Liran Gorp (1982) as follows:

> ... bright yellow, general plumage is a pastel shade, the head is a dull blue, eyes red, breast and abdomen a golden colour, the red of the wings and rump is a very bright red. The outer webs of the flight feathers are bright blue.

Range/Habitat: The Swift Parrakeet inhabits south-eastern Australia, also Tasmania and islands in the Bass Strait.

It is a migratory species, breeding only in Tasmania and the Bass Strait islands, where it arrives in August and September and stays until between January and May. It is irregularly dispersed and nowhere plentiful over its wide wintering range. As flowering trees are its main food source, the Swift Parrakeet is found in most types of low-altitude timbered country, including gardens and parks, even in cities. Its habits are similar to those of lorikeets in that it moves around in noisy flocks, feeding on blossoms in the tree tops. The flight is exceptionally rapid. In addition to pollen and nectar (especially that of eucalyptus), fruits, seeds, berries and insects and their larvae are eaten.

Aviculture: This species was exported to Europe in the nineteenth century and was first exhibited at London Zoo in 1863. In 1880, a dealer in London received 53 pairs. Most of these went to Germany where they were sold for the equivalent of £4.50 per pair – a large sum. Then called Swift Lorikeets, they were fed like lorikeets and some, from a consignment which arrived 'fit and healthy' in 1882 in England, were fed on seed and boiled rice, sweetened with honey or sugar, and greenfood. They were reported to do equally well on seed alone, although this was refuted by Dr W. Hamilton of Adelaide in 1928. It was his experience that:

> Swifts fed on seed will die for no apparent reason. They seem in the best of health, and when picked up dead are as fat as butter and with no sign of disease.

> I have lost them on seed, but never since using bread, milk and sugar.

Early breeding successes were recorded by A. Rousse in France in 1882 (three reared), 1883 (five) and 1884 (three and four). In Australia, R. Lewitzka reared one in 1935. Three eggs were laid; two chicks hatched, one died at 12 days and the survivor left the nest when 32 days old.

In Britain, the first breeder was the Duke of Bedford in 1936: three young were reared. In 1937, he started the season with one pair housed on their own which reared two young and an adult pair and three young birds in a colony aviary. The adult pair promptly changed partners. The young female bred when only one year old and the young male came into breeding condition in advance of the adult males. The two females, which treated each other with 'becoming forbearance' reared two and three young.

The 12th Duke of Bedford recorded (1937) of male Swifts:

> On finding an alluring nest-hole they warble excitedly and shiver their wings and later go inside and inspect the premises, but should a hen wish to enter they at first drive her away and only admit her some days later, with an apparent show of reluctance, when they are *quite* sure her intentions are serious.

The 12th Duke of Bedford noted, as have other breeders, that newly fledged young are seldom nervous; indeed, his would feed from his hand a few days after leaving the nest.

At the time of writing, this species has only rarely been bred in Britain and the USA. In 1970, three young were reared at San Diego Zoo. In Europe, a few breeders are consistently successful; indeed, an Australian aviculturist who visited me in 1978 after touring European collections thought that more Swifts were being bred there than in Australia.

In Germany, the first breeding did not occur until 1967 when W. Gote of Hildersheim and A. Woestendiek of Hilden were successful. J. Schumacher has bred the Swift Parrakeet since 1972 and recommended it without reservation (1975) as a quiet bird with a pleasant call, friendly – not timid – and requiring a dry enclosed shelter but not a large aviary.

Schumacher found that several pairs could be kept in a single aviary provided that it measured at least 6 × 1 m (20 × 3¼ ft) and all the birds were placed inside at the same time. His Swifts were fed on sunflower, millet, oats, wheat, niger, hemp, sponge cake moistened with honey, fresh corn-on-the-cob and half-ripened wheat (deep frozen for year-round use), sprouting sunflower, apple, orange and soft fruits such as strawberries and raspberries. He noted that his birds seldom went to the ground and thus were rarely found to have worms. Nest-boxes used had a diameter of 15–18 cm (6–7 in) and a height of 30–40 cm (12–16 in). The clutch usually consisted of four or five eggs which are incubated for 18 or 19 days. Chicks have white down and resemble 'balls of fluff'. The female only feeds the young for the first 12 to 15 days. The young leave the nest before they are six weeks old and are independent three weeks later.

A request for information on this species in an Australian avicultural magazine was kindly answered by Mr P. D. Shuttler of Kettering, Tasmania. He provided me with the following notes:

I obtained Swifts accidentally when cutting down trees for firewood. One tree cut contained a nest with three almost fully fledged youngsters. These were taken home and fed on a diet of arrowroot biscuits crushed up in warm 50/50 water and milk solution in which a little brown sugar or honey was dissolved. Two of the birds were successfully reared and were kept in an aviary with small finches, Budgerigars and Diamond Doves.

At first they would feed only on apples cut into quarters and would not look at seed but by cutting the apples fresh and dipping them into mixed Budgie seed they were gradually induced on to a seed diet. Later in the season when apples were not available they lived exclusively on seed, showing no interest in any greenfood supplied but really enjoyed themselves when supplied with fresh gum tips and particularly gum blossoms when available. They also formed a liking for fuchsia flowers at the fading stage when they were filled with nectar.

The young birds proved to be a pair and the following year the female disappeared into the log in late October, occasionally being fed by the male at the entrance but hardly appearing during observation until late January. When I inspected the log there was no trace of eggs or young. The log was about 47 cm (18 in) high, with the inside diameter 15 cm (6 in) and a 5 cm (2 in) entrance hole about 10 cm (4 in) from the top.

During that year I found a nest from which the young had flown and it was of interest to note that it was a vertical stump only about 1.8 m (6 ft) high on the edge of a small bank overlooking a bay. In view of this the following year I tried to simulate this by providing logs with an inside diameter of 13–15 cm (5–6 in), open at the top and very slightly inclined. The hen chose one of these in preference to the log of the previous season, again entering in late October. In the following February she emerged with two youngsters. Investigation of the log showed one infertile egg and a dead youngster nearly large enough to emerge.

Again I was fortunate enough to have a true pair of young and the following season both pairs went to nest. The original pair reared two more young, despite being disturbed when I moved house, and again these were a true pair. With three pairs in the aviary and no disturbances they produced five, four and three young. I then had a total of 18 birds and lost two.

They are all housed in a large aviary with a pair of Major Mitchell Cockatoos, a pair of Cockatiels, a pair of Golden Pheasants and six California Quail.

Until a sugar and honey solution was placed in the aviary for a Musk Lorikeet, the Swifts would not sample nectar but thereafter they took it eagerly. Occasionally jam was added to the mixture and, on one occasion, fermented jam was used inadvertently. The result was that 'the birds all got drunk and were on the aviary floor unable to fly'. Fortunately, there were no ill effects.

Their diet also included a constant supply of fresh gum boughs (preferably peppermint or white gum). When a garden sprinkler was placed on the roof of the aviary, the birds would bathe in the gum branches although they were most reluctant to bathe in a container on the aviary floor.

Mr Shuttler found that: 'Having a flock of Swifts in the aviary attracts large numbers of wild Swifts to the gum trees and some of these have become very quiet, allowing us to walk within about 6 ft of them'.

As references to the exact form of the Swift Lorikeet's tongue are vague, I am indebted to Mr Shuttler for complying to my request to examine the tongue. He described it as follows:

The outer part of the tongue resembles about two thirds of a tube with a blunt end. Lining the inside of the tube are the brushes which really look more like the tentacles of a sea anemone. The end of the tongue is quite smooth. The brushes would appear to be about 1 mm to 1.5 mm in length and about 0.5 mm in diameter. It would appear that the tongue can be opened out flat or completely rolled into a tube.

Cyanoramphus
Cyanoramphus

Some aviculturists are puzzled by the absence, even in specialist books, of information on New Zealand parrakeets, or Kakarikis as they are better known. The two species widely available, the Red-fronted and the Yellow-fronted, are now so much a part of aviculture that newcomers are surprised when told they were not available prior to the early 1970s. They are such free breeders that, within about five years, they were readily available at a price within the range of the less expensive Australian parrakeets. And their charm, vivaciousness and confiding ways have won the hearts of many breeders who normally look no further than the latter birds.

On seeing these birds for the first time, no one can fail to notice their mode of progress: they move rapidly in a manner which is unlike that of other parrakeets. Their long legs and the way they run up *and down* wire netting immediately attract attention and they scratch in an earth floor for all the world like chickens! Many aviculturists find them immediately attractive for they display none of the aloofness of Australian parrakeets. Most are relatively fearless and will learn to take favourite items of food from the hand. They are extraordinarily active and make very interesting aviary inhabitants, especially in contrast to the more leisurely ways of most psittacines.

As Kakarikis are extremely prolific and are neither noisy nor destructive, they can be thoroughly recommended, with one proviso: their lifespan is seldom long and sudden deaths are common. Many deaths may be due to not keeping them free of parasitic worms. Worming should be carried out twice a year. If young are retained for breeding, their numbers will be maintained, of course, but it is extremely disappointing for the novice to have sudden losses which often cannot be explained. Despite this, the readiness with which most pairs nest will be encouraging to the beginner, for nothing is more heartening than seeing young on the perches.

As Kakarikis are not expensive to purchase, it is advisable to buy two unrelated pairs at the outset; allowing for losses, one pair at least, possibly two, will breed, and one need look no further for a change of blood. The temptation to sell the young must be resisted and the wise breeder will retain at least two, preferably four, which will put him in a strong position for the next breeding season, or indeed even for that one. I doubt whether any other species of parrot, even the Budgerigar, can rear healthy young at an earlier age. Numerous instances could be quoted of young being reared by birds well under six months old, including that of a Red-fronted Kakariki hatched in March which was paired up in June and was feeding youngsters when it was four months old. While I feel that, in order to maintain the stamina of the strain, Kakarikis should not be allowed to rear young before they are six months old, the above examples do illustrate the remarkable fecundity of these birds.

Feeding: Feeding presents no problems. Some Kakarikis prefer sunflower and show little interest in other seeds, but this need not cause any concern if the diet is otherwise a varied one. These birds are extremely fond of greenfood, both cultivated and wild kinds. A favourite item which provides amusement as well as food is a fresh turf of grass; the roots will be eaten in addition to the blades, and minerals and even small insects will be found in the earth. If Kakarikis are kept in aviaries with concrete floors, the regular provision of turves will be greatly appreciated: boxes of earth in which grass seeds are sown can be placed in the aviaries when the shoots start to appear.

Fruit is sampled but not all Kakarikis will eat it with enthusiasm. In addition to apple, pear and grapes, soft fruits such as strawberries and redcurrants can be offered, and berries of hawthorn and elder will be taken. Mealworms will also be enjoyed, especially when there are young in the nest, and some Kakarikis will eat greenfly.

Kakarikis often have nests of five or six and so ample forethought must be given to the provision of rearing foods such as soaked seed. Bread and milk and similar rearing foods should be offered well in advance of the breeding season. Proprietary rearing foods manufactured for Budgerigars and Canaries will be eaten eagerly and can be given throughout the year.

These parrakeets are most enthusiastic bathers and should be given fresh water for bathing daily. Containers must be shallow when young birds are in the aviary.

Accommodation: An aviary for a pair should be about 3.6–4.2 × 1.2 m (12–14 × 4 ft) × 1.8 m (6 ft) high. Kakarikis will rear young in smaller aviaries but they are such active birds that they will utilise every inch of the enclosure, including the floor. Some kind of safety fastening should be used on any feeding hatch because Kakarikis are very quick to find their way out of an opening; however, they are usually equally adept at finding their way back. In a predator-free environment, they would make good liberty birds but they are too full of curiosity, and have too little fear for breeders even to consider releasing them into the wild.

Breeding: Kakarikis should be discouraged from breeding during the winter by the removal of the nest-box; egg-binding is likely to occur if hens are allowed to lay during cold weather. The box should be introduced during March and removed when the second nest of young have fledged. The hen may already be on eggs and could be allowed to rear a third round if fewer than six young have been reared in the first two clutches. It would be easy to sap the hen's stamina by allowing her to rear too many young, so it will often be necessary to remove the nest-box and the eggs and the female will then probably start to moult.

A suitable nest-box for these birds measures about 23 cm (9 in) square and 31 cm (12 in) high. When it is introduced, it is usually the male who makes the preliminary investigation and tries to entice the female inside. Having accepted the nesting site, the female will spend long periods inside the nest-box and will roost there at night.

Large clutches are usual: between five and nine eggs are laid, either on alternate days or with a longer interval between the eggs. The incubation period is 19 days. Newly hatched Kakariki chicks have white down

which soon changes to grey except for the white spot on the nape; their eyes open when they are about eight days old. When aged between five and six weeks, they leave the nest and then resemble the parents except for the horn-coloured bill. At this age, they can usually be sexed by the size of the beak, head and body. The hen is usually incubating the eggs of the next clutch so it will be the male's duty to feed the newly fledged young. When he becomes intolerant towards the young – or, more specifically, towards the young males – they should be removed, provided that they have been seen to feed themselves. One aviculturist bred from a trio of two males and one female. Both males fed the female and the young.

These birds probably average larger clutches per pair than any other parrot regularly bred in captivity. A pair owned by a New Zealand fancier illustrates the prolificacy of this species: they reared 14 young in two nests and were in the process of rearing six more when they were killed by rats. Another pair, in a twelve month period, between December 1977 and December 1978, hatched and reared 33 young. The eldest male in the first two nests was killed by the adult male and another was killed in an accident. The rest reached maturity.

Leslie Rance (1982) bred from a ten month old female who laid ten eggs. All hatched – in a box 25 cm (10 in) square. The five youngest were moved to an identical nest; the male fed them immediately. All were reared. A third nest-box was provided and the female laid six eggs; six young were reared. In 1980, six pairs belonging to Mr Rance produced six young and also fostered five Princess of Wales' Parrakeets and one Red Rosella.

Mutations of Kakarikis have been recorded in the wild but are very rare in captivity. At the time of writing, there are five Lutinos in New Zealand, described as 'fantastic golden yellow and scarlet'.

Red-fronted Parrakeet
C. novaezelandiae

Description: It is an attractive shade of deep green with the crimson of the forehead, crown and a patch behind

the eye a pleasing contrast. There are also patches of crimson on each side of the rump and the flight feathers are rich dark blue. The beak is a shiny bluish grey in colour. The male is slightly larger and bolder in appearance. The iris of the eye is ruby red. Length: 27–29 cm (10½–11½ in). Weight: 110 g (3$\frac{9}{10}$ oz).

Immature birds have less red on the head and a shorter tail. The iris is pale brown.

Range/Habitat: This species inhabits North and South Islands of New Zealand and outlying islands, also Norfolk Island and New Caledonia. It is rare on the mainland and there confined to the larger areas of forest; however, it is well established on outlying islands. On Norfolk Island and New Caledonia it is rare. It adapts its habits to suit its environment: in forest areas, it seeks food in the tree tops or in shrubs and seeks seeds on the ground; stunted shrub is the preferred habitat on small islands and, on Macquarie Island, which lacks trees, this species is completely terrestrial. It feeds on seeds, berries, fruits, blossoms, leaves and nuts.

Aviculture: Before World War I, Red-fronted Kakarikis were frequently exported but aviary-bred strains were not established and this species was lost to aviculture. It was persecuted by farmers in New Zealand, leading to a large decrease in its native population. At the time, it was an offence to keep native birds there but, perhaps because of its declining numbers, permits were issued to a few aviculturists to enable them to keep Red- and Yellow-fronted Kakarikis. In 1958, a census showed that there were 103 Red-fronted Parrakeets in collections in New Zealand; they bred so well that six years later the total had risen to 2,500.

Successful re-introductions of captive-bred stock to the wild have taken place since the early 1970s. At Mount Bruce Native Bird Reserve, 70 Red-fronted Kakarikis were bred which were released on to the islands of Ziri Ziri and Cuvier as an experiment. This proved successful, so other liberations followed from birds bred by private aviculturists on North and South Islands. The New Zealand Government paid a nominal sum for the birds supplied for release.

Red-fronted Kakarikis *(Cyanoramphus novaezelandiae)* – male left, female right.

Yellow-fronted Kakariki (Cyanoramphus auriceps).

British aviculturist Professor J. R. Hodges (1968) paid tribute thus:

The Red-fronted Parrakeet is a delightful aviary inhabitant. In addition to its beauty and attractive mannerisms, it is hardy, easy to keep, easy to breed and extremely intelligent. On one occasion, the feeding hatch of the aviary of the adult pair was accidentally left open. Within seconds both the male and female were apparently enjoying their newfound freedom and exploring the neighbourhood. After about half an hour's exercise, during which they came off worse in an altercation with the local Blackbirds, they flew back to the garden. They found their aviary with no difficulty, even though it is one in a group of identical compartments, and returned sedately through the feeding hatch.

Professor Hodges later discovered that his birds, privately imported from New Zealand, belonged to *C. n. hochstetteri.*

Yellow-fronted Parrakeet
C. auriceps
Description: This bird is about 2.5 cm (1 in) smaller than the Red-fronted. It has a red frontal band and the entire crown yellow but otherwise resembles the Red-fronted Immature birds have the tail short and the iris brown.
Range/Habitat: This parrakeet is found on North and South Islands, Stewart and Auckland Islands and offshore islands. Its habits and habitat are similar to those of the Red-fronted except that it is more arboreal.

The two species *C. novaezelandiae* and *C. auriceps* will hybridise with ease but this *must* be avoided. Both are readily available and the young might be used for breeding. This happened in the past and today there are a number of Kakarikis of doubtful ancestry. These have even been incorrectly advertised as 'Orange-fronted' Parrakeets.

Orange-fronted (or Alpine) Parrakeet
C. malherbi
Description: This parrakeet can briefly be described as a duller version of the Yellow-fronted. It measures only 20 cm (8in) and has an orange frontal band and pale yellow crown.

Immature birds have duller orange on the forehead.
Range/Habitat: This parrakeet is a rare inhabitant of the South Island of New Zealand. In 1965, it was seen after a lapse of 30 years in the Nelson Lakes National Park. Its habit of frequenting alpine scrub led to its being known as an Alpine Parrakeet.
Aviculture: Although the Orange-fronted Parrakeet is unknown in present-day aviculture, it was imported into Britain in the late nineteenth century. It is reputed to have been bred in France by Delaurier in 1883.

A nest of this species was located in October 1982. The female was captured and her three eggs were taken. All of them hatched, and the chicks provided the nucleus of a captive breeding programme. By 1984, breeding results indicated that *malherbi* is almost certainly a colour morph of *auriceps*.

Antipodes Island Green Parrakeet
C. unicolor

Description: The plumage of this species is of various shades of green with crown and facial area bright emerald, olive-green above and yellowish on the rump and under parts. The tail feathers are margined with yellow and the under surface is dull yellow olive. The outer webs of the flight feathers are blue. The bill is bluish grey, dark grey towards the tips. The iris is orange. Length: 31 cm (12 in).

Range/Habitat: This bird inhabits an environment of which penguins are more typical than parrakeets. The inhospitable Antipodes Islands lie 770 km (480 miles) south-east of South Island, New Zealand. The main island is only 8 km (5 miles) long and 5 km (3 miles) wide. The parrakeet is completely terrestrial and lives among tussock grass, feeding upon the seeds and apparently also on carcases of penguins. In the latter respect it differs from the race of Red-fronted Kakariki (*C. n. hochstetteri*) which also inhabits the island.

Aviculture: The Antipodes Parrakeet is virtually unknown in aviculture and very few specimens have left their native islands alive. London Zoo received one in 1831 and four during 1894 and 1895. The single bird received by the Duke of Bedford in the 1930s was procured by someone on board a small ship which stopped at one of the islands. It was possible to catch it from the shore by knocking it over with a stick and this fearlessness is typical of the species.

This parrakeet has been bred in New Zealand at the Mount Bruce Research Station. A. G. Caley, who worked there for six years, supplied me with the following information about these interesting parrakeets. In June 1971,

when he started work at Mount Bruce, there were four males and one female of this species. By 1973, 14 had been reared. Captive-bred birds appeared to take three years to mature. Although hens would lay when one year old, they would not incubate and usually broke their eggs. Red-fronted Kakarikis were therefore used as foster parents for the eggs of first-year females. During the second year, the Antipodes females would incubate their eggs, but Mr Caley wrote:

The hens seemed to be at a loss as to know how to feed the young. The chicks had the toes, belly, neck and wings bitten and were either squashed or left to die. By the third year, the parent birds would do everything right and would successfully fledge their youngsters. This was not only my experience as after the Department gave the zoos in Wellington and Auckland pairs of this species, the same difficulties were experienced.

As the birds came from a rugged island habitat, we kept them on a fairly simple diet – mainly sunflower with a variety of other seeds such as canary, panicum and white millet, rape and linseed. Fruit given was mainly apple although pears were given from time to time. Carrots and greenfood were enjoyed, especially when youngsters were in the nest. Rock salt was made available as in the wild these birds probably obtain a relatively high salt intake from salt-sprayed foods. I believe that the incubation period in this species is 26 days.

Eunymphicus
Eunymphicus

The single member of this genus is closely related to the *Cyanoramphus* parrakeets and has hybridised with them. In the opinion of Swiss aviculturist Dr R. Burkard, who has extensive experience of *cornutus* and *uvaeensis*, the two forms of *Eunymphicus* are sufficiently different in behaviour to be considered as separate species. The former is not a difficult bird to keep and breed whereas the latter is; *cornutus* is vivacious and playful while *uvaeensis* is quieter and less inquisitive. Their voices differ.

This unusual crested parrakeet is an avicultural rarity and, in the first edition of this book, was included in the

chapter for such birds. Now that there is more information on its behaviour, and there are enough birds in captivity in Europe for its captive future to seem quite hopeful, it seems more appropriate to include it with *Cyanoramphus*. This has been done at the suggestion of Dr Burkard to whom I am indebted for especially informative notes on *Eunymphicus*.

Horned Parrakeet
E. cornutus cornutus

Description: The outstanding feature of this species is the crest, formed of two elongated feathers from the centre of the crown, the male having at the tip two spatules of brilliant red. They measure 8 cm (3 in) in the male, being longer and wider then in the female, and lay more in the form of an 'S' on the head. In the female, they curve upwards. The crown and forehead are deep scarlet and the ear coverts and a small area behind the eyes are black, deeper in the male. There is a wide nuchal collar of rich yellow. The upper parts are rich green and the under parts are light green, yellowish on the upper breast. Flight feathers and the lower half of the upper surface of the tail are blue; the under side of the tail is pale brownish. There is some golden-green on the rump. The beak is black, larger in the male, and the iris orange. Length: 35 cm (14 in).

Immature birds have the facial markings less extensive and greyish, but darker in the male; the feathers of the forehead and forecrown are black, tipped with red. Ear coverts are pale green and the hindneck is olive green. The bill is horn-coloured.

Range/Habitat: Found in New Caledonia, in the western Pacific it is still common in the Haute Yaté Reserve but has declined in recent years, due to loss of habitat. Heinrich Bregulla, who lived on New Caledonia for 20 years from 1960, believed that the population was not endangered. Fortunately, its nests are not easily accessible. Two to four eggs are laid, usually in November or December.

Aviculture: The Horned Parrakeet was fairly well known in the nineteenth century but, judging by the records, it rarely reached Britain. The naturalist Layard brought Horned Parrakeets

Horned Parrot (*Eunymphicus cornutus cornutus*).

from New Caledonia in 1882; they were exhibited at London Zoo. They proved short-lived, even in the hands of such an experienced aviculturist as the 12th Duke of Bedford. He described them as intelligent and easily tamed, with a 'gentle voice' and the same habit of scratching on the ground in search of food as the *Cyanoramphus* parrakeets. Like the latter, they must be wormed regularly.

This species was bred by Baron von Cornely in 1881; one was reared. In France, Maillard bred five in 1889 from five eggs. Since the 1970s, it has been bred regularly in Switzerland and Germany. The first breeder in recent times appears to have been P. Schauf (1972) of Cologne. In New Caledonia, Heinrich Bregulla bred Horned Parrakeets regularly from the beginning of the 1970s.

In 1976, Dr Burkard received ten pairs. They commenced to breed one to two years later; third generation young have been reared to date. They mature at between two and three years old. One female owned by Dr Burkard laid at one year but the eggs were infertile. Usually two chicks are hatched, occasionally three and only once four. One pair was double-brooded in two years, producing six and seven young. The incubation period is believed to be 22 to 23 days. Chicks have grey down and a white nape patch. The young spend six weeks in the nest and can fly well on emerging. If they leave the nest at five weeks, as sometimes happens, they are unable to fly and are fed on the ground by the parents. They can remain with them for a long time as the adults are not aggressive and continue to feed them. Sometimes the youngsters are seen to feed each other, and this also occurs in the aviary, measuring 7 × 9 m (23 × 30 ft) which may contain as many as 20 young birds. Breeding pairs are kept in aviaries measuring 4 m (12 ft) square with an indoor enclosure 3 m (10 ft) square.

Dr Burkard informed me:

These are the most intelligent parrakeets I know. They are extremely curious and inspect everything with their beaks, each screw, each twig on the floor. They fly towards me as soon as they see me approaching with greenfood and soon learn to take it out of my hand. They are cold weather birds and love the daily irrigation with water, even at only a few degrees above zero. I have to pay special attention to worms because they spend so much time on the floor, grubbing in the sand and inspecting everything with their tongue.

They are fed on the usual seeds, plenty of fruit, carrots and other vegetables and greenfoods. They relish mealworms and other insects, also meat, cheese and yoghurt.

The French aviculturist, Dr H. Quinque, also obtained permission to import birds from New Caledonia, realising that captive breeding is imperative for this species. Several pairs were kept in a large enclosure to choose their own mates; pairs were then transferred to 12 m (40 ft) long flights with a shelter of 2.5 × 1.2 m (8 × 4 ft). Nest-boxes used measured 25 cm (10 in) in diameter and 50 cm (20 in) high and were partly filled with peat.

Dr Quinque (1980) described the male's courtship as:

... a series of pendulum movements of the head in a vertical direction with outspread head feathers and raising of the short feathers of the crown. The two large spatular feathers of the crest are not erectile and remain laying flat on the head or flutter about with the bird's movements.

The male's courtship song is deeper than that of the Uvaean Parrakeet. In rhythm with the song, he rapidly contracts and dilates the pupil to expose the brilliant reddish orange iris.

The first youngster bred by Dr Quinque was reared almost exclusively on mealworms for the first ten days. It left the nest at the age of 34 days when its colours were nearly as brilliant as those of the adults; the crest was absent; the first crest feathers appeared ten days after it left the nest.

Uvaean Parrakeet
E. c. uvaeensis
Description: Less striking than the Horned, this race is distinguished by

the lack of yellow on the head and the green ear coverts and nape. The red is confined to the centre of the forehead. The crest is composed of six curved dark green feathers. It is slightly smaller.

Range/Habitat: This subspecies has the doubtful distinction of possessing the smallest range of any parrot: an area of 4 or 5 km (2½ to 3 miles) on the 15 km (9 mile) long island of Ouvea in the Loyalty Islands. In recent years, the mature forest on which the bird relies has been greatly reduced by felling and by fire. Removal of young from the nest is also reducing the population, estimated to be 200 or fewer in 1974 by H. Bregulla. A more recent census indicated a higher figure – but this parrakeet must be considered as highly endangered.

Aviculture: This race is extremely rare in captivity. Heinrich Bregulla regularly bred it in Noumea, New Caledonia and, in 1980, obtained permission to bring three pairs to Europe. Dr Burkard received five of these birds, having previously obtained three pairs from a consignment of ten pairs which reached Belgium in 1975. All these proved extremely difficult to establish; on post mortem, they were found to be suffering from anaemia and rickets. It has not yet been possible to establish the reason. Another problem with the Uvaean Parrakeet is that it is very susceptible to stress (unlike *cornutus*). Dr Burkard believed that a genetic weakness might be involved. This seems very likely as, being endemic to such a small area, the population of birds must be very inbred.

Dr Quinque owned two tame male Uvaean Parrakeets for many years with little hope of obtaining females. He eventually paired one to a female Red-fronted Kakariki. In 1972, the first hybrids were reared. Twenty were produced before it was discovered that the hybrids were fertile – and any further breeding was stopped.

The young were beautiful birds, with a reddish purple cap of thick and silky feathers – but not long enough to form a crest. The voice exactly resembled that of the male parent. The hybrids were fierce and several were killed in fights; eventually one killed its mother.

13
Asiatic Parrakeets

Psittacula
Psittacula

The captive history of the *Psittacula* parrakeets goes back many centuries; indeed, the earliest parrot ever described was probably a Plum-headed Parrakeet. The Indian subcontinent is the centre of distribution of the members of the genus described in this chapter: eight of the ten species are found there. The Derbyan Parrakeet is found in China and the Long-tailed in Malaya, Sumatra and Borneo.

These birds are found in small groups which assemble in large, or immense, flocks to roost, and where food is plentiful. They feed on seeds, cultivated grain, wild and cultivated fruits, nectar and blossoms. In some areas, they are serious pests because they cause so much damage to crops. They are essentially arboreal.

All members of this genus have the bill red, black, red and black or, more rarely, yellowish. All males, and the females in some species, have either a ring encircling the neck or a wide black moustache mark. Body size varies from about 15 cm (6 in) in the Plum-head, whose total length is about 33 cm (13 in), to 25 cm (10 in) in the Derbyan, whose overall measurement is about 50 cm (20 in). The tail is as long or longer than the body in most species, though it is shorter in Layard's Parrakeet. This results in a group of extremely elegant birds – and this applies even to the large species which, proportionately, have very large bills.

The two large species, the Alexandrine and the Derbyan Parrakeets, are notable for their intelligence and can be rated in this respect with the larger parrots.

Feeding: Fruit and seed form the main items of the diet; greenfood is also eaten. Bread and milk can be offered the year round, but especially when young are in the nest.

Accommodation: For this purpose, the genus can be divided into two groups: the ultra-destructive and those with smaller bills. In the first group are the Alexandrine and the Derbyan, which should be housed in the manner described for cockatoos because anything made of wood is speedily reduced to sawdust. Alexandrines obtained when young make delightful pets but no one should consider caging this species unless they can provide a new wooden perch daily: its need to gnaw should not be thwarted. Alexandrines and Derbyans should be housed in flights not less than 4.2 m (14 ft) long and 90 cm (3 ft) wide. A pair of any of the other members of the genus require an aviary not less than 3.6 m (12 ft) long and 75 cm (2½ ft) wide. An enclosed shelter is imperative because *Psittacula* suffer more than any other parrots from frost-bite; they must be persuaded to roost in the shelter on winter nights, thus reducing the risk of mutilated feet. The latter can result in birds which are useless for breeding purposes because they are unable to keep their balance when attempting to mate. And of course, it is most unkind to subject these birds, or any others, to this painful condition.

Breeding: In few parrots is the male's fear or caution of the female so well marked. This is most noticeable in pairs which have been together only a short time. The notes on breeding behaviour found under the Ringneck Parrakeet apply also to the other species, about which much less is known. Some have not frequently reared young in captivity, despite the fact that they are, or were, commonly imported. It is the opinion of one experienced breeder that Asiatic parrakeets do not tolerate as much interference as Australian species.

Many pairs are early nesters, commencing in February or early March, as this is the time they would be nesting in the wild. They are single-brooded except occasionally when the eggs are removed or fail to hatch. Clutch size varies from two or three in the Alexandrine and Derbyan to four or five in the Ringneck. Incubation period is longer, about 28 days, for the two large species, and 23 or 24 days for the smaller ones. Young remain in the nest for about seven weeks.

Sexual dimorphism is marked or slight – but all adult birds can be readily sexed. In several species, the bill colour is different in male and female. Shortage of females is a major problem in attempting to breed most species; this is particularly frustrating when a 'female' moults out and proves to be a male. Behaviour of immature birds should be studied closely, for males start to court when only a few months old.

Females, unlike males, will sleep in the chosen nesting site for several months before breeding commences and, in captivity, many use the box in which to roost so it should be left in position throughout the year.

Display is pronounced in males: it is a sort of ritual necessary to overcome their fear of the female. It is sometimes carried out on the ground where it is most amusing to see the male walk with head held high, suddenly making small jumps into the air. Eye-blazing, bowing and head-swaying are other features of the display. Courtship feeding is preceded by exaggerated swirling of the head.

These beautiful birds were for many years under-rated by aviculturists, undoubtedly because some were very common and inexpensive, having been imported in large numbers. As has so often happened, their virtues were not appreciated until they were imported less often and the prices rose. This occurred during the 1970s.

Indian Ringneck Parrakeet (*Psittacula krameri manillensis*) – male.

Ringneck Parrakeet
P. krameri
Excluding Australian species, there can be no parrakeet which is better known to bird-keepers throughout the world. With one form endemic to India and another found in Africa, it has the widest distribution of any parrot species. It is known to ornithologists as the Rose-ringed Parrakeet.

Indian Ringneck
P. k. manillensis
This subspecies is much more common in captivity than the African.
Description: It is a soft shade of green, brightest on the cheeks, more yellowish below. The male has a black ring encircling the neck, widest where it meets the lower mandible and narrowest at the back of the neck where it is edged with pink. There is a black line from the cere to the eye. In some birds the nape is tinged with blue. The central tail feathers are bluish. The upper mandible is dark red, tipped with black,

and the lower mandible is black. The iris is yellowish white. Length: about 40 cm (15 in). Weight: 115 g (4 oz).

Females and immature birds are entirely green, except for a faint black line from the cere to the eye. The female's central tail feathers are shorter than the male's and, in immature birds, they are shorter still. Immature birds have the bill much paler in colour. Males usually assume adult plumage when they are about two and a half years old but this may occur at only 18 months.

P. k. borealis
Description: In this race from northwestern Pakistan, the lower mandible is red, sometimes marked with black.

African Ringneck
P. k. krameri
Description: This bird is smaller than its Indian counterpart and even more elegantly proportioned; in-

deed, it is one of the most superbly graceful of all parrakeets. It is readily distinguished by the colour of the bill; the upper mandible is very dark red, darker than the Indian Ringnecks, tipped with black or almost entirely black. The bill is smaller in proportion.

More mutations have been established in the Indian Ringneck than in any other parrakeet, excluding the Budgerigar. The best known is the Lutino, a sex-linked mutation. It is pure bright yellow, with the eyes pink, the feet flesh-coloured and the bill red, as in the Normal. In the male, the neck ring is white instead of black and the pink ring is retained.

As in the Budgerigar, an autosomal recessive (non-sex-linked) mutation of the Lutino is known; it is rare, perhaps non-existent at the present time. Alfred Ezra had birds of this type, as well as the sex-linked mutation; in 1938 and 1940, this Lutino pair reared six young, all of which were green.

African Ringneck Parrakeet (*Psittacula krameri krameri*) – male.

The sex-linked mutation has been known for perhaps as long as 200 years; in Britain, it was not established until after Alfred Ezra imported several specimens in the 1920s. It was eight years before the first Lutinos were produced, in 1934. Five years later 20 had been bred and these were the nucleus from which nearly all the Lutinos now in Europe were derived. Probably they were rarely exported before Ezra, who spent much time in India, brought them back, for the reason that Indian princes were willing to pay large sums for mutations.

The Duke of Bedford attempted to breed from a Lutino in 1918, or even earlier, but was not successful in rearing one to independence until 1931. The first Lutinos did not reach the USA until 1949, when F. H. Rudkin visited England and took two pairs back to California. By May 1950 he had two nests of four young. The Lutino mutation has been bred in larger numbers since the 1970s and no longer commands very high prices.

One of the most beautiful mutations known in any bird is the Blue Ringneck Parrakeet. A particularly lovely shade of powder blue, the male retains the neck marking, in the form of a grey ring edged with white; the female is entirely blue. The blue is most vivid on the crown and forehead, making a pleasing contrast to the deep red bill. Immature birds have the bill salmon-coloured. As in all Blue mutations, its manner of inheritance is autosomal recessive.

Most of the blues in Europe and the USA originate from a wild-caught pair obtained by the Duke of Bedford in 1950. They reared three Blues in 1951, four in 1952 and four in 1953, thus founding the strain which was to make this beautiful bird available to aviculturists throughout the world. By the end of 1953 there were at least 14 Blues, four of which the Duke of Bedford had sent to California. One of the first breeders there was David West, who reared two in 1955.

The Blue is still scarcer and more expensive than the Lutino; nevertheless, it is being bred in increasing numbers and can no longer be considered as rare.

Several other mutations have been established, none of which is likely to attain the popularity of the Lutino or the Blue.

It is explained in Chapter 7, in which the expectations for the various Ringneck mutations are given, that when a Lutino and a Blue are available, it is only a matter of time before an Albino is produced. The first one was bred at Keston Foreign Bird Farm in 1963. Unfortunately, it did not reach maturity. In Europe, the Albino was first bred in Germany, then in Belgium in 1969, in the collection of Dr and Mrs Swaenepoel, and in the USA where the first breeder was F. Rudkin of California. His first Albino was killed by its parents soon after its pin feathers opened. Another was hatched in 1968 and this was reared. The Albino has nothing to commend it, beyond its rarity, being pure white with pink eyes.

The Cinnamon or Isabelle has rather subtle colouration and, in poor light, could be mistaken for a Normal. It is light green with the flight feathers cinnamon; the eye is normally coloured. It is not yet known whether the male has a cinnamon neck ring; all the birds produced so far in Britain have been females.

This mutation was bred as long ago as 1935 by Alfred Ezra, but it was not established. Apparently it is not uncommon in the wild for it has been imported on quite a few occasions. The first breeder in Britain was probably E. M. Beale of Sussex in 1972.

The Grey mutation is not well known. As in the Budgerigar, it is dominant in its manner of inheritance and, when paired to a Normal, should produce Grey Green young. Khaki in colour, it has black tail and flight feathers. According to G. A. Smith (1978c), about four specimens have been imported into Britain since 1974 and, in the second generation, when paired with a Blue, Greys will be produced.

There is also a recessive Grey mutation which was first bred by David West of California in about 1978. A softer shade of grey than the dominant, it is the first mutation (rather than a combination of mutations) of the Ringneck Parrakeet to be produced in captivity.

G. A. Smith owns a Fallow Ringneck, which was imported from India. Its pale green plumage is slightly darker than that of a Cinnamon; the head is greenish yellow. The eyes are pink and the feet flesh-coloured. This rare mutation is sex-linked.

The Par-Blue mutation is of a sea-green shade with the tail blue and the head partly blue. In Europe it is sometimes referred to as Pastel Blue but this is incorrect because the ground colour is darker than in a Normal bird. As yet rarely bred, this mutation is an autosomal recessive.

Range/Habitat: The Indian Ringneck has a very wide distribution over almost the whole of India and Pakistan, Nepal, central Burma and Sri Lanka.

The African Ringneck inhabits a wide area including Guinea, Senegal, southern Mauritania, Uganda, Sudan and Ethiopia. It has been introduced to other areas, including Zanzibar, Egypt, Aden, Kuwait, Iran, Iraq, Hong Kong, Singapore and Mauritius. It is also found in China and Indo-China.

This is the most numerous member of the genus, extremely common in parts of its range in Africa and India and certainly the most numerous parrot in India, where it inhabits cities and gardens as well as woodland, scrubland and cultivated areas. Usually seen in small groups, it may congregate in immense flocks where food is plentiful. Seeds, fruits, berries, blossoms and nectar form the diet; it does much damage to cultivated grain and fruit crops in India, where it is a serious pest.

Immense numbers roost in the vicinity of some towns; in Delhi flocks estimated to contain 1,200 or 1,500 birds can be seen flying just before dusk.

Aviculture: The Indian Ringneck has a captive history which dates back very many centuries; in all probability, like the Plum-headed Parrakeet, it was known several centuries BC. In India, Ringnecks were considered sacred because of their ability to mimic human speech.

An early breeding record in modern times was in 1833 when the African

Ringneck was bred in Paris. In Germany, Otto Wigand reared the Indian Ringneck in 1872. In England, Dr W. T. Greene bred it in 1874 but this was almost certainly not a first success. It has been bred regularly in Europe since the early years of the twentieth century and has proved to be one of the most free-breeding of all parrakeets.

Males only two years old and still in immature plumage have been known to breed, but it is more usual for this species to start breeding when three years old. As they are slow to form a pair bond, a male and a female Ringneck should be put together several months before the start of the breeding season. This species is an early nester, females usually laying between mid-February and mid-March.

The courtship sequence is described by George Smith (1978c). Courtship feeding commences in the late autumn or early winter. Prior to this the male has cautiously preened the feathers of the female's nape and the wing butts. 'In preening he stands some little distance and only by stretching his neck to the maximum of his reach can he touch the hen.' After preening the female:

> . . . he pulls himself upright with the wing-butts held far from the body; but with the wing-tips in place. His eyes blaze. So far back, and high, does his head move that his near-side foot lets go of the perch to give the head more movement backward. The raised foot 'salutes' with a quick waver in the air and then his head is shot rapidly forward for another pecking-kiss of a preen.

Copulation starts several weeks before egg-laying. The usual clutch in this species is four or five, occasionally six; young hens usually lay only three eggs. Incubation commences towards the completion of the clutch. The incubation period is 23 or 24 days.

George Smith (1978b) recorded a most interesting case of two newly laid eggs of a Ringneck being placed under a Budgerigar (adding 'A chicken sitting on a pair of Ostrich eggs might be compared to the Budgerigar with its foster-eggs'). The eggs took 28 days to hatch, presumably because the small body size of the Budgerigar was not able to generate as much heat as that of a Ringneck.

The newly hatched chicks are almost naked, possessing a few very short white bristles which soon rub off. They weigh about 5 g. At five days, the back starts to darken as the down follicles appear under the skin. The eyes open at about ten days and, at about this age until about 15 days, chicks can be close-ringed. They usually leave the nest at about seven weeks but have been known to spend as long as 60 days in the nest. Young weigh about 120 g when weaned.

Ringnecks are normally single-brooded if they are successful in rearing young. If chicks die at an early age they might nest again and will usually do so if their eggs are removed for some reason. In this case, eggs will be laid between two and three weeks later. This is because copulation occurs during the incubation period, thus the male does not have to re-start courtship activities.

A male who is mated with a female of a striking mutation, such as a Lutino or Blue, may take longer to commence courtship if, in previous years, he has had a green partner.

Dead-in-shell is, unfortunately, not uncommon in early nests of Ringnecks because the females are easily alarmed from the nest; apparently, this is especially true when they are kept on the colony system and react to the alarm notes of other birds in the colony.

Ringnecks usually make conscientious parents, probably rearing a higher percentage of the young hatched than most parrots.

Another advantage of this species is that it can be kept on the colony system with others of its own species. Single birds usually prove harmless in mixed collections of small birds but it would not be safe to include a breeding pair, for when their young emerged from the nest they have, in some cases, proved murderous towards other species. Perhaps because the female is the dominant member of the pair and a male would not dare to attack a strange female, these birds usually agree well in a colony.

They are hardy in the extreme but, like other members of the genus, must be protected from frost-bite. However, a male with badly frost-bitten toes need not be considered hopeless as a breeding bird. I know of one, a Blue, which despite the fact that it has mere stumps and not one complete toe, invariably manages to fertilise the female's eggs.

Ringnecks often prove to be extremely long-lived; it is not at all unusual for them to reach their twenties. There is a remarkable and authentic record of an African Ringneck, imported in 1901 by Dr E. Hopkinson, which was in his daughter's possession for a day under 50 years.

The main disadvantage in keeping Ringnecks is the fact that so often, birds believed to be female moult into male plumage after a year or so. It is as well to watch the behaviour of young birds as this will provide an indication of their sex. At five months old, males will start to display.

Another small disadvantage of this species is the harsh voice and the fact that females can be destructive to woodwork although, if the nest-box is left in position all the year round, they will gnaw this rather than the aviary framework.

These points are minor ones when weighed against their many assets, especially their beauty and prolificacy.

As a general rule, Ringnecks do not make good pets – and this applies even to hand-reared birds – because of the nature of the species. The pair bond is not strong: there is none of the affectionate behaviour found in species in which the pair bond is maintained throughout the year.

Unscrupulous dealers will often sell adult Ringnecks as 'talking parrots' to be cooped up in a cage. To confine such active birds which, in captivity, should be kept only in an aviary, is thoughtless and unkind. It often led to purchasers of such birds releasing them, on the discovery that they would not become tame or learn to talk and, even worse, had a harsh voice.

In the days (as recent as the early 1970s) when a male Ringneck could be purchased for £1, released birds might have been the origin of some of the colonies of Ringneck Parrakeets to be found in various parts of Britain. For the most part, they consist of males and while a few breeding successes occur, the potential dangers of large flocks of this species, misguidedly reported by the media, are highly exaggerated. Indeed, it is doubtful

whether they could survive a winter without being fed by admirers.

Feral Ringnecks have been known in Britain for many years. In 1931, they reared young on Lord Lilford's estate, in cavities in trees. It is of interest that, in 1930, *The Gardeners' Chronicle* recorded that several parrakeets, said to be either Ringnecks or Alexandrines, lived on the edge of Epping Forest, now a suburb of London. Several young were reared. At the time of writing, Epping Forest is the home of a group of feral Ringnecks, one of the best known such colonies in the country. Some local householders encourage their presence by feeding them.

Attractive as these birds are when living free, people who live in fruit-growing areas should refrain from releasing them, for they do much damage to fruit. As is the habit of most parrots, they will take a bite out of each fruit, then drop it or leave it for another.

In many states of the USA, it is not permitted to keep birds at liberty. In Britain, under the Wildlife and Countryside Act (1981), it is an offence to release non-native species (see Appendix).

Ringneck Parrakeets have delighted bird lovers for centuries – but perhaps none more so than a male which Alfred Ezra bought in Calcutta in 1910. The bird performed in front of huge crowds for money, having been taught various tricks by an Indian. Included in his repertoire were twirling a stick which was lighted at both ends, using a bow and arrow, drawing water in a small wooden bucket, threading tiny beads, loading and firing a cannon which went off with a loud report and retrieving any small object thrown across a room.

Alfred Ezra recorded his death when he was at least 25 years old. He commented on this remarkable bird:

> . . . only kindness and coaxing with a grape or a nut used to make him do his tricks quickly. Once, when in a hurry, I was rather impatient with him, with the result that he refused to do anything, and flew away each time I brought him on to the table (Ezra, 1929).

The Ringneck Parrakeet has hybridised with the Alexandrine, Long-tailed and Moustache Parrakeets.

Mauritius Parrakeet
P. echo

Description: This bird is considered as a subspecies of the Ringneck Parrakeet by some taxonomists. A darker shade of green, it has the crown and nape tinged blue. It is a larger, heavier bird with a shorter, broader tail. In the female the bill is entirely black. Length: 42 cm (16 in).

Range/Habitat: This parrakeet is found only on the south-western part of Mauritius in the Mascarene Islands. Its numbers are perilously close to extinction mainly due to habitat destruction. The flock of eight observed in December 1983 was the largest group seen since 1977.

The status of this and other endangered species on Mauritius has been monitored since the early 1970s by a full-time biologist (currently Carl Jones) who has instigated successful captive breeding programmes. Unfortunately this has not proved possible for *echo*.

Moustache (Banded or Pink-breasted) Parrakeet
P. alexandri fasciata

Description: The male is recognised by his wide black moustache and by the dark pink breast, which has a lilac tinge to it. The upper parts are green, the median wing coverts being greenish yellow and the nape bright green. The head is bluish grey and there is a narrow line of black from the cere to the eye. The lower part of the abdomen is green, tinged with blue. The central tail feathers are blue tipped with yellowish green and the lateral tail feathers are bluish green; the under side of the tail is yellowish. The iris is light grey, almost yellow. The upper mandible is red, the lower mandible black. Length: 33 cm (13 in); the tail is much shorter than in the Ringneck. Weight: 110 g ($3\frac{9}{10}$ oz).

The female is easily distinguished by her black upper mandible. The head is bluer and the greenish yellow on the wing coverts is less pronounced. The pink of the breast continues upwards to form a narrow stripe on the side of the head.

Immature birds are mainly a soft shade of green with black moustache

Moustache Parrakeet (*Psittacula alexandri fasciata*) – male.

Moustache Parrakeet (*Psittacula alexandri fasciata*) – female.

markings and eye streak and the area between grey. On leaving the nest, both mandibles are red, of a paler shade than the male's, but darken to black in a few weeks, and eventually become red again in the male. The tail is much shorter in young birds. When E. N. T. Vane (1953) bred this species, he recorded that the young bird's bill started to darken ten days after leaving the nest; a month later it was almost entirely black.

At least eight races have been described. In the nominate form, the Javan Parrakeet (*P. a. alexandri*), the blue tinge on the head is less pronounced, the under parts are lighter pink, and the female has the bill pink.

In the other races, the distinctions are subtle, being mainly those of size and the depth of the blue suffusion on head and under parts.

Range/Habitat: This parrakeet has a very extensive range from northern India and Nepal, through Assam, Burma, the Andaman Islands, southern China and Indo-China to Java, Bali and the islands off western Sumatra; it is also found in Borneo where it was probably introduced.

It is common throughout much of its range. Although it is usually seen in groups of up to about 50 birds, occasionally it congregates in large flocks. Writing in 1945, one ornithologist recorded seeing a huge flock which he estimated to contain more than 10,000 birds. They were feeding on a plain where rice was grown, so must have been responsible for serious damage to the crops. They are noisy, calling loudly both in flight and when perched. Their favourite habitat is lowland plains and foothills and their flight is less swift than that of other members of the genus.

Aviculture: Common and inexpensive, the Moustache Parrakeet was formerly imported in large numbers. However, it did not always prove easy to establish in captivity and losses, especially among young birds, were undoubtedly high. In recent years, however, it has seldom been available.

Breeding successes with this species are lamentably few. In England, it may have been bred by Osbaldeston in the last years of the nineteenth century but the first documented success was that of E. N. T. Vane in 1953. His pair was imported in the previous year, when the female laid but deserted the nest due to interference. As is usual in *Psittacula*, the female was not the most amiable of birds and Mr Vane described her as 'a perfect shrew where the cock was concerned; he was not allowed on the same perch and whatever perch he chose that was the perch on which she wanted to be'.

Nevertheless, she nested in a large nest-box constructed of thick timber, filled from ground level to a depth of 60 cm (2 ft) with earth and topped with peat. The male began to display in March, standing on the perch beside the hen, drawing his head backwards and upwards and bowing while 'uttering a song which can hardly be called a warble, indeed it can hardly be called a song'.

The first of three eggs was laid on April 4; two were infertile. A chick was heard on May 3 which was brooded closely. It was described, at 25 days, as being 'downy and without any proper feathers'. On June 17 it was seen looking out of the nest-box and flew on June 23, when it was at least 51 days old. The male was never seen to enter the nest or to feed the young bird. Food offered consisted of sunflower, buckwheat and canary seed, oats, millet and hemp, apple, pear and 'brown bread rusked up and fed crumbly moist'.

In the USA, the first breeder was I. D. Putnam in California who bred this species consistently from 1929 until at least 1949. The male of the pair was tame and talking.

The nominate race, the Javan Parrakeet, was bred in Australia, in Adelaide Zoo, in 1936–37. Four young were reared in three nests. And at Taronga Zoo, Sydney, one *fasciata* was reared in the 1937–38 season and three in the following year.

Currently there are few breeders in Britain or Europe. P. A. Neachell (1977) recorded success with a pair obtained only weeks previously. The male was bought on January 17, 1977 and the female on April 4; she laid at the beginning of May. On June 8, apparently after 23 days, three half eggshells were found beneath the nest-box. For a period of about ten days, after the young were two weeks old, the parents were seen to mate each evening – a curious point in the breeding cycle. On July 25, a young bird was seen to look out of the nest and emerged on August 2. A second young one left later. Unfortunately, both died during October as a result of heavy infestation of worms.

In 1977, Brian Davis (1977) reared a single youngster from a pair obtained in June of the previous year. They bred in a large cage inside a greenhouse where they had been housed for the winter. The female laid at the beginning of March and the young bird left the nest on May 19. It was described as having 'a pale buffish mask and the Moustache and eyebrows are less intense than in the adult hen'. It otherwise resembled the female except for the reddish orange bill.

In Italy, P. Bertagnolio reared three Moustache Parrakeets in 1977 and two in 1978.

No mutations have been established in this species.

Mention must be made, however, of a unique bird in the possession of P. Done of Ellesmere Port, England. In 1973, he sent me colour photographs of his tame Moustache which, in one moult, became almost completely yellow, except for a few black feathers of the moustache; the yellow was tinged with pink on the breast and with blue on the lower breast and tail. Almost a year later more colour photographs showed the complete transformation into a bird of tremendous beaty. Of a rich golden yellow, set off by the deep red beak, the breast and head retained the pink tinge. The mask and the upper side of the tail were pure white. Transformation to a true Lutino was complete for the feet had become pink and the eye light reddish brown, almost pink. This must have been caused by some change in the bird's metabolism.

Blyth's Nicobar (Grey-headed) Parrakeet
P. caniceps

Description: It is entirely green but for the wide black moustache markings and a broad black line from the cere to the eye. Upper cheeks and ear coverts are yellowish grey merging into dull mauve towards the hind-neck. Central tail feathers are tinged with grey and tipped with yellow. The lower mandible is black; upper mandible is red in

the male and black in the female. The female has the crown and nape tinged with grey. Length: 56 cm (22 in). The iris is said to be orange-red; if so, it is unique in the genus.

Immature birds have yet to be described.

Range/Habitat: This species is found in the Nicobar Islands in the Bay of Bengal.

Aviculture: This parrakeet was exhibited at London Zoo in 1902; I know of no other instance of its being kept outside its native islands and it seems to be unknown in aviculture.

Slaty-headed Parrakeet
P. himalayana himalayana

Description: As is suggested by the name, in both sexes the head is dark grey tinged with blue. There is a narrow black moustache and neck ring – about the same width as in the Ringneck Parrakeet. The rest of the body plumage is green, with a blue tinge on the breast, upper parts and hind neck. There is a maroon patch on the wing coverts which is absent in most females. (E. N. T. Vane once examined definitely-sexed apparently adult birds at the British Museum: of the 26 females and 52 males, only two females had wing patches and two birds labelled as males had no wing patches.) The upper mandible is red with the tip yellowish; the lower mandible is yellow. The iris is white. Length: 40 cm (16 in).

The only mutation known so far is the Dilute or Par-Yellow owned by E. M. Beale in which the body colour is lime-yellow and the head a delicate shade of silver-grey. The moustache is brown and the red shoulder patch brighter than in the normal Slaty-head.

Immature birds have the head green, the cheeks being brownish green. The two central tail feathers are missing or very short. The bill is pale yellow or horn-coloured. Full adult plumage is attained at the age of two and a half years.

Range/Habitat: The nominate race is found from eastern Afghanistan, to northern India, Nepal and Assam. This species is found in small flocks or family groups, congregating in large numbers where food is plentiful. Forshaw (1973) states:

Slaty-headed Parrakeet (*Psittacula himalayana himalayana*).

A flock in flight is an attractive sight; the birds twist and turn through the trees in unison and with remarkable agility, and then suddenly swing upwards to alight in the uppermost branches of a tall tree.

This common bird inhabits highland areas throughout much of its range.

Burmese Slaty-headed (or Finsch's) Parrakeet
P. h. finschii

Description: This race is readily distinguished by the tail. Whereas in the nominate form the two central feathers are broad (about 13 mm/ $\frac{1}{2}$ in) along their entire length and the tip of the tail is yellow, in *P. h. finschii* the tail feathers are longer and narrower (tapering to between about 3 mm and 6.4 mm, $\frac{1}{8}$ and $\frac{1}{4}$ in, at the tip, which is yellowish white). The base of the tail is violet-blue in *finschii* and greenish blue in the nominate form. In *finschii*, the head is a purer shade of grey.

Range/Habitat: This race inhabits the southern part of Assam, Burma, northern Thailand, Laos, Vietnam and northern Yunnan in south-western China.

Aviculture: It is not well known in captivity, perhaps because it has no bright colours and is eclipsed by the Plum-head, *P. cyanocephala*. Nevertheless, it has a definite beauty, with the same graceful proportions as the latter species.

The Slaty-headed Parrakeet was exhibited at London Zoo as long ago as 1879 but has never been plentiful in collections.

The Duke of Bedford bred hybrids from a male paired to a female Blossom-headed Parrakeet on a number of occasions from 1932. In 1949, M. Bruyneel informed A. A. Prestwich that he had reared this species.

T. H. Alston (1967) of Swindon obtained a pair in 1965. In his breeding account he described the eye colour of this species as brown. His female lacked the red wing patch. She laid her first egg by April 2, 1967. The birds were then observed closely and the male was seen to display 'with a series of sharp drops to the left and down, always tail first. This was always to the left – not once did I see him go to the right ...'. The female laid five eggs, 'one every day from 2nd April'. (This is a rare occurrence for only in the tiny Hanging Parrots is it known for eggs to be laid on consecutive days.) There was a newly hatched chick in the nest on April 26, and another on each of the two following days. The fledging date is not given but the young were described as being very small with the head very light grey and the bill pale yellow. They were reared on canary seed, sweetened bread and milk and dandelion heads. No fruit was taken until the young were four weeks old, grapes then being preferred.

P. A. Neachell of Tamworth bred the Slaty-headed Parrakeet in 1975. The pair had been purchased in 1973. It was believed that incubation commenced on April 26. A chick was heard on May 26; two were hatched and they left the nest on July 4.

The Par-Yellow bird, of the race *finschii*, described above, produced two young for E. M. Beale in 1977; one fledged but unfortunately died during the following winter.

Plumhead Parrakeets (*Psittacula cyanocephala cyanocephala*) – male right, female left.

Intermediate Parrakeet
P. intermedia

Description: This bird resembles *P. h. himalayana* except for the forehead and area around the eye which are reddish pink, and the slaty-purple shade of the head. Female and immature birds are undescribed. Length: 36 cm (14 in).

Its name arose from the fact that it is intermediate in plumage between *himalayana* and *cyanocephala*.

Range/Habitat: It is said to originate from the Himalayan region of northern India. It is a mysterious bird, either a natural hybrid or a species with a very small and local distribution.

Plum-headed Parrakeet
P. cyanocephala cyanocephala

Description: This is one of the most beautiful of all parrakeets with its exquisite colours and elegant form. A lovely feature of the male is the plum-coloured head with the bluish purple cast, described by George Smith as 'the colour of a most perfect, luscious, plum'. The black moustache mark diminishes into a very narrow collar of black behind which is a band of bluish green. The body colour is green, more yellowish on the under parts and mantle. Rump and under wing coverts are bluish green; there is a maroon bar on the lesser wing coverts. The long, narrow, central tail feathers are dark blue, broadly tipped with white. The upper mandible is yellowish and the lower mandible is black. The iris is yellowish white. Length: 33 cm (13 in). Weight: 70 g ($2\frac{1}{2}$ oz).

The female has the head dull bluish grey with a dull yellow collar; the red patch is missing. The upper mandible is pale yellow.

Immature birds have been described as duller green than the female, the head yellowish grey-green and the tail the same length as the hen's. Males can be distinguished by their behaviour at about five months when they begin to display. At this age, males and females moult, resulting in the head becoming silvery grey.

Range/Habitat: The Plum-headed Parrakeet is found over most of the Indian subcontinent, the eastern part of West Pakistan, Nepal, Bhutan and West Bengal.

The Plum-headed Parrakeet is common throughout much of its range, particularly in forests near cultivation. Communal roosting sites are used by large numbers of birds which are said to screech and chatter long after nightfall.

Blossom-headed Parrakeet
P. c. rosa

This is treated as a separate species by some taxonomists. (Forshaw (1973) calls it *roseata*, pointing out that *rosa* is a synonym of *bengalensis* which seems inseparable from *cyanocephala*. But it has been known as *rosa* since 1783.)

Description: The male differs from the Plum-headed Parrakeet in having the forecrown, cheeks and ear coverts pink and the crown and nape more lilac than purple. The central tail feathers are blue, tipped with pale yellow. Length: 30 cm (12 in).

The female differs from the female Plum-head in having a small maroon patch on the wing.

Immature birds would appear to be indistinguishable from those of *P. c. cyanocephala.*

Several mutations are known but none is well established. Two are very beautiful: the Lutino (illustrated in E. J. Boosey's *Foreign Bird Keeping*) and the Par-Yellow (*Lovebirds and Related Parrots*).

Boosey's male Lutino was pure yellow with the head of a bright shade of red and the black neck ring and moustache replaced by white; the red wing patch is retained. This is surely one of the most beautiful mutations to be found in any parrot. A second male obtained by Boosey eventually was exported to California. Boosey had seen several and stated that they were usually marred by green feathers.

At least two Lutino Blossom-heads have been kept in Britain; Alfred Ezra exhibited one at a show in London in 1913 as did Lord Tavistock in 1922.

There is a Par-Yellow in the possession of G. A. Smith at the time of writing. The head is of a redder shade of plum than in the Normal. The body colour is a delicate, pale blue-green and the flight feathers are very light in colour. This mutation is an autosomal recessive.

Cinnamon and Blue mutations have also been recorded but are not known in captivity at the present time. Birds mottled with yellow, usually males, are not uncommon.

Range/Habitat: Distribution of the Blossom-head is continuous with the Plum-head; it is found in West Bengal and Assam, east to Indo-China. Its habits are similar to those of the Plum-head.

Aviculture: This species is notable for the fact that it has been kept in captivity for centuries and for many years was imported into Europe in thousands – and yet, until the 1970s, had only rarely been bred in captivity. As long ago as 1876, 400 were seen in a shop in Trieste, according to Greene.

Russ claimed to have bred the Blossom-head in Germany in the 1870s but stated that they bred up to three times each year and nested more readily than almost any other Parrot. While they lay readily, it is rare for a

second nest to be laid – let alone a third. However, he certainly bred this species, perhaps to the third generation as he claimed – for in 1877 he exhibited a young pair and their parents at the Crystal Palace bird show. As George Smith stated (1978c):

> In my experience better success is had when the birds are prevented from breeding until mid-March for Plumheads seem extremely unwilling or perhaps they are unable to lay a second clutch if the chicks are lost or when the eggs are removed.

One female Plum-head which was not provided with a nest-box in February, because of the bitter weather, burrowed a hole in the ground which led under the concrete floor of the aviary shelter. It stayed there all night in 12 degrees of frost, before the hole was blocked up.

Plum-heads and Blossom-heads were bred in Europe on several occasions between the 1870s and 1890s; thereafter there is a dearth of reported breedings until the 1930s when the Duke of Bedford bred a small number of young after many trials and tribulations. In 1927, he had written that the Plum-head would 'nest readily, in a cage as well as in an aviary' but had reason to revise his opinion to 'the hardest of all Parrakeets to rear to healthy maturity and others have had a similar bad luck with them'.

His young were rickety or short-lived and some were killed by stoats. Losses in the nest appear to be higher with this species than with other *Psittacula*, partly due to the fact that the female stops brooding at an early stage and, if the weather is cold, the young die as a result.

The experiences of Sheila and Tom Rogerson (1969) with the Blossom-headed Parrakeet are of interest. They summed them up as 'such gentle, quiet and pretty birds that it is a pity they are not more widely kept'. Unusually, for *Psittacula*, they were:

> ...most devoted to each other and have never shown the slightest degree of bad temper. Everything is shared, from the smallest perch to the choicest food....
> They are fairly active birds making good use of their outside flight. They love to scramble about on a springy branch and although they nibble at the twigs and sometimes the perches, it is

interesting to note that they are not destructive in any other way, leaving the wood structure of the flight and shelter alone. Flowers also grow in their aviary and the grass grows to the point of seeding. Then the Blossoms enjoy the fresh seeds, taking them while in flight as they hover over the grass. They also use the long grass as a joyful means of bathing after a heavy dew or a shower of rain.

Being such amiable birds, they have lived peacefully with a variety of birds yet seemed equally happy when they were the sole occupants of an aviary. It would be inadvisable to put them with any bird of uncertain temper as they are too timid to fight for their rights.

It is a comment on the gentleness of this species that it has often been kept successfully with the smallest finches.

After several years during which the chicks died in the shell or soon after, the Rogersons' pair hatched a chick after an incubation period of 27 days; two days later another chick hatched and on the next day the first chick died. On the third day the female ceased to feed it so it was transferred to the nest of a Bourke's Parrakeet which had a chick of the same age. For the next ten days, its crop was well filled by the Bourke's and at 13 days it was larger than the Bourke's chick. Two days later it was found dead with an empty crop.

As the Rogersons commented:

The fact that the Bourke had taken to the chick in the first place was remarkable as it was so unlike her own chick. Instead of a soft down on the body, the Blossom was completely naked and shiny. Its voice was extremely harsh and quite different in tone to the Bourke. As it grew, the call increased in harshness and volume and by its tenth day, the Blossom chick was covered with tiny black quills. At the time of its death, these quills were very pronounced. Its eyes had not yet opened but the Bourke had opened its eyes two days previously.

This pair are not altogether typical for, in describing the display of this species, George Smith states:

The fear that males have for hens is particularly noticeable and courtship may be described as a lot of wonderful noise about very little. The threat-jump is particularly evident in the Plumhead. Males stand very tall with the nape feathers to the head raised so that the black throat stripe, where it meets the nape of the neck, forms a corner.

The clutch usually consists of four eggs, occasionally five. Incubation period is usually described as about 23 days. Newly hatched chicks weigh about 4.6 to 5 g (about ⅕ oz). The young spend seven weeks in the nest. When weaned they weigh about 85 g (3 oz).

In the USA, *cyanocephala* was first bred by Dr Ralph Woods, probably in 1934. In 1947 he reported that his pair had produced young in 12 out of 15 years.

The Plum-headed Parrakeet has hybridised with the Slaty-headed Parrakeet.

Long-tailed Parrakeet
P. longicauda longicauda
Description: This is an extremely beautiful bird with the head most strikingly coloured. The male has the head, from between the wide black moustache mark (which does not narrow into a nuchal collar) and the black line from cere to eye, a lovely shade of rose-pink. The top of the head is emerald green. The rump is a soft shade of blue and the mantle is grey-tinged yellow. The rest of the body plumage is green, more yellowish on the under parts. The two deep blue central tail feathers are extremely long and narrow and are tipped with yellow. The upper mandible is red and the lower brownish. The iris is yellowish white. Length: 42 cm (16 in). Weight: 97–116 g (3⅖–4 oz).

The female is distinguished by the dark green moustache stripe, darker green crown and by the colour of the cheeks which is more orange than pink and the area less extensive. Upper and lower mandible are brownish. The tail is much shorter than in the male. Weight: 120–135 g (4¼–4¾ oz).

Immature birds have the side of the head marked with orange; they are otherwise mainly green, darker on the crown and cheeks. The tail is short and the bill brownish. The rump is said to be tinged with blue in males and the orange on the cheeks is more extensive.

Five races are recognised which show minor differences, except *nicobarica* from the Nicobar Islands, which is larger with the cheeks bright red. Sexual dimorphism is less pronounced.
Range/Habitat: Range of the Long-

Long-tailed Parrakeet (*Psittacula longicauda longicauda*) – male.

tailed Parrakeet is the Malay Peninsula, Borneo, Sumatra and adjacent islands, and the Andaman and Nicobar Islands.

This species is said to prefer open country or the edge of high jungle, where it is noisy, swift in flight and continuously active. It congregates in large numbers to roost.
Aviculture: There is a record of the Long-tailed Parrakeet being imported into Britain in 1864 but it has never been common in the trade and con-

signments normally consist of small numbers. It has a reputation for being short-lived which is probably correct; indeed, in 1973, John Yealland thought that a five-year old bird at London Zoo had set a longevity record for this species. The Duke of Bedford even described it as unable to tolerate a temperature lower than 15°C (60°F); this has proved to be incorrect but this species is especially susceptible to frost-bite. George Smith (1970) described a female housed in a wooden shed during the winter which lost most of its toes, probably because it: 'had to clamber down the netting of her inside flight to get her food, which was placed on the floor.... It was definitely not caused by having snow or hoar-frost gathering on the perches – often stated to be the cause of this injury'.

George Smith thought that losses with this species were caused by a) their not eating if watched – 'Newly imported parrots, in my opinion, often die of sheer starvation, even when in the midst of plenty'; b) psychological stress due to being kept near to disturbing factors; c) diet – 'As they may partake of very few forms of food once they do settle down this may predispose towards deficiency disease'; d) parasitism, especially microfilariae (larval bloodborne worms) – 'The worm probably lives in the peritoneal cavity or air sacs of the bird "pushing" its infective larvae (microfilariae) into the blood. Thromboses or "clots" of microfilariae may feasibly cause death through, say, coronary thrombosis; but the adult worm is not involved'.

Six years later George Smith wrote:

Although these birds are usually picked up [dead] in the very pink of condition, I believe that they have died of hypertension: a far too abrupt rise in an already high blood pressure system from excitement. I have autopsied five, two of which were mine. Both of mine had an atherosclerosis of the major arteries and all five were in seeming perfect feather and very good, indeed a fat, condition. Two had filarial worms in the air sacs and one had been despatched live by rail and was dead on arrival.

There are few instances of successful breeding of the Long-tailed Parrakeet in captivity. In Rhodesia, E. Green (1979) obtained a pair in 1977. In the following year, the female was incubating four eggs by December 29. After February 5, the female started to leave the nest for quite lengthy periods. Three chicks were reared and left the nest between March 7 and 10. They resembled the female but for their smaller size. Their beaks were reddish and their tails without the long central feathers.

In Denmark the Long-tailed Parrakeet was bred by Jorgen Jenson of Stroby in 1982. A pair which he bought in 1980 were moved to an outdoor aviary, measuring 2.5 × 2 m (8 × 6½ ft) × 2 m (6½ ft) high, with shelter attached, during the following summer. Two eggs were laid, one hatched and the chick died at an early age. In June 1982, the female laid five eggs, all of which hatched, the first on July 1. One chick died at one week old and another at four weeks. A third died at six weeks. Two youngsters left the nest, the first on August 28. The rearing food included mealworms (about 20 three times a day), a mixture of grated carrot, sprouted sunflower seed and eggfood, sprouted millet, corn-on-the-cob, fruit, greenfood and seed (Them, 1983).

This species has hybridised with the Ringneck, also with the Moustache Parrakeet. The latter cross occurred in the collection of B. Brownfield of California in 1974. A year later, their colours were starting to appear. The believed male hybrid had the crown dark green, the breast reddish, moustache black and the bill red. The believed female had the bill and moustache black, with colour starting to show on the breast.

In Britain, George Smith has had clutches laid (in April, May, June, July and October) on a number of occasions. The male's display is very pronounced:

The whole body, but more particularly the head, is gracefully weaved in front of the hen so that first one cheek and then his other is brought into her immediate gaze (Smith, 1978c).

The eye is blazed until it becomes a circle of white, then regurgitatory feeding occurs.

During this, as with so many birds of this subfamily, the head appears to be swirled around two or three times. When the movement is closely observed the head is seen to get its swirling movement because of combining the movements of normal vertical up and down head-regurgitation with head swaying.

Dignified walking and jumping are included in the display.

Five of the clutches laid by his birds consisted of three eggs and four of two eggs. He described the chicks as having long, thin white down.

One point to which the keeper of this species should be alerted is the very curved toenails. This results in the birds easily becoming hooked up on wire netting.

Malabar Blue-winged Parrakeet
P. columboides

Description: This species has the elegant proportions of the Ringneck Parrakeet and an even more pleasing colour scheme. Those who appreciate subtle colouring will find the male one of the most beautiful of all parrakeets. Perhaps the most striking feature is the very bright, slightly bluish green band behind the black nuchal collar. The head, breast and mantle are a soft

Malabar Blue-winged Parrakeet (*Psittacula columboides*) – male.

shade of grey and the rump is bluish grey. The forecrown is tinged with blue and the lores and the area surrounding the eyes are green. The wing coverts are dark green with yellowish margins. The long narrow tail feathers are dark blue tipped with yellow. The upper mandible is red, tipped with yellow and the lower mandible is brownish. The iris is yellow. Length: 38 cm (15 in).

The female is distinguished by her broad black nuchal collar (not followed by the bluish green collar) and moustache mark, the entirely grey head and the black upper and lower mandible. The tail is shorter.

Several writers have extolled its beauty. In 1916 Dr Lovell-Keays described the male as 'perhaps the most beautiful' of the genus. In his opinion 'the exquisite greens and delicate tracery of the wing feathers must be seen to be realised' and more recently George Smith described it as 'an incredibly beautiful bird' which is underrated by aviculturists.

The Duke of Bedford described the young birds on leaving the nest:

> The areas of the plumage, which are grey in the adult, are heavily washed with green in the nestling, giving a more uniform green tint to the whole body. The black ring of the adult is quite clearly indicated by a dark line widening under the lower mandible.

The bill was red and two of the four young had a small dusky patch below each nostril. He found that adult plumage was assumed with the first – not the second – moult.

Range/Habitat: The Blue-winged Parrakeet has a fairly limited distribution, being found in the Western Ghats strip in south-western India from about 19°N latitude, north of Bombay, south to Kerala. It is an inhabitant of tropical evergreen and moist deciduous forests, being most abundant in the hills between 450 and 1,000 m (1,450–3,300 ft). Generally found in the wetter areas, it associates with Plumhead Parrakeets in parts of its range and replaces them in other areas. Figs are a favourite item of food; it also consumes other fruits, berries, nuts, nectar, pollen and cultivated crops.

Aviculture: It is not known when this species was first imported into Europe

but there are no mentions of it in the avicultural literature prior to 1916. The first breeder was the Duke of Bedford, then Lord Tavistock. Dr L. Lovell-Keays had a pair, the female of which laid in 1916, at the beginning of March. One of the two eggs hatched; when the chick was two weeks old tragedy struck: the female was found dead beneath the nest – killed by a Mealy Rosella.

Lord Tavistock's pair hatched a chick in 1926 which was killed when the nest-box fell to the ground. In 1927, the female was slow in taking up her domestic duties, resulting in the male going for her 'tooth and nail'. It occasioned Tavistock (1927b) to remark:

> One of the strangest, most interesting and most amusing things I have observed with breeding Parrakeets is the anger and distress the cocks often display when their partners will not settle down in an eligible residence that has been provided for them. This annoyance is not due to thwarted sexual instinct, as it is displayed just as much when the hen is willing to pair; neither is it irrational, for it is hardly ever shown when there is no nest within reach and the birds are in breeding condition.

The female laid four eggs, all of which hatched; the young birds left the nest during early August. He described the voice of the hungry young as:

> . . . a quavering cry – a series of squeaking chirps – uttered in a lower and softer key than most young Parrakeets employ. The voices of the adults are, however, most unmelodious – a succession of short, harsh screeches, or, when displaying or investigating nesting-places, a more prolonged screech in a somewhat deeper tone.

In 1933 Alfred Ezra reared two Malabars; he and Lord Tavistock were the only consistent breeders of this species before World War I. After the war it was bred at Keston Foreign Bird Farm in 1950 and possibly not again in Britain until D. Curr (1971) was successful in 1971. He believed the incubation period to be 27 days – but incubation may not have commenced with the first egg. Another breeder records the incubation period as 23 days. When the chicks hatched, the adults consumed increased quantities of hemp and cuttlefish bone, also Budgerigar

mixture, which was previously untouched, and they almost ignored the sunflower seed. The first chick had hatched about May 3 and by June 13 the female was brooding the young at night only. They left the nest on June 21, 27 and 29. The female would not permit the male to enter the nest but he fed them when they emerged. At the beginning of July, he started to chase the eldest and, on July 4, the second youngster was found dead. The male was therefore removed. Forty-five days after leaving the nest the bill of the first youngster had started to darken. Three months later it had the bill reddish black, while that of the other was red.

In Ceylon, E. D. W. Jayewardene bred the Malabar Blue-wing in 1963. Obtained as fledglings in 1960, they first attempted to nest in January 1962, when four infertile eggs were laid. A year later the female hatched chicks. The male was not seen to enter the nest until they were six weeks old. Four young were reared, also at Delhi Zoo in India 1981.

In the USA, this species has been bred at San Diego Zoo on several occasions since 1970. A more beautiful sight than an aviary there containing a number of surplus males would be hard to imagine; they paraded on the floor in their erect and proud fashion, every so often jumping into the air – although there was no female to impress with this memorable performance.

Layard's (Emerald-collared) Parrakeet
P. calthorpae

Description: This bird is closely related to the Malabar Blue-wing but lacks the Malabar's elegant proportions for it has a much shorter tail. The head is dark bluish grey, the forehead, lores and the region around the eyes being suffused with green. There is a black moustache stripe, a blue nuchal collar and a broad band of emerald green between the grey of the head and that of the mantle. The rump is grey, tinged with violet. Wings are green with the lesser coverts grey and the median coverts yellowish. The rich blue tail is tipped with yellow. The iris is yellowish white. The lower mandible is brownish in the male, the upper mandible being red; in the female the beak is black. The female has the grey areas duller and the mantle of a greener shade of grey. Length: 29 cm (11 in).

Immature birds are almost entirely green with a brighter shade of green on the neck and the rump greyish blue. The bill is orange-red.

Range/Habitat: This species inhabits Sri Lanka (Ceylon), being found mainly in the hills up to about 1,600 m (5,000 ft or so). They are found in well-wooded country in pairs or small flocks; their flight is swift and direct.

Aviculture: This is one of the least known of the genus and was virtually unknown to aviculture before the 1930s. The first breeding occurred in 1935 in the aviaries of Mrs I. Darnton of Sissinghurst, Kent. Two young were hatched in June and both were reared.

Lord Tavistock made an attempt to establish this species but found it difficult to breed. In 1934, three young were hatched but died when a few weeks old; in the following year five were hatched, four of which were reared. A second pair reared one. In 1936, only one of the three pairs reared young – a nest of four, one of which was 'somewhat lutinistic'. In 1937 two were reared and in 1938 three.

At Keston Foreign Bird Farm, there were two pairs in 1954, one of which had clear eggs; the other pair hatched one youngster which died in the nest during a cold spell. In 1955, four were reared. Boosey (1956) recorded of them:

> Layard's are full of character, and once they get to know their owner show a tendency to become tame. As you approach their aviary a cock will often draw his plumage very tight and sleek while slightly leaning forward – this being part of the display. Both sexes are what I suppose would be called noisy, though personally I find their weird and very varied repertoire of strange cries attractive, save for the more raucous ones.

In Ceylon, G. P. Jinadasa bred two young in 1961 from a pair collected as nestlings. In 1960, four clear eggs were laid in an indoor enclosure. In 1961 they nested in an outdoor aviary.

Few Layard's Parrakeets have been imported into Britain; the best known individual must be the female which resided in the Parrot House at London Zoo for many years.

Alexandrine Parrakeet
P. eupatria

Description: This is the second largest member of the genus in body size and the longest on head to tail-tip measurement. Despite its huge bill, it is an elegant bird for its exceptionally long tail is at least the same length as the body. I measured a moulted central tail feather from a male and found it to be 36 cm (14 in) long.

The male is mid-green, brighter on the head and much lighter on the under parts. A prominent black ring encircles the neck, widest where it meets the lower mandible and narrowest at the back of the neck where it is edged with pink. The crown and cheeks are faintly tinged with greyish blue and a faint black line joins the eye and cere. There is a dark red patch on the secondary coverts. The under side of the tail is yellow. The deep red bill is much larger in proportion to its body size than that of the Ringneck Parrakeet. The iris is yellowish white. Length: about 60 cm (23 in).

The female lacks the black and pink neck ring, being mainly green with the wing coverts red; the tail is slightly shorter than that of the male.

Immature birds resemble the female but have much shorter tail feathers. One breeder recorded that three weeks after leaving the nest the young bird's tail was 10 cm (4 in) long.

Several mutations are known in this species but none is well established. There are a few Lutino specimens in Europe and in the USA. In this most attractive, clear yellow, red-eyed mutation, the red patch on the wing coverts is retained. The manner of inheritance is sex-linked recessive.

The first captive Lutino outside Asia may have been the female brought from India by Alfred Ezra in 1923. It was not until 1935 that Lutinos, two, were reared from this bird, when she was paired with one of her sons. These Alexandrines were probably lost during World War II.

Almost pure Lutino Alexandrines can theoretically be produced in three generations by mating a male Alexandrine to a female Lutino Ringneck. However, attempts may result in infertile eggs because the male has difficulty in keeping his balance when pairing. The experiment was success-

fully carried out at Keston Foreign Bird Farm. In 1946, E. J. Boosey hatched three young from this cross, two of which were reared. When a male hybrid moulted into adult plumage three years later, Boosey described it as 'hardly distinguishable from an ordinary cock Alexandrine except for his slightly smaller size and rather less massive head and beak – the latter a distinct improvement'.

One of the hybrids was then paired with an Alexandrine to produce a Lutino which was only one quarter Ringneck. There is an excellent photograph of one such bird in *Foreign Bird Keeping* (Boosey, 1956); it differed from the Alexandrine Parrakeet in having golden-brown patches on the wing.

Even rarer than the Lutino is the Blue mutation. Alfred Ezra brought one from India in 1923. Although it reared young over a period of 20 years, it was ten years before the first Blue was produced; only two more were reared and the mutation was lost. In 1943, the original Blue died. A coloured plate of this beautiful bird was published in the *Avicultural Magazine*, 1927: 17.

At the time of writing there are at least two Blue Alexandrines in Europe; it is to be hoped that they will be the founders of a Blue strain. In this recessive mutation, the colour is a soft powder blue with the wing patches retained as areas of white.

The Cinnamon or Isabelle mutation is, apparently, not rare in the wild – but it is seldom exported. However, there is a very small number in European collections.

Range/Habitat: The Alexandrine Parrakeet has a very extensive distribution, from Thailand, Laos, Cambodia, Vietnam, Burma, Assam to East Pakistan, India, West Pakistan, Afghanistan and the Andaman Islands and Sri Lanka.

Five races are recognised; there is little difference in the plumage but considerable difference in the size, and size of the bill.

The Alexandrine Parrakeet is uncommon throughout much of its range but is common and widely distributed in the lowlands of northern India, including some urban areas. Like Ringnecks, they are seen in small flocks during the day but congregate in hundreds or thousands to roost.

Aviculture: The history of the Alexandrine as a captive bird goes back centuries, probably to the time of Alexander the Great. Some historians believe that it was the first parrakeet to reach Europe.

It has always been readily available yet has never attained a great degree of popularity. This is almost certainly because of its large bill, which gives it a slightly fearsome appearance and accounts for its exceptional destructiveness. This species is a great favourite of mine, partly because it is one of the most intelligent of all parrakeets, comparable in this respect to the larger true parrots. It is an extremely handsome bird with its pastel colours, smooth plumage and long tail. Furthermore, it proves a willing and consistent breeder in captivity.

While I hesitate to suggest that such large and active birds should be caged, if they are given regular outings in a room, they can make wonderful pets if obtained young, becoming strongly attached to their owner and learning to repeat a few words.

There is no better testimony to this fact than the account of Edward Boosey (1956). While staying with Lord Tavistock in the 1920s, he was warned not to touch an Alexandrine which was reputed to be most savage and ill-tempered. However, it appeared to like him and he found that he was able to handle it. Shortly after returning home he received a box marked 'Live Bird'. Much to Boosey's pleasure, it contained the Alexandrine. It proved so tame and affectionate that he decided to keep it at liberty.

Boosey recalled how the bird:

> . . . used to roost in a large old yew tree opposite my bedroom window. As soon as I called in the morning and the curtains were drawn he would, while I was still in bed, fly on to the open casement window. Then he would perch on the bottom of my bed and walk sedately up the blankets to have his smooth and glossy head stroked, which he adored. Unfortunately, these morning visits eventually had to be discouraged as he took to flying up on the wardrobe while I was shaving and playfully removing and chewing up large hunks of it with his enormous beak.

The moment I went out of the house he would fly down on my shoulder, and if I went for a walk in the woods he would fly from tree to tree overhead – following as faithfully as any dog.

My own experiences of a liberty Alexandrine were of a very different nature. One Christmas Eve, above the pre-dusk cacophony which will be heard in any collection of parrots, I detected an unfamiliar voice. I soon sighted an Alexandrine flying towards the neighbouring garden. I therefore placed some sunflower seed on the roof of an aviary below a large apple tree. At dawn on Christmas Day, the Alexandrine was roosting in the tree and soon clambered down to feed. Tired and hungry, he spent most of the day eating and sleeping. The weather was cold and his tameness led me to believe he might have come from a cage. During the next two days, he spent most of his time in the tree, occasionally taking short flights. He looked so magnificent on the wing I was tempted to let him keep his liberty. However, such birds can be a disturbing influence on parrots which are breeding. Additionally, a liberty Alexandrine is an extremely conspicuous bird and I feared that some gun-happy individual would put an end to him.

I therefore decided to catch him. This was easily accomplished using a rough cage-shaped structure from welded mesh. An apple was placed inside and the Alexandrine could hardly wait to enter. He was soon installed in a spare aviary, of which he was the first occupant. Within three weeks he had caused so much damage that I reluctantly caged him. It was then that I discovered the endearing intelligence of this species. No attempt was ever made to teach this adult bird to speak yet within a few months he learned to say 'Hello'. After a year I felt that a continuous caged existence was unfair to this bird, which had become a great favourite, and I gave him to a friend. He was paired with a Lutino ringneck but was unable to keep his balance while pairing, resulting in clear eggs. After a while, a hen Alexandrine was found for him.

Alexandrines are bred only in small numbers and this must be because few attempt to breed them. The most successful breeder in Britain was Captain R. W. Veitch of Garforth. He owned a remarkable pair which reared every youngster they hatched during a period of 20 years, breeding almost every year. The female ceased to breed when she was 24 years old.

From these birds, Captain Veitch established a strain of Alexandrine Parrakeet which he described as 'bigger and finer than any imported birds' he had seen. Two birds which he bred produced 18 young in six years. Whereas the original pair reared two or three chicks in every nest, as is usual for this species, their young were successful in rearing four young on two occasions. They too raised every chick which was hatched.

Captain Veitch's Alexandrines were housed in aviaries 4.8 m (16 ft) long and they nested in the covered part. while the young were being reared, the parents were offered bread and milk and biscuits in addition to the usual seeds, peanuts and greenfood. Liberal supplies of fruit were available at all times.

The incubation period is 28 days and young birds spend about seven weeks in the nest. On fledging they resemble the female, except for the short tail which measures about 10 cm (4 in). Adult plumage is assumed at about two years or a little more.

Another prolific pair is in the collection of Mrs J. Blunden (1978) of Suffolk. The female lays two or three eggs in each clutch, at the end of January or the beginning of February, according to the weather. The chicks have grey down and their eyes open when they are about three weeks old. Their nestbox is placed in the shelter and the base is filled with sawdust.

W. Shore-Bailey (1918) commented on the hardiness of this species. The female of his pair dug a hole in the ground and nested inside – and then snow fell. No young were reared on that occasion but the pair later reared four, one of which became a good talker.

Among the earliest breeding successes in Europe are those by C. Christensen of Copenhagen, Denmark, in 1884 and by unknown breeders in England in 1899 and France in 1904.

Alexandrines are very easy to feed. My own bird had no interest in any seed other than sunflower until he discovered the attractive flavour of pine nuts when I offered him one by hand. Then he ate them ravenously. Other items enjoyed are fruit, especially apple and grapes, celery, carrot, toast crusts and the berries of elder and hawthorn. They can also be offered canary seed, hemp, peanuts and millet sprays.

The Alexandrine has hybridised with the Ringneck Parrakeet, as described, also with the Derbyan Parrakeet. The latter cross occurred in the collection of W. J. Sheffler of Arizona in 1951. The Alexandrine was the male parent and three young were reared.

Derbyan Parrakeet
P. derbyana

Description: This is one of the most magnificent of all parrakeets. It is readily distinguished by the entirely mauve under parts (not, however, the deep, almost violet shade as portrayed in *Parrots of the World*, but more lilac). There is a very wide black moustache mark and another black band from the cere to the eye. A large yellowish olive patch decorates the wing.

Derbyan Parrakeet (*Psittacula derbyana*) – male.

The central tail feathers are blue. The head is lilac, except the forepart of the crown and the cheeks, which are bright blue. The upper mandible is red, with the tip yellowish; the lower mandible is black. The iris is yellowish white. Length: 50 cm (20 in). Weight: 320 g (11¼ oz).

The female is readily distinguished by the bill which is entirely black.

Immature birds are dull green with the bill red. Rudkin (1953) recorded that after about three weeks out of the nest, the bill turns black. At the first moult, the bill of a young male becomes red again. K. A. Norris (1954) observed that this colour change was completed at 15 to 18 months and that there is a gradual colour change of the plumage which commences earlier than the beak change. He could determine sex of immature birds less than 12 months old. He noted that:

> In the adult female there is a very distinct pale pink ring around the neck forming a border to the grey hood. This ring is absent in the male at any age, but begins to develop on the young hens with the partial moult, which occurs not long after the birds leave the nest, and is followed by the appearance of a pink suffusion on the upper breast feathers.

Young males of approximately the same age or older have the black moustache and forehead stripe contrasting with the bluish grey of the head markings.

Range/Habitat: The Derbyan Parrakeet is found in western China in north-western Yunnan and the mountains of western Szechwan, Tibet and north-eastern Assam.

It inhabits coniferous mountain forests and feeds on the seeds of pine, fruits, berries and cultivated crops. One ornithologist reported that it normally breeds in mid-June.

Aviculture: This species has been exported on few occasions and in small numbers; however, it is better known than some exported in large numbers – no doubt because it is so handsome and noisy that it commands attention. Unusually, the type specimen, a female, was a captive bird; it lived in the collection of the Earl of Derby in 1850. In June 1899, the Hon. Walter Rothschild received two females, which he deposited at London Zoo. At this time a pair was at Berlin Zoo.

In Britain, the first breeder was Alfred Ezra. He obtained six of eight birds imported in 1929 and bred from one pair in 1933. The Duke of Bedford reared this species in 1936, 1937 and 1938. He described the display of the male (1931b):

> The cock begins by drawing himself up and turning his head sharply to right or left, tilting one eye slightly towards the heavens. Then he makes as though he were about to rub his beak on the perch and repeats both actions, frequently turning round as he does so. As he works himself up to a greater pitch of excitement he begins to squirm about in an extraordinary fashion, standing first on one leg and then the other, and clawing at the back of his neck with his disengaged foot.

In the USA, the first breeder was Dr Leon Patrick of California in 1930; this was probably the first captive breeding. The pair produced two more young in 1931 and, in 1932, a male bred in 1930 produced three young. A number of other aviculturists were successful in the 1940s in the USA, including F. H. Rudkin, Mrs Vance Wright, I. D. Putnam and Dr Wood. It is doubtful whether there are as many successful breeders there at the time of writing. In Germany, the first breeder was Mez of Marbach in 1963. In South Africa, J. M. Horn of Upington reared two in 1973.

J. N. Birch's pair were housed in a 5.4 m (18 ft) outdoor flight. In display, the male threw back his head almost as far as his rump. The final part of the display seemed to take place in slow motion, the male moving from side to side and dipping the body almost to a vertical position from the perch, with his tail pointing towards the sky. In 1980, the nest-box was placed in position in April and was entered immediately by the female. Three eggs were laid between May 13 and 18. Two chicks hatched; the first was heard on June 7. They left the nest on July 24 and 29. By August 11, their beaks had become black. The male did not enter the nest during the rearing period (Birch, 1980).

The incubation period is about 26 days. Newly hatched chicks have some white down. The second down is grey and dense, giving a woolly appearance.

The young spend seven weeks in the nest.

Mr Horn's young were reared on germinated sunflower seed, carrot, paw-paw, green maize cobs and ground nuts. Because of their destructive habits, the aviary was clad on the inside with 5 cm (2 in) chain link and, to exclude vermin, with 13 mm ($\frac{1}{2}$ in) wire netting on the outside.

In Britain, Claude Payne bred this species in 1955; while rearing young they ate large quantities of hemp, also bread and milk, lettuce, spinach, groundsel, apple and parrakeet mixture.

It is regrettable that few Derbyan Parrakeets are being bred in Europe at the time of writing. A consistent British breeder is Jim Hayward of Oxfordshire. A pair which reared young for Bob Clark (1982), fed them on strawberries and blackcurrants, also various other fruits, seed and green-food. The sexes of the young could be identified when they were 15 months old. In 1980, three eggs had been laid. In 1981, there were three but only one chick hatched.

This species has been bred consistently at Chester Zoo. Other successful zoos in recent years include Harewood Bird Garden in Yorkshire, Penscynor Wildlife Park in Wales, Tropical Bird Gardens, Rode, Somerset, also West Berlin (Germany) and Peking (China).

14
Crimson-winged and King Parrakeets

The birds which comprise this group are extremely showy and handsome with long, broad tails. They are in the region of 38 cm (15 in) in length. Kings have lustrous red, blue and green plumage and are boldly marked. Crimson-winged Parrakeets are a lighter shade of green with red only on the wing.

Feeding: These birds require a varied diet of the usual seeds with peanuts, pine nuts, spray millet, fruits and greenfoods. The greenfood should be increased when they are rearing young, and bread and milk and corn-on-the-cob should then be added to their diet. Other items taken by these parrakeets include Canary-rearing food, or a home-made eggfood consisting of hard-boiled egg and ground oats.

Accommodation: Kings and Crimson-wings need a flight which is at least 4.5 m (15 ft) long if their beauty is to be appreciated to the full. Also, they tend to be lethargic in a small enclosure. They bathe in rain, not in standing water.

Breeding: The Kings and Crimson-wings are closely related and hybrids between the two have been bred; they have also hybridised with *Polytelis* species. With the exception of the Shining Parrots, which have on rare occasions reared young in captivity, no other parrots are related closely enough for hybrids to occur.

The aviculturist can experience problems with these species, for male and female may quarrel fiercely or even fatally. Vane (1961) wrote of the 12th Duke of Bedford:

> He drew an interesting analogy between the two genera *Aprosmictus*, Crimson-wings, and *Alisterus*, Kings, emphasising that each included one species of mainland location in which the sexes were dimorphic yet tolerably well disposed towards each other; as opposed to which, each genus contained a species in which the sexes were alike and extremely bad tempered, both being of insular location. This is supported by the following avicultural observations: 'Between the species of *Alisterus* in which the sexes are alike and those in which they differ in appearance there are fairly marked points of resemblance and also fairly marked points of distinction. In voice the former group are definite Kings, but in temperament both sexes are fierce birds, addicted to murder,

which the Australian King is not (Bedford, 1950).

This, however, may not be everyone's experience. Miss M. Diekmann in 1958 aimed to overcome the problem of incompatibility in Australian Kings by housing an immature male with two young females, thus allowing him to choose his future mate. A more immediate remedy is to cut the flight feathers of one wing of the male, slowing it down sufficiently to allow its mate to escape.

Crimson-winged Parrakeets
Aprosmictus

The two species recognised, one from Australia and New Guinea (which is sexually dimorphic) and the other from Indonesia (monomorphic) are very close in appearance, behaviour and voice.

Crimson-winged Parrakeet (Red-winged or Blood-winged)
A. erythropterus erythropterus
Description: The male is the only parrakeet which has the mantle shining black. Head and neck are brilliant apple green, tinged with blue, and the under parts are a paler green. The upper surface of the tail, which is square, is dark green, narrowly tipped with yellow; the tail is dark grey below. There is a crimson patch on the wing from the shoulder to the secondary coverts. The lower back is blue, the bill is coral-red and the iris is orange-red. Length: 32 cm ($12\frac{1}{2}$ in). Weight: 130–145 g ($4\frac{3}{5}$–$5\frac{1}{10}$ oz).

The female is less brightly coloured, being dull green with only a small strip of red on the lower edge of the wing. The black mantle is absent. Under side of the tail is paler and the lateral feathers are margined with pale pink on the inner web. The iris is pale brown. Weight: 115–150 g (4–$5\frac{3}{10}$ oz).

Immature birds resemble the female. On fledging the bill is yellowish and the iris is brown. In its second

Australian Crimson-winged Parrakeets (*Aprosmictus erythropterus erythropterus*) – male right, female left.

or small flocks; large groups are rare. The nesting site is a hollow limb of a tree; often the entrance is at a great height but the nest is near the base.

A. e. coccineopterus
Description: The hind crown and nape are strongly tinged with blue and the plumage is paler throughout. Weight: M 120–146 g ($4\frac{1}{4}$–$5\frac{1}{10}$ oz); F 149 g ($5\frac{1}{4}$ oz).
Range/Habitat: This race inhabits northern Australia, including the Cape York Peninsula and some offshore islands.

A. e. papua
Description: It is not easily distinguished from *coccineopterus* but it does have the feathers of the mantle tipped with green.
Range/Habitat: This race inhabits southern New Guinea.

Aviculture: The Crimson-wing was exhibited at London Zoo in 1861. The first recorded breeding in Europe took place in France in 1881 by Delaurier. The female nested on the ground and reared one youngster. In the Netherlands, F. Blaauw was successful in 1887. The first breeding in Britain is unknown but was probably Mrs Morshead's in 1901. The 12th Duke of Bedford bred this species consistently for over 30 years, except during World War II. In the USA, the first breeder was probably I. D. Putnam, in the 1930s.

When Crimson-wings were first bred in captivity, they more often than not nested on the ground, perhaps because the nest-box was unsuitable. This species seems to prefer a nest with a long climb-down, almost to ground-level.

The Duke of Bedford (1928b) wrote on the subject of Crimson-wing behaviour with his customary charm and keen observation:

Individual cocks vary enormously in disposition: some are scandalously promiscuous in their amours; others are at least faithful: the worst are incorrigible hooligans, but even the best can hardly be termed polite. You can never tell what will happen when you introduce a healthy cock to a female. Sometimes he will pursue her furiously about the aviary with open beak and torrents of

plumage, the male has some black on the mantle; this has led some aviculturists to pluck the mantle feathers from young birds in the hope of discovering their sex when the feathers are replaced; however, this ruse is not always successful. Some young females are slightly larger than immature males. Adult plumage is usually attained in the third year or at the second complete moult.
Range/Habitat: The nominate race inhabits northern, north-eastern and

eastern Australia, as far south as the New South Wales border and the north-eastern corner of South Australia. It is common except on the periphery of its range. Its food is obtained from flowering and seeding trees and consists of seeds, nuts, insects, nectar and berries. It rarely descends to the ground. Open eucalypt forest, arid acacia scrub and casuarina groves are among its varied habitats; along the north coast it is also found in mangroves. It occurs in family parties

Billingsgate [strong language, as might come from the London fishmarket of that name]. In more hopeful cases he will mingle the pursuit and the abuse with a certain amount of display, and if really in love with the lady he will do more showing off than cursing, though he will never entirely forego the latter exhibition of masculine talent.

Crimson-wings will start to breed when two or three years old. The display is not very marked: the male shivers his wings, draws his plumage tightly and slightly depresses the shoulders to reveal the blue rump. He also flies to and fro, chortling. Courtship feeding occurs rarely and is accompanied by head-swirling. The female solicits to be fed with a whining noise.

The clutch often numbers four eggs, but varies from three to six; many pairs are double-brooded. The incubation period is about 21 days. On hatching, chicks have thick white down which is replaced by a second grey down at about ten days. When the young are about two weeks old, the female usually starts to leave the nest for longer periods and the male will enter the nest and increase his share of the feeding duties. Females usually brood the young every night until they fledge at the age of six weeks.

J. T. Walton (1969) owned a pair which reared 26 young in nine seasons before dying when aged 21 or 22 years. Since the early 1980s, the species' popularity has increased. Many pairs are proving more prolific than was generally the case with the Crimson-wing in the past.

It has hybridised with all three *Polytelis*, with the Australian King Parrakeet and the Sula Island King.

Timor Crimson-winged Parrakeet
A. jonquillaceus jonquillaceus
Description: The male is readily distinguished from the Australian form by the dark green feathers of the mantle which are edged with blue; also, the wing coverts are yellow and the area of red smaller. The green is of a more yellow shade. The female lacks the yellow in the wings and the blue edges to the feathers of the mantle.

Immature birds resemble the female except for the brown iris.

Timor Crimson-winged Parrakeet (*Aprosmictus jonquillaceus jonquillaceus*) – male.

Range/Habitat: Timor, Lesser Sunda Islands, Indonesia.
Aviculture: The Timor race was most uncommon in aviculture until the early 1970s, when it was quite often imported into Europe. The first breeder in Britain was probably Peter Paris of St Buryan, Cornwall, in 1975. Two young were reared, although both parents died due to strongyloid worms in the intestines despite the fact that they were regularly wormed. The high mortality rate in newly imported birds was due to tapeworm infestation. Dr Burkard found that 18 of his 21 imported birds had tapeworms. He cured them with Panacur (Hoechst).

Also in Germany, this species has been reared at Vogelpark Walsrode, since 1977. Breeding successes have been too few to establish the Timor Crimson-wing in aviculture, except in Germany and Switzerland. Dr Burkard has bred them to the third generation and has found that, unlike *A. scapularis*, they prefer a small nest-box.

Wetar Crimson-winged Parrakeet
A. j. wetterensis
Description: This race has the green wing coverts only slightly suffused with yellow and less red in the wing.

It is slightly smaller. The female lacks the yellow on the wing coverts.
Range/Habitat: Wetar Island, Indonesia.

King Parrakeets
Alisterus

King Parrakeets are easily recognised by their intensely coloured and lustrous red, green and blue plumage and by their long, broad tails. They do not breed in large numbers and have always been expensive to purchase.

Amboina King Parrakeet
A. amboinensis amboinensis
Description: Head and under parts are red, of a darker shade than the Australian King; the wings green; the back, rump and underside of the wings deep blue, and the mantle glossy violet-blue. The long, broad tail is blue above, greyish black below, the outermost feathers being edged with dull pink. The upper mandible is coral-red tipped with black and the lower mandible is black. The iris is orange. Length: about 36 cm (14 in). Weight: 150 g ($5\frac{3}{10}$ oz).

Amboina King Parrakeet (*Alisterus amboinensis amboinensis*).

Blue-winged King Parrakeet (*Alisterus amboinensis hypophonius*).

Buru King Parrakeet (*Alisterus amboinensis buruensis*).

Dr Burkard has found that: 'In all races with a red beak, the sexes can be determined by the beak. The black on the lower mandible of the female extends upwards; in the male the lower mandible is red' (pers. comm., 1985).

Burgess (1976) who had kept three pairs saw that the male had a 'long, flat head with greater distance between the eye and cere, while the hen is completely different with a small round head'.

Immature birds have the mantle green, although not all hatched in captivity show this feature. The bill is orange-yellow, then becomes brownish black. The iris is brown and the periorbital skin is white, not dark as in the adult.

Range/Habitat: The nominate race inhabits the islands of Amboina and Ceram in the southern Moluccas, Indonesia. It is found in lowland and mid-mountain forest and is observed singly or in pairs. The diet consists of fruits, seeds, berries and buds. Several races from other Indonesian islands are recognised.

A. a. sulaensis
Description: This race has a variable green band across the mantle and lacks the pink edging to the tail feathers.
Range/Habitat: The Sula Islands, Indonesia.

A. a. versicolor
Description: This race differs from *sulaensis* in its entirely blue mantle and smaller size.
Range/Habitat: Peleng Island, Indonesia.

Buru King Parrakeet
A. a. buruensis
Description: Differs from the nominate race in having a variable green band across the mantle. The outermost tail feathers are broadly edged with pink on the under side of the inner webs. The bill is entirely grey black. The periorbital skin is black.
Range/Habitat: Buru Island, Indonesia.

Blue-winged King Parrakeet
A. a. hypophonius
Description: The wings are deep blue and there is no pink on the tail feathers.
Range/Habitat: Halmahera, north-ern Moluccas, Indonesia.
Aviculture: This subspecies has proved extremely difficult to establish. Of two consignments which reached Europe in the late 1970s, most died within a short time. Dr Burkard found that his continually fell sick at intervals of three to four months.

Laboratory work resulted in the discovery of a causative organism, specific to the species, which was resistant to the usual antibiotics. Three birds were saved by treating them with a certain sulfonamide. One female laid three fertile eggs but was killed in the nest by the male. The last surviving male was placed with an Amboina King but the pairing was not successful. The male proved very aggressive (Burkard, pers. comm., 1985).

Salawati King Parrakeet
A. a. dorsalis
Description: This race differs from the nominate in its darker shade of red, and in lacking pink on the tail.
Range/Habitat: Western Papuan island, north-western New Guinea and the Weyland mountains and West Irian.

Aviculture: This species was rare and little known in aviculture until the early 1970s, since when the nominate race has been imported quite often and become fairly well known. The other races have been available in the past on rare occasions only. Probably the most distinctive is *hypophonius* with its wings of uniform deep blue. This beautiful bird is exhibited at Vogelpark Walsrode, Germany, at the time of writing.

In Britain, the first breeding was that of the Salawati King (*dorsalis*), which occurred in the 12th Duke of Bedford's collection; two chicks had hatched by June 20, 1940 and left the nest on July 24 and 25. Food supplied was wheat, oats, maize, sunflower, hemp, white millet and canary seed, greenfood, apple and tree branches. The female nested in a hollow log in the open flight.

During 1972, probably 100 or more *amboinensis* (of two races) were imported into Britain, most of which were young birds. In 1976, at least six breeders were successful in Britain and, in 1975, C. J. Hewson had reared two young in South Africa. The first clutch contained three infertile eggs. In 1975, several British aviculturists had eggs from their pairs, including William Carey (1977). Two hatched in June after an incubation period of 21 days; the chicks survived only one week. In January 1976, the birds fought, resulting in the male losing the toes on one foot. On three occasions it was attempted to reunite the pair – but each time the female would not tolerate his presence. They were finally placed together in June when the female had been seen inviting copulation; two weeks later she had laid a single egg. The resulting chick was removed for hand-rearing when 13 days old as it appeared not to be receiving adequate food.

Another pair which bred in 1976, that of T. H. Alston of Swindon, used a box measuring 30 cm (12 in) square × 1.8 m (6 ft) high; it was facing north. One of the three eggs hatched and the young bird left the nest after about nine weeks. Both parents fed it, on sunflower, hemp, pine nuts and soaked millet sprays. Three apples daily and large quantities of greenfood were eaten.

Another early breeder in Britain was S. Burgess. In 1976, the first clutch was deserted. A newly hatched chick from the third clutch, in April, was found dead and injured. The remaining egg, containing a live chick, was placed under a pair of Mealy Rosellas who had hatched a chick that day. Two days later, the male Amboina attacked the female (presumably wanting to nest again) who was removed for 48 hours, then returned. As it grew, the young Amboina stood in the nest while the Mealy Rosella remained in the crouched position. When 14 days old, both chicks were removed and hand-fed on baby cereal and honey, strained apple baby food being added after a few days. The Amboina's eyes opened when it was about 17 days old. Red-tipped tail feathers were then growing. The diet was varied to include carrot, soaked, crushed sunflower seed and spinach. When fully feathered, the red tips to the tail were noted. The young bird's parents nested for a fourth time.

The female of the pair of Amboina King Parrakeets owned by J. Hayward (1978) of Carterton Breeding Aviaries showed no interest in a hanging nest-box, apart from gnawing around the entrance. A ground nest was therefore provided – a box measuring 25 cm (10 in) square and 90 cm (3 ft) high. The bottom was covered with rotten crumbled wood mixed with sand. The female showed her approval by entering the box soon after its provision and laying the first of three eggs on May 15, 1977.

Incubation commenced when the second egg was laid and two chicks hatched on June 7, a third on June 9. On hatching, they were covered with fluffy white down. When seven weeks old the first chick left the nest. The young were at first put back in the nest at night, but later roosted with their father. The female brooded them until they left the nest. Their colouration was as vivid as the adults' but the blue mantle was less extensive and less brilliant. By October, their eyes were almost orange, the periorbital skin was dark and their bills were becoming dark. The second clutch of two eggs hatched six weeks after the first young left the nest and the latter were then removed. Jim Hayward is one of the very few breeders to have consistent

success with this species. He has reared to the third generation.

In Germany, the Amboina King has been bred at Tropicana, Neuweid, on several occasions since 1974. In Czechoslovakia, young were reared at Drur Kralove Zoo in 1978.

The experiences of the above breeders show that the usual clutch is three eggs, the incubation period is 21 days and young remain in the nest for seven to eight weeks.

In Denmark, *dorsalis* has reared young in the collection of Palle Blønd of Fredericia, Jutland, since seven adults were obtained in 1979.

King (or Australian King) Parrakeet
A. scapularis scapularis

Description: This species is sexually dimorphic. The male has head, neck and under parts scarlet, a narrow line of blue feathers on the hind neck and wings, and mantle dark green with a narrow line of pale green formed by the inner upper wing coverts. The rump is dark blue, shading into black; the long tail is blue-black, above and below, and the under tail coverts are scarlet, with black centres to the feathers. The bill is scarlet, paler at the tip. The iris is yellow. Length: 43 cm (17 in). Weight: M 209–227 g ($7\frac{2}{5}$–8 oz); F 220–275 g ($7\frac{3}{4}$–$9\frac{3}{4}$ oz).

The sexes can be distinguished at a glance; in the female the head, nape, wings, mantle and upper surface of the tail are dark green. The rump is blue, merging into the green of the upper side of the tail. Throat and upper breast are dull green tinged with red and the abdomen is scarlet. The pale green wing stripe is usually absent, but occasionally developed and to varying extents. The under tail coverts are green, attractively margined with scarlet. The bill is black.

Immature birds resemble the female but soon after leaving the nest the female's bill darkens, whereas the bill of the male is yellowish at this stage. Young females have less red on the abdomen. Lendon (Cayley & Lendon, 1973) states, 'Adult plumage is acquired by a slow moult, which starts when the bird is something over fifteen months of age and is not completed for a further twelve months or so'.

Australian King Parrakeet (*Alisterus scapularis*) – male.

Australian King Parrakeet (*Alisterus scapularis*) – female.

Females tend to be more slender with smaller heads.

In 1971, a Yellow (not Lutino) mutation occurred in Germany, apparently simultaneously in two collections, and, in 1975 in Denmark, two more Yellows appeared. This mutation is reported as being extremely beautiful.

An unusually coloured wild-caught bird had the wings yellowish lime green with no other alteration to its colouration.

Range/Habitat: This species inhabits the coastal and adjoining mountain areas of eastern Australia from northern Queensland to southern Victoria. Common throughout most of its range, it has disappeared from areas where eucalyptus trees have been cut down. Tropical rain forest, dense scrub and eucalyptus woodland to an altitude of about 1,600 m (5,300 ft) are the preferred habitats. Immature birds tend to be nomadic, while adults are sedentary. Diet includes seeds, especially those of eucalypts and acacias, fruits, berries, nuts and nectar. Kings will also raid orchards and maize crops and feed on spilled grain.

A. s. minor
This is the only recognised race, and is said to be smaller. It is found in north-eastern Queensland.

Aviculture: The Australian King Parrakeet was exhibited at London Zoo in 1859. It was bred in Europe as early as 1880 in Weissenfels in Germany by A.

Köhler and in the same year in France by Rousse. In the USA, I. D. Putnam of San Diego reared 11 young between 1928 and 1939. In Britain, the first consistent breeder was the Duke of Bedford, who reared young for many years from 1924.

In display, the male erects his head feathers, draws his body plumage tight, displays the green wing bar and, according to the Duke of Bedford (1928b):

> ... shakes his head, gives his wings a quick, shivering flip, makes a nibbling motion with his beak and after uttering his 'Crashek! crashek! ' call loudly goes off into a singular kind of song in a minor key interspersed by sounds not unlike a hen announcing the arrival of her egg. This is accompanied by blazing the eyes and scratching the head.

Four or five eggs are laid and incubated by the female for 21 days. Newly-hatched chicks weigh about 9.5 to 10 g ($\frac{3}{10} - \frac{2}{5}$ oz). Young leave the nest at about eight weeks.

This species is bred in small numbers in Britain and with more success in Europe.

The Australian King has hybridised with the Barraband's, Crimson-winged and Green-winged King Parrakeets.

The King × Crimson-winged Parrakeet is a hybrid of special interest, as unlike many hybrids, it could pass as a good species. Indeed, the nineteenth-century ornithologist, John Gould, believed it was a true species, perhaps from New Guinea, and named it *insig-*

nissimus (most distinguished), the Beautiful King Parrot. His painting of it can be compared with photographs of two aviary-bred hybrids. The three birds are identical. This hybrid has the side of the face, including the ear coverts, and a line on the nape green; the rest of the head is red, as are the under parts. There is a large yellow patch on the wing, some of the feathers being margined with red. Lower back and rump are blue; the rest of the plumage is green. The iris is yellow and the legs are grey. (Photographs of different hybrids of this cross appeared in *Singapore Aviculture*, Vol. 2, No. 2, and in the *Magazine of the Parrot Society*, August 1983).

In Australia, young have been bred from King × Crimson-wing hybrids.

Green-winged King Parrakeet

A. chloropterus chloropterus
Description: This species is also sexually dimorphic. The male has the head, neck and breast rich crimson. There is a patch of brilliant dark blue on the upper part of the mantle which merges into a small patch of blue on the nape. The mantle is greenish black. There is a pale yellowish green band across the wing coverts, the wings being otherwise greenish black. Back, rump and upper tail coverts are mauve-blue, and the under tail coverts are scarlet with dark blue bases. The tail is blue-tinged black above, grey-black below. The

upper mandible is orange tipped with grey-black and the lower mandible is grey-black. Length: 26 cm (14 in).

The female is mainly dull green with the throat and breast olive green with brownish red tips to the feathers. Her tail is tipped with black and suffused with blue. The upper mandible is brownish, rather than orange. The female may be distinguished from the female Australian King by the deeper blue rump and the darker reddish wash on the under parts. Under tail coverts are blue at the base, edged with red whereas those of the Australian King are green at the base.

Dr Burkard has observed that the plumage of his six pairs varies considerably in individuals, especially the extent of the blue on the neck and the yellowish green on the wings.

Immature birds resemble the female but lack the brownish red on the throat and breast feathers. The bill is brownish black with the tip paler. The iris is brown.

Range/Habitat: The nominate race inhabits eastern New Guinea.

A. c. callopterus
Description: The male can be distinguished by the narrow blue band across the upper mantle which does not extend to the nape. Weight: M 167–173 g ($5\frac{9}{10}$–$6\frac{1}{10}$ oz); F 155–170 g ($5\frac{1}{2}$–6 oz).
Range/Habitat: Central New Guinea.

A. c. moszkowskii
Description: The male is almost

Green-winged King Parrakeet (*Alisterus chloropterus chloropterus*) – male.

similar to *callopterus* yet the female is like the male: they have the blue band across the mantle absent or only faintly indicated according to Forshaw. Billet (1983) states that this is incorrect and that males are blue on the back like Amboina King Parrakeets.

Immature birds have the yellowish green band on the wing coverts narrower and duller. The breast is marked with green. Lower mandible and the top of the upper mandible are horn-coloured.
Range/Habitat: Northern New Guinea.

Aviculture: This species has always been rare and expensive in captivity. It was first exhibited at London Zoo in

1909 and is now virtually unknown in Britain. It is better known in Europe.

In Britain, the first breeder was Alfred Ezra in 1945. The pair had occupied their aviary for nine years before rearing a single youngster and then on nothing but oats and buckwheat. Single chicks were subsequently reared in 1951, 1953 and 1955 and two in 1954. On the death of Alfred Ezra, they went to Ireland, to the collection of Sir Crawford McCullagh. Some of them, or their offspring, were obtained by Alfredo Marques of Bedfordshire who reared young from them. More recently, in Switzerland, this species has been bred in several collections, including that of Dr Burkard.

In 1949, one Green-winged King was bred at London Zoo. E. N. T. Vane reared hybrids between the Green-wing and the Australian King and he retained one which was almost indistinguishable in appearance from the Green-wing.

The race *moszkowskii* has been bred on several occasions in the Netherlands by C. F. M. Billet. His pair was double-brooded; the clutch consisted of two or three eggs.

In Denmark, it was bred by Palle Blønd of Fredericia, Jutland. He obtained seven birds in 1979 and had reared seven by 1983. The male attacked and killed one of the youngsters after it had left the nest; thereafter female and young were removed to a neighbouring aviary after the young had left the nest. Rose hips and rowan berries (kept in a freezer) were fed throughout the year.

15

Eclectus and Tanygnathus Parrots

The two genera which are the subject of this chapter are very closely related and alike in temperament, although while the Eclectus are admired for their beauty and their willingness to breed in captivity, the less spectacular *Tanygnathus* parrots have few admirers. The smaller members of the latter genus are closely related to *Psittacula* parrakeets and bear a marked resemblance to the Ringneck Parrakeet, except that they lack long tails.

Eclectus
Eclectus roratus

Description: In Eclectus Parrots, sexual dimorphism is more marked and more striking than in any other parrot: the male is shining emerald green and the female is scarlet and maroon, in most cases with a large area of violet or blue on the under parts. The contrast between male and female is one of exceptional beauty.

The quality of plumage, too, is unlike that of other parrots, with a tight interlocking of the hair-like feathers producing a fur-like appearance.

Eight to ten races are recognised, the males of which are difficult or impossible to distinguish. All are mainly green with the under wing coverts and the sides of the body red. The bend of the wing is bright blue and the outer webs of the primaries are dark blue;

the outer tail feathers are suffused with blue. The under side of the tail is grey-black, tipped with yellow. The upper mandible is orange, tipped with paler yellow but is entirely yellow in some captive birds. The iris is orange.

Males of the various races differ in their size, in the shade of green and in the amount of yellow and blue in the tail. Without knowing a male's origin, it is impossible to ascertain its race. Length: 35–38 cm (13–14 in). Weight: 440–590 g ($15\frac{1}{2}$–$20\frac{4}{5}$ oz); F 465–615 g ($16\frac{2}{5}$–$21\frac{3}{5}$ oz).

The females vary considerably and can be divided into two groups. The first comprises those with a narrow ring of blue feathers surrounding the eye: the Red-sided Eclectus (*E. roratus polychloros*) from New Guinea and the western Papuan Islands; the larger *E. r. macgillivrayi* from the Cape York Peninsula of Australia, and the smaller Solomon Island Eclectus (*E. r. solomonensis*).

The second group comprises those which lack the feathered blue ring around the eye and have yellow or partly yellow undertail coverts. I find birds of this group more beautiful for, with the yellow on the tail, their red plumage is even more startling. The race *vosmaeri* is especially pleasing with its broad band of yellow at the tip of the tail, yellow under tail coverts and mauve lower breast, abdomen and upper mantle. The upper parts are dark red with the primaries and the bend of the wing dark mauvish blue.

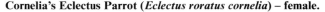

Cornelia's Eclectus Parrot (*Eclectus roratus cornelia*) – female.

Red-sided Eclectus (*Eclectus roratus polychloros*) – female left, male right.

It may be several years before adult eye colour is attained. The beak colour changes gradually and, in the male, is usually pale orange before the bird is a year old, with the exception of a small dark area at the base of the upper mandible. The bill does not become deep orange until about three years of age. Immature females have a yellowish tip to the black bill.

There are at least three examples of abnormal colouration in Eclectus Parrots. A Lutino specimen was obtained by the late Sir Edward Hallstrom. In 1954, the same aviculturist bred a female with the head orange and red and the wings mottled with yellow. The third example is, to the best of my knowledge, unique among sexually dimorphic parrots. In 1976, R. Sperber in Australia bred a female Eclectus which showed the colouration of male and female, the dividing line being very neat: one wing was red and one wing green with the corresponding body plumage red and purple, and green. The head was mainly red and the beak black.

These birds have a very interesting range of calls, quite unlike those of most parrots. The sound most often made by the male when in breeding condition is a deep 'konk konk konk'; at the same time his beak is rapped against hers. Courting females make an extremely attractive almost metallic sound.

Eclectus Parrots will learn to repeat a few words or may even acquire quite an extensive vocabulary.

Although they can be noisy under certain circumstances, such as when a pair is separated or there is a cat near the aviary, they do not have prolonged and regular periods of screaming, as do Amazon Parrots, for example. Their voices are loud and harsh but are not used frequently. However, if a number of Eclectus are kept on the same premises, they are likely to call to each other and their voices will be heard much more often than if a single pair is kept.

Range/Habitat: Eclectus Parrots inhabit New Guinea, the islands of Indonesia and the Solomons, and the eastern side of the Cape York Peninsula of Australia. On some Indonesian islands, they may have declined due to habitat destruction.

The head is bright red. Under side of the tail is dusky orange. The bill is black and the iris is yellow. *E. r. vosmaeri* comes from the islands of the Moluccas and is one of the most frequently imported races.

Although the females of each race do vary it is impossible to discover whether a male is of the same race unless it is known that the birds were collected in the same locality or bred from such birds. In selecting prospective mates, all the aviculturist can do is to match the male and female for size as nearly as possible.

The most distinctive females are of the races *riedeli* and *cornelia*. Both are mainly red, brownish red on wings and mantle, with the primaries and secondaries dark blue and under tail coverts yellow. Both have the tail tipped with yellow, more broadly in *cornelia*, which is smaller than *riedeli*. Mid-way in size is the Grand Eclectus (*E. r. roratus*), which has red and yellow under tail coverts, dull purple on the abdomen and mantle and the tail narrowly tipped with yellow.

Immature birds can be sexed as soon as the feathers on the mantle appear, usually when aged between three-and-a-half and four weeks. The plumage is duller than that of the adult. The bill is brown and the iris dark grey. In females, the red feathers on the wings may be partly green and a male I bred emerged from the nest with some brownish red feathers in the wings. I have heard of more extreme variation in immature plumage, such as a female which was more orange than red in shade, with bronze tail feathers.

Aviculture: Eclectus Parrots have been bred in a number of countries throughout the world during the 1970s. Since the 1980s, importation of this species has virtually ceased and those available are aviary-bred.

The first captive breeding in Europe was probably that which occurred by Frenzel in Freiberg, Germany, in 1881. In Britain, the first breeder was Miss R. Drummond in Scotland, in 1912. In the USA, Mrs Bonestell of San Francisco reared two in 1937 and, in the same year, Dr Osman Hill was successful in Ceylon. In Australia, Sir Edward Hallstrom bred Eclectus in 1948. In 1970, Eclectus were bred in Denmark by P. Nielsen (one) and in Sweden by E. Ekman of Malmö (two). Zoos which have had consistent success include Basle in Switzerland, Chester, East Berlin and San Diego. Eclectus have been reared in zoos in many countries from New Guinea (at Mount Hagen) and Indonesia (Djakarta) to Mexico (Chapultepec). The race *solomonensis* is bred by Dr R. Burkard in Switzerland.

Feeding: There is one point of which the prospective owner of Eclectus Parrots must be aware: their great need for Vitamin A. The most important item of their diet is fresh vegetables; carrot is particularly good for its high Vitamin A content, and corn-on-the-cob, celery, peas in the pod or cooked peas, spinach beet, lettuce and tomato should be offered as often as possible. The diet should consist of at least 30 per cent vegetables. The usual wild greenfood, such as chickweed, seeding grasses, sowthistle and young dandelion leaves and roots will also be eaten.

These birds cannot remain in good health on an all-seed diet and they are seldom as fond of sunflower seed as other large parrots: many show a preference for white millet or canary seed. They will also eat pine nuts and peanuts and they relish spray millet.

Most Eclectus Parrots prefer vegetables to fruit, with the exception of grapes from which the pips are speedily removed, and pomegranates which can be offered as a treat when they are in season. Eclectus also like cherries and will crack the stones to remove the kernels. Apple, pear, orange and other fruits can be offered as well as the berries of hawthorn and elder, various nuts, cracked or shelled, especially walnuts, sweet corn, sweetened rice pudding, toast crusts, cake, cubes of cheese and meat.

(For suitable rearing foods see Pets and Breeding below.)

These birds are susceptible to moniliasis (see p. 60) and failure to provide a varied diet and sufficient Vitamin A will aggravate this. As it is easy to persuade these birds to take the more beneficial items of food, or to add a multivitamin preparation to the diet if necessary, there is no excuse for failing to keep these lovely birds in good health.

Some aviculturists have found Eclectus their *bête noire*, almost certainly because the birds were incorrectly fed. For several years, I have kept a minimum of ten Eclectus and their health has never caused me a moment's concern. However, most of these are of my own breeding: imported birds were a very different proposition.

Pets and Breeding: Generally speaking, male Eclectus make better pets than females because they have a more gentle temperament. However, I do not like to see Eclectus caged. Anyone who has a tame bird would be advised to house it in an aviary for at least part of the day.

An aviculturist who is able to construct really large aviaries could consider keeping and breeding these birds in a colony. They would make a magnificent display and would constitute a great attraction at any zoo. At Taronga Zoo in Sydney, Australia, 14 pairs were kept in a very large enclosure. However, a major problem was that the parents lost contact with the young after they left the nest. The young birds therefore, when they left the nest, had to be hand-fed.

In Switzerland, Dr Burkard bred from six females in an aviary measuring 6 × 3 m (20 × 10 ft) with an outdoor enclosure of the same size. The dominant male mated with all the females. The bird proved compatible as long as the males submitted to the dominant male. The problem was that, after two to three weeks, the females ceased to feed the young (when the male would normally assist or take over) and they had to be removed for hand-rearing.

Another advantage of colony breeding is that birds can choose their mates, for obtaining compatible pairs is a major difficulty. This is partly due to the fact that, except during the short period of courtship, the female is the dominant partner and the male remains in fear of her. Males usually have a much more docile temperament and females can be most aggressive, bad-tempered and even vicious towards their mates; thus it is not surprising that some males take a long time to overcome their fear of the female. If this has not occurred after a pair has been together for two or three years, consideration should be given to obtaining another male or female. In such cases, the female may lay, regardless of the fact that the male cannot even pluck up courage to feed her, let alone mate with her. If this occurs, the female should be allowed to sit for the full period, then the nesting site should be removed for a while because some hens will spend so much time inside that the male does not have a chance to court her.

Because these birds take about three years to become sexually mature, most aviculturists will want to obtain adult birds for breeding purposes. However, the wisest course is to obtain a male and a female bred in the same year from different parents. If they are allowed to grow up together, problems are much less likely to occur; in fact, I have had a year old male feeding a female of similar age and inspecting a nest-box with her.

These birds require a fairly large nest-box approximately 30 cm (12 in) square and 1.2 m (4 ft) high with a peat-filled base.

Eclectus Parrots normally lay two eggs, clutches of one or three being very rare. The incubation period varies between 28 and 30 days. Usually there is an interval of two or three days between each egg but the interval can be as long as six days. When an established breeding pair are re-united after a period of separation, eggs will be laid between two and three weeks later, although the female may spend most of this time in the nest. Newly hatched chicks weigh about 16 g ($\frac{2}{3}$ oz).

In one of my breeding pairs, the male feeds the chicks, possibly from the time they are hatched and certainly

When these two Eclectus chicks were removed from the nest aged about 8 and 10 days, they weighed 20 g and 80 g (¾ oz and 2⅘ oz) respectively. The smaller chick made only small weight gains and, for reasons unknown, died at 20 days.

from the age of three or four days. He is so tame he allows me to watch this. Corn-on-the-cob is the favourite rearing food. Celery, cheese, tomato and carrot are also eaten at this time, plus bread and milk with wheat germ cereal added. Until the young are three weeks old very little seed is taken. No two pairs have the same preferences, of course; rearing foods of other pairs have included boiled rice pudding, boiled potato, apple, chickweed, lettuce, marigold and forget-me-not leaves and flowers, wheat, peanuts, soaked raisins, bananas, peas, seeding grasses and soaked wholemeal bread with a vitamin additive.

I know of several pairs of Eclectus in which the feeding of the young is carried out entirely by the female; the male is not allowed to enter the nest and feeds the female at the entrance.

On hatching, Eclectus chicks have a few wisps of white down; within a couple of weeks they are covered in dense dark grey down. My females do not spend any length of time away from the nest until the young are about two months old and they roost inside with them every night until they leave

the nest when aged about 72 to 80 days. I have not known the young to return to the nest for roosting but one breeder recorded that a young bird slept inside the nesting log for ten nights after leaving the nest.

When they fledge, the female may prove very aggressive towards the young birds, so much so that it may be necessary to remove her until the young are independent. The young birds can then be taken from the aviary and the female returned. However, the female is sometimes so impatient to start on the next round and will be spending so much time inside the nest, that it is preferable to remove the male and young. On one occasion when I did this, I caged the two young males and their father separately. Because of the tameness of the adult male, I could take him on my hand and place him inside the cage containing a young bird for him to feed it occasionally, although both had started to feed on their own. There is much to be said for breeding from birds which are so tame.

On another occasion, after the young were independent and had been

removed from the aviary, the female appeared not to want to nest again, but persecuted the male. When I entered the aviary the male came to me for protection and I carried him out. He was not returned for a few weeks, when the pair started to nest again. A major cause of loss in male Eclectus could be avoided and is unfortunately due to the owner's ignorance of the fact that a female in an aggressive frame of mind will keep the male away from the food; it is for this reason that food must be provided at both ends of the aviary for pairs which are newly introduced or are not entirely compatible.

Eclectus Parrots are continuous nesters; one clutch follows another, regardless of the season. A hen will not even stop breeding to moult, but will shed her feathers while incubating. To prevent winter-breeding and over-breeding, the male should be removed for several weeks. The only disadvantage of doing this, in my experience, is that the female will call very noisily for her mate; on one occasion I had to return the male after a couple of weeks for fear of disturbing my neighbours. However, only rarely have my females hatched chicks during the winter.

Winter-hatched chicks are hand-reared, using an easily prepared food of equal parts of two kinds of Heinz tinned baby foods: pure fruit and bone and beef broth with vegetables. After about ten days, ground sunflower seed is added. The fresh vegetable content accounts for about one third. To one feed daily, a vitamin/mineral powder is added.

A predominance of chicks of one sex is not at all unusual in Eclectus and it is more common for the chicks to be all males. One pair in my possession produced ten males before a female fledged.

In most parrots, the sex of young birds cannot be determined until after the first moult; as young stock is often disposed of before then, perhaps hatching of chicks of one sex, especially males, by one pair is less rare than is thought. In Eclectus the fact is soon apparent; in other birds it is not. A pair of Eclectus at Chester Zoo reared about 30 youngsters before a female was produced!

Male Eclectus chick being hand-fed at 7 weeks old.

The gold-edged black median wing coverts are the most beautiful feature of this parrot. Head and upper tail coverts are a pleasing shade of light green and the back and rump are bright light blue. The tail is tipped with greenish yellow and the under parts are entirely of this colour. The bill is red (smaller in the female) and the iris is yellowish white.

Plumage and bill colour are said to be identical in male and female, but the 12th Duke of Bedford described his female as having less distinctive black and blue markings on the wings and the blue area confined to the rump; also the female had a smaller head and bill and more slender body. Length: 41 cm (16 in). Weight 260 g ($9\frac{1}{5}$ oz).

Immature birds have little or no black on the wing coverts and narrower and paler yellow margins to the feathers.

Range/Habitat: This species inhabits the western Papuan, Tanimbar and Lesser Sunda Islands, the Moluccas and islands in the vicinity of Celebes in Indonesia. It is found on the Philippine island of Balut, possibly having been introduced there. Its main habitat is small islands and coastal areas of larger islands. Locally common, its favourite fruit, at least in Ceram, is the large green fruit of *Sonneratia alta*. In Timor, it was recorded some years ago that hundreds of birds were seen each evening flying to the mountains to roost. Nuts, various fruits and, when available, cultivated crops such as corn, comprise the diet.

Aviculture: This handsome bird was exhibited at London Zoo as long ago as 1856, and Lord Tavistock kept his pair at liberty. It is now rarely available to aviculturists and it would appear that it has yet to be bred in captivity. The Duke of Bedford, when Lord Tavistock, described (1928b) the vocal performance of the female of his pair as not so powerful as the male's but stated that she was his equal in repertoire. He described the male's song as 'startlingly deep and unbird-like' with 'indescribable screams, varied by thin, finch-like pipings'.

Dr Burkard informed me: 'They are quiet, amiable birds which – in contrast to *T. lucionensis* – easily become tame and like to take fruit from the hand'.

Great-billed Parrot (*Tanygnathus megalorhynchos*).

Tanygnathus
Tanygnathus

The largest member of this genus, the Great-billed Parrot, resembles the Eclectus in size and shape; the smaller members bear a resemblance to a female Ringneck Parrakeet except for the tail length and shape. In size, members of this genus range from 41 cm (16 in) to the Blue-naped Parrot which is about 30 cm (12 in) in length.

Tanygnathus parrots are not imported often because there is little demand for them. Comparatively little is known about them in captivity and breeding successes have been few. Their care in confinement should be the same as for the Eclectus.

Great-billed Parrot
T. megalorhynchos

Description: This striking and handsome bird is well named and in fact this feature gives it a slightly top-heavy appearance. Its plumage is mainly green but quite different in colour and quality from that of a male Eclectus. However, if one sees males of both species sitting side by side, the resemblance in other respects is noticeable.

Blue-naped (Philippine Green) Parrot
T. lucionensis

Description: Its bill is proportionately smaller than that of the Great-billed. Its plumage is not dissimilar apart from the fact that the nape is blue and the tail is not tipped with yellow above. The rump is brilliant green and there is black on the bend of the wing. Length: 31 cm (12 in). Weight: 170-200 g (6-7 oz).

According to G. A. Smith (1984): 'Hens have the gold on their coverts muted to dull brass; they have less blue both to the wing and nape, and the black is reduced and duller'.

Immature birds are described by George Smith as follows:

> The bill is muddier and duller red; there is no blue to the nape and only a little to the back; the wing markings are very dull and indistinct. The tail feathers are pointed, not rounded as in the adults, and the eyes are black.

Range/Habitat: This species inhabits the islands of the Philippines, those of northern and eastern Borneo and those north of Celebes, Indonesia.

Aviculture: Lord Tavistock recorded (1927a) that he had recently received a bird of this species:

> . . . which is perhaps new to aviculture, although, strange to say, it figures in Levaillant's quaint old book on Parrots.
>
> Unlike a captive Greatbill which is usually sluggish and morose, the Lucon Parrakeet is active and friendly. He talks in a somewhat husky and indistinct voice, and displays to a human friend in the usual manner of the genus by throwing up the head and elongating the neck. Occasionally he utters a series of short screeches like a *Palaeornis* [*Psittacula*] Parrakeet or Conure, which have no counterpart in the Greatbill's repertoire.

John FitzGibbon of Essex kindly provided me with the following notes:

> I have kept a few specimens only. I found them to be easy to establish, taking quickly to a diet of mixed seeds and grain, peanut kernels, apple, orange, grapes, cherries, carrot and spinach beet. They are very hardy when properly acclimatised, easy to sex (the male being more boldly and brightly marked, especially on the wings) and quiet, using their loud voices very infrequently.

The first breeding success was that of

Blue-naped Parrot (*Tanygnathus lucionensis*).

Mrs Bonestell (1937) of California, who obtained several pairs while in the Philippines in 1935. She housed them together in a large aviary and when two of them formed a pair they were moved to a separate enclosure. Provided with a nest-box measuring 76 cm (30 in) cubed, they entered it immediately. About two weeks later, the female laid two eggs, both of which were infertile. Two months later she laid two more, one of which hatched after four weeks. After two weeks, the parents deserted the chick so it was hand-reared by the owner but it was a poor specimen and lived for only four months.

In the following year, 1937, two eggs were laid. Both hatched on June 12, the 28th day. The parents fed their young on sunflower seed, hemp, canary, millet, nuts, corn-on-the-cob, peas in the pod, celery, watercress, soaked wholemeal bread, oranges, figs and grapes; lime was added to the drinking water.

When the chicks were six weeks old, they were well-feathered and lively but had badly swollen toes; one had lost a nail, apparently as the result of an infection. Mrs Bonestell bathed their feet in a weak solution of iodine and, every few days, soaked their feet in warm olive oil. After three weeks of this treatment the youngsters left the nest and after a month their feet were normal.

Both parents fed the chicks and the male was never observed to feed the female. The male slept in the nest after the chicks hatched. It had been suggested that the colour of the iris differed in male and female but in this pair the iris colour was the same: brown with an outer ring of grey.

Mrs Bonestell also provided the information that this species is a favourite pet of the Filipino and Moro, learning tricks and making quite a good talker. She found that their 'gentle disposition make them a delightful addition to an aviary'.

Mrs Bonestell's pair was successful in rearing two more young in 1938. In June 1979, I heard of the hatching of a single chick in the collection of Penny Luczak of West Virginia, USA.

In Germany, the Blue-naped Parrot was reared at Leipzig Zoo in 1981.

The first UK breedings occurred in 1983. George Smith (1984) wrote:

When approaching the hen the courting male (this is also noticeable in *Psittacula*) held himself, penguin-like, bolt upright with eyes blazing and a very slight drooping of the wings and flaring of the tail. He marched gradually forward (his legs stretched clear of the body) with long, gliding deliberate steps.

An unpaired female belonging to George Smith laid annually in May or June. In 1983, a male was obtained on loan from Kenneth McKenzie. The female laid on May 3 and 6. The eggs were removed to an incubator. A second clutch followed quickly, eggs being laid on June 2 and 5. These were left with the female and hatched on June 29 and July 1 (26-day incubation period). The single chick hatched in the incubator was placed in the nest of a Ringneck Parrakeet which had one three day old chick. They differed in

appearance only in the thin sparse down of the Blue-naped; Ringneck chicks are naked. This vestigial down remained after three weeks. The chicks' eyes opened at 12 days and at three weeks they were covered in the dark grey second down, the follicles of which had been visible at 11 days. At 29 days old, the green colouration of the secondaries and larger wing coverts was visible. The Ringneck-reared chick was removed for hand-rearing by Mr McKenzie when it was 40 days old. The other two left the nest when 56 days old.

In 1984, three chicks were reared. On hatching, they weighed 10.08, 10.5 and 10 g (about $\frac{2}{5}$ oz); weaning weights were 185 g, 192 g and 190 g ($6\frac{1}{2}$ oz, $6\frac{3}{4}$ oz and $6\frac{7}{10}$ oz).

When reporting this breeding, George Smith (1984) estimated the British population of this species to be 14 to 20 birds, including the two bred by David Alderton in 1983.

Müller's Blue-backed Parrot
T. mulleri mulleri (or T. sumatranus sumatranus)

Description: This is approximately the same size as the Blue-naped Parrot but has no blue on the head and no black in the wings. It is mainly green, more yellowish below and on the mantle; the back and rump are blue. The tail is tipped with greenish yellow. Adult birds are easily sexed as the beak is red in the male and white in the female. The iris is white. Females are darker green on the mantle with less blue on the margins of the wing coverts.

Immature birds resemble the female.

Length: about 32 cm (12 in), Philippine birds being larger than those from the more southern part of the range.

A number of races are recognised, including *T. m. everetti* which is darker green, especially on the head, and has a yellowish green collar around the neck. The feathers of the mantle are green, tinged with black and the back and rump are a deep blue.

Range/Habitat: The Blue-backed Parrot inhabits the Philippine islands of Talaud and Sangir and nearby islands in Indonesia.

Aviculture: George Smith of Peterborough obtained four of these birds in 1977 and found them extremely destructive though they were quiet with a pleasant voice. In Rome, in the collection of Paolo Bertagnolio, three chicks were hatched in 1981 but were not reared.

Black-lored Parrot
T. gramineus

Description: It measures 40 cm (16 in) and is predominantly green with the crown bluish grey and the lores black. The bill is red in the male and greyish white in the female.

In immature birds, the beak colour changes from the sides inwards, finally creating a narrow white line running down the culmen. In the males, the beak is tinged with pink before becoming red. It takes about six months for the complete colour change.

Range/Habitat: This bird inhabits the Island of Buru, Indonesia. Despite 20 per cent deforestation which has occurred there, there is no evidence to suggest that it is rare.

Aviculture: Has been kept on Buru.

Loriculus
Loriculus

The smallest of the parrots available to aviculturists, Hanging Parrots are quiet, inoffensive to other birds and not destructive to growing vegetation. They are therefore ideal inhabitants of a planted aviary for small species. In this respect they are more like small softbills, thus differing from all the other parrots.

Newly imported birds need very careful treatment and losses regrettably are high. This may be due partly to the stress caused by housing many together with dominant birds, which may keep them away from the food. Importers might reduce losses by housing two to four birds together. This can present another problem, however, for no parrots make more mess when caged; they throw fruit in all directions and their plumage becomes sticky and soiled, as does the interior of the cage and the perches. A shallow dish for bathing is essential and, provided that this is always available, Hanging Parrots will keep their plumage immaculate. Except in a small cage, they have a marked dislike of descending to the floor, so it is essential that the bathing receptacle is hooked on to the side of the cage or aviary at perch level. If the birds refuse to bathe, they should be sprayed. The food should also be placed at perch level. Perches for caged Hanging Parrots should be cleaned or renewed daily. Several layers of newspaper should be placed on the floor to absorb the liquid droppings, which are squirted some distance, resulting in the area immediately outside the cage becoming sticky. For this reason, although they are beautiful and quiet, Hanging Parrots are not suitable as ornamental indoor birds.

They acquired their name because they normally roost hanging from the perch by the feet, head downwards. They often rest in this position during the day. At all times, their breathing is much faster than that of other parrots. Because of the roosting position, it is vital that the claws do not become overgrown. If this happens, injuries could result when a Hanging Parrot tries to fly off when hanging from wire.

Feeding: These small birds require a varied diet, the basis of which is fruits and nectar. Fruits offered can include apple, pear and grapes and those in season, such as strawberries, raspberries, blackberries and redcurrants. Nectar should always be available and sponge cake with nectar can also be offered. Some Hanging Parrots will drink pure fruit juices, juice from tinned fruit (also the fruit) and evaporated milk.

A Blue-crowned Hanging Parrot lived for ten years in the Parrot House at London Zoo on a diet of canary seed, millet and fruit. At death, a few grains of grit were found in its stomach; seed-eating Hanging Parrots should therefore be provided with fine grit; that marketed for Budgerigars would be suitable. Any small seeds can be offered but canary and spray millet are most likely to be taken.

Lack of breeding success in the past was almost certainly due to inadequate diet: Hanging Parrots must have protein in some form if their young are to be reared and, in fact, may require protein to stimulate them to breed. When kept in a mixed collection of small softbills, they invariably take softbill mixtures and maggots (well cleaned) and so these foods should be supplied as a matter of course. Any acceptable protein foods can be offered, such as eggfood made for Canaries.

Accommodation: These birds have often been kept outdoors throughout the year in unheated aviaries but they do not thrive in damp conditions. If an attempt is to be made to winter them without heat, they must be provided with a strongly built shelter, which is completely dry and draught-proof. Although they can tolerate temperatures below freezing, such conditions usually adversely affect the stamina of any small bird. Ideal accommodation for Hanging Parrots is a tropical house (such as few private aviculturists can set up) which is kept slightly heated, or a planted aviary with a heated shelter. Unlike most parrots, they do not damage plants, although the females will tear strips from leaves as nesting material. Without a doubt, they are shown to their best advantage in a planted aviary.

Breeding: Generally speaking, it was

not until the early 1970s that Hanging Parrots began to breed in captivity. Up to that time, in Britain they were eagerly sought as exhibition birds and few attempts were made to breed from them. However, two zoos, Busch Gardens, Tampa, Florida, and Berne Zoo in Switzerland bred these birds during the 1960s.

When obtaining immature birds which are not in colour, a fairly good indication of sex will be given by the head which, viewed from the front, is larger and flatter in the female. Adult birds are sexually dimorphic in plumage and, in some species, in eye colour.

In captivity, they will nest in a small nest-box or natural log. Although under normal circumstances they dislike descending to the ground, a female Philippine Hanging Parrot I know of nested in the base of a hollow tree in a planted aviary. These birds line their nests with a thick pad of green leaves; the leaves are torn off lengthways along the midrib. In the wild nests have been found lined to a depth of 12 mm ($\frac{1}{2}$ in) with leaves. When George Gradwell's Vernals reared young, the female lined the nest to a depth of 37 mm ($1\frac{1}{2}$ in) with the leaves of cotoneaster. The nest of a Blue-crowned was described by F. N. Chasen (1939):

> The bird had filled up this large cavity, to above six inches below the entrance hole, with a pile of fronds of bracken and green leaves, torn up into pieces roughly an inch square. The leaves at the bottom were partly dry, but those at the top were still green. The three white eggs were much stained . . .

Female Halmahera and Worcester's Hanging Parrots in the 12th Duke of Bedford's collection carried grass into the nest-box, tucking it into the feathers of the rump and flanks. Dr Osman Hill recorded that his Ceylon Hanging Parrot carried nesting material beneath the upper tail coverts, as did the female Ceylon which bred at Chester Zoo. The female Blue-crowned in the same aviary at Chester would use only freshly picked leaves of trad-escantia for her nest.

Danish aviculturist, Jan Eriksen, specialises in breeding Hanging Parrots. In 1983, for example, he reared a total of 20 (Vernal, Philippine and Blue-crowned). He kindly provided the following notes:

> I keep my Hanging Parrots in relatively small aviaries about 2.3 m in length. Four species are kept together, even in the breeding season and no serious fights occur. When the females are about to lay their eggs and when the eggs have hatched the males show some aggressive tendencies towards other males – but never towards the females, for which they show a certain respect.
>
> When they incubate, which is carried out by the female only, the male calls the female from outside the entrance hole, where she is fed by the male. The male does not enter the nest-box while she is sitting but as soon as the eggs have hatched he enters to feed the youngsters and the female. The female normally leaves the nest-box twice a day to feed and to collect fresh leaves, especially from bamboo and ivy (*Hedera helix*) which she carries back to the nest-box every time she comes out. She rubs her feathers with the juice from the leaves.
>
> During the breeding season I check the nest-boxes every day and not one of my ten breeding pairs has ever left a clutch. As soon as I am out of the aviary they go back to their nests. When the chicks are about ten days old I change the nesting material to keep the flies away and to protect the chicks' feet.
>
> They use a lot of animal food, such as ant pupae, well-cleaned maggots and mealworms, to feed the youngsters. They eat a great amount of seed, too, especially sprouted sunflower and shelled oats (groats), if the livefood is short.

An interesting feature of the male's courtship is the manner in which he feeds the female. An excellent description of this behaviour in the Blue-crowned Hanging Parrot was recorded by R. T. Bloom (1960):

> He ran up and down the perch with slightly drooped wings, bobbing his head and rapidly moving his beak until the regurgitated food was worked into a mass of foam. He was able to protrude this out of his beak rather like a blob of bubble-gum and this was offered to the female who would suck it in, using the same quick movement of the beak. On any occasion when she did not accept the food he was able to suck it back into his own beak.

Such behaviour has not been recorded in any other group of parrots. Hanging Parrots lay three or four eggs; the incubation period is 20 days. They are exceptional among parrots in they sometimes lay on successive days.

Vernal Hanging Parrot
L. vernalis

Description: Vernal refers to the shade of green of this species, which is the fresh light colour of new leaves. It is brightest green on the head and paler on the under parts. There is a blue patch on the throat, the extent of which is more likely to be an indication of age than sex. The rump and upper tail coverts are bright red. The under sides of the flight feathers are greenish blue and the under side of the tail is bluish. The bill is orange-red with the tip yellowish; the legs are pale orange. The sexual distinction is the iris, the male having the iris white and the female brown. Length: 13 cm (5 in).

Immature birds have been described as having the forehead and cheeks dull green, the rump green and the bill pale orange. The iris is brown and the legs pale brownish. G. D. Gradwell of North Shields, England, stated that the young from his pair were very much like the parents but without the sheen to the plumage.

Vernal Hanging Parrot (*Loriculus vernalis*).

Range/Habitat: The Vernal Hanging Parrot has an extensive range from south-western India, south to Bombay, along the eastern coast to Bengal and the eastern Himalayas from eastern Nepal to Assam, east through Burma and Thailand to the Malay Peninsula, Cambodia, southern Laos and southern Vietnam. It also inhabits the Andaman Islands and islands in the Mergui Archipelago.

It is common in most parts of its range and is found in various habitats – deciduous jungles, open evergreen woodland, plantations and bamboo thickets, being observed in family groups and small flocks. Fruits form the main part of the diet and berries, nectar and small seeds are also eaten. The flight of this species is extremely rapid.

Aviculture: The Vernal Hanging Parrot does not appear to have been bred in captivity prior to the 1960s. One of the earliest records is of E. Nørgaard-Olesen of Janderup, Denmark, who reared Vernals on several occasions from 1968 (also a Blue-crowned in 1972).

In Britain, the first breeder was probably Gradwell (1975). His pair was kept with two female Blue-crowned Hanging Parrots (one of which later repeatedly attempted to enter the Vernal's nest but was driven off) and small softbills in a planted aviary measuring 6.3 × 2.1 m (21 × 7 ft). They nested in a box with an 11 cm (4½ in) internal diameter and a length of about 106 cm (3½ ft). The box leaned against the side of the aviary at an angle of about 45°; at the bottom, cotoneaster leaves formed a layer about 3.6 cm (1½ in) deep. The female had collected these from bushes growing in the aviary. She carried them to the nest in the feathers of her breast and, less often, her rump.

The female was obtained in 1965. In 1974, she laid three eggs which proved to be infertile. A second clutch of three produced three chicks which lived for 11 days. Three more eggs were laid on July 3, 4 and 5 or 6 and three chicks had hatched by July 27. The male was not allowed to enter the nest until August 1 but fed the female perched on the rim of the entrance and roosted in the inside flight. The chicks had dark reddish skin and were getting

grey down by August 4; by the next day their eyes were starting to open. On August 6, they were no longer brooded continuously during the day. Two days later their eyes were fully open; by August 10, the weather was colder and wetter and the male ceased to feed the young. By August 12, the wing quills of the chicks were visible and three days later the green wing feathers were partly out of their sheaths.

The nest became very wet and the female carried in more leaves to rectify the situation. At this time the male was anxious to nest again but the female attacked him when he attempted to mate. By August 26 she was feeding the young at the entrance.

They left the nest on August 30 but were returned because the weather was wet and foggy. Next day they again left the nest and were put in the shelter for the night with their parents. That night, one of the young birds roosted in the characteristic hanging position.

The birds were fed on sponge cake and nectar, various fruits, tomato, cheese, maggots, millet and sunflower seed. While rearing, they would eat the cambium (inner bark) of silver birch logs in the aviary. Maggots were provided when the second nest of chicks hatched.

Zoos which have bred this species include San Diego and, in Germany, Walsrode and Krefeld.

Ceylon Hanging Parrot
L. beryllinus
Description: It differs from the Vernal in having the forehead and crown scarlet and the nape and mantle tinged with golden-orange. The legs are orange-yellow. It is not known whether there is a similar variation in the colour of the iris as in the Vernal. Length: 13 cm (5 in).

Immature birds have the forehead greenish grey; the green crown is tinged with orange and the mantle is green. The throat is tinged with blue. The bill is pale orange and the iris is brown.
Range/Habitat: This species is confined to Ceylon (now known as Sri Lanka) and is most common in the south-west of the island. It is found in gardens and plantations and in wooded coun-

try. In addition to the usual fruits, berries, nectar and seeds, these birds feed on the toddy of the coconut palm which has an intoxicating effect on them; in this condition they are easily caught.

G. M. Henry (1962) described the display of the male in the wild which 'indulges in amusing attitudinisings, puffing out his blue throat patch and erecting his scarlet rump feathers, while he advances along a twig towards his lady with stilted little runs and hops, squeaking and twit-ing'. Henry recorded that, on one occasion, he 'took a fully fledged and healthy youngster out of a very wet and insanitary cavity' in a tree stump and observed that 'the mass of slowly decaying green leaves supplies this (from the human viewpoint) highly unhygienic environment'.
Aviculture: It would appear that the only captive breeding recorded is a hybrid one: by a male Blue-crowned and a female Ceylon at Chester Zoo in 1959. Three Blue-crowned and a pair of Ceylons were housed in a large aviary consisting of a flight 6 × 2.4 m (20 × 8 ft) and a 2.4 m (8 ft) cube indoor section; both parts were planted. Two males – a Ceylon and a Blue-crowned – displayed to the female but the former was far more energetic, fluffing up his red bib and the red feathers of the rump and tail.

The female accepted food from both males. She laid four eggs and did not use any nesting material. On the 22nd day, two chicks hatched; two eggs were infertile. A week later the male Ceylon died. Six days later one chick was thrown out of the nest and the second died a day or so later. On September 3, the female laid again. This time she collected grass and leaves after laying the first egg. By September 6, she had four eggs and collected more nesting material on her twice daily excursions from the nest. All four eggs hatched between September 22 and 25. Two chicks had died by September 27. By October 7, the Blue-crowned was seen feeding the young. They left the nest on October 27 but continued to return to it at night. By November 10, they were hanging and fed themselves ten days later. By eight weeks the young birds were exact replicas of their mother (Bloom, 1960).

Javan (Little or Yellow-throated) Hanging Parrot

L. pusillus

Description: It has an orange-yellow patch on the throat, much reduced in the female. The rump and upper tail coverts are red. The bill is orange. The iris is yellowish white and the legs are dusky yellow. Length: 12 cm (4¾ in).

Range/Habitat: It inhabits the islands of Java and Bali in Indonesia.

Aviculture: This species is extremely rare in captivity. Walter Goodfellow collected four and brought them to Britain in October 1926.

At a similar period, there were three in the collection of Dr Derscheid in Belgium. John Yealland (1940) described them as:

> Terribly wild; they were always fastidious about their appearance, keeping themselves very clean and, it seemed, never having a single barbule of a feather disarranged.
>
> I remember them especially for the charming song which the male would sometimes render during the quiet of the late afternoon.
>
> The song, a melancholy but not unmusical arrangement of a few Finch-like notes, was scarcely audible at more than a few yards distant.

The only breeding of this species which I can trace occurred in 1968 at Wassenaar Zoo in the Netherlands. Two young were reared. Two chicks hatched at Vogelpark Walsrode in Germany in 1978 but these were not reared.

Philippine Hanging Parrot (*Loriculus philippensis*) – female.

Philippine (Luzon) Hanging Parrot

L. philippensis philippensis

Description: This is the most colourful of the Hanging Parrots imported these days but it is available only rarely. It is an extremely beautiful little bird.

In the nominate race, the forehead and forepart of the crown are bright red bordered behind with a narrow yellow line and on the occiput by a dusky yellow patch. There is a golden-orange band on the nape and a red patch on the throat and upper breast. Rump and upper tail coverts are bright red with pale blue markings on each side of the rump. The bill is orange-red, legs orange, and iris brown.

The female lacks the red patch on the throat and breast and the lores are tinged with blue.

Immature birds differ from the female in having little or no red on the forehead.

At least eleven races have been described, most of which are unknown in aviculture. They are recognised by the lack of or amount of yellow on the crown. In *L. p. apicalis* and *L. p. dohertyi*, male and female have the entire crown scarlet. The race from Cebu Island, known as the Golden-backed Hanging Parrot (*L. p. chrys-onotus*), which is believed to be extinct, must have been one of the most beautiful. The male had the entire hind crown, nape and upper back rich golden-yellow; the female had the upper back green, tinged with golden orange.

Range/Habitat: It inhabits the Philippine Islands, including the Sula Archipelago.

Aviculture: The Golden-backed was exhibited at London Zoo as long ago as 1871. During that year, a Golden-backed chick was hatched by a Budgerigar but it was not reared. Walter Goodfellow collected twelve for an

English aviculturist in 1928. The specimen exhibited at London Zoo until 1943 may have been the last captive one. Deforestation resulted in the loss of nine Cebu Island bird forms.

The 12th Duke of Bedford kept a pair which were inoffensive and easily bullied. The male possessed a low whispering and chittering song with an occasional soft, sweet note interspersed. The performance, like that of a male Budgerigar, was kept up for some time. He kept another race, *L. p. worcesteri* (Worcester's Hanging Parrot), which has the entire crown scarlet, becoming orange on the nape; the mantle is tinged with orange. The female has the crown and cheeks scarlet and the upper throat pale blue but lacks the red throat patch. This subspecies was imported to Britain in about 1921 and perhaps not since.

The Duke of Bedford's pair showed signs of nesting but the male escaped through a small hole in the wire netting. A male Golden-backed was introduced into the female's aviary; he displayed by turning round and round, giving an occasional bob and curtsey, and opening and shutting his beak. The female disappeared into the nest for three weeks but no eggs were found. In July she laid three eggs; a second clutch of four eggs were laid. All were infertile.

Later, the female Worcester's was paired to a Sclater's and for two seasons she incubated her eggs on the sand tray in the aviary shelter – but without result.

According to de Grahl (1974), London Zoo bred a Philippine Hanging Parrot as long ago as 1871. This was reported in *Die Gefiederte Welt* in 1894. No more breedings were reported until the 1960s when Busch Gardens, Tampa, Florida, reared three in 1964 and one in 1965. At Berne Zoo, in Switzerland, three pairs were kept in an outdoor aviary and the results were as follows: 1967, three reared; 1968, two; 1970, two; and 1971, two. A Philippine Hanging Parrot was bred at the Hong Kong Botanic Gardens in 1975 and 1976.

The second British breeding occurred in the aviaries of Mr and Mrs G. W. Sharratt (1977) of Chellaston, Derby. They had purchased four birds in 1975 and fed them on nectar, slices of orange sweetened with sugar, sliced apple, a fine-grade insectivorous food and millet spray. On December 1, 1976, one female laid an egg in the corner of her cage. The egg was placed in a small finch nest-box and this was readily accepted by the female. The second egg was laid on December 3 and the third on December 5. A chick hatched on December 25. The pair was then offered a thicker nectar made from honey, condensed milk and Farex; sponge cake soaked in Stimulite nectar was also provided. On January 1, a full pot of maggots was consumed; maggots had first been offered during incubation. On January 3, the chick died. Its beak was brownish, it had no down on its body and its eyes were still closed.

The three eggs of the second clutch were laid on January 17, 19 and 21. Their contents dried up and they were removed on February 12. Eggs were laid on March 1, 3 and 4, followed by another clutch, laid on April 13, 14 and 16. Chicks hatched on May 2, 3 and 5, giving a definite incubation period of 20 days. By May 11, the male was roosting in the nest-box at night. Two days later grey down was apparent on the eldest chick. On May 14, the second chick was dead.

The eyes of the remaining chick opened on May 16. The female was then carrying torn up newspaper into the nest, presumably as a substitute for leaves. Sponge cake soaked in Stimulite nectar and maggots were favoured rearing foods. The eyes of the youngest chick opened on May 19. Mealworms were offered for the first time and the adults quickly learned to eat them and to discard the skin. On May 22, green feathers could be discerned on the back of the eldest chick, and red feathers on the rump and orange on the nape were visible a few days later. The nest had become so wet that it was necessary to put in fresh shavings. The female showed no sign of being disturbed by this.

The chicks left the nest on June 5 and 6. Their eyes were dark, and their beaks dark yellow with black marks near the base; their legs were grey. Plumage colouration was not described. Just over a week after leaving the nest, the young birds were seen to eat apple.

Halmahera (Moluccan) Hanging Parrot
L. amabilis

Description: This tiny bird is rich dark green, more olive on the mantle. The male has the forehead, crown and throat and also the edge of the forewing crimson. The female has the crown green with reddish spots on the forehead and throat. In both sexes, rump and upper tail coverts are crimson. The extremely small beak is black and the legs are orange. The iris is whitish in the male, brown in the female. Length: 11 cm ($4\frac{1}{2}$ in).

Four races are recognised. In Sclater's Hanging Parrot (*L. a. sclateri*), from the Sula Islands, male and female have the feathers of the forehead green with reddish brown bases; the crown is green and there is a triangular orange patch on the back. It is larger than the nominate race. The 12th Duke of Bedford kept a single male Sclater's which is otherwise almost unknown in captivity. He wrote of it: 'I never saw a handsomer little Parrot' and that it was 'a truly gorgeous little fellow'.

Range/Habitat: The Moluccan islands of Great Sangi, Sula, Peling and Banggai, Indonesia, are inhabited by this species.

Aviculture: At least one specimen of this little known species has been imported into Britain in the 1980s. It has been exhibited by Mr and Mrs Sharratt. A pair of Halmahera Hanging Parrots owned by the Duke of Bedford made an unsuccessful attempt to nest in 1931. The female carried the grass into the nest-box in the feathers of her rump and flanks. Three infertile eggs were laid. The male had the habit of vibrating his tail rapidly when inspecting the nest. In addition to nectar and grapes, the pair took flowering grass heads.

Red-crowned (Celebes) Hanging Parrot
L. stigmatus

The first reference to this bird in captivity is that of the Duke of Bedford who obtained a pair of Hanging Parrots in 1929 which he believed belonged to this species; however, from their description and small size, it would appear that they were *amabilis*: he described them as 'decidedly smaller then any Parrot-like bird I have seen alive'. The Red-crowned is 15 cm (6 in) long and also differs from *amabilis* in that the female has the forehead green, sometimes with red bases to the feathers.

In 1984, Danish aviculturist Jan Eriksen informed me that, a year previously, a consignment of 40 *stigmatus* was received in Denmark. Unfortunately only eight survived. He obtained three and described them as being very active, flying more than Hanging Parrots. They were apparently all females – and had fed the young of other Hanging Parrots in the same aviary. Two males were in the possession of another Danish aviculturist, Leif Rasmussen, and co-operation resulted in breeding success.

Blue-crowned Hanging Parrot

L. galgulus

Description: This species, with the Vernal, is the best known of the genus. An extremely dainty bird, it is the second smallest Hanging Parrot, measuring only 12 cm (5 in) and distinguished by the dark blue patch on the crown. There is a triangular patch of tawny gold on the mantle. The throat, rump and upper tail coverts are scarlet, lower back is yellow and the remainder of the plumage is green, paler on the under parts. The bill is black; the iris is dark brown and the legs are buff-brown.

The female lacks the red throat patch and the yellow band on the lower back. The blue on the crown and the golden-yellow on the mantle are only faintly indicated.

Immature birds are dull green with dusky margins to the feathers; the forehead is grey tinged with blue and the rump dull red; the remainder of the plumage is green. The bill is pale horn-coloured and the legs pale flesh-colour.

Several instances have been recorded of the females acquiring the red throat patch. Two cases were reported by E. Nørgaard-Olesen (1968). Both birds were obtained in 1965; both laid eggs in 1966. After moulting in autumn 1966, one female had a dark red throat

Blue-crowned Hanging Parrot (*Loriculus galgulus*) – male.

patch and the other acquired one a year later.

Range/Habitat: The Blue-crowned Hanging Parrot has a wide distribution from the Malay Peninsula, south of latitude 10°N, on Singapore, Anamba Islands, Borneo, Riau Archipelago, Bangka and Belitung Islands, Sumatra and outlying islands. It is common throughout many parts of its range; generally it prefers lower altitudes and primary forest rather than heavy jungle. It also inhabits gardens, orchards and plantations.

Aviculture: This species has been regularly available for many years. It was first exhibited at London Zoo in 1869. An unsuccessful breeding attempt occurred as long ago as 1907 in Berlin or Moscow when a pair belonging to a Frau Prowé laid four eggs and commenced incubation on February 16. A chick hatched on March 9 but died after three days. Eggs of the second clutch hatched on April 21, 24 and 27: the female unfortunately died when the chicks were four weeks old; the male continued to feed them for a week, after which two died. An attempt was

made to hand-rear the third but it too died.

Success with this species was not recorded until 1968 when E. Nørgaard-Olesen of Janderup, Denmark, reared two young. The female laid three eggs in a small tit nest-box. When the young were first examined they had a small amount of dark down and light, flesh-coloured skin. The female was found dead on February 20. The male continued to feed the young, two of which left the nest on February 24; the third was found dead in the nest. One died on March 27; the other was reared to independence. Nørgaard-Olesen was still breeding this species in 1972.

In Britain, the Blue-crowned was bred by L. J. Farrow of Wisbech, Cambridgeshire, in 1975; four young were reared. Mrs G. H. Horridge of Hampshire bred two in 1977. An unmated male helped to feed the young. K. Wardle of Helston, Cornwall, reared three young which left the nest in August 1977; the pair had two more chicks in the nest in March 1978. A second pair in the aviary helped to feed the 1977 young and both females would feed the young in the nest.

In the USA, Catherine Tyler (1975) of New Jersey purchased four immature Blue-crowned Hanging Parrots in January 1971. One male died in August 1971 and the other male in November 1973; three days later, one female laid the first of four eggs. Another male was obtained and placed with the female on December 23, 1973. The two birds ignored each other for a week; however, on January 13, the male was seen unsuccessfully attempting to mate with the female. The first egg was laid on January 17; the total clutch was five, laid on alternate days. On February 14, one chick hatched; it was described as shiny, transparent and naked. When the nest was inspected on February 18, the chick was cold and its breathing shallow. It was removed to an incubator, then to a hospital cage set at 35°C (95°F). The chick was fed every hour round the clock because it would take only a drop of food at a time. Its eyes opened on the 13th day. On the 19th day it was making preening movements. At 39 days it was drinking nectar and hanging. It took its first bath at six weeks and it ate seed, oats and apple at this age. A second nest of three young were reared by the parents and, in February 1975, two more young were reared.

Also in the USA, San Diego Zoo has reared Blue-crowns since 1975.

Hybrids from a male Blue-crowned and a female Vernal were reared by S. G. Eade (1977a & b) of Farnham, Surrey, in 1977. They nested in a 1.8 m (6 ft) elm log of 60 cm (2 ft) diameter. Lawn mowings, peat and straw to a depth of 1.2 m (4 ft) occupied the bottom of the box. The young left the nest in June; they resembled Vernals with grey beaks and foreheads. In August, three more fledged. They were darker green than the Vernal with the yellow and red rump markings of the Blue-crowned.

*   *   *

The two other species of Hanging Parrots (see Identification Table below) are unknown in aviculture. They include Wallace's Hanging Parrot (*L. flosculus*). Forshaw (1973) described this as a mysterious bird about which almost nothing seems to be known and it has even been suggested that it may be extinct. However, the reason for its obscurity is that few ornithologists have visited Flores, the only island on which it is found. It does still exist: it was seen by W. H. Timmis, former Curator of Birds at Chester Zoo when he visited the island in the early 1970s.

Identification of Hanging Parrots (*Loriculus*)

All are bright green, paler below with greenish blue under side to wings and tail. The tail is very short. The rump and tail coverts are red.

Species	Beak (Adults)	Distinctive colouring	Length in cm (in)
vernalis	red	blue throat	13 (5)
beryllinus	orange-red	blue throat; nape and mantle suffused with golden-orange	13 (5)
pusillus	orange	orange-yellow throat; mantle tinged yellow	12 (4¾)
philippensis	orange-red	male red upper breast; female no red. Golden-orange band on nape	14 (5½)
amabilis	black	red throat. Female with reddish spots on forehead	11 (4½)
stigmatus	black	throat red in male; green in female. Crown blue; mantle golden-yellow	15 (6)
exilis	coral-red	red spot on throat in male; reduced or absent in female	10.5 (4)
flosculus	red	red spot on throat in male; reduced or absent in female	12 (4¾)
galgulus	black	dark blue patch on crown, triangular patch of tawny gold on mantle	12 (4¾)

Lovebirds
Agapornis

With Australian parrakeets and Cockatiels, Lovebirds form the best known group of parrots. They are widely kept and can be universally recommended for the beginner. Except the Black-collared and the Red-faced, all Lovebird species have at one time or another been freely available although not all have proved prolific in captivity: the Red-faced has seldom reared young. That the Madagascar and Abyssinian are not free-breeders under confined conditions has been shown by the fact that soon after importations cease, they are rare and expensive. The same has applied to the Nyasa, although why this should be so is uncertain. The species which are readily available because it has not been necessary to rely on importations to sustain their numbers are the Peach-faced, Masked and Fischer's and, of these, the Peach-faced is the most common. Even in Australia (where no importations of birds have occurred since 1959) it is freely available.

Because of their comparatively low price, hardiness and readiness to breed, one of these three species is chosen by many beginners who have no previous experience of keeping psittacines. The most common mistake is to try to house them with other birds, usually Budgerigars or small finches. From the outset, it should be emphasised that Lovebirds are not suitable companions for any other species, let alone other small psittacines such as Budgerigars. By nature they are quarrelsome and, when breeding, vicious. (The exception is the Red-faced Lovebird which, in any case, is a rarity.) Although there are cases of Lovebirds co-habiting peacefully with other birds, the beginner would do better not to tempt fate in this respect because disillusionment with bird-keeping can so easily follow losses – and these are often incurred among newly fledged young of other species by Lovebirds.

Feeding: Lovebirds are very easy to feed. The basic diet will consist of canary seed and white and panicum millet. They can also be offered niger and sunflower. The use of hemp is probably best restricted to the colder months when it will be most beneficial. Spray millet will be relished and can be offered soaked to birds which are rearing young. The usual greenfood will be welcomed, especially seeding grasses and chickweed. The use of the various parts of pussy willow for Lovebirds is referred to on p.31.

Accommodation: Ideally, each pair of Lovebirds should be kept in a small outdoor enclosure measuring about 180×90 cm (6×3 ft) $\times$ 180 cm (6 ft) high. Colony breeding is often practised but this almost invariably leads to disappointment and cannot be recommended. If it is possible to house an equal number of males and females in known true pairs, bloodshed might be avoided; a single, unmated bird should never be allowed to remain in a colony and a female will try to enter the nest of another female, perhaps killing her or her young. To prevent squabbling, all nest-boxes should be hung at the same height and should be of identical design. There should be more nest-boxes than the number of pairs and even a single pair should be provided with two boxes as the hen may lay another clutch before the previous young have fledged. Nest-boxes should be left in position throughout the year as Lovebirds use their boxes for roosting. Incidentally, blocking the entrance hole after the birds have entered for the night and taking down the box is a good method of identifying or removing a true pair.

Because the nest-box is left permanently in position, Lovebirds will breed throughout the year and young could fledge in any month. Removal of boxes will not necessarily stop a female from laying and, as many Lovebirds seem capable of rearing healthy young during the winter months (provided that they are offered a nutritious rearing food), there is little point in trying to prevent them from breeding.

Breeding: The three commonly available species, Peach-faced, Masked and Fischer's, are impossible to sex on sight, as are the Nyasa and the Black-cheeked. This is unfortunate and can result in many wasted months or even years, during which it is attempted to breed from two birds of one sex. If it is possible to buy four birds at the outset, to keep them together and allow them to choose their own mates, the chances of obtaining a true pair are far greater. If necessary, two can be sold when a true pair is identified. Behaviour is a guide to sex in the species in which the plumage is alike because only females normally carry material into the nest. Also, a very large clutch might indicate that a pair consists of two females, both of whom have laid.

The nest-building Lovebirds require a slightly larger box than one would normally provide for birds of their size but there is no point in providing a really large box as the birds will attempt to cram it with nesting material, making nest inspection impossible. Materials provided can include willow branches and grasses. As an approximate guide, the box can be about 23 × 15 cm (9 × 6 in) × 17 cm (7 in) high. The entrance hole should be larger than provided for similar sized birds to prevent loss of nesting material carried in the feathers. A removable lid allows inspection. (Specialised nesting requirements which breeders of the Red-faced Lovebird have met are described under the notes on that species. It should also be noted that the Abyssinian Lovebird does not build a bulky nest and prefers a small nest-box.)

Lovebirds will breed in a cage, in which case the nest-box should be attached to the outside to facilitate inspection without disturbing the birds. A cage for a breeding pair should be not less than 90 × 36 cm (36 × 14 in) × 36 cm (14 in) high. Failure to provide a caged pair with a nest-box may well result in their trying to roost or even to nest under the paper which is used as a floor covering.

It is also likely to lead to feather plucking through sheer frustration at being unable to breed. This is not to say, however, that those provided with nesting facilities will not indulge in plucking themselves or their mates but it is less prevalent under these conditions. While housed indoors for the winter, a female Red-faced Lovebird in my possession so severely denuded the male's body feathers that the two birds had to be parted until they had grown again.

The number of eggs laid by Lovebirds varies according to the species, but the average is about five. Abyssinians lay smaller clutches, usually of three eggs, and Madagascars lay the largest, seven or eight being known. The incubation period is about 23 days and young spend six or seven weeks in the nest. They should be replaced in the nest at night for a few days if they fledge during cold weather. They start to moult at about 14 weeks. Lovebirds have produced fertile eggs as early as 16 weeks old.

Ringing Lovebirds to keep track of their parentage, which is a necessity for those breeding the various mutations, is something of a problem. These birds have strong beaks and are capable of removing plastic and aluminium rings. Only heavy gauge rings should be used as the birds can bend and tighten those made of a light material, possibly resulting in serious injury to the foot. A watchful eye should be kept on ringed Lovebirds to ensure that this has not occurred.

If these birds are ringed with closed rings bearing the year of hatching, there can be no mistake regarding their age. Lovebirds are sexually mature before they are a year old, thus can be used for breeding during the year following that in which they were hatched. It is difficult to state how long their breeding life is, as individuals vary, but generally males can be used longer than females. Best results from the latter are likely to be achieved up to the age of four years.

Breeders should retain young from the first nest for breeding purposes as they will be fully mature by the following breeding season. Although males as young as five months have been known to fertilise eggs, breeding with such young birds is not recommended. Once they start to breed, they should not be allowed to do so for months on end without a break, as their vitality will be affected. They should be prevented from rearing more than two or three clutches in a year. This will be difficult to control in a colony – another reason why controlled breeding is preferable.

Rather than remove a clutch of eggs from a female, which will merely have the effect of making her lay another clutch unless the box is removed, it is better to render each egg useless by puncturing it in several places shortly after it has been laid. The act of laying and incubating will not sap a female's strength as does rearing the young.

It is not at all uncommon for young Lovebirds to be very poorly feathered on leaving the nest. Often this is due to the fact that the parents have plucked the young in the nest but the problem is sometimes caused by a deficiency in the diet. Whatever the reason, they usually feather up rapidly on being removed from their parents. This can take place about two weeks after they have left the nest; they can remain much longer with their parents in a spacious aviary but, unless ringed, should be removed before they moult into adult plumage or it may prove impossible to distinguish the breeding pair. Poorly feathered young which have the misfortune to leave the nest during winter will have to be put back in the nest at night or shut in the shelter if they are not to die of exposure.

When young are in the nest, the diet should be supplemented with bread and milk, as the all-seed diet is seriously deficient in lysine, essential for good growth, which is found in milk. Soaked oats can also be offered.

Bathing facilities are especially important for Lovebirds when they are breeding. Some birds will soak nesting material before taking it into the nest and others will bathe when they are incubating; both actions help to maintain humidity in the nest.

Breeders should take care to retain only the most desirable birds for breeding: they should be judged not only by appearance but also by whether they are bred from pairs which do not pluck their young and have a low percentage of chicks which die in the shell; both these defects could be hereditary in some cases. It is not enough, in comparatively free-breeding species, such as Peach-faced and Masked Lovebirds, merely to breed from these birds; the aim should be to produce healthy, virile birds whose markings and size are typical of their species.

Mention should be made of the practice of hybridising Lovebirds. This should be strongly discouraged, even though some quite attractive birds can be bred. The danger is that they will be used for breeding purposes and will spoil existing pure stocks. Before World War II, so much crossing had been carried out by British Lovebird breeders that it was difficult to obtain pure Masked and Black-cheeked Lovebirds. It would be highly regrettable if a similiar situation ever occurred again. Because of the difficult trading relations with some African countries, large-scale importations of Lovebirds are not made, thus it is important to keep aviary-bred strains entirely pure.

The Masked, Fischer's, Black-cheeked, Nyasa and Peach-faced Lovebirds will interbreed freely. There are no hybrid records for the other species.

An explosion of interest in the colour breeding of Lovebirds occurred in the 1970s, when many more mutations than previously became available. Next to the Budgerigar, whose mutations and their combinations number hundreds, more mutations have been developed than in any other species. This aspect is still being developed and many more mutations will occur. Indeed, for anyone who is interested in genetics who does not wish to breed Budgerigars (the genetical behaviour of whose mutations is well understood, with a very few exceptions), the Lovebird will be of exceptional interest.

The high cost of some birds will preclude many from acquiring any but the more common mutations, but as specialist breeders succeed in increasing the number of the rarer mutations prices fall.(Recommended reading on the subject is Jim Hayward's *Lovebirds and their Colour Mutations* which describes the breeding of mutations in detail.)

Madagascar (Grey-headed) Lovebird

A. cana cana
Description: The male is unmistakable with the entire head and breast pale grey; the under wing coverts are black. The tail is green, the lateral feathers being marked with yellow and, near the tip, barred with black. The plumage is dark green above, yellowish green below. The female is a plain green bird which could almost be mistaken for a parrotlet. The bill is pale grey and the iris is dark brown. Length: 14 cm (6 in). Weight: 40 g (1⅖ oz).

Immature birds resemble adults, except in the colour of the beak which is yellowish with black marks at the base of the upper mandible.

A. c. ablectana
Description: It is a darker, more bluish green, especially in the wings and back, providing a stronger contrast between the light green of the body and the grey of the head, which is paler, more lavender in shade.
Range /Habitat: This race is found in the south-western arid zone of Malagasy Republic.

Range/Habitat: This species is found naturally in the Malagasy Republic (Madagascar) and has been introduced to Rodriguez, the Comoro Islands and the Seychelles, also to Mauritius and to Zanzibar and Mafia Island off Africa's east coast, where it is probably no longer present.

Madagascar Lovebirds are found in groups, usually up to 20 birds but larger flocks have been reported. They feed mainly on the ground; seeds of grasses are their principal food and they have difficulty in coping with a seed as large as sunflower.
Aviculture: This Lovebird has a curious avicultural history. It was probably first imported into Britain in 1860 when a pair was exhibited at London Zoo. At the end of the nineteenth century, pairs could be obtained for about 3*s* (15p). In 1900, F. W. Oats reared four young and this would appear to be the first recorded breeding in Britain.

During the early years of the present century, the price rose to about 4*s* 6*d* (22p) and was maintained until just before World War I when it dropped to 2*s* 6*d* (12p). After the war, the species was in short supply and fetched 25*s* (£1.25) per pair in 1925. Then it became available again so that the price had dropped to 10*s* (50p) by the time the ban on the import of parrots was imposed in 1930.

By the 1950s, it was an avicultural rarity. It was imported into Britain in 1959 when I obtained a pair for £5 – a low price as two or three years previously pairs were fetching £15 to £18.

When some importations occurred in 1975, they consisted mainly of males. The reason for these fluctuating prices is that the Madagascar Lovebird has never been established in captivity and, although many breeding successes have occurred, aviculturists have neglected to build up aviary-bred strains.

Exceptions are Mr and Mrs R. Hill of Devon who, by 1985, had bred this species to the sixth generation. Another problem with this species has been air-sac mite in newly imported birds, which causes severe respiratory disease and death in many instances. The mite can be eliminated if the birds are housed in a cage near to which should be placed a dichlorvos strip, such as Vapona. The complaint is most infectious.

Considering the large numbers of Madagascar Lovebirds which have reached Europe during this century, breeding successes have not been numerous. One reason may be that these birds often prefer to nest in late autumn or early winter and their attempts have proved much less successful than the unseasonable nests, for example, of Peach-faced and Fischer's Lovebirds.

Female Madagascar Lovebirds carry material into the nest tucked into the body feathers before and during breeding operations. They nibble leaves into the shape of a 'C'. It is common for five to seven eggs to be laid, a larger clutch than in other Lovebirds. The incubation period is 22 to 23 days. On hatching, chicks are sparsely covered with white down.

Young Madagascars can be sexed as soon as they feather, the males having grey on the head. They fledge at the age of six weeeks.

A small nest-box will suffice for these birds as only the base is lined with nesting material. They will nest readily in cages and a pair I had used a double-breeding cage of the type designed for Budgerigars with the nest-box attached to the outside. As a bulky nest is not made, nest inspection presents no problems.

Twigs with the leaves attached should be offered as nesting material. An aviculturist who bred this species as long ago as 1912 described the manner in which the nesting material was used:

Madagascar Lovebird (*Agapornis cana cana*) – female left, male right.

After preparing the strips of laurel, and oak leaves, she tucked them into the feathers of the rump and lower back, erecting the feathers of these parts almost perpendicularly, and when fully loaded up, she had a most absurd, almost hedgehog-like appearance (*Bird Notes*, 1912:50).

A. MacIntosh (1982) described the successful breeding of a female who laid her first egg when she was four months old, in a cage measuring 180 × 31 cm (6 × 1 ft) by 38 cm (15 in)

high. Three eggs had been laid by September 6; the first of these chicks hatched on September 26. Two males and one female, they were removed from their parents on November 30.

The male of a pair belonging to F. C. Barnicoat (1980) reared six young after the death of the female when they were four weeks old. The male was described as 'wonderfully devoted'. He would 'carefully shepherd all six – four daughters and two sons – into the shelter each evening'.

In Mr Barnicoat's experience, Madagascar Lovebirds:

. . . succumb somewhat suddenly and unexpectedly when in good health, and they seem to be particularly nervous and sensitive birds which panic at the slightest disturbance. This causes a high proportion to be lost as the result of night frights.

A pair of Madagascars belonging to K. Suckley (1980) reared 12 young in five years in a 1.8 m (6 ft) cage in a brick outhouse maintained at 10°C (50°F). Four male chicks hatched in that period but died when they fell out of the hawthorn log nest which had rotted. Mr Suckley emphasised the importance of providing soaked seed, especially spray millet, when young were being reared. They also ate brown bread soaked in honey, water and milk and dried figs sprinkled with SA37 (vitamin/mineral additive).

An aviculturist with limited accommodation, yet anxious to make a worthwhile contribution to bird keeping, could do no better than devote himself to building up an aviary-bred strain of this species.

Red-faced Lovebird
A. pullaria

Description: This species is an especially pleasing shade of light green, slightly darker above. The forehead and facial area is orange-red and the rump is light blue. The tail is green, barred with black and with a large area of red and yellowish green on the lateral feathers (these feathers are among the most beautifully marked of any parrot: yellowish green at the base with quite half the feather orange with a broad black V pointing towards the pale green tip of the feather). In the male, the under wing coverts are black; in the female, they are green. The orange on the female's head is paler and less extensive than in the male. The bill is of the same shade of orange as the head. Length: 14 cm (5½ in). Weight: 38 g (1$\frac{3}{10}$ oz).

Immature birds are a dull green and have the red on the head replaced by orange-yellow and less extensive in area. The bill is described as reddish brown, lightly marked with black near the base of the upper mandible. Young birds can be sexed by the colour of the under wing coverts.

Range/Habitat: The Red-faced Lovebird inhabits central and central-western Africa: it is found in Angola, Guinea, Sudan, Ethiopia and Tanzania. It frequents woodland and lightly timbered and open grassland, being a lowland species, normally found in flocks of 15–20. As a ground feeder, grass seeds are the principal item of its diet; fruits, berries and buds are also taken. An arboreal termi-

Red-faced Lovebird (*Agapornis pullaria*) – male.

tarium is the usual nesting site; sometimes terrestrial termitaria are used.

Aviculture: This is perhaps the least typical member of the genus, in its colouration, twittering finch-like voice, small size and proportionately small bill. It is by far the most difficult of the Lovebirds to breed in captivity and few successes have occurred. Until the late 1960s, the Red-faced Lovebird was common and well known in captivity; today it is rare and extremely expensive. Newly imported birds should be treated with great care. Arthur Prestwich, the first breeder of this species in Britain, had 'hundreds during a period of 35 years' and found newly imported ones to be 'incomparably the least hardy and most timid of all the lovebirds known to aviculture'. In his experience, they were 'very subject to cerebral haemorrhage, brought on by fright'. He found that the sudden opening of a door or window, or the entry of a visitor to the birdroom,

was enough to cause fatality. Even established birds proved just as susceptible to shock. In October 1953, Prestwich decided, with the onset of ground frosts, to take the Red-faced Lovebirds inside for the winter. Twenty birds were caught up by helpers and 'within a week half had died from concussion, cerebral haemorrhage, and pneumonia consequent on shock'.

There are a number of reports of breeding successes which date from the late nineteenth century but in view of the reluctance of the Red-faced to nest in captivity, the earlier records must be questioned. Perhaps, in some cases at least, there was confusion over the common names and records may have referred to the Peach-faced Lovebird. According to the literature, it was bred in Germany, France and Britain in the 1870s and 1880s, and in the USA between the 1880s and the early years of the twentieth century. However, since that time, perhaps only a dozen aviculturists have been successful. The most widely quoted success is the breeding by Arthur Prestwich which gained the Avicultural Society's medal for the first breeding of this species. Prestwich built a large aviary, three sides of which were made of asbestos. He suspended four peat bales in the centre. Ten pairs of Red-faced Lovebirds were released into the aviary; they bored into the peat – and straight out again. It was later found that these birds tunnel until they meet a firm surface; they then bore a nesting chamber to one side.

After wintering 31 birds indoors, they were released into the aviary. Small barrels were provided as nesting sites and these were packed with peat which had been made damp and pressed down. The result was 14 eggs laid in cavities in the peat. The Lovebirds wintered outdoors and in the following year, 1955, they were provided with smaller barrels, only 35 cm (14 in) deep. All excavation work was carried out by the females who burrowed tunnels 15–17 cm (6–7 in) long which terminated in a nesting chamber the size of an orange. On December 3, a single young one was found clinging to the aviary wire. The following year brought similar results – one youngster which left the nest on October 5. It died one month later after a severe frost. The food taken was mainly soaked millet sprays and apple (Prestwich, 1957).

Aage Nielsen, a Danish aviculturist, kept a pair with other birds in a large aviary in a cellar which was connected to a planted outdoor flight. In August 1960, the Lovebirds nested in a horizontal wooden box measuring 40 × 17 cm (16 × 7 in) by 17 cm (7 in) high with a 7 cm (3 in) diameter entrance. Five eggs were laid between August 1 and 11. At the beginning of the incubation period, the Lovebirds consumed as many as 200 mealworms daily. Eventually four eggs were found to contain chicks dead-in-shell and the fifth egg was damaged. The female laid again on September 26 and the clutch was completed at irregular intervals, the second egg being laid after October 1; by October 10 there were five eggs. When the nest was inspected on November 4 there were three chicks. One died on November 7 or 8 and

the headless body of the second, which had seemed weak, was found in the nest. The eldest chick died the same day, aged 13 days. Because of this experience, Nielsen provided them with a very large variety of foods, including all the usual seeds, apples, pear, oranges, grapes, bananas, figs, lettuce, cabbage, dandelion, plantain, stinging nettles, grass seeds, fresh grass turf and branches of fruit trees and sponge cake with glucose. The female laid again during July. Two chicks hatched; a week later mealworm consumption had reached an amazing 490–500 daily. The eldest youngster fledged on September 13 and the youngest on September 15. Their beaks were black at the base and their heads were orange-yellow where their parents' were red. The following year the male died, aged 12 or 13 years.

In South Africa, the Red-faced Lovebird has reared young successfully on several occasions. In 1958, a pair belonging to David Dale of Cape Town hatched two chicks (in a cork nest) which died. During the following year, in a new cork nest, they burrowed, forming an opening about 4 cm (1½ in) in diameter, and a tunnel, culminating in a chamber above the tunnel. It is of interest that the male was seen carrying small pieces of the creeper *Ipomoea purpurea* (morning glory) into the nest in the feathers of his mantle. A chick fledged on May 30, a second on June 3 and three more on June 6, 11 and 14. The breeding coincided with one of the wettest periods for years and the nest was exposed to a continuous downpour for days on end. Disputing the theory that a nutritious diet, after a suitable nest, is the factor most likely to lead to success with this species, this pair reared their young on millet and canary seed and the leaves of morning glory.

The Red-faced Lovebird has also been bred in Portugal by A. Coelho (1977). During 1976–77 he had 14 pairs, 13 of which started to breed between October and December 1976. The first youngster left the nest on December 25, about 90 days after the female started excavating. Two more young fledged, one of which died in heavy rain a day after leaving the nest. Other pairs hatched young which died.

The nests contained a central block

of cork 14 × 20 (or 15) × 20 cm (6 × 8 (or 6) × 8 in). The central block was covered on all six sides with 5 cm (2 in) panels of high density cork (harder cork conglomerate) and Mr Coelho stressed that the insulating panels must fit together well to prevent the escape of warm air from the nest chamber. This he felt might be the secret of successful breeding of the Red-faced. Elastic glue was used to fill gaps around the nest between each panel. To facilitate inspection of each nest at the end of the season the top was sawn off. The main problem with this method is that eggs may become buried in the cork residue; an inspection door is therefore desirable.

An outstandingly successful breeder of the Red-faced Lovebird is Reinhard Blome of Bremen, Germany. He first bred this species in 1974; by January 1979, he had reared about 40 young. An unusual feature, which may have accounted for his success, was the use of a heat pad beneath the nest-boxes. These measured 20 cm (8 in) square and were of 18 watts to keep the temperature of the nest at 30°C (86°F).

Herr Blome believed that the heating pads played an important part in his successes, since the behaviour of *pullaria* differs from that of other Lovebirds. Other species disappear into the nest at the first sign of danger, whereas the Red-faced stays only in the vicinity of the nest. This behaviour can result in chicks becoming chilled and thus the heat pad is of vital importance. Timing of its use is also important; it is not switched on until the young hatch as it can cause the eggs to dry out. Maintaining humidity is not of importance, despite the fact that the Lovebirds breed in indoor cages, because the incubating females bathe just before the eggs are due to hatch and return to the nest with the feathers still wet.

Nest-boxes used measure 35 × 10 cm (14 × 4 in) × 20 cm (8 in) high. They are filled with peat which the female excavates using her bill and feet. The first female which hatched young, in 1973, was seen to take pieces of bark into the nest in her feathers and to carry willow leaves in the bill.

The first of five fertile eggs was laid on October 17; two chicks hatched on November 13, and one each on

November 14, 16 and 18, giving an
incubation period of 24 days. None
survived longer than 16 days and all
had full crops at the time of their
deaths. Nest inspection was possible
because the female's nesting chamber
was luckily right below the inspection
lid. The female laid four more eggs, the
first on September 1. They were
marked: the first was infertile and the
others hatched on September 27, 28
and 30, giving an incubation period of
24–25 days. Chicks had rose-coloured
down. One died at two weeks but the
others developed quickly; wing quills
were visible at 20 days. They were both
females and left the nest at 50 days.
They had dark markings at the base of
the bill and the orange mask area was
less extensive than in the adult female.
Rearing food consisted of carrot,
apple, honey, a proprietary rearing
food and syrup made into a crumbly
moist mixture.

Herr Blome felt that the important
factors for success were nesting
material in which they can excavate,
thus stimulating breeding, and maintaining the nest at 30°C (86°F). Before
attempting to breed these birds in outdoor aviaries, an answer would have to
be found to the problem of the abrupt
change in temperature experienced by
young emerging from a heated nest
into an unheated aviary.

In Switzerland, E. Zurcher of Oster-
mundigen was successful in breeding
this species in 1976, after three successive years in which young were
hatched but died. In January 1976, two
chicks were hatched; they had light
rose-coloured down. After ten days,
the male shared the duty of feeding the
young. At 17 days, their eyes were
open. At 25 days, green feathers were
appearing on the wings and they
weighed 28 and 32 g (1 and 1⅛ oz). The
older, a female, left the nest at 50 days.
The youngest was a male.

Emil Zurcher attributed his success
to the fact that the female was able to
excavate the nest and that the temperature inside was maintained at 26°C
(78°F). The female was a keen bather,
thus the eggs were moistened by her.
The temperature of the cage was kept
at a minimum of 20°C (68°F).

The only mutation of the Red-faced
Lovebird recorded to date is a Lutino,
in a European collection.

Peach-faced Lovebirds (*Agapornis roseicollis*).

Peach-faced (Rosy-faced) Lovebird
A. roseicollis roseicollis
Description: This is perhaps the best
known member of the genus. It is immediately recognised by the salmon
pink facial area which extends from
the lores, cheeks and throat to the
upper breast.

The rump, also the upper tail
coverts, are bright blue and the tail
feathers have a subterminal band of
black, and red patches at the base. The
remainder of the plumage is green.

The bill is light horn-coloured and
the iris is dark brown. Length: 15 cm
(6 in). Plumage of the sexes is alike.
Weight: 55 g (1⁹⁄₁₀ oz).

Immature birds have paler pink
faces and the plumage has a softer
appearance. The upper part of the
upper mandible is blackish.
Range/Habitat: The nominate race is
found in south-west Africa, usually in
dry country within the vicinity of
water. It is seen in small flocks which
congregate to become hundreds where
there is an abundance of food. They
eat mainly seeds, berries and grain.

A. r. catumbella
Description: The head is deeper pink

and the plumage is brighter overall.
Range/Habitat: This subspecies inhabits southern Angola.

Aviculture: More mutations have been bred and established in the Peach-faced Lovebird than in any other parrot excluding the Budgerigar. The best known is the Pastel Blue, which would be better termed Dilute Blue. Its pastel shades are extremely attractive: the body is sea-green and the facial area palest peach. The rump is blue. This is a recessive mutation. It originated from a pair owned by a Dutch breeder, P. Habats, in 1963, when two of the five young were Pastel Blue. This mutation is among the most common of all Lovebird varieties.

The Pied Peach-face has the plumage broken with areas of yellow. It is dominant in its manner of inheritance. One strain probably originated in California in the 1960s and another was evolved from a wild-caught bird by South African aviculturists.

The 'Golden Cherry' mutation originated in Japan. It is a recessive Yellow (rarely golden) with dilute blue rump, pink face and white primaries. It occurred in the aviaries of Masuru Iwata in 1954. Most of those imported into Europe were weak birds, probably as a result of continued in-breeding.

The Lutino mutation (sex-linked) is particularly beautiful for the peach facial colouring contrasts with the bright yellow of the rest of the plumage. It probably originated in the USA in the 1970s.

The Olive can be compared with the Olive Green Budgerigar in that it has two genes for the dark factor. It originated in Australia and is now well established.

More than one mutation can be combined in one bird. As in Budgerigars, the Pied mutation can be combined with Normal (in which the plumage will have areas of bright yellow) or with the Blue to give Pied with pale yellow.

The Olive can be used to produce a greyish blue bird with a grey rump when paired with a Blue. When a Blue is paired with a Dark Green, a dark blue bird with a deep blue rump is produced.

The Orange-faced mutation appeared in the aviaries of well-known California Lovebird breeder, John A. Biggs Snr, in 1980. In 1981, this bird was proved to be split for Blue. In 1982, the first Orange-faced young were bred from it.

A mutation known as Buttermilk results when a Yellow and a Blue are combined in one bird. Visually the Buttermilk is pale yellow with the face pale pink and the rump pale blue. A version whose colouration is diluted even further is produced when the factors for Blue and Lutino are combined in one bird.

Birds suffused with red in varying degrees, or with a few red feathers in their plumage, are not uncommon. One breeder produced birds with a red spot on the nape and others with red-laced wing feathers, but this colouration was not retained beyond one year. Other birds produced have retained red markings on the body and wings. Jim Hayward has bred two generations.

One of the more recent mutations is the White-faced.

In its natural habitat the Peach-faced Lovebird is a successful species, partly because it will utilise any nesting site, whether it is a hole in a building or the nest of a weaver. Holes with hard surfaces will be packed with nesting material, whereas in a weaver's nest less material is necessary. In captivity, plenty of fresh twigs should be provided, as small strips of bark are a favourite component of the nest. These are tucked into the ruffled feathers of the rump and back which are then sleeked into position to hold the bark. It is more difficult for a Lovebird to carry dry bark in this manner. Females which have been 'paired' have been known to carry nesting material on occasions but this behaviour has not been recorded in two males kept together, so presumably it is stimulated by watching the female.

Four or five eggs form the usual clutch; the incubation period is 23 days. Newly hatched chicks have dense reddish down until the age of about ten days, when it is replaced by a second down, which is dark grey. The young leave the nest at about six weeks of age.

It is a pity that the Peach-faced Lovebird is not a suitable subject for colony breeding for it is one of the prettiest when seen in an aviary; it is also one of the most spiteful and not to be trusted with other birds, whether of its own species or widely differing ones such as finches.

One advantage is the fact that it is a ready breeder and attractively coloured, but it is most difficult to sex and, of all the Lovebirds, it has the loudest and harshest voice. It can, however, be considered as quite suitable for the beginner.

There may be fanciers who would not agree with the maxim that this species is not suitable for colony breeding but I feel that it is better to make this suggestion for the sake of the beginner; the more experienced breeder will make his own decision. At the Tropical Bird Gardens, Rode, Somerset, there is a successful colony aviary of this species but all the occupants are the offspring of six original birds – no newcomers have ever been added – and this, feels Donald Risdon, the owner, is probably the reason why fighting does not occur.

Abyssinian (Black-winged) Lovebird
A. taranta
Description: This bird has two distinct advantages from the aviculturist's point of view – it can be sexed at a glance and it has a quieter voice than the other Lovebirds, with the exception of the Red-faced. Additionally it becomes steady and usually shows a greater degree of intelligence than other Lovebirds. Sometimes called the Black-winged Lovebird, this name is appropriate only for the male which has the under wing coverts and the flight feathers black. It is more readily distinguished by the red forehead and lores, also by the narrow line of red feathers encircling the eyes. The tail is barred with black and the rest of the plumage is green. The bill is red and the iris dark brown. The female has no red in the plumage and her under wing coverts are green; according to Forshaw (1973) they are sometimes marked with black. Length: about 17 cm ($6\frac{1}{2}$ in). Weight: M 44 g ($1\frac{1}{2}$ oz); F 53 g ($1\frac{4}{5}$ oz).

Immature birds resemble the female except for the fact that males have the under wing coverts black. The bill is

Abyssinian Lovebirds (*Agapornis taranta*) – male left, female right.

dusky yellow with black markings at the base. Adult plumage is assumed at the first moult at about four months.

In 1977 I saw a Cinnamon which had been bred that year. Possibly it was a descendant of a wild-caught male owned by George A. Smith which had cinnamon flight feathers and golden feathers on the head and body. It moulted out to differ from the usual bird in having a paler shade of red on the face, paler green body plumage and pale brown, not black, flight feathers. Ten males were bred from this bird, all of usual colouration.

Range/Habitat: The Abyssinian Lovebird inhabits the highlands of Ethiopia in the forested plateaux between 1,300 and 3,200 m (4,300–10,500 ft). It is found in small groups. Figs are a favourite food and the birds move to lower altitudes to feed on them. They also feed on the berries of juniper, which have a high Vitamin B content. At Cornell University, Professor Dilger found that a number of his Abyssinian Lovebirds were suffering from Vitamin B deficiency and concluded that they may have a particular need for this vitamin.

Aviculture: This species was first imported into Europe in the early years of the twentieth century; in Germany it was first seen in 1906 and H. Astley imported the first pair into Britain in 1909. From that time until 1923, it was rarely imported, then large consignments regularly appeared. It is said to have been bred in Austria in 1906 but the first breedings in Britain took place much later, in 1925. In the USA, F. Rudkin was the first breeder in 1930. Unfortunately, it has not been bred sufficiently often in captivity for aviary-bred strains to be established; thus, when imports cease it quickly becomes expensive.

Unsuitable nesting accommodation may be the reason why successes are relatively few, according to George A. Smith (1978c). This species does not fill the nest with material, thus reducing the dimensions of the interior, but uses 'less than a teaspoonful of bits and pieces, including feathers'. These are carried into the nest in the body feathers. The female may remove feathers from her mate for this purpose, also from her brood patch. George Smith's birds chose to nest in the smallest boxes provided, with internal dimensions of 7 or 8 cm (about 3 in) square.

Abyssinian Lovebirds are highland birds, found where freezing temperatures at night are common, thus the habit of roosting in a nest is an instinctive one; no doubt they would find the smallest possible hole for its additional warmth and protection.

Nest sites are invariably chosen by the female; birds of the 'gentler' sex (and, in Lovebirds, the dominant one) are extremely territorial over their nest-box, defending it vigorously; thus this species should not be kept on the colony system, as serious fighting between females is almost certain to occur. Males never join in these skirmishes and certainly would not fight a female which is by far the stronger sex; in fact, a female provides sanctuary for her mate from attack by other males. George Smith has found that a female is practically invincible inside her nest, but outside it, the further she moves from it the more this invincibility diminishes. At approximately a metre away from their nests, all females are equal.

In this species, the clutch numbers three or four eggs and the incubation period is 24 days. On hatching, the chicks have thick, short white down. Growth rate is slow and the eyes do not open until they are between two and three weeks old.

Young birds leave the nest when they are in the region of seven weeks old. Adults appear to be quite tolerant towards their young; a female belonging to George Smith incubated three eggs while the two nine-month old males from the previous nest were still with the pair and sharing the nest-box at night. Once the chicks had hatched the young males helped to feed them.

It would seem that this species is not a continuous nester, for it seldom proves double-brooded. A point of interest, which may be nothing more than coincidence, was recorded by one breeder. His pair showed no desire to breed when housed next to an aviary containing four pairs of Peach-faced Lovebirds yet nested immediately they were removed to a 1.2 m (4 ft) long flight inside a birdroom. The female laid four eggs in a box 25 cm (10 in) square; all hatched and three chicks were reared. The diet included dried figs. Generally speaking this species will sample a wider variety of foods than other Lovebirds.

Masked Lovebird (*Agapornis personata personata*).

Black-collared (or Swinderen's and incorrectly Swindern's) Lovebird
A. swinderniana swinderniana
Description: The Black-collared Lovebird is small, about 13 cm (5 in), with a black line around the hind neck. A yellow band below this merges into the yellow breast. Rump and lower back are mauvish blue; there is a black sub-terminal band on the tail and some orange on the outer tail feathers. Outer webs of the flight feathers are black. The remainder of the plumage is green. The bill is black and, uniquely for a Lovebird, the iris is said to be yellow. The sexes are alike.

Immature birds lack the black collar and have only a few black feathers on the neck. The bill is pale grey marked with black at the base.

In the subspecies Zenker's Lovebird (*A. s. zenkeri*), a reddish brown collar replaces the yellow below the black collar.

Range/Habitat: Black-collared Lovebirds are found in Liberia, Ghana and possibly in the Ivory Coast; *zenkeri* inhabits Cameroon and Gabon east to the Central African Republic and the Congo; *emini* (which has less extensive reddish brown markings on the neck and head) is found from central Congo to western Uganda.

This species inhabits lowland evergreen forest; it is sometimes found in deciduous forests. Figs would appear to form the principal part of its diet. The much-quoted experiences of the Belgian missionary, Father Hutsbout, are that he tried mixing millet seed with wild figs – but the Lovebirds would not sample millet or even grass seed. They did nibble at palm nuts and peanuts but died after three or four days if not given figs. Due to their very particular feeding habits it has proved impossible to keep alive on the few occasions that this has been attempted.

Masked (or White Eye-ring) Lovebird
A. personata
The Masked, Fischer's, Black-cheeked and Nyasa Lovebirds which comprise this species are distinguished by the prominent area of white skin surrounding the eye and, though in the past they have been treated as separate species, there is little justification for such an approach as the differences lie rather in their appearance than in their behaviour.

It is interesting to note that, where feral populations of Fischer's and Masked Lovebirds have met in one area in Africa, hybridisation has occurred.

Masked Lovebird
A. personata personata

Description: The Masked Lovebird is immediately recognised by its bright yellow breast; this colour extends to the hind neck. The head is black or blackish, which sets off the red beak and prominent white eye ring. Upper tail coverts are pale blue and under wing coverts greyish blue and green. The tail is barred with black at the base and near the tip and marked with orange-yellow. The rest of the plumage is green. Length: 15 cm (6 in). Weight: M 50 g (1¾ oz); F 56 g (2 oz).

Immature birds are duller than adults; the upper mandible is marked with black at the base.

Range/Habitat: The nominate race inhabits Tanzania, being found on inland plateaux and at altitudes between 1,100 and 1,700 m (3,600 and 5,600 ft). It has been introduced to Nairobi, Kenya, and Dar-es-Salaam. In the northern half of its range, it approaches within about 50 km (30 miles) of the area inhabited by Fischer's Lovebird. It feeds mainly on seeds and a good food supply attracts large flocks. These birds can be a serious nuisance to farmers, for they attack growing millet and other cereals.

Aviculture: Several mutations of the Masked Lovebird have been established, the best known of which is the Blue. Those in Europe, and perhaps also those bred in the USA, originated from a single male imported by the London dealer, Chapman, in 1927. (A superb colour plate of this bird appeared in *Avicultural* Magazine, February 1928). Some Blue mutations are extremely beautiful – but there is nothing exceptional about the Blue Masked, the appearance of which is spoilt by the greyish white area of the collar and upper breast (which is yellow in the normal bird). Also, the beak is horn-coloured, so there is no bright contrast with the plumage. The head is black and the rest of the plumage is blue.

The bird imported by Chapman was purchased by London Zoo. By 1929 it had produced ten youngsters and, within a couple of years, the first Blue was bred when these youngsters were paired together. In 1935, a French aviculturist, M.

Morin, produced Blues from birds imported by Chapman which must have been split for Blue. In California, the first Blue was produced by Cross in 1932. The Blues there bred so well that by 1945 they were described as 'commonplace in California' whereas in Britain, according to A. A. Prestwich, 'only a few scattered birds' were left. (It is easier to breed Lovebirds in a warm climate.)

The Blue mutation is recessive in its manner of inheritance, as is the Yellow. The latter may have originated in California; Yellows bred by Mr Scheu in 1935 would appear to be the first recorded. This is a Dilute mutation, rather than one in which the plumage is bright yellow. The Yellow mutation also occurred in Japan and was established there, as well. It has never been popular, probably because of its dull colours.

When Blue and Yellow mutations are in existence, it is only a matter of time before the White mutation is established. However, in the Masked it is not particularly attractive as the blackish mask is retained, the body colour is off-white and the tail coverts are pale blue. The eyes are dark.

In 1971 a British breeder wrote to me that he had reared Blues with white flights, also Whites, from a pair of Blues.

The Masked Lovebird is extremely willing to breed in captivity, once one has overcome the problem of finding true pairs. Watching their behaviour is the most reliable guide for it is not usual – although not unknown – for a female to feed a male, and normally only the female carries material into the nest. If a group of birds are obtained, they should be marked in some way so that when they eventually form pairs, each bird's mate can be identified and surplus true pairs sold, if necessary. Probably the best way is to mark their yellow breast feathers with a felt-tipped pen.

The Masked usually lays four or five eggs but sometimes as many as eight. Chicks have dense reddish down on hatching unless they are of the Blue mutation, in which case the down is pinkish white. They leave the nest at about six weeks old.

Black-cheeked Lovebird
A. p. nigrigenis

Description: The Black-cheeked Lovebird is slightly smaller than the Masked, measuring about 14 cm (5½ in) and it lacks the yellow markings on breast and neck. The forehead is brown and the cheeks are brownish black. The throat and a small area of the upper breast are orange. The flanks are tinged with yellow and the central area is yellowish. Primaries are bluish. The four outer tail feathers have a patch of red. The rest of the plumage is green, darker above and olive green on the neck. The bill is red and the eye is encircled with white skin.

Immature birds differ only in the duller plumage.

Range/Habitat: The range of the Black-cheeked Lovebird is a restricted one in south-western Zambia along the Zambesi valley.

Black-cheeked Lovebird (*Agapornis personata nigrigenis*).

Aviculture: This bird was discovered only in 1904 by Dr A. H. B. Kirkman and three years later the first reached Europe. The first to be imported went to Germany and five of these reached Britain. They were obtained by two well known aviculturists, Hubert Astley and Reginald Phillipps. After being in Phillipps' possession for only two weeks, two of the three birds showed signs of wanting to nest. They were placed in a large box cage which was fitted with a nesting log in a screened corner. After a month, they were transferred to an outdoor aviary where they began to gather wood chips, hay, wheat and millet spray stalks as nesting material. Nearly a month later, four eggs were laid, all of which hatched. The young birds left the nest between August 22 and 28 and the female laid the first egg of the second clutch on about August 30. Three years later, Phillipps had third generation young and a total of over 20 Black-cheeks. He was not alone in finding this species prolific. Mathias recorded (1909) that 15 young were produced by his two pairs. Some of his hens started to lay when only four months old.

By this time, large numbers had reached Europe; perhaps it was for this reason that few aviculturists built up aviary-bred strains for when in 1926 Chapman imported these birds, their numbers in British aviaries were low. At the present time, a few aviculturists are breeding small numbers. In Sweden, however, this species is very well established.

In *Lovebirds and Parrotlets*, L. P. Luke wrote that he regarded the Black-cheeked Lovebird as being 'probably the most consistent breeder of the group' and Lord Tavistock (1928a) stated:

> Were it not for the fact that the eggs are apt to hatch badly in the unnaturally dry environment of a bird room or aviary shelter, the Black-cheeked Lovebird would exceed the Budgerigar in prolificacy, for, while the Budgerigar is apt to be a slow starter in a new home, no pair of these Lovebirds ever hesitated to endeavour to reproduce their species at the earliest possible moment with the least possible encouragement.

While Lord Tavistock's assessment might have slightly exaggerated the case, reports from breeders confirmed that it was very prolific and it is something less than a tribute to aviculturists that this species has not been established in captivity. Indeed, avicultural literature for the second half of this century, unlike that for the first half, contains scarcely a mention of it. It is therefore not surprising that no mutations have been reported.

Among the birds received by Chapman in 1926 were Black-cheeked and Nyasa Lovebirds, plus some which were said to be wild hybrids between the two. In captivity, the Black-cheeked has hybridised with the Peach-faced, Fischer's, Masked and Nyasa, according to various reports. An amazing claim by a Mrs Higginbotham was that she had bred four hybrids between a Black-cheeked Lovebird and a Budgerigar, reported in *Bird Notes* (1911:211) and, for this breeding, received the medal of the Foreign Bird Club.

Fischer's Lovebird
A. p. fischeri

Description: This bird is immediately distinguished from the Nyasa Lovebird by the blue rump and upper tail coverts. It has the forehead, cheeks and throat orange-red and the rest of the head dull green; the upper breast and a collar around the neck are yellow. The outer tail feathers are tipped with blue. The statement by Forshaw (1973) that the upper tail coverts are 'washed with pale blue', thus rendering it likely to confusion with the Nyasa Lovebird, is misleading. The bill is bright red and the bare white eye ring is present. Length: 14 cm (5½ to 6 in). Immature birds are duller than adults, especially on the face. The base of the upper mandible is blackish. Weight: M 49 g (1¾ oz); F 53 g (1⅘ oz).

Range/Habitat: Fischer's Lovebird inhabits Tanzania, in the south-east of Lake Victoria and southwards. Its range is not extensive and it is found mainly on inland plateaux where there are long periods of drought.

Thus it nests after the rains. Natural barriers of vegetation separate it from its relative – the Masked Lovebird.

Aviculture: Several mutations have occurred in captivity but none of these is as well known as the most popular mutations of the Masked and Peach-faced.

The first to occur was probably the Lutino. It originated in Toulouse, France, in the aviaries of M. A. Blanchard. This mutation has also been bred in the Netherlands by J. Postema, according to a report in *Avicultural Magazine* p. 215 (1972).

The Blue is said to be of a shade different from the Blue Masked and has the head pale grey. It is autosomal recessive in its manner of inheritance, like all Blues. It first occurred in the aviaries of Ronald Horsham in South Africa after he had separated and in-bred from birds which had some orange feathers on the breast. In one nest, there were three Blues and one Normal, in the late 1950s. At about the same time, the mutation also occurred in California. After five generations of in-breeding, Dr F. B. Warford bred one Blue.

The Yellow mutation (in effect a Dilute Green, with the breast yellow) occurred first in California, in the collection of David West, a well known aviculturist, and in the collection of Herr Heiser in Germany in the 1950s. It, too, is an autosomal recessive, and is now being bred in Europe.

The Albino Fischer's was first bred in California in 1983 by Lee Horton and Roland Dubuc (who also produced, in 1976, the first Albino Peach-faced). Albino chicks can be recognised in the nest by their white down and red eyes.

A very beautiful mutation is the Black-eyed Yellow which originated in Natal in 1980 in the aviaries of Willie Evans. Body plumage is yellow and the orange head and throat are retained.

Other mutations which have occurred but which are not yet established, are the Cinnamon, Dilute Blue and White. Pieds are occasionally bred.

Fischer's Lovebird (*Agapornis personata fischeri*).

The Fischer's Lovebird is extremely free-breeding in captivity; in *Guide to Lovebirds and Parrotlets*, E. N. T. Vane wrote:

... Fischer's are too easy. This, in fact, may be the very cause of their undoing. They seem over-eager to reproduce their kind. Many beginners think, therefore, once they have had a good season, that they are scarcely worth cultivating as they will not pay for their keep.

While this could have been the reason for the downfall of the Black-cheeked, it did not occur with the Fischer's which is numerous in aviaries all over the world.

In Britain, strains of Fischer's Lovebirds were kept going throughout the war years because they readily accepted substitute diets.

One breeder fed his on the seeds of wild weeds, cereals and stale bread.

Fischer's have been used to rear the young of totally different species. In one case, three eggs from a Golden-mantled Rosella were placed under a Fischer's. All three hatched; one chick died when six days old but the other two were reared. The Lovebirds, however, stopped feeding them when they emerged from the nest and they realised what strange young they had fostered. The Rosellas were then hand-fed until they were feeding on their own.

Fischer's Lovebirds, also Nyasas, are very prone to plucking their young in the nest. It sometimes helps to install two nest-boxes in the aviary so that the female can lay the next clutch in the second box and is therefore less likely to pluck the young in her anxiety to have them leave the nest.

Fischer's were first imported into Europe in 1926. Probably the first breeder in Britain was Herbert Whitley at Paignton; he had young leave the nest in November 1926.

Nyasa Lovebird
A. p. lilianae
Named in honour of Miss Lilian Sclater, it was occasionally known as Lilian's Lovebird.
Description: The Nyasa differs from the Fischer's in its slightly smaller size, being about 13 cm (5¼ in), and in the green upper tail coverts. The colour on the head is less extensive than in the Fischer's, the back of the head being yellowish green. Weight: M 38 g (1⅖ oz); F 43 g (1½ oz).

Immature birds are duller than adults, often with a blackish tinge to the cheeks.

Range/Habitat: This Lovebird is found in the Zambesi and Luangwa valleys, also in southern Tanzania and north-eastern Mozambique through Malawi and eastern Zambia to northern Zimbabwe.

Aviculture: It was not described until 1894; its presence was known 30 years earlier when it was assumed to be the Peach-faced. In 1926, when the first consignment reached Britain, the same mistake was made, until the birds were identified by a leading aviculturist, David Seth-Smith. It is easy to visualise them being mistaken for Fischer's Lovebirds but they are very different indeed from the Peach-faced.

As with the Black-cheeked, at first they proved extremely prolific; indeed, the medal of the Avicultural Society, presented for the first breeding, went to Captain Stokes. A young bird left the nest on May 18, 1926. As the first consignment did not reach Britain until February 11, this must surely have established some sort of record. In France, Madame Lécallier produced 40 young from 14 birds in 1926. However, during the war, the Nyasa almost died out in British aviaries and, when a census was taken in 1947, only five were counted.

In *Guide to Lovebirds and Parrotlets*, E. N. T. Vane wrote of this species:

> In temperament, they are much more tolerant of each other's company in captivity than other *Agapornis*. If a colony is gradually built up, the older birds seem to agree well together, and what is more, they keep the younger ones in order, more or less. There may be occasional squabbles when selection of mates is under consideration,

Nyasa Lovebird (*Agapornis personata lilianae*).

but it seldom develops into anything serious.

Unfortunately, very few aviculturists will have the opportunity to discover the truth of this as these birds are now rare in captivity in most countries, although established in Sweden and in California and especially in New Zealand where they have been colony bred for many years. There is more chance of establishing it in a warm climate as it is often a winter breeder.

The only mutation which has occurred to date in the Nyasa Lovebird is the Lutino. It differs from most Lutino mutations in being autosomal recessive, not sex-linked. It was reported as long ago as 1930 in Australia and some Lutinos were exported to Britain during the same decade. E. N. T. Vane obtained two of these and slowly built up a strain of Lutino Nyasas; however, by the end of World War II, only a single Lutino remained. In 1953, he obtained a male from the collection of the late Duke of Bedford and in two years produced 14 young. When one of these split Lutino youngsters was paired to its father, three Lutinos were produced, only one of which reached maturity. However, on Mr Vane's death these birds must have been separated and the strain lost. In the late 1960s, I saw a single bird in the collection of A. V. Marques and this was perhaps the last to be seen in Britain. At the time of writing, there are a few Lutino Nyasas in Europe, which have originated from Australian-bred birds. This mutation is also being bred at Houston Zoo in Texas. It is very beautiful for the pink face contrasts pleasingly with the golden plumage.

Guy R. Townsend of Mtoroshanga, Zimbabwe, has two aviaries of Nyasa Lovebirds which breed prolifically throughout the year. Young are removed to cages on the floor of the flight as soon as they leave the nest; the parents feed them through the bars. If left in the flight, they would be attacked by the adults with fatal results.

18
African Parrots

Africa is the largest continent in which parrots are found but contains the smallest numbers of species and from only four genera. In terms of numbers kept by aviculturists, only the Lovebirds are numerous and these warrant a separate chapter. Of the remainder, the Grey Parrot, the only member of the genus *Psittacus*, has the distinction of being the best known of all parrots (except in Australia and New Zealand where it is almost unknown). All the other species discussed in this chapter belong to the genus *Poicephalus*. The African Ringneck Parrakeet is the only *Psittacula* found in Africa and, as its needs are exactly the same as those of the Indian Ringneck, it is included in the chapter on Asiatic Parrakeets.

With the exception of the largest *Poicephalus* (the Cape Parrot), which is in certain aspects of voice and behaviour reminiscent of the Grey, in appearance *Psittacus* and *Poicephalus* are very different. The care and feeding of both genera are, however, the same.

Feeding: All these birds should be offered sunflower seed, peanuts and pine nuts, also hemp in moderation. The Cape Parrot, unlike most parrots other than macaws, is capable of cracking walnuts; large nuts given to the other species must, of course, be cracked first. Jardine's and Cape Parrots also enjoy cracking the stones of plums, cherries and peaches and removing the kernel to eat. *Poicephalus* and Greys like millet sprays and should also be offered the usual small seeds in loose form; however, the larger species may ignore these. Canary seed and white or panicum millet should be offered daily to small birds such as Senegal Parrots.

Many Greys are most reluctant to eat greenfood and fruit but one must persevere with them. This is especially true when birds are rearing young, when they may suddenly develop a taste for foods previously refused. A pair of Meyer's Parrots, for example, developed an insatiable appetite for peanuts. They were also provided with sprouting seed and bread and milk. Another pair took soaked oats, sweet apple, greenfood, peanuts and wholewheat bread while rearing young. A varied diet of boiled potato and carrot, stale bread soaked in sweetened milk and spinach beet and apple were taken by one pair of Senegal Parrots with young. Similarly, a pair of Greys consumed a bucketful of greenfood, chickweed and groundsel daily. All seed offered was soaked; safflower and hemp were favoured and sunflower, millet, wheat and oats were also eaten. Little interest was shown in apple or peanuts after the chicks hatched.

Another pair refused soaked seed after their chick was four weeks old. Hemp was their favourite seed and lettuce was eaten ravenously, a whole lettuce being devoured every two or three days. Chicken bones were relished and a little white fish was eaten.

Accommodation: Even the small species of African parrots can prove very destructive to wood; it is therefore advisable to cover the aviary framework with metal strips and to build the shelter of an indestructible material such as concrete blocks or reconstituted stone. Their need to gnaw should not be thwarted and fresh branches from trees should be provided as often as possible.

$1 \times \frac{1}{2}$ in welded mesh is ideal for all species; in no circumstances should $\frac{1}{2}$ in mesh wire netting be used; birds the size of Jardine's Parrot and above can crush this as easily as paper and the smaller species could destroy it if so inclined.

While they will undoubtedly breed in smaller aviaries, the minimum sizes suggested, including an enclosed shelter, are as follows:

Meyer's, Rüppell's and Senegal: 300×90 cm (10×3 ft) $\times 180$ cm (6 ft) high.

Jardine's, Cape and Grey: 360×120 cm (12×4 ft) $\times 180$ cm (6 ft) high.

If space and finances allow, 4.2 m (14 ft) flights will be appreciated by all these species.

Senegal Parrots have been bred in cages indoors; one cage used with success measured 45×60 cm (18×24 in) $\times 120$ cm (48 in) high. In another instance, a pair of Senegal Parrots reared young in a London flat next to a television set and yet another pair reared a chick in an indoor cage measuring only 33 cm (12 in) square and 56 cm (22 in) high.

Unless the birds are reasonably tame and many adults are not, generous aviaries 6 m (20 ft) long are not to be recommended, as the birds are less likely to become steady than when housed in a smaller aviary. Each pair should have an enclosure to itself and although a number of pairs will live together perfectly amicably out of the breeding season, they cannot be expected to do so when they have eggs or young.

Psittacus
Psittacus

The single member of this genus, the Grey Parrot, is the best known of the true parrots in most countries of the world and is renowned for its ability to mimic. The short, square red tail and the very large area of bare skin surrounding the eye distinguish it from all other parrots.

Grey Parrot
P. erithacus erithacus

Description: This bird has a simple colour scheme: the body plumage is grey, but this varies in shade from region to region and males are usually darker than females. The feathers of the head and neck are margined with very pale grey: the rump is so pale a grey as to be almost white, and the tail and adjacent tail coverts are scarlet. The beak is black and the iris is pale yellow. The feet are dark grey and the bare skin surrounding the eye is white. Length: 33 cm (13 in). Weight: about 320 g (11 $\frac{3}{10}$ oz).

Immature birds have the tail darker red and the iris dark grey.

Several Albino Grey Parrots have been described, in which the tail is red, in brilliant contrast to the white plumage. The eyes are pinkish red and the feet and beak light coloured.

One occasionally sees Greys which have areas of pink feathering and very many birds have a few pink feathers scattered throughout the plumage. However, D. Seth-Smith (1921) noted that Jean Delacour had acquired a Grey which was entirely pink, apart from a few feathers in the body and the quills, which were grey. What must surely be the same bird was described in *Avicultural Magazine* (1922) as:

...like a flamingo, each feather being bright pink with a lighter pink edge. The

Grey Parrot (*Psittacus erithacus erithacus*).

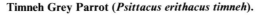

Timneh Grey Parrot (*Psittacus erithacus timneh*).

tail is crimson, the head light pink and white, the eyes and feet dark. She laid five eggs while with me last year. . . .

Some Greys with pink feathers in the plumage moult out normally.

Range/Habitat: The nominate race inhabits equatorial Africa from the south-eastern part of the Ivory Coast to western Kenya and northern Angola, the Congo and north-western Tanzania. Lowland forest is the major habitat of Grey Parrots. They are common in some areas and are even said to be extending their range in eastern Africa, while in other areas their numbers are decreasing due to habitat destruction. They are wary, seldom allowing a close approach. Their diet consists of seeds, fruits, berries and nuts, palm nuts being a favourite item.

P. e. timneh

Description: This race is very distinct having the upper mandible reddish, tipped with black, is slightly smaller and has the tail dull dark red.

Range/Habitat: Sierra Leone, southern Guinea, Liberia and the Ivory Coast is the range of *timneh*.

P. e. princeps

Description: The race *princeps* was separated on account of its darker plumage. However, it is virtually indistinguishable from the nominate race.

Range/Habitat: It is found on only two islands, in the Gulf of Guinea: S. Tomé and Príncipe. This race is classified as endangered and listed on Appendix I of CITES. However, Abbé R. de Naurois, who lived on Príncipe until 1973, did not consider it to be endangered. Much of the island had been deforested early in the twentieth century; deforestation had not been serious in recent years (de Naurois, pers. comm., 1983).

Aviculture: The Grey Parrot is renowned for its 'talking' ability; in mimicking the human voice, it has no rival among parrots. Not only can it acquire an extensive vocabulary of words, but it reproduces them with such accuracy of tone and accent that the teacher can be identified. The Grey Parrot, along with the Indian Hill Mynah (*Gracula religiosa*), and, to a lesser degree, certain

members of the crow family, are the best known 'talking' birds. Mynahs, which speak with great clarity, have the edge over Grey Parrots as talking birds, because they exhibit no signs of shyness, showing off their repertoire in strange places and for unknown people. A Grey will rarely oblige under such circumstances, being at its best when it is completely relaxed and in its own home.

Greys also learn to imitate the sounds around them, sometimes to the annoyance of members of the household who cannot distinguish between the ring of the telephone and the Grey's imitation. A bird in my possession would imitate to perfection the radio time signals and the squeaking of the door of a cooker. Many Greys are adept at whistling tunes, for whistling is part of their natural range of calls.

The Duke of Bedford (1930) recorded an instance of mimicry of sound and action. His aviaries were being dismantled for removal, involving 'much hammering on wood, wire and corrugated iron constantly going on, as the carpenters engage in their work'. He was surprised to hear, issuing from the aviary containing his Grey Parrots:

> . . . the typical sounds of carpentering proceeding therefrom, though no human agent was in view. Looking inside I saw the Parrot with her head bent right over, giving her perch five or six hard taps with the culmen of her beak, then turning to one side and repeating the action on the wire and iron to produce the necessary variation in sound. The time and rhythm were perfect in each case!

Greys are among the most perceptive and intelligent of birds but many are also rather sensitive and highly strung and a relatively small proportion become very tame. However, this is in many cases the fault of the owner as much depends on his or her patience and the amount of time devoted to the bird, as well as its age on acquisition. Nevertheless, there can never have been so many cherished pets among parrots as Greys. They can be the most delightful companions imaginable and their intelligence is a constant source of wonder.

No one should consider keeping one of these birds unless he or she is able to devote much time to it every day. This,

of course, applies to all tame parrots but a bored or neglected Grey will soon resort to feather plucking (see Chapter 2, Management) which is extremely difficult or impossible to cure. Under the same circumstances, Amazon Parrots, for example, rarely remove their feathers. The vast majority of parrots which remove their feathers are Greys, macaws and cockatoos and I feel it is significant that this problem occurs most frequently in the most intelligent species.

Until comparatively recently, most of the Greys exported from Africa were destined to become pets, only those which proved impossible to tame going to aviculturists. In the latter category are birds known as 'growlers'. Their fear of people is so great that whenever someone approaches their cage, they make a continuous growling sound. It is almost impossible to tame adult birds which are growlers and as it causes such birds great stress to be closely confined, they are suitable only for aviaries. Young growlers can be tamed but it is a long process and one which requires long suffering patience. The average person does not have the ability or patience to tame such a bird and should not allow a dealer to persuade him or her otherwise.

From the mid-1970s the number of Greys and other parrots exported from their native countries decreased greatly, so that the demand for young Greys as pets could not be met, with the inevitable result that the prices of these birds and other parrots reached record peaks.

The number of young bred increases annually but remains comparatively small. There is scope here for the aviculturist prepared to specialise. One of the main difficulties in breeding Greys, i.e. obtaining a true pair, has been removed with the advent of surgical sexing. In the days before this procedure was known, I placed five birds in an aviary measuring 3.6 × 1.2 m (12 × 4 ft) × 1.8 m (6 ft) high. For several years no pair formation occurred but on the introduction of what later proved to be a male, he immediately selected one of the females, and not long after she laid. The other birds, two of which later proved to be a true pair, were later removed – but their removal should have occurred before the female laid. It may have been their presence which caused the incubating female to leave the eggs too often, thus resulting in addled eggs. In five years, she produced a number of clutches (laying, in one season, before and after the moult) but did not hatch a chick until July 1979, not long after being moved to a smaller aviary. The male preferred sweet foods, feeding the chick on banana, orange and sponge cake with nectar; bread and milk and cheese were also taken.

The aviculturist with several birds has a fair chance of eventually being able to supply the pet market with a useful number of birds annually. The record produced by one pair of Greys must surely be that held by the late Mrs Velma Hart of Long Beach, California, a renowned breeder of parrots. Her pair produced 87 chicks between 1962 and 1974. This number was, of course, achieved by removing the young for hand-rearing, thus inducing the female to lay again.

Breeders should note the advice which Mrs Hart wrote to me:

Those who intend to breed parrots must have patience. The birds must be given good food and privacy – and nature seems to take care of the rest. For African Greys, I provide nest-boxes 31 cm (12 in) square and 61 cm (2 ft) deep.

Many people cannot wait for the birds to breed. They move them or change the nest. They try to improve things but only upset the birds and delay them nesting. I never move nest-boxes out after the breeding season. The nest is cleaned and fresh shavings are placed inside. The box is left in place throughout the year for the birds when they want to breed.

I feel that this is especially good advice where Greys are concerned because these birds are very suspicious and dislike change of any kind.

One of the problems in introducing two Greys as a potential breeding pair is that, even though they may be of the opposite sex, they will not necessarily prove compatible. Some of the larger parrots are extremely discriminating over the choice of a mate.

A guide to sexing these birds was offered by E. J. Boosey, who received the Avicultural Society's medal for the first breeding of this species in Britain, in 1945. He suggested that in the

female the head feathers are usually ruffled, whereas they are usually sleek and flat in the male; that the male's eyes appear round and wide open and the female's are slit-eyed; that the female's beak leaves the skull at a slightly outward angle.

Courtship behaviour in Grey Parrots consists mainly of head pumping; sometimes they will run along the perch with wings lowered, to display the red tail, and head down. When they come into breeding condition, the temperament of tame birds in aviaries can alter drastically towards their owner.

Greys lay three or four, more rarely five, eggs, with an interval of two or three days between the laying of each egg. The incubation period is 28 or 30 days.

The first youngster I bred commenced to sit in the nest entrance when aged about ten weeks; it left the nest at 12 weeks. Before it left, the male would spend long periods sitting on the nest-box perch, usually with an item of food in his foot, such as a piece of apple or millet spray. Evidently he was teaching the young bird how to feed as it was able to feed itself on its first day out of the nest.

The death of the male was a great and unexpected loss. It was some months before I was able to find a suitable replacement. He arrived when the lone female was sitting on eggs. She was so keen to breed that she laid despite the absence of a mate. As often happens with parrots which have been deprived of a companion, they were immediately compatible. Shortly after introduction they were seen locking beaks, a form of greeting I have observed only in Greys.

The pair produced chicks only eight weeks after being introduced. It was only then that the great worth of the previous male became apparent. He had fed the young. Neither bird of this pair fed the chicks. Also, initially, the new male was extremely nervous. Indeed, not until they had been together for four years was it possible to stand in front of the aviary and observe the birds. Previously they would enter the nest at first sight of anyone approaching.

To ensure their survival, all young from this pair are removed from the

nest on the day they hatch. Newly hatched Greys weigh 12 to 14 g ($\frac{2}{5}$–$\frac{1}{2}$ oz). They are among the most appealing of all parrot chicks. They are small balls of fluff, covered in dense white down which is longest on the upper parts. The bill is brown with a darker cutting edge and contrasting white egg tooth. The lower mandible is at first shovel-shaped and overlaps the upper mandible. The toenails are usually black. By the age of one week most of the white down has been lost and their appearances is less attractive.

Typical of the development of chicks is that of two hatched on August 31 and September 2. By September 12, most of the down had been lost. On one chick, the black pin points of feather tracts forming were just visible. They weighed 34 g and 37 g ($1\frac{2}{10}$ and $1\frac{3}{10}$ oz). By the following day, the ear opening was just apparent in the eldest chick, the size of a pin head. The egg tooth had almost disappeared in the eldest, which had the beak almost black. By September 19, the tip of the pink tongue had become black in the eldest chick; after several weeks the tongue was almost entirely black. The white second down was coming through. Weights were 70 g and 68 g ($2\frac{1}{2}$ and $2\frac{2}{5}$ oz). By September 20, the body of the eldest chick was grey with developing feather tracts, while the young one still had a pinkish appearance. Weights were 130 g and 115 g ($4\frac{3}{4}$ and 4 oz). By September 28, the lower mandible no longer had a shovel appearance; the egg tooth was still visible on close inspection. The second down was short, white, woolly and unevenly spaced. Within a few days, their nails were so sharp that they punctured the skin when handled.

By October 2, the head (except for the nape, one of the last areas to feather) of the eldest chick was grey with erupting feathers. In the youngest, head feathers were just starting to erupt. By October 6, the chicks weighed 230 g and 210 g ($8\frac{1}{10}$ and $7\frac{2}{5}$ oz). The red tail feathers were apparent by October 15. By October 23, the eldest chick's wings were fully feathered, except for some of the primaries which were still in their sheaths. The under parts were sparsely feathered. As the tail developed, the tip (the outer margins of the outer feathers and the area around the shaft in the central feathers) was dark grey. This colour is retained until the first moult and is a sure guide to immaturity. The rest of the tail is scarlet.

On October 25, pomegranate was offered and eaten enthusiastically, also soaked sunflower seed. Pear, apple and sweet corn were sampled but with little enthusiasm.

The eldest Grey was removed from the unheated brooder to a small parrot cage at the age of ten weeks. From being timid and reserved it suddenly became an attention-getter. After being fed it made it very clear that it wished to have its head scratched, seemingly hinting by performing this itself. When the obliging head-scratcher paused, it objected strongly. At this stage, it was still being fed every three or four hours. The youngest chick was much less mature; its slower rate of food assimilation may have been responsible for retarding its growth slightly.

The eldest chick flew for the first time when 80 days old. For the previous few days it had vigorously exercised its wings while feeding or playing on the table. It was starting to make muttering sounds. The youngest chick did not make its first flight until it was 99 days old. Its behavioural development was about four weeks behind that of its sibling.

Those young believed to be males are more assertive and, from an earlier age, have a tendency to strut about and show off. They are more inclined to nip at this stage; the believed females are far more gentle and affectionate. One chick weighed 330 g ($11\frac{1}{5}$ oz) when it took its first flight. The weight of two chicks peaked at 375 g and 410 g ($13\frac{1}{10}$ and $14\frac{1}{2}$ oz); fledging weights were 320 g and 360 g ($11\frac{3}{5}$ and $12\frac{7}{10}$ oz). Others weighed 290 g and 350 g ($10\frac{1}{5}$ and $12\frac{3}{5}$ oz) at fledging.

The earliest breeding record for this species is quoted by Buffon (*Histoire Naturelle des Oiseaux*, Vol VI). A pair belonging to a M. de la Pigeonière in France had reared young for five or six consecutive years in the early 1770s. Four eggs were invariably laid, one of which would be infertile.

The first success described in Britain took place in 1843. A nest of flannel was made for the female and put in a copper near a fireplace. She incubated

for exactly four weeks and one chick was hatched and reared (Workman, 1916). Since then Grey Parrots have been bred in many countries throughout the world but very, very few aviculturists have established aviary-bred strains. Females lay readily in captivity and this applies equally to caged pet birds as to those in aviaries.

The subspecies *timneh* has been bred, at Busch Gardens, Tampa, Florida, and by Tony Silva in Illinois, USA. K. W. Dalton of Worcestershire, in England, reared a youngster from a *timneh* male paired to a female of the nominate race. When it left the nest at the age of 13 weeks it had the reddish brown tail of the male parent. This race has also been bred at Vogelpark Walsrode, Germany. In 1977 a pair reared two young in a large mixed aviary of African parrots in the parrot house. Young have also been reared in Rostock Zoo, in East Germany.

The affection of Grey Parrot pairs is demonstrated by an incident concerning a pair of Greys which were regularly offered one or two sugar-coated chocolate drops each. The owner would call the incubating female out of the nest so that she did not miss this treat. However, when a chick hatched, a female failed to appear for her chocolate. Rather than eat his mate's share, the male carried one to the nest hole and passed it to the female.

The Grey has never hybridised with another species. *Poicephalus* appears to be its nearest relative and the Cape Parrot the only one which approaches it in size. It would be interesting to pair a Cape Parrot with a Grey. Fertile eggs from such a mating might show that the two genera are more closely related than is apparent at first.

Poicephalus
Poicephalus

There is no uniformity in size or colouration among the members of this genus. They range in length from about 22 cm (9 in) in the Meyer's Parrot to the huge-beaked Cape or Brown-necked Parrot which is mainly green with the head of most unusual

colouration and is almost as large as a Grey Parrot.

Poicephalus parrots make attractive aviary birds, if obtained young, and they also make excellent pets. The smaller species are especially suitable on account of their size and price, which is generally much less than that of Amazon parrots. It is only since about the late 1950s that they have regularly been kept in pairs for breeding purposes. Before this period, the Senegal was the only species freely available and was almost invariably kept as a pet. Thus there is much to learn about breeding the members of this genus, some of which have reared young in captivity only on rare occasions. There can occur marked sexual dimorphism, the female being the more brightly coloured bird in at least one species. In others, sexual dimorphism is slight or absent and the size of the beak, usually more massive in the male, may be the only hint of the sex.

Poicephalus parrots are not especially noisy when compared with other parrots of similar sizes. Included in the vocabulary of Cape and Jardine's Parrots are some most unusual and attractive sounds. A pair of Jardine's I kept were rather quiet, uttering an owl-like 'whoo' and I have found the Cape Parrot only occasionally noisy, and never in the irritating manner of, for example, Amazon Parrots.

Senegal Parrot
P. senegalus senegalus

Description: It has the head and face blackish grey; lower breast, abdomen and under tail coverts are bright yellow, deepening to orange at the centre of the abdomen. The tail and primaries are dark brown washed with olive green. The upper parts, thighs and a shield-shaped breast band are bright grass green. The iris is yellow. Length: 24 cm ($9\frac{1}{2}$ in). Brightness of colouration is no indication of sex. Weight: about 115 g (4 oz).

Immature birds have the breast pale yellow and are of a duller shade of green; the head is more brown and washed with olive. The iris is black, changing gradually to grey, then to greyish yellow. The beak is blackish grey in adult birds and brownish grey tinged with pink in young ones.

Senegal Parrot (*Poicephalus senegalus senegalus*).

Range/Habitat: The nominate race of the species is found from Senegal and Gambia to Guinea and southern Mali.

Open forest and savannah woodland are the main habitats of all races of Senegal Parrot. In some areas it is common; in others its numbers fluctuate according to the food available. It is observed singly, in pairs or small groups. Its flight, with full wing-beats, is said to be less swift than other *Poicephalus*. Favourite foods are figs and the seeds of various trees; it also eats buds, grain and fruits.

P. s. versteri
Description: It varies from the nominate race in having a red abdomen.
Range/Habitat: This race comes from the Ivory Coast and Ghana, ranging to western Nigeria.

P. s. mesotypus
Description: The green of the upper parts and breast is paler and extends further down than in the nominate race. The abdomen is orange.
Range/Habitat: This race occurs in eastern and north-eastern Nigeria, northern Cameroon and south-west Chad.

Aviculture: During the first part of the twentieth century the Senegal had a reputation as a pet *par excellence*, and of becoming exceptionally tame and learning to repeat a few words. Undoubtedly it is true that if one can obtain a young bird, it will make a delightful pet; however, wild birds caught as adults very seldom lose their fear of man and are suitable only as aviary birds. Like Greys, they will 'growl' when approached. Even with young birds, taming may be a long process requiring much patience and understanding – but, once tamed, a Senegal makes an ideal pet. Maud Knobel, former secretary of the Avicultural Society, had a Senegal which was her constant companion during a long illness. It would lie on her neck while she was in bed, remaining there for as long as she chose.

Another famous aviculturist, E. J. Boosey, founder of Keston Foreign Bird Farm, also had a greatly cherished Senegal. He obtained it when it was very young and it lived for 21 years. He wrote (1956):

> Polly was one of the tamest and sweetest things I have ever possessed. She would lie motionless on her back in my hand and would even allow me to put her head in my mouth. . . .

As it happens, Boosey's breeding of this species in 1957 was probably the first in Britain, if one discounts a claim for a breeding in 1886 which may or may not have been achieved. His pair was very shy and secretive, thus little could be recorded about the breeding. On fledging, the three young were calm and steady, in complete contrast to their parents. While rearing, they were fed on the usual seeds with additional hemp, plus boiled potato and carrot, bread and milk and apple and spinach beet. Boiled white fish was refused. The birds nested in a box which measured 25 cm (10 in) square and 60 cm (24 in) high.

Senegals lay three or four eggs which are incubated by the female for 28 days. Down colour of the chicks is grey. Nervous pairs can prove difficult to breed as they desert the nest at any disturbance. After successfully rearing one chick, when the male was 10 years old and the female 15, a pair belonging to J. B. Baker of Princes Risborough, Buckinghamshire, UK, deserted their chick at about seven weeks old after being upset by the deafening noise of a chain saw which was used nearby on two occasions. The chick was removed for hand-rearing and fed on Complan (Farley Health Products), Farex (Farley Health Laboratories), sponge cake, honey and Abidec (Parke Davis). By the age of 12 weeks, it was eating ground sunflower seed and sponge cake.

Mr Baker's pair had reared young for four consecutive years before they proved double brooded for the first time. Winter breeding was usual for this pair. In 1976, the first of three eggs was laid on January 13 and there were two chicks by February 12. In 1977, the first of two eggs was laid on January 10 and two chicks had hatched by February 6. In November of that year, the female laid three eggs by November 15 and there were three chicks by December 11. As soon as the chicks were reared the female nested again; the first of two eggs was laid by March 23. One egg was damaged and the remaining egg hatched on April 21. The next clutch was commenced on November 30. The average incubation period was thus 27 days.

Eric Callaghan from County Dublin noted that no mutual preening occurred between two males which were kept together but it took place immediately male and female were introduced (two pairs) – and not since.

In his opinion, the most definite indication of sex in an individual was threat behaviour:

> I have only ever been threatened by a cock bird, never by a hen. Threatening behaviour consists in the bird leaning backwards slightly, shrugging the wings outwards at the shoulders while doing so, this being accompanied by a raising of the head feathers, gaping the beak and producing a crackling sound within the beak. Even newly fledged young have been tentatively sexed from the fact that those which appeared more masculine looking in other ways have threatened me when approached too closely whereas a believed young hen has never done so (Callaghan, 1982).

There was a high degree of synchronisation in laying in the two hens. Their two cages faced one another across a room. They usually nested in winter, in spite of relatively uniform conditions of light throughout the year. The chicks were described as being sparsely covered with white down with noticeably fleshy swellings on the lower mandible. The young spent 67 or 68 days in the nest. They were seen to eat soaked sunflower seed within two days of leaving the nest and dry sunflower after 10 days.

The breeding life of this species is a long one. There is a record of one pair which had eggs when the male was known to be at least 40 years and the female 25 years.

In Denmark, H. Petersen was the forerunner of European breeding successes, in 1956, and C. Madsen's pair reared young in the same year. In three years, seven young were reared from 14 eggs. In Britain, E. J. Boosey's success in 1957 was the first. In 1961, T. Brosset, of Gothenborg, Sweden, reared a single youngster and, in 1967, W. and P. Ebert in Leipzig, East Germany bred this species.

Senegal Parrots have been bred in zoos in a number of countries, including the USA, India (Ahmedabad Zoo), Germany (Rostock Zoo) and France (Villars Zoo). However, considering how often this species has been imported, successes have not been numerous. It used to be so inexpensive that few attempted to breed from it, but since the mid 1970s attempts and successes have been far more frequent.

Meyer's Parrot (*Poicephalus meyeri meyeri*).

Meyer's Parrot

P. meyeri meyeri

Description: Predominantly dark grey-brown with the rump and under parts bluish green, all adult Meyer's have yellow on the bend of the wing, thighs and under wing coverts. The tail is brown. The iris is orange-red and the beak is dark grey. Length: 22 cm (9 in). Weight: M 121 g ($4\frac{1}{4}$ oz); F 112 g (4 oz).

Immature birds have much duller plumage; they lack the yellow markings and are mainly grey with the rump blue-green.

Range/Habitat: The nominate race is found from southern Chad and northeast Cameroon through northern Central African Republic to southern Sudan and western Ethiopia. The species inhabits most types of timbered country, but is seldom found far from water. It is common or locally so. It is said to roost in holes in trees and to nest in holes made by woodpeckers and barbets.

P. m. saturatus

Description: It has the rump washed with light blue.

Range/Habitat: This race inhabits Uganda, Rwanda, Burundi, western Tanzania and Kenya.

P. m. matschiei

Description: It has the rump bright blue and the under parts washed with blue.

Range/Habitat: This race is found from south-eastern Kenya to northern Malawi, Zambia and south-eastern Congo.

P. m. reichenowi and *damarensis*

Description: The distinctive feature is that the yellow on the crown is missing.

Range/Habitat: These races are found in Angola, Congo, South West Africa and north-west Lesotho.

P. m. transvaalensis
Description: Paler brown above.
Range/Habitat: Its range includes Mozambique, Zimbabwe and eastern Lesotho and the Transvaal.

The races are described to show that rump colouration or lack of yellow on the forehead, for example, is not a means of sexing these birds. Understandably, aviculturists have been misled when obtaining one bird with a yellow forehead and another without into believing they must constitute a true pair.
Aviculture: Meyer's Parrot was not well-known in aviculture until the late 1960s, since when it has been been fairly regularly available, and has been bred not infrequently. According to Barnicoat (1983), it was bred in South Africa by Jack Rough nearly 50 years previously and was still being bred by that aviculturist, who specialised in members of this genus. In the USA, the first breeder may have been William Hawkins of California. In 1970, his female produced three infertile eggs. In February of the following year, three more eggs were laid. All hatched, despite a severe earthquake during the incubation period on or about February 21. The youngest was not keeping pace with its siblings and was removed for hand-rearing on May 7. The other two left the nest about three weeks later. Sadly, they were so nervous that within 24 hours both had broken their necks in dashing about in flight. In October, three more fertile eggs were produced. The three chicks were removed for hand-rearing in December due to impending cold weather. This was successfully accomplished. The young birds were very gentle but also nervous. Also in California, Betty Byers hand-reared Meyer's and Senegal Parrots and described them as being very quiet and undemanding as chicks. On hatching, they have creamy white down about 6 mm ($\frac{1}{4}$ in) long. Meyer's chicks weigh about 5 g ($\frac{1}{5}$ oz) and 124 g ($4\frac{2}{5}$ oz) on fledging.

When this species was bred in England by Raymond Franklin of Chesham, Bucks, he recorded that two chicks had hatched by June 16 and a third later; they left the nest on August 10, 13 and 15 but returned to the nest log for several days. Meyer's Parrot has also been bred in zoos in East London, South Africa (1969 – two) and, in the USA, in Oklahoma (1972 – four) and Sacramento, California (1973 – one).

Rüppell's Parrot
P. rueppellii
Description: Sexual dimorphism is apparent in adult birds, the female being the most brightly coloured. The male is predominantly dusky brown with silver frosting on the crown and ear coverts and a slight green suffusion on the back. The rump and under tail coverts are tinged with blue. The shoulders, edge of the wing and under wing coverts are yellow and the thighs are yellow and orange. The beak is grey-black and the iris is orange-red or bright red. The female has the lower back, rump and upper tail coverts bright blue and the lower abdomen and vent dull blue. Length: 22 cm (9 in). Weight: about 115 g (4 oz).

Immature birds have the rump blue – of a brighter shade than the female, although possibly less extensive and less brilliant in immature males. The yellow may be confined to the under wing coverts or there may be a few yellow feathers on the shoulders. The beak is grey.
Range/Habitat: This species comes from a comparatively small area, south-west Africa from southern Angola to South West Africa, and has no subspecies.
Aviculture: It is a most attractive little bird which has only been sporadically exported and not in large numbers. Little has been recorded about it in captivity and it has reared young on few occasions.

In Britain, Rüppell's Parrot was bred in 1979 by Mr R. Gale of Essex. This species was bred at London Zoo in 1981 (Olney, pers. comm.). The pair was received in January 1973. In December 1980, the female laid three eggs; a chick was seen on January 9. Bread dipped in lorikeet mixture was then added to the diet of fruit and seed. The youngster left the nest on March 6. The female laid again late in the year but the eggs did not hatch; neither did the four eggs laid in December 1983. Four more eggs were laid in June 1984, three of which hatched. The young birds left the nest on August 27, September 1 and 5.

The breeding took place inside the Parrot House in an enclosure measuring 1.8 m × 1.2 m (6 × 4 ft) × 2.3 m (7$\frac{1}{2}$ ft) high. The nest-box used was 46 cm (18 in) high and 25 cm (10 in) square. The entrance hole was about 5 cm (2 in) in diameter.

When Rüppell's Parrots were bred by Allan F. Manning (1982), the parents consumed greenfly and blackfly on leaves of a privet hedge in a corner of their aviary. The pair were obtained in 1979 and placed in an aviary measuring 3 × 1.5 m (10 × 5 ft) × 1.7 m (5$\frac{1}{2}$ ft) high. The first egg was laid on April 6, 1981. One of the four eggs was infertile; two had hatched by May 6. As soon as the chicks hatched, the parents started to consume the livefood. Mealworms were also offered; the ration was reduced to 60 g (2 oz) per week after the chicks were ten days old.

When the nest-box was inspected, a chick could be removed without the parents attempting to attack as long as it remained within the parents' sight. Once, when the chick was hidden from the male's view, he 'went into a kind of panic display that was very distressing to watch'.

On July 6, the parents started to pluck the chicks' ear coverts 'in an attempt to get them out of the box'. They left the nest on the following day but returned at night. At this stage, mealworms were refused by both the young and the adults. The youngsters were observed feeding themselves on July 15 and were removed four days later. Mr Manning described Rüppell's Parrots as being 'wonderful birds to keep as they are quiet, intelligent, steady, placid'.

In the USA, Busch Gardens, Tampa, Florida, reported breeding this species on several occasions from 1965, also hybrids between a male Meyer's and a female Rüppell's.

Brown-headed Parrot
P. cryptoxanthus
Description: This is the least interesting of the genus in colouration. It can briefly be described as resembling a Senegal and differing in having the

under parts entirely green, also the rump. The head and neck are dusky brown and the ear coverts are silvery grey. Most of the wing feathers are dark green with lighter edges or with the inner webs brown. Under wing coverts are yellow, also the iris. The upper mandible is grey, the lower mandible white. Length is 22 cm (9 in). Weight: 123–156 g ($4\frac{1}{5}$–$5\frac{1}{2}$ oz).

Immature birds are said to be duller with the crown and neck suffused with yellowish olive.

Captive-bred young were described as having the head darker than in adults, the beak and cere pinker and the iris dark brown (Harris, 1984a).
Range/Habitat: This species is found in south-eastern Africa, including eastern Transvaal, Mozambique, Zimbabwe, Malawi, Tanzania and Kenya. It is locally common and favours acacia scrub and woodland.
Aviculture: It has always been rare and little known in aviculture, presumably because of its drab colours. First exhibited at London Zoo in 1870, since then few have reached Britain. In 1968, a small consignment arrived and the birds were offered cheaply.

The first breeding was reported by Mr and Mrs M. Collett of Hemel Hempstead, Hertfordshire. While in Swaziland in 1976, Mr Collett obtained a pair. He described the male as being slightly larger than the female, with noticeably larger head and a few yellow feathers on the crown.

In 1977, they were placed in an outdoor aviary with an angle-iron frame and many twigs and branches. In June, they were provided with a nest-box of chipboard which measured 25 cm (10 in) square and 45 cm (18 in) deep; an inverted turf and some peat were placed in the base. They showed immediate interest and, within a few days, mating occurred. During copulation, the positions were sometimes reversed, so that it was doubted that they were a true pair. It was not until October 18, when the female had spent longer than usual inside the nest-box, that examination revealed a single egg. The male fed the female inside the nest and called loudly and appeared agitated whenever she left the box.

After 26 days, the male spent most of the time in the nest and it was assumed that the egg had hatched. A few days later, using a torch, the box was examined and an almost naked pink chick with a sparse covering of white down was seen. Three days later, the amount of down on the chick had increased. The nest-box was kept immaculately clean and the female was seen to remove droppings and other debris.

By the time the chick was nearly a month old, the white down had been replaced by the second down, grey in colour, and judging by the amount of food taken by the male, he was doing most of the feeding. A favourite food was an insectile mixture provided for the Pekin Robins which shared the aviary. Parrot mixture, foreign finch mixture, fruit and carrot were also consumed.

The young bird was in the nest during the prolonged bitterly cold weather of January 1979; however, the female rarely emerged from the nest and the male, too, spent much time inside. At ten weeks old the chick was fully feathered, but for some down which remained on the rump and the shorter tail. It started to look out of the nest entrance when 11 weeks old and finally emerged from the nest at 12 weeks. Because of the cold and snow, it was returned to the nest for several days, where it was always joined by its parents. After it left the nest, it was fed only by the male and, when it was aged nearly 16 weeks, it started to feed itself.

In the USA, the Brown-headed Parrot was bred by Mr and Mrs F. Harris in 1983, in a cage measuring 91 × 47 cm (36 × 18 in) × 47 cm (18 in) high. Two eggs were laid and removed to an incubator because the female was not incubating conscientiously. The first egg hatched 24 hours after being placed in the incubator. The second egg hatched on the following day. The chicks had light grey down and were quite fluffy; toenails were grey; upper mandible dark grey; lower mandible pink. The chicks weighed 5.9 and 5.4 g (about $\frac{1}{5}$ oz) on hatching. At one month, weighing 35 g ($1\frac{1}{4}$ oz), they had second down of two shades – medium and dark grey. At two months, they weighed 85 g (3 oz) each. They were hand-fed on the food described for conures (see p.325). At 13 weeks, they were eating sunflower and safflower seed, Budgie mixture and fruit and vegetables (Harris, 1984a). In 1984, this species was bred in England by G. A. Smith. Two newly hatched chicks weighed 6 g ($\frac{1}{5}$ oz) each; at weaning, they weighed 124 g and 188 g (about $4\frac{2}{5}$ oz).

Niam Niam Parrot
P. crassus
Description: The Brown-headed Parrot's yellow under wing coverts distinguish it from this rarely imported bird which has the iris red and the under wing coverts green. The upper mandible is dark grey and the lower mandible whitish. Length: 25 cm (10 in).

Immature birds have the crown and nape greyish brown, marked with olive-yellow; the under parts are yellowish green. The bill is yellowish with a dark grey tip to the upper mandible.
Range/Habitat: The Niam Niam Parrot inhabits central-western Africa: eastern Cameroon to south-western Sudan.
Aviculture: The dullest coloured member of the genus, it is almost unknown in aviculture. A few were imported into Britain in 1978. The first (and perhaps only) recorded captive breeding was that described by João and Brickell (1981) in Mozambique. Four birds were obtained in 1967, one of which died soon after receipt. They were very nervous. Banana leaves were placed around the sides of the aviary for privacy. They were fed on sunflower seed and canary, apple and orange, boiled corn-on-the-cob, beans, peas in the pod, cabbage stalks and indigenous weeds.

The extra female was removed and the true pair was provided with a nest-box. Four eggs were laid and incubation commenced with the fourth egg. The male spent long periods in the nest beside the incubating female and roosted there at night. Three eggs hatched, the first after 27 days. On hatching the chicks were covered in fine greyish white down; the second down was a darker grey. The young left the nest within an hour of each other when 13 weeks old. They returned to the nest at night. The only extra rearing food provided was maize meal with water added.

Red-bellied (Abyssinian or Red-breasted) Parrot
P. rufiventris

Description: Adults can be sexed at a glance by the feature after which they are named; the lower breast and abdomen are deep orange in the male. In the female the feathers in this area are greyish brown tipped with pale bluish green. Under wing coverts are deep orange in the male and greyish brown in the female. The rump and under tail coverts are pale green and the rest of the plumage is dark brown. The beak is black and the iris is orange. Length: 22 cm (9 in). Weight: 125 g ($4\frac{1}{2}$ oz).

Immature birds resemble females but males can be distinguished by their orange wing coverts and orange markings on the abdomen.

Range/Habitat: The Red-bellied Parrot inhabits mid-eastern Africa; it is found in Ethiopia, Tanzania and Somalia, frequenting lowland thornbush and acacia scrub, particularly where there are baobab trees. In places, it ascends to 2,000 m (6,500 ft) to feed on figs.

Aviculture: this parrot was almost unknown in aviculture until the 1980s. In the 1920s, a few were imported into Britain. David Seth-Smith stated (1931a) that it:

> ...has the reputation of being difficult to keep in captivity. Indeed, a small collection of three which reached this country a few years ago appear to have all died soon after their arrival. They were extremely shy, and evidently captured as adult birds.

A hand-reared bird, taken from a nest in Somaliland in 1901, proved much longer-lived. It was presented to London Zoo in 1927 and lived there until at least 1931 and probably much longer. Wild-caught *Poicephalus* adults are very nervous, thus this species' suitability to aviculture should not be judged by the three birds sent to London Zoo.

In the early 1980s, a number of Red-bellied Parrots were imported into Europe. Prices were not high. In 1984, several hundred were imported into Sweden. Many pet shops were offering this species at the equivalent of US $150–200 per pair.

This species was bred in Mozambique by A. João and Neville Brickell (1981) in the mid- or early 1970s. The

Jardine's Parrot (*Poicephalus gulielmi gulielmi*).

pair obtained was semi-tame and soon settled down in an aviary. They bred seven months later. Three eggs were laid and incubation commenced with the first egg, which hatched after 28 days. Both adults incubated after the first week. The three young left the nest at 12 weeks old and were fed by the male for the next three weeks. The young birds were duller than the adults and the two males had a faint pinkish red frontal band.

Swiss aviculturist D. Ferrari (1983) reared one youngster in 1982. The species is also being bred in Germany.

Yellow-faced Parrot
P. flavifrons flavifrons

Description: This species is larger than those described previously; it is mainly green, paler and brighter on the rump, lower under parts and under tail coverts. The feathers of the upper parts and breast have bright green edges. The forehead, crown and upper part of the cheeks are yellow and the thighs are marked with yellow in some birds.

The tail and flight feathers are olive brown. The upper mandible is dusky horn colour and the lower mandible whitish. The iris is red. Length: about 29 cm ($11\frac{1}{2}$ in).

Immature birds are yellowish olive-green on the head instead of yellow. The under wing coverts have broad, yellowish green edges.

Range/Habitat: Little is known of this parrot's wild life. It inhabits the highlands of Ethiopia and has often been observed in the company of Abyssinian Lovebirds. It is found in flocks of up to about 20 individuals.

P. f. aurantiiceps
Description: There is orange on the head where it is yellow in the nominate race.
Range/Habitat: This race is from north and central Ethiopia.

Jardine's Parrot
P. gulielmi gulielmi
Description: This is a solidly built bird with a large beak. It is most attract-

ively marked, being mainly dark green with touches of orange in its plumage. The feathers of the upper parts are black, broadly edged with rich dark green. The lores are black and the feathers of the head are black with green edges. The crown, shoulders, thighs and inner edge of the wing are rich orange. The wings are black, each feather being broadly edged with green and the feathers of the underparts are rich green with a blackish centre. The flight and tail feathers are black. Length: 28 cm (11 in). Weight: about 250 g (8 oz).

There are three subspecies which vary slightly in the shade of orange on the crown and the width of the green margins of the feathers of the upper parts. A race formerly recognised was *P. g. aubryanus*, known as Aubry's Parrot. In an attempt to differentiate the two, I examined a number of skins in the British Museum (Natural History), to find one bird which carried a *P. g. gulielmi* tag on one leg and an *aubryanus* label on the other! A fair comment, I thought, on just how distinct they are.

Jardine's Parrot has a conspicuous area of white skin surrounding the eye. The iris is brown or reddish brown. When more is known about this species, it may be found that males invariably have reddish brown eyes and females brown eyes. (This is true of the two proved pairs of John Stoodley, see below, and of another proved pair.) The upper mandible is horn-coloured with a black tip or mainly blackish. The lower mandible is black.

Immature birds have the forehead dusky brown; the crown is buff-brown, the feathers being narrowly tipped with greenish. The thighs, wings and head are without the orange markings.

Range/Habitat: This species is found in Central Africa, in Cameroon and the Central African Republic to northern Angola, Kenya and northern Tanzania. It is more common in the east of its range, inhabiting forests up to about 3,500 m (11,500 ft).

Aviculture: It is available from time to time but has never been common. In the past, the few birds imported were usually kept as pets. They can be shy and difficult to tame but the confiding birds are very appealing. For many years, there were two in separate cages

Cape Parrot (*Poicephalus robustus*) – female.

in the Parrot House at London Zoo. They loved to have their heads scratched but if you looked away for even a second one would slyly remove part of your finger. A pair I kept, which were not at all tame, would stretch themselves, shake their heads, ruffle their head feathers and utter their soft appealing 'hoo' call note.

In Britain, Jardine's Parrot was first bred, in 1978, by Mr and Mrs J. Stoodley of Hampshire. The birds nested in a log in a fully enclosed aviary. John Stoodley took a unique photograph inside the nest. It showed not only the light grey down of the chick but the differences in the plumage colouration of male and female. The male is darker green, the female more yellowish green. The young bird was duller than the adults with only a small amount of orange-red in the plumage. Incubation period was believed to be 26 days. Average clutch size of this and another pair in the Stoodley's collection was four eggs.

In Czechoslovakia, this species was bred by Mr Nezblecha in 1984 for the fourth time (Hylas, pers. comm.).

Cape (or Brown-necked) Parrot
P. robustus robustus

Description: Despite its huge beak this is a handsome bird. In the nominate

race the forehead is greenish brown to yellowish brown flecked with darker brown and dull green. Both sexes have orange on the forehead but the female has more. The feathers of the back and wing coverts are black, broadly edged with dark green. The rump and under parts are green, suffused with dull blue and/or grey. The thighs and outer edge of the wing are orange and the tail is blackish brown. The iris is dark brown and the beak pale horn-coloured. Length: 32 cm (12 in). Weight: M 295–401 g (10½–14 oz); F 280–364 g (10–12¾ oz approx.).

The plumage of immature birds varies, perhaps according to the subspecies. Those bred in Basle Zoo, Switzerland, were said to have no orange on the thighs or wing; the head was brownish olive, sometimes marked with pink. However, Dr E. Hopkinson, who lived in Africa, was very familiar with this species and had kept a number of young birds. He wrote (1910) that the young were more brightly coloured than the adults and that he had 'often watched the change from the red-headed stage of the youngsters to that of the grey-headed, red-winged, and -thighed adult'. One young bird which he took from the nest had the 'whole crown from forehead to nape bright brick red'. It also showed a 'pale wash of the same colour over the rest of the head, the ground colour of which is brownish-grey as in the adult'. This head colouration, he found, is lost at the first or second moult when the bird had no orange at all in the plumage. This stage was followed by adult plumage (Hopkinson, 1916). It should be borne in mind that he was familiar with the race from Gambia, *fuscicollis*, which also occurs in southern Senegal to northern Ghana and Togo.

Range/Habitat: The nominate race is found in extreme south-eastern Africa from Knysna and eastern Cape Province to Natal, western Zululand, western Swaziland and eastern Transvaal. A locally distributed bird of forest and thick bush, it is uncommon throughout most of its range and is seen in small flocks. It feeds mainly on fruits and berries. The clutch is said to consist normally of four eggs.

P. r. suahelicus

Description: Hubert Astley wrote (1915) of the strange head colouration 'it is no more brown than it is blue or yellow'. The bird which Astley knew was evidently *suahelicus* for he described its head as 'silver-grey, suffused with dull rose-pink, that is to say, each dull pink feather seems to have a silver-grey edging'. The effect is one of most unusual beauty and entirely unlike the colouration of any other parrot. In *suahelicus* the female has the forehead and part of the crown orange; this colour is missing in the male. Weight: M 326 g ($11\frac{1}{2}$ oz); F 320 g ($11\frac{1}{4}$ oz).

Range/Habitat: this race inhabits Mozambique, Zimbabwe, northern Lesotho, northern South West Africa to Angola, southern Congo and central Tanzania.

The numbers of this species are increasingly giving cause for concern, although its exact status in the three areas in which it is found must be difficult to determine.

Aviculture: This has always been a rare bird in captivity; probably the main reasons are that it is not common in the wild, that its large beak deters aviculturists and that it is not easy to establish. Dr E. Hopkinson found adults almost impossible to keep alive for any length of time without ground-

nuts. Young birds were more easily established.

London Zoo exhibited two specimens as long ago as 1869. This species has never been imported in anything but small numbers and I know of only two importations in Britain consisting of more than a handful of birds, the largest being of 18.

In voice, behaviour and character, this species has a lot in common with the Grey Parrot. It is quite capable of being noisy and of emitting a harsh scream – yet seldom does so. And the female in my possession is an extremely quiet bird, never screaming and making soft 'hoo' sounds like a Jardine's Parrot. Hubert Astley said of his tame male that he had never once heard it scream. Cape Parrots can learn to talk and whistle and tame birds are every bit as delightful as a Grey and equally as intelligent.

One of the most charming birds I have ever owned was a male *robustus*. He had been kept as a pet for three years before he was offered to me. It so happened that at that time a dealer had been advertising a female for sale but because of the scarcity of this species, and especially of males, he had been unable to sell it. After several months he parted with it to another dealer – on the day before I telephoned him! He did not know the name of the buyer, only that he occasionally took birds to a well-known Sunday morning bird market. The next day was a Sunday and by an enormous stroke of good luck my husband was able to track the bird down and purchase it.

The two birds were caged side by side for a while and, on introduction, proved to be completely compatible. It was several months before it was possible to place them in an outdoor aviary. The female proved to be rather shy and would disappear into the nest-box on sight of people. But the male was quite the reverse and soon established himself as a firm favourite. When excited, he would rapidly rap his beak on the side of the aviary and also make a noise like distant machine-gun fire.

During their first year outside, the male constantly fed the female, with elaborate pumping of the head, and also attempted to mate. Regrettably, he entirely lacked a tail and this never

grew, so whether he was ever completely successful I do not know. During the following year, the female laid two clutches, the first egg of each clutch being laid on August 10 and September 12. The nest was inaccessible but the dates were accurate because I have never seen a parrot which was more obviously about to lay. The nesting site was a narrow log which supported a large nest-box. The birds gnawed through the base of the box into the log.

Only a few days later the male was horribly injured by a predator, probably a fox, which pulled his leg through 25 mm (1 in) welded mesh and bit it off at the top of the thigh. Not surprisingly, the shock and resulting loss of blood led to his untimely death.

The Cape Parrot was first bred in captivity in Basle Zoo, Switzerland. Consistent success has been achieved since 1964. Between 1964 and 1968, 15 young were reared in seven clutches.

The breeding pair was received in 1955 and lived with other *Poicephalus* and Grey Parrots until 1964. One was attacked by a Meyer's Parrot, a dwarf in comparison. Not surprisingly, the Cape Parrots made no attempt to breed until the other birds had been removed from the aviary. A chick was hatched on April 16 and left the nest 74 days later. In 1966, it was presented to San Diego Zoo with a young bird from a later clutch. In October 1964, another chick was hatched but died after a few days. During the following year, the female laid on the floor and a keeper transferred the egg to the nest, where the female incubated, then deserted. Another clutch resulted in three chicks hatching by August 10, which left the nest between October 4 and 16 (55 to 67 days old). In 1967, the young spent 72 to 79 days in the nest and, in 1968, they left the nest when aged between 65 and 68 days old.

The young birds were described as showing brick red on the forehead which disappears at the age of about five months to be replaced, in the female, by a bright red band. The young birds' heads were plucked by the female but the feathers grew when they were separated from her.

In 1978, Vogelpark Walsrode generously gave me a male Cape Parrot. When visiting this fine collection in the previous year, I had seen two males in an enclosure containing a nest-box with a female and two chicks. In the middle of May, he was placed in a small outdoor aviary measuring 1.8 m × 76 cm (6 × 2½ ft) × 1.8 m (6 ft) high, with the female. They were instantly compatible and, on the first day, mutual preening and courtship feeding were observed. She laid in August but the clutch was unsuccessful. She laid again during the end of October. A chick was heard on November 28. Anticipating cold weather, the whole family was transferred to an indoor flight on December 12. The youngster seemed to grow well; however, as it made no attempt to leave the nest, I removed it on March 1. It was then apparent that it was abnormally weak and it died the next day. A post-mortem examination revealed that it was severely afflicted with rickets. The problem had been that although the diet was not deficient in calcium, this was unabsorbed due to lack of sunlight and vitamin D.

The pair was returned to their outside aviary the following spring but made no attempt to nest that year. In 1981, the female laid during the middle of May. One chick was seen on June 21: a second was present but hidden from view. By July 7, the chicks had a covering of very short white down, in evenly spaced tufts. Six days later the down colour had changed to yellow. There was an orange blush on the forehead where the feathers were coming through; wing feathers were also erupting. By July 21, they were covered with dense yellow down, with a ruff of white down framing their heads. The bills were pale pink with the sides of the upper mandible slightly raised. The first chick was seen out of the nest on September 4 and both had left by September 7. They were very shy and returned to the nest when anyone was near, also at night (Low, 1982).

Both were as large as the female, differing from the adults in the pinker beak and cere and in the absence of orange feathers on the bend of the wing. They otherwise resembled the female except for the reduced area of orange on the head and the dark grey feathers on the lores. Their first moult commenced in March. Previously one had a considerable amount of orange on the back of the head which was not present when it left the nest. Both proved to be males. They lived amicably with their parents until the following January. They remained extremely timid for a long time. In April 1983, one was presented to London Zoo to pair with a female which had been donated. In January 1985, Birgitta Ullman of Stockholm generously presented me with her female as a mate for the second male.

The Cape Parrot (nominate race) was bred in South Africa by Jack Rough in the 1970s.

In the USA this species has been raised by Bob Nelson of Oregon since 1982. He described his hand-fed young (pers. comm., 1983) as:

> . . . very nice, quite precocious, affable, and perpetual comics and acrobats – so active, happy and in general a constant delight. Their 'human speech' is quite good also – good deliberate diction.

In Sweden, Birgitta Ullman obtained a female Cape Parrot and, unable to acquire a male, paired it with a male Jardine's Parrot (Ullman, pers. comm., 1984). The resulting young had the large bill of the Cape Parrot, which they resembled more than the male parent. The young could be divided into two types. Type I had very little red or yellow in the plumage; the head feathers were mainly grey-brown with occasional dark red feathers. Type II had varying areas of red and yellow on the head, and also on the body. One male had an entirely yellow mantle and large yellow patches on breast and abdomen. It seemed that areas which were poorly feathered on the young-

sters later became red or yellow. There was no difference in appearance between the first generation hybrids and those produced by pairing the hybrids together.

One second generation hybrid female lived with a Grey Parrot, probably male. An old female Grey in the same cage was ignored by the Grey. The male and the hybrid preened and fed each other but the female was not then old enough to breed.

Birgitta Ullman described the hybrid chicks as having white down, sparse and rather long. In one youngster, the down had been lost by the time it was 12 days old. There was no second down in these young.

In West Berlin, G. and H. Isert have bred the Cape Parrot since 1976. The two birds were put together in September 1976 and were observed mating on November 6. Two eggs were laid, the first on November 26 and the second three days later. The first hatched after 28 days, the second two days later. They left the nest at the ages of 82 and 85 days. At six months old, both had lost the orange colouration on the forehead. At nine months old, the young female acquired two or three red feathers on the forehead; at ten months there was a 5 mm (⅕ in) wide band of orange on the head. At ten months the young male acquired the first red feathers on the thighs and the bend of the wing. They were independent at 98 and 100 days old. At the end of 1977, two more young were reared, with two more in 1979 (Isert and Isert, 1980).

Their diet consisted of walnuts, hazelnuts, pine nuts, peanuts, sunflower seed (dry and soaked), apple, banana and grapes, also carrot, egg yolk and corn. My own birds have an almost identical diet but for the hazelnuts and banana; they refuse the latter. Favourite items of food are walnuts, the stones from cherries, plums and similar fruits, sweetcorn, and hawthorn berries.

Cockatiels

Nymphicus hollandicus

The only member of the parrot family known to aviculturists which is not covered fully in this book is the Budgerigar (*Melopsittacus undulatus*) mentioned in Chapter 11. It has become the best known of all cage birds, kept and bred in millions and in colour varieties and combinations which number hundreds. Yet less than 50 years ago, it was exhibited in foreign bird classes at shows and only three or four mutations were known. If any other member of the parrot family is to attain such great popularity that it, too, is no longer considered as part of the foreign bird fancy, that bird will surely be the Cockatiel.

The Cockatiel is an aberrant member of the cockatoo family. It used to be thought of as a link between the parrakeets and the cockatoos but in actual fact it has nothing in common with the former except for the long tail.

This bird has everything to commend it to the breeder and pet-keeper. It never ceases to amaze me that so many people acquire expensive parrots which are entirely unsuitable as pets, never likely to become tame or learn to talk and which, in many cases, should never have been removed from their natural habitat when, for a very modest sum, they could have purchased one of the most enchanting and long-lived of pet birds which can be tamed with ease.

The Cockatiel has every virtue an aviculturist could wish for and not a single fault. It is easy to breed, easy to sex when adult, naturally steady, neither noisy nor destructive and does not need large or expensive accommodation.

And yet it was not until the late 1960s and the early 1970s, when several mutations became generally available, that the Cockatiel began to be extensively kept in Europe, although its popularity in the USA as a pet was never in doubt.

Description: The Cockatiel is unmistakable, with its yellow and grey crest and orange cheeks. The only other crested long-tailed parrot is the Horned Parrakeet (*Eunymphicus*), which is rare in aviculture. Cockatiels are mainly grey; the male is generally darker but the depth of colour varies in individuals. There is a very prominent patch of orange on the ear coverts which is much brighter in the male and partly edged with a narrow border of white. The rest of the head and crest is yellow, this colour being much brighter and more extensive in the male. The crest is tipped with grey or, in the female, may be entirely grey. A broad band of white decorates the edge of the wing. The rest of the plumage is grey, except the under side of the tail which is black in the male and barred with grey and yellow in the female. The beak is grey, also the cere; there are some black hairs on the lores which are more pronounced in the male. Length: 32 cm (12 in). Weight: M 80–102 g ($2\frac{4}{5}$–$3\frac{3}{5}$ oz); F 89–92 g ($2\frac{9}{10}$–$3\frac{1}{4}$ oz); newly hatched chicks about 4 g to 4.6 g (about $\frac{3}{20}$ oz); weaning weight about 70 g ($2\frac{1}{2}$ oz).

Immature birds resemble the female but have the tail shorter and the cere pinkish. They cannot be sexed until the first moult which occurs when they are about five or six months old. However, males usually start to warble from the age of three months – and this is the best indication of their sex before the moult.

The Lutino mutation (sometimes incorrectly referred to as Albino or White) is extremely beautiful. The orange cheeks and yellow face and crest are retained; the rest of the plumage is white, or white and pale yellow below or, if depth of colour has been selected for, quite deep yellow below. Breeders who wish to produce richly coloured birds should retain for breeding the young which show most yellow on the under parts.

This mutation is difficult to sex until the bird is taken in the hand; in the adult female and in young birds of both sexes the under side of the wings and tail are faintly barred with yellow. Males have a few yellow marks but these are irregular.

At the time of writing, the Lutino is the most popular and the most inexpensive of the mutations. The others which have been bred to date are less striking.

The appearance of birds of the Pearled mutation is variable; the areas of the plumage most affected are the

Pearl Cockatiels (*Nymphicus hollandicus*).

paler, as if they were slightly soiled with excrement.... Another curiosity is that split males can be picked out from normals because they have pale streaks of feathers under the wing near the shoulder joint, giving a mottled effect.

In Pied mutations of any bird, the effect is variable and unpredictable; two well-marked Pieds might produce young which are disappointing in appearance. In this mutation, the plumage is irregularly marked with patches of white. If it is evenly marked, a Pied can be of pleasing appearance, especially if the overall areas of white and grey are approximately equal. Some Normals bred from Pieds show a white patch on the nape.

A mutation which is not of striking appearance is the Cinnamon (Isabelle, in the terms of Continental fanciers). The mutation can have such a slight effect that in poor light a Cinnamon could be difficult to distinguish from a Normal. However, males are usually darker cinnamon than females.

As George Smith (1978a) has stated:

> Melanin is still produced but the granules produced are brown, not black, and may be slightly smaller than are the granules in the normal black form. The cinnamon melanin, because it does not absorb so much light, gives the feathers a pale, brownish-grey colour. If the yellow background is intense then the cinnamon cockatiel is a most beautiful pale foxy-brown. With a light yellow background to the feathers, the bird is a very pale cafe-au-lait....

All the mutations described above are sex-linked in their manner of inheritance, with the exception of the Pied and the Red-eyed Silver which are autosomal recessive. The latter is equivalent to the Fallow mutation in the Budgerigar. The plumage is light silver and the eyes are pink. (Information on the theoretical expectations from the various mutations is given in Chapter 7.)

The Pied was the first mutation to appear, originating in the USA before 1950. The Cinnamon was the second mutation to occur, making its appearance in a New Zealand aviary about 1950. The third mutation was the Lutino which originated in Florida in 1958 and was firmly established by the late Mrs E. L. Moon, for which she won world-renown among avicultu-

neck, mantle and the wings, sometimes also the upper breast. In a Normal Cockatiel, these areas are grey; in the Pearled, the feathers are white or pale yellow, edged with grey and with a small grey area in the centre of the feather. This can result in a very attractive scalloped pattern but in some birds the effect is less definite, giving a spotted appearance.

The curious feature of this mutation is that male birds lose their scalloped markings when they moult until they

are almost indistinguishable from Normals.

To quote from *Encyclopedia of Cockatiels*:

> This happens because one of the secondary sexual characteristics of male Cockatiels is to lay down a higher density of melanin than do females or immatures. The extra black melanin of maturity therefore obscures the pearled effect, but not quite completely, for if close examination is given it will usually be found that the shoulder feathers look

Normal or Grey Cockatiel (*Nymphicus hollandicus*) – male.

rists. As in all new mutations, the price at first was very high; Mrs Moon sold pairs for $750.

Until the early 1970s, Pieds and Lutinos were the only mutations generally available. That decade was an eventful one in Cockatiel history for the price of Lutinos dropped as they were bred in increasing numbers and several other mutations put in an appearance, notably the Pearled. Still rare and yet to be firmly established, is the Red-eyed Silver.

The breeding of Cockatiel mutations is in its infancy and, during the next few years, it would be surprising if further mutations did not occur.

Range/Habitat: Cockatiels are very common in Australia where they are distributed over almost the entire continent except most coastal areas.

Ground-feeding birds, they exist almost entirely on seeds, and this is the reason for their success in captivity. It

is no accident that some of the most successful species of aviary birds which have been captive-bred for generations – the Budgerigar, Zebra Finch and other grassfinches – originate from a similar environment. All are Australian species which feed mainly on the seeds of grasses and which breed following the rains when these seeds are abundant. It is for this reason that in captivity they are capable of breeding at any time of the year – when food is plentiful – rather than during a certain season.

Feeding: Cockatiels favour the smaller seeds and should be offered canary, white millet, panicum millet and niger in separate containers; oats, wheat and buckwheat can also be provided. Some Cockatiels will eat sunflower or safflower; others show no interest in it. All relish millet sprays which can be offered regularly.

The usual wild greenfoods such as

seeding grasses and chickweed should be offered and lettuce, spinach beet and apple will be eaten by some Cockatiels. They can remain in good health for years on this rather frugal diet which must be supplemented with bread and milk during the breeding season. An all seed diet cannot be expected to produce young of the best quality.

Accommodation: Unlike most other parrots they are usually inoffensive towards other birds and can be kept safely with the smallest finches, provided that the aviary is of a reasonable size. A suggested minimum for several pairs of finches and a pair of Cockatiels is 3×1.8 m $(10 \times 6$ ft$) \times 1.8$ m $(6$ ft$)$ high. In such an aviary, three or four pairs of Cockatiels only could be kept for breeding purposes but the results are unlikely to be as good as when each pair is housed separately.

If the one pair per aviary principle is

adhered to – and this is essential when breeding from the various mutations if one is to control the pairings – each pair should be provided with an aviary approximately 3 m × 90 cm (10 × 3 ft) × 1.8 m (6 ft) high. To this should be attached a fully enclosed shelter in which the birds will roost. If the shelter is small, a half depth one with the floor about 90 cm (3 ft) above ground level will be appreciated more by the birds. As Cockatiels spend much time walking about the floor of their aviary, a shelter can thus be built without encroaching on the ground space.

Pets and Breeding: Cockatiels are sexually mature well before they are a year old and will breed successfully in the year following that in which they were hatched. Whether it is required for a pet or for breeding, a young bird should be obtained. The advantage to the breeder is that he or she knows the age of the bird and that it has not been discarded by the previous owner because it has proved unsatisfactory as a breeder. Therefore, as long as the bird is in nest-feather, that is, before its first moult at about six months of age, it will be suitable for breeding purposes. But if destined as a pet, it should be very young. The best way to obtain such a bird is through a breeder. In the northern hemisphere, Cockatiels are normally allowed to breed from March or April until the start of the moult in late summer or early autumn. Thus young birds suitable as pets will be available from April until about September. When a young bird is eating on its own, usually one to two weeks after leaving the nest, it can be removed from its parents.

This is the ideal age to start taming a young Cockatiel. At first it will be very nervous but it will settle down and become tame more quickly than an older bird. A pet Cockatiel can be appreciated to the full only if it is tame enough to let out of its cage, thus it should be made finger-tame before its first outing in the room. A tame Cockatiel is one of the most enchanting pets imaginable and will, with care and a little luck, bring years of joy to a family. Hardy and long-lived, many Cockatiels reach their mid-twenties and females will even lay when over 20 years old, although at this age the eggs are not likely to be fertile. As Cocka-

tiels are among the least expensive of pet birds, they can certainly be considered as superb value for money.

Males have a warbling song and the normal call note may be a little shrill. Both sexes can learn to talk but males usually make the best talkers; however, it is not possible to sex young birds. Cockatiels can also be taught to whistle tunes.

As aviary birds, they are generally much steadier and more confiding than most Australian parrakeets and certainly much more so than Lovebirds. As they nest readily and most pairs are successful in rearing young, Cockatiels are the ideal species for the newcomer to parrot keeping and breeding.

The nest-box should be hung in the flight. In the northern hemisphere, it can be hung up in March or April and removed after two nests of young have been reared or when the birds start to moult.

Pairing two young birds together should be avoided; a bird which has not bred before should be mated with one which has. It is not necessary to separate the sexes out of the breeding season, thus if a pair proves to be satisfactory breeders they can be kept together for the rest of their lives. Males may be ready to breed at almost any time of the year, but winter breeding – with few hours of daylight in which to feed the young – is best avoided. Cockatiels will breed indoors and, under these conditions, when artificial light can be provided, they can be allowed to nest at any time as long as they are rested and not allowed to breed continually.

Cockatiels should not be introduced to each other in March and expected to breed immediately. They should be put together four or five months before, although it often happens that two newly introduced birds will breed within a few weeks.

Where several pairs are kept, they should be provided with nest-boxes at the same time in the hope that they will breed simultaneously so that, if problems occur, chicks or eggs can be transferred to another nest.

Nest-boxes for these birds should measure approximately 18 cm (7 in) square and 30 cm (12 in) high. The entrance should be only just large enough to admit the birds, that is,

about 6 cm (2½ in) in diameter. A small amount of sawdust can be placed inside before the eggs are laid. When the chicks hatch, the addition of a little sawdust every few days will help to keep the nest dry.

The Cockatiel is one of the few species of parrots in which incubation is shared; generally, the male sits during the day and the female at night. The clutch usually consists of five eggs; however, sometimes very large clutches are laid. As it is impossible for the birds to incubate more than about six eggs properly, it is advisable to remove those laid after this number, either placing them with another pair of Cockatiels or in an incubator. Even if incubation of all the eggs was successful, as the eggs are laid on alternate days and incubation usually starts when the second or third egg is laid, the age and size difference between the first and last hatched chicks would be so great that the youngest would have very little chance of survival.

In Cockatiels, as in the white cockatoos, male and female share incubation and both feed the chicks from the time they are hatched. Occasionally one comes across a male who refuses to take his share of incubation; if he is young it may be due to inexperience and the bird should not be pronounced as useless for breeding until two years old. If the habit persists, finding a new male is the only course.

Cockatiels can be quite as discerning as the large cockatoos where choosing a mate is concerned and poor breeding performance by male or female could simply be due to the fact that the pair is not compatible. Mrs E. L. Moon, in *Experiences with My Cockatiels* shows quite clearly how strong is the preference of many Cockatiels for the mate of *their* choice. This being so, placing a number of unmated birds, males and females in equal numbers, in one aviary, should be the best way of finding compatible pairs.

The average clutch size is five. When the Parrot Society took a census among breeders of Cockatiels in 1969, the information supplied by members produced the following interesting figures: 41 pairs laid 430 eggs in 86 clutches (average of five per clutch). The largest clutch was seven (in six cases) and the smallest two and three (seven cases). Of the eggs laid, 58 per cent produced chicks. In only three of the 86 clutches were all the young reared. The nest-box size most commonly used was 25 cm (10 in) square and 46 cm (18 in) high. The highest number of young raised in one year was 14 (three clutches of five, four and five); the second largest was 11. The oldest parent was a 19 year old male (*Magazine of the Parrot Society*, February 1970). Miss N. Trayler reported (1978) that her pair had reared 68 young in five years; perhaps not a record but a most creditable total.

The incubation period is 19 days under normal circumstances but could be longer in cold weather. Because incubation seldom starts when the first egg is laid, more than one chick may hatch on the same day. The chicks are generously covered with long, wispy yellow down.

At about eight days old, their eyes begin to open and it is just possible to discern the feather tracts under the skin. When disturbed by nest inspection, they will rock from side to side and hiss in the same way as an adult will in defence of its nest.

Losses are most likely to occur when the chicks are about ten days old and in the pin-feather stage. The parents then cease to brood them continuously and if the weather is cold they could succumb to chills. This is also the age at which they can be ringed, if desired; internal diameter of the rings used should be 5 mm ($\frac{1}{5}$ in).

It quite often happens that, because of the difference in the ages of the chicks, the youngest does not always receive its fair share of the food; it gradually lags behind in growth and may die. By intervening before this happens, it can be removed for hand-rearing, producing a ready-made pet. Inexperienced birds not infrequently let the chicks die one by one and, if there are no other Cockatiels with young of a similar age, hand-rearing is the only way to save the chicks.

Sometimes the young die through no fault of the parents but due to inadequate feeding, or because the adults feed sunflower seed to very young chicks. In addition to their usual foods, they need bread and milk while rearing young, seeding grasses if available and, if sunflower is offered, it should be soaked for 24 hours then left another 24 hours until it has started to sprout. These foods will be much easier for the young to digest than hard, dry seed.

A common cause of death in Cockatiel chicks is the failure of the parents to brood the young at night, before they are old enough to maintain their body temperature. Some birds cease to brood when the chicks are only about 12 days old. A watch should be kept at dusk to ensure that the female returns to the nest at night. If she does not, the nest-box can be taken into a warm place at night and returned next morning, or the chicks can be removed for hand-rearing.

When retaining young for future breeding, it is wise to keep those from good parents, noting qualities such as brooding young until they are fully feathered, because such desirable attributes can be bred into a strain as well as variable features such as colour, size and good markings.

Cockatiels leave the nest when between four and five weeks old. The breeder should not despair if the young, on fledging, have had the crest or head feathers removed by the parents. These will soon be replaced when the birds are separated from their parents. Occasionally, the plucking is serious and extends to the body. If the young cannot be fostered or hand-reared, the best procedure is to place them in the shelter, on the floor, provided that the floor does not extend to ground level, in which case the parents could ignore them.

On leaving the nest, they will solicit the male for food, by bobbing up and down and making a whining noise. By this time the female may have laid the first egg of the second clutch. Two weeks after they have left the nest, the young can be removed from the aviary, provided that they have been seen to feed themselves.

If they are to be sold as pets, they should go at once to their new home. If not, they should be caged, at least for a short period, so that they lose their nervousness. In this way they will soon become tame and lose their fear of people and, whatever their future, as breeder or pet, their life will be almost free of stress.

Cockatiels mature quickly and are quite capable of breeding when only six or seven months old. Birds retained for breeding should be those from the most prolific strains in which there are no possibly inherent defects such as serious feather plucking. In the case of the mutations, only the best marked or most attractively coloured birds should be retained, except in the case of Pieds where the actual pattern of the markings is not inherited.

Finally, mention should be made of the Cockatiel as a liberty bird. It is not generally considered to be suitable for this purpose and some aviculturists have tried and soon abandoned the project. However, J. Strutt, from an unspoiled area of the Lake District, found them to be highly satisfactory at liberty because they look wonderful in flight and have a considerable range. Not only were they acrobatic when on the wing but they seemed to enjoy pursuing wild birds.

The Cockatiel has been well established in European aviaries for well over 100 years and can now be found in every country where aviculture is pursued. The year it was first imported is not known but it was bred in captivity as long ago as 1845 and is said to have been well established in European aviaries 40 years later. The Cockatiel, or Quarrion, as it is known in Australia, has given pleasure to thousands and with the growing popularity of breeding mutations is surely destined to become even better loved in the future.

20

Cockatoos

To the layman, cockatoos are among the best known and most easily recognised of the parrots; indeed, it would be difficult to mistake the white species for anything else. In addition, there are four species of black cockatoos and these are little known in aviculture.

Feeding: Some cockatoos are conservative feeders; nevertheless, one should persevere in offering foods for which little enthusiasm is shown. Two seed containers should be provided; one should be filled with the larger grains such as sunflower, also pine nuts and peanuts (kernels or unshelled), and the other with canary seed, white millet and hemp. If, after several days, certain seeds are ignored, it is advisable to offer them in a separate container to avoid wastage. If they remain untasted, they should be removed and similar seeds offered after a long period has elapsed, as some birds will ignore one kind of seed for months and then feed on it readily.

Some cockatoos which are reluctant to sample foods other than seeds, show a marked liking for foods in the ear such as millet sprays, corn-on-the-cob, wheat and peas-in-the-pod. Many cockatoos cannot be persuaded to sample fruit. If they still refuse it, there is little cause for concern as long as they will eat fresh vegetables, greenfood or sprouted seeds. Seeding grasses, chickweed, persicaria and dandelion (all parts) can be offered, in addition to spinach beet and other cultivated greenfood.

Dr R. Burkard of Zurich, who keeps 13 species of cockatoos, emphasises the importance of a diet which is not only varied but keeps the birds occupied for long periods, thus reducing the risk of feather plucking. All species relish green corn cobs, the nuts of cembra pine (expensive) and hazel nuts. His Slender-billed Cockatoos make a small hole in the nut and extract the kernel from it piece by piece with the long bill.

Fruits include apple, orange, plums, raspberries and grapes, plus the berries of mountain ash and pyracantha. Carrots, cucumbers, courgettes, aubergine, celery, peas and beetroot are included among the vegetables fed. The roots of dandelions collected in the spring are a particular delicacy for the Slender-billed Cockatoos. Branches of willow and birch containing buds are greatly enjoyed; juice is squeezed out of the bark.

The protein requirement of cockatoos is greater than is generally assumed. These birds do not gnaw simply to be destructive but because they are seeking beetles and larvae. After a long period of perseverance, Dr Burkard has persuaded his cockatoos to take raw mincemeat, as well as chicken bones; they are particularly fond of the marrow. The exception is the Palm Cockatoo which is virtually vegetarian. The other species are offered dog and cat food (meat and fish) in cubes and layers' pellets. Two to three day old mice are a special delicacy. Mealworms are given in moderation because they can prove too stimulating for the males (which might then attack the females); cheese, curd and yoghurt are also offered.

Accommodation: A cage for a pet cockatoo should be as large as possible, even though the bird is regularly let out. It should not be kept on a stand, which was formerly the most common method of keeping large parrots. Really large commercially produced cages are extremely expensive; as an alternative one should be specially constructed using welded mesh of the heaviest gauge obtainable.

It is worth putting some thought into the construction of such a cage. To facilitate cleaning, it should be made in sections which screw together. At regular intervals it can be dismantled and thoroughly cleaned. The wooden edges of the cage should be lined with metal, preferably in the form of removable metal inserts – again to facilitate cleaning. For the body of the cage, heavy gauge 25 mm (1 in) square welded mesh is the most satisfactory; for indoor use only, 50 mm (2 in) square mesh could be used. A removable metal tray is essential. Metal food and water containers should slot into a hinged door on the front of the cage and swing outwards for removal. The design has the advantage that the cockatoos are unable to throw containers to the ground or use them as playthings and that, as some cockatoos will playfully – or otherwise – grab at the hand which feeds them, it will remove the possibility of the owner being bitten.

Similar containers, on a larger scale, can be used in an aviary.

An outdoor enclosure for cockatoos is expensive to construct because of the additional safety features which are necessary, i.e. the strongest gauge wire or chain link available and metal strips to line any timber used. Ideally, the framework should be made of angle iron. Alternatively one can buy welded mesh panels which are clipped together.

Reconstructed stone or concrete are the best materials from which to construct the shelter. Wood should be avoided since there is no kind that a cockatoo cannot reduce to sawdust!

Most cockatoos prefer to roost in the open part of the aviary, no doubt because of their habit in the wild of having special roosting trees from which they remove all the foliage. Leadbeater's Cockatoos, for example, choose the tallest trees in the area and strip the top branches. Only one or two trees are chosen and the same ones will be used for many generations. Roosting in this manner must add to their sense of security which presumably is why some dislike sleeping in an enclosed shelter. Nevertheless, if a light and spacious shelter is constructed and the birds are driven inside before dusk every night, this will be of advantage during the winter, as cockatoos do not usually roost in their nest-boxes. Most cockatoos are extremely hardy when acclimatised and do not appear to suffer any ill effects from roosting in the open during bad weather. If necessary, additional protection can be provided during cold weather with the use of heavy duty plastic sheet or PVC on a frame which can be buttoned into position. This will shelter the birds from cold winds.

Cockatoos must be regularly provided with fresh branches for gnawing. Failure to do this will result in them destroying anything they can put their beaks to; some will even pull the staples out of the welded mesh.

The floor of the aviary *must* be made of concrete since these birds will burrow through turf or earth, possibly arriving in the adjoining aviary with fatal results to the occupants.

In a built-up area, some thought must be given to the siting of the enclosure. Because of the loud voices which cockatoos possess, the aviary should be placed as far as possible away from neighbouring houses. The birds may also be a source of annoyance to the owner's family, if placed too near the house.

The large species, such as the Moluccan and the Umbrella, require an aviary which is not less than 4.5 m (15 ft) in length. Although they have been kept – and even bred – in smaller enclosures, for the greater enjoyment of birds and owner, a flight of this length is desirable. It is a magnificent sight to see these lovely birds in flight. This applies especially to Leadbeater's Cockatoos, with their exquisitely coloured under wing coverts, the beauty of which can be seen only in an aviary of adequate length. The smaller species, such as Goffin's, can be housed in an aviary only 90 cm (3 ft) wide but for the large species the width should be 1.8 m (6 ft). An ideal aviary for large cockatoos would be 6 m (20 ft) in length as long as the birds are not nervous; cockatoos will steady down more quickly in a smaller aviary, preferably situated where they will have plenty of contact with people. However, one great advantage of a long aviary for certain cockatoo pairs is that the female has a better opportunity to escape attack by the male.

Pets and Breeding: Cockatoos in captivity present some special problems, thus one should not lightly undertake the acquisition of these beautiful and very intelligent birds. Having seen what an exceptionally attractive pet a tame cockatoo can make, many people long to acquire one of their own. After doing so, all too often it is not long before problems start to occur, mainly because the new owner does not understand sufficiently the needs of a cockatoo.

A tame young bird will make an enchanting pet and perhaps a life-long companion – provided that much time can be devoted to it. An adult bird is not likely to become tame enough to enjoy being closely confined and could, out of frustration and boredom, start to remove its feathers. The same is true of a very tame bird which is neglected. There are few more demanding pets than tame cockatoos – or macaws – and unless one is prepared to devote several hours daily to such birds, their purchase should not even be contemplated.

Perhaps only those who have the misfortune to be house-bound are truly competent to look after a very tame cockatoo which can demand as much time and affection as a child. In addition to plucking themselves, neglected birds could develop into screamers which emit ear-splitting yells immediately they are left alone. This is especially true of the large and intelligent birds, such as the Moluccan, which can become desperate for attention and affection.

Unfortunately, it can be a long and difficult process to 'rehabilitate' such birds. Owners of cockatoos often fail to seek advice until their bird is badly plucked, by which time it is difficult to help it. The owner of any tame bird which starts to pluck itself must try to ascertain the cause. Often it is because the bird is not receiving as much attention as formerly; if this is the case, to be fair to the bird it should be found a good home where it will be cherished and fussed over for hours every day.

If the bird is not tame and has not seriously plucked itself, there is a solution which usually proves successful: to place the bird in an aviary with another of its own species and of the opposite sex. Feather plucking is discussed more fully in Chapter 2.

Keeping a pet cockatoo is only rewarding if every thought is given to its welfare and much time is spent with it. Under these conditions, there can be few more enchanting pets. The small species, especially the Lesser Sulphur-crested, make the best house pets; the large cockatoos are too noisy – often unbearably so – and, as already mentioned, almost intolerably demanding.

Buying an adult, untrained cockatoo for a pet is a very common mistake, usually made by people who have no previous experience with birds and who do not know to whom to turn for advice. It is unusual for such birds to become tame; indeed, closely confining a nervous cockatoo causes it untold stress. Such birds should be kept in an aviary with a member of their own kind.

Young but slightly older birds can be distinguished from adults in good light by the eye colour. In small cockatoos and most of the large white species, the iris of the eye is usually, but not invariably, black in the male and brown or reddish brown in the female. Young birds have the eyes dark grey – which can be mistaken for black in poor light. Many have a few grey feathers in the plumage.

Other young cockatoos may be nervous and taming may take a long period – but will eventually be achieved. Taming nervous adult birds is another matter; I feel it is unfair to cage such birds and that only in an aviary are they likely to thrive.

It should be pointed out that cockatoos give off much white dust from their feathers; some people are allergic to the dust from parrots, and cockatoos are most likely to prove troublesome in this respect. They possess powder down feathers for maintaining the plumage in good condition. These modified down feathers grow continuously and disintegrate at the tips, producing the powder. Regular spraying of cockatoos kept indoors prevents this becoming a problem.

Breeding cockatoos is seldom easy. Perhaps more than most parrots, they have the tendency to neglect or desert their young. This may be due to the fact that they are not receiving the correct diet, but it is difficult to ascertain what that is in view of their reluctance to sample new foods. Rearing foods can include corn-on-the-cob and wheat and barley in the ear. Dry wholemeal, or stale bread, white or brown, soaked in honey and water or milk, is often relished. It may be that in difficult cases they require more animal protein, or it may be that these intelligent birds are particularly sensitive to disturbance.

It is so common for cockatoos to desert their young that aviculturists who have chicks in the nest should prepare for the necessity of hand-rearing. In Britain, only a few cockatoos are reared by hand but in the USA there are many breeders who are practised in the art of hand-feeding cockatoos and achieve very encouraging results. Not surprisingly, the majority of hand-reared birds are sold as pets.

The breeder of cockatoos must have unlimited patience. Young birds will take several years to mature and some adult birds will take a similar period to settle down. However, there are numerous instances of adult cockatoos going to nest after they have been together only a few months, usually birds which have been several years in captivity. There are also cases of aviary-bred cockatoos rearing young when only two years old – but these are exceptional.

Sexing adult cockatoos is a problem in some white species; even those in which the eye colour differs can present problems as the difference is not always pronounced and may even be misleading or incorrect. Surgical sexing has shown that there are black-eyed females in the small species and brown-eyed male and black-eyed female Roseate Cockatoos. Adult black cockatoos, except the Palm, are sexually dimorphic, although dimorphism is slight in some species.

Another problem in breeding cockatoos is compatibility. This is not only a question of two birds learning to accept each other; unfortunately, many female cockatoos in captivity have been slain in a vicious attack by the male – and the reverse has been known. It is for this reason that particular care must be exercised when introducing two adult cockatoos. If necessary, the male's flight feathers should be cut on one wing, so that the female can fly away from him if he attacks her.

A further problem is the habitual destruction of the nesting facilities provided. Many cockatoo aviaries are so well reinforced that the nest-box or barrel is the only destructible object. Little wonder that it is speedily reduced to splinters! An ingenious answer to this problem was found at Busch Gardens, Tampa, Florida. Nests are made of concrete to resemble hollow tree trunks, with an inspection door at the base.

It is difficult for many aviculturists to procure logs or branches on which cockatoos can work out their destructive urges but this is so important for their well-being that it is a factor which should be considered *before* cockatoos are purchased. Anyone who has witnessed the great enjoyment these birds derive from gnawing up part of a tree will feel that making an effort to obtain one occasionally is well worthwhile. When a huge limb of an apple tree crashed down under the weight of the apples one autumn, it was manoeuvred into the flight containing Roseate Cockatoos and they spent many happy hours destroying it.

The outside of a nest-box or barrel for cockatoos should be partly reinforced. Metal strips can be used to line the entrance hole as this is usually the most vulnerable area. The whole outer surface can be encased in welded mesh and the inside of the nest can be similarly lined. However, a cockatoo's urge to gnaw while incubating should be taken into account and large pieces of hard wood should be tacked on to the inside. These can be renewed as necessary.

Natural logs are often more attractive to cockatoos than nest-boxes and it is therefore worth attempting to obtain suitable logs. For large cockatoos, especially the black species, part of a tree trunk will prove ideal and this should be manoeuvred into position *before* construction of the aviary is completed, if possible. A log with an outer diameter of about 60 cm (2 ft) and an inner diameter of 25 to 31 cm (10 to 12 in) is suitable. The bottom of the log should be closed off with metal or $\frac{3}{8}$ in wire netting to prevent access by mice. If the birds fail to use the log, mice may breed inside and the log should therefore be inspected regularly. If the log does not contain a natural entrance a hole should be made about 15 cm (6 in) from the top. The diameter should be only just large enough to admit the birds. If there is a natural hole which is too small, the birds will enlarge it.

Such activity could stimulate nesting activity – another reason why natural logs are of value. The top of the log should be closed to the weather by fitting it with a removable lid when used for *Cacatua* cockatoos; black cockatoos prefer the top left open. This will aid inspection in a short log. In a tall one, a clever carpenter could cut out an inspection door near the level of the nest. This will prove invaluable in an emergency, especially if it is necessary to remove the chick or chicks for hand-rearing. Without an inspection door, it will be very difficult to discover what is happening.

The white cockatoos share incubation between male and female, it being usual for the male to incubate during the day and the female at night. In the Black Cockatoos, incubation is carried out by the female only and the clutch consists of one or two eggs. The incubation period is recorded as being from 25 to 30 days in the white species. In the *Calyptorhynchus* Black Cockatoos, the minimum incubation period is 29 days.

Breeders with no previous experience with cockatoos often become very optimistic when they see their birds mating. In many pairs, however, this would appear to be a way of maintaining or strengthening the pair bond and does not mean that eggs are imminent.

In many birds, the pair bond is maintained by courtship feeding, yet this does not occur at all with most cockatoos that share incubation. One exception I know of is a pair of Lesser Sulphur-crests. Courtship feeding does occur in the *Calyptorhynchus* species, in which only the female incubates.

When the chicks hatch the breeder's problems start; as already stated, providing the correct diet for adequate growth can be difficult.

Australian cockatoos remain in the nest for the short period of eight or nine weeks; for other white cockatoos the period is ten to 12 weeks. Black Cockatoos spend between 11 weeks and three months in the nest. Unlike most parrots, the chicks of cockatoos do not have a second down.

On fledging, cockatoo chicks may return to the nest at night, with their parents, for a few days. It is advisable to remove them fairly soon after they become independent for there are so many cases on record of one adult persecuting or even killing its young – those of the same sex being the usual target.

Prosciger
Prosciger

Palm Cockatoo
P. aterrimus aterrimus

Description: The single member of this genus is easily recognised by its large size, entirely greyish black plumage and by the form of the crest which

Palm Cockatoo (*Prosciger aterrimus aterrimus*).

consists of long, narrow feathers which project beyond the nape of the neck. Indeed, it is the largest of the cockatoos, varying in length from about 80 cm (31 in) to only 70 cm (26 in), according to the locality from which the bird originates. It has a massive strongly curved black bill. The large red naked cheek patches provide the only touch of bright colour and these 'blush' even redder when the bird is excited. It also provides an indication of health; in birds in poor condition the cheeks are pale pink. The black-tipped red tongue is visible through the gap between the upper and lower mandibles. The iris is dark brown and the legs are grey. Plumage is alike in male and female; the female is smaller and the upper mandible is longer in the male. Weight: (wild-caught) 760 g (27 oz).

Immature birds have the feathers of the under parts and under wing coverts edged with pale yellow. On fledging, the beak is edged with white and the periorbital ring is white.

Two subspecies are recognised; *P. a. goliath* is distinguished by its larger size and *P. a. stenolophus* by its narrower crest feathers.

Range/Habitat: The Palm Cockatoo inhabits the Aru Islands, New Guinea and offshore islands and the Cape York Peninsula in northern Australia. It is apparently fairly common throughout New Guinea, except in the vicinity of towns and villages where it has become scarce due to persistent hunting. It is a conspicuous bird, seen singly, in pairs or in small parties, perching on top of tall trees or flying above the forest canopy. In New Guinea, its habitat is forest and dense savannah woodland, up to an altitude of about 1,300 m (4,250 ft), while in Australia it is found in the zone between dense rainforest and eucalyptus woodland in the Cape York Peninsula. It feeds on nuts, seeds, fruits, berries and leaf buds, occasionally on the ground but usually in trees.

Its nesting habits are unique among cockatoos for it builds a platform of twigs inside the nest.

Aviculture: Palm Cockatoos have always been expensive to purchase and infrequently imported. However, from the noise aspect, they are more suitable for private collections than the white cockatoos. Their normal call note is quite unlike that of any other parrot, being a quite attractive whistle. The 12th Duke of Bedford's male used its voice only in moments of excitement, when it resembled that 'of a kitchen-maid when similarly elated'. A few years later he described the sounds made by his pair as a 'rattling chatter, like a Magpie's, and a very loud, sudden, harsh sound, not a screech...'.

In display, male and female face each other with crest erect. They stamp their feet and bow low, a performance which is fascinating to observe. The bare skin on the face 'blushes' deep red during the display.

Those who are familiar with this cockatoo in captivity invariably stress its gentle disposition. One owner of a Palm Cockatoo said that it was impossible to make the bird bite. This I can believe for a friend who had a pair delighted in guiding the finger of every admirer of the female into her beak, confident that she would do them no harm.

Palms are more easily stressed than other cockatoos. Dr Burkard has found that, after being moved, even to a different aviary, they may refuse food for some days and the bare skin on the cheeks becomes pale.

To date, Palm Cockatoos have bred successfully in collections on very few occasions. In Sydney, Australia, a pair obtained by R. T. Lynn, in 1968, when they were at least 30 years old, reared a youngster to independence in three successive years. Taronga Zoo, in Sydney, has also been successful. One pair was housed in an aviary 7.6 × 2.4 × 2.1 m (23 × 8 × 7 ft) and a second pair occupied a 6.1 × 3 × 2.4 m (19 × 10 × 8 ft) aviary on display. Each enclosure had a concrete shelter at one end, the flight being constructed of wire on a pipe frame. The off-exhibit pair were provided with a hollow log 1.5 m (5 ft) high and 38 cm (15 in) in diameter. The sawn-off end was set into a closely fitting cylindrical metal bin and placed on the ground in the shelter.

Wood chippings to a depth of about 30 cm (12 in) were put in the bottom of the cavity. The log was soon investigated and both birds chewed the twigs and branches into splinters and dropped them into the cavity where they formed a porous platform approximately 5 cm (2 in) deep. Exactly the same behaviour is found in birds in the wild, thus protecting the eggs of young from excessive rainfall, and allowing the chick's droppings to drain down through the sticks.

By the end of September, the female was spending most of her time in the log. A chick was heard on November 3. From this and subsequent breeding attempts, it was believed that the incubation period was 31 to 35 days. The male was never seen inside the log but he frequently fed the female.

In January, the male became ill with a *Candida albicans* infection of the crop. The adults and chick were therefore treated with Mycostatin; the adults responded quite quickly to the treatment but the young bird took two months to recover, only to die of psittacosis in April 1972. In 1974, another Palm Cockatoo was reared at Taronga Zoo and in the following year the first European breeding occurred in Neuwied in West Germany.

When the chick at Taronga was first seen, aged 60 days, it was covered with glossy black feathers, except for a bare area on the neck and crop. The primaries and tail feathers were still partly enclosed in the feather sheaths. A second pair at Taronga produced a chick which fledged in July 1973 after spending 100–110 days in the nest. (Previously, the female had laid eight single-egg clutches which had failed to hatch.) The young bird could not fly for two weeks after leaving the nest and was fed by its parents for six weeks.

In Britain, the first breeding of the Palm Cockatoo occurred in 1984 in the collection of Mr and Mrs R. Mann of Peterborough; the birds belonged to G. A. Smith. In the previous year, a chick had hatched in another collection but died at the age of ten weeks. The pair belonging to G. A. Smith were imported in 1977 and housed in an aviary measuring 5 m (15 ft) square and 2 m (6 ft 6 in) high. The nest-box was built of concrete blocks.

The first egg was laid in 1982 but was broken when found. Next year, another egg was laid and incubated by male and female. It was cracked about one week before it was due to hatch, patched up with nail varnish and placed in an incubator but the chick died before starting to pip. The nest-box was then cleared of sticks (Palm Cockatoos build a large nest), mouse nests, stones and the strips of plastic used in nest-building.

In 1984, the egg was laid on April 27; it measured 49.25 × 34.30 mm ($1\frac{9}{10} × 1\frac{2}{5}$ in) and weighed, after eight days of incubation, 30.92 g ($1\frac{1}{10}$ oz). The two eggs of a pair of Lesser Sulphur-crested Cockatoos were removed and replaced with the Palm Cockatoo's egg. It hatched after 34 days, four days after the chick commenced to pip. It was placed in a brooder at a temperature of 36.3°C (98°F) and fed 1.5 ml ($\frac{3}{10}$ teaspoon) of food every two hours. It weighed 18.47 g ($\frac{7}{10}$ oz) on hatching and was naked of down and its toes were clenched. The toes had opened out by the tenth day.

After five days the food was increased to 2 ml ($\frac{2}{5}$ teaspoon) every three hours. The initial rearing food consisted of Milupa 7-Cereal made

into a thin mixture with water; after six days, ground sunflower kernels were added. By day nine, the food consisted of two parts of Milupa 7-Cereal, one part of Milupa Mixed Vegetables and one part of ground sunflower kernels, with a little bone meal, mixed with water. From day 15, the food comprised equal parts of Milupa Mixed Vegetables, ground sunflower and the proprietary rearing food CéDé. The last feed was at 11.30 p.m. and the first at 5.30 a.m.

At 17 days, the chick's eyes opened, at 20 days feathers were apparent under the skin of the crown; the first feathers, those of the back, erupted at 28 days. The ears opened at 24 days. At 30 days, the cheeks blushed pink and two days later the bill was becoming black. By 43 days, the tongue was assuming a mauve colour and three days later the first feathers broke through the quills.

In common with other cockatoos (and contrary to Kerry Muller's account of the success at Taronga Zoo, made in 1975), the chick grew no second down. At 22 weeks it weighed 933 g (33 oz), approximately the weight of an adult. At five months old, it was fed only twice daily. A few weeks later it was as large as the male parent.

The female laid again on June 9; the egg measured 48.05 × 34.30 mm ($1\frac{9}{10} × 1\frac{2}{5}$ in) and weighed 30.35 g (about 1 oz) after an estimated eight days incubation. It was placed in an incubator and no water was added. It hatched after an estimated 34 days and was fed on equal parts of Milupa, CéDé and sunflower kernels with a little bone meal. It grew well but died at $5\frac{1}{2}$ months. George Smith (1985) stated:

> Autopsy showed its death to be consequent upon an enterotoxaemia *Clostridium perfringens (welchii)*. The liver and other viscera – except for the gizzard – were seemingly normal.

In his experience, this is a common cause of death in parrot chicks although it is never mentioned in the avicultural literature.

The crop of these chicks was described as:

> . . . particularly pendulous and hangs, not always emptying itself completely, loosely from the lower neck. As a large

The first Palm Cockatoo hatched in Britain by Mr and Mrs R. Mann and G.A. Smith.

capacity food reservoir, it indicates that the parents could feed their chick but once or twice during the day. I believe that the finely triturated (ground) diet fed by the hand-rearers aggravated this natural feature. This is partly borne out in the post mortem examination of the second chick . . .

In East Germany, the Palm Cockatoo was bred in Leipzig Zoo in 1981. One egg was laid on February 13. The height of the nest of twigs was raised to such a degree that, by the time the chick was eight weeks old, it could see out of the entrance. It left the nest at 12 weeks. The female laid again on August 2 and another chick was produced. This chick either died or was removed for hand-rearing because the female laid again on December 3. The resulting chick died at 14 days. In 1982, one chick was reared from three clutches (de Grahl, 1984). Also in 1984, a Palm Cockatoo was reared at Birdland, Bourton-on-the-Water.

All those who have kept Palm Cockatoos have remarked on their fondness for almonds. All nuts, even Brazils, are cracked with the same ease that a parrot cracks sunflower seed. Some nuts should be provided daily. At Taronga, the Palm Cockatoos would seldom eat fruit or greenfood; one bird would nibble at papaya and apple. A pair belonging to a friend are fond of raw onion. Sunflower seed, wheat and hard maize can be provided as the basis of the diet, with added vitamins for birds which refuse greenfood.

Calyptorhynchus
Calyptorhynchus

Outside Australia, members of this genus have always been rare in aviculture and, as has mainly been the case in the past, only mainstream zoos are likely to have the privilege of keeping these magnificent birds in the future. As with all Australian species at the time of writing, they are subject to the strict export regulations which allow only *bona fide* zoos to obtain them. In Australia, however, many private aviculturists keep these birds.

To my mind, there are few more interesting parrots: they are highly intelligent, strikingly handsome and their large size gives them a majestic appeal found in few other parrots.

The late Sir Edward Hallstrom made a most interesting discovery about their anatomy: they lack a gizzard. He discovered this fact during autopsy of a Glossy Cockatoo chick. Close examination proved that close to the crop was a receptacle containing food which was not a muscular gizzard. It was a parchment-like bag which was described as being like a secondary crop for the storage of food. In one part of the intestine were rudimentary muscles. It was noticed that a muscular portion of the bowel had two valves, and the outer one was easily blocked when the bird was fed with any substance containing fine bran. Bran of rice, oats, or wheat caused a stoppage.

Black Cockatoo
C. funereus

Range/Habitat: There are two widely separated areas of distribution: southwestern and eastern Australia including Tasmania.

Funereal (Yellow-tailed) Cockatoo
C.f. funereus

Description: The Funereal Cockatoo is mainly brownish black, with the feathers of the neck and under parts margined broadly with yellow; elsewhere the body feathers are narrowly margined with yellow. Ear coverts are yellow, brighter in the female. The tail is brownish black,

Yellow-tailed Black Cockatoo (*Calyptorhynchus funereus funereus*).

all but the two central feathers having a very broad band of yellow, freckled (more heavily in the female) with brownish black. The iris is dark brown, the bill dark grey in the male and horn-coloured in the female. The unfeathered area surrounding the eye is pink in the male, dark grey in the female. Length: about 65 cm (26 in). Weight: M (wild-caught) 749–760 g ($26\frac{1}{2}$–$26\frac{4}{5}$ oz); F (wild-caught) 840–900 g ($29\frac{1}{2}$–$31\frac{3}{4}$ oz).

Immature birds resemble the female; young males usually have dull yellow ear coverts and some grey on the bill. Very young birds have the bill white.

Range/Habitat: This race occurs in eastern Australia, from central Queensland south through New South Wales to easternmost Victoria. Funereal Cockatoos are noisy and conspicuous inhabitants of wet coastal woodlands and mountain forests and are seen in pairs or small flocks. They are uncommon or locally moderately common. They

White-tailed Black Cockatoo (*Calyptorhynchus funereus baudinii*) – female.

could be endangered by forestry practices, i.e. destruction of old trees bearing hollows suitable for nest sites.

C.f. xanthanotus

Description: It differs from the nominate race in being smaller and having a much shorter tail – only half the length in some birds. Weight: M 645–750 g (22¾–26½ oz); F 610–795 g (21½–28 oz).

Range/Habitat: Tasmania and the larger islands in Bass Strait, also Kangaroo Island and from south-eastern South Australia eastwards through much of southern Victoria.

White-tailed Black (Baudin's) Cockatoo

C.f. baudinii

Description: This distinctive cockatoo differs from the nominate race in having all the yellow areas replaced with white. In the male the ear coverts are greyish; in the female they are white. The bill is dark grey in the male, horn-coloured in the female. Weight: M 645–750 g (22¾–26½ oz); F 610–795 g (21½–28 oz).

Range/Habitat: This race is found only in the extreme south-western corner of Western Australia. A 1977

study indicated that the clearing of woodland and resultant fragmentation of the food supply is causing a decline in recruitment to the population. This race could be seriously endangered unless this warning is heeded and habitat is preserved.

C.f. latirostris

Range/Habitat: This race occurs in south-western Australia, from the coast, south of the Murchison River and inland as far as the Wongan Hills, Kellerberrin and east of Esperance. It is endangered by fragmentation of the food supply during the breeding season, resulting in a deterioration of parental care in some areas. A study carried out at Manmanning by the Division of Wildlife Research (CSIRO) revealed that the breeding success rate during the years 1970 to 1975 was one chick per pair every three years. Weight: M 540–760 g (19–26⅘ oz); F 560–790 g (19¾–27⁹⁄₁₀ oz).

Aviculture: This species has always been rare in captivity and few have been kept outside Australia. During the era when Australian birds were exported without restriction, a number of Funereals were obtained for a large private collection of parrots in Belgium – the Mosckicki collection. For the first

week the birds went on a hunger strike. Every imaginable kind of food was offered – to no avail. In a last desperate effort, woodlice were collected and sealed inside a hollow tree trunk. The trunk was placed inside the cockatoos' aviary and the woodlice could be heard quite clearly inside, even from a distance of several feet. Most cockatoos are very inquisitive birds and soon curiosity prompted one of them to investigate; it ripped open the trunk and consumed the woodlice as they crawled out. This ingenious idea saved the cockatoos' lives. They were fed on woodlice, mealworms concealed under rotten branches (20 per bird daily) and freshly cut wood and were gradually weaned on to the usual cockatoo diet.

John Courtney, who has kept some of his *Calyptorhynchus* Cockatoos for over 20 years, informed me that the Yellow-tailed and White-tailed differ from the Banksian and Glossy in several important aspects of behaviour. They will bathe in standing water, not only squatting in the container, flapping their wings and dunking their heads, but also rolling onto their sides in the water. Banksians and Glossies never do this – although incubating females will step into shallow water and wet the feathers of the abdomen before returning to the nest.

Yellow-tailed and White-tailed Cockatoos eat much greenfood. They rapidly destroy even thick grass until the aviary is quite bare. In contrast, one has to clip the long grass in aviaries containing Glossy and Banksian Cockatoos.

John Courtney noted that, compared with the latter two species, the northern race of the Yellow-tailed has a much more varied display. In full display, the normally pink periorbital area flashes bright red. In addition to the high-pitched squeaking notes, they utter rapid, high-pitched twittering notes; during this performance the tail is usually kept fanned out. Hand-reared birds are much more aloof and would never contemplate perching on a shoulder: 'Yellow-tails have no endearing qualities at all. They are friendly – but at a distance'. They are even more destructive to wooden perches and their frequent loud screams are audible for 1 km (½ mile) or more.

To the best of my knowledge, the

Funereal Cockatoo has yet to be bred outside Australia. What may have been the first captive breeding was achieved by G. F. Taylor. The clutch of this species sometimes consists of one egg but in this case two were laid. The precise incubation period has not been recorded but is probably the same as in the Banksian Cockatoo – 28 or 29 days. The chick hatched by Mr Taylor's pair left the nest when 76 days old. Chicks are completely covered in longish yellow down.

In Tasmania, the Funereal Cockatoo was bred at Westbury Zoo in 1967 and 1968 and, in 1967, success was also achieved with the Banksian Cockatoo. Both pairs were housed in relatively small aviaries measuring 4.5 × 1.8 m (15 × 6 ft) × 2.1 m (7 ft) high. They nested in 44-gallon petrol drums standing on the floor; 15–20 cm (6–8 in) of wood chips were placed on the bottom. The Funereal hatched three chicks from different clutches but only one was reared – and the Banksian female laid 14 eggs before the first fertile one was laid. Both pairs reared their young on nothing more than sunflower seed, oats and apple. This species has also been bred in Healesville in Australia since 1981.

The first recorded breeding of the White-tailed Black Cockatoo occurred under the auspices of the Divison of Wildlife Research (CSIRO) in Australia, with the race *latirostris*. The pair nested in an aviary measuring 4.9 m × 1.2 m (16 × 4 ft) × 2.4 m (8 ft) high; they had previously bred in the wild. The female first laid on October 24, 1973. A single chick hatched and died about six weeks later. In 1974, nearby work prevented the pair nesting. In 1975, two eggs were laid, the first on October 20. The female incubated and hatching of one egg occurred about November 18. The nestling was brooded continuously by the female for about two weeks after hatching (Saunders, 1976). After this period it was fed by the male as well as by the female. It left the nest on February 8 at the age of just over 80 days. During the breeding season, the birds were fed on sunflower seed, mature marri (*Eucalpytus calophylla*) nuts, *Banksia grandis* fruits and pine cones.

On hatching, White-tailed Black

Banksian Cockatoo (*Calyptorhynchus magnificus*) – female.

Cockatoo chicks may have yellow or white down; they are never naked but always well covered with down as the feathers appear.

Banksian (Red-tailed Black) Cockatoo

C. magnificus

Description: This bird is indeed one of the most magnificent of all parrots. In this species, sexual dimorphism is striking for the male is entirely black except for a broad band of scarlet on the outer tail feathers while the female is dotted (on the head) and barred with pale orange-yellow. The under side of the tail is barred with yellow and orange, or yellow only, in the same pattern as the tail feathers of a female Cockatiel. The Banksian Cockatoo has a wide range and there is considerable variation in its plumage. Weight: 660–870 g (23¼–30½ oz); F 620–850 g (21⅘–30 oz).

The Banksian has a crest which is not prominent until erected; the feathers are not elongated. In the male, the bill is dark grey and in the female it is horn-coloured. Length: 60 cm (23 in).

Immature birds usually resemble the female but have little or no yellow spotting on the head; however, it has been recorded that some males leave the nest with red tail bands. It would appear that males can be distinguished, even as fledglings, by the darker upper mandible.

Range/Habitat: The Banksian Cockatoo is widely distributed in eastern, northern and south-western Australia. It is more common and evenly distributed in the north of its range. It is rare in western Victoria and south-eastern Australia. Its habits are similar to those of the Funereal, except for the fact that the diet consists mainly of seeds, including those of eucalyptus, casuarina, Banksia and acacia; nuts and weeds are also eaten and probably grubs on occasions. However, the broad, blunt beak of this species suggests that it may be used for crushing hard seeds and nuts.

These cockatoos usually choose a eucalypt in which to nest, often on a river bank. The usual clutch is one egg; sometimes two are laid and it is said that if both hatch the second chick seldom survives for long.

Aviculture: In the past, a few private aviculturists were fortunate enough to keep this magnificent bird; today, outside Australia, it is likely to be found only in the larger zoos which have obtained them from Australian zoos in exchange. One of the few British aviculturists to have extensive experience with this species – and the only one to breed it – was the 12th Duke of Bedford. 'Dignified and charming pets' was how he described these birds taken when young.

It was the Duke of Bedford's experience that hand-reared males were useless for breeding because they much preferred the company of human beings to that of females of their own species. This was confirmed by the late Alan Lendon, Australian aviculturist and ornithologist of repute, who stated that most females lost their friendliness as soon as they become independent of human feeding.

In the early years of the twentieth century, when *Calyptorhynchus* cockatoos were fairly often available, Sir Charles Lawes-Wittewronge kept a number in a huge enclosure with other cockatoos. A visitor was impressed by a Banksian which flew on to his arm, climbed over his shoulder and rubbed its beak against his ears. He commented on the gentle and affectionate nature of these birds which rarely, if ever, used their powerful beaks as weapons.

Banksian Cockatoos have proved to be extremely long lived in captivity. One in the Parrot House at London Zoo has resided there for over 40 years; cataracts on both eyes indicate its advancing age.

The first captive breeding of this species was probably that which occurred in the 12th Duke of Bedford's aviaries. A single egg laid by the female on the floor of the shelter hatched on December 26, 1939. Despite the cold weather, the chick appeared to thrive for five weeks when it was found to have both legs and both wings broken due to rickets. It was therefore removed for hand-rearing.

Incubating female Banksian Cockatoo in the collection of John Courtney, Australia.

In 1945, two pairs of Banksian Cockatoos nested in Adelaide Zoo and each successfully reared one youngster. It is of interest that the male of the pair was at least 36 years old at the time. His female laid two eggs and the resulting chick left the nest after 96 days. It was first seen to feed itself four months after leaving the nest. The second pair hatched a chick on the floor of the aviary and it flew for the first time at the age of 75 days. Its plumage was more heavily spotted and barred than that of the other youngster (a male) and it eventually proved to be a female. The birds were fed on sunflower seed, hulled oats and boiled maize; pine nuts and lettuce were also eaten. The Duke of Bedford found that his Banksians ate smooth caterpillars greedily, also the small white grubs found inside oak apples. Wasp grubs, gentles and mealworms were usually refused.

This species has consistently reared young at Adelaide Zoo and it has been bred in most years since 1961. In November 1975, Fred Bohner, a keeper at the zoo, obtained a five year old pair. He kindly provided me with the following notes. The pair was provided with a log measuring 1.75 m (5¾ ft) with an inside diameter of 30 cm (12 in). It was hung inside the shelter at an angle of 30° and fixed at a height of 2 m (6½ ft). Moist rotted wood dirt was placed in the bottom to a depth of 30 cm (12 in).

The female entered the log in March 1975 and the first egg was laid on April 22. It was not incubated and artificial incubation proved that it was infertile. A second egg, laid 28 days later, was also infertile. In 1976 the first egg was laid on February 13 and hatched on the 28th day. The nest was inspected when the chick was three days old and resembled 'a small bundle of yellow down'. On the tenth day it 'had a blackish appearance, showing signs of feather growth under the skin'. Its eyes were only half open.

While the chicks were being reared the female took a strong liking to small clumps of 'blue panic grass' which were supplied daily. Sprouted sunflower seed, a few almonds and peanuts, were the basis of the diet, plus a quarter of an apple daily. When nine weeks old, the young bird ventured to the top of the log, from where the female fed it and spent much time preening it. If any sudden noise occurred, she would prod the youngster's head with her beak and send it to the bottom of the log.

The young bird left the nest when 3 months old. For the first four nights, the parents led it to the top of the log where they all roosted; then they took to the front perch of the aviary with the young bird in the middle. Its plumage resembled that of the female; its face was fairly heavily marked with yellowish spots and the rest of the body was slightly spotted. The mandibles were almost entirely white. On fledging, the young cockatoo was able to fly the full 8 m (25 ft) length of the aviary. It was still being fed by the female when 12 months old.

In 1977, the female laid on January 21, thus the young bird was left with the male who weaned it and led it to the food dish. Its call was still a 'soft squeak' and it rarely succeeded in imitating the screech of the adults. When the second youngster left the nest – this one at the age of 2½ months – the first was slightly rejected and was therefore moved to the adjoining aviary. The second bird's plumage was much blacker and lacked the yellow spots on the head; there were a few on the wings and body. The upper and lower mandibles were black with white tips. This fact, together with its louder voice, suggested that it might be a male.

In 1978, the egg was laid on March 9; incubation commenced the following day and the egg hatched after 28 days. The young bird left the log when 12 weeks old.

In 1979, incubation commenced on March 4 and again lasted for 28 days. The female's absence during incubation caused the previous year's youngster to squawk, resulting in the female hitting it on the head to quieten it. It was therefore removed as the annoyance to the adults could cause desertion (Bohner, 1984). The next chick vacated the log at the age of 13 weeks. The female laid again on December 11. A chick hatched on January 8, 1980, and left the nest 13 weeks later.

In 1981, the female laid on February 7 but the resulting chick was deserted, perhaps because of the presence of the previous year's youngster. Mr Bohner suggested that the ideal time to remove a previous youngster is when the female is in her third week of incubation. The female laid again: two eggs.

One hatched on April 26 and the chick left the nest when 11 weeks and three days old.

In 1982, two eggs were laid and incubation commenced on February 12. Both eggs hatched, the first on March 12. The second chick died. In 1983, a chick hatched on March 9 but died because of the presence of the previous year's youngster, which cried frequently. In the second nest, a chick hatched on April 1 and left the log on June 9.

Mr Bohner found that his young Banksian Cockatoos could be sexed when they left the nest – but not later when the beak colour changed. Males have blacker plumage, especially about the face, with fewer speckles on the head or face and sometimes none at all. The upper mandible is black, lower mandible black or white. The males seem to crave more attention from their parents and create more fuss at weaning than females. Males start to display at an early age, chattering and bowing before the red tail feathers appear at about two years and nine months.

Females have predominantly white or mainly colourless beaks on leaving the nest. The spotting on the face is fairly heavily spread, with more spotting on the body than males. The yellow barring on the lower throat is usually more pronounced. This information applies to the Western Australian race, *naso*.

The first successful breeding of the Banksian Cockatoo in the USA occurred at San Diego Zoo in 1954. The parents were reared in Australia by Sir Edward Hallstrom who had bred this species since 1943. Between 1955 and 1970, 15 Banksian Cockatoos were hand-reared at San Diego, where the incubation period, as in Hallstrom's collection, was established as 29 days. One pair in Hallstrom's collection hatched three chicks in one year when he removed the chicks on hatching for hand-rearing.

At Auckland Zoo in New Zealand, this cockatoo has reared young on several occasions since 1977.

In display, the male Banksian erects its crest and spreads out the cheek feathers to cover the beak. The tail is fanned to show the red area and the bird utters a soft note while strutting

along the perch and bowing to the female. In between bowing and fanning the tail, they sing a lengthy high-pitched song.

Glossy Black Cockatoo
C. lathami

Description: The Glossy Black Cockatoo is closely related to the Banksian. The male differs from the male of that species mainly in being smaller and having the head of a brownish shade. The female has the red tail band crossed with black bars and speckled with yellow; there is no spotting or barring on the body plumage. Some adults, especially females, have irregular orange-yellow markings on the head and neck. The beak is dark gun metal grey. Length: 48 cm (19 in). Weight: M 422 g (14⅘ oz); F 430 g (15⅕ oz).

Immature birds are spotted to a greater or lesser degree on the ear coverts, outer wing coverts and lesser under wing coverts. Barring is present on the throat, abdomen and the coloured portion of the tail and on the under tail coverts in some individuals (Courtney, in press).

Courtney pointed out that:

Despite the constantly recurring theme in most current literature (e.g. Lendon, 1973; Forshaw, 1978, 1981), the evidence here shows some males lose all spotted and barred body feathers by 1½ years, acquire the full mating display by less than two years, but retain some barred rectrices from 4½ to almost 5½ years old. Each successive yearly moult, when half the tail is shed in random pattern, produces feathers in which barring is reduced towards basal end of colour patch, the terminal part being clear. When such birds are momentarily glimpsed in flight, not examined in hand, it is easy to mistakenly conclude the tail is clear of bars, especially when many rectrices actually are plain.

He further points out that young birds cannot be sexed:

It is now shown that apparently all recently fledged young have spots; that some proven fledgling males are indistinguishable from same-age females, even to having yellow in the tail; and also that some young males may have yellow-mottled under tail coverts, a feature of adult females.

Range/Habitat: This cockatoo inhabits eastern Australia from central Queensland to eastern Victoria; it is also found on Kangaroo Island, South Australia. In the wild it is a specialised feeder, its diet consisting almost entirely of the seeds of the casuarina tree.

Aviculture: The Glossy Black Cockatoo is unknown in aviculture outside Australia. However, contrary to Hallstrom (1954), they do not have to be maintained primarily on casuarina nuts. At the time of writing, several Australian aviculturists keep and breed this species, including John Courtney. He stressed: 'It is most important for anyone keeping these birds to ensure that they have unlimited access to sunflower seed' (pers. comm., 1984). In addition, his birds receive four broken-up milk arrowroot biscuits daily and assorted nuts – but no casuarina seeds.

The first captive breeding of the Glossy Black Cockatoo occurred in the collection of Sir Edward Hallstrom in 1946. It has also been bred in Taronga Zoo in Sydney on several occasions since 1971. More recently, it has been bred by John Courtney and R. T. Lynn, among others.

Of two females in Mr Courtney's possession, one laid her first egg when she was three years and two weeks old and the other at the age of less than three years. In the latter case, the chick was successfully parent-reared. The female laid on March 1 or 2, 1984. The egg hatched on April 5 to give an incubation period of 34 days, or a minimum of 32½ days. The chick was observed the next day; it was 'covered in long, dense yellow natal down'. By April 12, it was able to sit upright some of the time; at 20 days it was standing and looking up when the nest was inspected. On April 26, its appearance was dark due to the tips of the black feathers showing through the down; these were not apparent on the previous day. By May 11, it was covered in short black feathers, with a tail estimated at 3–4 cm (1⅕–1⅗ in) long. It uttered loud, harsh growling noises when observed. By May 24, at seven weeks, it was two-thirds the body size of an adult; down was still clinging to the tips of some feathers. At eight weeks it was fully feathered but for the tail and would utter snorting hisses

and sway from side to side when observed. On July 3 and 4, driving snow covered everything and was up to a foot deep in places. The nest-log was situated inside the shelter and the young bird had not flown so it was not affected by the weather conditions. On July 17 (165 days) it was first seen flying but did not fly very much until August 5. For some time it would fly to the top of the log or even enter it at the slightest disturbance.

The female stayed in the log with the chick every night until it left the nest. The male would roost away from the nest until an hour after dark, when he would quietly go to the nest and roost at the entrance, tail outwards.

The food begging call of this chick, in common with that of other chicks of this species observed by John Courtney, was a brief repetitive, clear, high-pitched squeak, very similar to that of *C. magnificus*. As in that species (unlike *Cacatua* species), there is no food swallowing vocalisation. The begging call of the *funereus* birds is a harsh rasping sound and the chicks also utter a loud food-swallowing noise (Courtney, in press, and pers. comm., 1984).

In John Courtney's experience, Glossy Cockatoos differ from the other *Calyptorhynchus* species in flying very swiftly within an aviary. The enclosure of his pair measured 3.6 × 1.6 m (12 × 6 ft) × 2.1 m (7 ft) high. They frequently fly backwards and forwards and turn easily.

He described the song of the Glossy as differing from that of the Banksian in being softer and pitched higher. When displaying, the bow is not slow and dignified as in the Banksian; instead, the body is flung forward at the last moment, as if the bird's grip on the perch had slipped.

The Glossy and Banksian are similar in personality. John Courtney told me:

Hundreds of times my male Glossy and Banksian have sat on my shoulder and gently nibbled ears, cheeks, etc – so gently they can scarcely be felt. In between such friendly and affectionate behaviour, they chew holes in shirt and coat collars, and hat brims. I am always amazed at how they distinguish parts of me from my clothes!

In 1946, Hallstrom was successful in rearing the Glossy Black Cockatoo – a first captive breeding. The first chick

he attempted to rear died and with the discovery that it had no gizzard, he was able to rear the next one on the soft, oily kernels of casuarina seeds.

This species has since been bred in Taronga Zoo in Sydney. The chick hatched there in 1970 died but several have been reared since 1971.

Callocephalon
Callocephalon

Gang Gang Cockatoo
C. fimbriatum

Description: This bird, the single member of its genus, is one of the most distinctive of cockatoos with its mainly grey plumage and uniquely formed crest. It is the smallest of the dark-coloured cockatoos, measuring 35 cm (13½ in). The male is slate-grey with white edges to the feathers of the upper parts, excluding those of the primaries, secondaries and tail. The feathers of the head and crest are scarlet, the crest consisting of loosely formed, forward-curling feathers. The feathers below have pale, or even orange-yellow, edges and the wing coverts are washed with dull green. The bill is horn-coloured, the legs grey and the iris dark brown.

Gang Gang Cockatoo (*Callocephalon fimbriatum*) – male.

The female has the head and crest grey and the upper parts and tail are strongly barred with greyish white. The feathers of the under parts are broadly margined with orange and greenish yellow.

Immature birds mainly resemble the female. Males can be distinguished by the red-tipped crest and the red markings on the forehead and crown. The bill is dark grey. Weight: M 210–334 g ($7\frac{2}{5}$–$11\frac{3}{4}$ oz); F 240–300 g ($8\frac{1}{2}$–$10\frac{1}{2}$ oz).

Range/Habitat: The Gang Gang Cockatoo inhabits south-east Australia and Tasmania. It is common in south-eastern New South Wales and eastern Victoria, being less numerous elsewhere. Found in small parties, the birds perch close together in the topmost branches of tall trees and will suddenly take to the air, wheeling and twisting in all directions as though indulging in some kind of game.

A favourite food is the red berries of hawthorn. Gang Gangs will venture into the suburbs of Canberra and Melbourne in order to feed on hawthorn and congregate in flocks where the berries are ripe. They descend to the ground only to drink and to search for nuts and cones. The seed of eucalyptus and acacia trees, also insects and their larvae, form a large part of their diet.

This cockatoo usually nests at a height of 18 to 21 m (60 to 70 ft), often in a eucalypt and near to water. The breeding season extends from October to January. Usually two eggs, sometimes three, are laid and incubated by male and female for about 30 days.

Aviculture: A major problem with Gang Gang Cockatoos is feather mutilation. The eminent Swiss aviculturist Dr R. Burkard realises the importance of feeding these birds in a way which diverts their attention from their plumage and keeps them occupied for hours daily. He described (pers. comm., 1984) feeding ten fir cones daily, as long as supplies last. He wrote: 'This is very good occupational therapy for them as each scale is removed in order to find the small seed'. Rose hips, pyracantha berries and chicken bones are also provided. Sunflower seed is given only occasionally, the seeds consisting of small types such as millet. In this way, they are occupied with their food for three to four hours daily and with gnawing at fresh branches (birch, pine, hazel, etc.) for two or three hours.

Feather plucking can be severe in Gang Gangs which are not kept fully occupied; they damage the primaries so badly that they do not grow again.

The Gang Gang has been bred in captivity on rather few occasions. The first record occurred in France in 1921 in the collection of Madame Lécallier. Her pair used a five-gallon wine cask covered with thick boards and zinc and placed in the highest part of the aviary. Two eggs were laid; both hatched but one chick survived only one day. The surviving chick could be sexed at six weeks when the colour of the crest indicated that it was a male. It left the nest when 60 days old.

The first British breeding occurred in the aviaries of the Duke of Bedford, then Lord Tavistock, in 1938. His pair nested in a hollow tree trunk which was partly filled with peat and decayed wood. Two youngsters, a male and a female, were reared. Food provided was sunflower seed, peanuts, apple and bread and milk. An occasional piece of cooked beef fat was eaten.

The male of Lord Tavistock's pair was obtained on loan from London Zoo in 1937. It had been confined to a cage for so long it was unable to fly and, to make matters worse, it plucked itself. Nevertheless, that year the pair examined the nest and mating occurred. Months later, the male regained the use of its wings and, in the spring, the pair again showed an interest in a hollow tree trunk.

Lord Tavistock (1938) wrote:

Gang Gangs are quaint birds in that a mated pair, though really most devoted, love to engage in mock disputes accompanied by much bad language – *real* bad language, the same that is directed against an enemy. There is also much pretence at biting although not a feather is ever damaged.

On fledging, the young female resembled her mother but had a darker head and some white on the culmen and the tip of the upper mandible. The young male had the crest and the centre of the crown to the forehead red. The pair were still breeding in 1950 when a male and a female were reared.

In Australia, Gang Gangs were reared by Miss S. Merrifield of Jamestown, South Australia, in 1945. The birds were fed on sunflower seed, boiled maize, sweetened bread and milk, lucerne and branches of eucalyptus leaves; some mutton suet was given occasionally. The sunflower and bread and milk were favoured while the young were in the nest. In recent years, this species has been regularly bred in Adelaide and Melbourne Zoos and in several private collections. Chicks have pink skin and sparse creamy yellow down; the width of the mandible is startling (Courtney, pers. comm., 1984).

The Gang Gang Cockatoo was not bred in the USA until 1973 when the pair owned by Mrs Velma Hart of Long Beach, California, reared a male. In the following year, the pair passed into the possession of Dr J. M. Dolan, to whom I am indebted for precise data on incubation periods. The female laid on May 28 and 30 in 1975; chicks hatched on June 23 and 24, giving an incubation period of 26 and 25 days, or 25 days in both cases if incubation started when the second egg was laid. The eyes of the chicks started to open when they were 12 days old and were fully opened by the next day. A male and a female, they left the nest on August 5.

In 1976, the female laid on May 18 and 22, and incubation commenced on May 21. Chicks hatched on June 15 and 16, again giving an incubation period of 25 days. Both were males and left the nest on August 5. In 1977, the incubation period was 27 days and the young, two females, left the nest on August 4. During a three-year period, the dates on which the young fledged did not vary more than a day although eggs were laid between May 16 and May 30.

Also in the USA, this species has been bred at San Diego Zoo.

In recent years, the Gang Gang Cockatoo has been bred in Britain only by J. E. R. Robertson of Colchester. His pair nested in a parrakeet nestbox measuring 25 cm (10 in) square and 46 cm (18 in) high. Other boxes were destroyed. Incubation was carried out by the male during the day and the female at night. In 1976, his pair reared a single youngster, a female, which left the nest on August 25, aged eight weeks. It was removed from the aviary the following February when the female started to bicker with it. In 1977, two young were bred. Rearing food consisted of sunflower seed, bread and milk, bread and honey, spinach beet, banana and apple. In 1978, eggs were laid which disappeared and, in 1979, the pair did not nest.

A pair of Gang Gang Cockatoos owned by Australian aviculturist Keith Hocking (1983) reared young in 1980. Two eggs were laid and the incubation was shared by male and female. The two chicks could be sexed as a male and female as soon as the feathers appeared. The parents fed the young for five or six weeks after they left the nest and the young male begged for food as long as 12 weeks after fledging but was usually ignored towards the end of this period. Seven days after the young left the nest the female plucked their heads bare – but the feathers soon grew and were not removed again. In 1981, the female was paired to a different male. Both the young were females. The nesting site was an open-topped log, 45 cm (18 in) high and 30 cm (12 in) in diameter; other logs were not accepted. It was hung vertically in the corner of the aviary about 50 cm (20 in) below the roof. The female was the dominant member of the pair. Mutual vent preening, while the birds faced in opposite directions, often occurred.

The food consisted of sunflower, millet, canary seed, oats, safflower, milo, maize, gum branches with seed pods, pine tree branches with cones, separate pine cones, branches and berries of cotoneaster and hawthorn, plus pomegranate, apple and silver beet.

Sulphur-crested Cockatoo (*Cacatua galerita*).

Cacatua
Cacatua

The best known and most freely imported of the cockatoos, members of this genus are white (often referred to as 'white cockatoos') or, in three species, pink. Formation of the crest varies and in some species its colour forms a strong contrast to the body plumage. Length varies from 52–30 cm

(19–12 in); the tail is square and rather short. Most immature birds have some grey feathers in their plumage, which are lost at the first moult.

Greater Sulphur-crested Cockatoo
C. galerita galerita

Description: This is probably the cockatoo best known to non-fanciers, despite the fact that, as in the case of other Australian species, only zoos have been allowed to import it since

1960. However, they are very great favourites in zoos and, formerly, were not uncommon household pets.

This is the largest of the white cockatoos which has the crest yellow. The feathers of the crest are thrown forward like a fan in display or when the bird is screeching. When the crest is closed it looks not unlike a narrow yellow, backward-curving 'horn'. The other yellow areas of the plumage are the under side of tail and flight feathers, ear coverts and the bases of the feathers of the cheeks and throat.

The naked area of skin surrounding the eye is white and the iris is dark brown, almost black, in males, dark brown or reddish brown in females. The bill is dark grey. Length: about 50 cm (19 in). Weight: M 815–920 g ($28\frac{3}{4}$–$32\frac{1}{2}$ oz); F 845–975 g ($29\frac{4}{5}$–$34\frac{2}{5}$ oz).

Immature birds have the iris brown. Chicks have the skin surrounding the eye pale blue.

Range/Habitat: The nominate race inhabits northern, eastern and southern Australia and is common throughout most of its range. It was one of the first Australian birds to be sighted by an Englishman. Captain Cook's navigator, Sir Joseph Banks, wrote about the 'White Cockatoos' in his journal, describing them as the wariest birds met with. The first settlers shot parrots for sport but when they started to grow grain and the Greater Sulphur-crests descended on the crops in huge flocks, the persecution by farmers started, and has continued to this day. Yet after centuries of persecution, they remain abundant and are said, in some areas, to be as plentiful as they were when the first white man set foot in Australia. Each flock has its own roost to which its members return at dusk.

This handsome cockatoo feeds on the seeds of injurious weeds, such as burr and thistle. Fruits, nuts, berries, buds, roots, flowers and insects and their larvae also form part of its diet.

The usual nesting site is a hole in a tree or a hollow branch of a eucalypt, often near water and at a considerable height. The same nest site is used annually for a great many years. John Gould, the naturalist, reported over 100 years ago that thousands of these cockatoos nested annually in holes in the high limestone cliffs bordering the Murray River in South Australia. Possibly some still nest there; they certainly did so a century after Gould reported the use of this site.

The following three races are often referred to as 'Medium' Sulphur-crested Cockatoos.

Triton Cockatoo
C. g. triton
Description: It differs from the nominate race in having the skin surrounding the eye blue and in the formation of the crest feathers; the latter are more rounded and broader but resembling those of the Greater rather than the Blue-eyed Cockatoo.
Range/Habitat: This race inhabits New Guinea and the western Papuan islands and has been introduced to islands in Indonesia (Ceramlaut and Goramlaut) and to the Palau Islands in the Pacific.

C. g. eleonora
The race *eleonora* is generally called Medium Sulphur-crested Cockatoo in the USA.
Description: This differs from *triton* in having a smaller bill, narrower crest feathers and smaller size. In adult birds the periorbital ring is white (bluish in immature birds).
Range/Habitat: This race inhabits the Aru Islands, Indonesia.

C. g. fitzroyi
Description: This race is larger than the Triton and has little yellow on the ear coverts and the bases of the feathers of the cheeks and throat. The periorbital skin is pale blue and the bill is broader than that of the Greater Sulphur-crest. Weight: M 610–720 g ($21\frac{1}{2}$–$25\frac{2}{5}$ oz); F 600–780 g ($21\frac{1}{5}$–$27\frac{1}{2}$ g).
Range/Habitat: It inhabits northern Australia and the larger offshore islands.

Aviculture: Before the export of Australian fauna was prohibited the Greater Sulphur-crest was cherished as a pet by many; it was loved for its great intelligence and attractive personality. Today, the aviculturist is more likely to encounter the races from Indonesia and New Guinea. The *galerita* cockatoos make superb aviary birds, being hardy, showy and long-lived. As house pets they would be most appealing but for their extremely loud, harsh voices.

The Greater Sulphur-crested Cockatoo is famed for its longevity. The authenticity of some cases would be difficult to prove yet it would seem that some claims of centenarians are valid. The most famous of these was 'Cocky Bennett', reputed to be 119 years old at the time of his death in Australia. He was almost featherless for the last 20 years of his life. A photograph in a 1916 issue of *Bird Notes* depicts this ancient cockatoo after it had been preserved by a taxidermist: a grotesque sight with overgrown beak reaching to its breast.

In Europe, records of breeding successes with the Greater Sulphur-crested Cockatoo are not numerous. In England, Herbert Whitley of Devon bred from a pair which nested at liberty in an elm tree in 1915. The single chick died after it had been weaned. The parents were wintered indoors and released during the spring. They nested in the same elm and reared two young. These were removed when two months old and placed in an aviary with their parents. While at liberty, the parents were seen as far as five kilometres (three miles) from their home.

In the USA, this cockatoo was bred by W. Leland Smith on several occasions prior to 1936. Two who were consistently successful with this species were W. J. Sheffler and I. D. Putnam. In 1944, Mr Putnam hand-fed six young from two pairs, each female laying three eggs. One pair hatched the eggs consecutively, while the other hatched them together and the third later, thus in that case incubation did not start until the second egg was laid.

Among more recent successes with this species are those at Havana Zoo in Cuba, Fort Worth in Texas, Busch Gardens in Tampa, Florida, Los Angeles and San Francisco zoos in California, Gosford and Adelaide in Australia and Auckland in New Zealand.

In England, Colchester aviculturist J. E. R. Robertson reared a Greater-Sulphur-crested Cockatoo in 1974. His pair hatched a chick on July 1 which left the nest on September 16, aged 11 weeks. It was reared on bread and milk and glucose, bread soaked in honey water, a proprietary rearing food for Budgerigars, soaked oats, sunflower seed and peanuts. One egg laid by my female measured 42 × 32 mm ($1\frac{3}{5}$ × $1\frac{1}{4}$ in).

The Triton Cockatoo is fairly often imported into Europe and the USA but no reference to it can be found in the earlier avicultural literature, either because it was not exported or because it was not distinguished from the Greater Sulphur-crest.

The first breeding success of which I know is that which occurred at

Amsterdam Zoo in 1968. It has also been bred at Vogelpark Walsrode since 1979.

In the USA, Richard Schock of North Carolina purchased a pair in April 1974. They were spaciously housed in an aviary 7.2 × 3.3 m (24 × 11 ft) and 1.8 m (6 ft) high. On May 19, 1975, one egg was seen when the large nest-box was inspected. On June 19, a chick was heard; its voice was said to carry 23 m (75 ft). By June 25, it was covered with yellow hair-like down. It left the nest on September 10 when 12 weeks old. For two weeks it returned at night to roost. Rearing food consisted of soaked sunflower seed plus two or three oranges daily and whole beet tops. The young bird had deep brown eyes; those of the male were black and the female's were reddish brown – nearer red.

In 1976, two eggs were laid during April. On May 17, two chicks, aged two and a half weeks, were removed for hand-rearing. At the age of one month, one of the chicks was unable to digest food and a veterinary surgeon had to remove its crop contents. Its food was then mixed with the droppings of the thriving youngster; this was carried out three times daily and, within two days, the chick was 'eating like a horse'. Both were successfully reared (Schock, 1977).

In 1975, the Triton Cockatoo was bred in Canada. Robert McPeek obtained his pair in 1973. They were shy and spent much time in the nest-box. In April 1975, the sound of chicks being fed was heard. On the sixth day, the young were removed; both died soon after and it was found that their crops had been filled with whole sunflower seed. In mid-September, another chick hatched. Sunflower seed was removed and the chick was fed on dandelion and Swiss chard, canary seed and millet. At six weeks, sunflower seed was offered. On December 5, the young Triton left the nest; it was almost as large as its parents and was very tame.

In Britain, the Triton Cockatoo was bred by J. E. R. Robertson of Colchester in 1978. Two chicks hand-reared from a pair belonging to G. A. Smith weighed 16 g and 13.5 g (about $\frac{1}{2}$ oz) on hatching; one reached a weight of 450 g ($15\frac{9}{10}$ oz) before weaning and 380 g ($13\frac{2}{5}$ oz) at weaning; the other reached a peak of 510 g (18 oz) and weighed 470 g ($16\frac{1}{2}$ oz) at weaning.

Blue-eyed Cockatoo
C.g. ophthalmica
Description: This is the most distinctive of the races of the Greater Sulphur-crest. It differs from the Triton Cockatoo principally in the deeper blue skin surrounding the eye and in the formation of the yellow crest feathers. The latter are broad and resemble more nearly those of a Moluccan Cockatoo in that respect. Length: 50 cm (20 in)
Range/Habitat: The Blue-eyed Cockatoo is found in the islands of New Britain and New Ireland in the Bismarck Archipelago, New Guinea.
Aviculture: The first recorded breeding of this race appears to be that which occurred in 1951 in the aviaries of Sir Edward Hallstrom in Australia. Two eggs were laid and one chick was reared.

The second recorded breeding and the first in Britain took place in 1964. The breeder was A. V. Griffiths of Wales. Imported in 1963, the birds were placed in an aviary of 10.8 m (36 ft) long which was later reduced to 5.4 m (18 ft). The female became egg-bound on laying her first egg in October 1963 and again in the following May, one month after being reunited with the male. She laid two eggs in mid July, one of which hatched. The young cockatoo left the nest on November 10. In autumn 1965, another chick was hatched; it left the nest on December 31. While young were being reared, two handfuls of maggots were given daily, also apple, paddy rice and canary seed. Little interest was shown in sunflower or hemp seed.

At Chester Zoo in England, the Blue-eyed Cockatoo has been bred since 1973 when a pair was housed in an off-exhibit aviary. The youngster reared that year was a female and was paired with a male presented in 1975. Neither pair bred until 1979 when, in the aviaries attached to the Parrot House, they each reared one youngster – a male and a female. In 1981, both pairs nested again, each producing one male. In 1983, the youngest pair nested in mid-May. There were two chicks by June 20. In 1983, a pair of Blue-eyed Cockatoos were sent from Chester to Rotterdam Zoo on breeding loan.

At Chester, the diet of this species consists of parrot mixture, a varied selection of fruits and vegetables and, when young hatch, soaked seed, egg rearing food, boiled maize wheat-germ cereal and Vionate (Bloomfield, 1984).

At Clee Hill Bird Gardens in England, this species was hand-reared in 1981.

Lesser Sulphur-crested Cockatoo
C. sulphurea sulphurea
Description: This species is an almost perfect miniature of the Greater Sulphur-crest, measuring about 33 cm ($12\frac{1}{2}$ in). The plumage is mainly white, with the narrow backward-curving crest and the ear coverts yellow. The bases of the feathers of the neck and under parts are yellow and the under side of the flight and tail feathers is washed with yellow. The bill is grey-black, also the feet. The iris is dark brown to black in the male and brownish red in the female. Immature birds have the iris grey and the beak whitish.
Range/Habitat: Range of this species is Celebes, Sunda Islands and islands in the Flores and Java seas, Indonesia.

Timor Cockatoo
C.s. parvula
Description: This subspecies is considerably smaller than the nominate race and altogether more dainty in appearance. It has a smaller beak in proportion to the body and measures about 30 cm (12 in). There is a noticeable variation in the colouration, the ear coverts being faintly marked with yellow in some birds and bright yellow on the under parts.

A chick hatched by Elizabeth Butterworth's pair in 1982 was hand-reared. It weighed 25 g ($\frac{9}{10}$ oz) at nine days, 32 g ($1\frac{1}{10}$ oz) at 11 days, 42 g ($1\frac{1}{2}$ oz) at 42 days, 52.5 g ($1\frac{9}{10}$ oz) at 15 days, 110 g ($3\frac{9}{10}$ oz) at 23 days and 310 g ($10\frac{9}{10}$ oz) at 51 days.

C.s. djampeana
Description: This race, too, has a smaller bill than the nominate.
Range/Habitat: This comes from a number of islands in Indonesia including Djampea.

Aviculture: Lessers, and Citron-crested Cockatoos are very beautiful aviary birds. Perhaps they are seen to their best advantage when alarmed, when they will rock backwards and forwards, lift their wings and spread their crests.

Adult Lesser and Citron-crested Cockatoos are often extremely timid when newly imported and may take a long time to lose their fear. They are likely to steady down more quickly if housed in an aviary where they can fly away from the observer but taming may take many months if they are allowed to fly into their shelter every time they catch sight of a human 'intruder'.

In Britain, the first recorded breeding of the Lesser Sulphur-crested Cockatoo occurred in 1924. A pair belonging to M. T. Allen which had hatched a chick two years previously, had three eggs; one was infertile and the other two hatched. About one month after the young cockatoos left the nest one was literally torn to pieces by the male; the other was rescued only slightly injured. Such attacks are not uncommon in cockatoos and emphasise the necessity of removing the young as soon as they are independent.

A pair of Lessers belonging to R. Wilson of Luton hatched a chick (28 days after the second egg was seen) which died after two weeks due to an accident. The following year, 1969, the clutch again consisted of two eggs. Both hatched. The adults stopped brooding the chicks when they were aged between three and four weeks. On fledging they were described as being larger than their parents. Their eyes were brownish grey.

Since 1970, the Lesser Sulphur-crested has been bred on a number of occasions in Britain – yet few aviculturists have had consistent successes with this species.

A pair belonging to B. Scholz bred in 1978. Eggs were laid on May 26 and 28. Incubation commenced with the

Lesser Sulphur-crested Cockatoo (*Cacatua sulphurea sulphurea*) – female.

Timor Cockatoo nearly 6 weeks old.
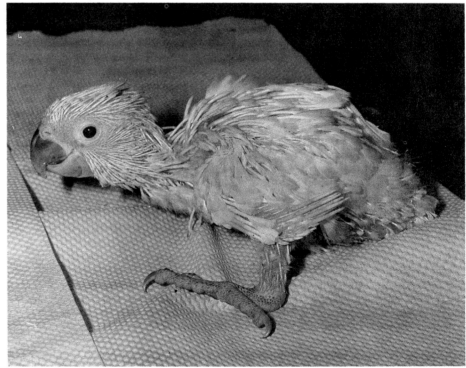

first egg and lasted 28 days. The male incubated for only half an hour each morning and evening when the female left the nest. A dead chick was seen in the nest on June 23. The female laid again on July 9 and 11 and a chick hatched on August 6. It had creamy fluffy down and left the nest at 72 days. Rearing food consisted of parrot mixture, maggots, apple and orange and up to five slices of bread soaked in nectar daily.

Betty Byers of California recorded an incubation period of 27 days for the Lesser and a hatching weight of 16 g ($\frac{3}{5}$ oz). She noted it was from four to eight months before the beak and feet started to turn from a brown colour to black, whereas in the Greater, Moluccan and Umbrella this occurred at about three weeks.

In Italy, Paolo Bertagnolio of Rome bred this species in 1976 (two), 1977 (one) and 1978 (two), and Ivo Ferrura did so in 1982. Successful European zoos in the 1970s included Arnhem (Netherlands), Wuppertal (West Germany), Leipzig, Mulhouse (France) and in Britain the Tropical Bird Gardens at Rode, Penscynor Wildlife Park in Wales and Chester Zoo. In Australia, it was bred at Crosford Zoo in 1981.

In the USA, it was bred by Mrs F. Eichwaldt in 1930 and 1931.

The clutch may consist of two or three eggs, incubated for 28 days. The chicks' eyes start to open at about 12 days.

The Lesser Sulphur-crested Cockatoo was, for many years, the most freely available of the cockatoos and, in Europe, was inexpensive until import controls came into operation in the mid 1970s. Before this it was more usually kept as a pet than in an aviary and few breeding successes had occurred in Britain.

Unfortunately, numerous cases of the feather disease which is so common in cockatoos have been reported in this species (see page 61).

When one considers the immense number of Lesser Sulphur-crested Cockatoos which have been imported over the years, and taking into account that most of these were destined to be kept as pets, remarkably little has been recorded about this species in captivity and few pairs are seen in collections. I

Citron-crested Cockatoo (*Cacatua sulphurea citrinocristata*).

suspect that the life span of many of these cockatoos is short and that it should not be assumed that these birds do well in captivity.

The Lesser Sulphur-crested has hybridised on a number of occasions. One of the most interesting crosses was with a male Roseate Cockatoo. It was bred in 1917 by Mrs M. A. Lee of Aylesbury. The hybrid was described as being pearl grey above with the inner part of the crest 'buff-yellow-pink'; the latter colour was repeated on the throat and cheeks and on a broad band across the breast. The parents nested in a hole which they had excavated between the roof of the aviary and the floor of the room above.

Citron-crested Cockatoo
C. s. citrinocristata
Description: This is the most distinctive subspecies of the Lesser Sulphur-crested with the crest orange and the ear coverts yellow – a very beautiful contrast with the white plumage.

A consistent breeder of this cockatoo, Dr S. B. Kendall of Surrey, stated: 'the male is typically slightly larger, has a considerably more massive bill and head, a markedly more richly coloured crest and, in the examples I have seen, more yellow on the breast and abdomen' (Kendall, 1955).
Range/Habitat: It is from the island of Sumba, Indonesia.

Aviculture: S. B. Kendall (1972) described two young he reared from a male Citron-crest and a female Timor as being 'indistinguishable from one of the Lesser Sulphur-crest races. They are bigger than the Timor with long elegant sulphur yellow crests'. On the third night after the young left the nest, the whole family was shut in the shelter because of a predator in the garden. That night the male killed the female, having previously killed the Citron-crest with which he was paired. However, he successfully finished rearing his two young.

The Citron-crested Cockatoo was first bred in Britain by S. B. Kendall who received the medal of the Avicultural Society for the first breeding of this cockatoo. It was well deserved – for one male Citron-crest in Dr Kendall's collection reared young from 1956 to 1976. This achievement demonstrates what consistent breeders cockatoos can be under favourable conditions.

On the first occasion on which Dr Kendall bred this species, a 15-gallon barrel was chosen in preference to a grandfather nest-box. It appeared that most of the incubation was carried out by the female and that the incubation period was 28 days. The two chicks fledged on August 22 and 26. A chick was first heard on June 16, giving a fledgling period of almost ten weeks. In November, the female youngster was bitten on the foot by one of the adults. Before they are independent young cockatoos are vulnerable to attack from a parent, usually the male who will attack the male young. Dr Kendall solved the problem by placing the father and daughter together, and, in a separate enclosure, the mother and son.

While rearing young, Dr Kendall's birds were supplied with hard-boiled egg and bread crumbs in the morning, and bread and milk at night, plus various fruits, especially apples and plums. They showed little interest in greenfood but relished hawthorn berries and corn-on-the-cob. The female was once seen taking apart a sparrow which she appeared to have caught and killed in the aviary.

In 1969, Mr and Mrs J. Robertson of Colchester reared one Citron-crest from a pair obtained in 1967. The rearing food consisted mainly of brown bread soaked in honey and an unlimited quantity of marigold heads. The young cockatoo stayed in the nest for about 12 weeks. The Citron-crest reared by Clifford Smith of Yorkshire in 1969 spent approximately 76 days in the nest. The experiences of these three breeders show that the length of time varies from ten to 12 weeks.

At Brean Down Bird Garden in Somerset a pair of Citron-crests nested for the first time in 1979. When the chick was about four weeks old it was necessary to remove the male because of his aggressive behaviour towards the female. She reared the youngster successfully, consuming much lettuce, apple and orange in addition to the usual seeds. When the pair were reunited, the male again attacked the female and they had to be separated again. Although the pair has subsequently nested every year, and reared young, continual vigilance is necessary. On one occasion, the male was caught in the act of attacking the female, and if there had been no immediate intervention, the female would certainly have been killed.

A pair of Citron-crests belonging to Elizabeth Butterworth (renowned worldwide for her paintings of parrots), nested for the first time during the late summer of 1979, after being moved to a new location. A chick was heard on September 17, after which the pair became much less conservative in their choice of foods. Spinach was offered three times daily and large quantities of this were eaten, also of hawthorn berries. In addition, soaked sunflower seed, millet spray and hemp were eaten. Bone meal was sprinkled on the seed.

When the chick was one week old, the nest-box was lowered to permit nest inspection. The parents did not return so the chick was removed and hand-fed. Next day, the chick was returned and the parents fed it. On September 26, both birds were out of the nest so the chick was removed permanently. Its eyes and ears had opened by October 1 (15 days). At 21 days, it was covered in unopened quills; two weeks later, by October 20, the feathers of the under parts were free of their sheaths. It weighed 269 g (9½ oz) on October 21 and 340 g (12 oz) seven days later. By November 4, it would erect its crest and open its wings in display. Its first flight occurred on November 20. At ten weeks, it was flying well and beginning to hold items in its foot.

In Canada, R. McPeek (1973) reared six young from his pair in three years. Their nest-box was made of 13 mm (½ in) plywood and covered and lined with 30 g galvanised iron. Rotted wood was placed inside which was chewed to a fine dust. The first chick hatched died at about 14 days. Future young were hand-reared. In 1973, two chicks were removed from the nest on May 20, the female laid again and two more chicks were heard on July 25. One of the young bred from this pair had the breast yellow and deep orange cheek patches.

In the USA, Mr and Mrs D. Mathews of Allinson Park, Pennsylvania, have hand-reared a number of Citron-crests.

This cockatoo has been reared in Warsaw Zoo (1972) and at Bird Paradise, Cornwall, in 1973. In Italy, Paolo Bertagnolio was successful in 1976 and 1977. Zoos which have bred this species since the 1970s include Natal Lion Park in South Africa, San Diego in California, Clères in France, Naples in Italy and, in Britain, Penscynor Wildlife Park and Harewood Bird Gardens. A hybrid between a male Citron-crest cockatoo and a Bare-eyed Cockatoo was reared in Cincinnati Zoo in 1975.

Umbrella (Great White or White-crested) Cockatoo
C. alba

Description: The most impressive feature of this species is the long, broad feathers of the crest. When alarmed, the Umbrella will react by slowly raising and lowering the crest (usually hissing at the same time). Its plumage appears almost entirely white but for the under sides of the flight and tail feathers which are suffused with yellow. The naked area of skin surrounding the eye is yellowish white; the iris is dark brown in the male and reddish-brown in the female. The bill is black and the legs grey. Length: about 46 cm (18 in).

Immature plumage does not differ from that of the adult.

Range/Habitat: The Umbrella Cockatoo inhabits the Indonesian islands of northern and central Moluccas: Obi, Batjan, Tidore and Ternate. It is known to feed on seeds,

Umbrella Cockatoo (*Cacatua alba*).

nuts, fruits, berries and insects.
Aviculture: Very little has been recorded of this bird although it cannot
be considered rare in captivity or in its
natural habitat. The Umbrella has
never achieved the popularity of some
of the other white cockatoos. It *is*
noisy and it *is* destructive – but so is
the Moluccan, for example; it is less
colourful than that bird but is, nevertheless, extremely handsome.

W. T. Greene (1887) thought that an
aviary for a pair 'would require to be
made of rods of iron of almost the
same strength as those employed in the
construction of a lion's den'. There
was more than an element of truth in
this; a friend whose Umbrella
Cockatoos destroyed the strongest
gauge welded mesh obtainable had to
resort to the use of the heaviest grade
of chain link.

The first recorded breeding of this
cockatoo in captivity occurred in 1960.
The nest barrel used by the pair,
owned by Paul Schneider in California,
was reinforced with a gross of screws!
A chick hatched on about June 26 and
left the nest on September 16. I saw it
nearly 18 years later – a magnificent
female. The favourite food taken while

the chick was being reared was quar-
tered oranges, canary seed, sunflower,
peanuts and wholewheat bread.

The first British breeding of the
Umbrella Cockatoo occurred at the
Tropical Bird Gardens, Rode,
Somerset. In the spring of 1968, the
pair was provided with a wooden barrel about 40 cm (16 in) in diameter and
51 cm (20 in) tall, filled to one quarter
of its depth with rotten wood and peat.
That year a chick was heard on July 30
and left the nest on October 1 when it
could be distinguished from its parents
only by its slightly smaller size.

Like many Umbrella Cockatoos, the
adults were rather nervous birds, yet
they nested in an aviary past which
hundreds of visitors streamed daily
throughout the summer. While the
chick was being reared, the adults
consumed a mixture of soaked bread
and chopped fruit, also brown bread
liberally smeared with butter and
sprinkled with a vitamin powder. The
usual seed mixture of sunflower,
peanuts and maize was available.

In Yorkshire, Clifford Smith's pair
reduced their large nest-box to a pile of
chippings within a week. The barrel
provided in 1967 was reinforced on the

outside with layer upon layer of timber
offcuts with bark attached, to form a
15 cm (6 in) protective covering – but
this too was eventually destroyed. The
pair finally nested in a natural log
90 cm (3 ft) in diameter and 1.8 m (6 ft)
high. The single egg in the first clutch
did not hatch. In 1968, a chick hatched
but died and in 1969, at the end of
August, a naked chick was found on
the aviary floor; it had fallen through a
hole in the nest. Repairs were effected
and it was returned to the nest. When
11 weeks old it was removed for hand-
rearing because it had been severely
plucked.

Another British breeding which
owed its success to hand-rearing was
that carried out by Mr and Mrs R.
Wallwork of Coventry. Two eggs were
laid in 1976, one of which hatched,
probably on July 14. Maggots were
relished then, four pints a week being
taken at the peak intake. At the
beginning of September, the male
became unwell and was removed to a
hospital cage. On that day there was
little food in the crop of the chick; the
latter was therefore removed for hand-
rearing. It was fed at first on Farlene
baby cereal mixed to a thin paste, then
on tinned strained baby food –
savoury being preferred to sweet kinds.

A breeding which occurred in
Germany, probably in 1972, is of particular interest. Two pairs of Umbrella
Cockatoos were housed in an aviary
measuring 18.4 × 14 m (66 × 46 ft) × 4 m
(12 ft) high which was built over part
of an orchard. The cockatoos shared
the aviary with ducks, pheasants and
touracos. A chick hatched after an
incubation period given as 33 days.
When eight weeks old, it was removed
from the nest and hand-reared on baby
food, cooked soft cereals, grated
peanuts and raw eggs. It became a
tame and beautiful pet.

In Czechoslovakia, Frances Novy
bred from a pair of Umbrella
Cockatoos imported in 1978 (Hylas,
pers. comm.). The female laid on
March 29 and April 2 but the eggs did
not hatch. She laid again on May 20
and 23. A chick was heard on June 18;
it left the nest on September 29.

In Sweden, Inge and Nancy
Forsberg hand-reared an Umbrella
Cockatoo in 1984. An egg laid on May
15 measured 35 × 45.5 mm ($1\frac{2}{5}$ × $1\frac{4}{5}$ in).

It weighed 26.5 g (nearly 1 oz) on May 29, 25.6 g ($\frac{9}{10}$ oz) on June 5 and 24.85 g (almost $\frac{9}{10}$ oz) on June 8. The egg was placed in an incubator with humidity 60%. The chick hatched on June 12, after pipping two days previously. Hatching weight was 20.6 g ($\frac{3}{4}$ oz). The chick's eyes opened on June 22 and two days later the bills and nails started to turn black.

In California, Betty Byers recorded an incubation period of 28 days, a weight of 24 g ($\frac{4}{5}$ oz) at three days and a weight of 607 g ($21\frac{1}{2}$ oz) at independence.

The Umbrella Cockatoo has reared young in zoos in Lexington, Santa Barbara, and Busch Gardens, Tampa, in the USA; Beira, Mozambique (1967 – two, 1969 – three); Auckland, New Zealand (1972 – two); since 1980, in Kaunas, USSR, and Peking, China; and since 1981 at Belo Horizonte Zoo in Brazil. In Britain it has also been bred at the Tropical Bird Park, Isle of Wight (1977 – one, 1978 – one).

Moluccan Cockatoo
C. moluccensis

Description: Although the Leadbeater's may be the most beautiful of the white cockatoos, this bird is surely the most magnificent. An imposing bird, it has a superb crest of long, broad salmon-pink feathers which can be raised and lowered at will. The plumage of the under parts varies in individuals from pink-tinged white to pale pink. The under side of the flight feathers is washed with deep salmon at the base and the tail feathers are pale orange on the under side. The area of bare skin surrounding the eye is white, tinged with blue. The bill is black and the legs are grey. The iris is black in the male and dark brown in the female. Length: about 50 cm (20 in).

Immature birds resemble adults; at first the eye is dark grey.

Range/Habitat: The Moluccan Cockatoo inhabits the Indonesian islands of Ceram, Saparua and Haruku in the south Moluccas, and has been introduced to Amboina.

It feeds principally on seeds, nuts including coconuts, berries and insects.

Aviculture: Because of the docile and affectionate nature of some birds of this species, Moluccan Cockatoos are

Moluccan Cockatoo (*Cacatua moluccensis*).

eagerly sought by those in search of an exceptional pet. However, not all birds have the desired temperament and even fewer are the enthusiasts who can spend enough time with a really tame cockatoo to keep it contented. Few birds have louder voices than a Moluccan Cockatoo and, if a tame bird is neglected, it will use its voice in protest – and the resulting ear-splitting yells would not be easily tolerated even by the most devoted owner. However, the temperament of some individuals is affectionate and trustworthy and such birds are among the most delightful pets in existence.

The first known captive breeding of this species occurred in San Diego Zoo in 1951, when a single youngster was hand-reared, after having been removed from the nest at the age of ten days. It proved extremely difficult to rear and was so nervous that any unusual noise would cause it to regurgitate its food. By three months old, it had started to feed itself and was spoon-fed three times daily. This success was repeated in the following year. The female laid two eggs and the incubation period was given as 30 days.

The Moluccan Cockatoo was not bred again until 1975 when there were three successes in Britain and one in South Africa. Mr and Mrs C. Wright

(1975) of London hand-reared a youngster from a pair which had been together since the end of 1972. The female laid her first egg in March 1974. In the following years, eggs were not laid until June. The incubation period was not determined exactly but was a minimum of 30 days. Two chicks, covered in long, wispy yellow down were seen in the nest on July 26. Thenceforth the parents refused apple, taking peanuts and raisins. Of the various foods offered, maggots became the favourite and were eaten in large quantities daily. When the chicks were about 30 days old, the parents resumed eating fruit; meat was ignored but seed was taken. On September 6, one chick died; the adults ceased to feed the other three days later. It was a difficult process to remove it from the nest for hand-rearing; a torch was used to dazzle its parents and the chick was removed with the aid of a wire loop. Its diet consisted of tinned strained baby foods until it started to crack seed when aged 86 days. At 104 days, it flew for the first time.

P. G. Leeves (1976) obtained a pair of Moluccan Cockatoos in 1970. The female laid two clutches annually from 1971 in an open-topped barrel about 60 cm (2 ft) in diameter and 75 cm (30 in) high. The eggs invariably hatched but the chicks died aged between a few hours and three weeks. In 1975, eggs were laid on June 2 and 6. Both chicks hatched; one died at four days, the other left the nest on October 17. It was reared on bread, milk and honey, greenfood, hemp, canary, millet and sunflower seed. Fruit was not accepted while the young were still in the nest.

In 1975, M. Wright hand-reared two Moluccan Cockatoos in South Africa. They were removed from the nest aged three and four weeks and, five weeks later, the female laid again, but the eggs were infertile. Also in South Africa, in 1976 and 1977, Mrs J. Rough of Rustenburg hand-reared one and two young respectively. Incubation period was found to be 28 days. On hatching, the chicks were covered in sparse yellow down. It was reported that their eyes opened at 14 to 15 days, in contrast with the chick reared by C. Wright, the eyes of which opened at about 29 days.

In Sweden, Claes-Goran Ahstrom obtained a pair of Moluccan Cockatoos in 1975 and housed them in a large aviary (Christian Lindstrom, 1978). He obtained an oak tree from which three nest-boxes were made. One measuring 1 m ($3\frac{1}{4}$ ft) high and 1.8 m (6 ft) in diameter was deemed desirable by the cockatoos when placed in position in December. Two eggs were laid and one chick had hatched by March 9. It left the nest on June 21.

In 1976, two eggs were laid in February, resulting in a young bird leaving the nest on June 8. The young were reared on a nutritious food: a milk extract for human babies mixed with porridge and unsweetened biscuit, vitamins and fruit sugar. Every day, the pair ate apple, orange, one third of a banana, a few grapes, one or two carrots, tomato, one third of a cucumber, peas, beans and corn-on-the-cob. Sunflower, soaked and dry, was also consumed. The incubation period was recorded as about 35 days.

In the USA, Betty Byers recorded the incubation period of this species as 29 days; chicks weighed about 20 g ($\frac{3}{4}$ oz) on hatching and 674 g ($23\frac{3}{4}$ oz) when independent. One reared by William Peratino (1979) had dense yellow down on hatching. It weighed 65.7 g

($2\frac{3}{10}$ oz) at 14 days and 781 g ($27\frac{1}{2}$ oz) at 115 days. The incubation period was 28 days and commenced when the first egg was laid.

In 1968, J. Brett of the Isle of Wight reported breeding two hybrid Moluccan × Umbrella Cockatoos, then aged two months.

It is of interest that an aviculturist who kept a pair of Moluccan Cockatoos at liberty reported that they never stayed out more than two hours; they would then fly back to their home and enter their cage.

One of the most famous cockatoos ever to have existed is 'King Tut' – the oldest resident of San Diego Zoo, imported in 1925. He whistles, sings and dances for the benefit of visitors, perhaps recreating roles he played in Hollywood films of years ago.

Leadbeater's (Major Mitchell's) Cockatoo
C. leadbeateri

Description: Leadbeater's Cockatoo is often considered to be the most beautiful of all cockatoos. Its crest is remarkable: salmon-coloured, tipped with white and with a yellow band through the centre; the latter is missing or merely indicated in the subspecies *mollis*. When the crest is opened, the 16 feathers form a beautiful fan; closed, it curves forward slightly. The forehead is dark pink, the rest of the head and under parts being salmon-pink, except the pink-tinged white crown. Under wing coverts are pink and the under side of the flight and tail feathers are marked with deep salmon-pink at the bases. The bill is white and the legs are grey. The iris is dark brown in the male and reddish pink in the female. Length: 35 cm (14 in). Weight: M 300–425 g ($10\frac{1}{2}$–15 oz); F 375–435 g ($13\frac{1}{4}$–$15\frac{3}{10}$ oz).

Immature birds have the iris pale brown and are usually paler than adults. According to G. A. Smith, the female's iris 'gets its brownish distinction' three to six months after leaving the nest – usually the former.

Colour is variable, some birds being deep pink, this colour extending further down the breast in some males. R. J. Berry, of Houston, a consistent breeder of this species for many years, informed me:

Leadbeater's Cockatoo (*Cacatua leadbeateri*).

Some of our specimens can be sexed by breast and crest coloration – even when they first develop pin feathers, the differences are so distinct. There are apparently subtle geographical differences in this species with regard to coloration, some specimens being a richer pink colour. The darker specimens cannot be easily sexed by breast coloration at an early age.

Similarly, there is variation in the eye colour of young birds. A very successful breeder of this species in England was E. N. T. Vane who had reared it to the fifth generation by 1959. He commented (1960) that the young of some pairs could be sexed from the time they left the nest: males had the iris black but 'hens all had much lighter irises, some were almond red, some were yellowish-hazel but they were always easily distinguished'.

The young of other pairs all left the nest with the iris dark which changed colour, in some birds after a few weeks, in others after nearly a year. Never, however, did the light iris of a young bird become black.

Range/Habitat: Leadbeater's Cockatoo inhabits the interior of Western Australia, the south-western part of the Northern Territory, most of South Australia, the south-western corner of Queensland, the western part of New South Wales and the north-western corner of Victoria. The subspecies *C.c. mollis* is known only from the Sarnamah area of Western Australia.

Leadbeater's Cockatoo is an inhabitant of mallee country – semidesert covered with mallee eucalyptus scrub – and of other sparsely wooded areas. Its numbers have decreased, especially in the eastern part of its range. In some localities it is common, but generally it is uncommon or rare. It appears to be mainly dependent on woodland and retreats from areas which have been cleared.

The Leadbeater's has to compete with the numerous Roseate Cockatoo for food and nesting sites; unlike the Roseate, it is never found in large flocks but in pairs or small groups. Its diet consists of various seeds, including weed pests, roots, fruits and berries, also cultivated nuts and cereals.

Mallee eucalyptus trees are small – average log size is 23 cm (9 in) thus the cockatoos start to enlarge a nesting hole many weeks before the start of the breeding season. One ornithologist observed how these cockatoos gnawed straight down into a mallee stump to a depth of about 30 cm (12 in). From the entrance of such a shallow hole they are able to feed their young; they cannot go deeper because there would be no turning room.

This explains why, in captivity, these birds start to prepare their nests several weeks before they lay and why they prefer small nest-boxes. Gnawing ceases after the eggs, two to four in number, are laid. The incubation period is 28 days; young spend eight weeks in the nest.

Aviculture: In aviculture, this has always been among the least numerous of the white cockatoos and is now by far the most expensive; indeed, it has become one of the highest-priced of all parrots. For this reason, outside Australia, it is rarely kept as a pet.

Leadbeater's Cockatoo was first exhibited at London Zoo in 1854. The first breeders were Mrs Johnstone and London Zoo, both in 1901. Mrs Johnstone's pair nested in a rotten tree, about 2.4 m (8 ft) high, boarded on one side for protection against the elements, as it was in an exposed situation. Three young were reared.

In Belgium, J. Bruyneel was successful in 1946; in Denmark, A. Husted of Shodsborg reared one in 1961 and, in Italy, P. Bertagnolio's pair reared young in 1976, 1977 and 1978. In Australia, this cockatoo was first bred by R. F. Bellchamber in South Australia in 1935. Four eggs were laid and three young were reared. Incubation commenced on September 11 and three chicks had hatched by October 11. Wheat, peas, green broad beans, almonds and thistles were among the foods offered. Australian zoos, such as Adelaide and Melbourne, have bred this species on many occasions. It has also been bred in zoos in Oklahoma, Brownsville, New York (Bronx) and, in Britain, at the Tropical Bird Gardens at Rode, Penscynor Wildlife Park in Neath, Wales, and at Bird Paradise in Cornwall.

The most consistent success has occurred at San Diego Zoo. Between 1932 and 1970, 56 chicks were reared, all by hand. In 1977, the development of a hand-raised chick was charted, after it was removed from the nest at 19 days. Two days later its eyes began to open. Pin feathers emerged between 25 and 27 days. By seven weeks its feathering was almost complete. This is the age at which young birds usually leave the nest. A week later it had started to eat finely chopped bread, lettuce, apple, sweet corn, millet, canary and shelled sunflower seed. Hand-feeding was reduced to twice daily. Three weeks later it was feeding well on its own and was fed only once daily (*Zoonooz*, October 1977).

One American aviculturist, W. H. Browning, deserves mention for his persistence. His pair, obtained in 1903, first reared a youngster to independence in 1940.

In South Africa, Phyllis Gale (1969) reared young from a pair obtained in 1963. They nested in a hollow log 90 cm (3 ft) deep with 20 cm (8 in) of rotten wood in the base. Chicks were

heard on October 16; on the previous day the male had flown at his owner with a scream of rage, thus she suspected they had young. The first fledged on November 28, the second on November 30 and the third on December 2. Rearing food consisted of white bread squeezed out in water and mixed with Pronutro. The parents consumed pounds of fresh peas. When reported, the pair had reared young for five years. The male severely injured the first youngster to emerge in the second year and it had to be destroyed. Subsequently he was removed from the aviary as soon as the young showed their heads at the nesting hole. Ms Gale wrote: '... when the babies are self-sufficient and are removed from their mother and the father is put back with his wife, it is quite pathetic to see the pleasure of their meeting again'.

In Australia, Keith Hocking (1981) described the inexplicable behaviour of one male. His three young left the nest at eight weeks old (returning at night). The male fed two of the young and was very possessive, not allowing the female near them. After a week, he drove away the third youngster which was fed by the female. The youngsters were left with their parents for four months. All three proved to be females; most aviculturists would have suggested that the one which was persecuted was resented by its father because it was a male.

Bare-eyed Cockatoo (Western Long-billed Corella)
Cacatua pastinator pastinator
Description: This cockatoo is white with the lores orange-pink, also the bases of the feathers of the head, nape, mantle, breast and flanks. The under side of the flight and tail feathers is tinged with yellow; ear coverts are pale dusky yellow. The grey-blue periorbital skin is more extensive beneath the eye. The elongated bill is greyish horn colour. Iris is dark brown. Length: 38 cm (15 in). Weight: M 665–860 g (23½–30 3/10 oz); F 530–750 g (18¾–26½ oz). Immature birds have the upper mandible shorter, the naked skin below the eye greyish (not bluish as on other parts).
Range/Habitat: There are two isolated populations in south-western

Australia. In one of these the range has overlapped with the Little Corella since the early 1960s. As the two forms appear rather different, are now sympatric and do not interbreed, there is reason for considering the western race to be a distinct species (Courtney, pers. comm., 1985; Ford, 1985). The nominate race declined markedly but this may have been reversed in recent times.

Aviculture: Bare-eyed Cockatoos are hardy and long-lived. Forshaw (1981) refers to one which had been taken from the nest in South Australia in 1911. It was a most accomplished mimic with an incredible repertoire that included Aboriginal dialect and camp sounds such as the clanging of pots and pans and the barking of dogs and the neighing of horses. The first recorded breeding took place at London Zoo in 1907, when one was reared. In the Netherlands, F. E. Blaauw was successful in 1926 and on several subsequent occasions.

San Diego Zoo had an incredibly prolific pair. Between 1929 and 1970 they produced 103 young which were hand-reared – surely a record number for a pair of captive cockatoos.

In California, Paul Schneider reared two Bare-eyed Cockatoos in 1971. In Italy, it was bred by Paolo Bertagnolio in 1975 (one) and 1976 (two). In 1977 the male killed the female when the two chicks hatched. The surviving chick was hand-reared.

Among the zoos which have bred this species are Adelaide and Melbourne, Australia; Wellington, New Zealand; Delhi, India and Mayaguez, Puerto Rico. In Britain there is a prolific pair at Clee Hill Bird Garden; it has also been bred at Whipsnade Zoological Park, in Wales at Penscynor Wildlife Park and in Ireland at Dublin Zoo between 1964 and 1972. In Europe, this species has been bred at zoos in Neuweid (Germany) and Rotterdam and Wassenaar (the Netherlands). In the USA, it has reared young in Busch Gardens.

Bare-eyed Cockatoos lay three or four eggs. When they are about nine days old chicks' eyes open; they fledge at nine weeks. Betty Byers in California recorded the incubation period as 27 days and hatching weight as 13 g (about ½ oz).

At Wroclaw Zoo in Poland, a female

Bare-eyed Cockatoo (*Cacatua pastinator sanguinea*).

paired with a male Roseate Cockatoo. They nested in the trunk of a 1.5 m (5 ft) high elm with a diameter of about 30 cm (12 in). The resulting youngster resembled the Roseate except for the bare area of skin surrounding the eye which was yellow. Hybrids between a male Bare-eyed and a female Slenderbill were reared at La Fleche Zoo, France, in 1976. The Bare-eyed has hybridised with the Citron-crested Cockatoo in Cincinnati Zoo.

Little Corella (Bloodstained Cockatoo, Shortbilled Corella)
C. p. gymnopis
Description: It differs in the shape of the beak, the upper mandible being short and strongly decurved. It is smaller. Weight: M 385–590 g

(13⅗–20⅘ oz); F 430–560 g (15⅕–19¾ oz)
Range/Habitat: It has a wide distribution from the interior of eastern Australia west to the central-western coast (where its range meets that of the nominate race). It is plentiful throughout most of its range.

C. p. sanguinea
Description: There is less orange-pink on the lores and on the bases of the head feathers than in *gymnopis*. The periorbital skin is paler blue – less greyish. It is slightly larger. Weight: M 466–626 g (16⅖–22 oz); F 370–540 g (13–19 oz).

Immature birds have the skin surrounding the eye almost white.
Range/Habitat: Northern Australia from the Kimberley division of Western Australia east to the south-western shores of the Gulf of Carpentaria. It is generally common and enormous flocks are seen.

Slender-billed Cockatoo (Long-billed Corella)
Cacatua tenuirostris

Description: It differs from the western Long-billed Corella in the deeper red-orange bases to the feathers of the head, nape, mantle, flanks and upper breast, also the orange-scarlet on the forehead, lores and throat. There are pale yellow-orange feathers above and below the eye. The bill is horn-coloured and the iris dark brown. Length: smaller about 35 cm (15 in). Weight: M 480–650 g (17–23 oz); F 550–600 g (19½–21 oz).

Immature birds have the upper mandible much shorter. There is less orange-scarlet on the throat.

Range/Habitat: It occurs in south-eastern South Australia to southern Victoria and south-western New South Wales. Compared with numbers at the turn of the century, there has been an enormous decline in this species as the result of drier conditions, land clearance and poisoning; this cockatoo is considered a pest by farmers as it attacks cereal crops. It appears that the decline has been arrested but its numbers remain low.

Aviculture: Before it was listed as a protected bird, it was trapped in large numbers and many were exported to Europe, where they often became cherished pets. Their pleasing characters, gentle disposition and ability to talk endeared them to many. Greene (1887) quotes a lady whose Slender-billed was a clever mimic of sounds *and* deeds.

> When first I had him, he knew about twenty sentences, and never misapplied them; now he has become a greater mimic than talker; daily he goes through the performance of pouring out tea. The sugar is first put into the cups – the action of putting it in, you understand – and then the tea is poured out; his beak being the spout of the teapot, and he makes the noise of pouring exactly, while pretending to do so.

> After watching a gardener clipping laurels, he imitated the whole procedure, giving his head a jerk with each imitation snip of the shears and making the exact sound.

> This bird was remarkable, for while mimicry of sounds is so common among captive parrots, mimicry of actions is rare indeed.

Slender-billed Cockatoo (*Cacatua tenuirostris*).

For many years, the Slender-billed Cockatoo has been little known in aviculture. Very few breeding successes have occurred. The first took place in San Diego Zoo, California, in 1959. The parents had been imported as young birds in 1951. To stimulate egg-laying, their diet was supplemented with snails and mealworms. The female laid a single egg in a wooden box 3.6 m (12 ft) from the floor of the aviary. K. C. Lint (1959) recorded that only the female incubated. A chick hatched after 29 days and was reared by the parents. Foods eaten daily were sunflower, whole corn, wheat, apple, carrot, sweet potatoes, bread, lettuce, corn-on-the-cob, pine nuts and peanuts. Subsequently the pair reared young in 1960, 1963 and 1964.

The next captive breeding occurred in the aviaries of Alan Lendon in Australia in 1968. The pair nested in a hollow log 90 cm (3 ft) above the ground. The three eggs were incubated by the male during the day and the female at night, incubation commencing after the second egg was laid. Two chicks hatched; one died at a week old and the other left the nest at seven weeks. The parents' favourite food while the chick was in the nest was nutweed, supplied in clumps of dirt, and seeding grasses. The young cockatoo was independent three weeks after leaving the nest.

This species has also been bred in New Zealand by Mrs C. Pullen of Wellington (eight hatched and seven reared during 1965–68) and in Australia in Adelaide Zoo and South Perth Zoo since the 1970s. The female in Perth Zoo could not be persuaded to use a nesting log. She laid two eggs in the food container where two chicks were hatched and reared only a few feet from the public. A survey carried out in the USA in 1980 revealed that only 15 Slender-billed Cockatoos were exhibited in American zoos – all wild-caught birds. At Birmingham Zoo, Alabama, a pair hatched chicks, which died, on two occasions prior to 1981. In that year, two chicks were hatched and reared – one by the parents; the other was hand-reared. In 1982, a single chick was reared by the parents (Pfeifer, 1983). There were probably no more than two breeding pairs in the USA at that time.

In Tenerife, one Slender-billed Cockatoo was reared at Loro Parque in 1981.

Goffin's Cockatoo
C. goffini

Description: This race is very closely related to the Bare-eyed. The close relationship is underlined by the appearance of the immature Bare-eyed which bears a marked resemblance to *goffini*. The latter differs from the Bare-eyed in its periorbital skin which is white and circular. It is smaller and less heavy in build. The lores and the bases of the feathers of the head are salmon pink. The eye is black in the male, brown in the female but this is apparent only in very good light. In most males, the head and area of periorbital skin is slightly larger in the male. The bill is greyish white. Length: 32 cm (12 in). Weight: about 370 g (13 oz).

Range/Habitat: Goffin's Cockatoo inhabits the Tenimber (Tanimbar) Islands of Indonesia. It is also found on Tual in the Kai Islands where it was probably introduced.

Little is known about its wild life. The Tenimber Islands were drastically deforested during the 1970s, resulting in the export of this cockatoo which was hitherto extremely rare in aviculture.

Aviculture: Large-scale export commenced in 1972. During the next decade thousands must have been exported. Indeed, the Goffin's unfortunately became the least expensive of the cockatoos. It did not prove suitable as a pet, for few birds settled down to cage life. The Goffin's is one of the most charming of cockatoos as an aviary bird and needs all the attention which aviculturists can bestow upon it. Comparatively few captive breedings have occurred and, because of deforestation, its wild population may find itself in a precarious position. Thus aviculturists had, and still have at the time of writing, the opportunity to aid the survival of this attractive little cockatoo. Unfortunately, it appears not to be among the easiest of the cockatoos to breed in captivity.

The incubation period is 28 days. Newly hatched chicks weigh between 9 g ($\frac{3}{10}$ oz) and 11g ($\frac{2}{5}$ oz). The first breeding occurred in 1975 but was not reported because the young bird was badly plucked in the nest and died of exposure during an unexpectedly cold night shortly after it left the nest.

The first fully successful breeding in Europe occurred in the Netherlands. The birds were obtained in March 1974 by E. G. B. Schulte (1975) of Eindhoven and housed in a large cage with a nest-box which measured 25 cm (10 in) square and 40 cm (16 in) high; they were so shy they disappeared into the box when anyone appeared. On June 15, three eggs were seen in the nest. A chick was heard on July 1; it was described as sounding like a Cockatiel chick. However, it was found dead on September 7.

By October 5 three more eggs had been laid. Chicks were heard on October 9; on November 1 two chicks

Goffin's Cockatoo (*Cacatua goffini*).

were seen. By November 23, they were fully feathered except for the tail. On December 18, the first chick left the nest, followed by the second on the next day. They resembled the adults and had the iris black. Three weeks later they were independent and soon after were removed to another cage. In May 1975, the pair nested again, hatching two chicks. Food taken by this pair consisted of sunflower, canary and hemp seed, oats, a softfood, soaked maize, bread and large quantities of chickweed.

In 1977, there were two breeding successes in Britain. Neil O'Connor (1977) of Surrey kept two pairs (both very shy), one of which reared a single chick.

Its parents had been together since April 1973 and mating commenced on the day they were introduced – before they were fully mature. The nest-box, which measured 57 × 39 × 28 cm (22 × 15 × 11 in) was first explored in April 1976. It was covered, inside and out, with welded mesh. Over one year

later, on May 17, 1977, one egg was seen in the nest. Eight days later, the birds deserted due to the presence of a cat. On June 2, the female laid another egg; it hatched on July 2. When the chick was inspected on July 4, it had primrose-coloured down. When it was about one month old, the parents ceased to brood it. At 80 days old it was seen to look out of the nest. Three days later it was found on the aviary floor and was returned to the nest. Six days later it re-emerged and perched in the flight. It was believed to be fully independent at about 16 weeks.

Sunflower, buckwheat and canary seed growing in the flight were consumed while the chick was being reared. Also offered were soaked sunflower seed, canary, buckwheat, wheat, oats and maize. Carrot was eaten in small quantities; bread and milk and corn-on-the-cob were refused. Spinach beet and dandelion were eaten with avidity.

Also in England, Mr and Mrs R. H. Day hand-reared a Goffin's Cockatoo in 1977. The parents were obtained in the previous year. Eggs were laid on May 6 and 9 and hatched on June 6 and 7. On the 30th day, the smallest chick died and the survivor was removed for hand-rearing. It was fed on flour made from sunflower, canary and millet seed placed in a liquidiser, with water added.

It would seem that, in this species, copulation is carried out to maintain the pair bond, for it occurs during most of the year, even in immature birds. This is true of my pair and of several other pairs of which I know. My own pair have been provided with a variety of nesting sites but seem afraid to enter a deep nest. An oblong box with a large entrance near floor level, and a natural log placed horizontally on the ground, have been entered. Noisy screaming accompanies the act of cautiously placing their heads inside nest-boxes which are not entered, as though fearful they contain a predator of some kind.

At first the four birds were kept together; I was looking after the second pair for the importer. After a few months, it was necessary to remove one male as the other had cornered it on the floor and would have attacked it. The story of the second pair, which went to a new home, is a sad one and contains a moral for all would-be owners of cockatoos. The birds took three days to gnaw their way out of their aviary and were never recaptured.

In 1979, my pair nested for the first time, after seven years in my collection; perhaps they were stimulated by the horizontal log placed on the ground. This was difficult to inspect but, judging by their behaviour, the first egg was laid on April 30 and incubation probably commenced one or two days later, the male incubating during the day and the female at night. On the morning of May 30, a hatched eggshell was seen outside the log and the sounds of a chick being fed were heard. Two days later I could hear two chicks.

The male spent all day inside, while the female was either seen in the flight feeding or was inside the log. The male was not seen to come out to feed until about 17 days after the first chick was heard. Their aviary was situated in a position where it was possible to keep a close watch on their movements and I saw the male out of the log only when he was called by the female to assist in 'shouting' at a ginger cat to whom they had taken a great dislike. When the chicks were being fed, they made a 'chip-chip-chip' sound which was clearly audible. Often the sound could be heard when only the male was in the log, thus there was no doubt that the male did much or most of the feeding. If the male was not feeding himself the female must have been feeding him. I was reluctant to accept that this was so, especially as courtship feeding does not occur in most cockatoos and was never seen in this pair.

The female fed mainly on corn-on-the-cob, spinach, millet sprays and sunflower seed. Corn and spinach were given every two hours or more often to try to ensure that the chicks were fed frequently. After the chicks hatched she suddenly became tame, clinging to the wire and 'asking' for food, while the male, who was rarely seen, remained more wary.

The pair did not normally leave the nest together except when they felt threatened by the presence of a cat. The mewing sounds of the chicks could then be heard more loudly than when they were being brooded.

Goffin's Cockatoos belonging to the author with youngster shortly before fledging. The nest site is a horizontal log.

On June 16, I became concerned at apparently hearing the voice of only one chick. Previously, using a torch and a mirror to attempt to see inside the log had proved unsuccessful. On June 17, my husband therefore took off the piece of wood nailed on the end of the log. He removed a large well nourished chick which had its eyes wide open and its crop partly full. Its weight was estimated to be at least 168 g (6 oz). The contrast between it and its sibling was astounding. The second chick was less than half its size, weighed 84 g (3 oz) and had no food in its crop. It was at once removed for hand-rearing.

It seemed advisable to let it take the food from the spoon with the same action it had taken it from its parent's beak; it then made the 'chip-chip-chip' sound as well as impatient noises between each spoonful.

On the evening of June 19, the male Goffin's left the nest at 8.30 p.m. Neither bird returned so the chick was removed for the night. It was returned the next morning and the male brooded and fed it throughout the day. That evening brought a repeat of the happenings of the previous one so the chick was removed and not returned.

Had the parents spent gradually increasing periods away from the nest at a slightly later stage, when the emerging pin feathers had opened, there would have been less cause for concern. But under the circumstances there seemed little chance of it surviving if left in the nest.

The rearing food for my two young Goffin's consisted of chopped spinach, corn-off-the-cob, grated carrot, Casilan (high protein milk powder), ordinary milk powder, sunflower kernels and wheatgerm cereal. To ensure that the chicks received adequate calcium, a small amount of bone meal and scraped cuttlefish bone were added. The dry ingredients comprised about two thirds of the mixture.

All these items were put in an electric blender with water to make a soupy mixture which was fed very hot while the chicks were young and slightly cooler as they grew. At six weeks of age, the oldest chick became increasingly difficult to feed. The larger particles of food would be retained in the mouth and chewed, indicating that the chick was willing to learn to eat harder foods. When offered sunflower seed, he was able to crack it but could not manipulate the kernels. That a chick of this age was even capable of shelling sunflower I found remarkable.

It was at this stage, when weighing about 336 g (12 oz), that he ceased to gain weight. Indeed, he behaved exactly as one would expect of a chick of about four weeks older which was on the point of being weaned.

The reaction of the parents to their eldest youngster which, at six weeks, resembled a miniature adult, was interesting. The female showed intense aggression, throwing forward her helmet crest and screaming. The male, on the other hand, made a brief regurgitatory movement of the head, indicating either that he recognised the chick or that it triggered his instinct to feed it.

Perhaps because of their considerable weight for their size, they were slow to learn to walk in comparison with some parrot chicks. Until they were about six weeks old, the Cockatoos tended to keep their four toes pointing forwards and the youngest usually had its feet outstretched in a manner which might have led some observers to believe that it was deformed.

At six weeks, the eldest became quite adventurous and started to plod across the table at feeding times. At first he had difficulty in controlling not only his large feet but also his direction. There was still a striking contrast in the size and development of the two chicks. The eldest was fully feathered, apart from the quills in tail and flights which were still within their sheaths. In comparison, the youngest looked two weeks younger. It was fairly well covered with feathers, but two thirds the size of its sibling. The tail sheaths were just appearing, while those of the eldest chick were 2.5 cm (1 in) long.

It was noticeable that the skin surrounding the eye was bluer than in the adults and that the skin on the top of the head was dark blue. The coral-red bases to the feathers of the head, including the crest, were extremely prominent and some of the breast feathers were suffused with pink. Indeed, the coral-coloured lores were so marked, the birds were reminiscent of Slender-billed Cockatoos in this respect.

By the time he was seven and a half weeks old, the eldest chick was a perfect miniature of the adults, except for the shorter tail. He perched for the first time and was capable of removing the bark from the perch with his strong beak. A week before, the baby Cockatoos had been moved from the heated brooder to a metal cage.

At this age he started to play, rushing about the table with crest erect, when the mood took him. The wire cage front was removed at feeding time and he would climb out on his own or go back when he was tired of playing.

When much younger, he had completely ignored his sibling, although her tiresome continuous crying and fidgetting when he was trying to sleep must have been annoying. Now, he would sometimes rush playfully at her, almost knocking her over. Often he would preen her but was somewhat lacking in gentleness, causing her to cry out when he was too rough.

The breeding success of a pair owned by J. H. Strutt of Kirkby Stephen, Cumbria, is of particular interest because it occurred at liberty. The pair was obtained in 1977; that year the female laid two fertile eggs which were deserted just before they were due to hatch. They were then released and, in 1978, reared two young in a Scots pine tree. The young fledged in the summer but one disappeared in January and the other in March, probably driven away by the parents when they wanted to nest again. In 1979, a single youngster left the nest in early July.

Mr Strutt kept other birds at liberty, including macaws, in the thinly populated area of the Lake District in which he resided. He was fascinated to observe how the Goffin's defended their territory against the macaws and against a wild Sparrowhawk and Carrion Crows. The Goffin's would fly beneath their target and suddenly lunge upwards and seize the unfortunate bird by its tail, pulling hard in a downward direction.

Goffin's Cockatoo is, without a doubt, a most destructive species. Wood should not be used in the construction of its aviary unless it is covered with metal, and small staples are removed from wood with consummate ease. Ideally, metal pipe and steel only should be used. The beak of this species is not large but it is extremely powerful and used with persistence. If a weak point is discovered in the aviary framework a Goffin's will keep working at it.

In display it throws forward its small helmet crest and bows low, then struts about shrieking. The crest is invariably erected as it lands on a perch. My pair can quite often be heard calling at night. However, unless disturbed by a cat, in which case the shrieks persist until the cat retires, they are not particularly noisy.

They were originally conservative in their choice of foods, showing enthusiasm only for corn-on-the-cob and millet spray. Staple diet consists of sunflower and canary seed and apple. Chickweed will also be eaten. Over the years, their diet has widened to include carrot, celery, all greenfoods, plus such favourites as walnuts and the berries of hawthorn and elder.

Zoos which have reared this species include Natal Lion Park, South Africa, and Walsrode, Germany.

In Czechoslovakia, Z. Markvard reared a hybrid between a Goffin's and a Lesser Sulphur-crested in 1979. It left the nest at ten weeks old; its crest was orange-yellow and its beak black.

Ducorp's Cockatoo
C. ducorpsi

Description: It differs from *goffini* in the fuller broader crest and in the colour of the skin surrounding the eye, which is blue (not white), and in having the lores white (not pink). There is some pale orange down below the feathers of the cheeks and upper breast. The iris is dark in the male and reddish brown or brown in the female. Length: 30 cm (12 in); male is slightly larger usually.

Range/Habitat: It inhabits the eastern Solomon Islands from Bougainville to Malaita but is absent from the San Cristobel group. Seeds, berries and fruits, buds, blossoms and insects form the diet.

Aviculture: Like most birds from the Solomon Islands, it is rare in aviculture. Since being exhibited at London Zoo in 1864, it has only rarely been exported. The first captive breeding would appear to be that which occurred in Hawaii in 1982, in the aviaries of Richard Hart and Hiroshi Tagami. The American Federation of Aviculture silver medal was awarded but no details published.

One of the few aviculturists with extensive experience with Ducorp's Cockatoo is Dr R. Burkard of Zurich. He also keeps Bare-eyed and Goffin's Cockatoos and believes that Ducorp's differs so greatly in its behaviour that it should not be classified with *sanguinea*.

His seven pairs are each kept in aviaries measuring a minimum of 16 m (about 50 ft) square. The secondary wing coverts of the males are clipped to one quarter or a third of their natural length to slow them down if they attempt to persecute the hens. He ceased to offer mealworms after finding the effect on the males was overstimulating. In this way, he aims to avoid an early experience in which a female with three young was killed by the male when the chicks were about ten days old.

Dr Burkard informed me:

Ducorp's is vivacious and surely has the most personality of the white cockatoos. It is intelligent and quickly learns to recognise the person who feeds it and to fly towards him when a delicacy is in view. It has the finest plumage of all white cockatoos. The plumage takes on a rose-red glimmer in sunlight (Goffin's and the Bare-eyed are a duller white and the Red-vented is more yellowish). Compared to Goffin's the crest is much higher.

Hybrids between a male Ducorp's Cockatoo and a female Bare-eyed were bred at Loro Parque, Tenerife, in 1984. The pair was housed in an off-exhibit aviary in the breeding complex. Eggs were laid on April 4 and 9 and measured 40×28 mm ($1\frac{1}{2} \times 1$ in); they were larger and with a more pronounced point than the eggs of other white cockatoos. Incubation was carried out by the male. During the incubation period increased quantities of vegetables, fruit and bread and milk were offered. The eggs hatched on April 29 and May 2. The chicks were fed mainly by the male and they left the nest on June 30.

Philippine Red-vented Cockatoo
C. haematuropygia

Description: This is another delightful little cockatoo which bears a resemblance to the Goffin's. It is immediately distinguished from all other cockatoos by its red under tail coverts. The under side of the tail feathers is yellow. It further differs from Goffin's in having the ear coverts tinged with yellowish pink and the bases of the feathers of the short crest yellow and pink. Length: 30 cm (12 in). The iris is dark brown in the male and brownish red in the female. De Grahl (1974) described the sequence of colours of the eyes of an immature female. For two years, they were greyish, then they changed to brownish and, at three and a half years, became brownish red. The skin surrounding the eye is white.

Range/Habitat: The Red-vented Cockatoo is found in the Philippine Islands, including the Palawan group in the Sula Sea.

Usually seen in pairs or in small groups, it feeds on seeds, berries, fruit and nuts and on corn crops. This habit has resulted in persecution by crop owners; this fact, together with extensive deforestation in recent years, has resulted in a decline in its population.

Aviculture: The Red-vented Cockatoo has never been common in captivity and little has been recorded about it. The first and, to date, most consistent breeder, was Calvin Wilson of Salt Lake City, Utah, USA. He reared three in 1974 and 1975, one in 1976, two in 1977, three in 1978 (hand-reared) and three in 1979 (hand-reared). The adult birds were so destructive it was necesssry to make two new nest-boxes annually. Their aviary was constructed from 13 mm ($\frac{1}{2}$ in) chain link on a pipe framework. Food consumed included sunflower seed, green fruit (including apricot, pears and apples) and pyracantha berries.

This species has also been bred at San Diego Zoo. The pair was obtained in 1969 and first bred ten years later. Eggs were laid on May 17, 19 and 21. Three chicks hatched, two by June 20; their eyes were open by July 5. By August 28, the adults were consuming more sunflower seed and peanuts and less corn-on-the-cob and bread than in the previous weeks. The three young left the nest on August 30; they had been plucked on the head. In the following year (1980), two more were reared. Subsequent breeding attempts were unsuccessful.

In Texas, Dr R. J. Jerome reared one youngster in 1983.

The first recorded breeding of the Red-vented Cockatoo in Britain was that which occurred in the collection of Mrs D. Eubele in 1984. The pair had been together for about three years when she obtained them in 1982. In 1981, when in the collection of Mrs S. Belford, who imported them, they produced two eggs with full-term chicks dead in the shell. Mrs Eubele housed them in an aviary measuring 2.7 m (9 ft) square and 2.7 m (9 ft) high. The nest-box provided was 31 cm (1 ft) square and 1.5 m (5 ft) high. Two eggs were laid which hatched, it was believed, during the beginning of June.

Rearing food accepted at this time was egg biscuit food with chopped hard-boiled egg, soaked sunflower seed and, relished above all, fresh corn-on-the-cob.

The nest was not inspected during the rearing period. The young were seen at the nest-hole between the first and second week in September and left the nest on September 22 and 24. Each parent seemed to look after one youngster. When disturbed, the female would retire to the nest followed by one of the young while the male would keep his charge alongside while deciding if it was necessary to follow suit (Hayward, 1984).

Hybrids from a male Philippine and a female Leadbeater's Cockatoo were reared in Busch Gardens, Tampa, Florida, in 1973. I saw these most attractive hybrids in 1974. Intermediate in size, they were mainly white with the crest and the bases of the flight feathers pink.

Roseate Cockatoo (Galah)
C. roseicapillus roseicapillus

Description: Its colour scheme – deep pink below and soft grey above – is unique among parrots. The top of the head, from the forehead to the nape, is pink-tinged white, the feathers having pinkish bases and being short. When closed, the crest is not visible; when raised, it is formed by all the feathers of the forepart of the top of the head. The rump is whitish grey, lower abdomen and under tail coverts are grey, the tail being of a darker shade. The narrow area of skin surrounding the eye may be almost smooth or very crinkled. In the nominate race, the periorbital skin is dark greyish red. The bill is horn-coloured and the legs are grey. The iris is usually dark brown in the male (almost black in some very mature birds) and deep red or reddish brown in the female. In males which are not fully mature the eye colour may be difficult to distinguish from the female's. Some misleading variations in eye colour are known to occur so it is unwise to rely on eye colour as a guide to sex.

The shape of the head, rounder and bolder in the male and dropping away more steeply in the female, can be a guide to sexing this species. Length:

about 35 cm (14 in). Weight: about 400 g (14 oz). A chick which hatched in my incubator weighed 12 g ($\frac{2}{5}$ oz) on hatching; weaning weight is about 290 g ($10\frac{1}{5}$ oz).

Immature birds are duller than adults and have the crown and breast washed with grey. The iris is dark grey. Adult plumage is assumed at about one year.

In a very rarely encountered mutation, the areas which are normally grey are replaced by white, making a beautiful contrast to the pink plumage. The Duke of Bedford obtained a pair of these birds in 1928. When paired with an 'Albino' (presumably the same mutation) they reared young – always normally coloured birds – until about 1947. The male died in 1953, after about 25 years in his possession.

A pair of Roseate Cockatoos of normal appearance in the possession of Northumberland aviculturist Arthur Lamb, produced two female youngsters which were white (presumably Albino). After the death of the female parent, the male was paired with one of his white daughters. Year after year they hatched white young which died in the nest.

Range/Habitat: The Galah is one of the most widespread and common of Australian parrots. It inhabits the interior of almost the whole of Australia.

Found mainly in arid regions, the Galah is extending its range into cooler areas, spreading rapidly in some places. It is one of the few species to have benefited from human settlement, for the provision of watering places has aided its increase.

It is ironic that it is not permitted to trap and export this cockatoo, on which a constant war is waged by farmers with gun and poison. Considered as little better than vermin in its native country, outside Australia it is one of the most expensive and sought-after of all cockatoos. Large flocks attack grain crops, thus it is not surprising that farmers fail to take into account the good it does in destroying certain noxious weeds. In addition to grain, growing or bagged, its food consists of roots, green shoots, seeding grasses and insects.

Plentiful in most types of open country, and frequenting gardens and park-

Roseate Cockatoo (*Cacatua roseicapillus*) – female.

lands, it is seen in small flocks or large congregations numbering 200 birds or more. They indulge in aerobatics as dusk falls and they sometimes fly at night.

C. r. assimilis
Description: It has paler plumage with the crown suffused with pink. The periorbital skin is greyish white.
Range/Habitat: This race is from western Australia.

Aviculture: Since 1843, when the Roseate Cockatoo was first exhibited at London Zoo, until 1960, when the export of Australian birds ceased, this species was the most frequently imported of all cockatoos. For many years it was so numerous in the trade as to be valued at a few shillings per bird. One hundred years ago Greene thought that it was 'very far from being accounted a desirable acquisition in the aviary' and that it 'rivalled even the peacock in hideous noisiness'. The latter is most unjust as it is not nearly as noisy as the large white cockatoos. Greene was amazed that his contemporary Gedney went to some trouble

in order to rear chicks of this species whose mother had died, describing them as 'unworthy subjects' for such care.

The breeding by Gedney is of interest not only because it is one of the earliest records of cockatoos breeding, occurring in 1876, but because of the strange foster mother. The female died, leaving two very young chicks. Gedney had a chicken which was broody and placed the chicks beneath her. He masticated their food himself.

Since that time the Roseate Cockatoo has bred in many countries throughout the world; there were few successes before the 1920s, probably because this species was so inexpensive to purchase.

In the USA, it was not bred until 1929, when F. H. Rudkin reared two young. The pair reared eight broods in ten years and went on to rear many more. In 1937, C. W. Travers reared young from a female hatched by Rudkin only two years previously. It has also been known for a two year old male to fertilise eggs.

The clutch usually consits of two to four eggs; five have been known. Male and female share incubation which lasts for 25 days. On hatching, chicks are sparsely covered with pink down which is soon abraded, leaving them naked until the pin feathers appear. They develop quickly and leave the nest when about seven weeks old. The parents will often entice them back into the nest for the first few nights. Roseate Cockatoos sometimes prove to be double-brooded.

The display consists of the male strutting towards the female, bobbing his head and raising his crest, these movements often being accompanied by rapid beak clicking.

In aviaries, Roseate Cockatoos spend much time on the ground, where plenty of branches must be provided for them to destroy. They are able to gnaw through the hardest wood with ease and keeping them supplied with perches can be a problem. A familiar sound in the vicinity of the aviary containing my pair of Roseates is the rubbing of their beaks on the concrete floor in order to keep the cutting edge in perfect working order.

They will fill their nesting barrel with all kinds of rubbish. It is amusing

Roseate Cockatoo (*Cacatua roseicapillus*).

to witness the male manoeuvring sticks which, because of the length, he has as much hope of getting in as he would a rolled umbrella. Small twigs, millet sprays with the seeds removed and the husks of sunflower seeds will be used to line the nest. One pair in California used 40 to 50 green eucalyptus leaves, as they would in the wild. A curious habit is the beating of nesting material, such as twigs, against a hard surface, for all the world as though killing it. Unfortunately, my male developed a lipoma which will almost certainly make fertilisation of the female's eggs impossible. Such growths have been removed successfully but when my Roseate was anaesthetised and placed on the operating table for this purpose he was found to have two huge lipomas which covered the entire surface area of the abdomen. Because of their extent, and the possible ill effects of such major surgery, it was decided not to operate. The lipomas were opened and pieces of tissue removed

for analysis. As is normally the case with such growths, they were not found to be malignant.

Lipomas are extremely common in this species, perhaps more so than in any parrot other than the Budgerigar. They usually appear in the region of the vent. Possibly the cause is the high fat content of sunflower seed. In a state of nature, Roseate Cockatoos exist on a rather poor diet and would not have the opportunity to store fat.

Paolo Bertagnolio informed me that he once removed 'a tumour as large as an orange from the abdomen of a male Roseate'.

The diet of this species should therefore be as varied as possible, with as much greenfood as the birds can be induced to take. While rearing young, they should be offered bread and milk and corn-on-the-cob.

When Roseates were inexpensive, many were kept as pets and learned to repeat a few words. Today, they are seldom kept for this purpose. Former

pets are sometimes used for breeding and, being fearless, will not hesitate to attack in defence of their nest or young. Tame birds are seldom to be trusted completely, delighting in giving a sly nip when, while having their heads scratched, the thoughtful person performing this service ceases to concentrate on that finely curved beak.

Although the voice of this species is harsh, it is seldom as penetrating or as persistent as that of most cockatoos. Roseates will often call at night.

This species has produced hybrids with several other cockatoos, including the Greater Sulphur-crested, Slender-billed and Leadbeater's. Reported in 1941, an Australian aviculturist reared two youngsters from a female Gang Gang and a male Roseate. They were described as having 'a quaint mingling of the contrasting colour schemes of their two parents'. An interesting cross was reared at East Berlin Zoo – Leadbeater's × Roseate. Four were bred in 1970 and two in 1971.

After producing a fertile egg in 1977, a Timor Cockatoo paired to a male Roseate in the collection of N. O'Connor of Surrey, reared a most beautiful hybrid in 1978. I saw it shortly after it left the nest when it nearly resembled a Roseate with the pink areas replaced with orange. It had the crest, cheeks and the small feathers of the cere orange, those at the side of the beak pale orange and the rest of the head and the breast orange suffused with grey.

It resembled the Roseate in its development, leaving the nest at eight weeks. Rearing food consisted of soaked sunflower seed, canary, millet, wheat, oats, carrot and the stalks of cabbage and cauliflower. Most cockatoos relish the latter.

21
Macaws

It might be said that even those with scant knowledge of birds can recognise a macaw, but while this is true of the large species which are readily identified by their long tails and huge size some of the smaller macaws are no bigger than large conures and here the feathered lores of the latter are the distinguishing features. Large macaws of the genus *Ara* have the lores (the area between the upper mandible and the eye) and the cheeks entirely bare or decorated with widely spaced, narrow lines of feathers. The blue macaws are the only ones in which the lores are feathered – but they could not be mistaken for any other type of parrot.

The large macaws are among the most fascinating of all living birds: their appearance is striking enough but it is their intellect which is truly remarkable. Even those who are not and never will be students of bird life quickly realise, when in the presence of a large macaw, that here is a bird which is very much apart from almost all others: its reactions are akin to those of an intelligent mammal.

The study and comparison of individual macaws is fascinating because there is such wide variation in their personalities. Becoming acquainted with them is a rewarding experience.

Feeding: Macaws require an abundance of fresh fruit and vegetables in their diet; most will sample a wide range without very much persuasion. The large species also relish nuts and can be offered uncracked walnuts, almonds, hazel and Brazil nuts, among others. Pine nuts and peanuts can be added daily to the sunflower seed, plus a small amount of wheat, maize and hemp. The smaller macaws should be provided with canary seed, also white millet, in containers separate from that in which sunflower is offered. Most macaws will relish spray millet although some large macaws merely destroy it.

While rearing young, macaws require a nutritious softfood of some kind. This is particularly important in the case of the large species. Some USA breeders use prepared monkey biscuits or dog chow with much success. Corn-on-the-cob will also be relished. Animal protein, such as cooked meat on a chop bone, is beneficial.

Occasionally problems are encountered in persuading large macaws to eat seed. A small group of Hyacinthines lived for some months on corn-on-the-cob, monkey chow and fresh coconut, resisting all attempts to persuade them to eat sunflower seed.

Accommodation: Some large macaws are very destructive, thus aviaries for these birds should be strongly reinforced. The comments on housing cockatoos (see Chapter 20) apply equally to the large macaws. The smaller species present fewer problems; however, a minimum of wood should be used in the construction of their aviaries. Fresh branches supplied regularly will help to distract their attention from the aviary woodwork.

Some of the smaller macaws will use a nest-box for roosting purposes; the larger species only do so occasionally.

A large, fully enclosed shelter should be included in the design of a macaw aviary, especially in a built-up area. The cries with which these birds greet the dawn are not universally appreciated and being able to shut noisy specimens into a shelter can help to reduce the carrying distance of such untimely sounds.

While the large macaws are often housed in small aviaries, housing a pair in such a way that they can thoroughly exercise their wings, looking magnificent in the process, will necessitate erecting an aviary not less than 6 × 1.8 m (20 × 6 ft) × 1.8 m (6 ft) high. The wing-span of these birds is the largest of all the parrots.

Breeding: The principal difficulty in breeding from macaws was that of sexing them. Surgical sexing has therefore greatly aided macaw breeders. While some males have the head, feet and beak more massive than those of females, this is by no means invariably the case and many breeders have wasted years attempting to breed from what eventually proved to be two birds of the same sex. In some of the large macaws, compatibility or otherwise cannot be taken as an indication of sex. Long established true pairs can fight quite viciously while, on the other hand, two of the same sex will live together on terms of great affection. On occasion, two females 'paired' together will co-ordinate their breeding cycles, laying eggs in such sequence that it may be believed that only one bird is laying. As some females may produce as many as six eggs in a single clutch, a large clutch size does not necessarily denote that both birds are females – a further source of confusion. A sure sign is when both birds consistently attempt to copulate with their tails in a vertical position.

A large aviary is not necessary for breeding macaws: extensive flying exercise is not required for them to attain breeding condition or to retain their fertility. In the USA, a male Scarlet Macaw which had been pinioned when young and had never flown, reared young for over 20 years. Single pairs of macaws kept in relatively small aviaries, about 3.6 × 1.5–1.8 m (12 × 5–6 ft) × 1.8 m (6 ft) high are more likely to breed than a number of birds housed in a very large enclosure.

The macaw breeding units at Parrot Jungle in Miami are of particular interest. This park of exceptional beauty which, at the time of writing, had a total of 200 large macaws, was the instigator of a unique method of breeding these birds. Their successes over the past 30 years have been consistent and one can see fifth generation captive-bred young although 'captive' is hardly an appropriate word in this context for a large number of the macaws fly at liberty and are free to choose their own partners.

When it is obvious that the female will lay shortly, pairs are confined to small metal compartments which are not unlike rows of kennels fitted with a single perch. The rear part of the floor is separated from the front by a low board, behind which is the nesting material on which the female lays her eggs. Breeding pairs are confined to these indoor units until the young have been reared.

Macaws will often nest on the ground out of choice; this is not surprising when one considers that, under natural conditions, some will nest in rock faces. At Newquay Zoo in Cornwall, for example, a pair with clipped wings which were free to wander over part of the zoo were not provided with a nesting site. They discovered a cement cave at the rear of a run intended for rabbits and guinea pigs, with an entrance at ground level. The macaws, a male Scarlet and a female Green-winged, ousted the rightful occupants and made a shallow nest in a layer of peat. In the first clutch, a chick died shortly after hatching; in the second, a chick left the cave when 103 days old.

More orthodox nesting sites for captive macaws are wooden barrels (capacity 30 to 40 gallons) or steel drums. However, they have certain disadvantages and are best hung in a horizontal position as young macaws seem to overheat easily and become extremely uncomfortable in temperatures of over 32°C (90°F). They lie prone and pant during hot weather and can easily be overcrowded in the nest chamber, to their detriment. Their plump bodies generate additional heat and they therefore need more floor space to allow them to spread out to dissipate their heat more easily.

A disadvantage which applies regardless of climate is that barrels and steel drums do not satisfy a female's need to gnaw before and during incubation. Large pieces of wood should be nailed to the inside of the barrel for this purpose. If this is not done the female may gnaw through the bottom of the nest. Two chicks of a pair of Blue and Yellow Macaws nearly met a tragic end when their parents gnawed through the bottom of the nest-box. It is for this reason that the base should be reinforced or constructed of wood not less than 8 cm (3in) thick. Dry wood, including lumps, should be placed in the bottom of the nest for the birds to reduce to a fine layer. Nestboxes for the large macaws should measure approximately 51 cm (20 in) square and 51 cm (20 in) high. For the small species, it can be 23–25 cm (9–10 in) square and 46 cm (18 in) high. When they become broody, some hens make a continuous groaning sound within the nest-box.

Eggs may be laid on alternate days or with an interval of two to four days. Clutch size varies a great deal; three or four eggs is the average for the large species. On hatching, chicks have some white down. The incubation period is usually 28 days in the large macaws and 25–26 days in the small species. The length of time the young spend in the nest varies from only eight weeks in the small Hahn's to 14 weeks in the large *Ara* macaws. In the large species, the iris of the eye starts to lighten at about six months; by 12 months it is as pale as in the adult.

Many breeders in the USA remove chicks for hand-rearing. Hand-reared macaws are the most affectionate, interesting and companionable birds it is possible to imagine, but also very demanding. The careful thought which needs to be given to keeping a large macaw indoors has been pointed out elsewhere. The 'dwarf' macaws, those the size of a Severe or less, are a different proposition: they are far easier to handle and to manage in a house or aviary.

The strength of the large macaws should never be forgotten and, no matter how friendly one might look, it is wise not to handle a bird whose temperament is not known. It should also be remembered that the large macaws can be treacherous towards each other. When introducing two, great care must be taken. These extremely powerful birds sometimes fight viciously, apparently intent on causing terrible harm. Introductions must therefore be closely supervised and should occur when the owner will be in the vicinity for a couple of days at least. Previously the two birds should have been housed adjacent to each other for several days. The talented parrot artist, Elizabeth Butterworth, told me that, when two of her Scarlet Macaws were introduced, they shared the same flight for eight hours without fighting, then a dreadful battle started and the two birds were parted only by means of coats and blankets.

Hybridisation: Hybrids between the large macaws (all possible crosses within the genus *Ara* except *rubrogenys*, also some *Ara* × *Anodorhynchus*) have been bred on numerous occasions. These macaws hybridise readily and even when they have their own species from which to choose mates, they have paired with other species.

Hybrid breedings are particularly common in the USA, especially between the Blue and Yellow and the Scarlet; this cross was given the name 'Catalina Macaw', after the birds of this parentage bred at Catalina Bird Park on Catalina Island in California in 1931. Jean Delacour described the original Catalinas as 'a lovely apricot colour underneath, pale greenish-blue above, much prettier than either parents'.

Since then many examples of this cross have been reared and many of them agree with the above description. However, the plumage of hybrids is never predictable and even nest mates may be totally different. I saw at Parrot Jungle, perched side by side, two hybrids from the same parents. One had the under parts clear yellow and the other pure scarlet.

In view of the dwindling wild populations of the large macaws, the export of which will cease entirely within a few years, I feel that hybridisation is an irresponsible waste of precious genetic material. It would be a deplorable situation, detracting from the credibility of aviculturists as conservationists, if in the USA macaws existed only as multi-coloured hybrids. Fortunately, in Europe, hybrids are seldom reared.

At Liberty: If properly trained, some macaws are ideal liberty subjects in a suitable area. However, not all macaws have the qualities required and some prove quite unsuitable. It must be remembered by those intending to keep macaws at liberty or in an aviary that macaws which have been caged for a long period will be unable to fly. It could take as long as 9 or 12 months of vigorous wing exercise, including flapping their wings while perched, before they regain their strength and confidence. When eventually released, they may get into all kinds of difficulties, mainly because of their fear of climbing or flying down from a high perch. A macaw which has not had the opportunity to fly for several years – or perhaps never previously, as most macaws are exported as youngsters – has to learn to fly. However – and this must be emphasised – other macaws which have been caged can fly strongly; thus a macaw should *never* be taken outside unless its wings have been clipped. Failure to take this into account has resulted in the loss of countless pet parrots.

Many bird gardens have macaws at liberty. They prove to be a major attraction which is not surprising, for I can think of no more beautiful sight than a macaw in flight. They have a tendency to swoop low – over a wide expanse of lawn, for example – a truly breathtaking sight. Most such macaws are released with the primaries cut and are returned to an aviary or barrel into which they can be confined, each night. It will be some months before enough flight feathers are moulted and replaced to allow the bird to make trial flights and about two years before most of the primaries have grown. During this period, the macaw will become thoroughly familiar with its surroundings and is less likely to stray when it starts to fly. Some birds, however, seem to have no homing instinct and have to be retrieved time and again before their owners eventually give up the attempt to keep them at liberty.

In some areas, members of the rook family will be a major menace because they attack free-flying macaws and may harass them until they become confused and lost. One breeder of macaws never allowed the young of free-flying parents to have their liberty until early summer; in early spring, rooks would persistently annoy the macaws; presumably by early summer they were too busy with their domestic duties to bother them. It is advisable to remove young macaws for hand-feeding if their parents are at liberty because of the difficulties of capturing the young and the problems the young could meet before they were self-supporting.

Macaws breeding at liberty have been observed 'grubbing' on lawns, so it is not unlikely that some insects are taken under these circumstances. This is almost certainly due to the fact that the quality of the protein offered to captive macaws is inadequate, for plant-derived protein may be lacking in certain amino acids. For this reason, dog chow or monkey chow, meat and cheese should be offered to breeding macaws.

Anodorhynchus
Anodorhynchus

The three large distinctive macaws *A. hyacinthinus, glaucus* and *leari* in this genus are entirely blue with yellow skin surrounding the eyes and at the base of the lower mandible.

Hyacinthine (Hyacinth) Macaw
A. hyacinthinus

Description: This is an unforgettable bird – entirely deep, rich cobalt blue with a high gloss to the plumage. The under side of the tail is dark grey. A surprising contrast is provided by the yellow skin surrounding the eye and conspicuously bordering the lower mandible; also the tongue is yellow with the tip black. The bill is dark grey, almost black, and the legs are dark grey. The iris is dark brown. In total length, including the long tail, this macaw measures about 100 cm (34 in), thus is the longest of all parrots. Weight: 2 kg (4½ lb approx.).

In immature birds, the tail is shorter.

An interesting fact – if one bird is typical – is that the skin of the body becomes yellow when exposed to sunlight. At Parrot Jungle, Miami, a Hyacinthine Macaw plucked the feathers from its under parts, revealing grey skin. The skin became yellow and was that colour when I saw it there.

Range/Habitat: The Hyacinthine Macaw inhabits a large area of southern Brazil in the states of Pará, Piauhy, Goyaz, São Paulo, Minas Gerais and Mato Grosso; it also occurs in extreme eastern Bolivia and extreme north-eastern Paraguay.

This species is seen in pairs or small groups and is said to be fairly common in some areas but is uncommon in others and has been extirpated from most settled regions, due to trapping and hunting.

It is most numerous in the Mato Grosso, but overall a substantial population decline has occurred. Its habitat includes forest, swamp, palm groves. Its diet consists of palm and other nuts, fruits and seeds.

Aviculture: Before the 1970s, the Hyacinthine Macaw was rare in aviculture and expensive. Its price remains high yet it is now by no means rare. Although this species has many, many admirers, its high price means that only the affluent can invest in these birds. Its powerful voice is another deterrent. A number of dealers who obtained consignments of these birds in the 1970s found that supply exceeded the demand for it, which had been satisfied by previous importations. Possibly this state of affairs was

Hyacinthine Macaw (*Anodorhynchus hyacinthinus*).

due to the 'opening up' of Brazil, brought about by the road constructed through hundreds of kilometres of the interior, resulting in the habitat of this species becoming more easily accessible. It has long been known that Indians use this bird for food; no doubt many of those exported would otherwise have been used for that purpose.

Much of its habitat may be lost as the result of settlement of areas which, until the early 1970s, were almost uninhabited. It therefore behoves aviculturists fortunate enough to possess these magnificent birds not to regard them as ornaments of aesthetic value only but to attempt to breed from them.

Breeding of the Hyacinthine Macaw in captivity had not occurred prior to 1967. A German avicultural journal reported that, in Poland, Poznan Zoo had bred from a pair on more than one occasion in a small indoor compartment. The birds nested in a wooden chest placed on the floor. In the following year, a Hyacinthine Macaw was reared in Kobe Zoo, Japan, according to the *International Zoo Yearbook*. The same source informs that, in 1969, three Hyacinthine Macaws were bred in Bratislava Zoo, Czechoslovakia; however, the curator in 1978 informed me that a chick was hatched in 1969 but lived for only two weeks. The female did not lay again until 1978.

Much of what is known about the captive breeding of this macaw can be attributed to Ralph Small of Brookfield, Chicago.

Mr Small's pair originally belonged to the zoo in Brookfield. The female was obtained by the zoo in 1949; its companion was not discovered to be a female until its death in 1966. In April 1967, the zoo purchased a male which had been imported in 1956. In April 1968, the two birds were introduced. In March of the following year, the female laid two eggs; both were infertile. Two more eggs were laid on May 13 and 16, one of which hatched on June 13. Three days later the chick had disappeared. In October 1970, the pair was purchased by Mr Small, a keeper at the zoo with a long interest in parrots. They were housed in his basement in an enclosure measuring 2.1 × 4.2 m (7 × 14 ft) × 1.5 m (5 ft) high. The nesting site the pair had used at the zoo, a 50-gallon steel drum laid on its side with the upper third of the top cut out, was provided. It was half filled with tan bark and about four litres of water were added to provide the necessary humidity. The temperature of the room was maintained at between 24 and 27°C (74 and 80°F).

Eggs were laid on January 5 and 9 and proved to be infertile. Of the next two eggs, laid on March 1 and 4, one hatched on March 30, giving an incubation period of 29 days. The chick was cold when found, probably shortly after hatching, and was removed for hand-rearing. This was successful.

The female laid a single egg in April and two more in December. A chick hatched on January 4, 1972. Four days later the female was observed feeding it: she held its entire head in the tip of her bill and gently moved her head up and down. At 41 days, the chick was removed for hand-rearing as the female had plucked it. The chick had been weighed from the time it hatched (18.6 g/$\frac{7}{10}$ oz) and its progress recorded as follows: two weeks, 156 g (5$\frac{1}{2}$ oz); three weeks, 302 g (10$\frac{7}{10}$ oz); four weeks, 464 g (16$\frac{2}{5}$); five weeks, 659 g (23$\frac{1}{5}$ oz) and six weeks, 643 g (22$\frac{7}{10}$ oz). The next chick to hatch was larger: two weeks, 189 g (6$\frac{7}{10}$ oz); three weeks, 347 g (12$\frac{1}{4}$ oz); four weeks 533 g (18$\frac{4}{5}$ oz); five weeks 668 g (23$\frac{1}{2}$ oz).

Two clear eggs were laid in March and, on May 1 and 5, the eggs of the third round were laid. One hatched on May 29, and the chick was removed for hand-rearing on July 27 because it had been plucked and was badly soiled with food. In May, October and December 1973, single chicks were hatched and hand-reared.

Also in the USA, two Hyacinthine Macaws were reared at Houston Zoo in 1975 and one in 1977. The parents were obtained in 1966 and housed in an indoor exhibit until 1972, when they were moved to an outdoor aviary which provided ample opportunity for flight. In the spring of 1975, the birds were given access to a nest-box and produced a single egg which proved to be infertile. They were then temporarily moved to a holding cage while the damage carried out during their three-year tenure was repaired. This cage was located in a storage building with a low intensity 24-hour light cycle. As copulation and courtship feeding were observed and the birds became decidedly aggressive, a hole was cut in the cage wire and their former nest-box was mounted at floor level outside the cage. They nested almost immediately, the female laying two eggs and rearing two chicks to independence without incident. The adults fed the young a great deal of corn-on-the-cob, soaked dog chow and peanuts, the latter being their favourite food.

Once the young were independent, the nest-box was removed. By this time, their aviary had other occupants and it was decided to move them back to their original home in the Tropical Bird House. Here the birds nested in a metal oil drum. A single egg was laid and the resulting chick was reared successfully. Adults and young were then moved to a series of specially constructed off-exhibit aviaries in the hope that second generation young would be reared. Also in the USA, this species has been bred at Oklahoma Zoo since 1978 and at Busch Gardens, Tampa, since 1981.

In Britain, the first breeding of the Hyacinthine Macaw occurred in 1983. Daphne and Walter Grunebaum obtained a pair in 1977 and placed them in an aviary 12 m (40 ft) long and 3 m (10 ft) high, with an attached shelter measuring 2.4 × 3.6 m (8 × 12 ft). After

two years, the female laid two eggs which disappeared. Two months later, two more were laid; they were fertile but the chicks died in the shell. The following year, the female died suddenly. After three months, another bird was obtained. At first she ate only Brazil nuts and white sunflower seed. By September 1982, she was eating sweetcorn, banana, apple, grapes, peas, broad beans, carrots, peanuts and walnuts. The male flew at liberty until March 1983 when he no longer wished to go out.

Two eggs were laid. On May 14 and 16 respectively two more were laid. A chick was heard on June 15. The nest was inspected on the following day and the chick was described as being black-skinned. The parents began to search for grit and a pile of ground-up limestone was placed in the flight. Much cuttlefish bone was also eaten. When the chick was six weeks old, the yellow skin surrounding the beak and eyes was evident and the tail was about 12.5 cm (5 in) long. It was nearly fully feathered.

The parents started to consume large quantities of cob and hazel nuts, even when green and unripe. On September 7, the chick was found on the floor and was returned to the nest. Two days later it was out again, but appeared listless and was nervous of climbing. It contracted a chill and had to be tube-fed with Complan and Farex, and was injected with Vitamin B_{12}. After being wrapped in foil and placed under an infra-red lamp it improved rapidly. After five days, the heat was removed and it was placed in a sunroom where it could see the other birds. It then started to feed itself on peanuts, half-shelled Brazil nuts, banana and apple. For ten days it was given three feeds daily – but milk-based foods had to be discontinued. After three weeks, it refused soft foods (Grunebaum & Grunebaum, 1984).

Also in the UK, a Hyacinthine Macaw was hand-reared at Birdworld, Farnham, in 1984, and this success was repeated in 1985. In Sweden, Hans Parnestam's pair reared a youngster in 1984 in a 2.1 m (7 ft) square indoor aviary.

In Germany, Gerd Volkeimer (1984) obtained a pair of Hyacinthine Macaws in 1981. Their aviary measu-

red 4 × 1.5 m (13 × 5 ft) × 2 m (6 ft) high with a shelter 1.75 m (5¾ ft) long. A wooden nest-box was provided. The entrance was 20 cm (8 in) square. The diet consisted of fruit, beef bones, corn, oats, wheat, hemp, sunflower and other seeds and peanuts. Calcium and minerals were added to the food.

At the end of May, both birds became defensive towards their nest-box. Sometimes they would sit together, nodding their heads while holding beaks and uttering loud rolling sounds. During copulation, the birds' tails were crossed.

Two eggs were laid but disappeared after two weeks. On June 2, another two eggs were found; they measured 50 × 35 mm (2 × 1⅖ in) and one weighed 20 g (¾ oz). The female incubated for 30 days. One chick hatched. It produced quiet noises for several weeks; then there was a period of silence before it became very vocal. Its eyes were open at two weeks and it left the nest at three months old. The plumage was duller than that of the adults and the skin surrounding the eye was paler yellow. Additional foods during the rearing period included sprouted oats, wheat, sunflower and corn and unripe corn-on-the-cob. In 1983, two pairs bred; one pair reared two young and the other pair one.

In the USA, the Hyacinthine Macaw has been hand-reared in a number of collections. These include Life Fellowship in Florida. Ramon Noegel obtained two feather-plucked Hyacinthines as a donation from Parrot Jungle. They were surgically sexed males stated to be incapable of breeding due to 'improperly formed testicles'. An 'immature sexed female' was also obtained. None of these descriptions proved to be accurate.

A male and the female were placed in a cage measuring 1.8 × 2.4 m (6 × 8 ft) × 1.8 m (6 ft) high suspended 50 cm (20 in) above the ground. It was constructed of 5 × 10 cm (2 × 4 in) 9 gauge galvanised welded wire. The nest site was a wooden whisky barrel mounted horizontally on an oil drum stand. On April 3, 1980, the first of three eggs was laid. The second was deposited on April 6. Because the female was nervous and came off the nest, the eggs were placed under a Cochin bantam. The second egg was fertile and, after 25 days, it was placed in an incubator. The egg seemed small and the chick occupied all the air space; it had a deformed head and had to be helped out of the shell. It lived only 16 hours. Two more eggs were laid on May 15 and 18 and were incubated by a Scarlet Macaw. One hatched on June 13, after 29 days incubation. The chick was removed when three days old and was reared without problem. It grew more slowly than a Scarlet Macaw and was weaned at nine weeks by placing crushed grapes in its mouth, moistened wholemeal bread, ripe banana and corn-off-the-cob. Within a week, the Hyacinthine, and a Hawk-headed Parrot which had been raised with it, were competing for food. The Hyacinthine would gorge itself so food had to be restricted.

In 1981, the female laid on May 15 and 19. The eggs were smaller than those of a Scarlet Macaw. They hatched on June 10 and 14 – one in the nest and one in an incubator. The female laid again on June 10.

Ramon Noegel commented that Hyacinthine chicks are more sensitive than those of Scarlet or Blue and Yellow Macaws. Their crops empty more slowly and must not be filled completely. They grow more slowly and require more heat until fully feathered than Scarlet Macaws.

Ramon Noegel's Hyacinthine were fed on dog chow, fruit, raw vegetables, sunflower seed, coconut, Cheddar cheese twice weekly and scrambled egg (including the shell). Wholewheat bread and peanut butter with added vitamins and wheatgerm oil were readily accepted.

As aviary subjects, Hyacinthine Macaws will give much pleasure to those able to provide suitable accommodation or fortunate enough to have conditions under which they can be kept at liberty. Because of the aptitude with which this species can demolish the strongest flight cage, and because of its size, caging a Hyacinthine should not be considered unless the bird is very tame and can be let out of its cage daily for exercise.

Many Hyacinthines are extremely gentle birds and more docile than the huge beak would suggest. It has been calculated (but I cannot say how!) that the biting pressure of this species is 300 p.s.i. David Chenault (1977) owner of five Hyacinthines estimated that he spent five to six hours every week welding back into place the bars of their enclosures. One bird alone, housed in an aviary constructed from chain link and steel pipe, would daily remove two or three of the aluminium tie bands, 'sit on the perch with a newly acquired tie and bite off a little at a time'. Nevertheless, its owner described this species as 'the most intelligent, alert, and loving' of all the macaws he had owned.

The Hyacinthine has hybridised with *Ara* species. A male, paired with a Blue and Yellow Macaw in Salt Lake Tracy Aviary in the USA, reared young on more than one occasion from 1965. I saw one of the resulting hybrids in the collection of Dr B. Levine of Miami in 1978. The size and shape of a Hyacinthine, it resembled that species, apart from the under parts which were yellow. In 1966, also at Salt Lake Tracy, two hybrids between a male Scarlet Macaw and a female Hyacinthine were reared.

Glaucous Macaw
A. glaucus
Description: It is greenish blue, more greenish below; the head and neck have a grey tinge and the throat and upper breast are suffused with greyish brown. The primaries and the under side of the tail, also the under wing coverts, are blackish. The bare skin surrounding the eye is yellow, that at the base of the lower mandible being a paler shade of yellow. The bill is grey-black and the iris is dark brown. Length: 72 cm (28 in).
Range/Habitat: The Glaucous Macaw inhabited Paraguay, north-eastern Argentina and south-eastern Brazil. It is now considered to be extinct in the wild (Ridgely, in Pasquier, 1981). It has been reported to have been kept in captivity in Brazil in recent years but there is no concrete evidence of this. The species obtained may have been *leari*. The reason for its decline or disappearance is not known.
Aviculture: It is almost unknown in captivity and nothing has been recorded about it. Australian aviculturist, the late Alan Lendon, informed me that there was a Glaucous Macaw in Australia for many years. Eventually it passed into the collection of the late Sir Edward Hallstrom.

Lear's Macaw
A. leari
Description: It is mainly dull cobalt blue, the head and under parts being tinged with green. The inner webs of the primaries, the under wing coverts and the under side of the tail are blackish. It otherwise resembles the Glaucous Macaw and has the tongue black with a yellow stripe on each side. Length: 75 cm (29 in).
Range/Habitat: The habitat of this species was discovered as recently as 1978; Raso de Catarina in northeastern Bahia, Brazil. The area is remote, extremely arid and inhospitable. Its population is believed to be in the region of 100, making it perhaps the most endangered of mainland neotropical parrots.
Aviculture: This macaw has always been an extreme rarity in aviculture. At the time of writing it is represented in collections in Birdland, England; San Diego Zoo, California, and Parrot Jungle, Miami.

The only breeding pair is that at Busch Gardens, Tampa, the male of which is on loan from Parrot Jungle, Miami. A chick hatched in 1982 was hand-reared at Parrot Jungle.

Cyanopsitta
Cyanopsitta

Spix's Macaw
Cyanopsitta spixii
Description: This single member of its genus is very different in appearance from the blue macaws already described and, in fact, from any other macaw. The comparatively small beak and the small area of naked skin on the face – which extends only from the lores to surround the eyes – makes this the least typical of the large macaws. The beak is black and the naked skin is dark grey, which gives prominence to the light yellow iris. Its soft colours are far less eye-catching than those of the members of the previous genus.

Spix's Macaw (*Cyanopsitta spixii*).

The forehead and ear coverts are grey tinged with blue, the head being otherwise greyish blue. The plumage is dark blue above, lighter blue below. The under side of the tail is dark grey. Length: 56 cm (22 in).

Immature birds are darker with the tail shorter. The bill is greyish black with horn-coloured markings along the culmen.

Range/Habitat: This extremely rare macaw is one of the least known of South American parrots. Virtually nothing has been recorded about it, other than the fact that it inhabits north-eastern Brazil, Southern Piauí, Southern Maranhão, north-eastern Golás and north-western Bahía. After Spix's discovery of it, there was no record of a further sighting until 1903, over one hundred years later.

Field work carried out in 1985 suggested that it is highly endangered. Only five birds could be found – but

possibly another population existed.

Aviculture: Few specimens have been kept in captivity. At the time of writing, there is a tame pair in the Parrot House at Vogelpark Walsrode in Germany and, in Italy, a single bird at Naples Zoo. It was bred by Alvaro Rossman Carvalhaes in São Paulo, Brazil, during the 1950s. Eight young were reared over a period of several years, most of which died when adult but without breeding. No other captive breedings have been recorded.

At the time of writing, there were probably about twenty in captivity in Brazil, including three in São Paulo Zoo, four in private collections in São Paulo and one in Parana. Outside Brazil, the number in captivity is even smaller.

Brazilian aviculturist, Nelson Kawall, informed George A. Smith (1983a) that three or four young (probably two nests) was the annual incre-

ment of young Spix's on the Brazilian market, but none had appeared since the murder of the man who supplied the birds.

Ara
Ara

Ara macaws vary in size from the well known giants, the Blue and Yellow and the Scarlet, which measure about 85 cm (33½ in), to the conure-like Noble Macaw, which is only 30 cm (12 in) in length. They are very closely related to *Aratinga* conures, and some of the latter are larger than the smallest macaws. All *Ara* species have the lores unfeathered or decorated with widely spaced lines of minute feathers.

Blue and Yellow (Blue and Gold) Macaw
A. ararauna

Description: This is one of the most magnificent of all parrots.

Rich sky blue above and golden yellow below, it cannot be mistaken for any other macaw. The primaries and tail are a darker shade of blue; the under tail coverts are light sky blue and the under side of the tail is dull yellow, the feathers having dusky edges.

The forehead and forepart of the crown are green, the ear coverts and the sides of the neck are yellow and the feathers of the throat and just below are black. The extensive white skin of the facial area is unfeathered except for several (usually three) narrow lines of tiny greenish black feathers. The beak is black and the iris is pale yellow. Length: about 85 cm (33 in), one half of which is accounted for by the tail. Weight: about 1400 g (3 lb).

Immature birds resemble adults, except for the dark iris.

Two mutants, both of which were devoid of yellow pigment, have been kept in captivity. In about 1973, a London dealer received one of these birds. To my eyes, its blue upper parts contrasting with white under parts made it less attractive than a normal bird; however, it was not in good feather when I saw it. A similar bird was exhibited at a small zoo in Entretat in France many years ago.

Range/Habitat: The Blue and Yellow Macaw has an immense range over almost the entire northern part of South America, except the western coast and northern Colombia and northern Venezuela. It is found from Panama, extending to Bolivia and is absent from the extreme eastern part of Brazil.

Due to trapping and deforestation, the Blue and Yellow Macaw has become less common or extinct in accessible areas but is still common in many remote locations.

Aviculture: Were it rarely imported, instead of being fairly readily available, it would almost certainly command a price in the region of that of the Hyacinthine Macaw. As it is, this species and the Scarlet are the most expensive of the parrots which can be considered common in captivity.

Prior to the 1970s, the Blue and Yellow Macaw was infrequently bred in captivity, probably due to the fact that the majority were isolated as pets. In recent years, there have been very many successes; some pairs nest readily and consistently produce young.

For example, a pair at Rode Tropical Bird Gardens in Somerset reared 17 between 1965 and 1972. Second generation young have been reared there; one pair which was hatched at Rode first nested when six years old but the eggs did not hatch.

The usual clutch is three eggs. Sometimes only two are laid and clutches of one and four have been recorded. The incubation period is normally 28 days although one breeder recorded that on one occasion it was 26 days. Newly hatched chicks weigh about 14 g ($\frac{1}{2}$ oz); one weighed 1100 g (nearly 2$\frac{1}{2}$ lb) when weaned.

Daphne Grunebaum (1976) noted of her pair, just prior to egg laying that: 'both smelled very strongly, the sweet sickly macaw smell'. After the eggs were laid, the macaws 'started to make a new call, a gentle call of two notes, the lower sliding up to the higher. This call was eventually taken up by all the family and only ceased when the babies were nearly feathered'.

The chicks of this species are naked

Blue and Yellow Macaw – lacking blue pigment and therefore appearing brownish black.

on hatching; down is then acquired and is lost when the quills appear. The wings and mantle feather up first, then the tail, head and body. At ten weeks, the young bird is fully feathered but the tail is considerably shorter than that of the adult. Young birds usually leave the nest when they are 13 weeks old.

It seems that even extremely close confinement will not deter this species from breeding successfully. In Chicago, a pair belonging to Erling Kjelland reared young in a shop, housed in a cage measuring 60 × 120 × 120 cm (2 × 4 × 4 ft). They nested in a metal box containing cedar shavings and wood chips. In the first clutch two eggs were laid, one of which was fertile. All three eggs of the second clutch hatched; one chick died when a few days old and the two survivors were removed for hand-rearing when they were well feathered. Corn-on-the-cob was the favourite food of the female.

Caninde (Blue-throated) Macaw

A. glaucogularis

Description: It differs from the Blue and Yellow Macaw in the colouration of the area covering part of the cheeks and ear coverts and beneath the throat which is blue instead of black. In Walsrode's specimen, the feathered

lines on the cheeks are broader, dark green and cover a wider area. The smaller area of bare skin adds to the beauty of this macaw. The size is the same or fractionally larger than that of *ararauna*.

For some years, the status of this little known bird was in doubt; there were suggestions that it was a subspecies or immature of a subspecies. It is now known to be a valid species.

Range/Habitat: The Caninde Macaw is restricted to Beni and Santa Cruz in Bolivia. Earlier reports that its range includes Paraguay and Argentina are incorrect. Its population has been estimated to be about 1000, or considerably less.

Aviculture: This macaw was unknown in captivity until the late 1970s when several consignments reached the USA. In the intervening years, virtually nothing has been recorded about it. A friend who has bred the Blue and Yellow for many years told me that behaviourally it differs in being much more active than that species.

The first breeding successes occurred in 1984 in the collection of Dr. B. Levine of Miami and at Loro Parque in Tenerife in 1984. The latter pair was obtained in 1981 and kept in an aviary measuring 4 × 3.6 m (13 × 12ft). A large tree trunk in the centre of the aviary is decorated weekly with fresh branches of pine or eucalyptus. The nest-box was situated in a sheltered corner of the aviary.

Blue and Yellow Macaw (*Ara ararauna*).

Caninde (Blue-throated) Macaw (*Ara glaucogularis*).

Caninde Macaw, aged 25 days (left) and 50 days (right), bred at Loro Parque, Tenerife, in 1984.

The female laid for the first time on July 10, 1984; a second egg was found on July 13. The eggs measured 44 × 34 mm ($1\frac{7}{10}$ × $1\frac{3}{10}$ in) and 42 × 32 mm ($1\frac{7}{10}$ × $1\frac{1}{4}$ in). The first egg hatched after 26 days. At the age of 15 days, the chick weighed 387 g ($13\frac{3}{4}$ oz) and at 25 days 510 g (18 oz). Its eyes opened after 14 days and its ears had opened by August 31. At the age of 38 days, it weighed 695 g ($24\frac{1}{2}$ oz); its head was completely feathered, also the wings; the tail measured 4 cm ($1\frac{1}{2}$ in). At 50 days, the chick weighed 760 g ($26\frac{4}{5}$ oz); its under parts were covered in yellow feathers. On the 56th day, when it weighed 768 g (27 oz), it was completely feathered except for the legs. At 71 days, it weighed 900 g ($31\frac{3}{4}$ oz). It left the nest at 90 days when it resembled the adults except for its slightly smaller size, dark eyes and darker blue on the upper breast (Kessling, 1985 and pers. comm.).

Military (Great Green) Macaw

A. militaris militaris

Description: The head is light green and the wings and back of an olive shade. The throat is brown. There is a bluish tinge on the hind neck and the greater wing coverts and the outer edge of the primaries are blue. The lower back, rump and upper tail coverts are light blue. The tail is maroon, deeply tipped with blue and the under side of the tail and flight feathers is olive-yellow. The large area of bare skin on the cheek is decorated with several narrow lines of black feathers. Bill and legs are grey-black and the iris is yellow. Length: about 70 cm (28 in).

Immature birds resemble adults but for the duller plumage and dark iris.

Range/Habitat: The Military Macaw is found in Mexico; in South America it is locally distributed in western Colombia, north-western Venezuela, Ecuador, northern Peru and Bolivia to north-western Argentina.

Buffon's (Grand Military) Macaw

A. m. ambigua

This is sometimes treated as a separate species from the Military, but

Military Macaw (*Ara militaris*).

it is here considered a subspecies.

Description: Buffon's Macaw differs from the foregoing principally in its larger size – about 85 cm (34 in) – and yellower shade of green. Immature birds are less brightly coloured than adults, with indistinct margins of yellowish green on the scapulars and also on the inner secondaries.

Both this race and the Military are easily distinguished from other Macaws by the combination of mainly green plumage and by the small, dense feathers of the forehead.

Range/Habitat: It inhabits Central America from Nicaragua, Costa Rica and Panama to western Colombia. Its range divides that of the Military Macaw. Habitat destruction has reduced its numbers in many areas.

Aviculture: Few breeding successes had been recorded until the late 1970s. A Military Macaw hatched at Wellington Zoo, New Zealand, in 1962 was not reared but the following year a successful breeding was achieved. In 1964, two Military Macaws were reared at Fort Worth Zoo in Texas. At Busch Gardens, Tampa, Florida, and at Tulsa Zoo, this species has been reared since 1978.

This macaw has also been bred by Paul V. Springman of Brownsville,

Texas, whose pair were housed in an aviary 6 × 1.8 m (20 × 6 ft) × 2.1 m (7 ft) high. They nested in a 55-gallon metal drum with half of one end cut out and doubled back (to prevent injury to their feet). The drum was laid on its side and filled with wood shavings, of which the macaws removed the surplus.

The same aviculturist also reared hybrids between a Military male and a Scarlet female for many years. As long ago as 1901, London Zoo received four hybrids between a Scarlet Macaw and a female Military. They had been reared in Milan Zoo.

The Grand Military Macaw bred at East Berlin Zoo in 1974; three chicks were hatched, two of which were reared. Young have since been reared on several occasions. The first British success occurred in 1977 at Bird Paradise in Cornwall. One was obtained in 1972 and another in the following year. They were established in a barrel about 3.6 m (12 ft) up a tree. At Bird Paradise, four or five pairs of

Buffon's Macaw (*Ara militaris ambigua*).

macaws were trained at liberty but the Buffon's proved complete failures, having no sense of direction. In April 1976, their wings were therefore clipped. Within two weeks, the female had taken to the smaller barrel placed on top of the roosting barrel. Two eggs were laid but after 12 days they were broken, following many noisy altercations between the male and female.

In 1976, the female laid two eggs at the beginning of May. Because of the fate of the previous eggs, these were removed; one was placed in an incubator and the other in the nest of another pair of macaws which had eggs. The latter hatched the Buffon's chick, together with one of their own, but both died after about three days. Five days after the Buffon's eggs were removed, she had laid a third egg. This was placed in the nest of a pair of free-flying Scarlet Macaws which had previously successfully reared young. A chick hatched which 'looked rather different from a young Scarlet. It was thickly covered in grey down, and seemed much plumper and rounder, and the general shape of the head seemed more solid' (Reynolds, 1977). When it began to feather at five weeks, it was apparent that it was a Buffon's Macaw. When it was ten weeks old, it was removed from the barrel to prevent it becoming lost or injured on fledging. Fed on a mixture of baby cereal and banana given in a syringe, it thrived. After two weeks, it was helping itself to bread and milk, fruit and sunflower seed. While the parents were feeding it, they had been provided with sunflower seed, peanuts, pine nuts, fruit and bread and milk, offered fresh four times daily.

In Zimbabwe, F. G. R. Townsend has been consistently successful in breeding from a pair of Military Macaws. In 1979 and 1980, three young were reared; in 1981, two; in 1982, three; in 1983, one – when the previous year's young were still in the aviary; in 1984, three were reared – a total of 15 in six years.

In 1975, Dr and Mrs Nathan Gale took two Buffon's Macaws from Panama to the USA, where they were kept separately as pets. In 1981, they were reunited in an indoor enclosure measuring 1.8 × 1.2 m (6 × 4 ft). The nest site was a barrel 69 cm (27 in) long

Red-fronted Macaw (*Ara rubrogenys*).

and 39 cm (15 in) in diameter. The first of three eggs was laid on March 28 1982; all were infertile. The first egg of the second clutch was laid on May 22. There were four eggs; two were broken. Two chicks had hatched by June 19. Their eyes were completely open by the 22nd day. The feathers of the forehead of one chick were plucked during the eighth week. The young macaws were looking out of the nest at two months old and both had left by 12 weeks (Gale, 1983). This was the first recorded breeding of Buffon's Macaw in the USA.

Red-cheeked (Red-fronted) Macaw

A. rubrogenys

Description: It is one of the least known of all the parrots of South America. Intermediate in length between the large macaws and the small members of the same genus, often known as dwarf macaws, it measures 60 cm (24 in). Its colouration is also distinctive, for it is mainly green (of an

olive shade which is closest to that of the Military) enhanced by areas of orange-red. The latter are found on the forehead, crown and a small area behind the eye and on the bend and carpal edge of the wing and the lesser under wing coverts and thighs. The olive green plumage is brightest on the head. Greater under wing coverts and the under side of the tail are olive-yellow. The tail is green above, tipped with blue, and the primaries and their coverts are greyish blue. The naked facial area is small; there are narrow lines of tiny black feathers on the lores. The bare skin around the eye is pink and the iris is orange. Bill and legs are dark grey.

Forshaw (1973) describes immature birds as having orange confined to the forehead, with pale orange on the lesser wing coverts and the thighs tinged with orange. This description conflicts with that of captive-bred birds which have the orange on the head confined to the ear coverts.

Plumage is variable in adult birds so that individuals can be recognised by the markings on the head.

Range/Habitat: This macaw was totally unknown in aviculture until 1973. The collector, Rolando Romero, saw it for the first time in 1970 and thought it might be a hybrid until he saw a skin in the British Museum. It took him almost three years to locate a wild population.

The valley where the only known specimens lived was difficult and dangerous to reach and it was there that he saw Red-fronted Macaws in the wild. They feed on corn and fruits, including cactus fruits. These macaws were usually seen in pairs and groups of more than 12 were rare.

Aviculture: What was probably the first bird of this species to reach Britain was obtained by macaw specialist John Halford (1974) of Hampshire in February 1973. It was in poor condition and had to be kept in a high temperature on arrival. In addition to seed, it was offered a variety of soft foods but would accept only corn-on-the-cob and boiled maize with multivitamin drops added. After a month, it started to vomit but recovered on being given antibiotics and increasing the temperature. Its food intake was so small that it was placed with a tame

Red-bellied Macaw; the two birds agreed well together and eventually the Red-fronted learned to eat seed and other foods.

During 1973 and 1974, a small number of Red-fronted Macaws reached Britain and the occasional small importation has taken place since then. The first recorded captive breeding occurred in Wuppertal Zoo in West Germany in 1978. Three young were reared. Subsequent successes include two in 1979, one in 1980 and three in 1981.

The first breeding in a private collection occurred in the USA. Juanita DeLoach's pair nested in a 15-gallon barrel. Three eggs were laid in May 1981 and three young reared.

At Tierpark Berlin (East Berlin Zoo), a pair of Red-fronted Macaws which were imported in 1974 nested ten years later. Three eggs were laid on the floor of the aviary in March. A chick hatched on April 29 but died at the age of four days. On May 20, the female laid again, this time in the nest-box. On June 13, the eggs fell from the box after the macaws gnawed a hole through the 5 cm (2 in) thick base. All contained well developed embryos. The box was repaired and the first egg of the third clutch was laid on June 30. Twenty-seven days later a chick was heard in the nest. Two hatched and both were reared.

In Britain, Harry Sissen of Yorkshire bred this species in 1984. The following year six young were reared from one pair, the first three hand-reared and the second nest parent-reared.

Scarlet Macaw
A. macao

Description: This macaw is perhaps the gaudiest of all parrots, yet some individual feathers show the most subtle and unusual colours. This magnificent bird is mainly scarlet; there is a broad band of yellow across the wing formed by the greater and median wing coverts. Part of this area is tinged with green in some birds. The flight feathers are dark blue and the lower back and rump and upper and under tail coverts are sky blue. The tail is scarlet, tinged with blue at the tip of the central feathers, the outer ones being almost

Scarlet Macaw (*Ara macao*).

entirely blue. The under side of the wings and tail is orange-red and brownish.

The large area of whitish skin extending from above the eye, across the cheeks and lores to the lower mandible, is transversed by minute lines of red feathers, scarcely visible from a distance. The upper mandible is white, tipped with black on the upper edge; the lower mandible is black. The iris is yellow and the legs are dark grey. Length: about 85 cm (34 in). Weight: about 1 kg (2¼ lb).

Immature birds have the lower mandible greyish and the iris brown. The tail is shorter. Some birds have more green in the wings than adults.

Range/Habitat: The Scarlet Macaw has a wide range, being found from Mexico south through Central America and in the Magdalena Valley of Colombia. East of the Andes it is found in the Guianas, Trinidad and south to eastern Peru, Bolivia and the northern Mato Grosso area of Brazil.

However, its numbers are being reduced due to habitat destruction and trapping, the later being carried out for export and by natives for their own use. In Mexico, for example, the population of this macaw has declined drastically during the past 50 years. In a report compiled by Robert S. Ridgely (1977), it was stated that the main reason for the decline was habitat destruction which 'in most areas probably is too far advanced for effective counter measures to be taken'. The Scarlet Macaw remains common in Amazonia and the Guianas but has declined seriously in the densely populated Central American countries.

Aviculture: The Scarlet Macaw is undoubtedly one of the best known of all parrots and has a long captive history; indeed, remains of this species have been found in prehistoric ruins in New Mexico and Arizona, meaning either that there was trade with the Indians of Mexico and those areas or, less likely, that its range once extended to the south-west. The birds were sought by Indians for their feathers which were used for decorative purposes.

The Scarlet Macaw is widely kept in captivity, increasingly in aviaries (rather than as a house pet) and is now reared regularly in many countries throughout the world. The first recorded breeding in the USA took place in California in 1916. In Britain, the Scarlet Macaw was first bred at liberty on Lord Lilford's estate. A young bird which fledged in 1933 died from internal injuries received on its descent from a nest in a tall elm tree. However, one macaw was reared in the following year.

Considering how numerous are the successes with this species, aviculturists have recorded very little about its breeding behaviour. One reason may be because it is more aggressive than, for example, the Blue and Yellow Macaw.

R. J. Berry, Curator of Birds at Houston Zoo, informed me of the Scarlet Macaws in his private collection:

They are much more nervous and aggressive than Blue and Gold Macaws when breeding, making it difficult to check the nest for incubation and rearing data. They do not develop as rapidly as the Blue and Gold and are approximately 16 weeks old before they begin feeding themselves when hand-reared. In our experience pairs scrap a lot and I would not believe they were true pairs from their behaviour if I did not know that they produced young every year.

They frequently show aggressive behaviour toward one another.

The Scarlets fly at those entering their aviaries during the breeding season and although the Blue and Gold Macaws threaten, they never become so overtly defensive.

As Blue and Yellow Macaws kept as pets generally seem to have a more docile temperament than Scarlets, it is quite feasible that this aggressiveness is typical of the species.

Clutch size is two to four eggs, incubated by the female; probably 28 days is the normal incubation period but, again, 26 days has been reported. The length of time the young spend in the nest may vary between about 80 and 104 days; 12 weeks is the average period. Volk and Volk (1983) recorded a mean incubation period of 24 days in a Marsh Farms Roll-X incubator and a minimum incubation period of only 21 days. Humidity requirements were between 50 and 70 per cent relative humidity; two days before hatching was anticipated, the relative humidity was lowered by 20 per cent. The temperature was 37°C (98.5°F). Chicks weighed about 24 g ($\frac{4}{5}$ oz) on hatching. Betty Byers recorded the weight at independence as 1,236 g (2$\frac{3}{4}$ lb). On hatching, chicks have a small amount of white down. Their eyes open when they are aged 10 to 12 days.

Buffon's Macaw (*Ara militaris ambigua*) – left, Green-winged Macaw (*Ara chloroptera*), right.

Green-winged Macaw
A. chloroptera

This bird was formerly often known as the Red and Green Macaw, also the Red and Blue Macaw; the latter names could apply equally well to the Scarlet. There is much confusion regarding old breeding records since it is not always clear which species was referred to. For many years it was not realised that they were two distinct species (and when it was, naturalists transposed the names). For example, Edwards (1743) attributed the variation in plumage to age factors.

Description: The Green-winged is easily distinguished from the Scarlet by the lack of yellow in its plumage, its darker shade of red (giving rise to yet another synonym, Maroon Macaw – although this is not an accurate description of its shade) and shorter tail, which results in a slightly disproportionate appearance. It is larger, with a larger head and beak. There is considerable variation in size, some Green-wings being extremely large and almost approaching the Hyacinthine in body size. It measures approximately 90 cm (35 in) and is the second largest macaw. Weight: about 1500 g (3 lb).

Head, under parts, under wing coverts and part of the mantle are crimson. The wings are green and blue, the median coverts, inner secondaries, tertials and scapulars being green and the secondaries and primaries blue. Back, rump and upper tail coverts, also the under tail coverts, are light blue. The tail is dark red, also the under side of the flight feathers. The otherwise naked facial area is adorned with half a dozen or more prominent lines of very small red feathers. The eyes are yellow. The upper mandible is mainly horn-coloured, being black on the upper part of the cutting edge; the lower mandible is black.

Immature birds have the dark areas of the beak paler and the iris brown. The tail is shorter.

Range/Habitat: The Green-winged Macaw had a wide distribution from Panama over almost the entire tropical region of South America, east of the Andes, and south to the province of Formosa in northern Argentina.

This species occurs mainly in humid lowland forest. It sometimes uses cliffs as nesting sites and has been seen digging burrows in cliff faces on river canyons. Uncommon or declining throughout much of its range, its numbers are stable in uninhabited regions.

Aviculture: The Green-winged Macaw has been exported for centuries, reputedly as early as the end of the sixteenth century. However, it has never attained the popularity of the Scarlet Macaw and is less often kept as a pet, probably because of its larger size and more massive bill.

The first captive breeding which definitely relates to this species was that which occurred in the aviaries of J. S. Rigge of Millom, Cumbria, in 1962. Between 1962 and 1977, they reared young every year, a total of 28. They first attempted to breed in 1960, when the three eggs were addled. In 1961, two chicks were hatched but died. From then onwards, every year was a successful one. Two or three eggs were laid but three young were reared only in 1968.

Because the death of the first chicks which the female hatched was thought to be due to the dust from the rotten wood at the bottom of the barrel, in the following year a large peat sod, 15 cm (6 in) thick, was placed at the bottom of the nest. An egg laid in April contained a chick which died in the shell. A second clutch was laid in June and a chick was heard on July 7. Five days later, there were two chicks in the nest. The female refused all foods but sunflower seed, a little hemp and spinach beet. When the young were nine weeks old, the family consumed nearly half a kilogram (one pound) of seed and five large spinach beet leaves daily. The first young macaw left the nest at 103 days and the second four days later.

One of the young macaws reared by Mr Rigge was obtained by Lt. Col. Norman Johnstone of Leicestershire. It flew at liberty with a pair of Blue and Yellow Macaws and a male Green-winged which had an interesting history. It was purchased cheaply because it was 'almost dangerously ill-tempered'. For six months, it had a strong chain around its leg and could be approached only with extreme care. Then:

> Overnight he changed into one of the most affectionate birds I have ever known, going for long walks with me cross country when he would alight on every gate waiting to be fondled.
>
> His periods of absence had to be curtailed when he took to arriving in my bedroom at first light with disastrous results to the furniture (Johnstone, 1972).

In Denmark, consistent success with the Green-winged Macaw has been obtained by Paul Calvert.

In the USA, the first recorded breeding of this macaw occurred in the collection of H. I. Gregory of Lytle, Texas. He obtained two females in 1966 and a male in 1967. Two clutches were laid early in 1972; all the chicks died in the shell. In April, only one female was left with the male; she laid three eggs, the first on May 9. All hatched, the first on June 5, giving a definite incubation period of 27 days. After three or four days, the parents stopped feeding the youngest, which was transferred to a pair of Scarlet Macaws which had young. After three weeks, it was removed for hand-rearing. The other two chicks were removed from the nest at five weeks. They perched when 11 weeks old.

These macaws nested in an aviary measuring 1.8 × 3.6 m (6 × 12 ft) × 1.8 m (6 ft) high. The nest was a 55-gallon steel drum with a 25 cm (10 in) diameter entrance. It was situated about 1.2 m (4 ft) above the ground. Nesting material was dry wood chips and sunflower chaff. Normal diet of the breeding pair consisted of sunflower seed, monkey chow, peanuts and whole dry corn. Very little fruit or greenfood was provided (Anon. 1972). This species has reared young in zoological collections in many countries throughout the world since the mid-1970s; collections include Lodz in Poland, Novosibirsk in USSR, Seoul in Korea, Montreal in Canada, Busch Gardens, Tampa, in Florida, and, in Britain, the Tropical Bird Gardens at Rode and Whipsnade Zoological Park. One youngster was hand-reared at the Ostrava Zoo in Czechoslovakia in 1980. It made its first flight at 102 days.

Green-winged Macaws have produced hybrid young on numerous occasions. A hybrid Scarlet × Green-winged reared at Newquay Zoo, Cornwall, in 1971, resembled the male parent, except for the darker body colour, the tail colour of the Green-winged and the lines of small feathers crossing the bare facial area.

Dwarf Macaws

The remaining members of the genus are often known as dwarf macaws. They make extremely attractive pets, being intelligent, affectionate and playful and of a size which is much more convenient for the average house. They can also be thoroughly recommended as aviary birds. The smaller species such as Hahn's and Illiger's often prove to be very prolific.

Yellow-collared (Yellow-naped or Cassin's) Macaw
A. auricollis

Description: This bird is immediately recognised by the yellow collar encircling the hind neck, a feature found in no other macaw. The forehead, crown and lower cheeks are brownish black and the primaries, primary coverts and carpal edge of the wing are blue. The tail is blue above, brownish red towards the base and olive yellow below, the latter being the colour of the under side of the flight feathers. The naked facial area is creamy white and the bill is black, the upper mandible having a light horn-coloured tip. The iris is orange. Length 38 cm (16 in). Weight: about 250 g (8 oz). Immature birds have fainter and less extensive yellow markings. Those bred at Bristol Zoo, England, had the feet grey; the colour started to change at about three months.

Range/Habitat: Despite its wide distribution, from the state of Mato Grosso, Brazil, through parts of Bolivia and Paraguay to north west Argentina, this species was a rarity in aviculture until the 1970s. It is described as 'common, conspicuous and ecologically adaptable' (Ridgely, in Pasquier, 1981).

Aviculture: A pair of Yellow-collared Macaws brought back from Bolivia by Walter Goodfellow in 1920, were the first seen in Britain and possibly the last for many years. A single bird at Wassenaar Zoo in the Netherlands in 1967 was the first of this species I had seen. In 1970, a further pair had been added to that collection and that year two pairs arrived in England. Since then this macaw has been imported into Europe and the USA in small numbers.

Yellow-naped Macaws obtained when young make the most delightful pets. Don Mathews (1977) described this species as inquisitive, intelligent, extremely affectionate and quick to learn to talk. In 1974, he and his wife obtained six Yellow-collared Macaws which were housed in couples. There was no sign of breeding activity so, in August 1976, the six birds were placed in one aviary. Within a few weeks, two of the original 'pairs' changed partners and it was eventually proved that they had consisted of birds of the same sex. In October, the birds were separated with their chosen partners and, by the end of December, one female was incubating three eggs, one of which was removed to an incubator after ten days. (The incubator was set at 36°C/96.6°F; humidity was between 60 and 70 per cent.) This proved to be a wise move: the other two eggs hatched and the chicks were left with their parents and lived for only two days.

The chick in the artificially incubated egg started to pip the shell by 5.30 a.m. on January 16 and had hatched by noon. It was transferred to a hospital cage in a temperature of 35°C (95°F). It had no down; it was noted that its toe nails were black and that it possessed a voice which 'would shake the shingles loose on an outhouse'. It was fed every two hours around the clock until the age of 14 days. During the third week, it was fed every three hours, the fourth week every four hours and, from the eighth week, every six hours. Fine grit was added to the food every three days after the age of three weeks.

At ten days, the chick's bill colour began to change from horn to black. At 24 days, it was so responsive that it could imitate the number of sounds, one, two or three 'wah' cries, made to

Yellow-naped Macaws (*Ara auricollis*).

it. At 26 days, the bill was entirely black and, two days later, the first yellow feathers were forming on the nape.

At seven weeks, the young macaw was offered a variety of foods, including soaked corn and sunflower seed, oats, sunflower kernels and mixed fruit and vegetables. It started to say 'Hello' when only nine weeks old.

In November 1977, the pair had three fertile eggs which failed to hatch. Two more fertile eggs, which had been buried, were discovered in February 1978.

In the USA, Janet Fuqua (1981) obtained a pair of Yellow-collared Macaws in October 1979. They were housed in a flight measuring 2.4 × 1.2 m (8 × 4 ft) × 2.4 m (8 ft) high. The first egg was laid on April 25, 1980, but it was thought that incubation did not commence until two days later. Three eggs formed the clutch. On May 20 – 48 hours after pipping – the first chick hatched. By May 23, there were two chicks. By June 4, both chicks had their eyes open. They were plucked by the parents and were therefore removed from the nest for hand-rearing on July 7. By July 24, the eldest was saying 'Hello'. On July 30, the female laid the first egg in a clutch of three. One chick had hatched by August 24, two by August 27 and three by August 28. On September 5, the

Severe Macaws (*Ara severa*).

three chicks were therefore moved to the nest of the Blue-crowned Conures until the youngest macaw chick was one week old, when all three were removed for hand-rearing. In 1983, the macaws again showed no inclination to feed the newly hatched chicks, which were removed from the nest each evening and fed and returned each morning. This was a successful ploy as eventually the macaws started to feed the young and three were reared (Harris & Harris, 1984b).

The first breeding of this species in Britain occurred at Bristol Zoo in 1976. Two chicks were hatched and were first seen out of the nest-box on August 26. In 1977, three chicks had hatched by May 19 and all had left the nest by July 20. In the following year, the pair nested early, during a cold spell, and the three eggs all contained chicks which were dead-in-shell. Also in Britain, this species has been bred consistently at Marwell.

The Yellow-collared Macaw has also been bred at Vogelpark Walsrode since 1977, at Natal Lion Park since 1978 and at Busch Gardens, Tampa, since 1979.

A hybrid Yellow-collared × Illiger's Macaw chick was hatched in an incubator by Don and Pat Mathews on April 23, 1978, exactly 12 hours from the time the egg started to pip. The chick was fed by a pair of Cockatiels for three weeks and was then hand-reared. Hatching weights of chicks from a pair owned by G. A. Smith were 12.04 g ($\frac{2}{5}$ oz), 11.87 g ($\frac{2}{5}$ oz) and 13.1 g ($\frac{1}{2}$ oz). Weaning weights were 250 g ($8\frac{4}{5}$ oz), 244 g ($8\frac{3}{5}$ oz) and 256 g (9 oz).

Severe Macaw

A. severa

Description: This is one of the least distinctive of the macaws; it can be recognised by its chestnut-coloured forehead, which has given rise to the alternative name of Chestnut-fronted Macaw. A prominent feature is the red on the bend of the wing and on the lesser under wing coverts. The head is green; the crown may be blue or tinged with blue. The large area of bare skin on the face is creamy white, decorated with lines of very small black feathers. The feathers of the chin and the mar-

oldest chick died and the other two were removed for hand-rearing. At the age of seven months, the feet of these youngsters were still partially black – not pink as in the adults.

In 1982, Fred and Robbie Harris of California reared Yellow-collared Macaws after using Blue-crowned Conures as foster-parents. The macaw had not fed the first chick hatched. The gin of the cheeks are chestnut in colour. Outer webs of the primaries are dull olive. The tail is reddish brown above with green towards the base; it is tipped with blue. The under side is pinkish red. Length: about 48 cm (19 in).

Immature birds have yet to be described.

Range/Habitat: It has an extremely wide distribution over almost the entire northern part of South America. It is found from eastern Panama to the Guianas and south to southern Bolivia and Bahía in Brazil. Among the foods it is known to favour are figs and the seeds of the jabillo tree (*Hura crepitans*). It is common over much of its range and tolerates forest clearance well. However, it has declined in Ecuador.

Aviculture: Although this macaw cannot be described as rare in collections, it is imported irregularly and never in large numbers.

The first recorded breeding of the Severe Macaw took place in Copenhagen in the collection of Otto Hirthe in 1954. In this case, the chestnut colour on the forehead was more pronounced in the male. Purchased in the previous year, the pair was provided with two nest-boxes constructed from 3.8 cm (1½ in) boards, which measured approximately 30 cm (12 in) square and 77 cm (30 in) high. A layer of moist earth was placed on the bottom of the box, with peat above it. The birds did not roost in the boxes, one of which was placed in the shelter, and eventually nested in the box in the outdoor flight. Three eggs were laid in August, two of which hatched. One chick lived only three days and the other left the nest when about seven weeks old. The pair reared another young bird in 1955 and three in 1956.

In Britain, the first breeding was probably that which occurred at Whipsnade Zoo in 1961, by a pair which belonged to P. H. Maxwell. The single chick was reared although the male died when it was about one month old. In India, P. Mullick bred the Severe Macaw in 1968. At Marwell Zoo in Hampshire, Severe Macaws have bred since 1978. Two eggs were laid and hatched after an incubation period of 28 days. In the USA, this species has been bred at Cincinnati Zoo (in 1970), Van Nuys, California,

and at Busch Gardens, Tampa, Florida. At Busch Gardens, three young were reared in 1977 and subsequently (1978, two; 1979, three; 1980, four).

Naples Zoo in Italy obtained a pair of Severe Macaws in 1977. The first nesting attempt occurred in July 1977 when two eggs were laid; one was fertile. In 1979, three eggs were laid. Two chicks had hatched by July 13; they left the nest on September 22 and 24. In 1980, two eggs were laid; one hatched but the chick died at about three weeks old. The following year, three chicks had hatched by August 6 and two were reared. In 1982, the clutch again comprised three eggs; two young left the nest on September 13. In 1983, three chicks had hatched by September 22. All three fledged but two were found dead on January 27, 1984. That year the adults made no attempt to nest.

Red-bellied Macaw
A. manilata

Description: This species is mainly green with the lower abdomen and ventral area maroon. There is a large area of naked dull yellowish skin on the face. The feathers of the crown are blue with blackish bases; the primaries, primary coverts and outermost greater wing coverts are blue, edged with green. The feathers of the throat and upper breast are edged with pale blue-grey, shading into light greenish yellow on the under parts. The under wing coverts are blue-green, tinged with yellowish or yellow. The rather small beak is black and the iris is dark brown. Upper parts, including the tail, are green; the under side of the tail is olive yellow. Length: about 48 cm (19 in). Weight: 280 g (10 oz).

Immature birds are undescribed at the time of writing. A possible indication of immaturity according to John Halford is the blackish or brownish feathers on the head.

Range/Habitat: This macaw has a very extensive distribution over northern South America, from Venezuela and the Guianas, Colombia east of the Andes, Ecuador to Peru, Mato Grosso and Bahia in Brazil; it is also found in Trinidad. It is common and conspicuous in some parts of its range,

including Guyana. Palm swamps are a favoured habitat; this macaw is also found in parklands, plantations and savannah country. It feeds extensively on the fruits of mauritia palms.

Aviculture: The Red-bellied Macaw, one of the most abundant in the wild, is decidedly rare in captivity, presumably because it is difficult to establish. John Halford of Hampshire, who specialises in macaws, considers it to be the most difficult species to adapt to captivity.

He provided me with the following information:

> I do not find these macaws hardy in winter. They will not roost or perch willingly at night but prefer to cling to the wire. Unlike all my other macaws who live out (save a few pet ones), the three Red-bellieds that I have now are kept inside. Even in summer with no warning I have had them die outside, but the ones inside seem all right. They have not become sick before dying. The cause of death was reported on autopsy as interstitial nephritis. This species has a very distinctive call which is more like a little shriek which is repeated.

Candy Mills (1983) wrote of a pair that 'dropped dead off their perch when someone let the aviary door slam'.

Her own pair nested within three weeks of being given a nest. The eggs were exceptionally round. The birds were quiet, rarely indulging in the sunrise and sunset vocalisations of other macaws. They bathed three or four times daily.

Illiger's Macaw
A. maracana

Description: This bird is immediately distinguished by the scarlet forehead and by the patches of red on the abdomen and lower back. The crown is blue and the rest of the head is bluish green. The primaries, primary coverts and the secondaries are blue; some of the upper wing coverts are tinged with blue. The tail feathers are blue, tinged with reddish brown at the base; the under side is olive yellow. Remainder of the plumage is green. The bill is black, the naked facial area is very pale yellow and the iris is reddish brown or dark brown. Length: 43 cm (16½ in). Weight: 250 g (9 oz).

Illiger's Macaw (*Ara maracana*).

Immature birds are said to have the red on the forehead paler and less extensive. The young produced by B. R. Aldred's pair differed from the adults only in their slimmer build and deeper yellow facial skin. In 1975, the young bred had twice as much red on the head as the adults. Both Aldred and Hauters (1973) recorded that, in the young bred, the upper mandible had a light stripe down the centre.

A pair of Illiger's Macaws owned by G. A. Smith produced, in 1978, a single young bird which was of a Dilute Yellow mutation with the forehead of a delicate shade of pink. The parents, bred by B. R. Aldred, were brother and sister.

Range/Habitat: This Macaw has a wide distribution over the eastern central part of South America, from eastern Brazil south to Mato Grosso and Rio Grande do Sul, and through Paraguay to Misiones in north-eastern Argentina. Habitat destruction has caused its decline or disappearance in many areas.

Aviculture: The first recorded breeding of Illiger's Macaw was that which occurred at London Zoo in 1931; two young were reared in an aviary attached to the Parrot House. Another breeding in Britain was not recorded until 1974 when B. R. Aldred of Ipswich reared three young. The female incubated three eggs in a hollow tree trunk. Young were heard on June 22; the nest was inspected on July 4 as no sounds had been heard for a week. The female had a habit of covering her young with her wings and it could not be ascertained whether there were two or three. On July 16, two chicks were seen with pin feathers approximately 3.8 cm ($1\frac{1}{2}$ in) long; their skin was almost black in colour. By September 9, three young had emerged, aged about 14 weeks. From that day the young birds were seen to feed themselves on hard seed and grapes. Seed husks and fruit skins were found in the nest, thus it appeared that the adults had been taking food inside; similar happenings have been recorded with other neotropical parrots in captivity. While the young were being reared, cooked maize and apple were ignored but large amounts of greenfood, including spinach, were taken.

In 1975, the pair reared two young from three eggs laid in March and three young from three eggs in August. In 1976, they were again double-brooded, rearing two nests of three young, making the notable total of 14 young reared from 15 eggs.

When the young hatched in April 1975 the weather was very cold, with heavy snow, and Mr Aldred noted that for the first time both parents brooded the young. The latter left the nest on June 14; they were removed only six days later and the hen laid again during July. Three chicks hatched, probably between August 7 and 11.

In Belgium, E. L. Hauters obtained five Illiger's Macaws in 1969. He believed that he could sex them as the females were 'somewhat smaller and prettier' with 'less pronounced and duller' colours (Hauters, 1973). Due to the presence of rats, they were moved to a 1.2 m (4 ft) long cage in a dark, moist and cold situation in October 1971. A dark environment suits many neotropical parrots from rainforest environment; it suited the Illiger's and one female had laid three eggs by January 27; the first egg was laid on January 21. By February 20, two chicks had hatched. On February 23, the third was assisted in hatching. Their down was white and about 20 mm ($\frac{3}{4}$ in) long. In addition to seed, rice with egg and bread and a protein food were eaten. The young spent three months in the nest.

In the USA, Ralph Small of Chicago hand-reared two Illiger's Macaws in 1973 and three which were taken from the nest in January 1975, when the eldest was 22 days and weighed 243 g ($8\frac{1}{2}$ oz). In August 1975 and June 1976 three more were removed from the nest on each occasion and hand-reared. Incubation period was given as 'about 26 days'. From the experiences of the other breeders related above, 26–27 days would appear to be the normal period.

Zoos which have bred Illiger's Macaw include Busch Gardens, Tampa, since 1976, the Tropical Bird Gardens at Rode in Britain since 1977, Rio de Janeiro in Brazil since 1978 and Duisburg in Germany in 1979.

Candy Mills (1983) who has kept all the dwarf macaws describes Illiger's as 'without a doubt the noisiest of all'. She commented that their vocabulary is greatly varied so that a single bird is tolerable – but several together can be unbearable.

Coulon's Macaw
A. couloni

Opinions vary as to whether this macaw should be treated as a full species or as a subspecies of Illiger's. David West (1959), well-known Californian aviculturist who owned a Coulon's Macaw believed Illiger's to be 'as vastly different from the Coulon's as an Elegant is from a Rosella'. John P. O'Neill, who is familiar with this macaw in its natural habitat, told me that its voice, unlike that of Illiger's, is 'very soft – a rasping grrrr, grrr'.

Description: In this species, the head is entirely blue, giving rise to the alternative name of Blue-headed Macaw. The primaries and primary coverts are blue and the secondaries and outermost upper wing coverts are blue edged with green. The tail is maroon above, broadly tipped with blue; under side of flight and tail feathers is dull yellow. Remainder of the plumage is

green. The bare facial skin is grey, the bill is black and horn-coloured and the iris is yellow. Length: 41 cm (16 in).
Range/Habitat: Coulon's Macaw inhabits eastern Peru and probably adjacent areas of western Brazil. It is locally common, although its total population is probably very small.
Aviculture: This species appears to have been unknown to aviculture until the early 1980s when a few were apparently imported into the USA.

Hahn's Macaw
A. nobilis nobilis
(formerly *A. hahni*)
Description: This is the most diminutive of the 'dwarf' macaws, smaller even than several species of conure. It has a small area of naked skin surrounding the eye – but the lores are naked, thus distinguishing it from the conures. It is predominantly green, more yellowish below, with the crown and forehead blue. The carpal edge, bend of the wing and greater under wing coverts are scarlet; under side of tail and flight feathers are yellowish. The naked facial skin is white and the iris is brownish red.

In the nominate race the beak is dark grey. Length: 30 cm (12 in).

Immature birds have less blue on the head and no red on the bend and carpal edge of the wing.
Range/Habitat: This species has a wide range north of the Amazon in eastern Venezuela, Guyana, Suriname, northeastern Brazil, possibly also French Guiana. It prefers partially open habitats, including sparse caatinga woodland and marshes.

Noble Macaw
A. n. cumanensis
(formerly *A. nobilis*)
Description: This race is distinguished from the nominate in having the upper mandible pale horn-coloured with a black tip. It is also

Hahn's Macaw (*Ara nobilis nobilis*) – pair with youngster (left).

slightly larger, being about 34 cm (13 in) in length.
Range/Habitat: It occurs south of the Amazon, in the interior of Brazil to south-eastern Mato Grosso and north-western São Paulo.

Aviculture: Hahn's Macaw was bred in Britain, probably for the first time, in 1963 at Birdland, Bourton-on-the-Water. Since then it has proved to be a consistent and prolific breeder in several collections. Two pairs bred at Birdland were 'returned' in 1964 to Trinidad, where the Hahn's Macaw became extinct in the early part of the twentieth century. In 1972, John Halford of Broughton, Hampshire,

sent six Hahn's to Tobago, the intention being to repopulate the island with this species. In 1974, he sent a further six, all bred in his collection. At the time of writing, his pair had reared 23 young. In 1978, the nest was inspected on March 17 when it contained one egg; there were two on March 21, three on March 24 and four on March 28. Two chicks had hatched by April 16; there were three on April 22 and one egg, giving a minimum incubation period of 25 days. Young normally spend eight weeks in the nest.

A. W. Bolton of Chalfont St Giles found that Hahn's Macaws could be bred successfully on the colony system; fighting had never occurred. He had also been successful in breeding from a pair in a flight as small as 1.8 m (6 ft). Nest-boxes used measured 46 cm (18 in) × 23 cm (9 in) square.

When E. N. T. Vane bred the Noble Macaw in 1949, the first British breeding, eggs were laid on June 10, 12, 16 and 18 and hatched on July 5, 7, 9 and 12, giving a maximum incubation period of 25 days. The eldest first made its appearance from the nest on September 3 but did not reappear until September 9 when all four young left the nest. By 1956, nearly 30 young had been reared by this pair.

In 1979, R. Taylor obtained three Hahn's Macaws. In 1980, two chicks were hatched but died within the first week. The three eggs from the second clutch were placed under a Golden-mantled Rosella. At six weeks old, the chicks were removed for hand-feeding. The two eggs in the third clutch were placed in an incubator. The chicks succumbed due to incorrect feeding. The two chicks from the fourth clutch were reared by their parents. In 1981, the parents reared four young in one nest, while the previous year's young were still in the aviary (Taylor, 1982).

Betty Byers in California, recorded the weight of this species at fledging as 159 g (5⅗ oz) It has also been bred at Busch Gardens in Tampa, Florida.

22

Neotropical Parrakeets

Devotees of conures and other neo-tropical parrakeets – those from South and Central America and the Caribbean – are not as numerous as those of Australian parrakeets. The birds are generally less brightly coloured, the voices of most species are loud and harsh (a serious failure from the viewpoint of many aviculturists); they tend to be more destructive to aviary woodwork, and the majority of those available will be imported birds rather than aviary bred. A number of species, such as the Sun, Jendaya, Queen of Bavaria's and Patagonian Conures are so attractively coloured that breeders are prepared to overlook the other disadvantages; but the less brightly coloured birds are never likely to attain a great degree of popularity, despite the fact that many have attractive personalities, being lively and inquisitive and often becoming tame or very confident.

For the average fancier who is not in a position to keep noisy birds, the *Bolborhynchus* parrakeets and *Pyrrhura* conures will be the most likely to appeal. They make an interesting addition to any collection, especially in contrast to Australian parrakeets, and some are equally free-breeding. In behaviour and appearance they are very different from the Australian species, with which most aviculturists are more familiar.

Feeding: Their diet is different in that these birds will sample and enjoy a wider variety of fruits; these form a large part of their natural diet (unlike Australian species which exist mainly on grass seeds) and are essential for their well-being.

Accommodation: The birds covered in this chapter range in size from 15 cm (6 in) to about 45 cm (18 in). Most parrakeets are strong fliers and will appreciate a long flight; a minimum of 3 m (10ft) is suggested for all the long-tailed parrakeets and flights of 3.6–4.5 m (12–15 ft) are more satisfactory for the larger species. Double wiring between flights is of vital importance; while small Australian parrakeets, for example, will not usually attack neighbouring birds, neotropical parrakeets will do so without hesitation, with the exception of the *Bolborhynchus* species. Most conures will require a nest-box for roosting.

Aratinga
Aratinga

Members of this genus are medium-sized to large long-tailed parrakeets ranging from 24–36 cm (9–14 in). The largest *Aratinga* are larger than the small *Ara* macaws, from which they are distinguished by the feathered lores and cheeks. In some *Aratinga* species, the naked periorbital ring is very prominent. Only the Queen of Bavaria's Conure has the heavy proportions of the true parrots and it and the Sun Conure, are the only *Aratinga* species which are not predominantly green. The more typical members of the genus have a contrasting colour or colours on the head – red, orange or blue – and lack the scaly markings on the upper breast and nape which the *Pyrrhura* conures have.

It is true that they have harsh voices, and some are very destructive to woodwork. Despite this, they have much to recommend them as aviary birds: many become very friendly towards their keeper; they are lively and entertaining and the larger species are especially intelligent (ranking with the small macaws in this respect); some species nest readily and prove prolific in captivity. Plumage is alike in male and female so sexing is not easy and surgical sexing is recommended.

Two to six eggs are laid and incubated by the female for 26 days. Young spend seven to eight weeks in the nest. Colony breeding is not recommended except in a very large aviary where each pair can defend the territory around its nest-box.

Some *Aratinga* make superb pets if obtained when young, being friendly and playful and learning to repeat a few words and to whistle. However, the harsh voice would deter many people from keeping them indoors.

The group of conures which follows causes identification problems for the aviculturist; all are green with varying amounts of red on the head and under wing coverts. Immature birds may be impossible to identify as some have less red in the plumage than adults, which adds to the difficulties of recognition. If their distribution is plotted on a map it can be seen that, with the exception of part of Venezuela, it covers the entire tropical part of Central and South America but nowhere does the range of any two 'species' overlap. They form a natural group, easily distinguished from other conures and it would be more logical if they were classed as conspecific.

Predominantly green, darker above and more yellowish below with the under side of the tail yellowish, and with the red markings already mentioned, they have a conspicuous area of white or whitish skin surrounding the eye (except *holochlora*), and a pale horn-coloured bill.

Mexican Green Conure
A. holochlora holochlora
Description: This bird is all green or has a few scattered red feathers on or below the throat. The iris is orange-red and the periorbital skin is greyish, not white as in most of the species in this group; it is small in extent and inconspicuous. Immature birds resemble adults. Size varies between the subspecies and ranges from 29 cm (11 in) to 36 cm (14 in).
Range/Habitat: This species inhabits Central America, from north-western Mexico south to northern Nicaragua. Some subspecies are numerous, others are quite uncommon.
Aviculture: The Mexican Green Conure is occasionally exported but is a little known species, the dullest coloured member of the genus. It was bred in the USA by W. J. Sheffler in 1934. One was reared at San Diego Zoo in 1979. The race *A.h. strenua* was bred in West Germany by Thomas Arndt in 1984.

Red-throated Conure
A. h. rubritorquis
Description: The red throat and foreneck distinguish it from the nominate race; there are variable red markings on the lower cheeks and the sides of the neck. It is smaller than *holochlora* with a length of about 30 cm (12 in).
Immature birds are all green.
Range/Habitat: It occurs in the mountains of eastern Guatemala, El Salvador and northern Nicaragua, mainly in pine forest, occasionally in

Red-throated Conure (*Aratinga holochlora rubritorquis*).

cloud forest. It is common.
Aviculture: This conure was virtually unknown in aviculture until the late 1970s. Arndt (1981) recorded of his pair:

> Once they are used to their keeper, they completely lose their shyness and will accept small titbits from the hand. As soon as they are tame, there is nothing that cannot be done with them. Their need for gnawing is slight, but they should still be offered fresh twigs at all times. They like to bathe. Initially they are very loud, but with increasing tameness they raise their voices less frequently.... Kept in an aviary they are shy, unfortunately. At any disturbances they retire to the farther end of the aviary, or, like the author's pair, immediately disappear into the nest-box when they see strangers.

The first recorded breeding occurred in the collection of Thomas Arndt in West Germany in 1976. The pair became very aggressive when breeding. Three or four eggs are laid. In Vogelpark Walsrode, the Red-throated Conure was reared in

1979. In the USA, the first breeding was achieved by the Reverend R. Noegel in 1982.

Finsch's Conure
A. finschi
Description: Even if one does not accept that all this group should form one species, it is difficult to see the logic of separating this bird from *holochlora*.
The crown and forehead are red; there is a red band or a few scattered red feathers across the throat, also at the bend of the wing. Length: 28 cm (11 in).
Immature birds have little or no red at the forehead and less red at the bend of the wing.
Range/Habitat: Central America from southern Nicaragua to western Panama. It is locally distributed and common.
Aviculture: It is not well known in aviculture.

Wagler's Conure
A. wagleri wagleri
Description: The forehead and crown are red and there is a red band or some scattered red feathers across the throat. There is no red in the wings except in the subspecies *A.w. frontata* and *A.w. minor* which have the bend of the wing, also the thighs, red.
Range/Habitat: Wagler's Conure has a wide distribution along the western coast of South America from northern Venezuela through Colombia to western Ecuador and southern Peru. Common throughout much of its range, some large flocks occur.
Immature birds have little or no red on the head. Its much larger size, about 36 cm (14 in), distinguishes it from *finschi*.
Aviculture: It is occasionally exported. Chester Zoo, England, exhibited a fine colony from 1969 until the mid-1970s. Third generation zoo-bred young were being reared in 1978.

Mitred Conure
A. mitrata
Description: This bird greatly resembles *wagleri*. It differs in having a

Wagler's Conure (*Aratinga wagleri frontata*).

Mitred Conure (*Aratinga mitrata*).

greater area of red on the head, extending over the forehead and forepart of the crown, the lores, part of the cheeks and sometimes part of the ear coverts. In some specimens, there are scattered red feathers over much of the plumage, except the wings. The iris is orange-yellow with an inner circle of grey. Length: 38 cm (15 in). Immature birds are all green.

Range/Habitat: The Mitred Conure inhabits central and southern Peru and southwards through central Bolivia to western Argentina. It is locally common.

Aviculture: Several large consignments were imported into the USA in the early 1980s and a few reached Europe. In Switzerland, Dr R. Burkard bred two or three young from two pairs every year between 1976 and 1982. Also, a hybrid between *mitrata* and *acuticaudata* was bred.

Red-masked Conure
A. erythrogenys
Description: This bird has the greatest amount of red on the head of any bird in this group and is undoubtedly the most handsome; in fact, adult birds are

extremely striking. Most of the head, except the hind part of the cheeks and part of the ear coverts is red and there are a few scattered red feathers on the throat. The shoulders, under wing coverts, edge of the wing and thighs are also red. The greater under wing coverts are yellowish olive. Length: 33 cm (13 in).

Immature birds have no red on the head; bend of the wing and outer under wing coverts are red.

Range/Habitat: This species inhabits the arid tropical zone of south-western Ecuador and north-western Peru. It remains common except in Ecuador, where it has declined.

Aviculture: It is occasionally imported.

It has been bred in the USA and in Denmark, by Hans Hansen in 1969; four young were reared. Zoos which have bred this conure include Riga (USSR), Naples (Italy), Walsrode (West Germany).

Hispaniolan Conure
A. chloroptera
Description: It is all green, with the outermost underwing coverts red. In some birds there are a few red feathers

on the head. The iris is reddish brown and a conspicuous area of white skin surrounds the eye. Length: 32 cm (13 in). Immature birds have less red on the wing.

Range/Habitat: This conure is confined to the island of Hispaniola (San Domingo).

Aviculture: This conure is very rare in aviculture. In the USA it is reputed to have been bred by Vance Wright in 1936; four young were reared. More recently it has been exhibited at Vogelpark Walsrode in Germany.

In Chicago, Tony Silva obtained a male in 1981. In the absence of others of its own species, it was paired with a Nanday Conure. After being together for two months, the female laid four eggs, three of which were fertile. Three chicks hatched; the first after 26 days of incubation. They were covered in white down; the second down was grey, differing from *chloroptera* chicks which apparently have the second down white (Silva, 1984a). The chicks were extremely aggressive and the eldest was injured by one of its siblings when four weeks old. At three months, the chicks differed slightly from the Hispaniolan Conure; the breast feathers carried a blue tinge and the thighs were partly red, a feature inherited from the Nanday. They had the crown dark green and reddish feathers surrounding the lower mandible. Under wing coverts showed traces of orange, the colour intensifying with age, as in *chloroptera*. Feet and tongue were dark grey.

Cuban (Red-speckled) Conure

A. euops

Description: It has scattered feathers on the head, neck and thighs, and sometimes on the abdomen and flanks. The smaller under wing coverts and the carpal edge of the wing are red. The greater under wing coverts are olive green, not yellow as in *leucophthalmus*. Length: 26 cm (10½ in).

Range/Habitat: This species is confined to Cuba.

Aviculture: Birds from Cuba are now virtually unknown in aviculture except to eastern European aviculturists. De Grahl (1974) gives details of a breeding in East Berlin in 1967 by H. Hähne. Four birds were kept in an outdoor aviary measuring 2 m (7 ft) in length. One female laid four eggs, the first chick hatched after 23 days. The oldest youngster left the nest at 48 days of age.

White-eyed Conure

A. leucophthalmus

Description: Scattered red feathers on the head and neck and red on the carpal edge of the wing are the distinguishing features, plus the yellow outermost greater wing coverts, which distinguish it from *chloroptera*. Length: 33 cm (13 in).

Immature birds have the carpal edge and the edge of the forewing yellowish green and the outermost under wing coverts green.

Range/Habitat: This conure has an immensely wide distribution over most of northern South America, except the western side; it inhabits the Guianas, Venezuela and eastern Colombia south to northern Argentina and northern Paraguay. It remains common and conspicuous throughout most of its range.

Aviculture: The White-eyed Conure is

White-eyed Conure (*Aratinga leucophthalmus*).

better known than others in this group although it has never been numerous in captivity. It has been bred in the USA on several occasions, three to five eggs forming the clutch. The first breeding there – and possibly in captivity – occurred in 1934. W. J. Sheffler's pair was double-brooded. The first young left the nest in April and three more in October.

In Britain, the first recorded breeding occurred in 1975 when a pair obtained in 1974 by C. Allaway of Norfolk reared young. In May 1975, four eggs were laid in a nest-box measuring 45 cm (18 in) high and 31 cm (12 in) square. The birds had added wood chewed from the aviary framework to the layer of peat moss. After 26 days the female deserted; all four eggs contained chicks. On August 12, she laid the first egg of the second and it was discovered that their feet were abnormal. The parents showed no further interest in them so they were removed from the aviary and fed by hand. The condition of their feet improved.

In Australia, Melbourne Zoo bred this species in 1937 and in South Africa R. J. Meise's pair hatched young on December 12, 13, 21 and 22, 1973. The youngest chick died and the three survivors left the nest at nine weeks of age. They were then marked with faint yellow, not red, at the bend of the wing and had no red specks on the head or throat.

Two of the following three conures (which are considered as separate species by Forshaw (1973) as well as by some other authors) are the most colourful members of the genus. They are here given subspecific status. Unfortunately, their voices are even less attractive than most *Aratinga* of similar size.

Golden-capped Conure
A. auricapilla auricapilla
Description: It is mainly green, darker above, with the forepart of the crown yellow and the sides of the head tinged with yellow. The area surrounding the eyes is tinged with red and the lower breast, sides and abdomen are dark red. Wings and tail resemble those of the Jendaya Conure. Length: 31 cm (12 in).

Immature birds have less yellow on the head and the red of the under parts is confined to the sides of the abdomen.
Range/Habitat: This conure is found in north-eastern Brazil, in northern and central Bahia. It is uncommon and has declined substantially due to habitat destruction.

Golden-capped Conure (*Aratinga auricapilla aurifrons*).

A. a. aurifrons
Description: In this bird, the sides of the head and upper breast are darker green than in the nominate species and without the yellow tinge. Also there are no red margins to the feathers of the rump and lower back.
Range/Habitat: This race inhabits south-eastern Brazil.
Aviculture: Since the mid-1970s, it

clutch. On September 11, a dead chick was found on the aviary floor. There was another chick in the nest; it was covered with white down. It left the nest on a cold, wet day – November 15. The plumage differed from that of the adults in lacking the red specks. The parents reared their young on the usual diet of sunflower, hemp, millet and canary seed, apple and pear, and other fruits on occasions.

In 1976, this species was bred by E. J. Taylor. His pair started to nest after only nine weeks in his possession. Two eggs were laid and both hatched. The chicks were reared on hemp, soaked brown bread, sunflower, millet and canary seed and when they were about two weeks old the adults started to feed chickweed to them. Later, groats and bread and milk were taken. At 76 days, the chicks emerged from the nest has been bred regularly by Dr B. Levine of Miami. The normal clutch is three eggs. In California, Ed Shoemaker bred 53 young in three years from seven birds by 1981, including a trio. There were two males, both of which sired young.

Mr and Mrs J. Spenkelink of Soesterberg became the first breeders in Holland in 1976 when four young were reared. In 1977, two nests of three left the box and, in 1978, two were reared.

Doubt surrounds some of the earlier reports, such as those in the *International Zoo Year Book*, of breeding in the zoos in Colombo, Sri Lanka and in Dublin; these were almost certainly incorrect, due to confusion over the common name. Likewise, in the USA, conures originally described as Golden-crowned and later corrected to Golden-capped were bred in California in 1930 and 1931 by S. Wigley.

Jendaya Conure (*Aratinga auricapilla jandaya*).

Sun Conure (*Aratinga auricapilla solstitialis*).

Jendaya (Yellow-headed) Conure

A. a. jandaya

Description: It has the whole of the head, neck and part of the upper breast rich, bright yellow, merging into the rich red of the under parts. The thighs are olive-green sometimes marked with a few red feathers. Upper parts are green except for the lower back which is orange-red. The flight feathers and the tip of the tail are bright blue, the rest of the tail being bronze-green and the under side blackish. The bill is black and the iris is greyish brown. Length: 30 cm (12 in).

Immature birds have the yellow or orange feathers paler, edged with green or occasionally replaced with some green feathers.

There would appear to be two forms of the Jendaya Conure, one approaching the Sun Conure in its brighter colouring and black periorbital skin. The latter area is pale coloured in the birds of the other form which are more yellow than orange on the under parts.

Range/Habitat: The Jendaya inhabits north-eastern Brazil. Locally common, it may even be increasing.

Aviculture: Its position in aviculture has changed in relation to that of the Sun Conure: now it is the Jendaya which is the rarer whereas formerly it was very common.

This species has been bred on numerous occasions in captivity. Three or four eggs are laid (occasionally five or six) and incubated for 26 days. The young leave the nest when about eight weeks old. The earliest breeding – in Britain – dates back to the 1890s when Mrs Hartley of Hastings was successful. Other first recorded breedings were as follows: Germany, W. Hoesch in 1926; USA, W. J. Sheffler in the 1930s; Portugal, Jorge O'Neill on several occasions between 1957 and 1961; Sweden, H. Hakansson in 1960; Denmark, Anker Christensen in 1964. The Jendaya has hybridised with the Nanday Conure on several occasions, and, reported in 1914, Lord Poltimore reared two hybrids from a Jendaya and a Golden-crowned Conure. In recent years, hybrids between Jendaya and Sun Conures have been bred on a number of occasions. This cross was bred by Mr and Mrs J. Bloom of Florida in 1976.

The newly hatched chicks had black bills and pink feet. When feathered, the breast colour was intense orange; the head colour was more like that of the Sun Conure. They were larger and prettier than the Nendaya but the wings were similar.

Sun Conure

A. a. solstitialis

Description: This is considered by most people to be the most striking of the small conures. It is a bird of quite exceptional beauty. The plumage is variable; it is mainly yellow and orange or a fiery shade of orange-red, with most of the yellow areas tinged with orange. Head and under parts are fiery orange and the wings are yellow with the secondaries partly green. Primaries are dark blue and the tail is olive-green, sometimes blue towards the tip and blue on the outer webs of the feathers. Under tail coverts are green tinged with yellow and the under side of the tail is dusky olive. The bill is black and the periorbital skin is whitish. Length: 31 cm (12 in).

Immature plumage is variable.

Young birds have less orange on the head and under parts, these areas being yellow. There is more green in the wings than in adults. Some young birds are mainly green and olive with patches of yellow and some orange on the head; others more nearly resemble adults with more green on the wings.

Range/Habitat: The Sun Conure is found in the Guianas and in north-western Brazil. Its wild status is uncertain – but there is no evidence of any decline.

Aviculture: This species was available more than a century ago and was bred in France in 1883 by Madame de Kerville in Rouen; two young were reared. In California, David West and I. D. Putnam bred Sun Conures in the 1930s. This species was almost unknown in Europe until 1971 when the first importation for many years created much interest. Subsequently many have been imported into Europe and the USA and have proved a welcome addition to aviculture. Not only are these conures beautiful but many pairs are prolific. As an example, an aviculturist in Zimbabwe reported breeding 17 young from one pair in 18 months (from four clutches).

In California, Ed Shoemaker bred from a trio – two males who took turns in breeding with the female. Fourteen young were reared in 1980 and 13 in the first eight months of 1981. By the late 1970s, this species was very firmly established in the USA and hundreds of young were being reared annually. It enjoys immense popularity as a pet (especially if hand-reared) and as an aviary bird.

In Britain the first breeder was A. Marques of Bedfordshire. In 1973, two young left the nest in June and three more hatched in August.

The usual clutch of this species is three or four eggs and the incubation period 26 or 27 days. Chicks have greyish white down. Eyes and ears open at about two weeks when the beak and feet start to darken. This also applies to the Jendaya Conure. Both weigh about 116 g (4 oz) on fledging (Byers, 1984).

Among the foods taken by pairs

Queen of Bavaria's (Golden) Conure (*Aratinga guarouba*).

rearing young are corn-in-the-ear, wholewheat bread, bread and milk mixed into a porridge with dog biscuit and a proprietary Canary egg food.

Queen of Bavaria's (Golden) Conure

A. guarouba

Description: Queen of Bavaria's Conure is rich golden yellow throughout, except for the green primaries and secondary flight feathers. The massive beak (light horn-coloured) and short, tapered tail contribute to the top-heavy appearance. Length is 36 cm (14 in).

Immature birds have scattered green feathers on the upper wing coverts and cheeks and are rather slimmer in build. At this stage, their close relationship to the Sun Conure is more apparent. However, immature plumage is variable. One aviculturist told me that of the two young reared in one nest, one was mainly green and the other was nearly all yellow.

Range/Habitat: This conure is found in north-eastern Brazil, south of the Amazon. Rare or uncommon, it has decreased due to habitat destruction.

Aviculture: In my opinion, it is one of the most desirable birds an aviculturist could possess. Not everyone would agree with that assessment. In shape and size, it is totally unlike other *Aratinga* conures, being much larger and heavier in build with a massive beak

which gives it a slightly top-heavy appearance. While it lacks the more slender form of the other conures, it has abundant intelligence and playfulness, in this respect resembling a young macaw, perhaps, rather than a conure. However, it has an unfortunate tendency to pluck itself, probably because, like the macaws, in captivity there is often not enough for these intelligent birds to occupy their minds with. A pair of Queen of Bavaria's Conures playing together in an aviary is one of the most pleasing sights imaginable. Like macaws, as pets they require more attention than the average person can provide.

In the USA, this species is bred by a few aviculturists and there is a tremendous demand for the young as pets. It is easy to understand their appeal for this purpose; nevertheless, it is to be hoped that breeders will not neglect to retain young for breeding. This is a species whose population has been affected by deforestation in Brazil; it is therefore vital to establish aviary-bred strains. Incidentally, one drawback of this species is its loud voice.

One difficulty in breeding this conure lies in sexing it; generally speaking, the upper mandible is larger in the male. They nest fairly readily and have been bred on a number of occasions in Britain and in the USA, also by Dr Osman Hill in Colombo who, over the years, had repeated success. These birds often become extremely aggressive while breeding. The usual clutch consists of three eggs. Chicks leave the nest after about ten weeks.

A nutritious rearing food is essential for these large conures. Among the items relished by one pair with young were corn-on-the-cob and bread-and-butter pudding.

At Busch Gardens, Tampa, Florida, young have been reared more consistently than in any other collection and from several pairs. The most successful breeder at the time of writing is in Britain: Jim Hayward of Oxfordshire. More than 20 young were hand-reared in 1983 and a similar number in 1984. Young have also been reared at Naples Zoo in Italy, at Walsrode in Germany and, in the USA, at Oklahoma Zoo. On one occasion five young were reared in one nest.

The remaining members of the genus are not of outstanding interest to the aviculturist. They do not have the attractive colours of the species already described to compensate for the harsh voice and destructive habits common to all *Aratinga* conures. Predominantly green, paler below, with blue in the secondaries; the under side of the tail is greyish yellow.

Aztec (Olive-throated) Conure

A. nana astec

Description: It has the throat and upper breast brownish olive and the abdomen yellowish to yellowish olive. In some birds, there is a narrow band of small orange feathers covering the cere. The iris is yellow. Length: 24 cm (9 in).

Range/Habitat: Its natural range is Mexico and Central America. It is of interest that W. H. Timmis, former Curator of Birds at Chester Zoo, has observed this species in Mexico nesting at an altitude of 900 m (3,000 ft). The nest sites, used for generations, were caves of soft limestone and the birds would fly without hesitation straight into the dark interior. It is common throughout most of its range.

Aviculture: This species was bred in Jamaica as long ago as 1903 in a cage. Soaked canary seed was the main rearing food. It is uncommon in captivity.

Jamaican Conure

A. n. nana

Description: This bird differs from the Aztec Conure in its slightly larger size and in the colour of the throat and upper breast which are dark brown, merging into dark olive on the lower breast. Overall, it is a pleasing shade of bright dark green. Length: 26 cm (10 in).

Immature birds are slightly duller than adults.

Range/Habitat: It is found in Jamaica in wooded hills and lower mountain slopes and has been recorded as breeding in termites' nests.

Aviculture: Like most Jamaican birds it is little known in aviculture. I have seen it only in Kingston Zoo, Jamaica.

St Thomas (Curaçao or Caribbean) Conure

A. pertinax pertinax

Description: The most colourful of the group, it has golden yellow-orange on the forehead, sides of the head and the chin. The crown is tinged with blue. The centre of the abdomen is orange. The under side of the tail is golden-olive. Length: 25 cm (10 in).

Range/Habitat: Endemic to the island of Curaçao in the Netherlands Antilles, it has been introduced to the island of St Thomas in the Virgin Islands, West Indies. Range of this species extends from Panama, to northern South America and the islands off the coast of Venezuela. While staying on one of the latter, Bonaire, I found that the race confined to that island, *A.p. xanthogenia*, was one of the most common, conspicuous and beautiful birds there. It fed mainly on cactus and nested in termitaria. This species is common and ecologically tolerant.

Aviculture: It is a rare bird in captivity.

pertinax races
In the past, dealers tended to give the name St Thomas Conure to several races of *pertinax*, especially *A.p. chrysophrys* from the Guianas which is darker than the other 13 races of this conure now recognised. Most of these vary only slightly in the shade of their plumage and have much less orange on the head than the nominate race.

Immature birds have the head green and brownish, occasionally showing a few orange feathers. The upper breast is tinged with green and the upper mandible is pale horn-coloured. This iris is light yellow. Length: 24 cm (9½ in).

There is so little interest in these birds that doubtless some, perhaps most, captive breedings have remained unrecorded. Several races have been bred in captivity. In Britain, W. Shore-Bailey bred *A.p. ocularis* in 1915; more recently, in 1971, two were reared at Penscynor Wildlife Park, Neath, Wales.

In the same year, eight birds were bred in Ahmedabad Zoo, India; and *chrysophrys* was bred by A. A. Prestwich in 1955. In the latter instance, two pairs were housed in 9 m (30 ft) flights and eight more birds were housed in another. Both of the former hens nested, laying four and five eggs. In the following year, one hen hatched two chicks after an incubation period of 25–26 days. They hatched on July 12 and 13 and left the nest on August 30 and 31. Both

Termitarium – nest site of Bonaire Conure.

Brown-eared Conure (*Aratinga pertinax chrysophrys*).

upper mandible is whitish, the lower mandible horn-coloured. Length: 25 cm (10 in).

Immature birds have the crown green, the throat and upper breast olive and the abdomen only tinged with orange.

It would more logically be classified as a race of *pertinax*.

Range/Habitat: This conure inhabits north-eastern Brazil in areas of low thorny scrub, ranging into deciduous woodland. It is fairly common.

Aviculture: It used to be freely imported into Europe, but has not been available in recent years, since Brazil ceased to allow the export of birds. The first recorded breeding occurred in France in 1883; Debray, of Paris, reared six young.

In England, Dr Lovell-Keays' pair reared three young from four eggs in 1914, and one in 1915. In Denmark, this species was bred in 1963. In Germany, Dietrich Kroner, of Schuttorf, reared three in 1973; six eggs were laid.

A yellow specimen has been kept by Nelson Kawall in Brazil.

Sharp-tailed Conure
A. acuticaudata acuticaudata

Description: Recognised by its dull blue head, in some birds the breast is also tinged with blue. The rest of the plumage is green, except the tail feathers which are brownish red at the base of the inner webs and the under wing coverts which are olive-yellow. The upper mandible is horn-coloured with a dark tip and the lower mandible is blackish. The iris is orange-red and there is an area of bare white skin surrounding the eye. Length: 36 cm (14 in).

Immature birds have the blue on the head confined to the forehead and crown.

Range/Habitat: This species inhabits a very wide area of South America from eastern Colombia and northern Venezuela south to Paraguay, Uruguay and northern Argentina. It is numerous over much of its range and tolerant of disturbed habitat.

Cactus Conure (*Aratinga cactorum*).

were slightly less brightly coloured than their parents. Seed and apple were the main rearing foods.

The most colourful race is *xanthogenia* which comes from the island of Bonaire. Some individuals have a slightly larger area of orange on the head than *pertinax*. The Bonaire Conure has been bred at Wassenaar Zoo in the Netherlands since 1979.

Cactus Conure
A. cactorum

Description: There is a slight tinge of blue on the crown; much of the head, also the upper breast, are pale brown. A yellow line below the eye and an area of bright orange on the abdomen are other distinguishing features. The

Blue-crowned Conure
A. a. haemorrhous

Description: Its distinguishing feature is the blue on the head which is paler and confined to the forehead and tinged with vinous. It is slightly smaller and has the upper and lower mandible whitish.

Aviculture: The first recorded breeding of the Sharp-tailed Conure in Britain occurred in 1971. A pair belonging to K. Bastien of the Isle of Wight reared three young after being in his possession for three years. Subsequently, they usually reared three or four young annually. Some of the young were sold as pets and became tame and affectionate, learning to talk a little and generally comparing favourably with the small macaws, which they greatly resemble. These large birds are among the most intelligent of the conures. The chief drawback is the loud and discordant voice. A few of the young birds had bright red spots on the shoulders or edge of the wing – a feature not present in the adult. In Denmark, the first breeder was Gert Funch of Vig, Nykøbing, in 1981.

The Blue-crowned Conure has been bred in the USA, first by G. Rayson Brown in 1950, and in Leipzig Zoo, Germany. This species is neither common nor rare in captivity which, together with the fact that the large *Aratinga* conures do not have a wide appeal, accounts for the scarcity of breeding successes. In Britain, a colony at Kilverstone Wildlife Park in Norfolk have produced young since 1976. In Switzerland, Dr R. Burkard reared young annually from two pairs between 1978 and 1982.

Hybrids between a male Blue-crowned and a female Golden-crowned Conure were reared at Brean Down Bird Gardens in Somerset in 1978. The three youngsters favoured the male in appearance, except for the golden forehead of two.

In Tampa, Florida, R. Kenny reared hybrids between the Blue-crowned and Finsch's Conures: one in 1977 and two in 1978; on fledging they were mainly green with yellowish under wing coverts. Two Lutino females were in the possession of Nelson Kawall in 1983. They were described as having the cap of a pleasing shade of apricot.

Weddell's (Dusky-headed) Conure
A. weddellii

Description: This species is recognised by the pale grey iris and the greyish blue appearance of the head; the feathers are greyish brown tipped with dull blue. There is a broad area of white skin surrounding the eye. The plumage is mainly green, more yellowish on the abdomen. The tail is tipped with blue and the outer webs of the primaries and secondaries are blue. The bill is black. Length: 28 cm (11 in). Immature birds resemble the parents but for the dark iris.

Range/Habitat: This is one of the few species of parrots with which I am more familiar in its natural environment than in captivity. On two visits to the Amazonas region of south-east Colombia, this was found to be the most common conure in the vicinity of the island on which I stayed at the southern tip of Colombia. It was found in groups of from about six to 20 birds. These conures were attracted to two palm trees near the edge of the flood-swollen Amazon. One afternoon I watched a group of seven birds; for half an hour I stood at the base of the tree filming them while they fed on its small fruits. The latter resembled miniature coconuts, being about 10 mm ($\frac{1}{2}$ in) across. The fibrous exterior concealed a hard nut. These were later identified as being a *Euterpe* species, probably, *E. oleracea*.

Weddell's Conure is found over a large area of the Amazon basin in Ecuador, Peru, Bolivia and western Brazil. A lowland species, it favours the edges of rivers. It is common over most of its range.

Aviculture: This conure first reached Britain in 1923. It was rare in aviculture until the mid-1970s. The first recorded breeding was reported by Herr Milling of Euskirchen, Germany, in 1976. In the Netherlands it was bred by Mrs Spenkelink of Soesterberg in 1978. In Denmark, the first breeder was Finn Bidstrup of Rønne in 1981.

In the USA, in 1978, one youngster was reared by Mr and Mrs M. Fischer of Mount Vernon, Washington. Three eggs were laid in April, one of which hatched on May 18; the other eggs contained chicks which died in the shell. When the chick was examined on June 3 it was covered with white down and its eyes were still closed. Its bill was black. On June 10, many pin feathers were present and its eyes were starting to open. Three days later its feet had become grey and the dark grey second down was apparent. Its eyes were fully open by June 18. It left the nest on July 22.

Also in the USA, Martha Medlar of Oxnard, California, has bred this species since 1981 when the young were parent-reared. In 1983, young were removed from the nest for hand-feeding on September 24; they were hatched on September 3, 5 and 8 and were independent by November 6. At the age of three weeks, their feet and legs were black; the feet had darkened by the age of two and a half weeks. These chicks were very amenable to handling. Martha Medlar (1984) wrote:

> As I'd pick them up to feed them I'd gently roll them over on their backs in my hand and they would relax and allow me to rub their tummies and seemed to enjoy this handling. Later I saw them tumble around and play in their cage with a green bean or a piece of bread and when one would be knocked off his feet he would calmly lie there on his back with those black feet and legs motionless and straight up in the air.... Later I was able to hold them on the head and shoulders rested on my palm and the rest of the bird went straight upward.

Martha Medlar described this species as 'relatively quiet' compared to other *Aratinga*, with absolutely no vices. 'Hand-reared chicks are a delight!'

R. J. Nichols agreed that this species is 'not too noisy unless disturbed by something'. His pair consumed various seeds, also blackberries, blackcurrants and gooseberries, when rearing young, also soaked sunflower seed and brown bread and milk. Seeding grasses, green dock, green cereals in the milky stage and lettuce were also consumed.

The pair, obtained in February 1982, were very nervous at first and hid behind their nest-box which measured 25 cm (10 in) square. The one in which they bred was 76 cm (30 in) high. At first they were afraid to descend but roosted on the nest-box perch or wire ladder. The first egg was laid on April 25 but the clutch was unsuccessful. The eggs of the second clutch were laid on May 30, June 1 and 3. The first chick was seen on June 23; it had pink flesh, whitish down and a black-tipped beak. The second chick hatched on June 26 and the third on June 28. On July 5, the chicks' eyes were open and the beaks were becoming blacker from the tip. On July 27, the brown head feathers were erupting. One died on August 9; two chicks were seen looking out of the nest on August 19 and left on August 28. They were returned at night. On September 1, one was found dead in the nest. By mid-September, the beak of the survivor was almost entirely dark, the iris becoming lighter grey (Nichols, 1984).

Petz's (Orange-fronted) Conure

A. canicularis canicularis

Description: Confusion with the Golden-crowned Conure will not arise if it is remembered that the bill is entirely black in the latter species while in Petz's it is mainly horn-coloured, the lower mandible being partly black. The forehead and part of the crown are orange and the hindcrown is blue. The secondaries are blue, narrowly edged with green. It is otherwise green, more yellow below and on the under tail coverts. Periorbital skin is yellow and feathered; the iris, too, is yellow. Length: 24 cm (9½ in).

Immature birds have less orange on the forehead; the iris is brown.

Range/Habitat: Petz's Conure inhabits the Pacific (western) side of Central America from Sinaloa, Mexico, south to western Costa Rica.

It is common throughout much of its range; in some areas, such as the lowlands of Honduras, it is the most common parrot. Fruits, especially figs, form a large part of the diet; blossoms, seeds, berries and nuts are also eaten.

Nesting sites are usually the occupied termitaria of the termite *Nasutitermes nigriceps*. Male and female conure excavate the nesting site; they make an entrance hole about 7 cm (3 in) in diameter near the bottom of

Petz's Conure (*Aratinga canicularis ebunirostrum*).

the termitarium and then tunnel upwards through the hard outer shell for about 30 cm (12 in), before tunnelling inward and downward into the softer interior. Here the nesting chamber, about 15–20 cm (6–8 in) in diameter, is excavated. The work is said to last about one week; on completion it is left unoccupied for the same period, perhaps to allow the termites to seal off the nesting chamber.

Aviculture: The Petz's Conure has long been a highly rated pet in the USA; however, in Europe, few are kept for this purpose. Unfortunately, its voice, no more pleasant than that of other *Aratinga*, must be a major reason for

not keeping it in the house. Those who disregard this factor find that, if obtained young, many Petz's excel as delightfully entertaining mimics and clowns. Anthony and Elizabeth Borge of Honolulu owned a 'Half moon Conure' which spent much time on a wooden playpen placed on top of her cage. Here she would 'sing' and talk and answer to the command 'dance!' by bobbing up and down. She was also able to whistle two tunes and to accurately imitate human laughter.

Breeding successes are scarce, particularly outside the USA. The first may have been that of Miss Palmer of San Francisco in 1929. In 1937, two were reared at San Diego Zoo. Birmingham Zoo, Alabama, bred two in 1967 and 1968 and four in 1970 and St Louis Zoo reared one in 1971.

Outside the USA, one was bred in Prague Zoo in 1971 and, in Britain, L. D. Guerin reported breeding two young in 1976. The female laid three eggs in a remarkably large nest-box (presumably the only one provided) which measured 36 × 30 × 62 cm (14 × 12 × 24 in).

In Italy, Umberto Cori-Carlitto of Albano, Rome, reared three Petz's Conures in 1977. They bred in a cage 1 m (3 ft 3 in) square. In 1978, Mr and Mrs J. Spenkelink of Soesterberg, in the Netherlands, also bred three. The incubation period was given as 24 days by one breeder.

Hybrids between a 'Halfmoon' and a Nanday Conure were reared at the Sunken Gardens, St Petersburg, Florida, during the 1960s, according to Roger Kenny, curator at the time. He told me that they were the size of the Nanday with 'washed-out grey heads' with six or seven yellow feathers on the forehead. In 1977 and 1978, he bred Petz's Conures in his own collection.

Golden-crowned (Peach-fronted) Conure

A. aurea

Description: This bird has a colour scheme which is similar to that of Petz's Conure (see above for distinguishing features). The forehead, part of the crown and a narrow ring of feathers surrounding the eye are orange. Hindcrown is blue and the cheeks and throat are olive-green.

Golden-crowned Conure (*Aratinga aurea*).

belonging to Captain R. Ward failed to hatch; in 1926, two eggs were laid and one youngster was reared – the first British breeding.

A more recent success was that of David Derrett (1973) of Norfolk. His pair was obtained in October 1972 and placed in a small outdoor aviary. In the following April, they entered the nest for the first time. A piece of turf covered by peat and dried bark had been placed in the box. The first egg was laid on about April 23. Three chicks, described as 'snowy white bundles of fluff', were seen in the nest on June 14. All were successfully reared on a nutritious diet consisting of turkey starter crumbs with chopped pear and the yolk of hard-boiled egg. The usual foods – seed, fruit, chickweed and poultry grower's pellets – were also available.

In Denmark and Germany, this species was bred in 1932 and, in Sweden, in 1959 by H. Hakansson. In the USA, the Golden-crowned Conure was bred in the 1930s by I. D. Putnam and more recently by Gene Hall of California in the late 1970s. His pair was double-brooded for five years, producing two nests of four young annually. In South Africa, E. F. Petsch hatched three in 1958; six eggs formed the clutch. Two chicks died shortly after leaving the nest, perhaps because of intense heat. In Australia, two were reared in Adelaide Zoo in 1963 and in 1970, and in Hong Kong Botanical Gardens three were reared in 1967.

Primaries are bluish, tipped with black. The rest of the plumage is dark green above and light green below, tending to yellowish olive on the breast and under side of the tail. Tail is green, tipped with blue. Bill is black and the iris is brown. Length: 26 cm (10 in).

Immature birds have less orange and blue on the head; the bill is pale horn-coloured and the iris greyish.

Those reared by David Derrett (1973) were described as being bright in colour but lacking the feathered orange ring around the eye and in having the upper mandible ivory-coloured – two features which would lend them an even closer resemblance to Petz's Conure.

Range/Habitat: The Golden-crowned Conure is found in Brazil, over almost the entire country, except the coastal areas and the south-east; it also inhabits a small area north of the Amazon. It is found as far south as eastern Bolivia, northern Paraguay and north-western Argentina. Semi-open country is its main habitat. It is very common over much of its range.

Aviculture: This species was regularly imported into Europe for many years and was bred in Danzig as long ago as 1880 by J. Wenzel. Unusually for early records, the correct incubation and fledging periods were given: 26 and 50 days respectively.

In 1925, three eggs laid by a female

Nandayus
Nandayus

From the avicultural viewpoints of behaviour and care, the Nanday Conure should be treated exactly as the *Aratinga* species. It is difficult to see how minor anatomical differences can justify placing it in a separate genus.

Nanday (Black-headed or Black-masked) Conure
N. nenday
Description: The feature which gives it its alternative names, combined with

Nanday Conures (*Nandayus nenday*).

the red thighs, immediately distinguished it from all other parrots. The throat and upper breast are washed with blue. The upper surface of the tail is green edged with blue, the under side being blackish. The outer webs of the flight feathers are blue. The remainder of the plumage is green, more yellowish below, also on the lower back, rump and under wing coverts. The bill is black and the iris is dark brown. There is a narrow circle of whitish skin surrounding the eye. Length: 31 cm (12 in), of which the long tail accounts for half.

Immature birds resemble adults, except for the shorter tail; within a short time of fledging, they are indistinguishable from adults.

Range/Habitat: It inhabits a relatively small area, about 200 km (125 miles) wide, in south-eastern Bolivia, Brazil, Paraguay and northern Argentina. It is often seen in very large flocks and, in some areas, has benefited from human settlement, feeding on crops of maize and sunflower and nesting in fence posts. It remains common in the wild.

Aviculture: Common in the wild and in captivity, this is one of the best known of the conures. It nests readily, will breed on the colony system and thrives at liberty. Under the latter conditions it can prove very free-breeding – as it often does in an aviary. However, its loud voice and destructive habits could make it very unpopular at liberty, especially in fruit-growing areas.

Always readily available, this species was bred in Britain as long ago as 1901 by Mrs N. Johnstone of Bury St Edmunds. Her pair nested in a hollow elm log which had the ends boarded up. The female was so wary she was never seen to enter the hole and the male always sat a few feet away, screaming if anyone approached. Three of the four young were reared.

Nanday Conures lay four or five eggs which are incubated by the female for about 26 days. On hatching, the chicks are naked but soon grow whitish down. Young leave the nest after about eight weeks.

Don Mathews, of Allison Park, Pennsylvania, USA, throws an entirely different light on the character of this sometimes maligned species. He wrote:

> They are by nature very noisy and squawky – and unpopular because of this one aspect. However, we have hand-raised a number of them and have found them to be an entity of their own. They are easy to feed, very loving and appreciative and make excellent pets. They do not seem to be nearly as noisy as their wild cousins and absolutely love to be handled. Our first pet was a hen Nanday and she was extremely quick to learn and very affectionate.

The Nanday Conure has hybridised with other *Aratinga* species, including the Jendaya Conure. One breeder of this cross produced young which were described as having the head dark grey, flecked with orange. The breast was marked with a V-shaped orange crescent and the thighs were green, black and gold. The rest of the plumage was green.

Pyrrhura
Pyrrhura

A group of delightful small conures which, at long last, are being more fully appreciated by aviculturists, are the *Pyrrhura*. Unfortunately, only the Red-bellied and, more recently, the Green-cheeked are fairly readily available. Of the 16 species, five are virtually unknown in aviculture. Their voices, although much louder than those of grass parrakeets, for example, are not as objectionable as those of most conures. Their two main assets are their endearing personalities (many are extremely steady, if not actually tame and they are very inquisitive) and their readiness to nest. Indeed, sometimes, they prove extremely prolific. All are easy to care for and can be highly recommended to the beginner and the experienced aviculturist alike.

Feeding: Inquisitiveness extends to the diet, and *Pyrrhura* usually prove willing to sample new items. The diet should therefore include a wide variety of fresh fruits and vegetables.

Accommodation: Due to their extreme inquisitiveness, which means that every corner of their aviary will be investigated – also that a nest-box will be entered within minutes – it is absolutely essential to ensure that an aviary containing these conures is carefully maintained and regularly checked for holes in the wire netting or mesh, or in the ground. I know of no birds which are quicker to leave their aviary if the opportunity occurs but, equally, if not frightened out of the vicinity, they are usually quick to find their way back. Any door in the aviary which could provide a means of escape should be fitted with a safety porch. Another point which should be noted is that they will attempt to nest underground by burrowing under the aviary floor. A pair of Pearly Conures in my possession were prevented from using a terrestrial site; however, the first breeding of the Green-cheeked Conure took place on the ground.

Breeding: In my experience, keeping *Pyrrhura* conures on the colony system is not successful. All may appear to be well, perhaps for a considerable period, then deaths will occur due to fighting. Also, where family groups are left together, the young may make no attempt to breed until housed separately. However, Mrs Spenkelink of the Netherlands, perhaps *the* most successful breeder of *Pyrrhura*, told me that no problems are experienced if each pair can defend a territory of 2 m (nearly 7 ft) around its nest-box.

Most *Pyrrhura* lay four to six eggs, except *leucotis* and *picta* which sometimes have as many as eight or nine. Incubation period is about 24 days and the young fledge after about eight weeks. They are then slightly duller than the adults, with lighter beaks, but they otherwise do not differ from the adults, except in the colour of the iris. Adults usually prove amicable towards their young which can be left with them until just prior to the next 'breeding season' – if such exists. They will nest in almost any month of the year and in a warm climate would almost certainly prove to be double-brooded. Perhaps leaving the young with them inhibits them from nesting again.

Pyrrhura will hybridise readily within the genus. I am firmly against hybridising unless it is carried out with some specific purpose in mind; nevertheless, I produced hybrid *Pyrrhura* by accident in 1972. A male Red-bellied and a female Black-tailed (*P. melanura pacifica*), inhabiting an aviary of un-mated birds, took over a nest-box 24 cm (9½ in) square × 50 cm (20 in) high. On July 8 I knew that the first of the five eggs had hatched because an old Ring-necked Parrakeet, the father of many chicks in his younger days, was seen sitting on the nest-box perch, looking into the nest – no doubt because he had heard a chick squeaking. Next day, inspection revealed one chick covered with long white down. The nest was then inspected daily and the chicks were handled from an early age. By July 15, there were four chicks; the last to hatch was three days younger than the third and its rate of growth was very much slower. It died when about two weeks old, when the other chicks were covered with dark grey down. The chicks' eyes opened when they were about two weeks old. Two of the young hybrids showed no distress at being handled while the third always struggled and even attempted to bite on some occasions. In nest feather, they resembled the male parent except for the colour of the bend of the wing which was red with a few flecks of yellow in two and orange in the other chick. By the beginning of September, this colour was almost lost in two. They had less maroon on the

Red-bellied Conure (*Pyrrhura frontalis*).

abdomen than the male. When adult, it was quite apparent that they were not pure-bred.

The young of *Pyrrhura* conures are generally easy to rear. Even when no greenfood was available, birds in my possession reared their young on soaked millet sprays, extra apple and carrot and sponge cake soaked in nectar with multivitamins added.

Red-bellied Conure
P. frontalis
Description: It has maroon on the forehead and an irregular patch of that colour on the abdomen. The crown and cheeks are dark green, also the nape, where the feathers have a lighter edge. The ear coverts are light buffish brown. The sides of the neck and the feathers of the upper breast are scalloped in the typical *Pyrrhura* fashion: olive on the breast, edged with yellowish, or, exceptionally, golden yellow. The feathers of the sides of the neck are tipped with whitish yellow. The tail feathers are maroon on the under side; the upper surface is green at the base, reddish in the centre in the nominate

race and golden-olive in *P.f. chiripepe*, which is known as Azara's Conure. The maroon on the lower breast is missing in this subspecies. Arndt (in press) states that *kriegi* is not a valid race.

A blue mutation (probably a single specimen only) has been recorded. The reddish areas on the under surface were replaced by a light buff or creamy colour.

Range/Habitat: This conure is found in south-eastern Brazil, south to Uruguay, north-eastern Argentina and eastern Paraguay. It is the most numerous of the parrot within its range.

Aviculture: The Red-bellied Conure was reared in Britain on numerous occasions during the 1970s. Before then it was commonly imported but only occasionally bred. The first breeder in Britain was W. Shore-Bailey who reared one youngster (*chiripepe*) in 1923. Two years later he reared four young of the nominate race. A. A. Prestwich bred this species in 1953 in an aviary housing four pairs. Even during the nesting period, the entire colony would roost in one box.

Red-bellied Conures have been bred by aviculturists in many parts of the world, including Australia, Japan and Denmark. Chicks weigh about 5 g (⅕ oz) on hatching.

Deville's (Blaze-winged) Conure
Description: It resembles a Red-bellied Conure but with the under wing coverts scarlet and the tail pale olive-green. Length: 26 cm (10 in).
Range/Habitat: This species is found in eastern Bolivia, northern Paraguay and south-western Mato Grosso, Brazil. It is unknown in aviculture.

Green-cheeked (Molina's) Conure
P. molinae
Description: It differs from the Red-bellied Conure in the feathers of the sides of the neck, throat and upper breast which are pale brown, some-

times tinged with green, each feather being broadly margined with pale greyish buff or dull yellow and tipped with dark brown. Also, the crown and nape are brown, the forehead reddish brown and the cheeks green. Upper side of tail is maroon. Length is 26 cm (10 in).

Range/Habitat: This species inhabits Brazil, in the state of Mato Grosso, northern and eastern Bolivia and north-western Argentina. It is common in the wild.

Aviculture: This species was rarely exported until the late 1970s. It has been bred by Swiss aviculturist Dr R. Burkard who reported (1974) that he kept 14 birds in adjoining aviaries. They gained access to the neighbouring aviary by gnawing under the floor boards in the shelter. One pair nested on the ground in a metre-long tunnel. When the young fledged, they differed from the adults in their slightly paler colour, lighter beak and in the whiteness of the skin at the base of the beak. This was the first reported breeding of Molina's Conure.

Shortly after it became available, a number of breeding successes were recorded. The first in Britain was that by George A. Smith. Four birds were obtained in 1978 which were described as being very wild. The first egg was laid on March 22, 1979; it measured 25.2 × 23.4 mm (1 × $\frac{9}{10}$ in approx.) but had vanished by the next day. On April 6 another egg was laid, which measured 26.6 × 21.9 mm. (Average weight of fresh eggs was 7 g/$\frac{1}{4}$ oz). Another egg laid on the following day proved that two females were laying. Four eggs placed in an incubator hatched after 22 days. Three left in the nest took 22 to 24 days to hatch. The two females incubated side by side and the males were equally friendly. All seven eggs hatched but the chicks disappeared. The hand-reared chicks were placed in the nest, plus a very young Hawk-headed Parrot. All were fed but the Hawk-head was removed for hand-rearing at 24 days. The Green-cheeked Conures left the nest at seven weeks. They differed from the adults in having less maroon on the abdomen and the red on the tail clearer and paler. This conure proved very prolific; in 1984, for example, 30 young were bred from two pairs (all young hand-reared).

Newly hatched chicks weighed about 5.6 g ($\frac{1}{5}$ oz); at weaning they weighed about 90 g (3 oz).

In the USA, Fred and Robbie Harris of California have bred this species since 1981. The first of four eggs was laid on January 14 and hatched on February 7. The chicks were removed at three weeks for hand-rearing.

In South Africa, Brian Boswell had bred 32 young from one pair by early 1982. In Hamburg, West Germany, Dr W. Merck bred this conure in 1982. Four eggs were laid in a log in the aviary shelter between March 28 and April 5; four hatched. The first youngster left the nest on June 11. All the young returned to the nest at night for the first few days. They were paler, especially on the ears coverts, with the cere lighter and the bill more brownish grey (Merck, 1984).

In California, Betty Byers recorded the incubation period for this species as 23 days and the hatching weight as 5 g ($\frac{1}{5}$ oz). She described the hand-reared young as 'very nippy' after weaning and unfriendly with birds of other species. This was in contrast to Red-bellied Conures which 'stay amicable' (Byers, 1984).

Red-eared (Red-rumped or Blue-throated) Conure
P. cruentata

Description: This is the largest and one of the most colourful members of the genus. The arrangement of colours on the head is most unusual: the feathers of the crown and nape being dark brown edged with dull orange, giving a streaky appearance on the nape. There is a patch of orange behind the brownish-red ear coverts. The cheeks are green and the lores maroon. The blue of the throat merges into an extensive blue area on the upper breast. A broad dark red area decorates the abdomen, also the lower back and rump. The bend of the wing is crimson and the tail is golden-olive above and brownish red below. Length: 28 cm (11 in). Immature birds are slightly duller in colour.

Range/Habitat: This rarely imported conure inhabits Brazil from southern Bahia and Minas Gerais to north-eastern São Paulo. It is listed as an endangered species because of extensive deforestation.

Aviculture: This species is rare in captivity; it was first bred in England by Herbert Whitley in 1937. Since the late

Red-eared Conure (*Pyrrhura cruentata*).

1970s it has been bred consistently in a few collections in Germany, the Netherlands, Denmark and Britain. A prolific species, which lays clutches of seven and eight eggs, there is good reason to believe it will be more securely established in aviculture within the next decade.

In the Netherlands, it has been bred by the Spenkelink family since 1977. Five young were reared in that year. In 1979, a young female laid infertile eggs; in the following year she reared young, Mrs Spenkelink van Schaik (1984) recommended a nest-box of very thick wood as nesting birds are very destructive. Her pair favoured a log 60–80 cm (about 24–30 in) high and about 20 cm (8 in) wide. The chicks' eyes open at 16 days and they are then ringed. After two months, all the young leave the nest within five days of each other, despite the size difference. For two weeks, they return to the nest at night. Usually seven or eight eggs were laid but only five or six would be fertile. The incubation period was 24 days or 26 days in cold weather. They were fed on paddy rice, oats, wheat, barley, hemp, linseed, buckwheat, canary seed, pine nuts, safflower, sunflower, and leaves from fruit trees. While breeding, sprouted seed and eggfood mixed with carrot and calcium was given.

In Britain, the most consistent breeder is Yorkshire farmer Harry Sissen. He obtained a pair during the mid-1970s. During the first breeding season the female laid 12 infertile eggs (Blackwell, 1982). The following year, five chicks hatched from a clutch of six eggs. The incubation period was 24 days. The chicks were removed for hand-rearing at about three weeks and four were reared. Since then young have been reared annually, some by the parents. In 1981, second generation young were bred, to give a total of more than two dozen young.

A pair which bred for the first time for George A. Smith in 1982 laid eight eggs. All hatched. The smallest chick died at an early age, three were left with their parents and four were hand-reared by my husband and me. Exceptionally noisy, the chicks, proved easy to rear and to wean but were very quarrelsome and could not be trusted with chicks of other species.

Pearly Conure (*Pyrrhura perlata*).

Pearly Conure
P. perlata

Range/Habitat: The Pearly Conure inhabits north-east Brazil. The nominate race was described from two specimens which have been shown to have been immature specimens of *rhodogaster* (Arndt, 1982). G. A. Smith (1983a) disputes this.

P. p. anerythra
Description: The forehead and crown are dark grey, the ear coverts being light greyish buff. The feathers of the throat and the sides of the neck are grey, edged with a lighter grey. The upper breast feathers are edged with blue. The lores are bluish green. The nape and the feathers surrounding the vent are blue. The upper surface of the tail is dull maroon, the under side blackish. The iris and beak are black. Length: 24 cm (9½ in). Immature birds resemble adults except for the paler bill.
Range/Habitat: This subspecies is found in Para, Brazil. It remains common in some areas but has declined overall due to deforestation.

Aviculture: Formerly occasionally available, it is now rare in aviculture.

In Britain, it has been bred on a number of occasions since 1963. In 1966 I bred from a pair obtained in the previous year. Three eggs were laid; all hatched and three young left the nest in October when they were between seven and a half and eight weeks old. They were then three-quarters the size of their parents which they resembled, apart from the lighter legs and bill. They fed themselves almost immediately on apple and hard seed. In 1967, the pair reared three more young. The female parent died that year and, in 1966, the male paired with his 1968 hatched daughter. No attempt was made to breed that year but they were successful in doing so in 1969. I kept the female until 1975 when she died in December from egg-binding. The male, at least 12 years old, died in 1976.

The first breeder of the Pearly Conure in Britain, B. M. Killick of Wellingborough, Northamptonshire, reared five youngsters in 1963 and 1966. He was then so successful that he parted with nearly all the young. Eventually he lost one of the parents and was unable to replace it. A pair belonging to Mr and Mrs R. W. Bridges (1974) of Stowmarket, Suffolk, reared three young in 1973. The proved incubation period was 25 days. The young left the nest in August and the female laid again three weeks later. Three of the four eggs hatched but the chicks lived only one week. In 1974, five eggs were laid; three hatched and two were infertile.

The three young died after three weeks, for reasons unknown. Three weeks later, the female laid the first of her six eggs, five of which hatched. The sixth was infertile. All the young were reared.

In Denmark, the Pearly Conure was bred by Albrecht Møller in 1960 or 1961 when two young were reared. In 1984, Jorgen Hare of Hvidore, Copenhagen, reared 14 in three nests. Due to lack of space, the first four remained in the aviary when the second clutch, also of four, hatched. As a result, ten birds roosted in the nest-box nightly.

In Sweden, it was bred by Nilsson in 1973 and in Switzerland by K. Mathys in 1980. In 1982, Mrs Spenkelink Van Schaik in the Netherlands bred the race *coerulescens*.

Crimson-bellied (Crimson-breasted) Conure
P. rhodogaster

Description: This must be considered as one of the most beautiful of all conures. It resembles a Pearly Conure with a crimson breast and, in my opinion, should be conspecific with *P. perlata*.

In the Crimson-bellied Conure, the whole of the lower parts from the upper breast to the vent are brilliant scarlet. The cheeks are yellowish green and blue. The feathers of the crown, nape, sides of neck, throat and upper breast are brown with a paler tip, giving a barred appearance. There is a variable blue collar surrounding the hind neck. The bend of the wing and the under wing coverts are crimson. The thighs, flanks and under tail coverts are blue. The tail is brownish red, marked with green at the base and tipped with blue above and greyish below. The bill is brownish grey and the iris dark brown. Length: 24 cm ($9\frac{1}{2}$ in).

It is of particular interest to record that the young which were bred at Chester Zoo in 1976 lacked the red breast whereas those reared in the following year exactly resembled the adults, except for the area of skin surrounding the eye which was dark – not white.

Range/Habitat: This conure is a native of Brazil, south of the Amazon River between the Madeira and Tapajos Rivers, south to northern Mato Grosso. Its present status is unknown.

Aviculture: It is extremely rare in aviculture. London Zoo received the first recorded importation in 1927 – a pair. The breeding at Chester Zoo in 1976 would appear to be the first success in Britain.

It is of interest that in the three years they nested, in an off-exhibit aviary, the female has always laid during the early part of June. The male died in 1980 of visceral gout. These birds have also been bred in the Netherlands and at Rotterdam Zoo. The first successful breeding there was in 1966 when three were reared. This was followed by four in 1971, two in 1972, two in 1975, three in 1976 and a further three in 1977. The young have been distributed to several European zoos.

Crimson-bellied Conure (*Pyrrhura rhodogaster*).

White-eared Conure (*Pyrrhura leucotis auricularis*).

White-eared Conure
P. leucotis

Description: The rich shade of dark brown on the forehead, lores and cheeks are the distinguishing features of this conure. The crown and nape are brown, suffused with blue on the forecrown in some subspecies. The hind neck is blue. Ear coverts are off-white. The feathers of the breast are edged with white and a narrow line of black which creates the typical scaled effect. There is a maroon patch on the middle of the abdomen and another from the lower back to the upper tail coverts. The bend of the wing is scarlet. Tail is maroon above, green at the base and coppery red below. The bill is brown, also the iris. Length: 21 cm ($8\frac{1}{4}$ in). Immature birds resemble adults.

Range/Habitat: It is of interest that the White-eared Conure, which is found in eastern Brazil, also occurs north of the Amazon in northern Venezuela. It is fairly common in some areas, rare and declining in others.

Emma's Conure
P. l. emma

Description: This is the most distinctive subspecies. The blue extends from the forehead to the middle of the crown. There is more blue on the throat, sides of neck and lower part of the cheeks than in the nominate race. The light edges to the feathers of the throat and upper breast are broader. It is slightly larger.

Aviculture: This was formerly the best known member of the genus but has seldom been seen in Europe since the late 1960s and is now virtually unknown in aviculture outside Brazil. It was regularly imported into Britain between the 1880s and the mid-1950s.

The White-eared Conure was bred in Europe as long ago as 1886 in Tours, France by M. Barnsby. Four chicks were reared. Seven eggs were laid and this would appear to be the normal clutch. The first recorded success in Britain occurred in the aviaries of an aviculturist who gained so many 'firsts' – E. J. Brook, in 1906. Eight eggs were laid, seven of which hatched. However, the record number in one nest must surely be held by a pair belonging to Danish aviculturist Carl Wentrup. In 1968 they reared nine. The youngest chick fledged a full month after the first. Previously the pair reared five in 1966 and then six in 1969.

Painted Conure
P. picta

Description: This is a most attractively marked bird. It has the crown and nape dark brown, suffused with blue on the crown in most of the seven subspecies recognised. There is blue on the lower cheeks and hind neck. The lores and the upper cheeks are maroon and the ear coverts are pale buff or, in *amazonum*, brownish buff, in *subandina* yellowish brown and in *caeruleiceps* greyish white. The feathers of the neck, throat and upper breast are dusky brown or green, broadly edged with greyish buff to give the usual scalloped effect. There is a maroon patch from the lower back to the upper tail coverts and another on the abdomen. The bend of the wing is green with red-tipped feathers. The tail is maroon above, coppery red below. Length: 22 cm (9 in).

Two subspecies have red on the head. In *P.p. caeruleiceps*, the lores and frontal band are red. In the beautiful *P.p. roseifrons* from north-western Brazil, the forehead, crown and nape and, in some birds, the upper cheeks, are scarlet.

Immature birds have the bend of the wing green with a few scattered red feathers.

Range/Habitat: The Painted Conure has a very wide distribution from the Guianas to Venezuela, south through the Amazon basin, to south-eastern Peru and northern Bolivia. It is also found in north-western Colombia. It is common over much of its range.

Aviculture: The Painted Conure is rare and little known despite the fact that a few consignments have reached Europe and the USA since 1974.

It was bred in France by Madame Lécallier in 1918 and by Jean Delacour, who reared six in 1920. In Germany, K. Müller of Bad Homburg reared 13 between 1962 and 1964. In 1976, Mr and Mrs J. Spenkelink in the Netherlands reared three young. In

1978 they reared ten – four of the nominate race and six of *amazonum*.

The subspecies *lucianii* was bred in France as long ago as 1866 by Jouet and Armand. In Canada, six eggs were laid and six chicks reared in 1960 by Lloyd B. Thompson of British Columbia. In 1961, ten young were produced.

In the USA William C. Wilson of Norshore Pets, Illinois, obtained six Painted Conures in 1981. Surgical sexing indicated that there were three males and three females. In July of the following year, one female laid seven eggs, six of which hatched. Five were reared – the youngest succumbing.

The other pair had made no attempt to nest but it was noticed that they were continually hanging on the sides of their flights squawking at each other. The idea occurred to Mr Wilson that they had paired up before he separated them and he had parted the chosen pairs. The partners were changed and both the new pairs nested in the following year. In 1984, one pair nested twice, raising six chicks on each occasion. That year the three pairs raised 21 young to maturity.

In Brazil, Nelson Kawall had bred 12 young from a pair of *P. p. roseifrons* by 1983. In Denmark, the nominate race was bred by Flemming Nielsen in 1984, and also by Bert Jørgensen.

In Sweden, *P. picta picta* has been bred by Sven Lennartsson in Rimforsa (between Stockholm and Gothenburg). He obtained five imported birds in 1980. During the winter of 1981–82, the temperature fell to −30°C (−22°F) and there was 60 cm (2 ft) of snow. The conures had access to a small outside flight in which they exercised daily, returning to a frost-proof shelter where their nest-box hung. In 1983, one pair produced four eggs, two of which hatched after an incubation period of 23 days. One chick died when aged between seven and ten days; the other left the nest when 40 days old. It was slightly smaller and duller than the adults, with the periorbital ring paler. In 1984, the female laid two days earlier. There were five fertile eggs, four of which hatched. Two chicks died at the same stage as the chick which was lost in the previous year; their crops were full when they died. The two survivors left the nest at 44 days. Young were

exchanged with another Swedish aviculturist who had bred the Painted Conure.

These conures were fed on a mixture of soaked seeds: safflower, sunflower, wheat, oats, hemp and buckwheat, in addition to a variety of fruits and vegetables, including carrots, corn-on-the-cob, cherries, hips and the seeds of various wild plants. Many of the food items were frozen and stored for winter use.

Black-tailed (Maroon-tailed) Conure
P. melanura melanura

Description: It has the feathers of the forehead brown; the crown feathers are brown with green edges, giving a mottled appearance when closely examined. The scaled markings on the upper breast are brownish green with narrow lighter edges; the remainder of the under parts are dark green, sometimes with a few scattered maroon feathers on the abdomen. The primary coverts are red, tipped with yellow. The upper surface of the tail is black, except at the base, which is green; the under side of the tail is very dark maroon. The bill is light brown and, except in the race *pacifica*, there is a prominent area of white periorbital skin. The iris is dark brown. Length: 24 cm (10 in). Immature birds resemble adults except for the fainter markings on the breast.

Range/Habitat: The Black-tailed Conure has a wide distribution over the western side of northern South America, in Colombia, southern Venezuela, Amazonas, north-western Brazil, through Ecuador to north-eastern Peru.

Ecologically adaptable, it is common throughout its range.

The nominate race inhabits north-eastern Peru, extreme eastern and southern Colombia, Brazil in north-western Amazonas and southernmost Venezuela.

P. m. souancei

Description: This race differs from the nominate in having more extensive red on the primary wing coverts and no yellow. The scaled feathers of the upper breast and the sides of the neck are much more

Black-tailed Conure (*Pyrrhura melanura melanura*) – female.

conspicuous, the feathers being broadly edged with buffish white.
Range/Habitat: It inhabits an area east of the Andes in Meta and Caqueta, Colombia, eastern Ecuador and northern Peru.

P. m. pacifica
Description: The feathers of the upper breast are dull green at the base and narrowly edged with pinkish buff. Maroon on the abdomen and yellow on the wing coverts is absent. The edge of the wing is scarlet. The forehead is green and a small periorbital area is greyish and barely noticeable. The bill is pale brown. Length: 24 cm (9½ in).
Range/Habitat: The only *Pyrrhura* found west of the Andes, it inhabits the Pacific slopes of the Andes in Narino, south-western Colombia.
Aviculture: This race was either rarely imported or incorrectly identified. In 1968, I picked out three *pacifica* from a consignment of *souancei*. A pair nested at the end of October 1970 and two chicks hatched which unfortunately died soon after.

P. m. berlepschi
Description: This is said to differ from *souancei* in having much broader light edges to the feathers of the throat and breast. However, Chapman (1917) described specimens of *souancei* with wider light margins than those of *berlepschi*. Ear coverts are said to be lighter green, tinged with olive, and the blue of the primaries is purer and brighter and the green of the upper parts has a yellow tinge. The maroon patch on the abdomen is more distinct. There is some doubt regarding the status of this form which possibly relates to aberrant specimens of *souancei*.
Range/Habitat: It is described from eastern Peru and is known only from the Huallaga River valley.
Aviculture: It is probable that most imported birds described as *berlepschi* were in fact *souancei*.

In 1977, Mr and Mrs J. Spenkelink in the Netherlands bred what they described as Berlepsch's Conure. Four eggs were laid and four chicks hatched. One died at 17 days and the rest were reared. In 1978, they reared the creditable total of 19 *melanura* – eight *berlepschi* and 11 *chapmani*.

P. m. chapmani
Description: This race has the feathers of the upper breast dark brown and broadly edged with whitish. The crown is dark brown with a small amount of green. The ear coverts are partly green and there is little maroon on the abdomen. The sides of the tail are green at the base. It differs from *souancei* in the colour of the upper breast and in having a bluish tinge to the green feathers between the nape and the mantle. There is less green on the crown and at the base of the tail.
Range/Habitat: It is found on the eastern slopes of the central Andes of Colombia from Belem, Caqueta, north to Gaitania, Tolima; it inhabits the sub-tropical zone between 1,600 and 2,800 m (5,250 and 9,200 ft).
Aviculture: First bred in the Netherlands by Mr and Mrs J. Spenkelink in 1976. Three young were reared.

Aviculture: The Black-tailed Conure was rarely imported into Europe until 1967 when quite large numbers of the nominate race and of *souancei* appeared. At that time I kept two subspecies, *melanura* and the rarely imported *pacifica*. Neither had the confiding nature of the other *Pyrrhura* species, although Mrs Spenkelink told me that this was not true of her various *melanura*. However, this species did not achieve any popularity during the few years it was available and comparatively few breeding successes occurred. At the time of writing, it is almost unknown in Britain.

The first breeder in Britain was Mrs B. Rhodes of Yorkshire, who bred the subspecies *souancei* in 1970. The pair was obtained in 1968 and housed in an indoor flight 91 cm (3 ft) long and 106 cm (3 ft 6 in) high. Four eggs were laid at the beginning of February 1970, a chick was heard on February 26 and two chicks fledged when seven weeks old. The pair nested again in December 1970. Four of the five eggs hatched and all the chicks were reared. At four weeks old they were covered with dark grey down. In Sweden, K. Hansson of Malmö reared four in 1969 and three in 1970 and, in Germany, Ruth Fanselau of Hanover reared *melanura* in 1971. The Black-tailed Conure has also been bred in the Netherlands and Denmark.

The following *Pyrrhura* species are unknown or rarely represented in aviculture. So little is known about some that immature plumage has yet to be described.

Red-eared Conure
P. hoematotis
Description: Forehead and forehalf of the crown are brown, the nape olive-green and the ear coverts brownish red. The feathers of the sides of the neck are edged with brownish grey (lacking in *immarginata*, the only subspecies described). The feathers of the upper breast are faintly tipped with grey and tinged with olive. Centre of the abdomen is suffused with maroon. The tail is maroon, tipped with olive-green. The bill is brownish grey and the iris is brown. Length: 25 cm (10 in).
Range/Habitat: This species is found only in the coastal mountains of northern Venezuela. It is common over much of its small range.

Santa Marta Conure
P. viridicata
Description: This is one of the least typical of the *Pyrrhura* in colouration.

It lacks the scalloped breast markings but has the abdomen variably marked with orange-red, also yellow in some birds. The bend of the wing and the under wing coverts are also variably marked with orange, scarlet and yellow. There is a narrow red frontal band and the ear coverts are reddish. The tail is green above and dusky reddish brown below. Bill is pale horn-coloured, dusky at the tip. Length: 25 cm (10 in).
Range/Habitat: This conure is known only from the subtropical zone of the Santa Marta mountains in northern Colombia. It is fairly common within its limited habitat.

Demerara (Fiery-shouldered) Conure
P. egregia
Description: The most beautiful feature is the under wing coverts which are yellow and orange; the bend of the wing and the carpal edge are red. There is a narrow brown frontal band and the feathers of the top of the head are brown edged with green; the ear coverts are reddish brown. Feathers of the sides of the neck, throat and upper breast are green, narrowly edged with yellow or yellowish white. The centre of the abdomen is variably suffused with brownish red. The tail is dark maroon above, greyish below. The bill is horn-coloured and the iris is said to be hazel. Length: 25 cm (10 in).

Immature birds have less yellow and orange on the bend of the wing; the carpal edge and lesser wing coverts are green.
Range/Habitat: This species inhabits south-eastern Venezuela and adjoining regions of western Guyana and extreme north-eastern Roraima, Brazil. It is apparently common within its small range.

Rock (Black-capped) Conure
P. rupicola
Description: This bird can be distinguished by the broad white or buff-white edges to the feathers of the lower breast. The sides of the head are green and the feathers of the crown are brown edged with green; on the hind

neck the feathers are brownish black, narrowly edged with buffish white. There are a few maroon feathers on the abdomen. The carpal edge of the wing and the primary coverts are red. The tail is green above and blackish brown below. The bill is grey and the iris brown. Length: 25 cm (10 in).

Immature birds have the carpal edge of the wing green with a few red feathers.
Range/Habitat: The Rock Conure inhabits central and south-eastern Peru, northern Bolivia and extreme north-western Brazil. It is believed to be fairly common.
Aviculture: This conure was probably unknown until 1980 when a few birds of the race *sandiae* were imported into the USA. Three were obtained by Tom McCoy of California and, in 1981, two were reared. Another successful breeder is Tom Ireland in Florida. In Switzerland, Mr Leumann obtained five in 1980 and reared young in 1982.

Flame-winged (Brown-breasted or Beautiful) Conure
P. calliptera
Description: It can be distinguished by the yellow carpal edge of the wing and the greater wing coverts; the lesser wing coverts are orange. The crown and nape are dusky brown, tinged with blue and green; ear coverts are maroon and the abdomen is tinged with this colour. On the sides of the neck, throat and upper breast the feathers are brown, tipped with reddish-brown. The tail is maroon on the upper surface, duller below. The bill is horn-coloured and the iris is yellowish brown. Length is 23 cm (9 in).

Immature birds have the primary coverts green.
Range/Habitat: This bird inhabits the Eastern Andes of Colombia. It has declined due to habitat destruction but remains common in some areas.

White-throated (White-necked) Conure
P. albipectus
Description: It has the frontal band reddish brown and the crown feathers brown streaked with green, with paler edges. The ear coverts are orange and

there is a broad whitish collar encircling the neck – which distinguishes it from all other conures. The throat and upper breast are pinkish white without any scalloping, shading to yellow on the lower breast. The primary coverts are scarlet and the tail is maroon, the central feathers being edged with green. The bill is greyish brown and the iris is brown. Length: 24 cm (9½ in).
Range/Habitat: This most attractively marked conure inhabits south-eastern Ecuador. It is uncommon in the wild.

Rose-headed (Rose-crowned) Conure
P. rhodocephala
Description: It is the only member of the genus with scarlet on the crown which also lacks the barred breast and throat marking. There are a few maroon feathers on the abdomen, and the ear coverts and the tail are maroon. Carpal edge of the wing is orange tinged with white and the primary coverts are white. Bill is horn-coloured and the iris is brown. Length 24 cm (9½ in).

Immature birds have the crown green tinged with blue and with scattered red feathers. Primary coverts are blue.
Range/Habitat: This species is known only from the mountains of the subtropical zone of western Venezuela. It is fairly common despite habitat destruction in some areas.

Hoffmann's (Sulphur-winged) Conure
P. hoffmanni
Description: The green feathers of the head are tipped with yellow on the primary coverts, inner primaries and outer secondaries. The tail is reddish olive above margined with green and brownish red below. The bill is horn-coloured. Length: 24 cm (9½ in). Immature birds are similar to adults.
Range/Habitat: This conure inhabits the mountains of southern Costa Rica. It is common over much of its limited range.
Aviculture: This species may have been unknown in aviculture until Dr Nathan Gale acquired several birds of the subspecies *gaudens* while living in

Panama in 1980. One pair was kept in the collection of Chris Rowley in Arizona. The female laid the first of four eggs on May 5, 1981; after 30 days, they were removed and found to be infertile. In 1982, copulation was observed to commence in mid-February. Six eggs were laid on alternate days, the first on March 5. All were fertile but two of the embryos died at an early age. Chicks hatched on March 29, 31 and April 6. The fourth had to be helped out of the shell but did not survive. On April 20, the youngest chick died. The survivors left the nest on May 20. This breeding occurred in a cage measuring 91 cm (3 ft) square and 91 cm (3 ft) high (Rowley, 1984).

Deroptyus
Deroptyus

The Hawk-headed Parrot, the only member of this genus, has long baffled most taxonomists and naturalists regarding its relationship with other parrots. Anyone with experience of keeping and breeding *Pyrrhura* conures and other neotropical parrots can have few doubts regarding the close relationship of the Hawk-headed Parrot to *Pyrrhura*. It differs only in its larger size, correspondingly louder voice and in its ornamental ruff. In behaviour, it resembles the *Pyrrhura* in every way.

Hawk-headed Parrot
D. accipitrinus
Description: This bird is a bizarre beauty. When displaying its erectile ruff it is totally unlike any other parrot and its appearance is so surprising that it could well have the intended effect of frightening away a predator. The dark red feathers of the neck, which are broadly edged with blue, are erected to frame the head like a Red Indian's headdress and the bird sways menacingly from side to side, emitting a high-pitched whine.

The feathers of the forehead and crown are white in the nominate race and dusky brown in the only subspecies, *D.a. fuscifrons*; however, this distinction is not always well defined.

Hawk-headed Parrot (*Deroptyus accipitrinus*).

The feathers of the top and side of the head are brown, shaft-streaked with pale buff (shaft-streaking is found in some species of *Pyrrhura* conures and in no other South American parrots). The colour scheme of the ruff is repeated on the under parts (red feathers edged with blue), and the under side of the tail, also the inner webs of the tail feathers, are black. There is a maroon spot at the base of the under side of the tail feathers in the nominate form. The remainder of the plumage is dark green. The bill is black and the iris is yellow. Length 31 cm (12 in). Weight: 300 g (10½ oz).

Immature birds have some green on the crown and the feathers of the breast are usually edged with greenish blue. The iris is brown.
Range/Habitat: The Hawk-headed Parrot is found from the Guianas and northern Brazil west to south-eastern Colombia and north-eastern Peru. The nominate race occurs north of the Amazon; *fuscifrons* is from south of the Amazon. This species is locally distributed in many parts of its range

and is common in very few areas. It is found in pairs or small groups. In flight, the spread tail distinguishes it from other parrots, also its habit of flying low through the forest instead of above the canopy. Food consists of fruits and berries as well as nuts and seeds.

Aviculture: Since export restrictions have operated from most parts of its range, it has become rare and very expensive in captivity; few South American parrots command a higher price. Previously it was expensive and has never been imported in other than small groups.

I have long had a special affection for this species. It is a charming bird: strangely beautiful, playful, intelligent and, behaviourally, fascinating. Certainly, in captivity, other species of parrots appear alarmed at the display. The heroics in which it indulges are not always for effect; the male of my present pair has to be distracted with a grape or some other delicacy at feeding times because he is all too ready to attack, unlike his aviary-bred female who always retreats. However, the female of a pair belonging to a friend is even more ready to attack than the male. It is usual for male Hawk-heads to be more assertive in their behaviour – to swagger and dominate.

A number of theories have been put forward on sexing this species by plumage colouration, none of which has proved reliable. There is considerable variation among individuals in the colours of the plumage.

Despite its great appeal, the Hawk-headed Parrot is not an ideal subject for captivity. In many individuals, nervousness manifests itself in feather plucking or biting or, much worse, in self mutilation.

Hawk-heads are exceptionally noisy birds and, in the absence of a sound-proof room, pairs have to be kept outdoors. While one bird in the house is just tolerable, more than one severely tests one's endurance.

An outdoor aviary with nest-box permanently in position for roosting is the only satisfactory way of keeping these birds. They normally retire to the box at night well in advance of other birds. The aviary is best placed in a tree-shaded area or should be largely enclosed; Hawk-heads need the quiet

and feeling of security which such situations provide.

Large amounts of fresh fruit, vegetables and berries should be included in their diet. Most kinds will be sampled and the berries of hawthorn will be favoured above almost all other foods. They are more frugivorous in captivity than many parrots. Bread and milk is readily taken, in addition to all the usual seeds.

George Smith (1976b) described additional features of the display: 'If really excited, the body feathers are sleeked, the tail is widespread and the wings held away from the body as the bird writhes a little, blazes the eyes and suddenly starts and hisses at the same time'. When threatening, the male 'lowers the head and raises the feathers of the chin, cheek and body slightly, but not the ruff, and the head is raised and lowered once or twice.... Such a display is entirely silent'. He then walks purposefully along the perch with head held low.

The Hawk-headed Parrot has been bred with conspicuous success by only two men: Ralph Small of Chicago and Ramon Noegel of Seffner, Florida. Both hand-rear the young and in Ramon Noegel's collection, between 1976 and 1980, for example, 32 were reared. They were independent at about 110 days. In 1978, the pair's breeding activities were temporarily suspended when another pair, newly acquired, were moved near to them, hoping it would stimulate the new pair to breed. However, the breeding female was so upset by her new neighbours and became so wild, that her next clutch was infertile and the new pair had to be moved.

In Britain, only three aviculturists have recorded successes: Mrs N. Howard in 1972; George Smith of Peterborough in 1976 and Harry Sissen of Yorkshire on several occasions since 1975; both the latter hand-fed the young reared. Mrs Howard's adults were so nervous that the entire range of aviaries was closed except to Mrs Howard and her husband. The pair bred when the male was six years old and the female eight. Two eggs were laid, one of which hatched after 28 days. The young bird left the nest when nine weeks old. Rearing food consisted of baked bread-and-butter

pudding made with eggs, milk, sugar and raisins; the usual diet, consisting of large amounts of fruit – and the usual seed, was also eaten.

George Smith's first 'pair' proved to be two females; copulation had been observed. One laid three eggs but it was noted that the other female did not feed her. A male Hawk-head was obtained on loan and the female laid on February 5, 1975, the first of three eggs which failed to hatch; the chicks were dead in the shell. The first of three eggs in the second clutch was laid on October 4. These were broken by the birds, through no fault of their own.

Hawk-heads become extremely aggressive while they are nesting and when George Smith's female laid a third clutch, in March 1976, entering the aviary became a hazardous procedure. Both birds would attack together when the female was out of the nest. George Smith wrote:

> The only defence against such angry birds (my fear is inadvertently injuring them in self-defence) is to show them a catching net, but in the case of Hawk-heads this is a frail defence, for the cock would wrench this out of my hand while my attention was being given to the box; and a Hawk-head rapidly pulling tuft after tuft from my head always made me escape as fast I could.

Strips of wood were found inside the box, arranged to form a definite nest. The eggs started to hatch after 26 days. The chicks soon disappeared and the part-mutilated chick rescued from a pipping egg died. The next clutch of three eggs, the first laid on May 20, started to hatch after 26 days. The first chick was missing on the second day so the second was removed in the egg as it was pipping and hand-reared.

The chick's down was thin, white and rather long. When it was 17 days old it weighed 90 g ($3\frac{1}{5}$ oz) with the crop empty and 109 g ($3\frac{4}{5}$ oz) when it was full. If tickled it hissed, jumping as it did so; it is interesting to note that it would wrinkle the skin of the occiput to 'raise' its non-existent ruff.

George Smith commented. 'One live chick from thirteen eggs demonstrates the inefficiency of my Hawk-head breeding ...' but I feel it demonstrates the difficulty of breeding this nervous species and the advisability of hand-

Thick-billed Parrot (*Rhynchopsitta pachyrhyncha*).

rearing the young when possible.

The first captive breeding of the Hawk-head occurred at Brookfield Zoo, Chicago, in 1965. Between that year and 1970, 13 young were reared, some by the parents, others by Ralph Small. In 1965, three chicks, each from a different nest, were reared by the parents, plus one more in 1966.

In the USA, the late F. H. Rudkin of Fillmore, California, reared one Hawk-head in the late 1960s by placing the chick under a Ringneck Parrakeet, then hand-feeding it from about two weeks. This is one of the most difficult of all parrot species to rear from the egg. Where possible, day-old chicks not hatched by the parents should be fostered to another species.

Rhynchopsitta
Rhynchopsitta

The single species of the genus consists of macaw-like birds.

Thick-billed Parrot
R. pachyrhyncha pachyrhyncha
Description: In shape and size and in the proportions of the head, bill and body, it is not unlike the Yellow-eared Conure. In colouration it is entirely different, being dark green with the forehead, forecrown and a stripe above the eye crimson. The under wing coverts are bright yellow and the bend of the wing, the carpal edge and the

thighs are red. The bill is black and the iris and periorbital skin yellow. Length: 38 cm (15 in). Weight: about 750 g (1 lb 11 oz).

Immature birds lack the red stripe above the eye; they have the bend of the wing and the carpal edge green, with less red on the thighs. The bill is horn-coloured. Despite the slightly top-heavy appearance created by the proportionately short tail and heavy bill, this is a most attractive bird with a pleasing gloss to its plumage.
Range/Habitat: This bird inhabits the highlands of western Mexico. Until the early 1900s, it was a regular visitor, usually during winter, to the mountains of southern Arizona and southwestern New Mexico and thus was the last member of the parrot family to occur naturally in the USA. Clearance of pine forests in Sonora and Chihuahua, in Mexico, will probably prevent the Thick-billed Parrot from ever again moving into the USA. Now uncommon and local, its numbers have declined substantially in recent decades due to destruction of trees (live and dead) used for nesting sites.
Aviculture: The Thick-billed Parrot was probably unknown to aviculture until the 1920s when it was represented in several collections in the USA. When these birds did become available, they found little popularity with aviculturists, partly because of their large beaks and destructive habits. In the 1970s, however, when parrot imports into the USA became fewer, Thick-bills were eagerly sought by some collectors, despite legislation whch prevented them crossing the border.

This species is, perhaps, found as often in zoos as in private collections. The first captive breeding occurred in San Diego Zoo in 1965. The adults were obtained ten years previously and had been provided with a variety of nesting sites. The female chose a box situated at a height of 3 m (10 ft); it measured 36 cm (14 in) wide and 61 cm (2 ft) long. Only one egg was laid and it hatched after 28 days. After 16 days, the chick was removed from the nest for hand-rearing.

The Thick-billed Parrot has since been bred in a number of collections in the USA and in Britain. At Los Angeles Zoo, young were reared

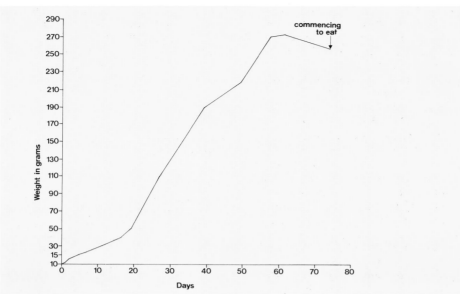

Graph showing development of Thick-billed Parrot (*Rhynchopsitta pachyrhyncha pachyrhyncha*). Hand-reared.

in1965 and 1966. At the Arizona-Sonora Desert Museum, one Thick-bill was obtained in 1963 and another in December 1965. One egg was laid, probably on July 10; it hatched on August 7. On September 14, the chick left the nest prematurely – perhaps as the result of being weighed on the previous day. It was returned to the nest where it stayed until October 5. Also in the USA, the Thick-billed Parrot has been reared in zoos at Sacramento, Brownsville and Honolulu, Hawaii, since 1977.

In California, Fred and Robbie Harris, known for their many breeding successes with conures, bred the Thick-billed Parrot in 1984. All young are hand-reared. One chick weighed 10 g ($\frac{2}{5}$ oz) at hatching. Its development is shown on the accompanying graph. At 57 days it said 'Hello'. Weaned youngsters weigh between 260 and 280 g (9 and 10 oz).

This species was first bred in England in 1973. A pair owned by K. W. Dolton of Worcestershire reared one youngster which left the nest on November 4. Subsequently, in 1974 a chick was hatched in this collection but not reared. Mr Dolton informed me that his Thick-bills always nest late in the year – August or September. They spend much time on the ground and have to be wormed three times a year.

In 1977 B. Higgs of Clee Hill Bird Gardens, Kidderminster, reared four Thick-bills.

At Jersey Zoo, where this species was first reared in1973, it also proved to be a late nester. Six specimens were obtained from Mexico in 1968. Two young were hatched in 1970 but lived for only nine and 13 days. Two more were hatched during the following year and lived for 21 to 22 days. Of the two chicks hatched in 1972, one died at 17 days and the other was removed at four days for hand-rearing. It was then sparsely covered with white down. Food provided closely resembled that used with success at San Diego Zoo: $\frac{1}{4}$ cup Froment, $\frac{1}{4}$ cup porridge oats, two fresh egg yolks, one teaspoonful of golden syrup, $\frac{1}{2}$ teaspoonful of scraped cuttlefish bone and one drop of Abidec. These items were mixed with water to a sloppy consistency and cooked for 45 minutes. The chick progressed well until the 29th day when its condition began to deteriorate. It died on the 37th day. Autopsy revealed liver abscess, necrosis of the muscle and severe osteomyelitis. It was concluded that the diet was deficient in calcium phosphate so in 1973, when three chicks hatched, the diet was changed. Two did not survive longer than five days; the third was removed for hand-rearing when two days old.

It then weighed 30 g (1 oz), had white down, longest on the lower back and nuchal area and quite dense on the head and wings. The food given differed in that Farex was substituted for Froment and two cups of Collo-Cal D for the cuttlefish bone. A chick from the second pair was removed for hand-rearing at 39 days just after it had begun to develop a similar condition to that of the chick which died in 1972. Its left leg was swollen, hot and splayed and the right shoulder joint was also affected. One drop of Ledermycin was given three times a day before feeds for 14 days. It was believed that this cleared up an infection which killed its nest-mate and which may have started as a result of feather plucking by the parents. Both chicks were successfully reared in 1973 and another in 1974.

Thick-billed Parrots have also reared young at Bird Paradise in Cornwall. From April 1973, two pairs were housed in an aviary 4.2 m (14 ft) long and 3.3 m (11 ft) wide. When one female laid two eggs, the second pair was removed from the aviary. The single chick died when aged about 16 days. The following year the pair was moved to a more secluded aviary; they made no attempt to nest so were returned to their original enclosure. A screen was built, behind which the nest-box was placed.

Two chicks were hatched and pine nuts, which had not previously been offered, became the most important item of the diet. Sunflower seed, banana, grapes and bread and milk were also eaten. On leaving the nest the young birds had horn-coloured bills; the red on the head did not extend beyond the eye.

Maroon-fronted Parrot
R. p. terrisi

Description: Differs from the Thick-billed Parrot in the maroon rather than scarlet forehead, grey (instead of bright yellow) under wing coverts, darker shade of green and slightly larger, heavier build. Length: 40 cm (16 in).
Range/Habitat: North-eastern Mexico: the highlands of the Sierra Madre Oriental in central west Nuevo-Leon. It is limited to an area of conifer forest about 300 km (185 miles) in length. As

Yellow-eared Conure (*Ognorhynchus icterotis*).

there are few large trees in the area, holes in limestone cliffs are used as nesting sites. It is threatened by destruction of its habitat.
Aviculture: This species is unknown in captivity. Any imported in the past could have been mistakenly identified as Thick-billed Parrots.

Ognorhynchus
Ognorhynchus

The single member of this genus is a particularly interesting bird for it is more reminiscent of a macaw than a conure. The distinction, in any case, is a tenuous one and depends mainly on the fact that basically macaws have the lores and, in some species, part of the cheeks unfeathered.

Yellow-eared Conure
O. icterotis
Description: It was interesting to compare Cooper's illustration in Forshaw's *Parrots of the World* (drawn from a skin) with a live bird. The first point that was obvious was that the yellow

ear coverts do not stand away from the head as is portrayed. Neither are its proportions quite as pleasing as the plate indicates; its tail would need to be longer. Another important difference is that the naked skin surrounding the eye is black.

The plumage is dark green above, greenish yellow below. The feathers of the forehead, lores and cheeks are yellow, those of the forehead being bushy and reminiscent in this respect of those of some macaws, such as the Military. The under wing coverts are pale greenish yellow and the primaries are greyish yellow on the under side and pale yellow on the inner edge of the upper surface. The under side of the tail is pale maroon with a pronounced sheen. Bill is black and powerful with a sharp, narrow tip. The iris is reddish brown. Length: 42 cm (16 in). Weight: 285 g (10 oz).

Immature birds have yet to be described.
Range/Habitat: Known only from the Andes of Colombia and northern Ecuador, in the sub-tropical and temperate zones, it is found in areas where there are wax palms. It has declined seriously during the past 50 years, due to extensive deforestation.
Aviculture: Little is known about the bird; thus I was very pleased to have the opportunity to look after a single bird belonging to G. A. Smith. On receiving it, I was interested to discover that there is an area of flesh-coloured bare skin at the side of the lower mandible and that this 'blushes' when the bird is excited; in the large macaws the bare cheeks redden under similar circumstances. This being so, the Yellow-eared Conure has as much bare skin on the face as, for example, the Spix's Macaw. It has a massive bill, as would befit a macaw. I have little doubt that it would be better named the Yellow-eared Macaw.

It had a delightful personality, marred only by its horrific voice and annoying habit of shrieking incessantly when I was in the room. I found that pine nuts and hawthorn berries were among its favourite foods. After a few months with me it was returned to its owner to live in an aviary with a Yellow-naped Macaw. The two agreed well together. Eventually, it was presented by George Smith to Vogelpark

Walsrode. This Yellow-eared Conure was probably one of two received on different occasions by a London dealer in about 1965. At the time of writing, there is reported to be another specimen in Switzerland.

Leptosittaca
Leptosittaca

The single member of this genus would appear to resemble a large *Aratinga*; presumably it has been classified separately only on account of the tuft of feathers above the ear coverts. It is unknown in captivity.

Branicki's (Golden-plumed) Conure
L. branickii
Description: Mainly green with a narrow orange or yellow frontal band. The feathers of the abdomen are orange in the centre, giving a mottled effect. The name Golden-plumed is derived from the narrow plume formed by the elongated yellow feathers above the ear coverts. The lores and a line of feathers below the eye are also yellow. Tail feathers are green with dull red on the inner webs. The bill is horn-coloured and the cere partly feathered. The iris is orange. Length: 35 cm (14 in).
Range/Habitat: This is one of the least known of South American parrots. It inhabits the Andes and has been found in the Central range in Colombia, south-western Ecuador and the province of Junin in central Peru. It has rarely been observed and little is known about it.

Enicognathus
Enicognathus

The two species in this genus are closely related to *Pyrrhura*; their plumage is almost identical and bears a marked resemblance to that of the Red-bellied Conure (*P. frontalis*) except for the cere which is thickly feathered. The two were formerly placed in separate genera but there is no doubt that they should share a genus, for their behaviour and appearance are so similar, the beak of the Slender-bill being the main distinction.

Both are rare in aviculture and were imported into Europe in 1976 by a Dutch dealer – probably the first commercial importation. Few birds are exported from Chile and the usual source of parrots from that country is the seaman. I am very fortunate in owning examples of both species and find them to be delightful birds.

Magellan (Austral) Conure
E. ferruginea

Description: This bird is dark green above, with the feathers of the head heavily edged with black and with less prominent black edges to those of the back. The under parts are green, slightly olive in shade, with very faint black margins to the feathers. The forehead and lores are dark brownish red; the centre of the abdomen and the tail are maroon. Primaries and primary coverts are green tinged with blue. The cere is feathered. The upper mandible is black and the lower mandible brownish grey. The iris is reddish brown. There is a small area of bare dark grey skin surrounding the eye. Immature birds have less maroon on the abdomen. Length: about 35 cm (14 in) in the nominate race and about 31 cm (12 in) in the Chilean Conure (*E. f. minor*).

Range/Habitat: This is the most southerly of all parrots in its distribution. It is found from Colchagua, Chile, and Neuquen, Argentina, south to Tierra del Fuego. It is a common inhabitant of beech forests, often being found in large flocks.

Aviculture: This species has dense plumage. The thick feathering is utilised in display when the feathers of the head are 'puffed out', making the bird look very much larger. This species has reached Europe on very few occasions. I first saw it in 1971 when visiting East Berlin Zoo, where there were six examples of *minor*. The first captive breeding would appear to be that in East Berlin Zoo in 1973, when four were hand-reared. Three more were reared in 1975.

Austral Conure (*Enicognathus ferruginea*).

Slender-billed Conure (*Enicognathus leptorhynchus*).

In the USA, the first breeder was Tom Ireland (1981) of Lake Worth, Florida. He obtained a pair in 1979. They were housed in a suspended cage made of 26 × 13 mm (1 in × ½ in) welded mesh, measuring 1.2 m (4 ft) square × 91 cm (3 ft) high. Copulation commenced in mid-January of the following year and eggs were laid in April. The clutch consisted of six eggs. Three were fertile and hatched after about 26 days on May 4, 6 and 8. Rearing foods included corn and a mixture of crumbled wholemeal bread, grated carrot and chopped endive sprinkled with vitamins. The chicks were removed for hand-rearing when the youngest was about three weeks old. Three weeks later the female laid five more eggs but they were infertile. Since this success, Tom Ireland has reared Austral Conures annually.

He generously sent me two females in late 1983. They were placed with my males (including the one bred in East Berlin) in April of the following year. One female laid only three weeks later: five clear eggs. The other female laid with similar results. In Britain, chicks were hatched by Brian Higgs at Clee Hill Bird Gardens in Worcestershire in 1983.

This species remains rare in aviculture but as it can prove prolific there is a good chance that it will become established.

Slender-billed (Long-billed or Slight-billed) Parrakeet
E. leptorhynchus

Description: Its unmistakable beak, which is very narrow and only slightly curved, distinguishes it from all other parrakeets. The upper mandible is as long below the lower mandible as above it.

Most of its feathers are dark green with a faint dusky edging to them, or heavily marked with black on the crown. The forehead and lores and an indistinct area surrounding the eye are maroon. There is a patch of the same colour on the abdomen and the tail is maroon with a greenish tip. The primaries are bluish green. The iris is orange and the skin surrounding the rather small eye is grey. Length: about 41 cm (16 in), of which the tail accounts for about 17 cm (7 in). Weight: 230 g (8⅕ oz)

Immature birds have the beak marginally shorter and smaller. On leaving the nest, young produced by my pair had the plumage brighter and more glossy than the adults, with the red on the abdomen brighter and tinged with yellow. The inconspicuous area of bare skin surrounding the eye is white instead of grey.

Range/Habitat: This species inhabits central and southern Chile. It has declined in recent years but it is believed to be still fairly common.

Aviculture: It had seldom been kept in captivity outside its native country until 1976. However the first breeding occurred as long ago as 1913. Dutch aviculturist, F. E. Blaauw, obtained the pair during his stay in Chile in 1911. Two years later the female laid four eggs. Two youngsters were reared in a roomy log and in 1916 four more were bred.

No further breedings were reported until after commercial importation occurred in the mid-1970s. In December 1978, Tony Silva of Riverside, Illinois, USA, bred this species and gave the following details: incubation period 26 days; chicks have white down and 'the bill is tipped with white until the age of a year or so'. Young are independent at the age of about eight weeks. He stated: 'Males have red on the thighs; the female does not' – but this may not be a consistent feature. The young soon became good talkers and were very tame and gentle. The pair bred in an enclosure which measured only 1.2 m (4 ft) square and 60 cm (2 ft) high.

The Slender-billed Parrakeet was bred in Sweden in 1978 by H. Hammerich. Three birds were imported in 1977, one of which died. The surviving pair was housed in an indoor cage measuring 91 × 60 cm (3 × 2 ft) × 91 cm (3 ft) high. It was placed in the living room where the Slender-bills soon became used to the presence of cats and a dog. The female laid her first egg on May 12. The clutch consisted of three eggs. They hatched on June 7, 9 and 12. On August 2, two young left the nest and returned at night. The third chick was helped out on August 10. It was not as well developed as its nest-mates and died at the end of October. The young were reared mainly on hard-boiled egg – three to four eggs being consumed daily. No difference in plumage was noted in the adult male and female.

Blaauw noted that his Slender-bills delighted in digging up the turf in their aviary. In the wild they are known to forage on the ground for seeds and to dig up bulbous roots. Acorns are said to form part of the diet but my Slender-bills have shown no interest in them.

I was extraordinarily lucky to obtain two of these interesting birds which, at the time, were the only pair in Britain and possibly in Europe. The original bird, a female, was obtained by the late Mrs N. Howard of Wolverhampton.

Two years later a male was obtained on loan from London Zoo, but he proved to be an egg-eater. After commercial importations commenced I obtained two more, in 1981, plus an aviary-bred bird, a gift from Tony Silva. Surgical sexing proved all three were males. Sadly, my original female had died in 1979.

In 1981, the first breeding of the Slender-billed Conure occurred in Britain, at Chester Zoo. Three were reared and I bought one of the surgically sexed female youngsters in October 1983. When she was compared with the four males, her smaller head and bill were obvious features. In March of the following year, she was moved with one of the imported males to an aviary which measures about

180 × 91 cm (6 × 3 ft) × 180 cm (6 ft) high. Both birds were wormed and the male passed about 20 *Ascaridia* worms; the female had none.

The female had laid four eggs by June 18, one of which was broken. I had never seen the two birds show any interest in each other – but the eggs were fertile. When the nest was inspected on July 7, there were two chicks; the third hatched on July 9 or 10. For the first few days, the female rarely left the nest and growled like a Grey Parrot when the inspection door was opened. I heard no sound from the chicks until they were about six weeks old; their food soliciting call was then not unlike that of an Amazon Parrot, but quieter. However, they had been heard to chorus in unison on several occasions when the nest was inspected at an earlier age.

During the second week of their lives, the weather was so warm that the female sat outside the nest during the day. Inside the nest, the heat caused the chicks to separate into the corners. The hot weather continued and, in the third week, the chicks were not even brooded at night.

The chicks resembled those of *Pyrrhura* conures, except for the slightly elongated upper mandible, and the denser down. The bill was dark on the

Slender-billed Conures, three young (left) and their parents, bred by the author.

upper mandible with the raised pads and the tip horn-coloured; the lower mandible was horn-coloured and grey. The second down was light grey, except at the point where the preen gland would be where there was a very small area of brownish yellow down with a white tuft in the centre.

The chicks were well fed with crops bulging at all times. Food consumption by the adults was enormous: large quantities of soaked sunflower seed, sprouted mung beans, sweetcorn and wholemeal bread and milk with Collo-Cal D added. Smaller quantities of apple, celery, peas-in-the-pod and Cheddar cheese were eaten.

By July 21, the secondary flight feathers and tail feathers had started to erupt in the older chick and the feathers of the forehead and scapulars were on the point of erupting. The red colouration on the forehead was apparent in the first two chicks by July 31.

The chicks were a joy to handle, never attempting to bite or struggle. By August 8, they were well covered with feathers and the barred markings on the forehead were apparent in the eldest. The youngest still had the feathers of the nape and part of the mantle enclosed in their sheaths. The first chick left the nest on August 22. Quite fearless, it would nibble my fingers. The second youngster left the nest on August 29 and the third three days later. The last two appeared in the aviary only briefly until the second week in September when they remained out all day. They returned to the nest at night.

Also in 1983, Chester Zoo reared 11 young from two pairs. In Czechoslovakia, two were reared in Prague Zoo (Hylas, pers. comm., 1984).

It is interesting to watch this species drink for it tips the head right back with a movement which is reminiscent of a pigeon drinking. The water container needs to be wide and not too shallow.

Hybrids from a male Slender-bill and a female Nanday Conure were bred in 1977 in the aviaries of Francis Wenke of Bellingham, Washington, USA. He obtained the Slender-bill in Chile in 1972 and kept it as a pet.

In the late summer of 1976, he introduced it to the Nanday. Later, the birds were transferred to a large out-door cage with a nest-box measuring 31 cm (12 in) square and 41 cm (16 in) high. The Nanday laid the first of two eggs on December 7; both proved to be infertile. On February 4, 1977, the female laid again and two more eggs were produced at two-day intervals. Chicks hatched on March 1 and 3.

Despite the difference in the shape of the beaks of the two birds, the male had no difficulty in feeding the female. When the chicks were well feathered the female started to pluck them – and herself. This was apparently done to line the bottom of the nest for, when shavings were placed in the bottom of the box, the plucking ceased. The young hybrids left the nest when 60 days old, on April 29 and May 1. While they were in the nest the adults took the usual seeds and greenfood, also sweet corn and a small portion of Granola (mixed cereal containing nuts, etc.).

Photographs of one hybrid, taken when it was about one year old, show that it resembled a Slender-bill to such a degree that in a black-and-white photograph it would probably be mistaken for this species. However, its plumage was entirely different. The forehead was red, brightest near the lores and the crown was dull blue. The primaries were blue and the tail green with a bronze tinge. The rest of the plumage was green, more yellowish below, with a mere hint of red on the thighs. A large area of bare white skin encircled the eyes.

Cyanoliseus
Cyanoliseus

The only member of this genus, the Patagonian Conure is a large and beautiful conure of elegant proportions. It cannot be confused with any other bird. Unlike most conures, it has the cere feathered.

Patagonian Conure
C. patagonus

Description: The head, neck and back are dark olive-brown tinged with green; the throat and breast are greyish brown, with some white on the upper breast. There is an area of bright red and yellow on the abdomen: the centre and the thighs are orange-red, the rest of the abdomen, also the rump and upper tail coverts being yellow. The wings are olive-green with the primaries and primary coverts blue. The upper surface of the tail is olive-green, the central feathers having a bluish tinge along the middle; the under surface is brown and the under tail coverts are olive-yellow. The beak is black and the iris is white. An area of bare white skin surrounds the eye.

Immature birds have the upper mandible white and the iris pale grey. The beak colour changes from the sides, inwards, finally creating a narrow white line down the culmen.
Range/Habitat: This species is known from central Chile, northern and central Argentina and may also inhabit Uruguay.

In some parts of its range, its numbers have been drastically reduced by the activities of man. To make matters worse, in Chile, the chicks of this species are regarded as a delicacy, and chicks too young to eat and eggs are destroyed by the hooks on poles used to remove chicks from their nests. In Chile, it is now protected by law but is still persecuted in other parts of its range. Italian aviculturist Paolo Bertagnolio (1973) wrote:

> Argentine economy, beside cattle breeding, is largely based on growing wheat, maize and sunflower and orchards to which Parrakeets such as the Patagonian and the Quaker represent a constant menace.
>
> For this reason the extermination of the birds is carried out at every level and with every medium under the supervision of a government Central Committee for the 'Fight against the Parrakeets'.

Thus the Lesser and Andean Patagonian Conures have also had their numbers drastically reduced.

Lesser Patagonian Conure
C. p. patagonus
Description: The whitish markings are usually confined to the sides of the upper breast. Length: about 43–46 cm (17–18 in).

Patagonian Conure (*Cyanoliseus patagonus*).

make a most worthwhile project of building up aviary-bred strains of this lovely bird. Its pleasing colouration and proportions make it, in my view, one of the most desirable of the parrakeets from South America; regrettably, its loud, harsh voice makes it undesirable for many collections.

Patagonian Conures will breed on the colony system, but results are more likely to be obtained from pairs housed individually. At Rode Tropical Bird Gardens, England, Donald Risdon has found that in a colony only one or two pairs lay and the young are attacked by the other occupants of the aviary as soon as they leave the nest. When kept on their own the original breeding pair – the parents of all the other birds – rear three or four young.

Many visitors to Rode have seen the tame Patagonian Conure at liberty. It was attacked when it left the nest and had to be removed from the aviary. Mr Risdon (1975) wrote:

My wife took it over and under her care it has become an affectionate if noisy pet. It takes daily flights around the garden and returns to her wrist when called, as well behaved as a trained falcon. Incidentally, these birds have a remarkably hawk-shaped silhouette when in flight.

Patagonian Conures are such friendly and intelligent characters that I had long cherished the notion of letting our colony of nine fly at day liberty. Accordingly a special trap section was designed in part of their aviary so that one bird at a time could be released and could return without letting the others out. I was thankful that we took this precaution, for the first one made two circuits round the tree tops and disappeared and was located two days later 60 miles away.

In their natural habitat, Patagonian Conures utilise holes in sandstone cliff faces for nesting. In captivity, they will use a nest-box or a natural log. Two or three eggs are laid. R. Nelson of Oregon, USA, recorded that the two eggs produced by the female of his pair in 1972 were laid, exceptionally, seven days apart. In display, the male drew himself up and snapped his beak loudly. He would then strut along the perch. The female also indulged in beak-snapping. The male was not seen to enter the nest until a chick was heard. Four days later, the chick was

Greater Patagonian Conure

Description: In some specimens, the white on the upper breast forms an almost unbroken band and is usually more extensive than in the Lesser Patagonian Conure.

The yellow and red on the abdomen are usually brighter and the yellow more extensive. It is the largest subspecies, measuring about 53 cm (20 in).

Andean Patagonian Conure

Description: This race has little or no yellow and less red on the abdomen and no white on the upper breast. The plumage is duller. It is approximately the same size as the nominate form.

Aviculture: This conure usually proves willing to nest in captivity, thus aviculturists in the fortunate position of having no close neighbours could removed for hand-rearing. It was described as responding like a baby macaw, never being moody or nipping as do some hand-reared parrots when they reach the weaning stage. Subsequently, it made a delightful pet. In 1973, three young were reared.

In Britain, the Patagonian Conure was first bred by W. R. Partridge of Evesham. His pair destroyed the nest-boxes supplied in 1961 and 1962. The following year they nested in a 75 cm (29 in) high hollowed-out log of very hard wood. The inside measured approximately 23 cm (9 in) in diameter and was lined with chippings chewed from the log. Three eggs were laid and the incubation period was believed to be 24 or 25 days. The eldest two youngsters left the nest when they were about eight weeks old; the third two days later. In this case also, it was recorded that the male did not enter the nest until the chicks hatched. The only addition made to the usual diet of sunflower and canary seed and apple was bread and extra spinach beet. R. Nelson's pair consumed bread, groats, soaked corn and fresh corn-on-the-cob, while feeding young. Fruit and vegetables remained untouched. The normal seeds – sunflower, safflower, cracked corn, wheat, oats, millet and canary seed – were also eaten.

In 1973, a pair owned by Paolo Bertagnolio of Rome hatched three young. The third was hand-reared because of its small size. Four birds were housed together in a flight measuring 5 × 1 × 2.5 m (16 × 3 × 8 ft). The pair reared two more in 1974, three in 1975, six (one hand-reared) in 1976, three in 1977 and four in 1978. Three young reared in 1973 and one reared in 1974 produced two young in 1976 and two in 1977. It is of interest that young bred by Dr Alberto Guerra, another Italian aviculturist, produced chicks in the year after they were hatched. Patagonian Conures have reared young in a number of zoos in recent years, including Chester (England), Arnhem (Netherlands), Magdeburg and West Berlin (Germany), Loro Parque (Tenerife), Vienna (Austria), Prague (Czechoslovakia) and San Diego (California). In Italy, Paolo Bertagnolio has reared two races – *patagonus* and *byroni*.

Betty Byers (1984) recorded the weight of this species on hatching as 10 g ($\frac{2}{5}$ oz) and on fledging as 225 g (9 oz). Also in California, Ed Shoemaker believes that the Patagonian Conure should be classified with the Dwarf Macaws. He hand-reared this species simultaneously with the Yellow-collared Macaw and found it difficult to distinguish the two species until they started to feather.

Myiopsitta
Myiopsitta

The single member of this genus, the Quaker Parrakeet, is distinguished by its grey breast, feathered cere and robust bill. It is, perhaps, the best known of all the parrakeets from South America.

Quaker (Monk or Grey-breasted) Parrakeet
M. monachus

Description: It has the lores, throat and cheeks grey and the grey feathers of the breast are tipped with white; the abdomen is greyish green. Upper parts are a medium shade of green, brightest on the wings and tail. The forehead and most of the crown are pale greenish grey. Primary feathers are blue and black. The under wing coverts are pale grey and pale bluish and the thighs are bright green. Under surface of the tail is pale green, with pale blue on the outer edge. The bill is pale brownish and the iris is dark brown. Length: 29 cm (11 in). The upper mandible is usually broader in the male and the head noticeably bolder. Weight: about 150 g ($4\frac{3}{10}$ oz).

Immature birds have the grey forehead tinged with green.

There is a most attractive Blue mutation which is well established in captivity; like the Blue Ringneck Parrakeet, it commands an extremely high price. Most of the Blues in existence today are descendants of those bred by Belgian aviculturist, M. J. Bruyneel. On his death in 1959, nine Blues were sold for the total sum of £53. At the time of writing, a single Blue would command many times that figure.

Those attempting to breed from this

Quaker Parrakeet (*Myiopsitta monachus*).

mutation should note that poor results – or none at all – are obtained when it is attempted to pair together two Blues.

Blue Quakers are a pleasing shade of soft blue except for the cheeks, throat and upper breast which are white. The bill is pale orange.

The Yellow mutation is even rarer than the Blue. It first occurred in Berlin Zoo before World War II. Good examples are very beautiful, being pure yellow above with the forehead and under parts greyish white. The primaries are greyish and the underside of the tail is bluish green. The beak is pinkish brown.

Range/Habitat: It is found in central

Bolivia and from southern Brazil to central Argentina. This is the only parrot which invariably builds its own nest, due to the scarcity of trees over much of its habitat. A very sociable species, it nests in large colonies. The nests are skilfully constructed from lengths of twigs which are firmly woven, suspended from the ends of branches. No lining is used. The entrance to the nest is usually on the under side; if at the side, a protective eave is added. A number of pairs will build on the original nest until the structure houses many pairs and can weigh as much as a quarter of a ton. A common bird, it is often found in large flocks.

M. m. luchsi
Description: Of the four races recognised only this one differs markedly in lacking the barred effect on the upper breast.
Range/Habitat: Cochabamba Province in central Bolivia is the extent of this bird's distribution. It is said to be locally distributed and rare.

Aviculture: This species has a long history in aviculture and has always been inexpensive. In many ways it is most attractive but it is also noisy and destructive.

It has been bred in Europe for over one hundred years: in Vienna in 1867; at Berlin Aquarium between 1869–1873; in France in 1876 and in England in 1887. In the USA, San Diego Zoo bred Quaker Parrakeets in 1930; in Australia, Edward Hallstrom reared young in 1948.

Quaker Parrakeets can be bred quite successfully on the colony system if the aviary contains no unmated birds. Because of their nesting habits, a colony is of absorbing interest.

In captivity it is easy to persuade the birds to build a natural nest, a few twigs woven together and a wire mesh base as a foundation. A plentiful supply of cut twigs must be offered; willow and privet are suitable, being pliable. Alternatively, Quakers will use a nest-box – but twigs will still be utilised. One disadvantage of their nesting habits from the aviculturist's viewpoint is that nest inspection may be very difficult or impossible.

Five to seven eggs are laid. Young leave the nest when aged six to seven weeks. Quakers are prolific birds.

This species can be offered the usual seeds, fruit and fresh vegetables and greenfood. Canary rearing food and bread and milk can be offered to birds rearing young. Its voice is its principal drawback, otherwise it can be recommended to the beginner, being hardy and entertaining. In the USA, hand-reared birds are occasionally offered for sale and make most attractive pets. One such bird started to talk even before it was weaned on to hard seed. It should be remembered that because of their strong beaks, Quakers must never be housed in an aviary constructed of wire netting which can be destroyed with ease. Welded mesh, 16 gauge or stronger, should be used.

A number of aviculturists have found that Quaker Parrakeets thrive at liberty and have gained much enjoyment from keeping them in this manner. They have proved even more prolific than when kept in an aviary. However, in many areas this method of keeping them would not only arouse the disapproval of neighbours because of the damage they can do to trees and fruit crops but is also illegal.

In some parts of the USA, escaped birds have established feral populations, taking over the ecological niche left vacant when the Carolina Parrakeet became extinct in 1918. Breeding activities have been reported from colonies in south-eastern New York, New Jersey and Connecticut and nests have been found in Massachusetts, Virginia and Florida.

Bolborhynchus
Bolborhynchus

Of the five small, indeed tiny, parrakeets which comprise this genus, only the Lineolated Parrakeet is well known. The Aymara or Sierra Parrakeet is occasionally available and the remaining three are very rare in aviculture. Their small size and quiet voices make them ideal for even a flat-dweller and they rival all other parrots in this respect, with the exception of the Hanging Parrots, although even their

feeding habits cause problems when kept indoors.

The rather thick, swollen-looking bill is typical of the members of this genus. Only one species, *aurifrons*, is sexually dimorphic.

The members of this genus have aroused the interest of few British or American aviculturists; in Europe, however, especially Denmark, the Netherlands and Germany, repeated successes and second generation breedings have occurred. Dutch aviculturist, the late Mrs Spenkelink (1981) kept all the races of *lineola*, *aymara* and *aurifrons* during the late 1970s and early 1980s. She described *Bolborhynchus* as:

> . . . charming, small agile birds, always chirping softly. They go into their nest-logs before dusk and stay there overnight. This is very important in the winter, when there is always the possibility that their toes might freeze.

On the subject of diet she wrote:

> The *Bolborhynchus* feed on a mixture of seeds – millet – and like fruit and vegetables of all kinds.
> In addition to this, the Barred Parrakeet likes some sunflower seed, the Sierra Parrakeet likes hemp, and the Mountain Parrakeet likes weed seeds.

Aymara (Sierra or Andean) Parrakeet
B. aymara
Description: In size and shape it is not unlike a wild Budgerigar. Its colours are muted: forehead, crown and upper ear coverts are dark brownish grey; the cheeks, sides of the neck and upper breast and throat are whitish grey. Upper parts are dark green and the under parts are light yellowish green. There is a bluish tinge on the primary coverts, on the flights which are dusky grey and on the central tail feathers. The bill is whitish. Length: 20 cm (8 in). The tail is long. Weight: about 45 g (1½ oz).

Some aviculturists have noted that males have darker grey on the crown and that the breast is more silvery.

Immature birds resemble adults. It is worth noting that when Aymara Parrakeets were bred at Keston Foreign Bird Farm in 1964, W. D. Cummings stated that the young could be sexed more easily when they left the nest

Aymara or Sierra Parrakeet (*Bolborhynchus aymara*).

Golden-fronted or Mountain Parrakeet (*Bolborhynchus aurifrons*) – male.

establish this attractive and prolific little bird. Now that it is no longer imported, in Britain there is a demand for it which cannot be met. It has been established in Denmark; Flemming Nielsen, for example, reared 48 in four years up to 1984, producing fourth generation young. He knew of 50 young reared in Denmark in 1984.

Aviary-bred specimens have every possible virtue, in addition to being very willing to nest; they are quiet with a pleasant finch-like twitter and do not need a large aviary, although it is enjoyable to see them flying in an aviary of reasonable size.

In common with other parrots which come from the high Andes, this species does not adjust readily to a lower altitude. Losses with newly imported birds are high – yet another reason for those fortunate enough to own these appealing little parrakeets to make a concerted effort to breed from them.

Golden-fronted (Mountain) Parrakeet
B. aurifrons
Description: This is a dainty little bird. It is readily distinguished from the other members of its genus by the yellow in its plumage. The forehead, lores, throat and part of the cheeks are yellow in the male. The female is mainly green, being tinged with yellow on the forepart of the cheeks, the throat and the sides of the breast. The plumage is otherwise green, darker above; in the male the under parts are more yellow and the cheeks are emerald green. According to Mrs Spenkelink van Schaik (1981), this race can be distinguished by the 'yellow' legs with just a black tinge'.

In all races, the outer webs of the primaries are violet-blue and the tail is bluish grey below. The bill is horn-coloured and the iris is brown. Length: 18 cm (7 in). Weight: about 45 g (1½ oz).

Immature birds resemble the female.
Range/Habitat: Golden-fronted Parrakeets are found on coastal plains, high plateaux and Andean slopes to over 4,000 m (13,000 ft) in central and southern Peru, central Bolivia, northern and central Chile and north-western Argentina. These birds have been observed entering nesting burrows. Two burrows excavated in an

because the males had 'distinctive silver breasts and darker caps'.
Range/Habitat: The Aymara Parrakeet inhabits the eastern slopes of the Andes, being found between 1,200 m and 4,000 m (4,000 and 13,000 ft) in an area from central Bolivia south to north-western Argentina. One ornithologist recorded finding this species nesting in a hole excavated in an earth bank and Brian Woods (pers. comm.) observed about ten of these birds nesting in a 3 m (10 ft) high cactus. He wrote that: 'The nesting holes were neat, round openings in the body of the cactus which was surrounded by low spine bushes – a truly impenetrable combination'. This location was about 80 km (50 miles) from La Paz at the height of about 3,000 m (10,000 ft). A fairly common species, its habitat includes settled and cultivated areas.
Aviculture: In 1959 Gerald Durrell, now director of Jersey Wildlife Preservation Trust, obtained eight in a bird market in Mendoza where large numbers were offered for sale. He was quite unaware that they were unknown in aviculture. However, it was not long before dealers began to obtain them. In 1961, perhaps before, some specimens reached Europe and in that year

they were bred in Denmark by B. Stenstrup of Nysted. Aymara Parrakeets were reared in Jean Delacour's collection at Clères, France, in 1963 and in Germany by K. Müller of Bad Homburg in 1965.

In Britain, this species was reared in 1962 by A. V. Marques; one youngster left the nest. Subsequently, some pairs have proved most prolific. The usual clutch consists of seven to ten eggs and there are several records of six or seven young being reared in one nest. In 1976, D. Lewis of London reared eight young in one nest.

A female belonging to another aviculturist laid 12 eggs, eight of which hatched. The first four died and the survivors were 'bitten to pieces' by the male when they were four weeks old. Newly hatched chicks are lightly covered with whitish down; by the time they are two weeks old the down is thick and blue-grey. They leave the nest when seven weeks old, when they resemble the adults except for the shorter tail.

A nest-box for this species should measure about 23–25 cm (9–10 in) square and 31 cm (12 in) deep.

It is regrettable that aviculturists did not make more of the opportunity to earth bank were found to consist of an upward sloping tunnel about 2 m (6½ ft) long, leading to two chambers, the first containing the eggs. It is fairly common over most of its range.

B. a. robertsi
Description: The under parts of the male are darker green without the yellow tinge; the chin and throat are bright yellow. According to Mrs Spenkelink van Schaik (1981), who had kept all the subspecies, it is of a heavier build than the nominate race, the male has black legs and a yellowish bill and the female has black legs and a dark bill.
Range/Habitat: North-western Peru.

B. a. margaritae
Description: The notable fact about this race is that both male and female are similar to the female of the nominate race. It is the most heavily built of the three races. Mrs Spenkelink van Schaik (1981) describes it as having a shorter tail and lighter bill and legs than other races.
Aviculture: Vogelpark Walsrode has exhibited this race.

The first European breeding of this subspecies is that which occurred in Denmark during 1977. Originally the adults were incorrectly identified as *B. andicolus*. In January of that year, Jan Sorensen and Arne Sparrebo obtained a pair from a dealer. On February 13 there were two eggs in their nest-box, laid on sphagnum moss. The clutch consisted of five eggs, three of which contained dead chicks. In April the female laid again; young were heard in mid-May and a single chick left the nest four weeks later. Food provided consisted of seed (some germinated), carrot and various other items, including dog biscuit, chickweed and dandelion. Fruit was not eaten. It has also been bred in Sweden.

B. a. rubrirostris
Description: According to Mrs Spenkelink van Schaik (1981):

The mature cock has a reddish horn-coloured bill and the hen a dark grey horn-coloured bill. The legs of the cock are lighter than those of the hen. This subspecies has a dark blue-green back and a brighter, blue-grey front and abdomen. The bigger girth of the breast gives this bird a compact appearance.

Range/Habitat: It occurs in north-western Argentina, mainly on the eastern slopes of the Andes, and on the western slopes in central Chile.
Aviculture: After two years of observation, Mrs Spenkelink van Schaik reached the conclusion that *rubrirostris* has more in common with *aymara* than with *aurifrons* – in behaviour, outward appearance (both species have greyish blue in their plumage) and in their choice of foods.

In 1977, Mrs Spenkelink van Schaik bought five pairs of *rubrirostris*. By the spring of the following year, only one male and two females had survived. One female nested in a log, making a well-formed depression in wood chips. She was unfortunately found dead on two eggs, which were placed in an incubator. Within ten days, the male had paired with the second female who laid five eggs. She did not incubate very conscientiously so the eggs were placed under an Elegant Parrakeet, together with the two eggs from the incubator. Six chicks were hatched over a period of 16 days. When the eldest chick was 30 days old (that is, the age at which the Elegants' young would be leaving the nest), their foster-parents fed them less, so the *rubrirostris* chicks were transferred one by one to the nest of another pair of Elegants which had younger chicks, their own chicks being fostered among other Elegants. Two days later the youngest *rubrirostris* died, so the older chicks were given supplementary feeds to allow the foster-parents to cope better with the younger chicks. After 53 days, the eldest chick left the nest; the youngest three left the nest at 56 days. Five were reared. The female *rubrirostris* nested again; four eggs were laid and three chicks were reared. This occurred in an outdoor aviary as it was found that members of this genus breed better outdoors.

Aviculture: Few Golden-fronted Parrakeets have reached Europe and most of these have survived only a short time, such as the consignment of 30 birds which reached Sweden in 1972. Experiences suggest that this species is not suitable for aviculture and that it should not be exported.

A German aviculturist, Herr Streimer, was probably the first to breed this attractive little bird in captivity. His pair was obtained in a consignment of White-winged Parrakeets in 1967. He placed them in a cage where they instantly disappeared into a Budgerigar nest-box. Three weeks later an egg was laid – the first of three. Twenty-three days later a chick was heard. After five days, a dead chick was found on the cage floor. The two survivors were successfully reared. Nine days later, the female laid again – with even greater success; seven chicks were reared.

In Denmark, this species was bred by Erik Keszler. So small and inoffensive is it, that he kept his pair with finches and waxbills. They inspected a number of nest-boxes and were observed mating. Having read that the closely related *orbygnesius* digs deep tunnels into earth in which it nests, Keszler fixed a wooden tunnel 5 cm (2 in) square and 91 cm (3 ft) long to the front of the nest-box. The box measured 31 cm (12 in) deep and 15 cm (6 in) square. The upper section had a hole in one corner leading to the lower section. When they were presented with the box in January 1970 they failed to find the entrance; a hole was therefore cut in the upper side of the entrance tube, 25 cm (10 in) from the entrance to the box. Three days later they went inside and on February 27 a chick was heard. Four were reared.

Streimer fed his pair on hemp, sunflower and grass seed, apple, carrot, banana, orange and greenfood. Cod-liver-oil food and grated carrot were provided when the young hatched.

Lineolated (Catherine or Barred) Parrakeet
B. lineola
Description: It is immediately recognised by the barred markings, absent only on the forehead, cheeks, ear coverts, throat and under parts which are light green. The feathers are edged with black on the nape, the sides of the

neck, extending beneath the wings to the flanks and rump and the edges of the tail coverts. The black margins become broader towards the tail and on the rump, to give a pronounced barred effect. In some specimens, the feathers of the crown and ear coverts are narrowly edged with black. There is a black patch on the shoulders and the smaller wing coverts are broadly edged with black, the secondaries and primaries narrowly so. Faint barring marks the area of the vent and the flanks have a brownish tinge. The tail is short and pointed. Bill is pinkish flesh coloured and the iris is dark grey, giving the eye a bold appearance. Length 16 cm (6½ in). Weight: about 50 g (1¾ oz).

This species is not easy to sex and it would appear that the amount of barring in the plumage is no indication of sex; in some proved true pairs the plumage appears identical, or almost so, in male and female. In 1985, there was a Blue specimen in a collection in the Netherlands.

Immature birds are usually paler in colour and have a more pronounced bluish tinge on the forehead.

Californian aviculturist David West once possessed a Cinnamon bird of this species.

Range/Habitat: The Lineolated Parrakeet is found from southern Mexico south to western Panama (*B. l. lineola*) and further south in north-western Venezuela, the Andes of central Peru (*B. l. tigrinus*). The latter is darker in colour and more heavily barred. In Mexico this species is becoming scarce as its restricted habitat is gradually being destroyed. In some parts of its range it is very local in its distribution, being confined to cloud forest. It also occurs in sub-tropical forest, usually over 1,500 m (5,000 ft).

Aviculture: This is a charming little bird: quiet, inoffensive, attractively marked and very willing to nest when kept on the colony system. It is irregularly imported in small numbers. Despite the warnings of writers of the earlier years of this century, it proves hardy, even though it does not roost in a nest-box. An enclosed shelter should therefore be provided. A pair formerly in my possession went into ecstasies of delight at their first sight of snow, hanging upside down from the perch,

Lineolated Parrakeet (*Bolborhynchus lineola*).

flapping their wings, then opening them wide. They seemed to have an intense dislike of sunshine. This species has a habit of moving slowly and stealthily along a branch, carrying itself almost horizontally, which is fascinating to watch.

Lineolated Parrakeets will feed on sunflower, hemp, white millet, spray millet and canary seed. My birds had a great liking for apple but could seldom be persuaded to try other fruit. Some will readily eat soft pear and grapes; they also like nectar and sponge cake and nectar.

Lineolated Parrakeets should never be housed with other parrots or with birds of any kind larger than themselves as they seem incapable or disinclined to protect themselves. They are one of the few parrots which do well on the colony system, however, and one breeder I know who has been consistently successful with this species, R. Oxley of Essex, has adopted this method. Pairs which I kept on their own did not make any attempt to breed and while single pairs have bred

successfully on a number of occasions, it is probable that the stimulus provided by others of their own kind is an incentive to breeding.

Some Lineolated Parrakeets nest readily in captivity and prove to be prolific; what is more, they will breed in a cage. A pair owned by M. G. Stern of Ropley, Hampshire, reared 34 young between November 1972 and May 1975. The clutches consisted of four or five eggs. The adults reared all the young hatched, a remarkable achievement. They were fed on sunflower and panicum millet, and groats were offered until the chicks were weaned. Chickweed, seeding grasses, twiggy branches of hazel and hawthorn, especially in bud, were relished. This varied diet must have played its part in the excellent results obtained from this pair.

The most comprehensive report on the breeding of this species was that by R. E. Oxley (1978): in 1974, four were reared; in 1975, two were reared and, in 1976, two were hatched but not reared. In 1976, three unrelated birds were obtained to add to the five surviving. In 1977, 14 young were reared. Two females shared one nest-box and 14 eggs were laid inside in May. Three chicks hatched but died, probably due to the fact that two young from the previous year insisted on roosting inside. Eighteen young were reared in 1978. Four emerged from the nest quite naked, having been plucked, at the end of October. They were removed to a flight inside a birdroom with their mother (the male parent could not be identified).

Ron Oxley recorded that the average egg size was 22 × 17 mm ($\frac{9}{10} × \frac{7}{10}$ in) and the incubation period 18 days; this is a shorter period than given by some other breeders and is allied to that of parrotlets. The chicks were close-ringed at 12 days with rings one size larger than those used for Budgerigars. In addition to seed, his birds ate Madeira cake soaked in nectar, apple and grapes (preferred to other fruit), chickweed, hard-boiled egg and a nutritious soft food.

Lineolated Parrakeets lay from three to six eggs. Newly hatched chicks possess a small amount of white down. They leave the nest when about five weeks old.

This species was bred in Britain as long ago as 1913; the single youngster reared by Miss M. Baker's pair drowned after it left the nest but before it became independent. It was probably not bred successfully until 1953 when A. A. Prestwich, secretary of the Avicultural Soceity, reared a single youngster. In 1957, three more were reared.

In the USA, the Lineolated Parrakeet was bred at San Diego Zoo in 1938. European successes include that of J. Dalborg-Johansen in Denmark in 1955 (three reared), in Sweden that of K. Stenholm in 1968 and, in the Netherlands, young were reared by E. Wessels of Rotterdam in1964 and 1965 and subsequently by Mr and Mrs Spenkelink. A consistent breeder in Denmark, since 1972, is Jørgen Hare of Hvidore.

Andean Parrakeet
B. orbygnesius
Description: It resembles a Lineolated Parrakeet which lacks the black barring, being all green, or a lighter and yellowish shade on the under parts. Forehead and lores of the male are tinged with yellow. The bill is greenish. Length: 17 cm (7 in). According to H. H. Jacobsen (pers. comm., 1984), the adults of Verner Jespersen have dark beaks and pale feet and nails, and the young have light beaks and nails. The bare skin around the eye is blue in adults.
Range/Habitat: This species inhabits the Andes of Peru and northern Bolivia. It should not be confused with the Aymara Parrakeet which is sometimes known as the Andean Parrakeet.
Aviculture: This little bird would pass unnoticed and unidentified by most aviculturists; nevertheless, it would seem that it has been exported on very few occasions.

This species has been bred in Denmark by Verner Jespersen of Silkeborg since 1982. It first reached Denmark in 1980; earlier reports were incorrect and the birds were later identified as *B. a margaritae*.

Rufous-fronted Parrakeet
B. ferrugineifrons
Description: It can briefly be described as resembling *orbygnesius* but has a narrow frontal band, lores and area surrounding the base of the lower mandible rufous. Length: 18 cm (7 in).
Range/Habitat: It is known only from the Central Andes of the temperate zone of Colombia in Tolima and Cauca where it inhabits scrub-covered mountain slopes. Its range is small and it is said to be rare.
Aviculture: Unknown in captivity.

Brotogeris
Brotogeris

The members of the genus are small birds with gradated, short or longish tails; they are mainly light green with a small area of colour on the chin, forehead or primaries and, in one species, on the under wing coverts. For the aviculturist, the most notable point of interest is the rarity of captive breeding records, especially when considered in conjunction with the fact that the members of no other neotropical genus of parrots – and possibly no other genus in the world – have been exported in such immense numbers. For many years, until the early 1970s, hundreds of thousands of White-winged Parrakeets, for example, were exported annually from South America.

Many of these were tame, young birds, destined to be bought as pets; however, some species have such harsh, often used and irritating voices that they have never become popular house pets, yet might well have done so if their voices were more attractive. *Brotogeris* parrakeets can learn to repeat a few words, but, generally speaking, are not renowned for their talking ability. Tame birds have been known to mimic sounds, including the calls of other parrakeets.
Feeding: Fruit should form a major part of the diet; berries such as those of elder and hawthorn can also be offered. The area of bare skin between their lower mandible and the sides of the face probably indicates that much fruit is taken in the wild because, if this area were feathered, it would become soiled. Few *Brotogeris* parrakeets consume greenfood with enthusiasm; nevertheless, it should be offered so that they have the opportunity to take vitamins in that form. All the usual seeds should be offered, with a full range of the smaller seeds, including niger and linseed. In their natural habitat, these birds feed on fruits (wild and cultivated), blossoms, nectar, seeds and other vegetable matter.
Accommodation: These small birds are very swift fliers and will make full use of a large aviary: however a pair can be housed in an enclosure 2.4–3.6 m (8–12 ft) long and 90 cm (3 ft) wide. A light but fully enclosed shelter should be provided as hardiness of these birds seems to vary with individuals and some look most uncomfortable in cold weather. If they do appear uncomfortable, it is advisable to house them in a frost-proof building during the winter months. This applies especially to birds which do not roost in their nest-box. A box or log should be left in position throughout the year for this purpose but, unlike most species of parrots, *Brotogeris* are unpredictable in this respect: some always roost in a box while others never do so.

All Green Parrakeet (*Brotogeris tirica*).

White-winged Parrakeet (*Brotogeris versicolorus versicolorus*).

These parrakeets are extremely enthusiastic bathers and must always have the opportunity to bathe in clean water. They will then maintain themselves in immaculate condition with a fine sheen to the plumage.

Breeding: Captive successes were few until the 1980s when Fred and Robbie Harris in California succeeded with most species except *tirica* which was not available (Harris, 1985).

All-green Parrakeet
B. tirica

Description: This bird is green tinged with brown on the bend of the wing and the upper wing coverts, with bluish on the hind neck and mantle and with dusky bluish on the under side of the tail. The bill is brownish, becoming horn-coloured towards the base. The iris is dark brown. The long tail accounts for half the total length of 23 cm (9 in).

According to Forshaw (1973), immature birds have the primary coverts, primaries and secondaries tinged with blue; the tail is shorter and the bill is darker brown.

A Blue mutation occurred in birds bred at Schönbrunn Zoo in Austria before World War I. Of an unspecified number of young in the first nest, two were Blues; two of four in the second nest were Blues. Two survived to adulthood and were sold to a lady in Budapest; she reared seven Blues which, with their parents, came to grief during World War I. In the early 1970s, a Blue was reported from Brazil.

The Museu Paulista in Brazil has two Blue specimens collected earlier this century in the Serra do Cubatao in São Paulo. Alvaro Rossman Carvalhães received Blues from the same region in the 1920s, purchased from a native who trapped them there. Carvalhães (and others) reputedly reared Blue young and still has their descendants – but no Blues (Silva, 1984b).

Range/Habitat: The All-green Parrakeet inhabits eastern Brazil from eastern Bahía and southern Goias to Rio Grande do Sul. It varies from being common, especially in open country and parklands, to uncommon.

Aviculture: Like other species endemic to Brazil, it is virtually unknown to aviculturists; probably it was imported more frequently a century ago.

The first recorded breeding occurred in Germany: Pastor Hintz reared nests of two and four in 1882 and more young in the following year.

The only detailed breeding account in avicultural literature would appear to be that by Dr L. Lovell-Keays (1914) who was the first to report rearing this species in Britain. He obtained two newly imported birds in the spring of 1914. Four eggs were laid at the beginning of June: the incubation period was 26 days and all the eggs hatched. The chicks' eyes opened when they were about 14 days old. On August 14, the first youngster left the nest and was described as differing from the adults only in its dark brown beak and in the 'short and almost square' tail. Six weeks later the young were indistinguishable from their parents. The remaining chicks left the nest on August 15, 17 and 19, when they were about six weeks old. At first they slept in a bare oak sapling but soon learned to seek cover at night.

Other breeders in Britain were

Wesley T. Page (three in 1918), and L. J. Praill (four in 1957). In Europe, this species was often available at the end of the nineteenth century and a number of breeding successes occurred in Germany. *Die Gefiederte Welt* reported young reared in 1886 (G. Graeff, two young), 1894 (Von Prosch, seven young in two years) and 1932 (Charlotte Rieck, nine young in two clutches which left the nest after five or six weeks). In Denmark, this species was first reared in 1961; six young were bred.

White-winged (Yellow-winged) Parrakeet

B. versicolorus versicolorus

Description: The distinguishing features of the White-winged Parrakeets are a greyish olive shade and a bluish grey around the eyes and forehead. The first four wing primaries are green, the rest are white, secondaries are white and their coverts yellow. The lores are only partly feathered, and it is the larger of the two best known races at 23 cm (9 in). Weight: 65 g ($2\frac{3}{10}$ oz).

Immature birds have a smaller area of white in the wing, with green tips to the white primaries; the secondary coverts are yellow, edged with green.

Range/Habitat: This species has a wide distribution over most of the Amazon drainage area, the nominate race being found in eastern Ecuador, north-eastern Peru, south-eastern Colombia, northern Brazil and French Guiana. Its status varies from common to uncommon in different localities.

The White-winged Parrakeet has been introduced into Lima, Peru, and it is probably this race which has been introduced to the island of Puerto Rico in the West Indies.

When I first visited the Leticia area of southern Colombia and saw large flocks of White-winged Parrakeets, I was mystified as to why the species did not appear in de Schauensee's *Birds of Colombia*.

I soon discovered that, a few years previously, an exporter had been forced to release a few thousand birds when the USA suddenly placed an embargo on the importation of parrots. They were thriving and possibly this was affecting the population of the *Brotogeris* indigenous to that area –

the Tui Parrakeet.

Canary-winged Parrakeet

B. v. chiriri

Description: Forshaw (1973) puts forward the interesting view that *versicolorus* and *chiriri* may be specifically distinct because three *chiriri* captured in northern Brazil almost within range of the nominate race showed no tendency towards the latter in colouration. However, the possibility that they were birds which had been captured and escaped must not be discounted. The two races are often confused but, in fact, are readily distinguishable. The Canary-winged, with its brighter, purer shade of green, is far more attractive. There is no white in the wing. The primaries and secondaries are green and the secondary coverts are yellow. The lores are fully feathered in *chiriri*. Weight: 60 g ($2\frac{1}{10}$ oz).

Range/Habitat: The Canary-winged Parrakeet is found in eastern and southern Brazil, northern and eastern Bolivia, Paraguay and northern Argentina.

B. v. behni

Description: It differs from *chiriri* in having the under side of the tail bluish green, instead of yellowish green, and in being larger.

Range/Habitat: This race is found in central and southern Bolivia.

Aviculture: For many years, this species was one of the more freely imported and inexpensive of all parrots. The vast majority of imported birds were destined to be caged as pets, although I suspect that most people would fairly soon seek a quieter replacement. As aviary birds, however, they are extremely attractive, especially in a spacious enclosure where, in flight, their plumage is shown to its greatest advantage. Many become very tame, which only adds to their owner's pleasure.

However, they do not breed readily; it seems that the necessary stimulus is usually lacking for few even attempt to nest. The breeding successes I can trace are amazingly few. In the USA, R.

Schmidt raised one youngster of the nominate race in 1930 from two eggs; San Diego Zoo bred it in 1959, 1960 and 1962 and, in Pennsylvania, Pittsburgh Conservatory Aviary reared three in 1971 and four in 1972. The Canary-winged Parrakeet was first bred in Britain by the well-known aviculturist, E. N. T. Vane. Five young were reared each year between 1954 and 1956. Mrs G. Narraway of London reared one youngster in 1970. The pair reared another in 1972 which left the nest after ten to 11 weeks. Two other pairs, including the female reared in 1970, laid eggs, but none hatched.

In Australia, C. C. Burfield was successful between 1967 and 1968 with a pair which had been in his possession for ten years.

In Bermuda, Hamilton Zoo reared four young in 1971.

No details of most of those successes were published and all that can be gleaned from the published reports is that between three and six eggs were laid, more usually five. The incubation period is 26 days. Chicks' eyes open during the third week and the feathers start to open during the fourth week. The beak is white at first but dark by the time of fledging. One pair consumed large amounts of seeding weeds while rearing their young, also fruit; another pair reared on bread and butter, seed, soaked groats and fruit. Young birds become independent within three to four weeks after leaving the nest.

In 1977, Brian G. Davis (1979) reared a single youngster in a cage measuring 120 × 40 × 40 cm (48 × 16 × 16 in), with a nest-box built into an upper corner. Four eggs were laid between April 8 and 16. Two hatched, the first on May 8 or 9. One chick survived and was sparsely covered with white down. The bill was dark horn colour. It left the nest when 45 days old when the bill colour was changing to light horn.

Mr Davis noted that this point was at variance with other breeders. During the rearing period, groats soaked in milk and moistened dog meal was eaten in addition to the usual diet of seed, plantain heads, apple and grapes.

Orange-flanked (Orange-winged) Parrakeet

B. pyrrhopterus

Description: This bird, called Grey-cheeked Parrakeet by Forshaw (1973) is immediately distinguished by its bright orange under wing coverts; its build is more solid than other members of the genus and the bill more prominent. It is the only member of the genus which has the cheeks grey. The top of the head is bluish green and the forehead greyish. The bill is horn-coloured and the iris is dark brown. Length: 20 cm (8 in). Weight: 54 g ($1\frac{9}{10}$ oz). Immature birds lack the blue tinge to the crown.

Range/Habitat: The Orange-flanked Parrakeet has the most limited range of any member of the genus; it inhabits south-western Ecuador to north-western Peru. In Peru, it is said to be rare and local; in Ecuador it is more numerous.

Aviculture: Until the early 1970s, this species was readily available in Europe; hand-tame young birds were frequently imported and were inexpensive. They made most attractive pets. As long ago as 1919, Dr L. Lovell-Keays described a male in his possession which was so tame he would often take it outdoors. As so often happens, the tamest bird may be alarmed at a strange sound or sight; Dr Keays' Orange-wing one day took off and disappeared into an 800-acre wood. Finding a small green bird under such circumstances would appear to be as impossible as finding the proverbial needle in a haystack; however, the little Orange-wing came to hand when called.

This species was first bred in Britain in 1925 by W. Lewis. Five young were reared in an aviary measuring 3.6 × 1.8 × 1.8 m (12 × 6 × 6 ft), which contained three other pairs of *Brotogeris* parrakeets and two pairs of Lovebirds – an unlikely combination; however, two of the young were soon killed by Peach-faced Lovebirds. The three survivors were removed to a flight cage. On fledging, they were paler than the adults and lacked the blue on the head.

M. J. Cope bred this species in Britain in 1969 inside a shed. They were kept in an enclosure measuring

Orange-flanked Parrakeet (*Brotogeris pyrrhopterus*).

2 × 1.2 m (6½ × 4 ft). No interest was shown in the nest-box until it was positioned so that light from the window no longer entered it. Rearing food consisted of soaked and sprouted seed, in addition to large amounts of fruit, especially apple.

Die Gefiederte Welt reported a breeding of this species in 1902 which probably occurred in Denmark. This was almost certainly a reference to successes of a pair owned by bird dealer A. Kristensen of Klejtrup. They were at liberty in his shop and bred in a nest-box hanging on the wall as long ago as 1898.

In the USA, the Orange-flanked Parrakeet was reared by A. R. Hood in 1935. Eggs were laid on June 19, 21, 22, 24 and 27. By July 21 four had hatched. Two were removed for hand-rearing when five weeks old and the

other two left the nest on August 26. The adults were very spiteful towards their keeper, while breeding. In Germany, Herr Schenk bred this species in 1982. In a cage measuring 90 × 70 × 50 cm (36 × 29 × 20 in) the female laid five fertile eggs. The first hatched after 26 days. The eldest youngster – one of five – left the nest after seven weeks.

Tovi (Bee-bee or Orange-chinned) Parrakeet

B. jugularis jugularis

Description: The feature which gives it the alternative name distinguishes it from the other members of the genus. However, the subspecies *B.j. apurensis* (not recognised by all taxonomists), from the Apuré region of Venezuela, lacks the orange chin spot. The Tovi

Parrakeet has no other bright colours. There is a large brown patch on the wing, extending from the shoulder, formed by the lesser and median coverts. The plumage is a paler shade of green below and is tinged with olive on the mantle and with blue on top of the head, lower back and rump and the upper surface of the tail. The primary coverts are violet, the under wing coverts greenish yellow and the under side of the flight feathers are bluish green. The bill is horn-coloured and the iris is dark brown. Length: 18 cm (7 in). Weight: 58 g (2 oz).

Immature birds are similar to adults.

Over one hundred years ago, a Blue specimen (with white throat spot) was seen in a wild flock.

Range/Habitat: The Tovi Parrakeet is found from south-western Mexico southward to northen Colombia and northern Venezuela. It is common in many parts of its range and may be found in small groups which unite to form large flocks. Arboreal termites' nests are sometimes used as nesting sites. Tovis are sociable when breeding and a number of pairs sometimes nest in the same tree. They are prolific birds and Alexander Wetmore recorded seeing eight nestlings taken from one nest.

Aviculture: Formerly regularly available, young Tovis were easily tamed and made attractive pets (in their less vociferous moments). Export restrictions have altered their avicultural status; at the time of writing they were distinctly uncommon.

Few breeding successes have been reported. Frau Greiner reared two in 1873 and three in 1874. The incubation period was given as about 22 days. In Australia, G. Staunton bred this species in 1930. It may be significant that the only consistent breeders, Mr and Mrs Vance Wright, kept their birds on a colony system. They started to breed this species in 1934; four years later they possessed a colony of over 50 which had been reared in their aviaries. In 1934, one was raised by hand from a clutch of nine eggs. In 1936, second generation young were bred. One of these reared a nest of five when only one year old. In 1938, a four year old hen produced eight young in one nest and another female reared a nest of six.

This species was bred at San Diego Zoo in 1960 and 1962; also in 1960, in the USA, Mrs Ruby Hood bred from a pair which were introduced into an aviary already containing one pair – an introduction with an element of risk. Four young were reared on wheat, cracked wheat bread which was toasted then soaked in water, and on fruit and the usual seeds.

In Denmark, the Tovi Parrakeet was bred by Jørgen Hare of Hvidore in 1982. One chick hatched on August 1 and left the nest on September 4. Rearing food consisted of apple, pear, orange, banana, dry figs, eggfood, greenfood and various seeds. They bred in a cage with access to a small outdoor flight.

Forshaw (1973) treats *cyanoptera* and *chrysopterus* as separate species but there would appear to be a good case for considering *cyanoptera* (the Blue-winged Parrakeet) and *jugularis* as subspecies of *chrysopterus*.

Cobalt-winged (Blue-winged) Parrakeet
B. cyanoptera

Description: The orange spot on the chin and violet-blue primaries and primary coverts distinguish this species. It is otherwise dark green, bluish on the crown, with the forehead and lores yellow. The under side of the tail is yellowish green. The upper mandible is brown, paler at the base, and the lower mandible brownish horn-coloured. The iris is dark brown. Length: 18 cm (7 in). Weight: 65 g ($2\frac{3}{10}$ oz).

Immature birds have the plumage duller; the beak colouration is different for the upper mandible is dark grey, almost black, near the base, and pink towards the tip and the lower mandible is pink (Harris & Harris, 1984c). Weight of a recently weaned bird was 61 g ($2\frac{1}{5}$ oz).

Range/Habitat: It occurs in the western basin of the Amazon from southern Venezuela, north-eastern Peru, south-eastern Colombia and eastern Ecuador south to north-western Bolivia. A low-land species, it is common throughout much of its range.

Aviculture: This species is rarely exported and not well known. In California, Fred and Robbie Harris obtained

two pairs in 1981. One year later, one female laid five eggs. The eggs were placed in an incubator; the first hatched after 24 days. The period from pipping to hatching was 38 hours. Two chicks hatched and were fed by Bourke's Parrakeets until they were eight and five days old and weighed 15 and 6 g ($\frac{1}{2}$ and $\frac{1}{5}$ oz) respectively. The youngest chick died at eight days; the other was successfully hand-reared. At 12 days, it weighed 18 g ($\frac{3}{5}$ oz) and its eyes were open. Its voice was loud and similar to that of an Orange-flanked Parrakeet. No second down was acquired. It weighed 25 g ($\frac{9}{10}$ oz) at 14 days and 40 g ($1\frac{2}{5}$ oz) at 26 days when the wing and tail feathers were starting to erupt. The feet were light grey. At six weeks it was fully feathered and at seven weeks it was eating soft foods and seed.

Golden-winged Parrakeet
B. chrysopterus chrysopterus

Description: It is distinguished by its orange primary wing coverts and brownish or brownish orange chin spot. There is a blackish brown frontal band and the cheeks are bluish green and the upper side of the tail is tinged with blue. The primaries are violet, tipped with green, the under wing coverts are green and the under sides of the flight feathers are bluish green. The bill is pale horn-coloured and the iris is dark brown. Length: 17 cm ($6\frac{1}{2}$ in). Weight: 62 g ($2\frac{1}{5}$ oz).

Immature birds have the primary coverts green, instead of orange.

Range/Habitat: This bird is found in eastern Venezuela and the Guianas as far south as the Amazon.

Tuipara (Golden-fronted) Parrakeet
B. c. tuipara

Description: This is probably the most attractive race and has a narrow frontal band and chin spot of orange. The lateral tail feathers are narrowly edged with yellow.

Range/Habitat: It inhabits the southern side of the Amazon River in northern Brazil.

Golden Parrakeet

B. c. chrysosema
Description: It has the forehead and lores yellowish orange, the chin spot orange and the primary coverts yellow. Length: 20 cm (8 in).
Range/Habitat: This race is found in Brazil in the area of the Madeira River and its tributaries in Amazonas and Mato Grosso.

B. c. tenuifrons
Description: It differs from *tuipara* in having the frontal band much reduced and brownish.
Range/Habitat: North-western Brazil.

B. c. solimoensis
Description: This race has a reddish brown frontal band and yellowish brown chin spot but otherwise resembles *chrysopterus*.
Range/Habitat: It inhabits northern Brazil in the Codajas and Manaus districts.

Aviculture: This species is little known in aviculture. It was exhibited at London Zoo as long ago as 1878 – and in 1888. The next reference to this species I can find is that by A. A. Prestwich who obtained four in 1952. In 1971, a dealer in England received a consignment of about 20 of these birds but it appears that none of them reared young and, as a Brazilian species, it is not likely to have been imported since then.

Tui Parrakeet (*Brotogeris sanctithomae sanctithomae*).

Tui Parrakeet

B. sanctithomae sanctithomae
Description: It is readily distinguished from the other *Brotogeris* parrakeets by its yellow forehead and forepart of the crown and by the chestnut-coloured beak. The under parts and under side of the tail are yellowish green. The iris is orange. Length: 17 cm (7 in). Weight: 58 g (2 oz). A white bird, said to be of this species, was offered to the 12th Duke of Bedford.
Range/Habitat: The Tui Parrakeet has a wide distribution over the Amazon basin. The nominate form inhabits eastern Amazonas, Brazil, westwards through south-eastern Colombia and north-eastern Peru to eastern Ecuador and northern Bolivia. It is common.

B. s. takatsukasae
Description: It is readily identified by the yellow streak behind the eye, a feature which was mistakenly considered as a sexual distinction by some aviculturists. The iris is brown.
Range/Habitat: This race is restricted to the Amazon region of Brazil.

Aviculture: It breeds either in termites' nests or in holes in trees. Considering how common this species is in its natural habitat and in captivity, prior to export restrictions, this must be one of the most neglected of all parrots for very little has been recorded about it and I can trace no account of it breeding in captivity. A German aviculturist, Herr Streimer (1968), made passing mention of the fact that he had bred Tui and Tovi Parrakeets in his account of the breeding of *Bolborhynchus aurifrons*.

It has been suggested that this species is less noisy than other members of the genus – but this did not apply to the single specimen which I kept. It was a rather nervous bird.

Forpus
Forpus

Parrotlets were kept in a menagerie in France, at Chantilly-Vineuil, as long ago as 1682. In more recent times, during the period following World War II and until the early and mid-1970s, they were freely available to aviculturists at very low prices. Although a number of breeding successes occurred, very few serious attempts were made to build up aviary-bred strains. This fact was not felt until quarantine and export restrictions severely curtailed the numbers imported and it was realised how few captive-bred birds there were available.

Parrotlets are easy and inexpensive to maintain; they nest readily, and adult birds can be sexed at a glance. Furthermore, they are small, not noisy, and do not need large enclosures. In many respects, their care is similar to that of Lovebirds and they can be thought of as their New World counterparts; indeed, many years ago the Blue-winged Parrotlet, a species which was freely imported, was occasionally referred to as the Blue-winged 'Lovebird'. Although parrotlets would be a suitable choice for the beginner to parrot-keeping, this must be influenced by availability and, at the time of writing, parrotlets are not regularly available.

Habitat: Parrotlets are found in a wide variety of habitats, from arid areas to dense tropical rainforest, in north-western Mexico and most of the tropical northern parts of South America. They are usually seen in flocks numbering from about 10 to 50 birds. They are opportunists with regard to nesting sites, utilising such unlikely situations as telephone poles, pipes, woodpecker holes, rafters in houses, fence posts and the mud nests of ovenbirds. No nesting material is used. Of nests observed in the wild, it has been reported that young fledged when between 20 and 30 days old. If this is so, parrotlets fledge earlier than any other parrot.

I have seen parrotlets in their natural environment in two very different kinds of habitat: in the area of the Amazon where southern Colombia meets northern Peru (in this locality they are wary and not easy to observe) and at the foot of the Eastern Andes of Colombia. In the latter locality, the Spectacled Parrotlets allowed approach within a few feet in the grounds of a hotel where I was staying while a kilometre away on agricultural land they were more wary. As they flew, they made a finch-like twittering sound.

Description: Parrotlets are small, measuring from 12 cm to 13 cm ($4\frac{3}{4}$ to 5 in), with the exception of the Yellow-faced Parrotlet which is about 14.5 cm ($5\frac{3}{4}$ in). They have small heads and comparatively small beaks. Males are green, lighter below, with deep blue or light blue on the wings or wings and rump; one species has yellow on the face. Females are all green or have some yellowish green in the plumage. Immature birds resemble the adults. Parrotlets have very short tails. The bill is horn-coloured, with the upper mandible partly dusky in some species.

Feeding: The natural diet of these birds consists of seeds of grasses and other plants, berries and fruits. Seeds form by far the largest part of the diet of captive parrotlets since these birds can seldom be persuaded to sample green-food and fruit, although some birds will take seeding annual grass (*Poa annua*). In separate containers, sunflower, canary seed, white millet, hemp and niger should be offered. Millet sprays will also be eaten.

While rearing young, parrotlets have been recorded as taking seeding grasses, spinach, lettuce, sprouted seed and soaked wheat.

Accommodation: While some parrotlets will breed successfully in cages, confined accommodation may result in a bird killing its mate, a most unfortunate occurrence which is common among caged parrotlets. This seems less likely to occur among birds kept in outdoor aviaries. Ideally, a pair of parrotlets should be given an enclosure of about 180 × 90 cm (6 × 3 ft) to themselves. Although they can be kept in a mixed collection of larger species, they will bully birds which are not aggressive: a pair of Celestial Parrotlets in my possession ousted a pair of Cockatiels from a 90 cm (3 ft) high nest-box simply out of mischief.

In a really large aviary, parrotlets can be kept and bred on the colony system. I recall with delight the sight of a flock of these birds in a huge planted aviary at Wassenaar Zoo in the Netherlands. For the person of average means, however, one pair per aviary is the system which is most likely to lead to breeding success. While there have been cases of parrotlets rearing young while housed with Budgerigars, this is not to be recommended as serious fighting is likely to occur during the breeding season. This applies also to housing them with Lovebirds. All these small species are extremely quarrelsome.

Aviaries for parrotlets can be constructed from 13 mm ($\frac{1}{2}$ in) wire netting or 25 × 13 mm (1 × $\frac{1}{2}$ in) welded mesh. Unlike most small neotropical parrots, they do not roost in a nest-box. The aviary should therefore include a dry and draught-free shelter. If the floor is of turf, the parrotlets will bathe in wet grass. They will also bathe in a water container.

The only instance I know of parrotlets being kept at liberty is of Guianas and Blue-winged kept by the 12th Duke of Bedford who experimented with many unusual species as liberty birds. He succeeded in breeding parrotlets when they were free-flying. They were housed in aviaries during the winter.

Breeding: Parrotlets can be sexed when they fledge but, although one can easily obtain a true pair, it can be very difficult to distinguish the species in females. One should ensure, as far as possible, that two parrotlets of the same species are paired together and careful reference to detailed descriptions or, better still, examination of museum skins, is well worthwhile. If young males bred do not take after their father in colouration, it is almost certain that the female is a different species from the male parent.

Parrotlets will accept Budgerigar nest-boxes which provide a rather larger floor area than these birds would use under natural conditions. One successful breeder of parrotlets uses a nest-box with a base only 8 cm (3 in) square. No nesting material is provided but the birds gnaw slivers of wood from inside the nest and the eggs are laid on these. Alternatively, one can use damp peat pressed well down, or a mixture of sawdust and soil as nesting material. Some birds take any-

thing available, such as torn-up newspaper, into the nest-box.

Parrotlets lay clutches of between three and eight eggs but normally there are four to six eggs. The hen incubates them although the male spends long periods inside the nest during the day and roosts inside at night. If a clutch does not hatch, the first egg of another clutch is laid seven to ten days after the previous eggs have been deserted.

Recorded incubation periods vary between 18 and 23 days. The longer period recorded may be due to the fact that the earliest laid eggs did not hatch. Observations in the wild have shown that the incubation period is 17 days.

On hatching, parrotlet chicks are almost naked with only a few white wisps of down which are lost after a few days. Their eyes open when they are approximately 12 days old. Development is rapid; quills start to open when the chicks are about 10 days old and at 20 days they are well covered with feathers and can be sexed. They leave the nest when aged between four and five weeks old, the longest period recorded being 'about 40 days'.

Parrotlets have been seen to feed themselves the day they leave the nest and adult birds have taken seed into the nest-box which the unfledged young would eat.

A close watch must be kept on the behaviour of the parents towards their newly fledged young because the adults sometimes attack them, causing grievous injuries. It seems that this is most likely to occur in a cage and, under these circumstances, it is wise to remove the young as soon as they are seen to be feeding themselves.

One breeder of Celestial Parrotlets found that, by placing the young birds indoors in a busy room in a pet Budgerigar cage a week after they left the nest, they quickly became tame. As a result, they were more amusing and vocal than untamed birds. A young parrotlet tamed in this way would make an excellent pet although untamed adult parrotlets are suitable only for an aviary.

Parrotlets will rear more than one nest of young in a season, using the same nest-box, and a reliable breeding pair will prove most prolific. Parrotlets

nest readily but although large clutches are laid, it is comparatively rarely that more than three or four young are reared. If well cared for these birds should reach more than ten years of age and there is a record of a male Spengel's Parrotlet which reared young (in Sweden) when 18 years old.

Reference to all but the most modern literature on parrotlets will prove confusing due to the fact that the scientific names have been changed. The original generic name was *Psittacula* which has long been applied to the Asiatic parrakeets of the genus which includes the Ringneck. Not only did this mean altering some of the specific names, but modern taxonomists have rearranged *Forpus* further.

Blue-winged Parrotlet
F. xanthopterygius (formerly *F. passerinus*)
Description: This bird was once the best known of the genus and was frequently imported during the early years of the twentieth century. The male has rich ultramarine blue on the lower back, rump, outer webs of the flight feathers, wing coverts and under wing coverts. The rest of the plumage is green, brighter around the eyes and ear coverts. The female is entirely green, more yellowish below and tending to yellow on the forehead and cheeks. The rump is emerald green. The feet are bluish grey, distinguishing the female from certain other parrotlets.
Range/Habitat: This species ranges from eastern Brazil to Paraguay and north-eastern Argentina. In Brazil, Blue, Fawn, Yellow, Pied and Lutino mutations have been seen.

Mexican Parrotlet
F. cyanopygius
Description: It has the rump, lower back, greater wing coverts and under wing coverts turquoise, a feature which distinguishes it from other male parrotlets. The shade of green is brighter above, lighter and more yellow below and yellowish on the forehead. The bill is whitish and the legs are greyish. Females are entirely green, often more yellow below than males and yellowish

Mexican Parrotlet (*Forpus cyanopygius*) – male.

Spengel's Parrotlets (*Forpus passerinus spengeli*) – female left, male right.

Spectacled Parrotlets (*Forpus conspicullatus*) – female left, male right.

green in the area where males are blue. George A. Smith who breeds this species told me that when males are in breeding condition, the beak takes on a silvery bluish hue.

Range/Habitat: It inhabits north-western Mexico.

Aviculture: Only occasionally imported, this species has never been common in aviculture. At the Arizona-Sonora Desert Museum, in Tucson, USA, eight young were reared in 1981.

Guiana (Green-rumped) Parrotlet

F. passerinus (formerly *F. guianensis*)

Description: The male is bright emerald green on the forehead, cheeks, lower back and rump and a greyer shade of green on the back of the head. The edge and bend of the wing are blue. The under wing coverts are brilliant dark blue. The female is green except for the forehead which is yellowish green, almost yellow in places. The beak is whitish and the legs are brownish.

Range/Habitat: This species is found in the Guianas, also in Jamaica, where it was introduced in the early twentieth century, and on Trinidad, where it is a common species.

Aviculture: The Guiana and the sub-species *F.p. spengeli* were fairly often available in the past. Both have been bred in captivity. In Brazil, Nelson Kawall keeps Cinnamon and Lutino specimens. He has also bred Blues.

Spectacled Parrotlet

F. conspicullatus

Description: The male can be distinguished by the blue feathering around the eye and by the blue-grey tinge to the breast. The legs are brownish. The female is entirely green, the upper parts being of a brighter shade than in the male; the area surrounding the eye, the lower back and the rump are emerald green. Immature males are said to have the area surrounding the eye emerald green and the blue on the rump and wings mixed with green.

Range/Habitat: This species is found in eastern Darien, Panama, Colombia and Apuré in Venezuela. A common bird, it is said to have benefited from forest clearance.

Aviculture: This species is now seldom available to aviculturists. The first recorded captive breeding occurred in the collection of Mrs R. Hood in California in 1931. Also in the USA, Vance Wright bred this parrotlet in 1934 and 1936. The most consistent breeder was Danish aviculturist Walter Langberg who reared 30 between 1965 and 1973. In Sweden, E. Ekman of Malmö bred two in 1970 and, in Britain, W. G. Carpenter of Swanton Morley, Norfolk, reared two chicks from five eggs in 1975.

Sclater's Parrotlet

F. sclateri

Description: Male and female are distinguished from other parrotlets by the

much darker shade of green. The lower back and rump, wing coverts and secondaries are brilliant cobalt, also the under wing coverts. The upper mandible is dark grey and the lower mandible is horn-coloured. The legs are greyish brown. The female is entirely green, with greenish yellow forehead and cheeks and yellowish green underparts.

Range/Habitat: This species is found in eastern Ecuador, eastern Peru, in the tropical zone of Colombia and in northern Bolivia and through Amazonian Brazil to southern Venezuela, Guyana and French Guiana. Its status varies from common to uncommon.

Aviculture: Although it is known to have been imported into Britain, it is rare in aviculture.

Celestial (or Pacific) Parrotlet

F. coelestis coelestis

Description: This is, perhaps, the most attractive species of *Forpus*. The male is a soft, silvery green, darker above and bright apple green on the crown and cheeks, with a touch of light blue behind the eyes. The lower back, rump, wing coverts and under wing coverts are brilliant cobalt blue. The beak is horn-coloured and the legs are brownish. The female has a hint of blue behind the eye and the rump is slightly bluish. She is otherwise green, duller than the male, paler on the

Celestial Parrotlet (*Forpus coelestis coelestis*) – male.

Yellow-faced Parrotlets (*Forpus coelestis xanthops*) – male above, female below.

breast and brighter green on the crown and cheeks.

Range/Habitat: This species comes from Ecuador and Peru. It favours arid areas and is a common species.

Aviculture: This parrotlet was bred in Peru by R. F. Losky in 1938 and by Jean Delacour in France in 1958. Formerly rarely exported, it has become one of the best known of the parrotlets since it became available in the early 1960s. In Britain, one of the first breeders was Mrs W. Boorer of London in 1963. Her pair hatched six young in a cage in her kitchen. One was killed before it fledged and two were injured by the parents, thus the young were separated from them as soon as they left the nest. Since then the Celestial has been reared on countless occasions. European successes include those of W. Grote (West Germany) in 1963 and A. Jensen (Denmark) in 1964.

Yellow-faced Parrotlet
F. c. xanthops

Description: At 14.5 cm (nearly 6 in) it is the largest member of the genus. The male differs from the Celestial in having the crown, face and throat lemon yellow, merging into yellowish green on the under parts. The upper parts are greyish green and the upper tail coverts, in addition to lower back, rump and wing coverts, are deep cobalt. The female has the rump light blue and grey under wing coverts tinged with light blue.

Immature birds are slightly duller with a dark line on the mandible.

Range/Habitat: This race is found in northern Peru in the upper Maranon valley. It is believed to be common, with a stable population.

Aviculture: This beautiful bird was introduced to aviculture in 1979. In Denmark, for example, 50 pairs were imported in the first consignment, in January 1980. The first breeder there was Jan Sorensen of Bronshoj. In the Netherlands, Mrs Spenkelink van Schaik reared six in 1981. Roy Girdler and Graham Austin (1982) purchased eight males and four females and placed ten of these on loan to the Midland Bird Garden in Shropshire. One died soon after purchase and another was killed in December of that year. In the following spring, they were placed in an outdoor aviary measuring 5 × 2 m (16½ × 6½ ft) × 2.3 m (7½ ft) high, built into a grass bank at the rear. They proved to be much steadier in the aviary. Their diet consisted of a mixture of seeds, also fruit, mainly apple.

The first of six eggs was laid on June 19, 1980. They were then offered a mixture of brown bread and condensed milk, soaked corn, currants, chopped cabbage, Prosecto insectile food, apple and SA37. This was not eaten until July 13 when the first chick hatched. All six hatched and left the nest at about 30 days. They were easily sexed in the nest by their rump colour: four males and two females.

Three more eggs were laid in mid-September; the average measurements were 21.5 × 16.8 mm ($\frac{4}{5} \times \frac{7}{10}$ in). This clutch was abandoned on September 25. All three females laid during October and three chicks hatched but were not reared. The nest-boxes were then removed. A young male was found dead, leaving six males and seven females. A pair housed separately made no attempt to breed.

This parrotlet continued to breed at Midland Bird Garden until 1984 when the collection was dispersed.

It has also been bred by Tom St Vaughan (1983). He recommended a nest-box measuring 13 cm (5 in) square and 19 cm (7½ in) high, with an entrance hole 3.8 cm (1½ in) in diameter. His female laid the first of five eggs on June 29. Four were fertile and four chicks hatched between July 23 and 29. The incubation period was 22 to 23 days and the young could be sexed at 32 days. They were two males and two females but one of the latter died in the nest. The first fledged at 42 days old when it was considerably smaller than the adults. These birds were fed on sunflower, canary and safflower seeds, mixed millets, oats, hemp, buckwheat, apple, celery, chickweed, bread and milk and CéDé rearing food. All were accepted.

In the USA, Mr and Mrs J. Lannom of California gained the American Federation of Aviculture award for the first breeding of this species in 1982.

Identification of Parrotlets (*Forpus*)

	·Lower back, rump, wing coverts	Other features
Males		
xanthopterygius	rich ultramarine blue	
cyanopygius	turquoise	
passerinus	bright emerald green back and rump; brilliant dark blue wing coverts	edge and bend of wing blue; emerald green forehead and cheeks
conspicullatus	brilliant cobalt	blue feathers around the eyes; blue-grey tinge to breast; darker green below
sclateri	cobalt (darker than other species)	
coelestis	brilliant cobalt	silvery green below; bright green on crown and cheeks; light blue behind eye
c. xanthops	brilliant cobalt	upper tail coverts deep cobalt; larger size than nominate race; crown, face and throat lemon yellow
Females		
xanthopterygius	emerald green	yellowish forehead and cheeks; feet bluish grey
cyanopygius	yellowish-green	feet greyish
passerinus	bright green	yellowish on forehead; legs brownish
conspicullatus	emerald green	area around eye emerald green; feet brownish
sclateri	dark green	greenish yellow forehead and cheeks; yellowish green underparts; feet greyish brown
coelestis	green; bluish rump	bluish behind eye; feet brownish
c. xanthops	bluish rump	bluish behind eye; feet brownish; larger than nominate race

24

Amazon Parrots

Amazon Parrots
Amazona

For those who like birds with distinctive personalities, Amazon Parrots are among the most rewarding of subjects. Many are extremely intelligent and for this reason they are always interesting in an aviary. If sympathetically cared for they can also make fascinating pets. Indeed few birds are superior as pets provided that the initial choice is made with care and the owner is prepared to put up with the regular daily periods of screaming which are natural to all Amazons. This point may limit the number of aviculturists who can keep them in aviaries since close neighbours may justifiably complain about the birds' vocal habits.

As a caged pet, the Amazon must be given plenty of attention and a degree of freedom. Then it will blossom into a companion quite without equal. Individual personalities are very strongly marked. They can be affectionate, unreliable, intelligent, demanding, mischievous, strong-willed, noisy and even dangerous. It is unwise to generalise about these birds because the personality varies so much from individual to individual and also from species to species. But generally speaking, they are the noisy extroverts of the parrot world who love to show off and, unlike many parrots, will often 'talk' for complete strangers. They are very inquisitive and full of mischief.

It was not until the late 1960s and early 1970s that Amazons were kept in aviaries to any degree. Before then, it was the fate of the majority of the thousands imported annually to end up as pets. That many were unsuited to cage life, mainly due to their temperament, could be gauged by the large numbers offered to zoos every year. The great increase in the price in recent years means that it is now more likely that only those who are really enthusiastic about owning an Amazon are prepared to meet the expense.

If an Amazon is to be kept as a pet, the main essential is that it is a young bird. Before one year old the colour of the iris changes from dark grey to yellow, orange or red, according to the species. Thereafter there is no indication of age in an Amazon Parrot, except in the Double Yellow-headed which takes four or five years to attain the full head colour of the adult. An adult bird which is tame and friendly will make a good pet but, unless it can already repeat one or two words, it is not likely to learn to talk. Any young bird has the potential to learn to mimic.

It should be borne in mind when buying a tame adult that many Amazons show a decided preference for people of one sex – not necessarily the sex opposite to their own, as is usual with Grey Parrots. Very many Amazons show a marked dislike of men. I have one such bird which was not at all popular with the keepers at the zoo where it resided; in fact, one could say that it terrorised them! It still shows marked aggression towards men and yet it is completely docile with me and allows me to carry it about on my hand.

A tame Amazon is one of the most companionable and rewarding pets imaginable for an adult, although most are not suitable for children or for anyone who is nervous of a parrot's beak. Fully mature birds in breeding condition – and this applies especially to males – can be far from easy to handle, becoming extremely fierce and excitable and inclined to bite. Such birds can become a real problem and, if the owner no longer feels confident about handling such a bird, the best solution is an outdoor aviary where it can be placed with a mate of its own species.

Feeding: Amazons are always interested in their food and it is easy to teach them to take a wide range of items. In fact many would exist quite happily on the same diet as their owners – and this would do them no harm provided that the foods were chosen sensibly.

Seed should form no more than 60 per cent of an Amazon's diet; the remainder should be made up of fresh fruits and vegetables with the addition of such items as toast crusts, baked bread, and food which would otherwise have been thrown away, such as unwanted biscuits or cake, cooked meat and vegetables and, greatest of all treats, bones from chops and chicken with some meat still attached. Many Amazons seem to crave meat and it will not harm them.

The usual seeds, both large and small, should be offered. These can include sunflower, safflower, canary, hemp, white millet and millet sprays. Pine nuts and peanuts will be eaten by most birds.

Accommodation: The Amazons available to aviculturists vary in size from about 25 cm (10 in) to 37 cm (15 in). Pairs of the smaller species can be kept and even bred successfully in aviaries as small as 2.5 m (8 ft 6 in) long and 90 cm (3 ft) wide but, if the space is available, a minimum length of 3.6 m (14 ft) is desirable. For the larger species, a length of 4.5–6 m (15–20 ft) will show off the birds better and allow them to have plenty of exercise on the wing.

I have never found Amazons to be particularly destructive to woodwork and, if fresh-cut branches are provided regularly, almost no damage will be done to the aviary. While most parrots enjoy gnawing branches, this is particularly true of Amazons and a real effort should be made to provide them. Ideally, caged Amazons should be given a twig a day.

It is essential to incorporate a feeding hatch in an aviary for a pair of these birds. When breeding or in breeding condition, most pairs, or certainly the males, become so aggressive and protective of their nest that they will not hesitate to attack anyone who enters the aviary. For the same reason, nest-boxes must be positioned where they can be inspected from outside the enclosure.

Many birds of this genus spend much time walking about the aviary floor, unless the aviary is very small. Some will bathe in a heavy, shallow container (lightweight ones would be used as playthings) but most will prefer to rain bathe. During a heavy downpour they will hang upside down from the roof of the aviary with wings outstretched to catch every drop of rain. When wet, the plumage of most Amazons takes on a bronze hue which could alarm someone seeing this for the first time. If an Amazon is not sprayed or allowed access to rain, it will become very dusty, giving off clouds of dust when it shakes its feathers. This is unhealthy for bird and owner.

Breeding: The main difficulty in breeding these birds is in obtaining a true pair (with the exception of *albifrons* and *xantholora* which are sexually dimorphic). In some pairs, the male is larger, especially in the head and beak, and is bolder in appearance, but even where there are a number of birds for comparison, this is not an infallible guide. Surgical sexing is therefore recommended.

When they come into breeding condition, Amazons are even more voluble than usual; noisy calls are accompanied by flaring of tail feathers, dilating of pupils and lowering of wings. A single bird or one with an unwilling partner will emit a whining and wheezing sound which indicates its desire to mate. The more aggressive Amazons will lunge at anyone who passes their aviary or fly at speed at the wire and will usually attempt to bite the person who replenishes the food and water. If it is necessary to enter the aviary for some reason, the sight of a catching net *may* lessen their enthusiasm for attack but it may do no such thing, in which case it will be necessary to take a cage into the aviary and to catch up the offenders temporarily.

It is not unknown for an Amazon to lay when only two years old – a very early age when one considers the long life span of these birds. Three or four years is more usual. The eggs of the first clutch may be smaller in size and number than those of more mature birds. The clutch usually consists of three or four eggs; occasionally two. Very often, the first clutch is infertile. The incubation period is 25 to 28 days; incubation is carried out by the female who is fed in or outside the nest by the male. The usual type of upright nest-box will be accepted.

The female broods the young during the day until they are about three weeks old and at night until about three weeks before they fledge, at about eight weeks old. While the young are being reared, soaked sunflower seed should be offered instead of dry sunflower. A nutritious bulky rearing food, such as bread and milk with wheatgerm cereal added, is essential; unlike some parrots, Amazons usually take this readily. Extra greenfood will also be appreciated by some pairs but I feel that the emphasis should be on a cereal rearing food, plus fresh vegetables such as carrot, celery and corn-on-the-cob or sweet corn.

Amazons are never continuous nesters and are often single-brooded, even if the eggs fail to hatch. Seasonal nesters in captivity, pairs vary little regarding the date on which they start to lay. In a temperate climate this will usually be in May; in a warmer climate in April.

Black-billed Amazon Parrot
A. agilis
Description: This is the least typical of the genus in appearance. A rich shade of dark green not found in any other Amazon, the colour is darker and more bluish at the top of the head and the feathers of the neck are faintly edged with black. The blackish ear coverts and the bird's size and shape make this species slightly reminiscent of a *Pionus*, unlike other Amazons. The primaries are mainly black and the secondaries blue. Some primary coverts are scarlet; the presence or absence of scarlet does not indicate sexual dimorphism. The inner webs of the lateral tail feathers are also scarlet. The under side of the tail is yellowish green. The beak is greyish black. Length: 25 cm (10 in).

Immature birds are a less rich shade of green and have the primary coverts entirely green.
Range/Habitat: The Black-billed Amazon inhabits Jamaica, where it has a more restricted range than the Yellow-billed with which it sometimes associates. It is threatened by habitat destruction.
Aviculture: This species has always been very rare in aviculture. A female at London Zoo was, for many years, the only one in a zoological collection in Europe. It was paired with a male Spectacled Amazon in a small indoor flight in the Parrot House. The Black-bill laid in 1972. The following year, two eggs were laid and after 28 days a chick hatched. It lived only two days. In 1978, a number of Black-billed Amazons were imported into the USA – the first seen there for many years. They proved difficult to establish; postmortem examination indicated that they had bacterial infection and liver

damage before entering the USA. Regrettably, most proved short-lived.

The first captive breeding of the Black-billed Amazon occurred in 1978 in the collection of Ramon Noegel of Seffner, Florida. Two eggs were laid and one hatched at the end of April. The young bird left the nest on June 21. The display of this species is unlike that of other Amazons. The male charges at the female and sways from side to side with a stiff-legged jerky motion and occasionally jumps over the female.

Yellow-billed (Red-throated) Amazon Parrot
A. collaria

Description: It is a quietly-coloured bird (Cooper's illustration in *Parrots of the World* shows a specimen of exceptional colour) with extremely subtle head colouration. In this species, the forehead is white, also the lores in some birds, the white extending below the eye to the ear coverts. Part of the cheeks, the throat and sometimes a wide collar extending around the neck, are dull pink, most of the feathers being only partly pink and very delicately suffused with this colour.

The feathers of the crown and nape are distinctly edged with black. Ear coverts are dark bluish green and the forecrown is dull blue. Primaries and primary coverts are mainly blue. The tail has pink and yellow markings at the base and a band of yellowish green at the tip of the tail. Its shade of green is yellowish below and on the upper tail coverts, pale green on the lower back and rump and darker on the upper parts. Length: 28 cm (11 in). The bill is pale yellow. Immature birds are similar to adults.

Range/Habitat: This species is more widespread and common in Jamaica than the Black-billed. It inhabits the limestone forests of Cockpit Country, Mount Diablo and the John Crow Mountains. It is absent from the Blue Mountains from where I saw five birds fly into the Hope Zoological Gardens in Kingston in 1975. The curator told me that they were escapees.

Aviculture: Jamaica does not permit commercial exportation of its two species of Amazons, thus the Yellow-bill is rare in aviculture. However, for a period commencing in 1977, birds, totalling several hundred, were exported illegally.

The first recorded captive breeding occurred in the USA by Perry Linder of Petaluma, California. The pair

Yellow-billed Amazon (*Amazona collaria*).

hatched a chick in 1963 which was killed by a snake. They did not breed again until 1972. Three eggs were laid and all hatched. One chick died at three weeks and the other two were hand-reared. The death of one of the adults occurred before they could breed again.

In Britain, the first success was gained by Mr and Mrs J. Arman in 1982. They noted that a lot of bickering and beak sparring took place, which had not been observed in the larger Amazons; they flicked their wings prior to mating. In 1982, the first egg was laid on June 2; there were three eggs by June 7. One egg disappeared during the incubation period. A chick hatched on July 4. Next day both its feet had been mutilated, also one wing tip. It was removed for hand-rearing on July 8. By 74 days it was fully feathered and flying and was independent at 80 days (Arman, 1983).

In 1983, the pair hatched three young. One died at three weeks and the other two were reared. In 1984, three young were hand-reared from the age of ten days and in 1985 two were

Yellow-billed Amazons hand-reared by John and Josie Arman.

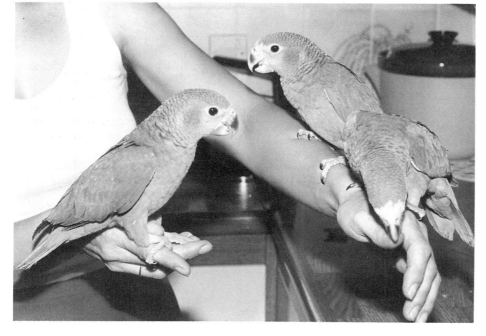

reared from the egg after being incubator-hatched. In the UK, this species has also been bred by Mr and Mrs A. J. Stoodley.

This species was bred in at least two collections in California in 1984. Gail Worth of Aves International bred from three pairs and Fred and Robbie Harris (1985) bred from one pair. The female of the latter was purchased in a badly feather-plucked condition a few months earlier. The habit ceased when she was placed with a male in a cage measuring 180 × 91 cm (6 × 3 ft) × 91 cm (3 ft) high. The nest-box measured 31 cm (12 in) square and 61 cm (2 ft) high and contained a 10 cm (4 in) layer of pine shavings. The female laid four infertile eggs soon after being placed in the cage. Both birds appeared to be overweight so the sunflower seed in their diet was cut down to a handful of sprouted seed daily. In the next clutch, three eggs were laid. Two were fertile and one hatched after 26 days. When the chick was four days old the parents were disturbed by an escaped conure and badly injured the chick's right foot. The chick was removed for hand-rearing. It then weighed 22 g ($\frac{3}{4}$ oz). At eight days it weighed 25.6 g ($\frac{9}{10}$ oz) and at 16 days 41.5 g ($1\frac{1}{2}$ oz). At three months it was eating on its own and saying 'Hello'.

In Switzerland, A. Fricker reared two young in 1983. They left the nest on June 22.

Cuban Amazon Parrot
A. leucocephala leucocephala
Description: This is one of the most beautiful of the smaller members of the genus. The white forehead and fore-crown and rich pink extending from the lores to the area below the eye to the throat or upper breast, distinguish it. The abdomen is irregularly marked with vinous red; usually the appearance is of a wedge-shaped patch of green extending from the breast into the vinous colouration. The primaries are blue on the outer webs, black on the inner webs. Tail feathers are most attractively marked with red, orange and yellow, the outer tail feathers having a pronounced bluish tinge. All the body feathers are edged with black, this being most marked on the mantle and head. Shade of green is dark. The

Cuban Amazon (*Amazona leucocephala leucocephala*).

periorbital skin is conspicuously white. Length: 32 cm (13 in). Immature birds usually show reduced areas of pink and white on the head.

Colouration is extremely variable in individuals, especially in the extent of the pink which may reach quite far down the breast in exceptional birds.
Range/Habitat: Little is known about the status of Cuba's birds, thus details of the population of the Cuban Amazon are unknown at the present time but there is no doubt that it has declined dramatically. However, this species has long had to contend with human predation, formerly for the pet trade, also as food.
Aviculture: The Cuban Amazon is rare in captivity but has been established in Florida and in eastern Europe. In the early years of the century they were occasionally available as pets. The dedicated aviculturist Edward Boosey was the first to rear it in Europe; two were bred in 1956. This remains the only British success.

In the USA, the first breeder was Mrs V. McDaniels (Hart) in 1960; two young were hand-reared.

The highest number of Cuban Amazons outside Cuba are found in the communist countries of eastern Europe. In East Germany there are probably over one hundred at the time of writing. Several zoos had bred Cubans: Rostock Zoo from 1977, Erfurt Zoo from 1979 and East Berlin since 1981 (all in East Germany), as well as several private aviculturists. It has also been bred in Czechoslovakia.

Much of what we know about the Cuban Amazon and its races is due to

Ramon Noegel in Florida. He has expended much time, effort and finance into studying its races in the wild and to establishing them in captivity. Between 1974 and 1984 over 100 *leucocephala* were reared in his collection – a record without precedent for an endangered Amazon. Third generation young had been bred, all removed for hand-rearing at an early age.

Isle of Pines Amazon
A. l. palmarum
Description: Males and females have deeper scarlet on the throat than the Cuban Amazon. The vinaceous colouration on the abdomen is richer and more pronounced and the white on the crown is more extensive.
Range/Habitat: This species is or was found on the Isle of Pines and the nearby area of western Cuba. It may already be extinct on the Isle of Pines; nothing is known of its status on Cuba.
Aviculture: There are few specimens in captivity. The only breeding success has been obtained by Ramon Noegel since 1976. Between that year and 1981 the female laid 17 eggs of which 12 hatched and eight were reared. Subsequently more have been bred. A pair which included a feather-plucking male taken from the Isle of Pines in 1946 produced young in 1980.

Grand Cayman Amazon Parrot
A. l. caymanensis
Description: It differs from the Cuban in having a turquoise wash to the rump and under parts. The shade of green is slightly lighter and the black edges to the feathers of the head and neck are less pronounced. The white on the forehead is often suffused with pink or has a yellowish tinge and the pink on the head is usually lighter in shade and less extensive.

Its build is stockier than that of the Cuba Amazon. The periorbital skin is greyish.
Range/Habitat: This species is con-

fined to Grand Cayman Island, situated 290 km (180 miles) west-north-west of Jamaica. The island is approximately 37 km (23 miles) long and averages 8 km (5 miles) wide. The parrots are confined to the eastern end and keep principally to the mangroves, of which there are over 7,200 hectares (18,000 acres). The island's tourist industry is expanding so quickly that the future of this race is far from secure.

Aviculture: This race has been established in aviculture by Ramon Noegel in Florida. Between 1974 and 1984, over 30 young were reared, including third generation young – a feat unequalled with any other endangered Amazon. The Grand Cayman Amazon is relatively lethargic and not easy to breed. It has yet to be bred in any other collection. Unable to tolerate low temperatures, it should be wintered in fully enclosed accommodation where necessary. Prone to obesity, it must be offered a large proportion of fresh fruits and vegetables in its diet and only a small quantity of sunflower seed.

Cayman Brac Amazon Parrot

A. l. hesterna

Description: It is considerably smaller than the Cuban. It differs in having a narrower head and in having the white usually confined to the forehead in females, more extensive in males. The vinous colouration on the abdomen is mauver in shade and often extends upwards on to the breast. The feathers throughout are even more heavily edged with black. The pink on the head is reduced in area, being confined to the cheeks, especially in females. The white or bluish skin surrounding the eye is more pronounced than in the Grand Cayman Parrot.

Range/Habitat: This race is now found only on Cayman Brac, an island of less than 7,770 hectares (19,000 acres), which is situated about 145 km (90 miles) north-east of Grand Cayman. Fieldwork carried out by Ramon Noegel and associates resulted in an estimate of

130 birds in 1976. In 1980, after Hurricane Allen hit the island, the Reverend Noegel believed that the population had been reduced to about 50. A road constructed across the small breeding territory of this sub-species will render its tiny population even more vulnerable.

Aviculture: It exists only in the collection of Ramon Noegel. A pair hatched in 1973 and obtained by him in 1975 attempted to nest in 1978 when two fertile eggs were laid but did not hatch. The same result was obtained in the next two years. In 1981 one of the two eggs was fertile and hatched after 26 days. The chick was hand-reared.

Bahamas Amazon Parrot

A. l. bahamensis

Description: This race differs from the Cuban in having the patch of white on the forehead extending round and behind the eye. Most specimens have more intense red on the face and upper breast and more pronounced black margins to the green feathers. The vinous patch on the abdomen is indicated by a few scattered red feathers or absent entirely. The tail is green except the two outer feathers which are edged with blue and have a small area of red. It is slightly larger, about 34 cm (13 in).

Range/Habitat: It occurs only on the Bahaman islands of Inagua and Abaco.

The destruction of pines on Abaco during the late 1950s and early 1960s was a major intrusion into the primary habitat of this Amazon; it is now confined to about 3,850 hectares (9,636 acres) at the south-eastern end of the island. The population is believed to be in the region of 300. In contrast, the Inagua population is undisturbed. On Abaco, the parrots nest underground in limestone cavities.

Export is prohibited and the Bahamas Amazon is unknown outside of these islands.

Sallé's Hispaniolan Amazon Parrot

A. l. ventralis

Description: This race can briefly be described as resembling a Cuban Amazon without the pink facial markings. Forehead and lores are white, also the very prominent area of white skin surrounding the eye. The upper part of the cheeks are blue, also the crown, and the ear coverts are black. The feathers of the head and mantle are narrowly but distinctly edged with black, also those of the upper breast, to a lesser degree. Length: 28 cm (11 in). Immature birds have little or no blue on the crown and the red patch on the abdomen is paler than in adults.

Range/Habitat: This Amazon is native to the island divided into the Dominican Republic and Haiti. It has also been introduced into Puerto Rico. Inhabiting an island which is large by West Indian standards this species is still fairly common in the Dominican Republic but now rare on Haiti, but its numbers are being diminished by land clearance. It was once widely eaten by the islanders.

Aviculture: Sallé's Amazon is rare in captivity; its export is restricted. It is comparatively dull in colour and there has never been any demand for it. What was almost certainly the first European breeding occurred at Jersey Wildlife Preservation Trust in the Channel Islands in 1971. The director Gerald Durrell obtained four young birds from a market on their native island. In May 1968, two were seen mating; the female had three eggs by the beginning of June. These were infertile. The following year the third of the three surviving birds was removed from the aviary as the pair were behaving aggressively towards her. The female laid the first of three eggs on April 5; one was fertile and the chick died in shell.

In 1970, all three eggs were fertile and the following year brought success. One of the three eggs was fertile and a chick hatched on May 15. It left the nest on July 15, aged 61 days. Its colouration differed from that of the adults in the larger white patch on the forehead, followed by a tinge of yellow (no dark blue) and in the orange-red patch on the abdomen. Favoured foods during the rearing period were canary seed, hawthorn leaves, yolk of hard-boiled egg, tomatoes, grapes, pear and banana. A month after fledging, the young bird occasionally begged food from its father and fed itself, a favourite food being hawthorn berries. In 1973, the pair was successful in rearing two youngsters. It is of interest that the female laid her first egg on April 17 or 18 on five of the first eight occasions on which she laid. In 1978, Jersey sold these birds to John Stoodley in Hampshire who has bred from them consistently.

In the USA, *ventralis* has been bred in aviaries more often than in Europe. Ramon Noegel reared young between 1973 and 1978 and consistent successes were achieved at the Patuxent Centre of the US Fish and Wildlife Service in Maryland, in conjunction with the programme to breed the Puerto Rican Amazon. In addition, it has been bred at the Field Station in Puerto Rico and used in various experiments concerned with the captive breeding of the native parrot.

In 1981, a pair of White-crowned *Pionus* were used as foster parents for a *ventralis* chick in the collection of Dr B. Levine of Miami. This Amazon was bred on several occasions in the zoo in the Dominican Republic in a large walk-through aviary containing 300 birds.

Spectacled Amazon (*Amazona albifrons albifrons*).

Spectacled (White-fronted) Amazon Parrot

A. albifrons albifrons

Description: With the Yellow-lored Amazon, it is distinguished from other members of the genus by the red, white and blue head colouration. The forehead and forepart of the crown are white, followed by an area of blue. The feathers on the lores and surrounding the eye are red, the latter area being considerably reduced in the female. The smaller upper wing coverts along the edge of the wing are red, also the primary coverts in the male. In the female, these areas are usually green; however, Italian aviculturist Paolo Bertagnolio has two female *albifrons*, both of which have laid, and one has

the wing green and the other has the alula and primary coverts partly red. The outer primary is black, the next four green at the base and blue towards the tips; the inner primaries and secondaries are mainly deep blue. The two central feathers of the rather short tail are tipped with yellowish green, the lateral ones being yellowish green with crimson bases. The rump is yellowish green, the remainder of the plumage being deep green; the feathers are heavily edged with black on the neck and mantle, less so on the upper breast. The bill is pale yellow. Length: 25 cm (10 in). The female may be considerably smaller.

Immature birds have an incomplete circle of red feathers surrounding the eye and the white forehead is reduced in area in some individuals and may be tinged with yellow.

Range/Habitat: This species inhabits a wide area stretching from Mexico to western Costa Rica. It favours arid country and is very common in some parts of its range.

A. a. saltuensis
Description: This subspecies has the green on the neck and head suffused with blue, and the blue on the crown extends further down the nape.

A. a. nana
Description: Birds of this race – if, indeed, it is a valid one – are very much smaller – the smallest of all Amazons.

Aviculture: Very little has been recorded about it as an aviary bird or as a pet although it is not a rare bird in aviculture. Its small size would appear to make it more suitable for the latter purpose than the larger species. One aviculturist observed that his Spectacled Amazons seldom drank water – an adaptation for existence in arid areas. The first recorded breeding of the Spectacled Amazon occurred in Japan in 1922 in the collection of Prince Taka-Tsukasa.

I. D. Putnam's pair reared young in the USA in 1949. The next reference to a captive success is that of H. Müller of Walsrode, West Germany. His account is contained in the Dutch magazine *Onze Vogels* (June, 1978). A comprehensive article includes a superlative series of colour photographs showing clearly the difference in plumage of male and female, including close-up pictures of the wings, together with photographs taken inside the nest of the two eggs and of the chick as it developed. At ten weeks old, the young bird can clearly be seen to have the skin surrounding the eye white, not greyish, as in the adult, and the iris whitish brown, not pale yellow.

This species has been bred in Europe more frequently than in Britain and was bred in Austria, Germany and Switzerland before any British successes were recorded. In 1978, two young were reared in Schönbrunn Zoo, Vienna, Austria. Early nesters, the female first laid in January 1977. The nest-box used was 25 cm (10 in) square and 45 cm (18 in) high. In Switzerland, the Spectacled Amazon has been bred in several private collections. The first successes occurred in 1979: Arthur Fricker of Villmergen (three young reared), Erwin Konig of Wohlen (three) and Gregor Boni of Hombrechtikon (two). In the latter case there were three eggs, measuring 38 × 36 mm ($1\frac{1}{2}$ × $1\frac{2}{5}$ in). Two hatched and the young birds left the nest at 50 days. They could be sexed as the male had red lores and the female green lores.

Since then, the Spectacled Amazon has been bred on numerous occasions in zoos (e.g. Moscow since 1977; Vienna 1978; Natal Lion Park, South Africa, in 1979) and in many private collections.

The first published account of a breeding in Britain was that by P. Clarke (1982). The pair was introduced in December 1979. Four fertile eggs were produced the following spring; three hatched in an incubator but the chicks were not reared. In 1981, the female laid on April 18, 21, 24 and 27. On the 25th day, a newly hatched

chick was found in the seed tray. One of its legs had been severed and it died soon after. The other eggs were removed to an incubator; they hatched on the 25th, 24th and 24th day of incubation.

Rearing food consisted of a runny mixture of Farlene baby cereal initially, then fruit-delight baby food and finely sieved ground sunflower was added, also scraped cuttlefish bone and a small amount of yoghurt, grit, Vionate and Vitapet (vegetable and cod liver oil). The saliva from a pet Eclectus who fed the padlock of his cage was added to the food of the middle chick; its crop cleared more quickly than that of the others, indicating apparently that the secretions from the Eclectus' crop assisted digestion. Henceforth it was added to the food of all three chicks.

Examination of the pin feathers before they erupted revealed that all three had red in the primary covert and alula areas: all were males. At first, the red on the face was restricted to the region of the lores; not until two months after the young birds were otherwise fully feathered did red feathers appear around the eyes.

Yellow-lored Amazon Parrot
A. xantholora

Description: It differs from the Spectacled Amazon in having the area of red more extensive below the eye and in the lores being bright yellow. In addition, it has black ear coverts. The female has little or no red on the head and wings; her crown is blue whereas the male's crown is white. Length: 25 cm (10 in).

Range/Habitat: It inhabits the Yucatan Peninsula in south-eastern Mexico. It is common in the centre of its range, less common towards the periphery. Unlike *albifrons*, this species prefers pinelands and areas of secondary growth.

Aviculture: This species is very rare in aviculture. The first recorded breeding occurred in the collection of André Meier in Switzerland in 1980. By July 22, four chicks had hatched from a clutch of five eggs. Between August 19 and 22, the chicks could be sexed as three males and one female.

The young female's crown was green, not blue as in the adult female. The young left the nest between August 30 and September 3.

The rarest of all neotropical parrots: Puerto Rican Parrot photographed at the entrance to its nest in the Luquillo rainforest.

In the USA, the Yellow-lored Amazon was bred in 1984 by Ramon Noegel – a first breeding in that country.

Puerto Rican Amazon Parrot

A. vittata

Description: The Puerto Rican Parrot is mainly dark green, with most of the feathers edged with black, most conspicuously on the head, neck and upper breast. There is a narrow band of red on the forehead and a patch of red on the inner webs of the outer tail feathers. The bill is yellowish and the iris is brown or yellow. Length: 29 cm (11½ in).

Immature birds are similar to adults.

Range/Habitat: This bird holds the doubtful distinction of being the most gravely endangered of neotropical parrots; only about 30 individuals survive in the wild. Puerto Rico is a part of the USA and the US Fish and Wildlife Service administers the 11,400 mountainous hectares (28,000 acres) of the Luquillo Forest, the last sanctuary of this species. Since 1972, the US Fish and Wildlife Service has been actively engaged in protecting and conserving this parrot (for detailed information see *Endangered Parrots* by Rosemary Low). It is battling for survival against a number of factors. Its chief problems were lack of suitable nesting sites and competition for them with the Pearly-eyed Thrasher. Biologists have aided the breeding birds by providing Thrasher-proof sites and repairing existing nests, resulting in an increased number of young fledging. At the time of writing, there were 23 birds in captivity at the Luquillo Forest Field Centre operated by the US Fish and Wildlife Service.

Pretre's Amazon Parrot

A. pretrei pretrei

Description: This species is green, darker above, each feather being edged with black – more heavily on the upper parts. It is dark red on the forehead, forepart of the crown, lores, area surrounding the eye, the bend of the wing and the carpal edge of the wing. The tail is broadly tipped with yellowish green and the thighs are red. The bill is pale horn-coloured. Length: 32 cm (12 in). Immature birds have less red on the head and the carpal edge of the wing is green.

Range/Habitat: Its numbers have declined seriously in recent years and the decline is believed to be continuing, partly due to deforestation. A reduction in range has also occurred. It inhabits south-eastern Brazil from southern São Paulo to Rio Grande do Sul and Misiones, north-eastern Argentina.

Aviculture: This bird is almost unknown in present day aviculture but was on occasion imported into Europe between the 1880s and 1930s. There are a number of pairs in zoos and private collections in Brazil. The zoological park at Sapucia do Sul, near Porto Alegre, had bred young from two pairs in 1981. In Europe, this species is represented in a private collection in France and in Loro Parque, Tenerife.

Tucuman Amazon Parrot

A. p. tucumana

Description: It differs from the nominate race in having the edge and the bend of the wing green, not red. The thighs are yellow and red. Immature birds have yellow flecks in the red patch on the forehead, or have this area orange. Length: 31 cm (12 in). Weight: 270 g (9½ oz).

Range/Habitat: Found on the eastern slope of the Andes in northern Argentina and south-eastern Bolivia, its status is uncertain. It may be at risk due to deforestation.

Aviculture: For many years this species was known in aviculture only by the single bird at Jersey Wildlife Preservation Trust. Then, in 1978, a few birds were imported into the USA. Since then, Tucumans have been available in the USA and in Europe in small numbers. They have proved to be a most delightful addition to the avicultural scene. Lively, friendly and vivacious birds, their personalities endear them to all who know them. Their small size and, in particular, the diminutive head and bill, lend them a special charm.

My own pair use every inch of their aviary; I have found that they fly more than is usual in other captive Amazons.

The first recorded captive breeding occurred in the collection of Ramon Noegel in Florida. In 1980, the female had laid three infertile eggs. In 1981, the first of three eggs was laid on June 14. Only one egg was fertile and it hatched on July 13. It was hand-reared from the age of seven days.

In Britain, the Tucuman Amazon has been bred by Mr and Mrs J. Stoodley since 1982.

Tucuman Amazons.

Green-cheeked Amazon Parrot
A. viridigenalis

Description: It is often known as the Mexican Red-headed Parrot as scarlet is the colour of the forehead, crown and lores, probably less extensive in females; the feathers are yellow at the base. The cheeks are a bright shade of green. There is a small patch of blue or lilac behind the eye and the feathers of the hind neck are tipped with lilac and black. The primaries are blue-black; there is a large patch of red in the secondaries, which are blue and green. A broad yellowish green band tips the tail (missing from Cooper's illustration in *Parrots of the World*). The shade of green is lighter below and the feathers of the upper breast are tipped with black. The bill is horn-coloured and the iris is yellow. Length: 33 cm (13 in).

In immature birds, the red on the head is restricted to the forehead; the crown is green or green with scattered red feathers.

A pair of Lutino Green-cheeked Amazons were owned by American aviculturist Jerome Buteyn. The birds were described as being 'a wonderful clear daffodil yellow, with red on the head, primaries and tail'.

Range/Habitat: This species inhabits north-eastern Mexico in lowlands and foothills up to about 1,200 m (4,000 ft). A large decline has occurred during the past few decades, due to loss of habitat and extensive trade; the latter has been curtailed.

Aviculture: The Green-cheeked Amazon has been imported into the USA in large numbers. It is much less common in Europe.

In the USA, it was bred at Los Angeles Zoo in 1970. A consistent breeder of this species in Texas is Paul Springman of Brownsville, who reared 36 birds between 1972 and 1980. The clutches usually consisted of two eggs – sometimes three. In 1976, second generation young were reared. It has also been bred at the Jackson Zoological Park, Mississippi (two reared in 1978), at Gainsville Zoo, by Greg Harrison in Florida (ten hand-reared from several pairs in 1980), and at Calgary Zoo in Canada in 1972.

In Europe, Mattmann in Switzerland reported breeding two in 1981, in which year Inge Forsberg bred two in Sweden. In Britain, it was first bred by David Spilsbury of Worcestershire in 1980 and has since been bred by Mr and Mrs J. Stoodley.

Other collections which have achieved breeding success include Natal Lion Park in South Africa, since 1976.

Finsch's (Lilac-crowned) Amazon Parrot
A. finschi

Description: This bird is closely related to the Green-cheeked Amazon. It differs in being smaller and more slender in build. The forehead and lores are deep maroon; the feathers of the crown, neck and the side of the head are mauve, narrowly edged with black. The iris is orange.

Immature birds are similar to adults but have the iris brown.

Range/Habitat: Found in western Mexico, it is common and widespread.

Aviculture: This species is occasionally imported into Europe but is better known in the USA where it has reared young on several occasions. At San Diego Zoo, a chick hatched in 1951 after an incubation period of 28 days.

Green-cheeked Amazon (*Amazona viridigenalis*) – male.

Finsch's Amazon (*Amazona finschi*).

When it was five days old, the parents stopped feeding it and it was removed for hand-rearing. Its eyes opened at 11 days. For three months, it was spoon-fed with the usual formula used at the zoo, consisting mainly of wheat hearts. The young Amazon was independent at four months. The adult birds were only three years old when the breeding occurred.

In two instances when young of this species were reared by their parents, one in the USA, the other in Canada, they left the nest when eight weeks old. In one case two chicks hatched – the first 26 days after the first egg was laid.

In Britain, the first recorded breeding occurred in 1978. The female of a pair belonging to Mr and Mrs R. Mann (1978) of Peterborough laid two eggs during the beginning of June, apparently one week apart. A chick seen on July 3, thought to be one or two days old, had a few strands of long white down, most of which were on the body. The eyes opened on July 15 and the ear when it was aged 25 days. By August 12, it was almost fully feath-ered and would scramble up to the entrance hole. It left the nest on August 29 when it differed from its parents mainly in having more red on the head.

In Czechoslovakia, Finsch's Amazon was reared by Charles Bar-tolshie in 1983 (Hylas, pers. comm.). The female laid the first of three eggs on May 6. A chick was heard on June 4 and a second four days later. The first left the nest on July 28 and the

second on August 8. Rearing food consisted of sunflower seed, egg, ears of wheat, corn and lettuce.

Yellow-cheeked (Primrose-cheeked or Scarlet-lored) Amazon Parrot

A. autumnalis autumnalis

Description: It is a beautiful bird and owes its beauty as much to the head colouration as to the large eyes with black eyelashes, surrounded by white skin. Scarlet is the colour of part of the crown, the lores and the lower part of the cheeks. The feathers of the upper part of the cheeks are orange-yellow with red at the base, those of the crown and nape of the neck being lilac towards the tip, with dusky edges. The wing speculum is scarlet and the pri-maries are blue-black and green. There is a yellow band at the tip of the green tail, which is blue on the outer edges. The bill is horn-coloured and dusky at the tip of the upper mandible. Length: 34 cm (13 in). The iris is brown or golden. In E. N. T. Vane's proved true pair, it was golden in the male and dark brown in the female.

Immature birds have less red on the forehead and lores. The feathers of the forehead lack the lilac tips. The iris is dark brown.

Range/Habitat: The nominate race inhabits the eastern slopes of Mexico, southward to Nicaragua where it inter-grades with *salvini*.

Found in forested and partially de-forested areas, it is numerous through-out most of its range but has probably declined in north-eastern Mexico.

Aviculture: It is quite well-known to American aviculturists but was seldom imported into Europe until the late 1970s. Those imported included wild-caught adults which were very nervous and took some while to adapt to captivity.

The first breeding in Britain occur-red in unique circumstances: the chick was reared by a Grey Parrot. A pair belonging to the British aviculturist E. N. T. Vane (1957) repeatedly produced fertile eggs. They failed to hatch so, when egg-laying coincided with laying by a tame Grey Parrot kept in a 46 cm (18 in) parrot cage, the three Amazon eggs were removed and given to the

Grey. She incubated them on the thickly sanded floor of the cage. One egg hatched after 25 or 26 days of incubation. The Grey Parrot reared her foster chick on dry and sprouted seed, bread and milk, soaked brown bread and greenfood. During the first 24 hours she made no attempt to brood or feed it.

The first feed was given on the sec-ond day. To feed the chick, she lifted it by the head, and inserted the point of her upper mandible into the small gap between the chick's mandibles at the rear. Later the chick instinctively raised its head and, taking the tips of its mandibles in her beak, the Grey then applied the usual pumping action to regurgitate food. At this early stage, the consistency of the food was that of milk. The chick was fed every two hours.

When it was about ten days old, its eyes began to open. At seven weeks it was fully feathered and just over a week later it climbed on to the perch. At that age its plumage was similar to that of the adult; its bill was blackish and yellowish and its eyes were dark. UK breeders in the 1980s include Mr and Mrs A. A. J. Stoodley and Mr and Mrs R. Mann.

Salvin's Amazon Parrot

A. a. salvini

Description: It differs from the Yellow-cheeked Amazon in being larger and having the cheeks and ear coverts bright green and the margins of the feathers of the crown and nape broadly marked with lilac; the bases of the lateral tail feathers are red on the inner webs.

Immature birds have less red on the forehead.

Length: 34 cm (13½ in). Weight: 500 g (17¼ oz).

Range/Habitat: This Amazon in-habits south-eastern Nicaragua and eastern and south-western Costa Rica south to western Colombia and extreme north-western Venezuela.

Aviculture: Irregularly imported into Europe, it was quite often available during the 1960s. Almost all the birds still in Europe date from that era. Since then a few have been im-ported into the USA.

In the Netherlands, Ronald van

Yellow-cheeked Amazon (*Amazona autumnalis autumnalis*).

Lilacine Amazon (*Amazona autumnalis lilacina*).

Salvin's Amazon (*Amazona autumnalis salvini*).

Dieten reared Salvin's Amazon in 1979.

In Britain, the first breeding occurred in 1980 when David Spilsbury hand-reared three young. Subsequently it has been bred by Mr and Mrs J. Stoodley.

This is a handsome bird, but rather too noisy to keep as a house pet.

Lilacine Amazon Parrot
A. a. lilacina

Description: It differs from Salvin's Amazon in having pale yellowish lime-green cheeks, the lavender feathers of the crown (not the nape) edged with pale reddish and a narrow crimson streak above the eye. The nape feathers are heavily edged with black. A distinctive feature is the black beak.

Length: 30 cm (12 in).

Range/Habitat: This prettily marked race inhabits the tropical zone of western Ecuador. Because of widespread deforestation, it has probably declined substantially.

Aviculture: This most attractive bird is rare in aviculture. Since the late 1970s a few have been exported – doubtless the result of destruction of habitat. In the UK, K. Duffett reported breeding this Amazon in 1984.

Diademed Amazon Parrot
A. a. diadema

Description: This race differs from the Salvin's in the small, almost hair-like, red feathers which cover the cere and nostrils. (In Salvin's Amazon, the nostrils are unfeath-

ered.) The forehead is crimson, becoming dark purple-red on the lores. The centre of the crown is green, the surrounding feathers being dark green edged with black. Length: 36 cm (14 in).

Range/Habitat: North-western Brazil is the home of this race.

Aviculture: It is very rare in aviculture. This race is kept in at least one Brazilian collection and also by Ramon Noegel in Florida.

Dufresne's (Blue-cheeked) Amazon Parrot
A. dufresniana dufresniana

Description: This species has a pretty and unusual arrangement of colours on the head. There is a very narrow line of colour on the forehead, varying from gold to orange which is the colour of the lores. The crown is yellowish green or green, the cheeks are mauve and the throat bluish or green. The breast is bluish. A patch of colour varying from fiery orange to yellow decorates the wing and the primaries are dark blue. The outer tail feathers are edged with mauve and the tip of the tail is greenish yellow. The rest of the plumage is dark green. The bill is dusky with red at the base of the upper mandible. The iris is orange. Length: 33 cm (13 in).

Immature birds are so far undescribed.

Range/Habitat: This Amazon is found in the Guianas, south-eastern Bolivia and Venezuela.

Aviculture: It is very rare in aviculture. A few have been exported from Guyana since the late 1970s.

Red-topped (Red-browed or Red-crowned) Amazon Parrot

A. d. rhodocorytha

Description: The feathers of the crown and forehead are variable, being usually scarlet with some green or yellow feathers. Compared with the nominate race, there is less blue on the cheeks, which may be merely washed with sky blue or as deep as mauvish blue. The wing speculum is red and the outer tail feathers have a patch of red on the inner webs.

Immature birds have less distinct markings on the head, which is quite brightly coloured.

Young bred by Ramon Noegel had a blue sheen on the under parts. The iris is dark.

Range/Habitat: This Amazon is found in eastern Brazil from Alagoas south to Rio de Janeiro. It is now rare and locally distributed due to extensive destruction of habitat.

Aviculture: It is regrettable that it is not permitted to export this endangered species; in Brazil, it is common and inexpensive in street markets (specimens were being offered for $20 in 1984) and there are reports that some birds are eaten. To the best of my knowledge, it has yet to be bred in Brazil and, until the early 1980s, there was no interest in it among Brazilian aviculturists – but this situation may be changing. Outside Brazil, it is exceedingly rare and cherished.

The first captive breeding would appear to be that which occurred in the collection of Mr and Mrs R. Mann of Peterborough, England, in 1980. Young have since been reared every year; chicks are removed for hand-rearing, resulting in a second nest in most years. The clutch usu-

Red-topped or Red-browed Amazon (*Amazona dufresniana rhodocorytha*) chicks bred by Mr and Mrs R. Mann in 1984.

ally consists of four eggs. The first young reared perched at 78 days and were independent at 100 days. Three chicks hatched in 1984 weighed 13.24 g, 14.10 g and 14.5 g (around $\frac{1}{2}$ oz).

In the USA, the first captive breeding occurred in the collection of Ramon Noegel in 1984. After three seasons of infertile eggs, four fertile eggs were laid between March 15 and 24. Two chicks had hatched by April 12. The third and fourth chicks were placed in the nest of a Double Yellow-headed Amazon until they were nine days old. They were then removed for hand-rearing but died when between three and four weeks old. Twenty-five other Amazons being hand-fed at the same time were thriving. The other two chicks were left with their parents until the age of four weeks. They were then removed and then successfully reared by hand (Noegel, 1984).

The adults, two males and five females, in Ramon Noegel's collection were gathered from various sources over a period of nine years. They are probably the only group of this species of any size in captivity outside Brazil and may prove to be of vital importance in the continued existence of this species.

This species is also kept at the Dominican Republic breeding centre

of Vogelpark Walsrode in West Germany and is reported to have bred there in 1984.

A hybrid between a male *rhodocorytha* and a female Finsch's Amazon was bred at Busch Gardens, Tampa, Florida, in 1972. Two young were reared. The male was subsequently acquired by Ramon Noegel.

Red-tailed Amazon Parrot

A. brasiliensis

Description: This is a distinctive and prettily marked Amazon. It has the top of the head and the lores pinkish red; the cheeks, throat, ear coverts and upper breast are dull greyish blue, dusky on or behind the ear coverts. The metacarpal edge of the wing is red and the wing feathers have pale or yellowish green edges; under tail coverts are yellowish green. There is no red wing speculum in this species. The tail is particularly unusual, with a band of yellow at the tip, followed by a band of carmine red and purplish blue towards the base.

Length: 37 cm (14 in).

Immature birds have yet to be described.

Cooper's attractive illustration of this species (in Forshaw, 1973) depicts a very colourful bird which is not typical of the species.

Range/Habitat: The range of this species in eastern Brazil has contracted due to deforestation. A major decline has occurred, causing it to become endangered.

Aviculture: In Brazil, the late Professor G. A. della Riva collected together a number of these Amazons and was successful in breeding this species before his death in 1978. This would appear to be the only captive breeding to date and indeed the birds are virtually unknown in aviculture outside Brazil. In 1983, G. A. Smith saw nearly 30 *brasiliensis* in four collections in Brazil.

Festive (Red-backed) Amazon Parrot

A. festiva festiva

Description: This is the only member of the genus which has a red rump. It has a narrow line of maroon from the forehead to the eye; the rest of the forehead is green and the head, especially the chin and area above the eye, has a distinct bluish tinge. There is no red wing speculum. The feathers of the lower back and rump are crimson, with the base yellow; the latter is not apparent until the feathers are parted. The plumage is mid-green, slightly darker above. The edges of the outer tail feathers are bluish and the tip of the tail is yellowish green. The iris is orange and the beak is black. Length: 34 cm (13 in).

Immature birds have less blue on the head. The lower back and rump are green with a few scattered red feathers.
Range/Habitat: The Festive Amazon occurs in eastern Ecuador, northeastern Peru and south-eastern Colombia, eastward through the Amazon basin to eastern Amazonas, Brazil. It is found along rivers, where it is common.
Aviculture: It is not well-known in aviculture; there are few pairs in collections.

The first captive breeding would appear to be that which occurred at Busch Gardens, Tampa, Florida, in 1980. One youngster was reared. A male paired with a Yellow-billed Amazon produced three young which took after the male in appearance. At Keston Foreign Bird Farm in England, a Festive Amazon paired with a Blue-fronted or Orange-winged produced young which, in immature plumage, were mainly green. In 1974, when four years old, one was described as mainly green with blue in the wings.

Bodin's Amazon
A. f. bodini

Description: In this race, the red on the head is more extensive and more crimson in shade; the feathers of the crown are red, green and blue. Primaries are bluish, rather than the rich dark blue of the nominate race, and the shade of green is lighter below and darker, more olive, above.
Range/Habitat: It is found in north-western Guyana and from central Venezuela west to the Meta River.
Aviculture: Rare in aviculture, it is represented in the collection of Ramon Noegel in Florida.

Bodin's Amazon (*Amazona festiva bodini*).

Yellow-faced Amazon Parrot
A. xanthops

Description: It is possible that two phases exist. One is probably usually smaller and much more colourful. Adult birds of the less colourful type have the forehead, crown and ear coverts yellow, the latter with an orange tinge; the upper breast feathers are yellowish green, broadly margined with dark green, merging into an orange patch on each side of the body. The feathers of the nape, hind neck and abdomen are green, broadly edged with dark green. The upper and under tail coverts are yellowish green and the larger wing feathers are edged with the same colour. The tail is green, the lateral feathers being banded with orange-red. The bill is horn-coloured; the iris is bright yellow – an unusual colour for an Amazon. Other strange features are the nostrils which are large and prominent and the cere which is bright pink with a swollen appearance. The feet are pale orange. Length: about 27 cm (10½ in).

Immature birds of the less colourful type have yellow on the crown, ear coverts, lores, cheeks and the area surrounding the eyes only. The feathers of the under parts are green with darker edges, and the upper parts are bluish green. There is a small patch of yellowish orange above each thigh.

Both colour phases are illustrated by Cooper in Forshaw (1973).

G. A. Smith (1983b) wrote:

> The general inference has been that the amount of melanin deposited in the lowest feathers would diminish with age. This has occurred in the otherwise greenish birds that I own.
>
> As there is a positive selection for Parrots to be sexually dimorphic, could it be that the two 'morphs' are sexual differences? A nest may contain both forms. This was demonstrated to me with nest-gathered youngsters of this year.

Range/Habitat: The Yellow-faced Amazon is found only in eastern and central Brazil, in open country. It is locally common.
Aviculture: This species is extremely rare in aviculture. In 1879, Karl Hagenbeck imported some into Germany and at least five specimens reached Britain during the 1930s. Vogelpark Walsrode, has exhibited three specimens since 1973, extremely neat and attractive birds when I saw them four years later and showing no yellow suffusion on the breast. While in Paraguay in 1977, F. Turner obtained two young hand-reared birds. A dealer there told him that in ten years he had had only about ten through his hands – and those in the latter years. There are few specimens in captivity and no breeding reported to date.

Yellow-shouldered Amazon Parrot
A. barbadensis

Description: This species has the feathers of the forehead white with the bases of a delicate salmon colour. The yellow on the head, the extent of which varies considerably in individuals, is suffused with blue on the cheeks. The forepart of the crown and the area immediately surrounding the eye is yellow. The shoulders and thighs are yellow and the red wing speculum is present. The green feathers of the

Yellow-shouldered Amazon, aged 22 days. (Eyes not fully open).

Seven-week old Yellow-shouldered Amazon hand-reared by the author – the first bred in Britain.

mantle and the upper breast are heavily edged with black. The tail is beautifully marked with red near the base and a broad band of yellow near the tip. The beak is pinkish horn-coloured and the iris is orange. Length: 31 cm (12 in).

Immature birds are less distinctly marked. The iris is brown. The race *A.b. rothschildi*, which supposedly differs in having less yellow on the head, is not a valid one.

Range/Habitat: The Yellow-shouldered Amazon has a small range, being confined to two small areas on the coast of Venezuela, where it is now rare, the island of Bonaire in the Netherlands Antilles (it is now extinct on Aruba) and the islands of Blanquilla and Margarita off the coast of Venezuela. It is locally common in Venezuela, uncommon on Bonaire; its current status on Blanquilla and Margarita are unknown.

Aviculture: These are rarely imported.

In 1982, the first recorded captive breedings occurred – in the collection of Ramon Noegel in Florida and in my own. In 1979, the Reverend Noegel acquired nine birds from different sources – private owners and zoos. When they were sexed, they proved to be eight males and one female. In

1981, a second female, an old bird, was obtained. That year she hatched two chicks which were not reared. Later that year, four birds were obtained which had been confiscated by US Customs and Excise; they were two males and two females. The following year one female laid three eggs – on May 13, 16 and 19. They hatched on June 9, 10 and 12. Another youngster was produced from the old female. Since that time, several more have been reared.

Also in 1982, a female in my collection which usually laid in May, previously without success, had shown no interest in breeding by that month. I therefore offered her a new mate, as I had two unpaired males. This change was much to her liking; his extrovert, cheerful personality matched her own and was unlike the almost morose character of her first mate. Within four weeks, she was incubating three fertile eggs.

The first hatched on July 15. My husband inspected the nest soon after the chick hatched and discovered that its head was bruised and that its wing tips and toenails had been bitten, but not seriously. The chick was removed immediately and placed in a brooder at about 35°C (95°F). It had some longish

white down on the upper parts only, from the nape to the lower back. The day after hatching it weighed 10g ($\frac{2}{5}$ oz) and for the first five days it gained only 1 g ($\frac{3}{100}$ oz) daily. During this period, the food consisted of a thin mixture of Heinz first weaning food (dry), the variety being bone and beef broth with vegetables (since discontinued in the dry form, now available in tins), plus Heinz tinned strained fruit dessert, blended with water and a little bone flour, and cooked. For the first five days, a small amount of yoghurt was given directly on the spoon at each feed. Three days later ground-up CéDé (a proprietary rearing food for Canaries) was added. Daily weight gains then increased.

The eyes started to slit on the 19th day but were not fully open until the 28th day. During the fourth week, the most marked changes occurred in the chick's appearance. The tongue, which was pink on hatching and later tipped with black, became entirely black. The first feather tracts appeared on the wings and, by the 26th day, feathers were visible over most of the body. At five weeks, the first feathers were erupting, on the wings and just above the flanks. The chick was removed to a brooder kept at a lower temperature, approximately 28°C (83°F). Thenceforth, feathering was rapid and completed by the end of August, except for the tail which was not full length. At 77 days, it flew for the first time, circling the room strongly. At 11½ weeks old it was independent, having been easily weaned on to soaked seed and pomegranates, and other fruit. At 11 weeks, the iris colour was orange, duller than in the adult but quite different to the indistinct brownish eye colour of the unweaned bird.

Most Amazons flare their tails in display: the Yellow-shouldered does this to great advantage since its tail is one of its most attractive features. On first sight this species might not strike one as being of particular beauty yet it repays close inspection.

Blue-fronted Amazon Parrot
A. aestiva aestiva

Description: This species has the forehead and lores blue. The crown, area surrounding the eyes, sometimes part of the cheeks, the throat and, in some individuals, even part of the upper breast, also the thighs, are yellow. There is a broad yellowish green band at the tip of the tail and a red patch at the base of the lateral tail feathers. Many of the feathers, especially those of the neck and upper breast, have black edges. The beak and cere are black, also the eyelashes. Length: 36 cm (14 in).

Immature birds have less blue and yellow on the crown which is usually duller in colour; in some birds the head is almost entirely green. Colouration of the crown in the young produced during several years by John Scott's pair was variable, some being mainly blue on the head, and others predominantly yellow.

Lutino mutants have been recorded on several occasions. The Duke of Bedford had one in which the areas which are normally green were deep golden-yellow, the blue areas were replaced by white and the red was retained. Cinnamon mutants and abnormally coloured birds of no recognised mutation have also been recorded.

Range/Habitat: The Blue-fronted Amazon is found in Brazil, Bolivia and

Blue-fronted Amazon (*Amazona aestiva aestiva*).

northern Argentina. The nominate race is found in eastern Brazil as far south as Rio Grande do Sul and southeastern Mato Grosso. It is common throughout most of its wide range, although in some areas its numbers have been adversely affected by deforestation.

Aviculture: This bird is one of the best long been popular as a pet.

It is one of the best mimics and, unlike the majority of Amazons, some individuals acquire quite an extensive vocabulary. It is probably for this reason that it was formerly neglected as an aviary bird.

The earliest recorded breeding of this species occurred in France in the 1880s. M. Renouard bred three young from a pair which he had obtained in

Buenos Aires. The eggs hatched after 30 days and the young remained in the nest for 62 days.

Another early success occurred in Switzerland in 1984. Dr Wyss of Hunenburg, had allowed his pair to fly at liberty for 20 years in the surrounding meadows and forests. They nested in a deep hole in a pear tree and four young were reared. They were again successful in 1895.

One of the most interesting successes occurred in the sawdust at the base of an ordinary parrot cage! The pair belonged to G. D. Smith of Aberdeen. In 1939, two chicks hatched from four eggs and were killed at the age of seven days. A chick hatched in 1940 died at 14 days and in 1941 a chick was successfully reared, partly by hand. In genus, including the Festive, Red-tailed, Yellow-cheeked and Yellow-fronted.

Yellow-winged Amazon Parrot

Description: It differs from the nominate in having the bend of the wing and the frontal edge of the wing yellow rather than red. Only the rear shoulder coverts are predominantly red, more or less mixed with yellow. The red is seen only when the wings are lifted.

Range/Habitat: This race is found in south-western Mato Grosso in Brazil, northern and eastern Bolivia, Paraguay and northern Argentina.

Aviculture: A prolific male Yellow-winged Amazon paired to a female Salvin's reared young annually for Mrs Yeats of Surrey. The young varied in appearance. In 1973, two chicks hatched but one was killed after Mrs Yeats inspected the nest. The survivor had the white eye ring and mauve-edged neck feathers of the Salvin's and the yellow and blue forehead of the Blue-front. The young were reared on chicken and lamb bones, cheddar cheese, peanut butter on bread, fruit, greenfood, sunflower, hemp, oats, elderberries and carrots.

Orange-winged Amazon Parrot

A. amazonica

Description: This bird is considerably smaller than the Blue-front, for which it is frequently mistaken. The horn-coloured beak (not black), smaller size, slimmer build and different arrangement of yellow and blue on the head, distinguish it. Other obvious differences are the orange wing speculum and the orange patch at the base of the tail feathers, these areas being red in the Blue-front.

In the Orange-wing, the forehead, lores and a stripe above the eye are mauvish blue and the chin is a paler blue. The crown is yellow, also the cheeks, which are usually of a deeper shade. However, as in the Blue-front, the head colouration is variable. The

Orange-winged Amazon (*Amazona amazonica*).

1945 and 1946 two young were fully reared by the parents.

At Keston Foreign Bird Farm in Kent, five young were reared in one nest in 1939, four in 1940 and one in 1941. Second generation young were not bred until 1950, when four young were reared. No nesting attempts were made by birds under four years old.

A pair which reared one youngster for W. H. Rose in 1957 nested in a hollow elm trunk. The first of three eggs was laid on about July 10; a chick hatched on August 11. It fledged at nine weeks. Since the 1970s, this species has reared young on very many

occasions in collections throughout the world.

In Sweden, it bred successfully in Stockholm Zoo in 1962 and, in Germany, young were reared at Walsrode Bird Park in 1977.

This species often proves to be long-lived. W. C. Osman Hill (1954) recorded life spans of 97 and 98½ years. One of these birds had been in one lady's possession for 70 years and both had spent most of their long lives with only two families, thus these records appear to be authentic.

The Blue-fronted Amazon has hybridised with several members of the primaries are black, deep blue and green and the feathers of the hind neck are edged with dark grey. The plumage above is mid-green, the feathers of the back being tinged with grey; the under parts are a greyish shade of green. The bill is pale horn-coloured with a dark tip. The iris is orange. There is an area of pale grey skin surrounding the eye. Length: about 30–33 cm (12–13 in). Size and colouration is variable, which is to be expected considering its immense range. Immature birds are similar to adults.

In 1960, I saw a pure yellow (almost certainly a Lutino) Orange-winged Amazon at Paignton Zoo, England, where it lived for several years.
Range/Habitat: This species is found over the entire northern part of South America, west of the Andes. It is almost certainly the most common and widespread of the genus. It is also found in Trinidad and Tobago.
Aviculture: Perhaps because the species is so common, little has been recorded about the Orange-winged Amazon in captivity. It probably rates with *aestiva* and *ochrocephala* among the three Amazons which have been exported in the greatest numbers. Relatively small and inexpensive, this species is often kept as a pet.

Despite its small size, the Orange-wing has a loud voice which can be quite as annoying as that of the larger species. Apart from that, it can be recommended as a pet.

In Britain, the Orange-winged Amazon was bred in unusual circumstances in 1979 – and this would appear to be a first UK breeding. Mrs Jane Davis of Gloucestershire kept a pair of Orange-wings and a male Green-cheeked free in her living room. The Orange-wings nested on the top of a toy cupboard. Six attempts during a three-year period resulted in infertile eggs. In 1978, a new male was obtained and the female laid three eggs in October. Two were fertile; one chick died in the attempt to hatch. The female laid again the following year, on September 18, 21 and 28. The second egg hatched on October 16; the chick was sparsely covered in white down. It left the nest at 47 days, perhaps slightly prematurely because of its close contact with human beings. At 55 days it flew for the first time. The pair

reared two more young in the following year.

This species has also been bred in the aviaries at Waddesden Manor, Buckinghamshire. The pair bred in a large display aviary containing other parrots, such as Senegals and Greys. They had to be removed; the Orange-wings would not tolerate their presence when they started to nest in 1982. Long-tailed parrots, such as Ringneck and Moustache Parrakeets were tolerated as long as they did not go near the nest log.

Two of the four eggs hatched after an incubation period of 25 to 26 days. The third chick was killed at about one week old when the other two were removed for hand-rearing.

In the USA, young have been reared since 1967 at Busch Gardens, Tampa, Florida. One pair has bred consistently in a suspended wire cage measuring about 180 × 91 cm (6 × 3 ft) × 91 cm (3 ft) high.

A pair belonging to Ramon Noegel of Seffner, Florida, reared young in 1975, and continued to do so from 1976 in the collection of Roger Kenny of Tampa. San Diego Zoo also bred this species during the 1970s.

Amazona ochrocephala complex

Difficulty often arises in the identification of the various races of *ochrocephala*. This is because ranges overlap and birds intermediate between two races occur. At the 1982 convention of the American Federation of Aviculture, Howard Voren gave some examples. The *ochrocephala* found in the area approaching the Colombian border differ from typical *panamensis* in having the beak darker and in their larger size.

On the Pacific coast of Central America, from Mexico to Costa Rica, are birds intermediate between *auropalliata* and *parvipes*. In addition, there is an unnamed subspecies from Honduras which has red at the bend of the wing, a large area of yellow on the nape and forehead, white beak and white cere. In Honduras, the people collect only nestlings – not adults. Immature birds have no yellow on the

nape but they do have yellow on the forehead. Importers shun these birds, because they have no yellow on the nape, and a light beak, unlike *auropalliata* for which there is always a large demand.

Yellow-fronted Amazon Parrot
A. ochrocephala ochrocephala
Description: It has the crown yellow, the rest of the head, including the forehead, being green. The upper surface is a medium shade of green, with the feathers of the neck and mantle faintly edged with black and those of the wings with pale yellowish green. The under parts are a more yellow shade of green, also the upper tail coverts. The wing speculum and the bend of the wing are pinkish red, also a patch at the base of each tail feather. A broad yellowish green band decorates the tip of the tail. The beak is dark grey, with a pinkish spot on the upper mandible in some birds. The iris is orange and the area of white skin surrounding the eye is most conspicuous. Length: 35 cm (14 in). Weight: 450 g (1 lb).

Immature birds usually have less yellow on the crown, sometimes none at all, and less red on the bend of the wing. The bill is dark grey or dull black and the iris is dark.

Recorded mutations of the Yellow-fronted Amazon include one which was described as 'almost a pure Lutino' and the very unusual Blue mutation of *panamensis* at Wassenaar Zoo in the Netherlands. The bird has the forehead white, the rest of the plumage being a soft powder blue.
Range/Habitat: The Yellow-fronted Amazon has a very extensive range from the eastern Andes of Colombia, to the Guianas and Venezuela. It also occurs on Trinidad.

Panama Yellow-fronted Amazon
A. o. panamensis
Description: It differs from the nominate race in having the forehead yellow, not green, with a distinct bluish sheen on the green feathers following the triangular shaped patch of yellow crown feathers. The

Yellow-fronted Amazon (*Amazona ochrocephala ochrocephala*).

During the breeding season the pair was fed on a mixture consisting of one part each layer pellets, wheat, peanuts (shelled and in the shell) and of hemp to four parts sunflower. Bread and milk and boiled potatoes were also eaten.

Newly hatched Yellow-fronted Amazon chicks weigh about 12 g ($\frac{2}{5}$ oz).

Natterer's Amazon Parrot
A. o. nattereri

Description: *A. o. nattereri* differs from *ochrocephala* in having a broad frontal band, cheeks, ear coverts and throat green strongly suffused with blue.

Range/Habitat: It is found in southern Colombia, eastern Ecuador, eastern Peru and the north-western Mato Grosso region of Brazil.

Marajo Amazon Parrot
A. o. xantholaema

Description: It has the crown, lores and cheeks yellow and some birds also have yellow extending to the nape and with red feathers over the yellow areas. The bend of the wing is blood red, the wing speculum is red and the thighs are green and yellow. There is a green band on the forehead, from 0.5 to 1 cm ($\frac{1}{5}$ to $\frac{2}{5}$ in) wide. The beak is larger than that of the nominate race; the upper mandible is horn-coloured and dark grey and the lower mandible is dark grey. (van Dieten, pers. comm., 1984). Judging from an excellent photograph of this race, its appearance is more reminiscent of *aestiva* than of *ochrocephala*. Perhaps it can be used as evidence that these two forms are conspecific. Its size is approximately the same as that of the Double Yellow-headed Amazon; the wing measures about 23.5 cm ($9\frac{1}{4}$ in) and the tail 12.3 cm ($4\frac{4}{5}$ in). Weight: 520 g ($18\frac{1}{4}$ oz).

Range/Habitat: It occurs on Marajo Island at the mouth of the Amazon in northern Brazil and in the vicinity of the Paru River. Several flocks of up to 25 birds were observed by van Dieten in 1984.

Aviculture: It was unknown in captivity outside Brazil until 1984 when a few were imported into Europe.

upper mandible is horn-coloured near the base, light grey at the top. The lower mandible is light horn colour. Most have the toe nails very light coloured. It is smaller at about 30 cm (12 in). This is not a well-defined subspecies; there are many intermediates between it and the nominate race.

Range/Habitat: This race is found in Panama and the tropical lowlands of northern Colombia east to the Santa Marta region.

Aviculture: A tame Yellow-fronted Amazon is one of the most delightful birds it is possible to own. They are excellent mimics of sounds and most learn a few words, even without any conscious effort to teach them. Especially talented at mimicking human laughter, this is an aptitude which can cause great amusement – especially as they may take their cue from the tone of voice rather than actual laughter.

The Panama race, in particular, has a reputation as an excellent mimic and entertainer. In the nominate race the patch of yellow is more oval. Some Panamas have the bases of the yellow feathers on the forehead pink.

The Yellow-fronted Amazon is now commonly bred in captivity. The first breeding reported in Britain occurred in 1967 in the aviaries of Clifford Smith of Yorkshire. He obtained two birds in 1961; in 1966, the female laid two eggs which failed to hatch. In 1967, a chick was heard in the nest on July 11; it fledged on September 23, to be followed by a second a week later. Their plumage was duller than the adults' with perhaps even more clearly defined black edges to the feathers of the mantle. The yellow on the forehead was less extensive. The pair reared more young in subsequent years; the average length of their stay in the nest was 74 days.

The Panama race was bred in the USA in 1945 by Mrs E. Davies, and in Denmark in 1963 (two), the same pair rearing three in the following year.

S. L. Drewery of Ormskirk, Lancashire, reared a single youngster from his pair of Yellow-fronted Amazons in 1977. The eggs of the first clutch were laid on May 5 and 7. When the female deserted on June 2 the eggs were found to be broken. The interesting aspect of this breeding is that the female laid again during August and it was believed that the chick hatched on September 11. It left the nest on November 19 and was fed by its parents until December 31.

Yellow-naped Amazon Parrot

A. o. auropalliata

Description: It is easily recognised by the large yellow patch on the nape. The cere and the hairs surrounding the nostrils are black and the bill is black or slate-coloured. There is no red at the bend of the wing. Length: 35 cm (14 in).

Immature birds have no yellow on the nape or two or three yellow feathers only. The iris is dark.

In 1942, there was a Lutino Yellow-naped Amazon at San Francisco Zoo.

Range/Habitat: This race inhabits southern Mexico, north-western Costa Rica and northern Honduras. It has declined due to modification of its habitat for agricultural purposes, yet is said to remain fairly widespread.

Aviculture: It has never been well known in Europe but is very highly regarded as a pet and talker in the USA. One bird which could speak Spanish, repeating songs and shouting orders for dinner in that language and eating mashed peas and gravy from a spoon, is typical of many Yellow-naped Amazons which have become much cherished pets.

The Yellow-naped Amazon was bred by Sir Edward Hallstrom in Australia; the breeding was reported in 1948.

Possibly the first and also the most consistent breeder in Europe is Heinz Martin in Sweden. The female commenced to lay in 1972; in that year and 1973 the eggs were infertile. Young have been reared every year since 1974. The female normally commences to lay in January or February; the usual clutch is three eggs.

In the USA, Velma Hart in California was one of the earliest breeders and possessed a prolific pair that bred during a ten-year period. Despite the large numbers in the USA, the Yellow-naped Amazon has reared young on relatively few occasions. It appears to be much more difficult to breed than the Double Yellow-head Amazon, for example.

A. o. parvipes

Description: It differs from *auropalliata* in the red on the bend of the wing and in the slightly smaller size. The most noticeable feature is the paler bill.

Range/Habitat: It is found in the Bay Islands of Honduras (Roatan, Barbareta and Guanaja) and the Caribbean slope (Mosquitia region) of easternmost Honduras and north-eastern Nicaragua.

Aviculture: This race is rarely exported or rarely identified. The first reported captive breeding occurred in 1982 in the collection of Mr and Mrs J. Stoodley in Hampshire (Stoodley, 1983); however, the birds concerned did not precisely match the description of *parvipes* and may belong to an unnamed subspecies. The first of three eggs was laid on April 23; average weight was 24.5 g ($\frac{9}{10}$ oz). One was infertile and the other two hatched in an incubator after 28 days. The chicks died in an outbreak of *Pseudomonas*. In the second clutch, three eggs were laid; two chicks hatched and both were reared. A second pair had two eggs; one hatched but the chick died. Subsequently more young were reared.

Double Yellow-headed Amazon Parrot

This name covers four races of *ochrocephala*.

A. o. oratrix

Description: It has the head and throat – but not the upper breast – yellow. In some birds some of the feathers of the nape are margined with red. The bend of the wing is red, or red and yellow; carpal edge of wing and thighs, or part of the thighs, also yellow. The bill is pale, almost ivory, and the cere yellowish. Length: 36 cm (14 in).

Immature birds have the yellow on the head confined mainly to the forehead. It takes about four years for full adult plumage to be attained.

Range/Habitat: This race is found on the Gulf slopes of Mexico, from southern Tamaulipas and Nuevo Leon to Tabasco and, on the Pacific coast, from Colima south to Oaxaca. This race has declined throughout its range in recent years due to the pressures of trade and habitat destruction.

A. o. magna

Description: It differs from *oratrix* in its larger size, and differs from *tresmariae* in the shorter tail and in lacking the blue sheen to the under parts. Birds with the yellow of the head extending well into the upper breast are probably attributable to this race – not to *tresmariae*.

Range/Habitat: It occurs on the Atlantic slope of Mexico from central Tamaulipas and extreme south-eastern San Luis Potosí south through Veracruz to eastern Tabasco.

A. o. tresmariae

Description: It has the entire head and neck yellow, paler on the forehead. This race has a bluish tinge to the pale green under parts and is the largest, measuring about 38 cm (15 in). The wing speculum, on five secondaries, is pinkish red and the bend of the wing is red, usually with a few yellow feathers. The upper parts are mid-green, the feathers of the mantle being faintly edged with dark green and the rest of the feathers narrowly edged with yellowish green. The thighs are yellow. The lower half of the tail, also the upper tail coverts, are yellowish green. The bill and cere are whitish, also the area of skin surrounding the eye which is not very conspicuous. The feet and nails are pale pink. Iris is orange with an inner ring of yellow.

A. o. belizensis

Description: The yellow on the head is confined to the forehead, crown, lores, ear coverts, upper cheeks and area surrounding the eyes.

Range/Habitat: It inhabits Belize.

Aviculture: The Double Yellow-head is one of the most magnificent of the Amazons. Despite its large size and loud voice, it is in demand as a pet, being an excellent mimic and possessing a very pleasing personality. In the USA, it has long been popular as a

Three young Double Yellow-headed Amazons just after leaving the nest. Bred by the author.

pet; it is less well known in Europe, especially since Mexico ceased to export birds in the early 1980s. This resulted in it becoming expensive and, by the mid-1980s, much sought after.

Although it is kept and bred in much smaller enclosures, a minimum aviary size of 3.6 × 1.2 m (12 × 4 ft) × 1.8 m (6 ft) high is recommended if its beauty (especially in flight) is to be appreciated to the full.

In the USA, it has been bred in many collections. One of the earliest successful breeders was Velma Hart in California, who produced 23 from one pair during the seven years from 1957. More recently, also in California, Ed Shoemaker reared 17 young between 1979 and 1981. On several occasions, the female laid as soon as three weeks after the young were removed for hand-rearing. In Zimbabwe, Mr and Mrs G. Wood had reared 22 young in the 16 years up to 1981.

In Europe, the first recorded breeding of the Double Yellow-headed Amazon occurred in Britain in 1970. A pair was obtained by Clifford Smith of Yorkshire in 1966; the female laid two infertile eggs in 1969. In 1970, four eggs were laid and two chicks were

reared. They fledged when eight weeks old.

One of these birds itself reared young in 1974 in the collection of K. Dalton of Hallow, Worcester. During the previous year one chick had hatched and died. In 1976, the female behaved strangely, laying her eggs from the perch and taking pebbles into the nest-box to incubate. In 1977, she reared three young but one became paralysed after fledging and survived only a few months.

Young have been reared at Zurich Zoo in Switzerland since 1972. In Sweden, a pair belonging to Sven Williamsson reared three young in 1975. In Texas, Paul Springman of Brownsville has a pair of *oratrix* which had reared young for the fourth consecutive year in 1977, one or two being produced each year. It is of interest that, in 1977, the first of two eggs was laid on March 31 and there were two chicks on April 26, giving a minimum incubation period of 24 days – presumably shortened by warm weather. The male of the pair has never been seen in the nest-box.

In 1980, my two *tresmariae* females (genuine *tresmariae* of the large size,

lighter yellow on the head and distinctive blue sheen on the breast) both proved their sex by laying. Ramon Noegel generously sent me two surgically sexed male *oratrix*. One was introduced to one of the females in October. The female laid the following April. Although the nest-box was situated in such a way that inspection could be carried out from outside the aviary, the aggressiveness of both birds made this virtually impossible. They refused to leave the nest when anyone was in the vicinity. A chick was heard during the last week in May. Only a few glimpses of it were obtained before it left the nest on July 31. It differed from the adults in having yellow from the forehead to the middle of the crown, down through the lores and cheeks to the forepart of the ear coverts. The eye and feet were greyish and the nails (white in adults) were black.

Rearing food consisted mainly of soaked sunflower seed and fruit, sprinkled with bone meal, cheese and, mainly during the early stages, hard-boiled egg. Even corn-on-the-cob was refused. A male, when adult it resembled the male and lacked the distinctive blue sheen of the female.

In 1982, the female laid the first of three eggs in February; one hatched and the chick left the nest in May. In 1983, the pair nested during a cold spell in January; three young were reared and the first left the nest on April 19.

Mercenary (Scaly-naped or Tschudi's) Amazon Parrot
A. mercenaria

Description: Mainly green, it is paler and brighter on the forehead and cheeks and yellowish green on the under parts. The feathers from the crown to the neck are tipped with dusky black. There is a dark red patch on the base of the outer three secondaries. The tail feathers are tipped with yellowish grey, preceded by a red band. The bill is dark grey except the base of the upper mandible which is horn-coloured. The iris is reddish brown. Length 34 cm (13 in).

Range/Habitat: This species is found in the mountains of western South America from Santa Marta mountains

Mercenary Amazon new to aviculture in 1983.

Mealy Amazon Parrot
A. farinosa farinosa
Description: This is the largest of the mainland Amazons. It has some yellow on the crown, the amount and even the position of which varies considerably. In some specimens, the yellow is extended to the forehead and the yellow feathers may be tipped with red. There is an indistinct grey patch on the hind neck, the feathers of which – and those of the mantle – are broadly edged with very dark brown or black. The carpal edge of the wing and the speculum are red. There is a broad yellowish green band at the tip of the tail. The upper parts are green with a greyish mealy appearance; the under parts are lighter green. The bill is pale horn-coloured. The iris is brown and there is a prominent area of white skin surrounding the eye. Length: 38 cm (15 in).

Immature birds have less yellow on the head – only two or three feathers in some birds.
Range/Habitat: Distribution of *farinosa* is southern Mexico and over most of northern South America east of the Andes to northern Bolivia and central eastern Brazil.

Throughout its very extensive range, it remains common where continuous forest survives.
Aviculture: These large handsome birds, with appealing personalities, had not been bred in captivity prior to the 1980s.

Plain-coloured Amazon Parrot
A. f. inornata
Description: This usually lacks the yellow on the head and is darker green. There is some doubt regarding the validity of this race.

Blue-crowned Amazon Parrot
A. f. guatemalae
Description: It has the whole of the top of the head to the nape blue, lighter on the crown and merging into darker greyish blue on the nape and mantle. The bill is grey with a yellow spot near the base of the upper mandible. The iris is reddish brown.
Range/Habitat: This race inhabits southern Mexico through Guatemala to Honduras.
Aviculture: It is rare in aviculture, perhaps because the people in the regions in which it is found do not take it from the nest because it is reputed to be incapable of learning to talk. In the same area, the Yellow-naped Amazon is highly regarded as a talking bird.

In 1984, *guatemalae* was bred in West Germany by Wolfgang Burkart of Benningen. He obtained six birds of this race in December 1980. In the spring of 1981, one pair was placed in a separate aviary. The female laid on April 5, 9 and 12. A chick was heard on May 2; three chicks had hatched by May 6. On May 23, they weighed 363, 348 and 236 g ($12\frac{4}{5}$, $12\frac{1}{4}$ and $8\frac{3}{5}$ oz), on May 29, 462, 424 and 360 g ($16\frac{3}{10}$, 15 and $12\frac{7}{10}$ oz) and, on June 5, 538, 476 and 450 g (19, $16\frac{4}{5}$ and $15\frac{9}{10}$ oz). Their eyes opened at about 18 days. At 30 days, green feathers were apparent, on the wings. The first youngster appeared at the nest hole at 52 days and left the nest at 61 days. The second and third left the nest five and seven days later. Photographs of the very handsome youngsters at ten weeks show them as being almost identical to the adults, except for the white edge of the upper part of the upper mandible.

The birds were kept in an indoor aviary with the temperature during the breeding period maintained at about 25°C (77°F). The humidity was between 60 and 90 per cent. They were fed on parrot mixture, germinated oats, wheat, barley and sunflower seed, bread and milk and much fruit, including apple, banana and cherries, also carrots and berries.

Costa Rican Amazon Parrot
A. f. virenticeps
Description: It differs from *guatemalae* in having the head mainly green, the forehead and crown being tinged with blue. There is little or no red on the edge of the wing.

in Colombia to Peru. It is believed to be uncommon but with a stable population in most areas.
Aviculture: The Mercenary Amazon was virtually unknown in aviculture until 1983 when a few specimens were imported into the USA. In 1984, Ramon Noegel in Florida acquired six. It is also kept by Alberto de Camargo Cardoso in São Paulo.

Mealy Amazon (*Amazona farinosa farinosa*).

Range/Habitat: It inhabits Nicaragua, Costa Rica and western Panama.
Aviculture: In 1985, Ramon Noegel reared two *virenticeps* × *guatemalae* hybrids.

Vinaceous Amazon Parrot
A. vinacea
Description: This is the only Amazon with a deep red beak; the tip of the upper mandible is horn-coloured. In adult birds the forehead, chin and lores are red. The elongated, erectile feathers of the hind neck (which, unjustifiably, have led to this species being confused with the Hawk-headed Parrot), are green, with a band of bluish grey near the black edge. The upper breast is purplish vinous, also the abdomen in some specimens; in others it is bluish green or green. The carpal edge of the wing is red, also the wing speculum. The tail is green, yellowish green at the tip, with a red patch near the base of the lateral feathers. The iris is orange-red. Length: 30 cm (12 in).

Immature birds have less vinous on the under parts, a duller shade of red on the forehead and yellow on the carpal edge of the wing. The iris is dark.
Range/Habitat: This species occurs in Brazil, from southern Bahía south to Rio Grande do Sul and westwards across Parana and Santa Catarina to Misiones in north-east Argentina and south-eastern Paraguay. It has declined greatly due to deforestation and is now uncommon and locally distributed.
Aviculture: This species was irregularly imported into Europe and the USA until placed on Appendix 1 of CITES. Certainly there are few pairs in aviaries, thus it has only rarely been bred in captivity. The first success in Britain occurred in 1977 in the aviaries of Clifford Smith of Yorkshire. Two were reared and left the nest at approximately ten weeks. They were fed on soaked sunflower seed, dandelion roots and leaves, chickweed, peanuts, apple, brown bread and milk.

Well-known American aviculturist, H. I. Gregory, of Lytle, Texas, was successful in breeding the Vinaceous Amazon in 1978. Four birds obtained in 1969, kept in two aviaries, made no attempt to breed so, after seven years,

Vinaceous Amazon (*Amazona vinacea*).

they were placed together in an enclosure measuring 3 × 5.4 m (10 × 18 ft) × 1.8 m (6 ft) high. In April 1978, one female laid three eggs, the first of which hatched after 28 days. The male took an equal part in feeding and caring for the young which were removed for hand-feeding when the eldest was 26 days old. The adults had fed their young on sunflower seed, monkey chow, apple, orange and carrot. The hand-feeding formula consisted of two parts of water to one part of monkey chow, plus a high-protein baby cereal.

In Belgium, J. Wierinckx (1975–76) was successful in 1975. He purchased two birds in 1971 and two more in 1973. During the summer, they were housed in a small outdoor aviary measuring 1 m (3¼ ft) square and 2 m (6½ ft) high. In the winter they were confined to a small indoor aviary where the temperature was controlled at 10°C (50°F). In 1972, two birds mated but were not provided with a nest-box until March 1975. On March 28, 1975 two eggs were seen in the nest-box (30 cm/12 in square and

40 cm/16 in high). By April 1 there were four eggs. The birds became very aggressive. One egg was infertile and one had hatched by April 27. By May 5, there were three chicks. The parents were eating large amounts of canary seed, sunflower and buckwheat. By May 26, the red feathers on the wings were apparent; by May 31, the young birds were aggressive and displayed when the nest was inspected. All three were fully feathered by June 4. Ten days later one was looking through the nest entrance. On June 16 one left the nest; two days later all three had left.

In appearance, they differed from the adults mainly in the colour of the iris which was slightly paler in colour; their bills were as red as the adults'.

The usual diet of these birds consisted of seed, banana, apple, tomato and greenfood, also bread sweetened with honey water.

St Vincent (Guilding's) Amazon Parrot
A. guildingii
Description: This bird is extremely variable in its colouration, more so than any other member of the genus. It can be predominantly green or mainly

St Vincent Parrot (*Amazona guildingii*).

orange-brown. One constant feature is the cream or whitish area on the forehead and crown, merging into yellow and blue on the rest of the head. The wing speculum is orange and there is a band of yellow at the tip of the tail. The remainder of the plumage is orange, green, gold and brown.

Whatever its combination of colours, it is unmistakable, an imposing parrot, which measures about 41 cm (15 in) in length. The iris is orange with an inner circle of yellow and the bill is whitish. Immature birds have the iris brown.

Range/Habitat: This species is confined to the central mountainous part of the island of St Vincent in the Lesser Antilles. Its population is believed to be in the region of 400 and either stable or declining slightly.

Aviculture: There are very few St Vincent Parrots in captivity outside the island and most of these are part of the consortium organised to increase breeding success. Co-operation between consortium members has resulted in birds being sexed and relocated. The first success occurred in Houston Zoo, Texas, in 1972. The zoo had exhibited a single specimen for several years and contact was made with three other zoos in the US in the same position; all agreed to lend their birds to Houston. This resulted in two of them pairing up; they were moved to a separate aviary. During February 1972 they became extremely aggressive. The female laid on March 28 and April 1. A chick hatched on April 25 and was successfully reared.

The next success was that which occurred in the collection of W. Miller in Barbados. In 1976 a single bird of the green morph was reared from a mainly orange female paired to a predominantly green male. Several more were reared in subsequent years. Several of Mr Miller's pairs were acquired by Ramon Noegel, who hand-reared one youngster in 1982 and another in 1985.

In Europe no Guilding's Amazons had been seen for many years until the mid-1970s when this species was acquired by three establishments; the Jersey Wildlife Preservation Trust, Bird Paradise in Cornwall and also Vogelpark Walsrode in West Germany.

St Lucia Amazon Parrot
A. versicolor

Description: This species has the forehead, lores and cheeks blue. The green feathers of the nape are heavily edged with black; on the remainder of the upper parts the feathers are narrowly edged with black. The scarlet wing speculum consists of a patch on the outer webs of four secondaries. The plumage of the under parts is most variable: the area of red on the upper breast may consist of a few feathers or an expansive patch. The feathers of the rest of the under parts are pale green or golden olive edged with black and usually blotched with vinous. There is a broad yellow-green band at the tip of the tail which is mainly green, with a concealed red patch near the base and some blue on the outer tail feathers. Length: about 43 cm (17 in).

Range/Habitat: This species is confined to an area of about 10,500 hectares (about 25,000 acres) on the island of St Lucia in the Lesser Antilles of the Caribbean. Its population is believed to be about 125 specimens. In recent years, the St Lucia government has done its utmost to protect this species and to educate the people concerning the importance of its survival.

Aviculture: Very few specimens have been kept in captivity outside their natural habitat. At the time of writing there are six at Jersey Wildlife Preservation Trust, received in 1976. The first captive breeding occurred there in 1982 when one was hand-reared.

Imperial (Dominican) Amazon Parrot
A. imperialis

Description: This is the largest of all Amazons. The Duke of Bedford described it as 'the emperor of all true Parrots', and no one who has seen it alive is likely to argue with this assessment. It is most distinctive, being dark purple on the head and under parts, where the feathers are edged with black. The upper parts are dark green and there is a crimson wing speculum. The tail is mainly reddish brown. The bill is dark horn colour and the iris is deep orange. Length: 45 cm (18 in).

Immature birds have yet to be described.

Imperial Amazon (*Amazona imperialis*).

Range/Habitat: This is the most endangered of neotropical parrots with a population believed to be in the region of 50 individuals (in 1984). Natural catastrophes (such as Hurricane David in 1979) have hastened its decline, caused by habitat destruction (especially that which has occurred since 1980) and shooting. Confined to the island of Dominica in the Lesser Antilles, it inhabits mountainous forests which are limited in area, thus its population has always been small.

Aviculture: Very few specimens have been kept in captivity outside Dominica. The last one seen in Britain was loaned to London Zoo by the Governor of the West Indies, Lord Hailes, in 1961. It was the first seen in Europe for over 20 years. The next were the three obtained by Vogelpark Walsrode. None are known at the time of writing.

Red-necked (Blue-faced, or Lesser Dominican) Amazon Parrot
A. arausiaca

Description: This handsome bird, is inaccurately named. It is mainly green, with the forehead, part of the crown, lores, cheeks and throat violet-blue. The middle of the lower throat and part of the upper breast is pinkish red, also the wing speculum. There is a broad yellowish green band at the tip of the tail. The bill is horn-coloured. Length 40 cm (16 in).

A Lutino specimen has been recorded in the wild.

Range/Habitat: Lower altitude forest is its habitat and it has been disturbed by clearance for banana culture and road building. Shooting is another serious threat to the survival of this species. It inhabits Dominica. Its population is small and therefore extremely vulnerable.

Aviculture: Always an extreme rarity in aviculture, probably fewer than a dozen specimens have ever reached Britain.

My first sight of this species was at Vogelpark Walsrode in 1978. Here two magnificent pairs are kept, one pair on exhibit. In both pairs, the believed female lacked the pink on the throat.

Although a large bird, the Red-necked Amazon is less bulky than the Imperial or Guilding's – and those at Walsrode certainly gave the impression of being more active. They seemed extremely fit and noisy and it was a pleasure to watch them chortling and flaring their tails.

In 1984, only three other captive birds were known: one on Dominica, one in the collection of Dr T. D. Nichols in Houston and one with Ramon Noegel in Florida.

25

Other Neotropical Parrots

The species covered in this chapter are small to medium-sized parrots from South and Central America; most are not well-known in aviculture and three genera, *Pionopsitta*, *Triclaria* and *Graydidascalus*, are rare. Only the Caiques and two or three species of *Pionus* are regularly offered for sale.

Little is known about the breeding behaviour of the more rarely imported species, any of which are worthwhile subjects for study by an aviculturist whose aim is to make a useful contribution to avicultural knowledge. The accelerating rate of destruction of neotropical rainforest is another incentive to study these birds. Some will have their habitats drastically reduced, possibly bringing them to the verge of extinction and then they will become forbidden subjects for the aviculturist.

Accommodation: Caiques often prefer to progress by climbing rather than flying so large aviaries for these birds are not essential. The reverse is true of the Purple-bellied Parrot; in flight, it is perhaps the most agile of all the neotropical parrots. The Short-tailed Parrot also enjoys a spacious area in which to exercise its wings. With *Pionus*, the beauty of their plumage is best seen in a long flight.

Pionus
Pionus

This genus of small parrots consists of seven species which would repay study by discerning aviculturists. Few genera have members showing such widely differing colouration, although all have red under tail coverts. The more unusually coloured are unique in their subtle colour combinations; they are also beautiful. Much quieter and more gentle (as pets) in disposition than Amazon Parrots, they seldom have the extrovert nature of these birds.

At the time of writing, Vogelpark Walsrode in Germany exhibits representatives of each species, probably being the only collection ever to do so concurrently. Despite their ideal size, they cannot be said to be very popular birds in captivity and few collections, private or public, have more than two species.

In England, Mr and Mrs J. Stoodley specialise in these birds and have bred most species to second and subsequent generations. Their results show that there is no reason why breeding successes should not be achieved by those willing to devote time and enthusiasm to the task.

There are two problems to be overcome in breeding these birds. One is sexing. One cannot rely on head shape as a guide, nor on behaviour of single individuals; thus surgical sexing is essential. Trial and error placing of birds together is the only way to obtain true pairs, apart from steroid analysis of the faeces.

The second problem is the aggressiveness displayed by birds in breeding condition. Some mated pairs show little of the affectionate behaviour towards each other which is typical of most neotropical parrots. If they do, mutual preening may become so aggressive that the head is denuded of feathers. The only case I have ever had of a bird killing its mate was a Massena's Parrot. In the collection of a friend who was not able to obtain a male, a female Dusky Parrot on the point of laying, entered the nest-box of another female Dusky which was incubating and killed her with a few swift bites on the head.

Aggression is demonstrated in *Pionus* by flaring the tail, after the manner of a courting feral pigeon (so that the red areas of the tail feathers are visible) and walking along the perch with head lowered and beak held against the perch. John Stoodley (1978) recorded:

> Mating is very much of communal interest, the birds becoming noisy and excited. The mating pair make a noise different from the usual calls and this brings immediate silence among the others, the noise being continued throughout the mating. The pair stand with both feet grasping the perch and they back toward each other, this position being held for some time and when the pairing is over the noise is discontinued and the neighbours become noisy again.

Pionus do not invariably mate in this position for I have seen the more usual method among neotropical species in my Bronze-winged Parrots, in which the male mounts the female but retains one leg on the perch.

Pionus do not normally roost in the nest-box unless breeding; females may roost inside for a long period before the eggs are laid. When breeding, the female may not be seen for literally weeks but when young hatch she may be seen looking out of the nest entrance; however, it is extremely difficult to catch her off the nest, making inspection or removal of chicks for hand-rearing very difficult. Eggs laid by *Pionus* are exceptionally large for the size of the bird, proportionately larger than any other parrots with which I am familiar. George Smith found that two new laid eggs of a Bronze-winged Parrot weighed 22 g and 23 g (about $\frac{4}{5}$ oz), while the weight of the adult female was 220 g ($7\frac{3}{4}$ oz); an egg 10 per cent the weight of the laying bird is very large indeed. Clutch size is usually three but may number two or four or even five. Incubation period is 26 days. Young leave the nest when about ten weeks old.

Because of the nervous disposition of some *Pionus*, resulting in their killing their young, success is more likely to be achieved if the young can be removed for hand-rearing, but this is a long job. If this is impossible, the aviary should be mainly enclosed, in a sheltered situation and as free as possible from outside disturbance.

When under stress, *Pionus* wheeze and gasp in a manner which is most alarming to those who do not know what it signifies. If left alone (and not treated for a respiratory disease which probably does not exist) the gasping will cease. However, some newly imported birds may be suffering from aspergillosis and it could be difficult to distinguish the wheezing symptoms of that disease from those of stress.

These birds usually accept quite a varied diet and, in my experience, are fonder of the small seeds, such as canary, than many parrots. They also relish spray millet, are fond of pine nuts and some have a great liking for peanuts. A wide variety of fruits and vegetable items should be offered as individuals vary somewhat in their preferences. Carrot, celery, sweet corn, the berries of elder and hawthorn and cracked walnuts are among their favourite items. Green-leaved vegetables such as spinach and kale are needed daily.

Blue-headed Parrot (*Pionus menstruus*).

Blue-headed Parrot
P. menstruus

Description: This is by far the best known member of its genus. Adult birds have the head, neck and upper breast blue, of a rich, dark shade. The ear coverts are blackish. The feathers of the throat are pink at the base, also on the outer edge in some feathers, thus producing an irregular pink patch. The feathers of the lower breast are green, tinged with brown and edged with blue. There is a bronze patch on the shoulders formed by the lesser and median wing coverts; the primaries are blue on the outer webs. The under tail coverts are scarlet and tipped with green to form a most unusual pattern. There is a large area of red at the base of each tail feather. The outer webs of the outer tail feathers are blue. The bill is dark grey with red markings at the base of both mandibles; iris is dark brown. Length: 28 cm (11 in).

Immature birds are much less colourful: the blue areas are replaced by dull green until they are about one year old. At this age they lose the red or orange fronted band which is usually a feature of immature plumage.

Colouration of this species is noticeably variable. Two races are recognised – *P.m. rubrigularis* has a more conspicuous area of pink on the throat and the shade of blue is duller; the upper parts are a darker green. The race *P.m. reichenowi* is darker blue and lacks the pink bases to the feathers of the throat; the feathers of the under parts are suffused with blue and the under tail coverts are tipped with blue.

This species is difficult to sex. In some individuals the male has the head and neck darker blue – but this is not a reliable guide.

Range/Habitat: The Blue-headed *Pionus* has a very extensive distribution over the greater part of tropical South America: from southern Costa Rica in Central America, also Columbia, Venezuela and the Guianas south to northern Bolivia and central Brazil. It is also found in Trinidad. It is common in many parts of its range and prefers dense forest in most localities. It has a far greater range than any other member of the genus, and is common and widespread.

Aviculture: Young birds make delightful pets and I have long advocated them as being far more suitable for the average household, especially where there are children, than Amazon Parrots. They are less noisy and usually more gentle in temperament and not capable of giving such a serious bite as an Amazon.

The earliest recorded breeding success was that which occurred in 1890, in France. The breeder was A. Maillard of Croisic. Four young were hatched.

The first recorded breeding in Britain took place in 1902; the breeder was the Reverend B. Hemsworth of Yorkshire. There was a conspicuous lack of further published records until the early 1970s. In England, Mr and Mrs A. J. Coulson of Whittlesey, Northamptonshire, purchased four young birds in 1971. At the end of 1973, these moulted into adult plumage and were then separated into pairs.

In 1974, one female laid four eggs; all hatched but none of the chicks lived beyond four weeks. In 1975, the pair which had hatched two chicks in the previous year hatched five young from five eggs, the first being heard on May 11. On May 28, one was dead and the survivors had empty crops. They were removed for hand-rearing; three fed readily from a syringe but the fourth died, after its crop continually filled up with air. From the time they were a few weeks old, they went through the motions of feeding each other and when the eldest two youngsters started to eat seed, they fed their younger nest mates by regurgitation. The second pair laid two clutches of four and three eggs, none of which hatched. The Coulsons reared two more Blue-headed Parrots in 1976 and four in 1977.

Blue-headed Pionus were reared from the egg by Mrs R. Hill in Devon in 1984 and 1985, using a mixture of cooked porridge oats, Milupa seven cereal, ground sunflower seed, wheat-germ cereal, tinned apple baby food, corn oil and, for the first 10 days, egg yolk.

Mr and Mrs J. Stoodley have reared this species consistently since 1975. It was bred in the USA by Mrs F. Hubbell of San Diego in 1958 and in South Africa in 1976, in the collection of Mr and Mrs B. Boswell of Natal Lion Park. Since these early successes, many others have occurred.

Sordid Parrot
P. sordidus sordidus

Description: It resembles a Blue-headed Parrot but with the head feathers green edged with blue. Regardless of the subspecies, it is generally called Coral-billed Parrot by aviculturists, although strictly speaking this name should be applied to the race *P. m. corallinus*, which is darker green than the nominate race with the forehead dark blue. The feathers of the breast are broadly edged with mauvish pink. There is a blue band on the throat in all races and the general colouration is olive-green with the primaries edged with blue and the feathers of the upper parts with olive-brown or dusky blue margins in most races (six have been described). The outer tail feathers are blue on the outer webs and red at the base. The under tail coverts are red, narrowly tipped with green. The iris is brown and the beak is coral red. Length 28 cm (11 in).

Immature birds have the head, throat and breast pale green, red on the forehead and the under tail coverts yellowish green marked with red. John Stoodley described the young Coral-billed Parrots which he bred, at 12 weeks old, as being:

> . . . beautifully coloured with blue, pink, golden-green and almost gold on the breast and about the head, but the brilliance of the colours seemed to fade, as did the facial red soon after the birds were separated from their parents.

Range/Habitat: The Sordid Parrot is found in mountain forests: in Colombia it inhabits the Santa Marta Mountains in the north, also northern Venezuela, and is found in the Andes of Colombia, Ecuador, eastern Peru and northern Bolivia. It is local in occurrence and common in some areas.

Aviculture: This species is rather rare in captivity, and probably remains un-identified in many instances or is mistaken for Maximilian's Parrot. This species has seldom been bred in captivity. In 1977, Mr and Mrs J. Stoodley bred from two birds obtained in 1975. They chose, from several nest-boxes, one measuring 45 × 20 cm (18 × 8 in) square and spent much time enlarging the entrance hole. Three eggs were laid

Sordid Parrot (*Pionus sordidus sordidus*).

and incubation commenced on April 27. The three chicks were first seen on May 24 when they were covered with creamy white down which abraded off. By 20 days, their eyes were fully open, pin feathers were appearing and the pink colour of the bill was becoming apparent. At 12 weeks old, they were independent and were removed from their parents. I saw them when they were a year old and as large and as handsome as their parents – if not more so. They were so bold that when I entered their aviary one soon settled beside me and sampled my finger.

Maximilian's (Scaly-headed) Parrot
P. maximiliani maximiliani

Description: The colouration is, perhaps, the least interesting of the members of the genus. The feathers of the head and upper parts are green, narrowly edged with dark grey. Forehead and lores are nearly black; the chin and a band across the throat are dull purplish blue (reddish purple in the race *siy*) and the feathers of the hind neck have whitish streaks – only visible when ruffled. The mantle and upper part of the wings are bronze-olive, the

Maximilian's Parrot (*Pionus maximiliani*).

bronze being most pronounced on the shoulders. The primaries, secondaries and tail are olive-green with a bronze tinge. The tail feathers have a patch of red on the inner webs, the outer webs being edged with blue; under tail coverts are red, the longest having yellowish green edges. The bill is blackish with horn-coloured edges. There is a prominent area of white skin above and below the eye, that at the sides being dull grey. Length: 29 cm (11 in).

Immature birds may or may not have a broken red frontal band which is lost at the first moult, and less blue on the upper breast.

Range/Habitat: Maximilian's Parrot is found over a large area of eastern South America from eastern and south-eastern Brazil to northern Argentina. It remains common over much of its range, being more tolerant of altered habitat than many parrots.

Aviculture: This species has never been imported in large numbers; it is available spasmodically but cannot be described as rare. Very little has been recorded about it in captivity and I know of no captive breeding before 1970. In that year, two young were reared in Beira Zoo, Mozambique. However, Sir Edward Hallstrom re-

ported breeding *menstruus* in Australia in 1958 but the distinguished aviculturist, Alan Lendon, informed me that he believed the species bred was Maximilian's. In Britain, the first breeding occurred at Birdworld, Farnham, Surrey, in 1974; however, both youngsters died shortly after leaving the nest. The parents were both tame birds which had been donated as unwanted pets. They nested fairly soon after being placed together. They did not become aggressive towards their keepers as tame birds often do; in fact, they allowed inspection of the nest.

In 1975, Mr and Mrs J. Stoodley reared two young and, in 1977, Herbert Murray of Brentwood, Essex, reared two. In 1978, his pair reared three, one of which had a red frontal band – unlike those bred in the previous year. Rearing foods included nectar, soaked sultanas, mealworms, maggot chrysalis, softbill food and seed.

In Europe, Maximilian's Parrot has been bred (Geil, 1978; Mathys, 1978) in West Germany and Switzerland. Both breeders reared two young from two eggs in 1977. Vogelpark Walsrode has also been successful since 1977. In 1978, in Belgium, Johan Ingels' pair hatched a chick from one of three eggs; it was successfully reared.

In South Africa, this species was among those bred by J. Rough of Parrots Paradise, Rustenburg. Since 1976, young have been reared consistently in the collection of Mr and Mrs B. Boswell of Natal Lion Park. The parents of the latter birds showed a marked preference for greenfood after the chicks hatched, even cropping the grass in their aviary. This was in contrast to the *menstruus* which bred in the same collection and ignored greenfood. Four Maximilian's were kept in the same aviary; the non-breeding pair was removed because the male bullied the breeding male but was not as aggressive as *menstruus*, more than one pair of which cannot be kept together, in the experience of W. Cummings who was caring for these *Pionus*.

In California, Betty Byers recorded the incubation period for this species as 26 days and the weight of a young bird on fledging as 197 g (6$\frac{9}{10}$ oz).

A hybrid between a Maximilian's Parrot (of the race *lacerus*, known as

the Yellow-billed) and a Blue-headed was bred in the collection of H. Whitley at Primley, Devon, probably about 1930.

P. m. siy
Description: The chin and throat are vinous red (not blue as in the nominate race); the shade of the body plumage is a more olive green.
Range/Habitat: This race is found in Mato Grosso, Brazil, central and eastern Bolivia, Paraguay (except in the east) and northern Argentina in Formosa and Chaco. It inhabits forested regions.
Aviculture: This race has probably been exported more frequently than the others in recent years; the nominate race is not likely to be encountered in aviculture. In Sweden, Mats Tell obtained a pair in October 1979. The following April, the female laid four eggs. Three were fertile and all hatched. A chick was first heard on May 22. The eldest left the nest on July 6 and the other two left five days later. They all had brick red frontal bands (Tell, 1983) and this was believed, incorrectly, to be an indication of their sex. Many, perhaps most, young *Pionus* exhibit a red frontal band and surgical sexing at an early age has shown that this is not a sexual distinction (Brawley, 1983). In 1981, Mats Tell's female laid five eggs. Four hatched, the first on May 17. The young left the nest on July 11, 16, 18 and 24 respectively. They had blackish frontal bands. Also in Sweden that year, a pair kept by Alf Sundstrom reared three young. Their food consisted of soaked sunflower, safflower, hemp and wheat, also fruit, greenfood, blackcurrants, hawthorn berries; the young were fed on softfood, soaked seed, green oats, seeding grasses and chickweed.

P. m. melanoblepharus
Description: It is larger and darker than the nominate race: chin and throat are darker blue and the under parts are darker green.
Range/Habitat: It is found in central Brazil, southwards to eastern Paraguay and to Misiones and Corrientes in north-eastern Argentina.

Yellow-billed Parrot
P. m. lacerus
Description: The throat band is bluish vinous and more extensive than in *siy*; overall size is slightly larger.
Range/Habitat: Salta and Tucuman in north-western Argentina.

Plum-crowned (Restless or Tschudi's) Parrot
P. tumultuosus tumultuosus
Description: This is a very beautiful bird with unique head colouration which is variable, being intense rich plum on the crown and forehead in adult males in breeding condition and duller in other birds. The centre of each feather is white, but this feature can be seen only when the feathers are parted. The nape is blackish green, the rest of the upper parts being dark green. The cheeks, throat and upper breast are an unusual mixture of pinkish maroon, white and dark blue and the feathers of the upper breast are edged with greyish pink and dark blue. The rest of the under parts, except the red under tail coverts which are edged with yellowish green and of a shade which nearly matches the head, are dark green. The tail is green above, with a red patch near the base; the under side is pinkish maroon, except for the green terminal band. The bill is yellow and the inconspicuous area of bare skin surrounding the eye is greyish. The iris is brown. Length: 29 cm (11 in).
Immature birds have the feathers of the nape and hind crown green, also the cheeks and breast. The throat is pink. Under tail coverts are yellowish green, marked with pink at the base.
Range/Habitat: The Plum-crowned Parrot inhabits the mountains of eastern Peru, west of the Andes in Cajamarca, and Bolivia in La Paz and Cochabamba. It is a bird of the forests of the tropical and sub-tropical zones. Although uncommon, its population is probably stable.
Aviculture: This species was unknown in captivity until 1974 when a few specimens reached Europe: their cost was about £350 per pair. It has since been imported on a few rare occasions and at a very high price.

The first breeding of the Plum-crowned Parrot in Britain, and perhaps anywhere in captivity, occurred in 1977, when a chick was hand-reared by Mr and Mrs J. Stoodley. Six birds were obtained in 1974 and were allowed to choose their own partners. One pair produced four infertile eggs in 1976. In April 1977, they nested in the same small log and four eggs were laid but not incubated. Two weeks later, the female started to lay again. Three of the four eggs were fostered to other birds and the fourth was placed in an incubator. It hatched after 26 days.

The chick was fed on Farex baby cereal and the ground-up kernels of sunflower seed. It was mixed freshly at each meal and once daily some green-food was liquidised and added to the mixture. At first the chick was fed every two hours during the day by means of a dropper.

By the time it was seven days old, the white down had abraded to leave it nearly naked. At 20 days, the eyes were open and pin feathers were appearing. However, there were a number of serious problems in rearing the *tumultuosus* which nearly died on several occasions. Once the crop contents soured and had to be removed and, later, 12 stitches were necessary to repair an injury to the crop and seven more to bring the outer skin together. Afterwards, its crop could hold only $1\frac{1}{2}$ ml of food, instead of 10 ml ($\frac{3}{10}$ instead of 2 teaspoonsful).

I saw the young bird when it was a year old, a most appealing parrot which responded to John Stoodley's voice by whistling and fluffing up its head feathers. At that age, its head colouration did not have the brilliance of that of the adults. The male parent was the most handsome *tumultuosus* I have seen and I was told that, when out of breeding condition, its head colour fades slightly.

In 1980, Raymond Sawyer's pair of *Pionus*, consisting of a male *tumultuosus* paired to a Dilute mutation of an unidentified species, reared three young. The mutant was mainly creamy yellow in colour. The young regrettably died before they were fully adult. Their appearance gave no clue as to the female's species.

On my first sight of this bird, my belief that Massena's Parrot should be considered as a subspecies of it was confirmed. Immatures of *tumultuosus*, which have much less colour on the head, differ no more in appearance from *seniloides* than do two races of *maximiliani* – the nominate and *siy*, for example. In voice and behaviour, *seniloides* and *tumultuosus* do not differ.

It has recently been discovered (John P. O'Neill and Theodore A. Parker, 1977) that the range of the two birds is almost continuous and further field work would establish whether the two make contact with each other. O'Neill and Parker state:

> After careful scrutiny of the specimens available to us we have come to the conclusion that the only difference between *P. seniloides* and *P. tumultuosus* is the amount of rose or plum color present in the plumage of the head and belly....
>
> We believe, in the absence of evidence to the contrary, that the two forms of *Pionus* under discussion do not differ enough morphologically or ecologically to warrant their being retained as separate species.

Massena's (Grey- or White-headed) Parrot
P. t. seniloides
Description: The feathers of the crown are dark grey, with the bases white and, of course, normally hidden. In some birds, the feathers of the crown are mainly white. Some of the feathers of the forehead are tipped with pink and some birds have two or three white feathers. The feathers of the lores, cheeks and throat are edged with dark grey, the centres being white or pinkish white. The large feathers of the nape are buffish white in some birds; ear coverts are dark grey. The whole of the upper parts, including the tail, are dark green. The upper breast is dark vinous or dark mauvish blue and in some birds the vinous-tinged feathers extend to the red of the under tail coverts. There is a reddish patch at the base of the tail. The small area of bare skin surrounding the eye is much less prominent than in most *Pionus* and is pale greyish in colour. The bill is pale yellow and the iris brown. Length: 28 cm (11 in).

Immature birds have the feathers of the head green with white bases, with little vinous colouring on the breast. The crown feathers are faintly edged with orange.

Range/Habitat: Massena's Parrot inhabits the mountains of north-western South America, from north-western Venezuela, west to the Central Andes of Colombia and south through western Ecuador. It has recently been discovered in Peru, south of the western Andes in the Department of Cajamarca and in the Eastern Andes. The Carpish region of Huanuco in central Peru apparently represents the most northerly part of its range so far discovered. Deforestation has almost certainly caused a decline in its population.

Aviculture: At the time of writing, one pair of Massena's Parrot can be seen at Vogelpark Walsrode, in Germany and another pair at Loro Parque, Tenerife. It is one of the rarest of its genus in captivity. The only other specimens I have seen were my own two and one in a pet shop in London during the same period. I refrained from purchasing the latter as it was not in good health. I obtained a young bird of this species in December 1969 from a trade stand at the National Exhibition of Cage Birds for the sum of £13. Thousands had visited the show but no one else was interested in her. Soon after, she began to take grapes from my fingers and to nibble playfully at my hand. After about two months, Pinky, as I called her, was allowed out of her cage. I well recall the first time: she circled the room two or three times, flying with much confidence before landing on the picture rail. Then she dropped almost vertically on to her cage and returned inside.

She proved to be a totally delightful pet being intelligent, inquisitive and full of mischief. She was gentle, too. She soon learned to come to me when she saw me holding a certain twig for it meant she was to have her head scratched.

I lived to regret the day when I obtained by great chance a mate for her. Having read something I had had published about this bird, a kind correspondent offered me the single bird of this species in his collection. It was heavily built and I felt that it was probably a male; autopsies eventually proved that they were indeed a true pair. The male was the only parrot I have ever had which never adjusted to captivity: it was frightened of people and would turn its head away as though to hide if anyone even looked at it. However, it was equally ill at ease with other birds and lived for about three years on varying terms with Pinky. Sometimes the birds seemed quite compatible: at other times the male was aggressive towards her. Early one morning in February 1973, I experienced one of the worst moments of my avicultural career when I found the female dead. The male had killed her. Subsequently I tried to keep other birds with the male but it proved impossible and they had to be removed for their own safety. I often wished that it could have been returned to its native habitat.

My Massena's Parrots relished fruit and greenfood of all kinds, in addition to the usual seeds, especially spray millet.

In 1981 and 1982, a few Massena's Parrots were imported into the USA.

This *Pionus* has yet to be bred in captivity.

White-crowned (White-capped) Parrot
P. senilis

Description: This is the smallest member of the genus. It is immediately distinguished by the pure white feathers of the crown and forehead. The rest of the head appears dark blue, darkest on the ear coverts, the feathers being white at the base, green in the centre and blue at the edges. There is a white patch covering the chin and throat and, in some specimens, a few coral pink feathers on the throat. The feathers of the upper breast are dark mauvish blue with brownish green centres; the lower breast is bluish green. Under tail coverts are pinkish red, each feather being tipped with yellowish green. The wing coverts are bronze. The rest of the plumage is green except the brilliant blue primaries and the blue-tipped tail with a red patch near the base. The skin surrounding the eye is dull pink: the bill is pale yellow and the iris is brown. Length: 24 cm (9½ in).

Immature birds bred in captivity were described (Zimmerman, 1983) as having bronze-coloured wings, blue flight and tail feathers and a little red around the vent; the feathers of the white cap were tipped with green. The rest of the plumage was bright green except for the blue ear coverts. The periorbital area was grey (not red as in the adults).

Range/Habitat: The White-crowned Parrot inhabits Central America from south-eastern Mexico, south to western Panama. It is common in some areas, being found in rainforest, savannah woodland and semi-open areas. It is probably most common in Costa Rica where it is even found on the outskirts of towns.

Aviculture: This species is infrequently imported. The first recorded breeding success occurred in the collection of the Duke of Bedford. In 1933, the pair hatched a chick which was killed by the male when one week old. The following year a chick was hand-reared from the age of a few days by John Yeatland, then curator of the collection.

In recent years there have been very few breeding successes due to the fact that only small numbers have been exported. In the USA, Richard Zimmerman of Michigan obtained young birds in 1975. Four eggs were laid by one female in April 1982; the first hatched about May 24. The four chicks made a harsh rasping noise when being fed. They had thin white down. The male was not seen to enter the nest-box until the young were feathered, when he commenced to feed them. They left the nest on July 17, 22, 24 and 31 and returned at night.

In the following year the first egg was laid on April 20. Two chicks hatched, the first on May 20. They left the nest on July 12. The pair bred in an aviary 4.8 m (16 ft) long with a small indoor flight to which they were confined from November until April. They were not subjected to a temperature lower than 10°C (50°F). Previously, two females had been kept together for one year. Both laid eggs in a small box and one bird sat on top of the other.

Corn-on-the-cob was the favoured rearing food; two cobs were eaten daily. They also consumed apple, cheese, carrots, spinach, peanuts, grapes, a mixture of Torula yeast and Gevral Protein and a little seed.

Other successes have been achieved at Natal Lion Park since the mid-1970s and by John and Pat Stoodley in the UK.

Bronze-winged Parrot
P. chalcopterus

Description: This species is distinguished by its predominantly navy blue colouration. Seen in poor light, it appears a sombre dark blue; in sunlight, its colours come to life and their variety and unusual combination can be appreciated. The head and under parts are dark blue, except for the white patch on the throat, below which is an area of feathers tipped with coral pink. The upper parts are blue, except for the wings which are bronze (every feather being edged with almost iridescent bronze) and the primaries which are brilliant deep blue. Under tail coverts are scarlet. The bare skin surrounding the eye is deep pink and at its deepest in birds in breeding condition. The beak is pale yellow and the iris is dark brown. Length: 28 cm (11 in). Weight: 220 g ($7\frac{3}{4}$ oz).

Immature birds may have the wing feathers edged with green to give a mainly green appearance, or they may have bronze wings. The feathers of the under parts are brown edged with dark green. The skin surrounding the eye is yellowish.

Range/Habitat: The Bronze-wing is a mountain species, inhabiting northwestern Venezuela, the upper tropical and sub-tropical zones of the eastern central and western Andes of Colombia to western Ecuador, northwestern Peru. It is locally common in some areas, much less numerous in others.

Aviculture: Bronze-wings are occasionally available but have never been common or imported in large numbers. While they can be kept and will even breed in a small aviary, to appreciate their beauty to the full, an aviary at least 4.5 m (15 ft) long is necessary, as the bright sky blue of the underside of the wings will then be seen as they

fly. The plumage of adult birds seen in sunlight is extremely beautiful and makes a contrast to that of any other parrot in a collection.

An unfortunate trait of this species is that, perhaps due to the stress of captivity, mated pairs tend to over-preen each other's heads; for this reason, on one occasion I had to separate my pair during the winter months to allow the regrowth of the head feathers. One bird then removed the feathers from its back and thighs. For a couple of years, the head of the other bird was completely bare, giving an unfortunate vulturine appearance. However, the feathers did grow when the birds were separated. One January, I had to separate the pair when the male attacked the hen's head; the pair was re-united after five or six weeks and then nested.

George Smith (1976a) also found that the male of his pair was over-enthusiastic in preening the female:

> The head preening, once it starts, is rather vigorous, for it breaks off the dark grey tips to the head feathers leaving huge white patches. It may be that this permanent revelation of the underlying white serves to signal to the preening bird that it is becoming too aggressive. If so, these white bases to the feathers may serve to inhibit aggression as does the white nape-patch of broadtailed parrots.

However, I find it difficult to believe that such aggressive preening would occur in wild birds; also, most *Pionus* have the bases of the feathers of the nape white and I do not know of this problem in other species.

In my experience, with seven individuals, it is a highly nervous species, becoming subject to stress in conditions under which an Amazon, for example, would not bat an eyelid. One night in January 1978, there was a noisy storm with high, whining winds; next morning a female Bronze-wing which had been in my possession over seven years was found dead on the floor, although the aviary was a sheltered one in an open-fronted brick building. Autopsy revealed that the bird was in perfect condition. The nervousness of this species means that it is far from easy to breed in captivity; both the Stoodleys and I have had chicks killed in the nest for reasons unknown.

The Stoodley's pair was housed in an aviary measuring 5.4 × 1.2 m (18 × 4 ft), a third of the length being occupied by the open-fronted shelter where the nest-box was situated. The birds were obtained in 1971 and fed on peanuts, carrots, spinach, rose hips and cooked rabbit. Seed was refused. Mating was observed during May 1973; eggs were laid on June 9 and 12. The female was not seen again until July 7 when there were two newly hatched chicks in the nest which were covered with creamy white down. During the incubation period, which lasted about 26 days, the male spent much of his time just inside the entrance to the nest, looking out. Foods taken were spinach, sweet corn, carrot, peanuts, hemp and canary seed. The adults objected to nest inspection so only occasional glimpses into the box were taken. On July 24, when the hen left the nest for a long period, it was found to contain one dead chick, with upper mandible and one foot missing. The surviving chick was cold and limp; it was fed baby porridge by syringe and placed in the nest of a Golden-mantled Rosella, which fed it. On August 3 the feathers were visible as minute black spots and from then on the feathering was rapid. On August 20, the Rosella ceased to feed the young *Pionus* which was then fed on peanuts ground in a coffee grinder and baby porridge.

Not only was she successfully reared but she reared two fine youngsters herself in 1977. In 1976, she had laid two clutches of four eggs, all of which contained chicks which failed to get out of the shell. Of the two young reared in 1977, one had greenish bronze on the wings and the other green.

In 1976 my pair of Bronze-winged *Pionus* nested in May, the first egg being laid about May 18. On June 17, a chick was heard: Bronze-wing chicks have a peculiar quavering cry. The female was not seen in the aviary until more than four weeks after the chick was heard, and I had not seen her for more than two months, except towards the end of this period when she was occasionally seen to look out of the nest entrance and the male would feed her from the nest-box perch. On July 18, she was sitting unconcernedly in the aviary in a manner which suggested she had deserted. My husband entered the aviary to inspect the nest, in case a deserted or mutilated chick could be saved and we were amazed to hear the loud and angry cries of a chick from within. A hasty retreat was made. Thereafter, the female spent increasingly long periods in the flight and the male was occasionally seen to enter the nest. On August 5, a young bird was seen at the entrance; thereafter it often looked out. Unfortunately, its head was almost bare of feathers, having been plucked by one or both parents. The plucking was so severe that the feathers on the crown never grew, except for a small amount of white down. At 7 p.m. on August 18 the young bird left the nest. Its under parts were plucked bare but the plumage which remained was different from that of the adults, the most noticeable feature being the green wings with a few brown feathers on the wing coverts. The naked skin around the eye was yellowish (that of the adults being red). When the under parts feathered, they were navy blue, as in the parents.

On the following day, I saw the female enter the nest and heard the sounds of another chick being fed. It was not seen to look out until August 24; it, too, had the head plucked naked. On August 26, when it fledged, the discovery was made that it had rickets. The joints of its feet were so badly swollen that it was unable to perch. Its parent seemed very concerned over its condition and even its nest-mate would occasionally fly down to it on the floor. The parents continued to feed it, yet it quickly learned to feed itself from food placed on the floor. It seemed to make good progress but died on September 17.

The other youngster was first seen to feed itself on August 30, although it called for food for several weeks after that date. During the rearing period, a wide variety of foods had been offered, the most favoured being celery, carrot, Cheddar cheese, tomato and spray millet. The usual items of the diet – apple, sunflower, canary seed, pine nuts and peanuts – were also eaten. Greenfood was seldom available but lettuce was occasionally offered.

In Belgium, at Meli-Park, Adinkerke, several birds were obtained

Dusky Parrot (*Pionus fuscus*).

from Dr and Mrs Swaenepoel in 1974; one pair had three eggs and reared two young that year. In 1975, the breeding pair was moved to another aviary: that year, and in 1976, no eggs were laid. In the USA, this species has been bred by Stan Carpenter of Arizona.

Dusky (Violaceous or Violet) Parrot
P. fuscus
Description: This parrot is as uncharacteristic in its colouration as the Bronze-wing and shows an even greater variety of colours, most of which are very subtle. There is considerable variation among the plumage of individuals, some being more brightly

coloured on the under parts. The head is slate-blue; ear coverts are black with the surrounding feathers pale buff or broadly edged with buff. Fine, hair-like red feathers surround the cere and some birds have a small red spot on each side, just above the cere. The feathers of the upper breast are dark brown, edged with buff to give a frosted effect. The breast varies from soft vinous pink, reddish vinous or even scarlet, to reddish brown. The more colourful birds are extremely beautiful. The upper parts are dark brown with reddish brown edges to the feathers; primaries are deep violet and the secondaries are greenish or brown. The under tail coverts are scarlet and the under wing coverts are deep, rich blue. Rump and middle of the tail are black, the terminal band being deep violet and the base of the tail red. Beak is black with a yellow patch on either side at the base; iris is brown and the small area of skin surrounding the eye is grey. Length: 24 cm (9½ in).

Immature birds are said to have the upper wing coverts edged with green and a greenish tinge to the secondaries.

Range/Habitat: The Dusky Parrot is found in a small area of north-eastern Colombia, also in a much wider area from southern Venezuela, the Guianas, northern Brazil, north of the Amazon, and south of the Amazon from Maranhao west to the Rio Madeira. Locally distributed and, in some areas, common, it is essentially a forest species.

Aviculture: This species is exported occasionally from Guyana, in small numbers. Unusually, females have predominated, resulting in few true pairs in collections. As George Smith commented (1977):

This complete confidence in humans, the very gentle behaviour towards each other – except when defending their nesting territory, and then they are merciless – and the most gentle-sounding conversational grunts and whistles which accompany their feeding make them especially attractive.

The first recorded captive breeding of the Dusky *Pionus* occurred in the collection of the Reverend R. Noegel in 1983 (Noegel and Moss, 1984). In 1980, six birds were obtained from a large importation of about 100 Dusky Parrots. They were found to be very susceptible to stress and many birds died of stress within one year of being received, as it was believed did one pair in Ramon Noegel's collection. When the post-mortem was carried out, no major disease could be found.

One pair nested in May 1982; there were four infertile eggs and one which contained a dead chick. In 1983, four fertile eggs were laid; there were two eggs by April 28. Three had been eaten by May 26, possibly as they started to hatch. The remaining egg was placed in the nest of the second pair, the female of which had laid her first egg on May 1. Four eggs were laid, one of which was infertile. This was removed. All four eggs hatched that week. The chicks were very well fed, the male taking anything offered, including large quantities of wholewheat bread, fruits, vegetables, seeds, scrambled egg, cheese and fresh corn-on-the-cob. At two weeks old, the chicks were removed for hand-rearing which was carried out successfully.

Mr and Mrs J. Stoodley paired their female Dusky with a male Maximilian's at a time when no males were available in the UK. In June 1978 a chick hatched and was removed for hand-rearing when fully grown; it took after the Maximilian's more than the Dusky in colour, being mainly green.

Pionopsitta
Pionopsitta

This genus consists of small stocky parrots, only one of which, the Red-capped, is known in aviculture. According to Forshaw (1973), this species differs from the others in its less projecting bill, proportionately longer tail and narrower tail feathers, and narrower and more pointed wings. Additionally, it is sexually dimorphic. I know of no records of the other species in aviculture, with the exception of the Brown-hooded Parrot and, albeit briefly, the Beautiful; thus they are not covered here. (Full descriptions will be found in Low's *Parrots of South America* and in Forshaw's *Parrots of the World*.)

Red-capped (Pileated) Parrot
P. pileata

Description: The male is green, darker above, and has the forehead, most of the crown, part of the lores (the remainder being unfeathered) and a narrow line below the eye, including part of the ear coverts, scarlet. The lower ear coverts are dull red. The bend of the wing, the carpal edge and the primary coverts are deep blue. The under wing coverts are bluish green and pale bluish; the tail is green, tipped with blue, the under side being yellowish green. The beak is dark grey and horn-coloured with a heavily bulbous lower mandible, and the iris is brown. An inconspicuous area of bluish skin surrounds the eye. Length: 22 cm (9 in).

Females lack the scarlet on the head but, as in males, have the ear coverts dull reddish. Some females have a small area of blue on the forehead.

Immature plumage is variable in males; two imported birds in my possession at first lacked red on the forehead, except a tinge on the ear coverts. The red appeared first on the forehead and crown. However, most of the immature males imported had some red on the head. Of the males bred by Paolo Bertagnolio, those hatched in 1973 exhibited a thin red frontal band, but the single male hatched in 1974 had an orange-yellow band in the middle of the forehead. They had hatched

---

Pionus identification
All have red under tail coverts. Length: 24–28 cm (9½–11 in).

	Head	Bill
menstruus	blue	black and pink
sordidus	green	red
maximiliani	green forehead; lores almost black	black and horn-coloured
tumultuosus tumultuosus	dark pink	yellow
t. seniloides	mixture of dark grey, pink and white	yellow
senilis	white crown	yellow
chalcopterus	dark blue	yellow
fuscus	bluish black and buff	black and yellow

Red-capped Parrot (*Pionopsitta pileata*), male.

in early July and early August and in both years the first traces of colour appeared on the forehead during the second half of October.

Range/Habitat: The Red-capped Parrot inhabits south-eastern Brazil from southern Bahía south to Rio Grande do Sul, eastern Paraguay. It is a forest bird, found in pairs or small flocks. Because of widespread loss of habitat in Brazil, it is considered endangered there.

Aviculture: This species was extremely rare in aviculture until 1969; from that time until about 1976 it was regularly imported into Europe. Then it was placed on Appendix A1 of CITES and its export ceased. However, the proportion of females imported was extremely small and it was the fate of the majority of males never to be kept with a female. Presumably the females were not exported because trappers believed that there would be no sale for these dull coloured birds.

I feel that this species cannot be considered as completely hardy and that, at least in Britain, Northern Europe and the USA, indoor accom-modation should be provided during the winter. If left outdoors, mine almost invariably seemed to have respiratory problems, breathing heavily and even wheezing audibly. They seemed uncomfortable during cold weather.

Not long after receiving them (1970) I wrote:

> They are very sociable little birds, rather like Budgerigars in their behaviour in that they constantly preen each other and warble in their soft, inoffensive voices; but, unlike Budgerigars, they are gentle, sweet-tempered and peaceable.
> . . . I doubt that a single pair would go to nest.

The latter speculation proved incorrect. However, as it happens, the first two successful breeders in Britain to date each had three pairs but, on one occasion, one of my pairs hatched a chick when I had no other Red-caps within earshot.

The first recorded captive breeding was achieved by Paolo Bertagnolio in Rome. In November 1969, he obtained four males and a single female. The female was kept with one of the males in a large community flight with par-rakeets and lorikeets. A second male had been removed after the first showed aggression towards it in the typical manner: walking with head lowered and beak almost touching the perch and plumage slightly ruffled. The two males never fought as the second invariably flew off.

The female laid her first egg on June 7; on June 15 there were three eggs and by June 26 there were four eggs. On July 4, a chick hatched; it was covered with abundant long white down. The other chicks hatched on July 6, 8 and 13. Loss of down began at two weeks; the body was pink and the cere lead grey. On July 18, the male was seen in the nest-box for the first and only time. On the following day, the oldest three chicks had their eyes open. From July 21 to 24, they were fitted with rings of internal diameter of 6 mm ($\frac{1}{4}$ in) and 4 mm (just over $\frac{1}{10}$ in) high. Very pale grey, short, thick down appeared on the chicks at the end of July. When inspected they assumed the same aggressive-defensive attitude as the incubating female: puffing the plumage, crouching and rolling slightly with semi-opened bill. On August 6, the first traces of green were seen on the crown and under parts. Three days later, a narrow red frontal band was apparent in the two larger chicks. The fourth was a female and left the nest first on August 20; she was replaced as she was unable to fly or climb. Two days later, she was perched in the flight with one of her brothers; the plumage was incomplete with traces of down. So calm were these youngsters that they allowed themselves to be lifted on to a finger, biting in a firm and painful manner. The parents showed concern when they were approached closely. The third chick fledged on August 27 and the last at the end of the month.

All the males had golden-yellow on the crown; the lesser wing coverts were greenish blue instead of ultramarine. The female had a faint bluish green forehead. Towards the end of October a few red feathers appeared on the crown in the males. The lighter part of the beak was still horn-coloured, instead of light grey. At the end of 1973, the red areas on the head had increased and the red eye ring was almost complete. Bill, feet and skin around the eye had assumed their final colour but the feathers at the bend of the wing were still bluish green, not dark blue as in the adult. The young birds were kept with their parents until mid-January 1974.

They were fed on sunflower, canary, millet, niger, oats, hemp and linseed, with greenfood in quantity, also apple and pear and, on occasions, raw minced meat, stale bread and biscuit (Bertagnolio, 1974 and 1975).

In 1974, the female laid four eggs from which a male and a female were reared. The male showed a very small area of yellowish orange on the middle of the forehead. No eggs were laid in 1975. In 1976, two chicks hatched but died due to lack of greenfood while Signor Bertagnolio was not present. In 1977, three chicks were reared and four were hatched in 1978. Three young reared in 1973 and one in 1974 produced two chicks in 1976 and in 1977.

Perhaps the highest number of young reared in one collection in one year was nine at Natal Lion Park, South Africa, in 1981, where this species has been bred consistently and with great success.

A number of disasters with this species befell Arthur Lamb of Northumberland. In 1976, young were hatched by two pairs; all died shortly before or shortly after leaving the nest. In 1977 a young bird fledged, only to die shortly after leaving the nest due to the attentions of a Sparrowhawk which caused it to panic. In later years, young were reared. Arthur Lamb informed me:

The parents lived in the same aviary for three years and never touched the cocksfoot or a poplar tree growing in the flight, both of which I had to cut each year, but as soon as the youngsters flew they kept the cocksfoot tufts down and have killed the tree. Even when the cocksfoot was white with frost they ate it with no ill effects.

However, 1977 was the year in which a successful British breeding was finally achieved – by George Smith of Peterborough. In a large aviary containing two pairs, a male and a female fledged. I saw them soon after; they were fine birds and the male had yellow on the crown. Both were later presented to Chester Zoo. In 1978, all three pairs laid but only one pair

hatched chicks. Two males were reared. Subsequently, George Smith has reared young in every year but one to date (1984); very few females have been hatched but 25 males have been reared.

Bertagnolio (1975) speculated on the relationship of the Red-capped Parrot to other neotropical parrots. He pointed out similarities and divergencies between it and the *Forpus* parrotlets. From my own observations I would doubt that it is any more closely related to *Forpus* than to other small South American parrots. He then compared it to *Triclaria*, the Purple-bellied Parrot. Very few aviculturists have had the good fortune to keep this totally delightful parrot. I had a male for ten years; during one period he was without a female and I considered giving him a female Red-capped Parrot as a partner but this would have meant depriving one of my male Red-caps. However, on showing the male Purple-bellied Parrot the female, he reacted to

her in the same way that he would to a female of his own species. (The two birds were not actually introduced as was implied in Bertagnolio's article.) For a couple of years, the male Purple-bellied was kept with a male Red-cap and the two birds agreed perfectly.

As Bertagnolio stated, there are similarities in display and voice, including the 'similar rasping-mewing sound' (an excellent description) uttered when frightened or excited. However, the male *Triclaria* was far more dominant and aggressive in courtship than any Red-cap.

Bertagnolio also notes that both species are forest birds with an almost identical distribution area. When I first kept *Triclaria*, I thought it quite different from any other neotropical parrot but over the years came to note the similarities between the two species. By coincidence, Paolo Bertagnolio sent me a coloured photograph of partly feathered *pileata* chicks which to my eyes bore a strong resemblance to *Triclaria*.

Brown-hooded Parrot (*Pionopsitta haematotis haematotis*).

Brown-hooded Parrot
P. haematotis haematotis
Description: Its colouration is unremarkable being almost entirely green, with the head brown, hind neck olive yellow and the upper breast pale brown. Ear coverts are reddish brown. Lesser wing coverts, carpal edge and outermost secondary coverts are deep blue; primaries are dull black. Sides of the body (hidden by the wings) are red. Tail feathers are tipped with dark blue and the lateral tail feathers are marked with dull red on the inner webs. Bill is horn-coloured and the iris is said to be yellow in adults. Length: 21 cm ($8\frac{1}{2}$ in). There is a conspicuous area of white skin surrounding the eye.

Immature birds are duller, especially on the head. The iris is brown.

Range/Habitat: The nominate race inhabits southern Mexico from Veracruz and Oaxaca, south to western Panama.

This species congregates in small groups up to about 20 individuals. It feeds on fruits, including figs, berries and seeds (also on corn crops) in the canopies of trees in forested areas and is even found in cloud forest, thus it is difficult to detect. This is probably why it is almost unknown in aviculture. It is common over much of its range.

P. h. coccinicollaris
Description: The lower foreneck and the upper breast are variably marked with red, forming a band in some males and usually less extensive in females.
Range/Habitat: This race is found in eastern Panama and north-western Colombia, east to Bolivia.

Aviculture: It appeared on dealers' lists in 1978 – yet probably none were exported, except those collected privately by Vogelpark Walsrode. When I visited Walsrode in October 1978, I saw a single female. I was interested in observing it to ascertain whether in behaviour and appearance it differed radically from *pileata*. However, all the time I watched it, it was dozing quietly and I never saw it move! It certainly seemed much like *pileata* and this was confirmed by the parrot-keeper, Klaus Trogisch.

Beautiful (Rose-faced) Parrot
P. pulchra
Description: Forehead and crown are dark brown, the feathers of the nape being brown margined with golden olive. The side of the face is conspicuously marked, the ear coverts, part of the cheeks and the chin being pinkish red. Hind neck is dull olive-yellow, extending to the upper breast. The feathers of the bend of the wing and the lesser wing coverts are orange and yellow; wing coverts are blue, violet and black. Under wing coverts are greenish blue and under tail coverts yellowish green. The tail is green, the central feathers being tipped with blue, the lateral feathers being red on the inner webs and broadly tipped with blue. The bill is horn-coloured and the iris yellow. Length: 23 cm (9 in).

Range/Habitat: It occurs in Pacific north-western South America, from north-western Colombia (northwards to southern Choco) south to southwestern Ecuador, to El Oro. It inhabits forest and forest borders, usually from 500 m to 1,200 m (1,600 to 4,000 ft), also occurring in adjacent lowlands and up into the lower subtropical zone to 16,000 m (5,300 ft). It is uncommon throughout most of its range. Much suitable forest remains in Columbia but it has probably decreased in Ecuador, due to deforestation. It has been described as quiet and inconspicuous (Ridgely in Pasquier, 1981).

Aviculture: An extreme rarity, the skin of a bird collected by Walter Goodfellow in 1914 is in the British Museum (Natural History). It is labelled 'E. J. Brook's Trustee' but whether it reached the collection of this aviculturist alive is not known.

In 1982, a German importer received nine specimens, most of which were very short-lived. Autopsies were carried out and the causes of death reported as pneumonia and inflammation of kidneys and bowels.

In the same year this species was also imported into the Netherlands but it is not known whether any birds survived for any length of time.

Triclaria
Triclaria

The single member of this genus is, in my opinion, one of the most attractive of all the parrots suitable for an aviary. It has several characteristics, including its thrush-like song, which are quite different from those of other parrots. It is a species for which I have a very special affection and very few birds have ever given me more pleasure than the male which graced my aviaries for ten years.

Purple-bellied Parrot
T. malachitacea
Description: The plumage of this species is a most attractive shade of glossy dark green; in the male, the centre of the abdomen and the lower breast is violet; in the female, this area is green. The primaries are dark blue on the outer webs; the greater wing coverts and the under side of the primaries are verditer blue. The iris is dark brown and the bill is whitish. The large eye adds to the beauty of this bird. Length: 30 cm (12 in); of which the long, broad tail accounts for approximately 12 cm (5 in). The area of bare skin around the eye is whitish.

Pair of Purple-bellied Parrots.

Immature males have only a small area of violet on the abdomen.

Range/Habitat: The Purple-bellied Parrot is found in south-eastern Brazil from southern Bahia south to Rio Grande do Sul. According to Forshaw (1973), it is quite common in the remaining forests and even occurs in woodlands and gardens on the outskirts of São Paulo. Its stronghold is the lower montane rainforest of the Sierra do Mar, an area too wet and too steep for agricultural use.

Aviculture: This is an extremely rare bird in captivity which is mainly due to the difficulty in establishing it. There are a few pairs in Brazilian collections. A friend in Asuncion, Paraguay, who visited a dealer there, was told that 'the Brazilero dealer did not like dealing in this species as they always died'.

Very few specimens have reached Britain; perhaps none between 1905, when Hubert Astley received a single bird, and 1961, when an Essex importer received a pair. Then Herbert Murray, of Brentwood, Essex, imported five birds for his own collection during 1964 or 1965. When he advertised a pair in 1968, I was the only person to answer the advertisement; evidently very few aviculturists were familiar with this species. I had often admired these birds in his collection. The pair cost me £30 – probably the greatest avicultural bargain in which I ever invested, for the male was one of the most beautiful and pleasing birds I have ever known. Today, were these birds imported, their price would place them well beyond the means of most private aviculturists.

Imported Purple-bellied Parrots which are thin on arrival have little chance of survival. Herbert Murray's birds thrived because they were placed in a large planted aviary and were provided every week with 2.4 m (8 ft) saplings cut specially for them. They fed on the bark and leaves in a 'frantic manner'. At first, they were reluctant to accept the usual foods and took fruit only if it was hung from a perch. After a while they were taking berries, seed and nectar. Nectar with added vitamins was given daily to my Purple-bellied Parrots, together with a small piece of spray millet, sunflower, peanuts, pine nuts, niger and canary seed. Fruit, berries and corn-on-the-cob were relished eventually, although at first I had to hang grapes from the perches in their aviary. Many items of food would be eaten held in the foot.

The voice of the Purple-bellied Parrot is just one of its endearing features. Apart from a harsh 'chack chack' given in moments of intense excitement, every note in its repertoire is mellifluous in comparison with other parrots. It is unique for its song, a term which is no exaggeration, for it is loud and thrush-like. Both male and female have a soft sub-song and the female sings, but with less intensity and less often. The clear notes of my male Purple-bellied were a feature of frosty winter mornings, and winter never seemed the same after he died. It is strange that cold weather should have proved a bigger incentive to sing than good weather; in fact, these birds invariably keep in the shade in warm weather.

The Purple-bellied is slimmer in build than most neotropical parrots, a graceful bird which shows great manoeuvrability in flight. Herbert Murray kept his in a very large aviary, such as few aviculturists can erect these days, and recorded that they hawked flies with the circular flight of a Spotted Flycatcher. This is one of the few true parrots which would use a large aviary. A pair in a free-flight aviary large enough for damage to vegetation to go unnoticed would be a superb sight.

Herbert Murray described his birds as being as playful as lorikeets, though I never saw that trait in mine, perhaps because their aviary measured only 4.5 m (15 ft) in length and because they were fully adult. He wrote:

> Several of them will get together and play, usually by finding the lowest twig which hangs from the branches that I have given them. Then, holding on to the twig with one foot, and gripping another bird with the other, they revolve very rapidly and apparently to their great enjoyment, for they flap their wings and call loudly.

Murray's pair hatched chicks on several occasion but the chicks never lived beyond a few days. My original hen died but was replaced when the male of the pair owned by Dr and Mrs T. Nichols of Texas died. The Nichols generously sent me their female. My male had been without a mate for almost two years; the female was received on April 12, 1975, and introduced to the male on the following day. He immediately flew at the female and pecked her briefly; to my delight, she showed no fear of him; in fact, she followed him about the aviary and after a short time mutual preening took place.

Three days later, mating was observed and, on the following day, the female was seen to enter the nest-box. She did not lay until nearly four weeks later, probably on May 12. When I inspected the nest on May 17 there were two normal eggs, measuring approximately 31 mm ($1\frac{1}{4}$ in) long, and one which measured only 20 mm ($\frac{3}{4}$ in). However, the male did not enter the nest to feed the female nor, apparently, fed her on the nest-box perch for, during the early days of incubation, the hen frequently left the box to beg food from him. He failed to respond and she had to feed herself.

On June 14, a chick hatched, giving a minimum incubation period of 29 days. The male was then seen searching the flight almost frantically for something I could not provide. I offered all kinds of extras, including a tray of seedlings of canary seed, planted a few days previously. He showed much interest in this and appeared to be eating the earth. However, success was not to be. On June 16 the chick died. Autopsy revealed a septic navel cord, an infection which is apparently common in chicks of domestic poultry. On removing the chick from the nest I noticed that the tiny upper mandible had been injured, perhaps by the female when the chick failed to respond to her attempts to feed it.

The pair never again attempted to nest, although in 1976 and 1977 mating occurred. As it so often happens that parrots which have been deprived of mates will nest immediately, I decided to separate the pair during the winter of 1977. However, in November that year, fate struck a cruel blow from which I smarted for months afterwards. One morning I found the male dead on the feeding shelf. The female, who looked perfectly well, was immediately brought indoors for observation. Next day she suddenly deteriorated and died within a few hours. Autopsies on both birds failed to reveal the cause of death.

This species has an interesting display in which the male walks jerkily along the perch with head lowered, 'pushing' its beak in front of it so that it is actually touching the perch. The feathers of the mantle are raised, the tail is spread and the male sings while shaking his head very rapidly, then rubs his bill on the perch. The female shakes her head and sings.

In the *Magazine of the Parrot Society* for November 1974, a photograph showing a very young chick with much light-coloured down and another of two feathered youngsters in a nest-box were published. The birds were in the collection of the late Professor G. A. della Riva of São Paulo, but whether they were successfully reared is not known. In 1985, one Purple-bellied Parrot was reared by its parents at Loro Parque, Tenerife.

Graydidascalus
Graydidascalus

The only member of this genus is a small all-green parrot which has only rarely been available to aviculturists.

Short-tailed Parrot
G. brachyurus

Description: This bird is almost all green, paler below and on the upper tail coverts. It is distinguished by the small size, very short, square tail and the yellowish green edges to the feathers of the wings which are especially prominent on the secondaries and secondary coverts. Part of the lores – a narrow line from beak to eye – are dark grey. The only other contrasting colour is the small area of dark red on the carpal edge of the wing and at the base of the tail. The large beak is black or very dark grey (in Forshaw's *Parrots of the World*, this species is wrongly depicted and described as having the beak 'greenish-grey'). The iris is dark red. Length: 23 cm (9 in). Immature birds lack the red in the tail.

Short-tailed Parrot (*Graydidascalus brachyurus*).

Range/Habitat: The Short-tailed Parrot is found in the tropical zone of south-eastern Colombia from Caqueta southward to eastern Ecuador, eastern Peru and eastward through the Amazon basin to the mouth of the Amazon River and the coast of the northernmost part of Brazil. It occurs in swampy or seasonally flooded areas along the larger rivers and is common in this type of habitat.

During two stays on a small island in the Amazon on the Colombian/Peruvian border, I watched this little parrot on numerous occasions. It was by far the most common parrot in the district. One area of creeks and tributaries of the Amazon invariably reverberated with the calls of this species, their short tails and butterfly-like flight (so different from the direct, flapping flight of other parrots) made them unmistakable. Always in the distance could be heard the far-carrying double call-note, as distinctive as their flight.

Aviculture: This is a rare bird in aviculture and this may be partly due to the fact that there is simply no demand for it. Natives who take birds from the nest to sell would probably not bother with this small parrot when, in the same area, brightly coloured Amazons abound.

The Short-tailed Parrot was exhibited at London Zoo as long ago as 1894. The well-known aviculturist Hubert Astley obtained one in 1910 of which he said, 'A gentler bird I never saw'. It has been imported on isolated occasions only and, when in 1973 a dealer imported three birds, perhaps the first to reach Britain since the 1930s, I was particularly interested in seeing them to inspect the tongue. In 1925, Maud Knobel had written that it was 'unlike that of any parrot. Instead of being round it is flat and large, flesh-colour in appearance with a black edge'.

The importer, Jim Hayward of Carterton Aviaries, caught one of them so that I could examine its tongue. What surprised me most was the shape, which was almost like a spoon. These birds were bought by George Smith of Peterborough. He found them to be noisy and the least destructive of parrots for their small size. His four lived together perfectly amicably but unfortunately proved to be all females. In 1978, each of the three surviving females laid one or two eggs. Previously these birds had been seen to display by flaring the tail and holding the wings away from the body to reveal the red carpal patch.

Short-tailed Parrots should be offered a similar diet to that suggested for *Pionus*.

Caiques
Pionites

Caiques are small parrots which have the breast white, a feature which immediately distinguishes them from all other parrots. In behaviour, they are closest to the *Pyrrhura* and *Aratinga* conures. The caiques have always been treated as two species but I believe that they should be considered as conspecific. Voice and behaviour are identical. *P. leucogaster* differs from *melanocephala* only in the absence of black pigment: it therefore has flesh-

pink feet and white bill. Immature birds more nearly resemble *melanocephala* for they have the legs, feet, and exposed skin black and the bill streaked with black, which colour is lost gradually during their first year. The blackish streaks on the head are lost at the first moult at about six months. It is of interest that two Pallid Caiques bred by Bertagnolio differed in the amount of dark pigment exhibited on fledging; one had the beak and feet entirely black, the other had light-coloured bill and toe nails and flesh-pink toes.

Caiques are extremely destructive birds and can do considerable damage to unprotected aviary woodwork. It is essential to provide them with fresh twigs or branches for gnawing in order to prevent their bills from becoming overgrown – a common tendency in these birds. The provision of branches will reveal an interesting aspect of caique behaviour, which I described in *The Parrots of South America*:

> An area of the branch is immediately stripped of bark and the body is rubbed, cat-like against it, first on one side, then on the other. So absorbed does the bird become in these vigorous, almost frantic, rubbing movements that I am invariably reminded of a bird anting. These movements are carried out equally enthusiastically on a twig completely stripped of bark, or on a dry but bark-covered one. If I held a twig vertically, my Pallid Caique would rub himself against it for minutes at a time, and would even sharpen the end to a point to obtain a more satisfying effect.

Caiques require plenty of fruit in their diet and should be offered a wide variety as most individuals seem to have varying preferences. Apple pips are relished but perhaps the favourite food of most caiques is walnut. They can also be offered nectar, or trifle sponge soaked in nectar. The usual seeds should be provided, although small seeds are seldom favoured, except hemp. Greenfood is not usually eaten with as much enthusiasm as fruit.

Caiques have a stance which is more upright than that of other parrots; this tends to give them a comical appearance. They are extremely appealing, playful and intelligent birds.

Black-headed Caique
P. melanocephala melanocephala
Description: It has the entire top of the head black; the lores and a line below the eye are green and the throat and cheeks are yellow. There is an orange band across the hind neck. The upper parts are dark green and the entire under parts are white except for the orange-yellow under tail coverts and orange thighs. The primary coverts and primaries are deep blue. The iris is bright red and the beak is black. Bare skin surrounding the eye is grey. Length: 23 cm (9 in).

Immature birds have the under parts yellowish white or pale buff and the plumage is paler than in adults. There is a blue tinge to the green on the wings. The bill is horn-coloured, marked with black. The iris is dark brown.
Range/Habitat: This caique is found north of the Amazon, from the Guianas and northern Peru, Brazil, west to southern Colombia, eastern Ecuador and north-eastern Peru. Found in forested and savannah areas, it is seen in small flocks of up to about 30 birds and is abundant in many areas. It feeds in canopies of trees on fruits, berries and seeds.

Pallid Caique
P. m. pallida
Description: It differs from the Black-headed in its paler yellow and orange plumage, with the thighs yellow.
Range/Habitat: This bird comes from southern Colombia south to north-eastern Peru and eastern Ecuador.

Aviculture: The Black-headed Caique has long been a favourite with aviculturists; in fact, one owned by a London dealer in foreign birds was described as long ago as 1751. It is fairly regularly available but never imported in large numbers.

Caiques have a charm which is entirely their own. No other parrot has a personality which is quite the same. A tame caique is irresistibly charming and many aviary birds become quite fearless. This fearlessness, combined with a natural talent for mischief,

Black-headed Caique (*Pionites melanocephala melanocephala*).

Having witnessed the frantic attempts of my Pallid Caique to reach another pair of Caiques, and its satisfaction when I gave way to its desire to be housed with them, I would never again consider keeping one of these birds as a pet unless it had been hand-reared.

The Pallid was eventually proved to be a male and the 'pair' two females. If a strange caique is released into the aviary of a true pair it would probably be killed or seriously injured.

A caique kept in a mixed aviary with no companion of its own kind will quickly form a bond with another species – sometimes with one quite unlike or much larger than itself.

Caiques are very difficult birds to sex. George Smith, the first breeder of *melanocephala* in Britain, found true pairs by introducing various birds – under supervision – and watching their reaction. In the USA, they have been bred at several establishments, including Busch Gardens, Tampa, and the Sunken Gardens at St Petersburg, both in Florida, by initially placing four or six birds in the same aviary. There are several reports of colony breedings which were entirely successful, with no fighting occurring. Neither beak size nor colouration are reliable guides in sexing these birds; but George Smith recorded that, on occasion, females mounted males and even fed them. He has bred this species since 1971.

Caiques usually lay three eggs; occasionally the clutch numbers two or four. The incubation period averages 25 days. Newly hatched chicks weigh about 5.8 g ($\frac{1}{5}$ oz); weaning weight is about 120 g ($4\frac{1}{4}$ oz).

Italian aviculturist Paolo Bertagnolio reared ten chicks from a pair of Pallid Caiques between 1972 and 1977, when the female died. Chicks were reared every year except in 1975 when they died in the shell. In 1978, a female bred in 1973 laid two eggs.

The Black-headed Caique has also been bred by Mrs Williams of Miami, Florida, who was consistently successful from 1958 onwards and reared 40 birds in ten years, and at the Tropical Bird Garden, Rode, England, in 1976, when three young were reared. The following year no breeding was attempted, perhaps because the young had been left with their parents (which could no longer be identified).

means that with many caiques one has to keep a close watch on their beaks at feeding time for they positively enjoy the sport of nipping fingers. For their size, they are rather noisy birds with an interesting vocabulary of piercing shrieks and calls. This is their only fault and they must be counted among the most endearing and interesting of all parrots.

The desire for the company of their own kind is stronger in caiques than in almost any parrot I know. For this reason, unless one of these birds is extremely tame and completely devoted to its owner, I feel that it is most unkind to deprive it of the company of another caique.

In *The Parrots of South America*, I wrote:

Long neglected by zoos, in 1981 this species was reared at three in the USA: Columbia, Columbus and San Diego, and previously in Jackson and Washington Zoos.

Hybrids between Black-headed and White-bellied Caiques have been bred. Lady Poltimore bred this cross in 1936; the single bird resembled the Black-headed except for its green thighs. The parents were in her possession for at least 34 years.

White-bellied (White-breasted) Caique
P. leucogaster leucogaster
Description: It is immediately distinguished from the Black-headed by the orange on the head, extending from the forehead to the nape. There is no green line under the eye. The thighs are green. Its plumage otherwise resembles that of *melanocephala*. The bill is whitish; the bare skin surrounding the eye and cere is pinkish white. Even the eye colour is 'diluted', the red of the iris being of a paler shade and the inner ring grey – not deep red and black as in *melanocephala*. Length: 23 cm (9 in).

Immature birds have the crown irregularly marked with black feathers. The wings are tinged with blue. The iris is brown.
Range/Habitat: This caique is found south of the Amazon, in northern Brazil, west to northern Bolivia, eastern Peru and eastern Ecuador. It occurs in forest and forest edges and is common over much of its extensive range.

Yellow-thighed Caique
P. l. xanthomeria
Description: It differs from the nominate race in having the thighs and flanks yellow, instead of green. It is common in Brazilian aviculture.

White-bellied Caique (*Pionites leucogaster leucogaster*).

Range/Habitat: This bird is found in Amazonas, Brazil, westwards to eastern Ecuador and south to northern Bolivia.

Yellow-tailed Caique
P. l. xanthurus
Description: It is paler throughout and has the thighs, flanks and under tail coverts and the entire tail yellow.
Range/Habitat: North-western Brazil.

Aviculture: *P. leucogaster* has always been much rarer in aviculture than *melanocephala*, probably because less trapping has been carried out in its range. Of the two, both of which I have kept, my preference is for the Black-headed; the sooty black cap sets off the plumage to perfection and, in comparison, the plumage of the White-bellied somehow seems incomplete. However, both are extremely attractive little parrots and a joy to keep.

For their size, they are long-lived. A Yellow-thighed Caique which died at London Zoo in 1944 was known to be at least 45 years old.

This species has been bred in the USA: by Gilbert Lee in 1932 (three young reared), at San Diego Zoo in 1934 (one reared) and at Cincinnati Zoo in 1969 (one reared). At Busch Gardens, Tampa, a *leucogaster × xanthomeria* pair were reported to have produced nine young by 1969.

An unsuccessful breeding attempt was made by a *leucogaster × xanthomeria* pair on loan from George A. Smith to Mr and Mrs R. Mann (1977). Three eggs were laid in the first clutch; one hatched 26 days after the first egg was laid. Two days later the chick had disappeared. The female laid the first egg of the second clutch on July 30. The weather was very warm, thus shortening the incubation period to 24 days in the case of one egg: chicks hatched on August 23, 26 and 29. The adults took bread and milk, Cheddar cheese, nectar, apple, orange, hemp, peanuts and parrot mixture. On August 4, the two smallest chicks had disappeared; the survivor was removed for hand-rearing but died due to an unfortunate accident.

Chicks hatched by G. A. Smith in 1984 weighed 6.95 g ($\frac{1}{4}$ oz) and 5.9 g ($\frac{1}{5}$ oz) on hatching. They were hand-reared and weighed 125 g ($4\frac{2}{5}$ oz) and 129 g ($4\frac{3}{5}$ oz) on weaning.

There is no reference to *xanthurus* in avicultural literature.

26
Lories
and Lorikeets

The special appeal which lories and lorikeets hold for me lies not in a single factor but in the combination of beauty, playfulness, willingness to breed in captivity and, in the larger species, intelligence. Their colours rivet the eye; perhaps in no other group of birds is such diverse and boldly marked plumage found. They are irresistibly playful and lively (greater time wasters than any birds I know) and one could spend hours watching their antics. The larger lories are among the most intelligent of parrots and, as pets, they are usually exceptionally affectionate. This is not surprising for the pair bond is extremely strong in these birds. Most true pairs attempt to breed and many pairs are consistent breeders.

With all these attributes why are lories not more widely kept? The answer must lie in their feeding habits. The natural food of lories is pollen and nectar; their tongues are specially adapted for this diet. Because of this adaptation, they are often known as the 'brush-tongued' parrots. 'Brush' refers to the cluster of elongated papillae on the tip of the tongue which are visible only when the bird is feeding or exploring with its tongue. They are shortened and compressed at other times.

Feeding: In captivity, the principal item offered is nectar, made up from a wide variety of ingredients. In fact, they will thrive on almost any liquid food which contains nutritious ingredients including sweet ones. The inclusion of a baby cereal or wheatgerm cereal and sugar in the form of glucose, or honey, is recommended and, in a cool climate, condensed milk. Milk-based invalid foods, such as Complan (Farley Health Products), are widely used. Using a liquidiser, all kinds of foods, including fruits, can be added, if required.

It should be borne in mind that pollen, the principal food of lories in the wild, has a very high protein content and that nectar has a high carbohydrate content. The latter is less important in captive birds as they do not have to expend much energy to obtain food; therefore, the carbohydrate content of the substitute nectar should be low and the protein content high.

To introduce variety into the diet, the ingredients of the nectar made up can be varied from day to day as the range of foods which can be used is almost endless. As an example of two nectar mixtures I describe that offered to my own birds and those at San Diego Zoo; the latter collection formerly bred more lories than any other.

That which I prepare is made by dissolving two heaped dessertspoonsful of glucose (or one of honey) and three of Milupa baby cereal (any one of the fruit flavours) in warm boiled water, then adding a dessertspoonful of malt extract and stirring until dissolved. Water is added to make 1 litre (35 fl oz) and a $\frac{1}{4}$ to $\frac{1}{2}$ dessertspoonful of condensed milk (omitted in hot weather) is added. It is given fresh twice daily (this is not essential). It is essential that nectar is made up fresh every day. I feel that it is better to reduce the quantity made up (the above would be too much for a single pair of lories for one day) rather than make a larger quantity which is kept in a refrigerator, for chilled nectar should not be used. Any taken out of a refrigerator should have boiling water added. Lories show a marked preference for freshly made warm nectar.

At San Diego Zoo, items used to make up nectar include cane sugar, Super Hydramin powder (a human protein-vitamin concentrate manufactured by Nion Corporation, Los Angeles), chopped apples, boiled rice, soaked raisins, ground carrots, bread, shredded lettuce, evaporated milk and water. If in doubt regarding the quantity of water to use, it is better to err on the side of using too much, for nectar which is too concentrated can damage the liver while that which is over-diluted will not have a harmful effect. This applies especially to newly imported lories, for whom it is advisable to offer a diluted nectar.

Some aviculturists will not keep lories because they believe their feeding involves a lot of extra work. While it does take a little more time than feeding seed-eating birds, this is negligible with a small number of lories and the pleasure of their company makes it well worthwhile.

Nectar dishes must be kept spotlessly clean; a second set will prove helpful. Fresh nectar should always be provided in a clean container, that is, not by topping up that already holding nectar. The best receptacle for the larger species is an earthenware dog bowl. These playful birds will easily unhook or upset any other type. For smaller lories, plastic hook-on drinkers or drinking tubes (of the kind used for pet birds) can be used. The latter are not suitable if the mixture contains condensed milk or in a warm climate as the contents will sour easily. These tubes must be cleaned before being refilled, using a discarded toothbrush.

The natural diet of lories includes fruits, buds and small insects ingested with the nectar. Small seeds are taken by some species. Use of seed should be strictly limited, especially for the larger species for they will thrive on a nectar and fruit diet. Small seeds, such as canary and spray millet, can be offered but sunflower is best rationed to a small quantity of soaked, not dry, seed, if it is given at all.

The usual fruits can be offered, those usually favoured being apple, grapes, pomegranate and soft pear. Much wastage will occur, thus it may be preferred to liquidise the fruit and add it to the nectar mixture.

Some lories also relish lettuce and spinach beet and most eagerly consume chickweed and seeding grasses. Celery and carrot can be offered but most lories show little enthusiasm for fresh vegetables. Mealworms are relished by some birds, especially when rearing young. At this time, bread and milk can be offered, but a preference may be shown for fresh milk on its own, which is an excellent extra when there are young in the nest. If seed is given then, it should be soaked first.

Sprays of blossom and flower heads are perhaps the greatest treat one can give a lory for these will contain the only natural food it is possible to provide in captivity – pollen. Care must be taken that the blossoms provided have not been sprayed with an insecticide. Berries of hawthorn and elder will be eagerly eaten by some birds.

If lories are obtained unexpectedly, an emergency food can be made up from sugar or golden syrup dissolved in warm water, milk or tinned fruit (the syrup and the fruit).

Accommodation: The diet is the principal point on which the care of lories differs from that of other parrots. However, the liquid droppings create problems indoors, which is why these birds are seldom kept as pets. Unless a lory is extremely tame, it will be much better off in an outdoor aviary with another bird of its own kind. If it is decided to keep a tame lory indoors, it is worth going to the trouble of having a large metal cage, fully enclosed except for the front, made for it. Lories are very active and playful and to confine one to an orthodox parrot cage is cruel, for this type of cage is entirely unsuitable. Any cage should be not less than 1.2 m (4 ft) long. A nest-box can be attached to the outside or fixed inside as these birds invariably roost in a box.

Even keeping lories in indoor aviaries presents problems and much extra work. Outdoors, rain will prevent the wire mesh or fittings from becoming sticky but indoors the frequent and tedious job of washing the wire and perches is essential. Newspaper is the best floor covering. Indoors or outdoors, the feeding shelf will need frequent washing and should be constructed of an easily cleaned synthetic material rather than wood or asbestos.

As most lories sleep in their nestboxes, an elaborate shelter is unnecessary. The nest-box can be placed in the shelter or in the flight. One in each position will provide the birds with a choice. A major problem in breeding lories is that the liquid droppings of the young birds quickly causes the interior of the nest to become damp and insanitary. It is a simple matter to renew the nesting material – peat or shavings – with some pairs but others are extremely aggressive and will not hesitate to attack anyone who enters their aviary while there are chicks in the nest. It is thus an advantage to place the nest-box on the outside of the aviary, preferably where a safety passage will prevent escape.

Alternatively, for such pairs, it is worth constructing a special nest-box. This should be longer than it is deep, to give a floor area which is larger than normal. The base of the nest should not be made of wood but of hardware cloth; above this should be small mesh wire netting, on which rests a layer of charcoal at least 2.5–5 cm (1–2 in) thick. The female lays her eggs on the charcoal and when the chicks hatch it will absorb the wet droppings.

Breeding: A major problem in breeding lories, as in so many parrots, is obtaining true pairs. With a few exceptions (species only rarely available), the plumage is alike in male and female – or sexual dimorphism is so slight as to be unreliable to those not familiar with the species.

Neither is behaviour a truly reliable indication of a lory's sex. Sometimes two birds of the same sex behave as affectionately as a pair, although copulation may be less prolonged and less regular. Lories are among the most affectionate of all parrots and when not playing or exercising, they spend hours sitting quietly side by side, preening each other. And when the female is incubating, some males will spend hours inside the nest-box with her. When attempting to select a true pair from a number of birds, the size and shape of the head and beak is the best guide. Usually males have a larger head, with more rise above the eye, and the upper mandible is broader. The male is usually broader in the body. It is often easy to sex young lories in the nest, if they are male and female, when the contrast is most noticeable.

Most true pairs attempt to nest, although with the larger species it may be several years before breeding commences, and most hens lay eggs sooner or later. Unlike many parrots, lories nest readily in captivity.

At no time are they to be trusted with other birds and must always be housed one pair per aviary. In instances where a pair has shared an aviary, the occupants have almost invariably been killed by the lories when their chicks hatched, if not before. And although colony breeding has been practised, this usually results in the young being killed when they leave the nest.

The male, and sometimes also the female, will be seen to display when the breeding season approaches. Some lories are seasonal nesters, whereas others are continuous nesters. In display, lories arch the neck, bow the head, bob the head or entire body rapidly up and down, hiss through an open bill, dilate the pupil and chatter excitedly. The performance varies according to species, often depending on the plumage and which feature of it is to be displayed.

The clutch usually consists of two eggs, occasionally three in some *Trichoglossus* species, especially the Perfect. An exception is found in the small *Glossopsitta* lorikeets from Australia which lay three to five eggs. Incubation is carred out by the hen only, except in the *Charmosyna* and *Vini* species and in the only member of the genus *Phigys*, the Solitary Lory. It lasts from 23 to 28 days. The female's high-pitched plaintive call for food from within the nest-box is usually an indication that the eggs have been laid.

Newly hatched lory chicks are sparsely or heavily covered in down, which may be white, yellowish or grey. This is replaced by a denser second down, which is dark grey. With the exception of the Australian *Glossopsitta* species which spend only about six weeks in the nest, sometimes even less, lory chicks fledge after eight to twelve weeks.

A common problem with lories is plucking of young in the nest, which may be so serious that the young birds are unable to fly on emerging. Where possible, it is advisable to hand-rear the young from pairs which make a habit of denuding their chicks. If this is not possible, the young should be removed from their parents as soon as they are independent – or the plucking may continue and the feather follicles be damaged so badly that proper feather growth will be impossible. Plucking of young in the nest may be averted by nailing strips of wood or bark inside for the adults to gnaw. When the nest becomes very wet, if no other material is available to use as additional nesting material, young will be plucked.

Hand-rearing is also advocated when lories nest in the winter, as many do, because they cease to brood the chicks after two or three weeks, and the chicks are likely to succumb from the cold.

After fledging, the young can remain with pairs which nest only once annually for some months, if necessary, but should be removed after a few weeks in the case of those which are continuous nesters.

Lories are extremely enthusiastic bathers; many will bathe on the frostiest winter day. The larger species should be provided with large earthenware water containers which are filled and cleaned daily. The very small species will bathe in the large plastic hook-on drinkers.

If bathing facilities are always available, lories will keep their plumage in immaculate condition. While that of some parrots has a matt quality, in lories it should be glossy and gleaming.

Most lories are hardy, once acclimatised, and can be kept outdoors throughout the year, provided that a nest-box is available in which to roost. Exceptions are the small *Charmosyna* and *Vini* species which should not be expected or allowed to tolerate a cold climate. They must be wintered in an indoor birdroom or provided with a heated shelter.

There are about 50 species of lories and lorikeets, half of which are well known in aviculture. The terms lory and lorikeet, like those parrot and parrakeet, are not precise ones but, as a general rule, lory (and parrot) apply to short-tailed birds and lorikeet (and parrakeet) to long-tailed species.

Range/Habitat: Lories occur in Australia, New Guinea, Indonesia and the islands of the South Pacific.

Out of the breeding season most are nomadic in their habits, congregating in flocks wherever trees are flowering. After consuming the pollen, nectar and even the blossoms, they move on to another area. Lories are observed in flocks which may be quite small or which may be many hundreds strong. Some species are persecuted for raiding cultivated crops of grain and fruit but it is doubtful whether the population of any lory has been endangered by human activity other than habitat destruction.

Certain species from small Pacific islands, such as the Red-throated (*Charmosyna amabilis*) from Fiji and the Ultramarine Lory from the Marquesas, may be endangered and, with rapid habitat destruction in Indonesia and other areas in which lories are found, many more species could fall within this category in the coming years.

Chalcopsitta
Chalcopsitta

The members of this genus are large birds, approximately 30 cm (12 in) in length with long tails. They are recognised by the area of naked skin surrounding the lower mandible (also a feature of the Dusky Lory) which is the same colour as the beak, except in the Cardinal Lory, and by the distinctive feathers of the back of the head and neck which are narrow and pointed. The members of this genus were largely unknown in captivity until the early 1970s.

Black Lory
C. atra atra
Description: The body plumage is entirely black with a purplish vinous sheen; the rump is tinged with blue. The under side of the tail is red and yellow and the upper surface is dark vinous. Beak and legs are black and the iris is dark brown with an inner ring of yellow.

Immature birds have a few small red feathers on the head, usually in the region of the ear coverts and sometimes on other parts of the plumage.

Black Lory (*Chalcopsitta atra atra*).

The skin surrounding the eyes and lower mandible is white – not black as in the adult.

It is of interest that San Diego Zoo bred a Black Lory which was mainly red in immature plumage. It is probable that this species evolved from a red bird. The down on the body of adults is very pretty, being grey with the tips of pink. Length: 30 cm (12 in).
Range/Habitat: This species inhabits western New Guinea in the Western Vogelkop, West Irian, also the islands of Batanta and Salawati.
Aviculture: It was rare in aviculture until 1971. During the following three or four years the supply exceeded the demand and the price fell to a low of £50 per pair at one stage. At the time of writing, it is seldom imported and, while available, did not prove a favourite with aviculturists, perhaps because of its mainly black colouration.

However, to me, a bird's personality is as important as its colouration – and personality is something which the Black Lory does not lack. Some birds soon become tame and their engaging characters, mischievousness and intelligence is then very apparent.

The Black Lory was first bred in captivity in 1909 by E. J. Brook of Hoddam Castle in Scotland. A single bird was reared. The pair was again successful in 1910. I believe that this species was not bred again in Britain until my own pair reared two young in 1977. For several years I had kept two females together. In 1975, I obtained a third bird which was much larger in size and build – and this is probably so in most male Black Lories. They bred in an aviary only 1.8 m (6 ft) long and 90 cm (3 ft) wide. The aviary has no shelter but is protected by trees.

None of the *Chalcopsitta* lories has a pleasant voice; indeed, those with close neighbours should think twice about obtaining them. In the spring of 1977, the Black Lories became almost unbearably noisy. The male became so bold and aggressive that it was necessary to construct a wire cage over the earthenware bowl containing the nectar, but not before he had taken a piece out of my finger.

The female laid her first clutch during the second week in May and deserted the nest on June 8 when it was found to be empty. The second clutch was laid during the second week in July. On August 5, a chick was heard. Nest inspection was impossible but from the volume of sound coming from the nest, it was soon apparent that there were two chicks. They were reared on the usual nectar with added wheatgerm cereal and a small drinker of milk daily. Occasionally ripe pear was taken; fresh corn-on-the-cob was refused.

After the chicks hatched the adults became much quieter. Before they were a month old it was necessary to enter the aviary on a couple of occasions to place new peat in the nest-box. The adults resented this intrusion so the aviary was not entered again until September 17 and then only through sheer necessity. The birds had gnawed the lid of the nest-box until it split in two and the chicks were exposed to the weather, which was cold. The inside of the nest had become wet with the chicks' liquid droppings, thus the adults had attempted to rectify the situation using the slivers of wood gnawed from the lid.

During the last week of September, the chicks were seen looking out of the nest-box, calm and unafraid, and it was evident that the parents were plucking them. The first fledged on October 17, aged 10½ weeks. That night one of the adults roosted on top of the nest-box with it. Next morning I saw it for the first time; it was three-quarters covered with feathers and looked well and confident. The following morning I experienced the kind of disappointment every aviculturist knows sooner or later and recalls ever more with a sinking heart: the young lory was dead beneath the nest-box. During the previous day it had been severely plucked by one of its parents and had probably died of exposure.

I therefore caught up the adults and gently removed the surviving youngster from the nest-box. The family was transferred to a large cage with nest-box attached in the house. Within minutes the young lory had found its way into the nest-box but from the following day entered only when its parents did. Four days later it was feeding itself and five days after that I returned the adults to their aviary.

The young bird's plumage differed from that of its parents in the presence of a few very small red feathers on the ear coverts and a few flecks of red in the body plumage. At just over 12 months old, the periorbital skin and that at the side of the lower mandible was still partly white perhaps because it had never been exposed to sunlight.

A female, she has remained in the same large cage indoors. I made no attempt to tame her and it was not until she was six months old that she became at all friendly. Now, she is the tamest and most gentle and affectionate bird it is possible to own. She delights in sitting on my shoulder and exploring my face with the brushes of her tongue. It is almost impossible to prevent her scrambling along my arm when the cage door is opened to remove the nectar-pot and when I carry her into the kitchen to refill it, she jumps on to the nectar jug and helps herself. Like all young lories, she is playful and inventive. I often give her a grape or a small green apple for the pleasure of seeing her lie on her back and juggle with it.

In 1985, a pair belonging to Andrew Coughlan of Surrey nested five times. Seven chicks hatched; three died in the nest at an early age and four were hand-reared.

The Black Lory has also been bred in San Diego Zoo, on a number of occasions since 1969, and in South Africa in the collection of Brian Boswell at the Natal Lion Park since 1976. Also in South Africa, a hybrid between a male Black Lory and a female Edwards' Lorikeet was reared by B. von Sorgenfrie. Described as a beautiful bird, it had the head, neck and tail black, under side of tail yellow, breast dark blue and the rest of the plumage green.

Red-quilled Lory
C. a. insignis
Description: This bird differs from the Black Lory in having the forehead, forepart of the cheeks, the thighs and under wing coverts red, with some red feathers on the abdomen. Under tail coverts are greyish blue and the rump is dull blue.
Range/Habitat: The Red-quilled Lory inhabits Amberpon Island in Geelvink Bay; Onin and Bomberai

Peninsulas and the eastern Vogel-kop, West Irian and New Guinea.
Aviculture: It is extremely rare in aviculture. A single specimen was exhibited for some years at Birdland, Bourton-on-the-Water, England.

Bernstein's Lory
C. a. bernsteini
Description: This bird is doubtfully distinct. It supposedly differs in having red feathers on the thighs and sometimes on the primaries. A bird answering this description in my possession gradually increased the areas of red in its plumage (when adult) before losing them entirely.

Duivenbode's Lory
C. duivenbodei
Description: This bird is of unusual beauty. Next to Stella's Lorikeet it is, to me, the most beautiful of all lories. Predominantly dark brown with a golden tinge, it has a well defined golden yellow ring from the lores, encircling the beak and throat; the forehead is also yellow. The narrow feathers of the nape and the sides of the neck are streaked with yellow. The entire under wing coverts are bright golden yellow, also the thighs. The under side of the tail is paler, more bronze yellow. Lower back, rump and under tail coverts are deep blue, tinged with violet. The feathers of the breast have the hidden portion yellow and the primaries are black with a large yellow patch on the inner web. Beak, cere and legs are black. The iris is dark brown with an inner circle of pale yellow. Length: 31 cm (12 in). Weight: 235 g ($8\frac{1}{5}$ oz).

Immature birds have the plumage duller throughout; the periorbital skin is white.

Range/Habitat: Duivenbode's Lory inhabits northern New Guinea along the coastal area. It is found in the lowlands up to 200 m (650 ft).

Aviculture: A single bird of this species reached Britain in 1929, shortly to be followed by two more. It would appear to have remained unknown in aviculture until 1973, since when it has been irregularly imported into Europe and the USA in small numbers.

In a large aviary, where the brilliant yellow under wing coverts can be seen in flight, this species is magnificent.

The first captive breeding I know of occurred at Vogelpark Walsrode in Germany; one was reared in 1977, two in 1978 and two in 1979. In the USA, it was first bred at San Diego Zoo in 1979; five were bred in 1980 from two pairs and three in 1981; in the same year, Chicago reared two. Also, in 1979, this species was bred by Mr and Mrs J. Longo of Kent, Washington.

In Britain, Duivenbode's Lory was not bred until 1983, first in my own collection and later by Mrs Patricia King in Cornwall (one youngster) and at Birdland, Bourton-on-the-Water (one). My male and female were introduced in November 1978. Copulation was first seen in 1981. In the following year, two eggs were laid; one chick hatched and died the same day.

In February 1983, the pair was moved to an aviary where the nest-box could be inspected from outside. This was essential because they became very aggressive when breeding. The aviary measured 210 × 91 cm (7 × 3 ft) × 180 cm (6 ft) high. By April 12, the female was incubating one egg. When the nest was inspected on May 5, I saw a chick; the female was momentarily away from the nest. I made an instant decision to remove it and did so as the female re-entered the nest. It was fluffy and had probably hatched on the previous day. Its weight was 9 g ($\frac{3}{10}$ oz). The second chick hatched the next day, weighing 8 g (almost $\frac{3}{10}$ oz), and was removed. For the first week, the chicks had quite long white down on the upper parts, the down being sparse elsewhere. The bill was dark brown with contrasting white egg tooth.

By the age of seven days, their feet had assumed a brown tinge and their bodies took on a darker appearance as the feather tracts of the second down became apparent. By about 20 days, the dark grey second down was erupting. Their eyes started to slit when they were about 12 days but were not fully open until three weeks. At about 24 days, the first contour feathers were erupting on the wings, shortly to be followed by the head feathers. Wisps of down remained on the head and back. By five weeks the body feathers had erupted – dull brown above and

yellow-tipped brown below. By then the area of white skin surrounding the eye was very prominent. The chicks weighed 130 and 140 g ($4\frac{3}{5}$ and $4\frac{9}{10}$ oz). At seven weeks they were transferred from the heated brooder to a wooden weaning cage (with hinged lid and wire mesh floor). They were then almost fully feathered, except for under the wings and the short (4 cm/1$\frac{1}{2}$ in) tail. When first offered nectar at the age of seven and a half weeks, they drank readily.

Rearing food from one to six weeks consisted of equal parts of tinned baby foods: fruit dessert and bone and vegetable broth. After that ground-up CéDé (proprietary Canary eggfood) was added. At the age of eight weeks they were transferred to a 1.8 m (6 ft) indoor flight.

Meanwhile the parents had nested again. The female laid on June 4 and 6. The eggs hatched on June 28 and 30, establishing the incubation period as 24 days. The chicks were well fed, with bulging crops, but as they grew the youngest gave cause for concern. At 21 days, it weighed only 41 g (1$\frac{1}{2}$ oz); at the same age, the hand-reared chicks had weighed 83 and 74 g (3 and 2$\frac{1}{2}$ oz approx.). By August 21, it weighed only 89 g (3$\frac{1}{10}$ oz) and was badly plucked, so was removed for hand-rearing. Nine days later, its weight had increased greatly to 140 g (4$\frac{9}{10}$ oz). It was successfully reared, as was the parent-reared youngster which left the nest at 11 weeks old.

In 1984 two eggs were laid in February. A chick hatched and was removed on March 3; it weighed 7 g (almost $\frac{1}{4}$ oz). It died on March 8 when it weighed 11 g ($\frac{2}{5}$ oz). The cause of its death was not apparent. The chicks of the second clutch hatched on April 29 and May 1. The eldest left the nest on July 17 and the youngest soon after. They had been plucked slightly but were completely feathered on leaving the nest.

The next clutch was laid during the middle of December 1984 and incubation occurred during bitterly cold weather, with temperatures permanently below or just above freezing at the end of the incubation period. One chick hatched on January 12 and was removed for hand-rearing two days later, because of the severe weather.

The second egg was infertile. It measured 34×25 mm ($1\frac{3}{5} \times 1$ in).

In Sweden, Duivenbode's Lory has been bred by Bengt Larsson. His female laid two eggs in March 1981. Both hatched. The chicks' eyes opened on the 14th day and the first feathers appeared on the 35th day. At 27 days, they weighed 200 and 140 g (7 and 5 oz). On the 63rd day, the young were heard flapping their wings inside the nest; seven days later the eldest chick left the nest, followed the next day by the youngest one. Neither had yellow thighs. This breeding occurred in an indoor aviary measuring 1.2 m (4 ft) square and 1.2 m (4 ft) high.

Yellow-streaked Lory
C. sintillata

Description: This is a most colourful bird. Two subspecies have been named but the plumage varies so much in individuals that it is a matter for speculation whether they are valid ones. The forehead, lores, thighs, under wing coverts and base of the under side of the tail are scarlet. The hind part of the crown, nape and ear coverts are black; the feathers of the neck and mantle are dark olive shaft-streaked with yellow, also the upper breast. In some birds, the underlying colour of the upper breast is orange and the streaks may be more orange than yellow. There is a yellow band across the under side of the flight feathers. The abdomen is green with yellow shaft-streaking. Lower back is sky blue or green, streaked with paler green and the under side of the tail, except at the base, is bronzy yellow. Wings, tail and under tail coverts are green. Shaft-streaking reaches its maximum development in this species. Feet and beak are black and the iris is dark brown with an inner ring of yellow. Length: 29 cm ($11\frac{1}{2}$ in). Weight: 195–210 g ($6\frac{4}{5}$–$7\frac{2}{5}$ oz).

Immature birds are altogether duller. One breeder noted that the red on the thighs was missing. Leif Rasmussen described his five young as lacking the red frontal band and having duller streaking on the chest.
Range/Habitat: The Yellow-streaked Lory inhabits the southern half of New Guinea and the Aru Islands.
Aviculture: Its avicultural history par-

Yellow-streaked Lories (*Chalcopsitta sintillata*).

allels that of the two members of the genus already described in that it was collected on a few occasions during the second and third decades of this century and then was almost totally unknown until the early 1970s.

It is a delightful bird to keep but although its voice is not quite as loud as that of the Black Lory, it is hardly pleasant on the ear. The male of my 'pair' (which may yet prove to be two males) loves to be noticed. He will approach the front of the aviary to display to me, bobbing his head up and down gradually more rapidly and hissing so close to me that I can feel the air he expels.

The first captive breeding success may be that of I. and H. Roth of Farum, Denmark in 1976. Two eggs were laid; two chicks hatched at the end of January and left the nest on April 29 and May 1. In the USA, Dr Ray Jerome of Dallas has bred Yellow-streaked Lories since 1981.

This species was first bred in Britain by R. Kyme of Boston in 1978. Continuous nesters, the pair hatched numerous chicks which survived only a few days, before successfully rearing two which fledged in September. The incubation period was 24 days. On hatching, the chicks were covered with thin, long whitish down which was very sparse over the head and neck. Chicks hatched on June 1 and 3 and left the nest on August 26 and 28. By November, the white periorbital area was darkening and a week later red feathers were coming through on the head (Kyme, 1979).

Probably the most consistent UK breeder to date is Mrs Patricia King, who first bred this species in 1980. Eggs laid on January 21 and 23 hatched on February 16 and 18. The colder weather was perhaps responsible for the slightly longer incubation period (26 days). The chicks were removed from the nest on March 19 after a bad storm; they weighed 184 and 141 g ($6\frac{1}{2}$ and 5 oz). At seven weeks, they weighed 227 and 198 g (8 and 7 oz) and at nine weeks 213 and 198 g ($7\frac{1}{2}$ and 7 oz). They were then more difficult to feed. They flew at ten weeks. At six months old they started to attain adult plumage (King, 1980).

Zoos which have bred this species are Natal Lion Park in South Africa, since 1976, and the nearby Pietermaritzburg Zoo in 1979, Vogelpark Walsrode in Germany since 1979 and Asson Zoo in France in 1980. In Denmark, Leif Rasmussen's pair reared five in three nests in 1984. The young were plucked in the nest. Mealworms were consumed while the young were being reared. The nest-box used was 25 cm (10 in) square and 50 cm (20 in) high (Rasmussen, pers. comm.).

Cardinal Lory
C. cardinalis
Description: It is almost entirely red, darker and more brownish on the back and wings; the tail is rusty red and the feathers of the under parts are edged with buffish-yellow. Bill is red with the base of the upper mandible black. Legs are dark grey. The naked area of skin surrounding the lower mandible distinguishes it from other red lories. The iris is red. Length: 31 cm (12 in).

Immature birds bred by T. Morford (1980) were described as having greyish yellow margins to the feathers of the under parts. The beak was reddish brown; there were light brown patches on the ear coverts.

Range/Habitat: This species occurs in the Solomon Islands where it is extremely numerous, being found in very large flocks.

Aviculture: It is rare in captivity because few birds are exported from the Solomons. Two birds were received by San Diego Zoo in 1944 and a small consignment imported privately by Swiss aviculturist Dr R. Burkard in 1976. Of the latter, two pairs went to Vogelpark Walsrode in West Germany. Loro Parque in Tenerife also exhibits this species.

Eos
Eos

Averaging smaller than the members of the preceding genus, the *Eos* lories have the plumage predominantly red, set off with black, mauve or blue. Immature plumage is obvious: in most cases the red feathers have dark tips, to give a mottled appearance.

Red (Moluccan) Lory
E. bornea bornea
Description: The plumage is mainly bright red, duller on the tail. The under tail coverts and the area surrounding the vent is blue. The pri-

Red Lories (*Eos bornea bornea*).

maries and secondaries are black and red and the greater wing coverts are blue. The bill is orange, the iris red and the periorbital skin black. Four races are recognised, three of which are distinguished mainly by size, which varies from about 25 cm (10 in) to 30 cm (12 in). *E. b. cyanonothus*, from Buru, with its darker shade of red, is the only one which the aviculturist is likely to recognise. Weight: 180 g (6⅗ oz).

Immature plumage is variable but most young birds have the red feathers edged with blue, the beak black and the iris brown. Some young birds have blue ear coverts.

Range/Habitat: This species inhabits the Indonesian islands of Amboina, Sapura, Ceram, Ceramlaut, Watubela and Kai Islands.

Aviculture: This is the best known of the genus. Being comparatively inexpensive and beautiful, it is ideal for the beginner with lories, its only disad-

vantage being the rather harsh voice.

The Red Lory has successfully reared young on many occasions in Europe and the USA. The incubation period is usually 24 days and the young remain in the nest for about nine weeks.

The earliest reference I can find to this species breeding in captivity is that relating to Herbert Whitley's collection in Devon. By 1940 it was reported to have bred there at least twice. Two other successes are of interest because they occurred in rather small cages. At Paignton Zoo, in Devon, a pair reared two young in 1967 in a cage which measured 90 × 70 × 150 cm (36 × 67 × 58 in). In South Africa, Dr A. J. Wright's pair reared a chick in an even smaller cage but they were allowed out twice daily for exercise.

In the USA, W. Sheffler bred this species in Arizona during the 1940s. It has reared young in many other

Blue-streaked Lory (*Eos reticulata*).

Violet-necked Lory (*Eos squamata*).

private collections, also in zoos in Rio de Janeiro (1967), Asson Zoological Park in France (1967), Wassenaar Zoo, the Netherlands (1970, 1972 and 1973), Jurong Bird Park in Singapore (1974) and Naples Zoo in Italy.

The race *cyanonothus* was bred by J. Hayward at Carterton (then Carterton Bird Gardens) in 1971. Two young were reared. This race has also been reared at Natal Lion Park in South Africa since 1976 (22 reared during 1976–1979) and at San Diego Zoo.

The Red Lory has hybridised with a number of other lories, including some in different genera. In San Diego Zoo, for example, a male mated to a Swainson's Lorikeet reared a hybrid in 1972. It had the crown red, the rest of the head and nape blue, wings and thighs green and under parts red with some blue on the lower breast.

Black-winged (Blue-cheeked) Lory
E. cyanogenia

Description: It is mainly black and red above (the wings being entirely black with a golden spot on the fifth primary), and red below. A violet V-shaped patch, with the V pointing towards the beak, covers most of the side of the face, the feathers being slightly elongated. The thighs and a spot on the flanks are black. Under tail coverts are red: central tail feathers are black with red inner webs. The bill is orange and the iris dark red with an inner ring of white. Length: 28 cm (11 in).

Immature birds have the red feathers of the head, neck and under parts irregularly margined with purplish black. The iris is brown and the beak is black.

Range/Habitat: The Black-winged Lory is an island species, being found in Geelvink Bay, New Guinea, on Numfoor, Biak, Manim and Mios Num.

Aviculture: This handsome bird is not frequently imported, but neither is it rare in aviculture. The musky odour, characteristic of all *Eos* species, is particularly strong in this lory.

It has only rarely been bred in captivity. The first success would appear to be that of Gilbert Lee in the USA in 1934. In Britain, it was first bred by Mr and Mrs C. Wright of Ealing in 1976. Two young were reared, and one more in 1977, when the youngster left the nest at 87 days; the first two had fledged at 75 days. While they were rearing young, the adults would attack anyone who entered their aviary. Also in Britain, Andrew Blythe hand-reared three youngsters from two pairs. In 1983, two females had been paired together; copulation had been observed and the birds took turns in laying eight or nine clutches. It was not until the spring of 1984, when four eggs appeared, that it was realised that both birds were females. In 1985, Mrs Patricia King of Cornwall hand-reared one Black-winged Lory; the pair had produced only infertile eggs in the previous five years.

In the USA, this species has been bred by Dr R. Jerome of Dallas, Texas, since 1980. In South Africa,

Peter Oderkerken reared two young in 1977. At Vogelpark Walsrode in West Germany, young have been reared on several occasions since 1977.

Blue-streaked Lory
E. reticulata

Description: This bird is distinguished by the feature which gives it its name – the bright blue streaks on the mantle and hind neck. The ear coverts are dark blue and the wings are irregularly marked with black except on the lesser wing coverts. The upper side of the tail is black, some of the feathers with red inner webs and the thighs are marked with black. The rest of the plumage is bright red and the beak is orange-red. The tail is longer than in other *Eos* species, giving a total length of 31 cm (12 in).

Immature birds have the feathers of the breast edged with blue-black and the bill dark grey.

Range/Habitat: The Blue-streaked Lory inhabits the Tenimber Islands in Indonesia and has been introduced to a few smaller islands.

Aviculture: This lory was fairly rare in aviculture until the 1970s when, like the Goffin's Cockatoo from the same islands, it suddenly became available – but not in large numbers. It was exhibited at London Zoo as long ago as 1862.

The first recorded breeding in captivity occurred in the collection of Mrs Bonestell in California in 1939. In Britain, R. Phipps of Maidenhead had a first success in 1972. A single chick left the nest about 14 weeks after hatching. Among the foods taken while it was being reared were maggot pupae (previously ignored), corn-on-the-cob and nectar with wholemeal breadcrumbs added.

Two young reared by W. Riley of Lancashire in 1973 left the nest when they were 12 weeks old during December. The weather was so cold that the liquid droppings froze as they emerged from the bottom of the nest-box!

The Blue-streaked Lory has also been bred in Britain by Mr and Mrs C. Wright of Ealing in 1977 (two) and in Zimbabwe by D. S. Edwards in 1973, by Martin Hansen of Denmark in 1974, and in 1976 when four were reared in two rounds, by Dr A. J. Wright of Durban in 1974 and in 1974 and 1975 at Pietermaritzburg Zoo in South Africa. Also in 1974, two young were reared in Naples Zoo, Italy and in 1975 at Asson Zoological Park in France. In 1976 Birdworld at Farnham, England, reared one. In the USA, Mr and Mrs J. Longo of Kent, Washington, has bred this species since 1978 and Dr R. Jerome of Dallas has reared young on several occasions. In California, Roland Cristo has reared Blue-streaked Lories since 1979.

Violet-necked (Violet-naped) Lory
E. squamata
Description: This is the smallest member of the genus, measuring 22 to 25 cm (9 to 10 in). The plumage is rather variable, being mainly red and dull purple. The latter colour is found on the neck, often with a wide band around the throat, and on the abdomen. The primaries and secondaries are marked with black and the upper side of the tail is purplish red, the under side usually being brownish red. The rest of the plumage is red and the bill is orange. The iris may be red, orange or yellow.

Immature birds have the feathers of the under parts edged with purple and the ear coverts tinged with purple. The iris is brown.
Range/Habitat: This species inhabits the Schildpad Islands and the western Papuan islands of Gebe, Waigeu, Batanta and Mysol.

Aviculture: It is quite well known in aviculture and was long one of the least expensive of the lories to obtain. The first recorded breeding would appear to be that which occurred in Chatillon, France, in 1926. M. P. Soudée's pair reared one youngster. In California in 1939, Mrs Bonestell's Blue-streaked Lories reared a single Violet-naped Lory with their own young.

More recently, Paolo Bertagnolio of Rome has been consistently successful with this species since 1972. Also in Italy, it has been reared at Naples Zoo on several occasions. In 1973, three Violet-naped Lories were reared in Pietermaritzburg Zoo, South Africa.

In Britain, there is no record of this species breeding before 1976. A pair belonging to Mrs L. Hutchinson of Eastbourne reared a single chick. Two eggs laid in March 1977 hatched and both chicks left the nest; one died two days later, perhaps as a result of injuring itself.

Two chicks hatched during December 1977 but after two weeks the female ceased to brood them, at a time when the weather was very cold. One died and the other was removed for hand-rearing but it died after a few days. While rearing young, this pair consumed large quantities of greenfood: heads of sowthistle, spinach, chickweed and grasses.

In 1977, the Violet-naped Lory was bred by Mr and Mrs C. Wright of Ealing. The female laid one fertile egg in February which failed to hatch. Two more eggs were laid on May 23 and May 26 and hatched on June 19 and 21. The young birds left the nest on August 22 and 24, when their plumage was very different from that of the adults, with an iridescent brown tinge to the flights and tail, brownish violet ear coverts and the collar only faintly indicated, dark edges to the feathers of the breast, blackish beaks and brown iris.

Unlike the Black-winged Lories in the same collection, the adults were not at all aggressive. The young were reared on nectar made up from baby cereal, baby rice, glucose, honey, Complan and Ostermilk, plus fruit, sunflower seed and milk mixed with honey.

Red and Blue (Blue-diademed or Blue-tailed) Lory
E. histrio
Description: It is distinguished by the very broad band of violet-blue which extends across most of the lower parts from the upper breast. A band of the same colour decorates the crown and there is a streak through the eye which meets the violet-blue on the nape and mantle. Scapulars, flight feathers and thighs are black and the wing coverts are tipped with black. The tail is reddish purple above and the under tail coverts are washed with blue. The rest of the plumage is red. The beak is orange, the cere white and the iris red. Length: 31 cm (12 in).

Immature birds are blue rather than violet on the head and nape. The under parts are variably marked with dusky blue and the thighs are mauvish blue.
Range/Habitat: Found on the islands of Great Sanghir, Siao and Talaud, Indonesia.

Challenger Lory
E. h. challengeri
Description: It differs from the nominate race in having the blue band on the breast less extensive and broken with red and the blue line through the eye not extending to the mantle. It is smaller, about 25 cm (10 in).
Range/Habitat: It inhabits the Nenusa Islands, Indonesia.

Aviculture: This handsome lory has always been very rare in captivity. It was exhibited at London Zoo as long ago as 1871 and San Diego Zoo had two specimens in the 1960s. Birdland, Bourton-on-the-Water exhibited a single *challengeri* obtained in 1972.

The only breeding success of which I know occurred in Denmark in 1965; the breeder was Carl Aage Jensen of Køge. A hybrid between this species and the Red Lory was exhibited at San Diego Zoo in 1937.

Ceram (Blue-eared or Half-masked) Lory
E. semilarvata
Description: Mainly bright red, it has the area from the beak to the ear

coverts violet-blue with a line of the same colour on the side of the neck. The primaries are black with a red speculum and the secondaries are tipped with black. The rest of the plumage is red. The bill is orange and the iris orange-red. Length: 24 cm (9 in).

Immature birds have less blue on the head and the feathers of the abdomen are edged with blue. The red areas are duller and the scapulars are brownish grey edged with pale blue.
Range/Habitat: This bird inhabits the mountains of central Ceram.

Lorius
Lorius

Several genera of lory are so closely related that they could perhaps be considered as a supergenus; indeed, it would be difficult to justify to a taxonomist how the Red Lory (*Eos bornea*) can be placed in one genus and the Chattering Lory (*Lorius garrulus*) in another. It seems that the *Lorius* species have been separated solely on account of their green wings and larger size.

They are most attractive aviary birds if their loud and sometimes persistent voices can be forgiven. They are certainly among the most intelligent of the lories and tame birds make wonderful pets. Some learn to talk quite well. These birds have thick-set bodies and short, rounded tails. They are weak, heavy fliers.

Chattering Lory
L. garrulus garrulus
Description: The Chattering Lory is almost entirely scarlet with green wings and thighs. The bend of the wing and the under wing coverts are yellow and there is a broad pinkish band across the under side of the primaries. The tail is green above, blue at the tip and the feathers of the under side are bronze-red with a red patch at the base. Length: 30 cm (12 in).

Immature birds have the beak brown and the iris dark brown.
Range/Habitat: This bird is found in the Halmahera and Weda islands.

Chattering Lory (*Lorius garrulus garrulus*).

Yellow-backed Lory
L. g. flavopalliatus
Description: This subspecies differs in having yellow on the mantle.
Range/Habitat: It inhabits the islands of Batjan, Morotai and Obi in the Moluccas.

Aviculture: Chattering and Yellow-backed are the best known and most frequently imported of the genus.

Relatively inexpensive, this is another species which is suitable for the beginner with lories. Its brilliant colouration and pleasing personality make it a favourite. Most Chattering Lories soon become tame or fearless, thus there is much enjoyment to be gained from keeping them close to the house, if one can tolerate their noisy calls. My own pair of Yellow-backed Lories are housed just below my bedroom window and I often hear them squabbling noisily in the middle of the night. They have remained in excellent health for 15 years or more on a diet of nectar, half an apple daily and a whole banana every morning and evening. To date they have consumed in excess of 13,000 bananas.

Chattering and Yellow-backed Lories have been bred in captivity on

numerous occasions. The incubation period is about 26 days and young remain in the nest for about ten weeks. In Britain, the first breeding of the Chattering Lory occurred in 1913 when Lord Poltimore's pair reared a youngster. In the USA, Mrs Bonestell of California fostered two under Swainson's Lorikeets in 1939 as the parents had previously killed their young. A varied diet was provided for the pair owned by J. F. Simoes in Lisbon, Portugal. In 1958, a single chick was reared on nectar, sunflower seed, carrots, tomatoes, various fruits, insectivorous food, mealworms and, indeed, earthworms. Had it not been for the intervention of an aviary attendant, the young bird would have been killed by the male as it left the nest.

Mr and Mrs R. Wallwork of Coventry were successful in breeding the Chattering Lory in 1977 and kindly provided me with the following details. Their first 'pair', obtained in 1973, produced four clear eggs annually; the two females were observed feeding each other and mating on many occasions. In June 1977, a male was obtained and put with one of the females for a few hours daily; after two weeks of minor squabbles they were left together and within five weeks the female had laid her first egg which measured 25×21 mm ($1 \times \frac{4}{5}$ in). The second egg was laid on July 13; by August 11 one chick had hatched and the other egg had disappeared. By the time it was ten days old, the young lory had a few wisps of grey down and 'big black feet'. As the parents did not object to nest inspection the chick was photographed weekly. By August 27, the chick's pin feathers were appearing and, by September 3, its eyes were fully open. By the time it was 38 days old, black, green and red quills were apparent and at 53 days its tail feathers were 1 cm ($\frac{2}{5}$ in) long; a week later they measured 2 cm ($\frac{4}{5}$ in). By the 67th day it was seen looking out of the nest hole. It left the nest at 76 days. The male parent became very possessive of it and even drove the female away. By November 11, it was feeding itself on nectar, maggots, fruit and greenfood.

The Chattering Lory has reared young in many countries throughout the world, including Canada (by Mrs

Engelsman, 1973 and 1974), France (Villars Zoo), the Netherlands (Amsterdam Zoo), East Germany (Leipzig and East Berlin Zoos), Poland (Wroclaw Zoo), South Africa (Natal and Amanzimtoti Zoos), Mozambique (Beira Zoo) and the USA. The Yellow-backed Lory has bred with equal frequency. At one time Paolo Bertagnolio of Rome had three breeding pairs which reared eight young during one year.

Hybrids between a Yellow-backed Lory and a Green-naped Lorikeet were bred in 1983 by Howard Kaplan in California. Photographs of the two young in immature plumage depict them as being like the Green-naped in shape, with the top of the head brown or mauve, the rest of the head and the under parts scarlet, back, wings, tail, thighs and under tail coverts green.

Black-capped Lory (*Lorius lory lory*).

Black-capped Lory
L. lory lory

Description: It has the forehead, crown and nape black, the under parts and the mantle dark blue and the wings green with a bronze patch; there is a broad yellow band across the under side of the flight feathers. A blue band decorates the hind neck, the abdomen is brilliant blue and the under tail coverts are pale blue. The rest of the plumage is red. The bill is orange and the iris is orange or yellow. Length: 31 cm (12 in).

Immature plumage would appear to be variable; under parts are dark blue and the bill is horn-coloured.

A number of subspecies are recognised. One of the most distinctive is *L. l. erythrothorax* which has the upper breast entirely red and less extensive blue areas on the abdomen and hind neck.

Range/Habitat: The Black-capped Lory has an extensive range over almost all mainland New Guinea, also the western Papuan islands and some of the islands in Geelvink Bay.

Aviculture: This species has long been popular in captivity and is probably the second best known of the genus but has become rarely imported and expensive. It has all the attributes of the Chattering Lory and the same failing: a voice which is harsh. However, young birds can be taught to talk and members of this species can become accomplished mimics, unlike most lories. It will also learn to imitate the sounds around it. One pair could mimic chickens, gulls, steam whistles and the yelping of a dog, among other sounds.

As an aviary bird, the Black-capped Lory has everything to recommend it and pairs nest fairly readily. In Britain, it was first bred in 1921 by Mrs Dalton Burgess. During the rearing of the youngster, the male became extremely savage.

The incubation period has been reported as from 23 to 26 days and the length of time the young have remained in the nest from only eight weeks to 10½ weeks. It has reared young on many occasions in captivity, including in Belgium in the collection of M. J. Bruyneel, reported in 1946, in Amsterdam Zoo (1965), Asson Zoological Park in France (1970) and in Britain at Birdland, Bourton-on-the-Water, Dudley Zoo and in the collections of D. G. Bloom (1972 and 1973) and Lady Lathbury (1972 and 1973).

In 1982, Mike Gammond of Devon obtained a female Black-capped Lory for the male which had produced 16 hybrid young in four years when paired with a female Yellow-backed Lory. At first, the female Black-cap was afraid of the male; mutual preening was observed for the first time in February 1983; two eggs had been laid by February 12. Fighting was heard in the nest-box on March 6; on the following day there was one chick; the egg had disappeared. On the 11th day after hatching, the female was found with her nails caught in the wire mesh ladder. She was successfully released – but the chick was cold. Hand-rearing was successful and the young bird was independent at the age of 74 days.

By July 19, two more eggs had been laid. The first chick hatched on August 8 and the second on August 11. They left the nest aged 63 and 60 days, completely denuded by feather plucking. They were removed, started to feed themselves three days later and had feathered up perfectly within a few weeks.

These birds were housed in an indoor aviary measuring 150 × 91 cm (5 × 3 ft) × 220 cm (7½ ft). In addition to nectar, they consumed carrot, green-food and fruit. When young were in the nest, mealworms and sweet corn were eaten.

In Denmark, this species has been bred by Leif Rasmussen. Other successful collections include the zoos in

Rotterdam (Netherlands), Wroclaw (Poland) and Jakarta (Indonesia). The race *erythrothorax* has been reared at the Natal Lion Park in South Africa since 1977. In the USA, it has been bred consistently at San Diego Zoo where a hybrid between a male of this species and a female *Eos histrio* was bred in 1932. Hybrids with another *Eos* species, *bornea*, were reared at Busch Gardens, Tampa, Florida – one in 1966 and four in 1967.

Purple-capped (Purple-naped) Lory
L. domicellus

Description: This is a very beautiful bird, possibly of more pleasing proportions than the Black-capped Lory. It has the forehead and crown black and the violet feathers of the nape are streaked and narrow. The wings are green with white and blue on the bend of the wing and a broad band of yellow on the under side of the flight feathers. A variable yellow band crosses the upper breast and the thighs are violet-blue. The rest of the plumage is crimson, darker on the mantle and brownish red on the tail. The bill is orange and the iris reddish brown to orange. Length: 28 cm (11 in).

Immature birds have a more extensive area of yellow on the breast, the under wing coverts margined with black and the beak black, changing to brownish. The iris is black.

Range/Habitat: The Purple-capped Lory inhabits the islands of Ceram and Amboina in Indonesia. It has been introduced to the island of Buru.

Aviculture: This species is a long-time favourite yet far less frequently imported than the Black-capped. It has been bred in captivity on a number of occasions. In Britain, the first breeder was Tom Spence in 1954. The first egg hatched after 24 days and the second after 26 days. On hatching, the chicks were covered in long white down on the back. The second down started to appear at three weeks and by the fourth week the surviving chick was covered in dense dark grey down. It left the nest on the 95th day.

Peter Oderkerken of the Transvaal, South Africa, bred this species in 1975 and 1976. The first two young left the nest when about nine weeks old while

Purple-capped Lory (*Lorius domicellus*).

that reared in the following year left the nest when 92 days old. His assessment of this species as extremely intelligent, endearing and well worth keeping is one which would, I feel, be echoed by all who have the good fortune to keep it.

In the USA, the Purple-capped Lory reared young in 1939 in the collection of Mrs Bonestell; since then it has been bred at San Diego Zoo and, since 1976, at Busch Gardens in Tampa, Florida. Zoos in Beira, Mozambique, Dhrangadhra in India, Naples in Italy, Walsrode in Germany, Amsterdam in the Netherlands and Loro Parque in Tenerife have all been successful. In Britain, successes have occurred at Birdland, Bourton-on-the-Water, and at Kelling Park Aviaries in Norfolk. In 1981, Dr R. Jerome of Dallas, Texas, produced a hybrid between a Purple-capped and a Chattering Lory. In immature plumage, it had a yellow collar, maroon head and body of the male parent, maroon-black cap and iridescent orange under the wings.

In the pre-war collection of M. J. Bruyneel in Belgium, a female Purple-capped Lory produced a hybrid when paired with a Red-collared Lorikeet after many years of producing young with a male of her own species.

Louisiade (Purple-bellied) Lory
L. hypoinochrous

Description: Briefly, this bird resembles a Black-capped Lory but without any blue on the nape or breast and with the back red. The cere is white, unlike that of the Black-capped Lory which is grey. Length: 26 cm (10½ in).

The plumage of immature birds is said to resemble that of adults. The bill is brownish.

Range/Habitat: This species inhabits south-eastern New Guinea, the eastern Papuan islands and the Bismarck Archipelago.

Aviculture: The breeding at Chester Zoo in 1973, recorded in the first edition, was in error. The species bred was *Trichoglossus haematodus aberrans*.

Yellow-bibbed Lory
L. chlorocercus

Description: It is nearest in appearance to the Purple-capped Lory from which it differs in the narrow yellow half-collar on the upper breast, bluish-black markings on each side of the neck and green-tipped tail. It lacks the purple patch on the crown. The broad band on the under side of the flight feathers is pinkish-red (not yellow as in the Purple-capped Lory).

Immature birds have little or no yellow on the breast and lack the black markings on the side of the neck. The bill is brownish and the iris brown.

Range/Habitat: Native to the Solomon Islands, except Bougainville.

Aviculture: It was exhibited at London Zoo as long ago as 1867 and at San Diego Zoo in 1944. More recently, it has been imported from the Solomons by Swiss aviculturist Dr R. Burkard. He informed me that his two pairs:

. . . do not have a loud voice but a pleasant pipe and whistle. They have an extraordinary capacity for mimicry, imitating numerous voices of birds. After one week they imitated the whistle I always emit when I enter the aviary. This is one of the most beautiful and pleasant of all lories.

It is very rare in captivity. At the time of writing, it is exhibited at Loro Parque in Tenerife and apparently is also kept in New Zealand.

This species has been bred by Dr Burkard. By 1984, from the original three breeding birds, he had increased the numbers to three pairs and three youngsters. When rearing they feed mealworms to the young. Throughout the year they eat sprouted wheat and sunflower, in addition to the two types of nectar mixtures, one having a higher protein content. All his lories have such a choice.

White-naped Lory
L. albidinuchus
Description: It has the forehead and crown black, with a white patch on the nape. Yellow markings on either side of the upper breast form a broken collar. The wings are green with a broad yellow band on the under side of the flight feathers. The rest of the plumage is red. The beak is orange and the iris yellow. Length: 26 cm ($10\frac{1}{2}$ in).
Range/Habitat: It inhabits the island of New Ireland in the Bismarck Archipelago.
Aviculture: This bird is totally unknown in captivity.

Dusky Lory (*Pseudeos fuscata*).

Pseudeos
Pseudeos

The single member of this genus could be used as a link between *Eos* and *Trichoglossus*. The Dusky Lory's closeness to *Eos* became very apparent to me when I kept one with a Red Lory. The two birds hardly differ in behaviour, only in colouration. On the other hand, photographed in black and white, a Dusky Lory looks very much like a larger *Trichoglossus* species.

Dusky Lory
P. fuscata
Description: The plumage is extremely variable; some birds are brilliantly coloured, others quite dull. The fiery orange of the brightest coloured is very striking but some birds have this colour replaced with yellow. The forehead, part of the crown and the ear coverts are black; the upper parts are brownish black except the secondary coverts, which are brown, and the

rump, which is silvery white or yellowish white. The crown is golden-bronze and there is a narrow collar varying from fiery orange to yellow between the upper breast and the throat and another above the abdomen, which is the same colour as the abdomen. The feathers of the upper breast are black with whitish edges. Under wing coverts are orange and there is an orange spot on the primaries. Under tail coverts are dark blue and the under side of the tail is pale bronze. The upper surface of the tail is bronze and blue with orange on the inner webs of some feathers. The prominent area of bare skin at the side of the lower mandible is orange, as is the bill. The iris is orange-red. Length: 25 cm (10 in). Weight: 143 g (5 oz).

Immature plumage is variable but the colours are duller and less well defined than those of the adults. The bill is brownish, the skin at the side of

the beak grey and the iris reddish brown. The rump colour too, is variable. In one young bird, each feather of the rump is brown, yellow and orange – more colourful than in any adult bird.

The colour of the rump appears to be an indication of sex in this species – although it may not be an infallible one. In the male, the rump is yellowish white, that of the female being silvery white. When a pair is seen together, the difference is most pronounced.
Range/Habitat: The Dusky Lory has a wide distribution throughout New Guinea, except the central part, in the Western Papuan Islands and Japen Island in Geelvink Bay.
Aviculture: The willingness to breed of this species makes it a fine avicultural subject. It remained rare until 1972, since when it has been frequently available. It has proved to be very ready to nest, a characteristic it shares

with some of the *Trichoglossus* lorikeets. In Britain, the Dusky Lory was reputed to have been bred in the collection of Herbert Whitley at Paignton, the success being reported in 1940 by E. Hopkinson. In recent years there have been numerous successes, several of which occurred during 1974.

My own pair have been consistent in hatching young since that year when chicks were hatched on two occasions but died after about two days.

Young are normally parent-reared, unless hatched in or after August (rarely). After leaving the nest, they are returned at night for the first few days. Thereafter, this is not necessary as they roost inside voluntarily. If the weather was bad and they did not return to the nest they could perish during the night. In 1980 my husband and I were abroad when two chicks left the nest on October 10. One was picked up dead the next morning. If youngsters are replaced in the nest and pop out again immediately, as may well happen, the solution is simple. The young are picked up in a towel, placed in a small cage and taken indoors overnight. The cage can be covered and left in a dark place. Next morning the young can be returned to the aviary.

Young have been reared from my pair every year since 1975, the minimum being one, and the maximum four, when young were removed for hand-rearing. Wheatgerm cereal is added to the nectar to increase the protein content while young are being reared; the food is otherwise the normal diet of nectar, spray millet and pear. Grapes and a little sweetcorn will also be eaten.

Most of the eggs laid by my female Dusky during an 11-year period have hatched. A very few have been infertile and two chicks died in the egg – one which pipped in September 1979 and another in August 1981 which had penetrated the air space.

They are usually good parents, the only problem being that the first chick is favoured and invariably receives more than its fair share of the food, while the youngest has very little food. In 1980, the youngest was so neglected that it had to be removed four or five times daily for supplementary feedings. The discrepancy in weight between the

siblings was marked. On May 16, when they were about three weeks old, they weighed 49 g ($1\frac{7}{10}$ oz) and (well below normal weight) 20 g ($\frac{7}{10}$ oz). Three days later the weights were 60 and 26 g ($2\frac{1}{10}$ and $\frac{9}{10}$ oz). By May 23, the eldest chick had forged ahead to 80 g ($2\frac{4}{5}$ oz) and the little one was only 30 g (1 oz). After June 2 (110/$3\frac{4}{5}$ and 48 g/$1\frac{7}{10}$ oz), the youngest gained weight more quickly. Both were removed from the nest at six weeks for hand-rearing and they were drinking nectar at seven weeks, before they were fully feathered. That year four young were reared.

During incubation, the male spends long periods inside the nest with the female, who ceases to brood the young for most of the day two to three weeks after hatching. She is a seasonal nester, laying in April or May and never during the cold part of the year.

Young birds spend in the region of 70 days in the nest. The incubation period is 24 days.

In the USA, the Dusky Lory was bred on several occasions by W. Sheffler in Arizona during the 1940s. He also reared a hybrid between this species and Swainson's Lorikeet.

The Dusky Lory has proved to be one of the most ready nesters of all the lories and has been bred in many collections throughout the world since the mid-1970s. Successful zoos include Los Angeles in the USA, Naples in Italy, Rotterdam in the Netherlands, Asson in France and in Hong Kong.

Unique hybrids between a male Solitary Lory and a female Dusky Lory were reared at Taronga Zoo in Australia in 1957 and 1958. The Dusky Lory has also hybridised with the Chattering Lory and Green-naped Lorikeet.

It is of interest that while birds of the orange phase produce only orange young, yellow phase birds produce yellow and orange young.

Trichoglossus
Trichoglossus

The members of this genus are kept and bred in captivity more frequently than any other lories or lorikeets. Some pairs are continuous nesters and

prove extremely prolific. Their voices, although harsh, are not as powerful as some of the larger lories. Nectar and fruit form the main items of the diet and some will also consume seed.

Most of the members of this genus can be recognised by the barred breast. The size is smaller and the build more slender than that of the lories described so far. The tail is long and pointed in most species. One of the best known of all lories, the Swainson's or Blue Mountain Lorikeet, belongs to a species in which more races are recognised than in any other parrot, making precise identification difficult or impossible. However, the races of *haematodus* are among the most suitable for the beginner with lorikeets and among the most frequently available. *Trichoglossus* species usually lay two eggs, occasionally three, and the incubation period is between 23 and 26 days.

Cherry-red Lorikeet
T. rubiginosus

Description: It is almost entirely dark red and the least typical of the genus in colouration. Primaries and tail are olive-brown and the feathers of the back and under parts are indistinctly barred with black. The under wing coverts are also black. Length: 24 cm (9 in). The bill is orange, paler in the female. The iris is said to be yellow-orange in the male and greyish white in the female. Immature birds are said to resemble adults but one would expect the bill to be brownish.

Range/Habitat: This species is found only on the island of Ponapé in the eastern Caroline Islands in the Pacific.

Aviculture: It is almost unknown in aviculture but has been bred at Kelling Park Aviaries in Norfolk in 1967 and at Los Angeles Zoo in 1970 and 1971.

Ornate Lorikeet
T. ornatus

Description: Brightly coloured and typical of the genus, this bird has the forehead, crown and ear coverts dark purplish blue and a patch of yellow behind each ear covert which do not join to form a collar, as in *haematodus*. The cheeks, throat and a patch on the side of the neck are red; the lower part

Ornate Lorikeet (*Trichoglossus ornatus*).

of the face and the breast is barred with red and blue-black, the latter colour being found on the edges of the feathers. Under tail coverts and the ventral area are yellowish green. The under wing coverts are yellow without the coloured band found in the other members of the genus. The tail feathers are green with red on the bases on the inner webs; under side of the tail is yellow. The rest of the plumage is dark green with variable yellow markings on the lower breast. The beak is orange and the iris orange-red. Length: 25 cm (10 in).

Immature birds have narrower blue-black edges to the breast feathers and more yellow on the abdomen than adults. The bill is dark brown.

Range/Habitat: The Ornate Lorikeet inhabits Celebes (Sulawesi) and the larger offshore islands.

Aviculture: Frequently available during the late 1960s and the early 1970s, it is now fairly rare in captivity, as it was previously. This species was bred in France as long ago as 1883. In the USA, it was bred by Mrs A. R. Hood

in 1932 (two nests of two). It has reared young successfully in a number of zoos, including Los Angeles, Cairo, Rotterdam and Naples. At San Diego Zoo, it proved most prolific and 40 were reared between 1968 and 1975. At Topeka Zoo Park in the USA, one pair reared five young in three clutches in just under one year. The first eggs were laid on April 5 and 9 and the first chick hatched on May 2 and the second by May 10. They left the nest on July 8 and 9. The second clutch was laid on August 7 and 11, the chicks hatched on September 2 and 4 and they left the nest on November 5. A chick which hatched on January 12 left the nest on March 13.

In Britain, this species was bred at Merley Tropical Bird Gardens in 1969 and 1970, by J. Bunker of Stratford-upon-Avon in 1970, at Chester Zoo since 1976 and by J. Hudson of Melton Mowbray in 1977.

It has reared young on several occasions at Naples Zoo and in 1974 nine were hatched and seven reared. Also in Italy, Paolo Bertagnolio has had several successes, the young fledging after 58 to 80 days in the nest, and N. Fiorentini of Merano reared one youngster in 1974. His pair accepted a varied diet which included spinach, carrot and radish.

In Denmark this species was bred in Copenhagen by Otto Hirte in 1936.

Vogelpark Walsrode, in Germany, has bred it since 1977. In Johannesburg, South Africa, a pair belonging to Luch Luzzato had reared 21 youngsters by 1983 and was estimated to be 18 years old. Another pair nested two or three times annually.

In South Africa, this species has been bred by Dr A. J. Wright. The male Ornate killed the female when she was incubating two eggs. The eggs were placed under Scaly-breasted Lorikeets. A few days later, the male Ornate died and it was then discovered that there was an abscess on his lung which must have caused the change in his behaviour. The Scaly-breasts reared the Ornate chicks. The latter first nested when they were three and a half years old. The first egg weighed 6.9 g ($\frac{1}{4}$ oz) and measured 26.5 × 21.5 mm ($1 \times \frac{4}{5}$ in). One egg was damaged and the other hatched after 26 days. The chick was removed for hand-rearing

when it was about two weeks old. When the Ornate chick was being fed, a Duivenbode's Lory in the same room became very agitated. When it was shown the chick, it started to regurgitate and fed the chick through the cage bars. The chick was afterwards introduced into the cage three times daily and was fed by the Duivenbode's. After a few days, it was left there and the Duivenbode's successfully reared it. In the next nest, the Ornates hatched two young and reared both of them (Wright, 1981).

The Ornate Lorikeet has hybridised with several other *Trichoglossus*, including Scaly-breasted, Swainson's and Red-collared.

Green-naped Lorikeet
T. haematodus haematodus
Description: It has forehead, forecrown and chin blue and the ear coverts and throat purple-black. The band on the nape, typical of this species, is greenish yellow. Feathers of the lower part of the throat and of the breast are bright red with purplish black edges, giving a barred appearance. The centre of the abdomen is green and the lower abdomen, flanks, thighs and under tail coverts are yellow with most of the feathers edged with green. The under wing coverts and parts of the flanks are red and there is a broad yellow band across the under side of the flight feathers. The back, wings and the upper side of the tail is green; the under side of the tail is olive, the outer feathers with yellowish inner webs. The bill is orange-red and the iris is red or orange in all subspecies. Length: 26 cm (11 in). Weight: M 127–142 g ($4\frac{1}{2}$–5 oz); F 116–124 g (4–$4\frac{2}{5}$ oz).

In all the races of this species, immature birds are duller than adults with the bill brownish or black.

Range/Habitat: The nominate race inhabits New Guinea, west along the north coast, east to Humboldt Bay and south to the Upper Fly River; the islands of Western Papua and Geelvink Bay; also Amboina, Buru, Ceram, Ceramlaut, Goram and Watubela.

Apart from the races described overleaf, a number of others are recognised (Low, 1977) the distinctions of which are subtle.

Mitchell's Lorikeet
T. h. mitchellii
Description: It differs from the nominate race in having the breast scarlet with bluish, green or yellow edges to the feathers. It has most of the head and nape dark chestnut brown and dark olive green feathers on the forehead. The abdomen is purplish black. Length: 23 cm (9 in).

Colouration of the breast may be an indication of sex in Mitchell's Lorikeet, those with the upper breast entirely scarlet being males and the birds with well-defined green or yellow edges to the breast feathers
Range/Habitat: This race inhabits the islands of Bali and Lombok in Indonesia.

Forsten's Lorikeet
T. h. forsteni
Description: *T. h. forsteni* differs from *mitchellii* in lacking the barring on the scarlet breast and in having most of the head, also the hind neck in some specimens, dark purplish. The abdomen is dark purple or mauve. Forehead and cheeks are streaked with violet-blue and the nuchal collar is light green. Length: 23 cm (9 in).
Range/Habitat: Forsten's Lorikeet inhabits Sumbawa in Indonesia.

Edwards' Lorikeet
T. h. capistratus
Description: It is recognised by its yellow breast. The forehead, cheeks and throat are dark blue with shaft streaks of almost the same colour; lower part of the throat and ear coverts are dark green, also a wide stripe above the eye which has shaft streaks of a lighter green. The nuchal band is yellow or greenish yellow. The abdomen is dark green; the sides and the thighs are dark green and yellow.

Under wing coverts are orange and yellow and the inner webs of the lateral tail feathers are yellow. The rest of the plumage is green. Length: 26 cm (10½ in).

The colour of the feathers of the upper breast can be an indication of sex. These are usually edged with red

in the male and with green in the female.
Range/Habitat: Edwards' Lorikeet is found only on the island of Timor in Indonesia.

Wetar Lorikeet
T. h. flavotectus
Description: It differs from Edwards' Lorikeet in lacking orange on the under wing coverts.
Range/Habitat: It inhabits the islands of Wetar and Roma, near Timor.

Rosenberg's Lorikeet
T. h. rosenbergii
Description: It is boldly marked and is distinguished from the nominate race by the very wide yellow nuchal collar. It has heavy blue-black barring on the breast. Length: 28 cm (11 in).
Range/Habitat: Biak Island in Geelvink Bay, New Guinea is the known extent of its range.

Massena's (Coconut) Lorikeet
T. h. massena
Description: It has the head dark blue with the cheeks blackish, the back of the head green and the nuchal collar yellowish green. The nape is rich dark brown. The feathers of the breast are red, narrowly edged with black and the abdomen is dark green, the lower abdomen being greenish yellow. Length: 25 cm (10 in).
Range/Habitat: This race inhabits the Bismarck Archipelago of New Guinea, the Solomon Islands and the New Hebrides.

Aviculture: The nominate race has been regularly available since about 1980 and has been bred in many collections. Most of the other races described above have been bred on numerous occasions in captivity except *flavotectus* and *rosenbergii* which are rarely exported.

In the UK, for example, the other four races mentioned are all being reared on a regular basis. Feather plucking of young in the nest

is a common problem. Recorded incubation periods vary from 23 to 26 days. The length of time the young remain in the nest also varies widely, from a reported 56 days to 89 days, both extremes being recorded in Swainson's Lorikeet. About 10½ weeks is usual.

Trichoglossus haematodus must have been bred in every country in the world where aviculture is pursued. It is reputed to have been bred in the collection of the Governor of the Cape of Good Hope in the eighteenth century, probably between 1781 and 1784. It must have reared young in captivity with greater regularity than any other lory or lorikeet.

Among the items of food which have been consumed by those rearing young are – in addition to nectar – canary seed, sunflower, spray millet, maggots, spinach beet, sowthistle, apple and other fruits.

This species matures quickly. G. Blundell of Southport told me that two reared by him nested when only 11 months old.

Hybrids between the various races and other species have been reared on countless occasions. However, such birds merely add to the confusion which even the identification of purebred birds causes, thus every attempt should be made to pair birds with the correct subspecies.

Swainson's (Rainbow or Blue Mountain) Lorikeet
T. h. moluccanus
Description: This lorikeet is perhaps the most beautiful of the genus. Vividly coloured, it has the head rich blue, almost violet, with blue shaft-streaking; the abdomen is the same colour. The nuchal collar is yellowish green. The breast is mainly scarlet or irregularly marked with red and yellow. The flank feathers are red and yellow, edged with green and merging into green on the thighs. The under tail coverts and the under side of the tail are yellow and green. Under wing coverts are orange. Eyes and beak are deep orange. Length: 30 cm (12 in). Weight: 115–157 g (4–5½ oz).

Development of a Swainson's Lorikeet (Day 1–57).

Day 1

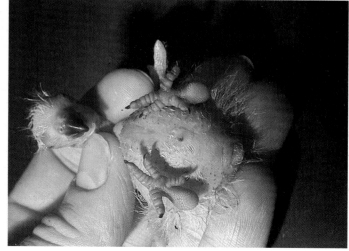

Day 7

Day 10

Day 16

Day 19

Day 20

Day 29

Day 57

Development of a Swainson's Lorikeet (continued).

Swainson's Lorikeets (*Trichoglossus haematodus moluccanus*).

Immature birds have more yellow than red on the upper breast. The bill is brownish.

An abnormally coloured bird was bred by W. Osbaldson in 1891 it was mainly 'bright chrome yellow' with some green feathers. The tail feathers were tipped with red and the feathers of the head were red with white edges.

Range/Habitat: This lorikeet inhabits north-eastern, eastern and south-eastern Australia, westward to the Eyre Peninsula, and Tasmania. It is common throughout most of its range and numerous. A popular visitor to gardens and parks, it is a huge tourist attraction at the Currumbin Sanctuary near Brisbane. Large flocks arrive to partake of honey-soaked bread. The birds have become so fearless that they climb over visitors.

Aviculture: Being Australian in origin, those available are the result of several generations of aviary-bred birds. (At the time of writing, Australia has prohibited the export of native fauna for many years. Swainson's is thus the only Australian lorikeet which is not rare in aviculture.)

Friendly and playful with an engaging personality, this bird has every attribute from the avicultural viewpoint.

Some pairs prove remarkably prolific and many are continuous breeders. The incubation period is usually 25 or 26 days and two eggs form the usual clutch. A chick hatched in my incubator weighed 4 g ($\frac{1}{5}$ oz) on hatching.

Given the opportunity, they will dig tunnels or nest on or in the ground. This behaviour was first recorded in 1882 at Blackpool Aquarium where a pair reared two young on the floor of their 1.5 m (5 ft) square aviary in full view of hundreds of visitors. Housing these birds in aviaries with earth floors should be avoided.

Hybrids with most other *Trichoglossus* species (and, of course, the subspecies of *haematodus*) have been recorded, in addition to such intergeneric crosses as Swainson's with the Musk Lorikeet, Violet-necked, Red and Dusky Lories. One Australian aviculturist had an interbreeding colony of Swainson's and Scaly-breasted Lorikeets. The resulting hybrids were fertile and reproduced their kind. This hybrid also occurs in the wild.

Red-collared Lorikeet
T. h. rubritorquis

Description: It is distinguished from Swainson's by its broad orange-red nuchal band, followed by an area of blue on the hind neck. Length: 30 cm

(12 in). Weight: (wild) 100–140 g ($3\frac{1}{2}$–5 oz); M (captive) 136 and 131 g ($4\frac{4}{5}$ and $4\frac{3}{5}$ oz); F (captive) 125 and 128 g ($4\frac{2}{5}$ and $4\frac{1}{2}$ oz).
Range/Habitat: It inhabits northern Australia from the Kimberley division of Western Australia east to the Gulf of Carpentaria, Queensland. It is common throughout most of its range.
Aviculture: Equally as attractive as the Swainson's, it is extremely rare in aviculture and is now represented in few collections outside Australia. At San Diego Zoo in one period, between February 1969, when it first reared young there, and 1976, over 40 were reared to maturity. The birds were then dispersed to private aviculturists. Several, such as Dr R. Jerome of Dallas, have had consistent success in breeding it. In Australian zoos, such as Adelaide, Melbourne and Sydney, and also at Jakarta Zoo in Indonesia, it has reared young on numerous occasions.

At Currumbin Sanctuary in Queensland, second generation hybrids between Rainbow and Musk Lorikeets have proved fertile. They took after *moluccanus* in appearance, except for the red ear coverts and forehead. Their flight resembled that of the Musk Lorikeet, making reckless flying and collisions in the aviary not uncommon. The incubation period was 22 days.

Natural hybrids occurring in the area are *T. h. moluccanus* × *T. chlorolepidotus* and *T. h. moluccanus* × *G. concinna*.

In Europe, it has been bred at Naples Zoo since 1976.

In the USA, it has been bred consistently in several private collections since the late 1970s; Roland Cristo of Auburn, California, has bred from two pairs since 1976.

During the earliest years of this century it was probably the most popular of all lorikeets in Europe. Four exhibited at London Zoo in 1900 were thought to be the first to reach Europe and in 1910 one youngster was reared in the Parrot House there.

A previous success must have been gained by E. J. Brook for, in 1916, he reported that he had been breeding these birds for eight years and that they were 'as hardy as Budgerigars and nearly as prolific'. At Keston Foreign Bird Farm, in the early 1930s, they bred 'steadily the whole year round'.

Weber's Lorikeet

T. h. weberi

Description: Very different from the races already described, it is entirely green, darker on the head, the feathers of which have brighter green shaft streaks; those of the forehead are tipped with blue. The nuchal collar is greenish yellow, also the upper breast, some feathers of which are tipped with dark green. The rest of the plumage is dark green with some light yellowish green on the thighs and abdomen. Under wing coverts are greenish yellow and the primaries are blackish with a yellow patch on the inner webs. The bill and iris are red. Length: 23 cm (9 in).
Range/Habitat: Weber's Lorikeet inhabits the island of Flores in Indonesia.
Aviculture: This species is rare in aviculture.

In Britain it was first bred by R. Kyme of Boston, Lincolnshire. In 1970 three eggs were laid at the end of January. Two chicks hatched but lived only three days. Eggs of the third clutch were laid on May 20 and 22 and hatched on June 15 and 17. When the young birds fledged on August 13 and 14, they were badly plucked on the back and breast. The pair bred subsequently on several occasions. In 1975, one Weber's Lorikeet was reared at Penscynor Wildlife Park in Neath, Wales.

In the USA, Jan van Oosten obtained three Weber's Lorikeets – two males and one female – in December 1982. The pair was kept in a 1.8 m (6 ft) long suspended cage attached to a building, where the nest-box was situated. The nest-box was L-shaped, 51 cm (20 in) deep and 36 cm (14 in) across the bottom. The nest litter consisted of pine shavings and orchid bark.

They favoured papaya and orange from a wide variety of fruits offered. Seed and nectar were also consumed. Copulation was observed on April 6 and the first of two eggs was laid on April 26. The female would leave the nest four or five times daily for three to ten minutes and occasionally the male would incubate. The first chick hatched on May 22 and was covered in light-coloured down. The second chick hatched on the following day. Fresh corn was readily eaten but no soaked seeds were taken after the chicks were seven days old. On June 12 the chicks were removed for hand-rearing; they started to eat on their own on July 18. By July 29, the eldest had a spot of colour on the beak; three weeks later it was bright orange-red. The beak of the youngest bird took six weeks to complete the colour change. On September 29, the first egg of the second clutch was laid. The incubation period was 27 days and the chicks were ringed at 10 days old (van Oosten, 1984).

Perfect (Plain or Yellow-headed) Lorikeet

T. euteles

Description: This is the only species which could be confused with the preceding one. The head is olive-yellow and the nuchal band is light green. Upper breast and abdomen are greenish yellow, the under side of the tail is dull yellow and there is a yellow band on the under side of the flight feathers. The rest of the plumage is green. The bill is orange-red and the iris is red. Length: 25 cm (10 in).

Immature birds are duller than adults and have the bill brownish or orange. In two prolific pairs belonging to M. Gammond, males fledge with the bill orange.
Range/Habitat: This species inhabits Timor and the Lesser Sunda Islands in Indonesia.
Aviculture: This species is occasionally exported; although it is one of the least colourful of the lories, it has much to recommend it, being attractive and prolific.

In Denmark, the Perfect Lorikeet was bred by C. Jensen of Køge, reported in 1964. Three eggs were laid and two young were reared. Also in Denmark, J. Aarestrup has bred this species since 1969. The normal clutch is three but on one occasion his female produced four eggs.

In Britain, the Perfect Lorikeet was first bred in 1970 by K. Russell of Wisbech. Three youngsters were reared, one of which was removed for hand-rearing, as all three were badly plucked. When these youngsters were only nine months old, Mr Russell was surprised to hear the sound of chicks from their nest-box. They reared two healthy youngsters.

A consistent breeder of the Perfect Lorikeet is M. Gammond of Exmouth. Four birds were acquired in 1980 and within one week two had paired up. They nested in a box measuring 20 cm (8 in) square and 36 cm (14 in) high made of 15 mm ($\frac{5}{8}$ in) plywood. Two eggs had been laid by February 13, 1981. A third egg was laid and three chicks had hatched by March 11; they left the nest on May 5, 11 and 12. They were removed from the aviary on June 5 and the female laid again on June 20. Three eggs were laid and there were three chicks by July 14. They left the nest on September 7, 10 and 12.

In 1982, seven chicks were hatched but three died when the female ceased to brood them. Six young were reared by this pair in 1983 and eight in 1984, when a second pair nested for the first time and hatched two chicks in November.

This species has bred consistently at San Diego Zoo. In one period of under two years, 17 young were reared from more than one pair. The Perfect Lorikeet has also been bred in Sweden by Inge Forsberg (1968), at Busch Gardens, Tampa, Florida (1965), and at Jurong Bird Park in Singapore in 1975, at Natal Lion Park, South Africa, since 1976, at Naples Zoo since 1977 and at Vogelpark Walsrode since 1977.

Scaly-breasted (Gold and Green) Lorikeet
T. chlorolepidotus
Description: This species is almost entirely green, of a rich shade, with the feathers of the under parts yellow, broadly edged with green. The crown is tinged with blue. The bases of some of the feathers of the mantle are yellow and those of the throat are tinged with

red. The under wing coverts are red and there is a band of the same colour on the under side of the flight feathers. The under side of the tail is yellowish. The beak is orange and the iris is orange with an inner ring of white. Length: 24 cm (9½ in). Weight: (wild) 82–89 g ($2\frac{9}{10}$–$3\frac{1}{10}$ oz); M (captive) 98 g (3½ oz); F (captive) 90 g (3 oz).

Immature birds have less well-defined markings on the under parts sometimes with yellow spotting on the abdomen. The bill is brownish.

Blue Scaly-breasted Lorikeets have been bred in Australia. The plumage is mainly dark blue with the yellow areas replaced by white.

Range/Habitat: This lorikeet inhabits north-eastern Australia from northern Queensland south to the Illawara district of New South Wales. It is common in the centre of its range, less common on the periphery.

Aviculture: Now rare in aviculture, before the ban on the export of Australian fauna it was quite well known. It was bred at Berlin Zoo as long ago as 1890, in Copenhagen by B. Christensen in 1891, and in Britain by a correspondent to *Notes on Cage Birds* who signed himself 'H.J.' in 1899. In France, it was bred by P. Soudée on several occasions from 1916 onwards. In South Australia, W. K. Penney bred this species in 1935 and in Ceylon, Dr Osman Hill had a pair which reared two broods annually during the 1940s. More recently, it has been bred consistently in various Australian zoos, such as Adelaide, Melbourne, Perth, Healesville and Currumbin. In 1978, at Chester, because of shortage of males, one was paired with three females, at least one of which had fertile eggs.

Since the mid-1970s, this species has been reared in San Diego Zoo, at Busch Gardens, Tampa, Florida, and at Natal Lion Park in South Africa. Also in South Africa, a pair belonging to Luch Luzzato produce two or three nests annually. At Currumbin Sanctuary in Queensland, the incubation period was 23 days and the young spent 50 to 52 days in the nest.

Two Lutino Scaly-breasts have been bred in New Zealand (Baird, pers. comm., 1984). They were reared one year apart in a colony of one dozen birds.

The Scaly-breasted Lorikeet has hybridised with a number of *Trichoglossus* species including Meyer's (at San Diego Zoo), Forsten's, Swainson's and Ornate Lorikeets.

Yellow and Green Lorikeet
T. flavoviridis flavoviridis
Description: At 21 cm (8½ in), the nominate race is slightly larger than *meyeri* but the species is the smallest of the genus. The feathers of the head and upper breast are olive-yellow. The feathers of the entire under parts are tipped with dark green to give a definite and regular scalloped effect. Ear coverts, lores, chin and part of the cheeks are dusky green and the nuchal collar is brownish. Under wing coverts are yellowish green, and the under tail coverts have yellowish green margins. The upper parts are dark green and the under side of the tail is yellow. The bill and iris are orange. It differs conspicuously from *meyeri* in the pinkish orange skin around the eye.

Immature birds are said to have the yellow markings more greenish. The bill is brownish.
Range/Habitat: The nominate race is found in the Sula Islands, Indonesia.
Aviculture: It is virtually unknown in captivity. There is no record of its having been imported into Britain since 1931 when it was probably new to aviculture. At the time of writing, a French aviculturist has a pair which were obtained in Borneo, and several specimens are exhibited at Walsrode where it has reared young since 1977. No doubt it is rarely imported because it is confined to small and seldom visited islands.

Meyer's Lorikeet
T. f. meyeri
Description: It is dark green above and below with the feathers of the under parts with greenish yellow bases to produce a neat scalloped effect. The crown is olive-brown with gold or a strong golden tinge on the forehead in males. The ear coverts are yellow, of a denser appearance and deeper colour in males. It otherwise resembles the nominate race, except for its noticeably smaller size. It is the smallest

member of the genus with a length of 17 cm (6¾ in). Weight: 50 g (1¾ oz).

Immature birds have the dark green edges to the feathers of the under parts less well defined and the yellow bases to the feathers of the mantle more conspicuous. Head colouration is variable, some birds showing as much yellow on the forehead as adult males, and others merely a tinge of yellow. The bill is brown, also the iris.

Range/Habitat: Meyer's Lorikeet inhabits the much larger island of Sulawesi (Celebes).

Aviculture: Meyer's Lorikeet was apparently not imported into Britain until the early 1960s when a pair was exhibited at Kelling Park Aviaries in Norfolk. In 1973, a small number was imported and I obtained a consignment consisting of nine birds. At first they were kept with success in a colony and looked most attractive. However, after two years they started to breed and to fight because males outnumbered females. Chicks were hatched but did not live beyond three weeks. Autopsy on four chicks showed no obvious cause of death in three and fatty degeneration of the liver in one. At the end of 1975, the three true pairs were each moved to a separate enclosure. These are very small, measuring only about 1 m (40 in) square and 1.8 m (6 ft) high, but have proved perfectly satisfactory for hatching these small lorikeets.

They are continuous nesters, invariably hatching young in the winter as well as in the summer. In 1976, two chicks were removed for hand-rearing when they were about one week old. They were reared without any problems and proved to be a male and female. The female nested for the first time in March 1978 with an unrelated male. A chick hatched in April when there was snow on the ground and lived for only two or three days.

Males as old as 11 years continue to breed. The incubation period is 23 or 24 days. Since 1976, many young have been reared, most by hand. They all grow up with other Meyer's and are not allowed to become too tame or imprinted – yet they retain

their lack of fear (ever after nibbling gently at fingers) and are thus ideal for breeding purposes.

The clutch invariably consists of two eggs. Chicks weigh 3 to 4 g (about 1/10 oz) on hatching and 50 g (1¾ oz) on fledging. Their nestling weights peak at 45–55 g (1½–2 oz).

This delightful little bird lives on nectar, spray millet, pomegranate and apple. Some will eat sunflower seed. Greenfood, such as lettuce and chickweed, is also eaten.

This species was first bred in San Diego Zoo in 1973 where young have since been reared in most years.

In Denmark, Leif Rasmussen obtained five imported birds in January 1984. Fighting occurred so one pair was removed to a cage measuring 70 × 40 cm (28 × 16 in) × 4 cm (16 in) with a nest-box measuring 20 × 12 cm (8 × 5 in) × 15 cm (6 in) high. One chick hatched and left the nest at seven weeks old. In this species, young usually spend 52–54 days in the nest.

Mount Apo (Mrs Johnstone's) Lorikeet
T. johnstoniae

Description: It resembles *meyeri* but with deep pink on the forehead, throat and forepart of the cheeks. A broad stripe of brownish maroon extends from the lores to behind the eye (said to be more pronounced in the male). The ear coverts are greenish yellow. Length: 18 cm (7 in).

Immature birds are said to have dull mauve instead of brownish maroon behind the eye and less pink on the cheeks.

Of those bred at San Diego Zoo, it was noted: 'Scattered over the breast are small, rusty orange spots, much more pronounced in juvenile males. This difference in colouration between the sexes also is noted in the adults, but to a lesser degree' (*Zoonooz*, September 1972). In immature birds, the beak is blackish and the periorbital skin is white (not grey as it is in adult birds).

Range/Habitat: The Mount Apo Lorikeet is found only in the Mount Apo region of the island of Mindanao in the Philippines. It feeds at altitudes

between 1,200 and 2,500 m (4,000 and 8,000 ft), descending to lower altitudes to roost.

Aviculture: This bird was first collected by Walter Goodfellow who discovered it in 1903. Because collectors seldom visit the area they are very rare in captivity. The first breeding occurred in Mrs Johnstone's collection in 1906. Two young were reared. The birds fed mainly on spray millet, sweetened bread and milk and half an orange daily. The next captive breeding would appear to be that which occurred at San Diego Zoo in 1941, when two were reared. It did not breed there again until 1971. Between December 1 and July 1972, ten chicks were hatched and most of these were hand-reared. Approximately 20 were reared to date. The incubation period is 23 days. Unfortunately, this lovely little bird has not been established in aviculture and is virtually unknown at the time of writing.

Iris Lorikeet
T. iris

Description: The scarlet forehead and crown and violet ear coverts distinguish this bird. The feathers of the throat and at the sides of the lower mandible are pink. The nuchal collar is greenish yellow, upper parts are dark green on the upper breast. Colouration of the crown is variable: red, red and green or violet. This species can often be sexed by the violet ear coverts which extend further downwards in the male, which usually has more pronounced barring on the upper breast. The beak is orange, also the iris. Length: 18 cm (7 in). Weight: 55 g (2 oz).

Immature birds have the barred markings on the breast less well defined. They are very much duller throughout, most noticeably on the head. Ear coverts are bluish green, not violet. The bill is black in nestlings and brownish in immature birds.

Range/Habitat: The Iris Lorikeet inhabits western Timor, Indonesia.

Aviculture: It has always been rare in aviculture and did not reach Europe until the 1930s. It was probably not seen again until 1971 when Mrs S. Belford imported a single pair. They came into my possession a few months later and are still with me. They set me firmly on the path of admirer of the small lorikeets, and, to me, the Iris is the most captivating of all.

For a few months during 1972 the Iris Lorikeet was available in the UK. Later in the decade the species was imported into Germany and the Netherlands. In 1983, a few were imported into the USA. It is now very rare in aviculture. In the earlier importations, some proved short-lived due to incorrect feeding as nectar alone will not sustain these birds. They take a more varied diet than any lorikeet with which I am familiar. Their diet more nearly resembles that of a large parrot, consisting of sunflower, spray millet, any small seeds such as canary and niger, almost any fruit or vegetable, including carrot and celery – and nectar.

The bill is strongly built in this small species, so that one wonders whether this is an adaptation for a special item of its diet. Like Fig Parrots, Iris Lorikeets have a very great need to gnaw and their beaks will become overgrown if this need is ignored.

This species was first bred in captivity at San Diego Zoo in 1970 and bred there until 1978. In Britain, R. Kyme of Boston was the first breeder. A chick which was hatched in 1973 died at four weeks. The following year two young were reared. The incubation period was 23 days. While the chicks were in the nest, huge quantities of raspberries were consumed by the adults, in addition to nectar. The young left the nest when 65 and 67 days old. They had been plucked but quickly feathered up.

At West Berlin Zoo, one or two young have been reared in most years since 1976. Also in Germany, Karl Bruck has bred this species since 1971 and Vogelpark Walsrode since 1977.

Eggs from one of my females measured 23×20 mm, 22×20 mm and 23×19 mm ($\frac{9}{10} \times \frac{3}{4}$ in, $\frac{4}{5} \times \frac{3}{4}$ in and $\frac{9}{10} \times \frac{3}{4}$ in).

The female of my original pair first laid in 1973. It was not until June 1975 that the first chick hatched.

When it was four weeks old the male unfortunately became ill and had to be removed from the aviary; to my intense relief and joy, he recovered, after being as near to death as one can imagine and so weak he was unable to hold up his head. Before he could be returned to the aviary, the chick died. Autopsy revealed haemorrhage of the head. Presumably this was caused by the female who had also plucked the chick.

In 1976 the pair was at last successful. A chick was heard in the nest on June 26 and it fledged on August 21, only slightly plucked on the nape. This pair hatched their last chick in 1984, when both were at least 13 years old. Subsequently eggs were infertile. Young have been produced by several pairs (including second generation), some hand-reared (in cold weather), others parent-reared. Young spend about eight weeks in the nest and weigh 52 to 60 g ($1\frac{4}{5}$ to $2\frac{1}{10}$ oz) when weaned.

Varied Lorikeet
T. versicolor

Description: A most attractive little bird, it has the forehead, crown and lores scarlet and the throat, cheeks and the back of the head greyish blue streaked with yellow. The ear coverts are yellow and the light green under parts are streaked longitudinally with yellow. The upper breast is vinous in colour. The upper parts are green streaked with greenish yellow and the tail is green, the lateral feathers being margined with yellow on the inner webs. The area of white skin surrounding the eye is most conspicuous in this species. The beak is orange and the iris is yellow or brown. Length: 19 cm ($7\frac{1}{2}$ in). Weight: 55–62 g (about 2 oz).

Immature birds are duller with the crown green marked with red.

Sexual dimorphism is marked in some birds and hardly apparent in others. In some proved true pairs, the male has been described as having the red on the crown darker and more extensive, more prominent colouration of the ear coverts and darker vinous or mauve colouration on the upper breast.

Range/Habitat: The Varied Lorikeet inhabits the tropical northern part of Australia from the Kimberley division of Western Australia, Northern Territory, to the coast of north-east Queensland.

It is common but its numbers are variable and its appearance irregular in many areas.

Aviculture: It used to be exported from Australia occasionally but today is almost unknown in aviculture outside Australia.

The first recorded breeding occurred at Keston Foreign Bird Farm in England in 1936 when a single chick left the nest during May. The rearing foods were nectar and stewed apple. The first recorded success in Australia took place in 1949. Two eggs hatched after an incubation period of 22 days and the young left the nest when 37 and 39 days old. They were reared on a breakfast cereal, milk, sugar, honey, apple and thistle. Another Australian aviculturist recorded that his two females laid clutches of four eggs and this larger number would appear to be normal for this species. When he succeeded in rearing a youngster, it left the nest after 43 days.

Probably the only pair in Europe for some years was exhibited at Chester Zoo from 1975 to 1982. (In the first edition it was incorrectly stated that they bred there.)

On the death of the male, the female was presented to me and paired with a male Iris Lorikeet. Much quieter and more gentle than the Iris, it was some months before the two birds were compatible. One clutch of eggs laid about one year later proved infertile. Unlike the Iris, the Varied eats no seed, nectar being the main item of the diet. She relishes grapes (steadied between beak and perch – not held in the foot) and sweetcorn.

The exquisite and delicate colouration of this little bird is admired by all who see her. The red on the head has a more brilliant quality than that of the Iris, while the softer colours are intricately blended.

Even in Australian zoos, the Varied Lorikeet is uncommon. It has been reared in Sydney Zoo.

An interesting case of longevity in this species was brought to my notice in September 1978 when I received a letter from I. Ramjean of Mauritius, who was lamenting the fact that his pet Varied Lorikeet was unwell. He had obtained it 25 years previously! During that period it had lived at liberty in his house and fed on 'all human foods except meat and fish'.

Goldie's Lorikeet
T. goldiei

Description: It is an extremely pretty little lorikeet with the forehead and crown scarlet, the crown and the eyes being bordered with mauve. The lores, cheeks and ear coverts are soft bluish pink and the dark green streaks of the under parts extend on to the lower cheeks. The streaked under parts are light green with broader streaks on the side and continued on to the nape of the neck, also on the under tail coverts. The upper parts are dark green. The small beak is black and the iris is dark brown. Length: 19 cm (7 in). Weight: 45 g (1½ oz).

The red on the crown and forehead is replaced by a dull plum colour in immature birds; this area is indistinctly streaked with black, as is the crown which is dull bluish. The streaking is less distinct in all areas. The cere is lighter than in adults and the beak is brownish.

Range/Habitat: Goldie's Lorikeet inhabits New Guinea from the Weyland Mountains near Geelvink Bay, West Irian, to south-eastern Papua.

Aviculture: This species was almost unknown in aviculture until 1977. Quiet, beautiful and easy to care for, it has proved a most welcome addition to the avicultural scene. In Britain, the first importer was Mrs S. Belford who received between 30 and 40 birds, some of which were in her possession for up to six months. During this period not a single bird died. Several aviculturists who had birds from this consignment during the autumn put them in outdoor aviaries where they wintered without any problems, proving remarkably hardy. I had eight birds but chose to winter them indoors as this species' reaction to an English winter was unknown. That they should prove so hardy is particularly interesting in view of the fact that most proved extremely reluctant to enter a nest-box.

In this respect and in others, their behaviour is totally unlike that of *Trichoglossus* lorikeets. They lack the boisterous personality and playful ways. When mine were housed in an indoor birdroom, I seldom saw them perched; they spent most of their time hanging head downwards from the welded mesh of which their flights were constructed. When moved into small outdoor aviaries, they usually perched in the normal manner.

In display, the male arches the neck and sways back and forth, clicking the beak or chattering, but not hissing. The feet are firmly anchored to the perch. He approaches the female closely, swaying his head on either side of the female's.

Nectar, spray millet and pear is the main food eaten by my birds; some also relish soaked sunflower seed.

This species was bred in Chicago Zoo in 1950. The pair had been exported from Australia in the preceding year, presumably together with a pair of Little Lorikeets with which they shared an indoor cage. There were three Goldie's, probably two females and a male. Two youngsters fledged during March when the unmated Goldie's was removed from the enclosure after it had been seen to annoy the young ones.

In the early 1950s, this species reared young at Taronga Zoo in Australia. In December 1978, the pair belonging to T. Buckell of Wiltshire nested. The first egg was laid on December 17. Both birds then remained in the nest-box during most of the day. Two

Parent-reared Goldie's Lorikeets aged seven weeks.

Goldie's Lorikeets (*Trichoglossus goldiei*).

chicks hatched but both died at a week old. The pair had been confined to a small indoor enclosure, measuring about 1 m square, for the winter. It was heated to a temperature of 10°C (50°F). During the previous spring the pair took nectar from the bluebells which covered the floor of their aviary.

It is interesting to compare the development of a chick hatched on January 1, 1981, which I hand-reared from the age of ten days, with two parent-reared chicks from the same pair (1984). The hand-reared chick weighed 10 g ($\frac{3}{10}$ oz) at ten days, 11 g ($\frac{2}{5}$ oz) at 13 days, 15 g ($\frac{1}{2}$ oz) at 16 days (ears open, eyes closed), 16 g ($\frac{3}{5}$ oz) at 18 days (second down apparent; by 20 days it was covered in light grey down, except on crown and cheeks); 22 g ($\frac{3}{4}$ oz) at 23 days, 27 g ($\frac{9}{10}$ oz) at 25 days, 34 g (1$\frac{1}{5}$ oz) at 27 days – taking 3 g ($\frac{1}{10}$ oz) at each feed; 27 g ($\frac{9}{10}$ oz) at 32 days (breast feathers and red feathers on forehead erupting; bill black, feet blue); 40 g (1$\frac{2}{5}$ oz) at 34 days – taking 4 g (1$\frac{1}{10}$ oz) at each feed; 40 g (1$\frac{2}{5}$ oz) at 38 days (under parts half feathered, very thick grey down, tail 6 mm/$\frac{1}{4}$ in long. Ate a piece of soft pear); 42 g (1$\frac{1}{2}$ oz) at 41 days, 44 g (just over 1$\frac{1}{2}$ oz) at 44 days (fully feathered but for nape; tail 2.5 cm/1 in long), 50 g (1$\frac{3}{4}$ in) at 48 days; 52 g (1$\frac{4}{5}$ oz) at 53 days (difficult to feed), 48 g (1$\frac{7}{10}$ oz) at 57 days; refused food on the 59th day; weighed 45 g (1$\frac{3}{5}$ oz) at 61 days. This bird was a female and reared her own young successfully from the age of two years.

In 1984, her mother reared her two young unaided. The parent-reared chicks (sex as yet unknown) were heavier than the one described above. The female did not show any concern when I removed the chicks to be weighed. They hatched on May 17 and 19. On May 30, one had its crop filled massively and weighed 17 g ($\frac{3}{5}$ oz); the other had the crop empty and weighed 13 g ($\frac{2}{5}$ oz). On June 13, the unfed chicks weighed 32 g (1$\frac{1}{5}$ oz); on June 19, both weighed 41 g (1$\frac{2}{5}$ oz), on June 23, 42 and 49 g (1$\frac{1}{2}$ and 1$\frac{7}{10}$ oz), on June 30, 56 and 60 g (2 and 2$\frac{1}{10}$ oz), on July 4, 60 and 61 g (2$\frac{1}{10}$ and 2$\frac{1}{5}$ oz), on July 7, both weighed 58 g (2 oz). They left the nest on July 16 and 18 (aged 60 days).

Within a decade, Goldie's Lorikeet

had become the most frequently bred and securely established of the small lories. The usual incubation period is 24 days but has been extended to 28 days in cold weather, and as short as 22 days in warm weather. The male has been known to take part in incubation in some pairs but it appears to be more usual for the female alone to incubate. The two eggs laid in one clutch measured 21 × 19 mm ($\frac{4}{5}$ × $\frac{3}{4}$ in).

Glossopsitta
Glossopsitta

None of the species included in this genus is well-known in aviculture. Characteristics of this group are the fine bill and the wedge-shaped tail feathers.

These little birds are delightful subjects for aviculturists. Indigenous to Australia, they differ from other lories in laying three to five eggs in a clutch and in having a shorter fledgling period.

Musk Lorikeet
G. concinna

Description: The forehead, lores and ear coverts are scarlet. The crown is blue and the paler blue feathers below the ear coverts are shaft-streaked with dark blue. A large area on the hind neck and mantle is olive-brown, the rest of the upper parts being dark green. The under parts are light green with an irregular patch of yellow on each side of the breast. There are orange-red markings at the base of the tail feathers, on the inner webs. The bill is blackish-brown tipped with orange and the iris is brown or orange-brown. The length is 23 cm (9 in). Weight: (wild) 52–65 g (1$\frac{4}{5}$–2$\frac{3}{10}$ oz); (captive) 86–108 g (3–3$\frac{4}{5}$ oz).

Immature birds are duller, with the red on the head duller and less extensive and the crown tinged with green. The bill is blackish.

Range/Habitat: The Musk Lorikeet is found in eastern and south-eastern Australia: throughout Victoria, in New South Wales and in South Australia as far north as Orrorro. It is widely distributed in Tasmania. It is common throughout much of its range and is unpopular with farmers for the damage it does to cereal and fruit crops.

Aviculture: This species was always rare in aviculture and at the time of writing is almost non-existent outside Australia. This is a pity, for the Musk is a most attractive little bird and one which is quite willing to breed in captivity. Early aviculturists found them difficult to keep alive, probably due to incorrect feeding. Like Iris Lorikeets they will take a varied diet which includes seeds. A pair which bred in the

Musk Lorikeets (*Glossopsitta concinna*).

Mosckicki collection in Belgium in 1958 were fed on raisins, muscat grapes, mealworms and grated sweetened carrot, in addition to more orthodox items.

The earliest captive breeding recorded took place in Germany in 1903. In Australia, Dr W. Hamilton bred this species in 1930. Since then it has reared young in Australian zoos, such as Adelaide, Melbourne, Westbury, Perth and Taronga (Sydney). It is also being kept in New Zealand.

In Australia, David Jonas of Port Lincoln, South Australia, bred Musk Lorikeets in 1979. Eggs were laid on August 11 and 13 and hatched on September 5 and 7, giving an incubation period of 25 days. The chicks were handled daily. They left the nest aged 52 and 53 days. One youngster had more yellow on the breast, also streaks of yellow and was more brightly marked. It was believed to be male. Rearing foods included nectar, apple, grapes, figs and a small amount of seed (Jonas, pers. comm., 1980).

At San Diego Zoo 11 Musk Lorikeets were hatched between November 1971 and June 1972, not all of which survived. This species has been bred there occasionally since.

In Denmark, Mr Nagel of Copenhagen bred this species in 1903. One youngster was reared in the Mosckicki collection in Belgium in 1958. More recently, Amsterdam Zoo in the Netherlands has two breeding pairs at the time of writing. They have reared their own young and chicks placed under Goldie's Lorikeets have also been successfully reared.

At the Currumbin Sanctuary in Queensland this species has been bred. Salisbury (1975) recorded the incubation period as 24 days. He observed that Musks sleep in their nest-boxes less often than other lorikeets. Young fledged two days apart at 52 days. In the pairs at Currumbin, sexual dimorphism was slight; the females have less blue on the crown, which is paler in colour; the ear coverts are also paler and less extensive. The name is derived from the musky odour exuded:

> This sweet, perfumy smell is most easily detected in the nest log, making inspection of this species much more pleasant than the Australian *Trichoglossus* species.

Nectar was rationed because these birds are prone to obesity.

A male Musk Lorikeet paired to a Scaly-breasted Lorikeet produced five youngsters in Perth Zoo, Australia, in 1970 and one in 1974.

Purple-crowned Lorikeet
G. porphyrocephala

Description: This tiny bird is exquisitely marked. The forehead and ear coverts are yellow and orange, the lores orange and the crown deep purple. Throat, breast and abdomen are bright powder blue. A yellow patch decorates each side of the breast. The mantle is olive, the wings dark green with the bend of the wing rich blue; under wing coverts are crimson. Thighs and under tail coverts are yellowish green and the tail is green with orange-red markings near the base. The small bill is black and the iris is brown. Length: 15 cm (6 in). Weight: 37–50 g ($1\frac{3}{10}$–$1\frac{3}{4}$ oz).

Immature birds are duller and have little or no purple on the crown.

Sexual dimorphism in this species is slight; the orange patch on the ear coverts is probably slightly less extensive in the female and perhaps also less brightly coloured.

Range/Habitat: The Purple-crowned Lorikeet is found in south-western and south-eastern Australia and is the commonest lorikeet in many parts of South Australia. Unlike Musk Lorikeets, they do not raid cultivated crops but play an important role as pollinators of eucalypts. They are common throughout much of their range.

Aviculture: Only Australian aviculturists have the pleasure of keeping this beautiful little bird. Always extremely rare in collections outside Australia, it is now entirely unknown.

In Australia and on board ship, in 1936, Dr W. Hamilton hand-reared two chicks taken from the nest of his pair, the male of which was very tame. It even learned to talk, copying words spoken by an Amazon Parrot in a clear but gruff voice. Another early success was achieved by J. Gregg of Croydon, Australia, in 1936. However, the total successes recorded are not numerous and little information can be gleaned from the published accounts. Clutches of three and four eggs are mentioned.

In England, the Duke of Bedford had disappointing results with this species in 1932. A pair wintered in an outdoor aviary with a heated shelter had three eggs; two chicks were hatched; one lived a very short time and the second for only three weeks.

This species remains uncommon in Australian aviculture. Little has been published about it and I am indebted to Lyn Williams of Western Australia for providing the following notes. She has been outstandingly successful with this delightful little bird – so much so that, by early 1985, her colony numbered about 55 specimens. Extremely gregarious, they agreed well together. They appear to enter each other's nest-boxes; some trios exist, presumably because males predominate. A lemon tree within their aviary is a source of enjoyment; they nibble the leaves, also the flowers when it blossoms. Two types of nectar are offered. The most favoured kind consists of Complan and honey mixed with water. The second contains high-protein baby cereal, wheatgerm, raw sugar and Denkavit (calf-raising formula).

Most females commence to lay at the same time and are double-brooded. In 1984, for example, they commenced to lay in August but in some years they will breed in April and continue through the winter. The clutch consists of four to six eggs, usually five. Fertility is good but some chicks fail to emerge from the shell. The time spent in the nest varies; those in deep nests may remain inside for two weeks longer than those which leave before they are able to perch properly. After the chicks are half grown it is necessary to renew the nesting material every second day. Unfortunately, losses among three-quarter grown chicks are high; apparently they are not fed sufficiently well. There are similar problems with hand-fed chicks if they are not given a midnight feed. Once independent, however, there are few losses.

Lyn Williams wrote:

> They are very friendly, inquisitive birds. There are several who land upon me when I enter the aviary. One always comes except when the hen of the pair with which he lives is laying and incubating. I can tell when the eggs have hatched as he reappears on my shoulder.

I do not believe he is the father and I don't think he feeds the babies but he is definitely a member of the trio.

Little Lorikeet
G. pusilla

Description: Almost uniformly green, it has the forehead, lores and throat red. There is pale green shaft-streaking on the ear coverts and the nape and mantle are bronze-coloured. The under parts are yellowish green, the upper parts being of a darker shade of green. The tail feathers are marked with orange-red at the base. The bill is dark brown and the iris orange-yellow. Length: 15 cm (6 in). Weight: 35–48 g ($1\frac{1}{5}$–$1\frac{3}{5}$ oz).

The female has duller and less extensive red on the face. Dr W. D. Russell noted that the golden-brown colour on the mantle and neck was more pronounced in the male of his pair.

Immature birds are duller in colour, especially on the face. The bill is dark olive-brown.

Range/Habitat: The Little Lorikeet is found in eastern and south-eastern Australia, also Tasmania. It is a common inhabitant of wooded country containing fruit-bearing trees.

Aviculture: In aviculture it is rare in Australia and almost unknown outside its homeland. It reached Europe as early as 1877 yet next to nothing has been recorded about it. Before emigrating to South Africa in 1970, Peter Oderkerken kept a pair in Australia. He informed me that he fed them on nectar made from honey, baby cereal, wheat germ and vitamin drops; they also relished apple, pear, carrot and soaked sponge cake. He also commented of all his *Glossopsitta* lorikeets:

They enjoyed being sprayed lightly with a hose, and hung on the wire, spreading their wings, ruffling their feathers and soaking up the spray. When I placed eucalyptus blossom in the aviary the birds used to hang on the branches in preference to the wire, while being sprayed, and rubbed themselves against the branches and leaves.

Peter Oderkerken's pair of Little Lorikeets were obtained by Dr W. D. Russell of Bryanston, South Africa, in March 1975. They had not reared young for the intervening owner, but with Dr Russell they nested in a small finch nest-box containing a layer of wood shavings. Dr Russell informed me that the male displayed by running up and down the perch, holding his head low and whistling. On reaching the female, he bobbed up and down.

The female laid the last of four eggs on August 19 and an egg-shell was seen on the ground on September 10. Three chicks hatched; one died at two days old and the two survivors left the nest when aged 38 and 42 days. Two chicks were reared in a second nest and a single chick in 1975.

In Peakhurst, Sydney, in 1948, the Little Lorikeet was bred by N. K. Bush in a planted aviary containing finches. The male had been hand-reared and the female had been caught as a young bird two years previously. Four eggs were laid and hatched about October 19. The young fledged about the middle of November and were eventually exported to the USA. In 1949, three more were reared. In addition to nectar, the parents consumed some canary seed.

Also in Australia, a pair owned by R. Rowlands nested in 1973 after they had been in his possession for four years. Four eggs were laid and the first chick hatched after 23 days. Four chicks hatched, one of which died after a week. Their nestling down was white and sparse. They fledged when about 52 days old.

This species has also been reared at Taronga Zoo, Sydney, between 1972 and 1974 in a colony of six birds in a planted aviary. They nested in logs. In 1974, Adelaide Zoo reared two Little Lorikeets. Perth Zoo has also bred this species.

Charmosyna
Charmosyna

The members of this genus are slender, graceful birds, ranging in size from 13 cm (5 in) to Stella's Lorikeet which measures 39 cm (15 in) including its extremely long tail. The latter is one of the most beautiful birds in existence. In some members of this genus, incu-bation is shared by male and female; or perhaps this applies only to the sexually dimorphic species.

Experience gained with two or three of the smaller members of the genus suggests that they are particularly susceptible to candidiasis; Vitamin A should therefore be added to the nectar.

Pleasing (Red-flanked) Lorikeet
C. placentis

Description: This is one of the few members of the Loriidae in which sexual dimorphism is well marked. The plumage is dark green above, yellowish green below. In the male, the cheeks and lores are scarlet, the forehead is lime green and the ear coverts are violet, streaked with a lighter shade of blue. The sides of the breast, the flanks and the under wing coverts are scarlet and there is a dark blue patch on the rump. A yellow band crosses the under side of the flight feathers. The upper surface of the tail is green, tipped with orange; the under surface is yellow with red and black markings at the base. The bill and feet are vivid red and the iris is orange-red. Length: 17 cm ($6\frac{3}{4}$ in). Weight: M 33–42 g ($1\frac{1}{5}$–$1\frac{1}{2}$ oz), average 35.5 g ($1\frac{1}{4}$ oz).

The female is entirely green, except for the yellow ear coverts which give a streaked effect, and the under side of the tail which is also yellow. Weight: F 26–36 g ($\frac{9}{10}$–$1\frac{1}{4}$ oz), average 32 g ($1\frac{1}{10}$ oz).

Immature birds of both sexes have red on the lores. Males have blue ear coverts, some of the feathers being tipped with yellow; females have yellow ear coverts, the yellow area being smaller than in adults. Males have the flanks red and the forehead yellowish green. The tail is shorter than in adults; the bill is blackish brown. This description derives from young bred by Leif Rasmussen, probably of the race *C.p. intensior*. The iris is yellow and the legs orange-brown.

Several races are recognised, the most distinctive of which is *subplacens* which lacks the blue patch on the rump.

Range/Habitat: This species has a wide distribution from the Moluccan Islands in Indonesia, throughout most

Pleasing Lorikeets (*Charmosyna placentis*) – female above, male below.

in 1982 (this race is darker, has the blue rump patch larger and, in males, a more extensive red throat patch). In 1983, she also reared *intensior*.

The subspecies *subplacens* has been bred by Dr R. Burkard (Landolt, 1981). Eggs measure 17.1 × 20.1 mm ($\frac{7}{10}$ × $\frac{4}{5}$ in). Only the female incubates. The newly hatched chick has fine down about 1 cm ($\frac{2}{5}$ in) long on the back, nape and crown. The beak is flesh-coloured with the egg-tooth white. At ten days, the eyes are beginning to open and the beak is becoming grey-brown. At three weeks the second down – short and dense – has grown and the bill, feet and iris are brown. At $5\frac{1}{2}$ weeks one chick weighed 38 g ($1\frac{3}{10}$ oz). It had the crown darker green than the adult male and the cheeks red. The area surrounding the eye was blue with yellowish white shaft-streaking. The tail feathers were 3 cm ($1\frac{1}{5}$ in) long and green with yellow tips. The young bird left the nest at eight weeks. Two weeks later its beak and feet were starting to become red and the dark brown iris was becoming yellow.

The feathers below the eyes were moulted when the young bird was four and a half months old. There were short shaft-streaks in the middle of the feathers. The red on the cheeks was then almost complete, but there was no red on the flanks and under wing coverts.

Striated Lorikeet
C. multistriata
Description: Another member of the genus which is predominantly green, it is more yellowish on the head. The hind crown is brown, also the nape which is spotted with orange-yellow. The under parts are dark green, streaked with greenish yellow and the ventral area is red. The tail is marked with red at the base. The beak is orange and grey and the iris is red. Length: 8 cm ($6\frac{3}{4}$ in). Male and female are alike. Immature birds are darker green on the head and have duller streaks on the under parts. Weight: 36–40 g ($1\frac{1}{4}$–$1\frac{2}{5}$ oz).
Range/Habitat: This species is found in western New Guinea on the southern slopes of the main ranges between the Snow Mountains and the upper Fly River.

of New Guinea, except the central part, the Bismarck Archipelago and Bougainville in the Solomon Islands. It has been known to nest in arboreal termites' mounds. In some parts of its range it is extremely common.
Aviculture: One reason why it is so rare in captivity would appear to be that it does not adapt well. While working for his doctorate from Liverpool University and collecting lories in Indonesia, James Serpell told me that he collected some Pleasing Lorikeets but released them when it became apparent that they would not survive in captivity.

In 1977 Mrs S. Belford imported a pair of these birds and some months later two females were received by another importer.

It is virtually unknown in Britain and the USA, yet is being reared in several European collections.

This species is exhibited in the collection at Vogelpark Walsrode in Germany. It was the only species in the entire collection which, on a cold October day, required the warmth of an infra-red lamp.

In Denmark, Leif Rasmussen has bred from two pairs of imported birds since 1983. One pair produced eight young by October 1984 (six males and two females) and the other pair four males. Two of the young were paired together and the female produced chicks when 7 months old; the male was 13 months old. The incubation period is 25 days and the young spend seven to eight weeks in the nest. Each pair was kept in a glass-fronted cage measuring 80 × 70 × 70 cm (32 × 28 × 28 in). Nest-boxes measured 18 × 10 cm (7 × 4 in) × 15 cm (6 in) high.

In Germany, this species has been bred by Karl Bruck, and Helmut and Marianne Michi of Gaggenau.

In the Netherlands, Mrs J. L. Spenkelink van Schaik bred an *ornata*

Aviculture: In 1977 it appeared on dealers' lists for the first time and late in the year this species was imported by Naples Zoo in Italy and was also exhibited by Vogelpark Walsrode in Germany.

This species has been bred in Switzerland by Dr R. Burkard (Landolt, 1981). The eggs measure 16.4 × 19.7 mm ($\frac{4}{5}$ × $\frac{3}{4}$ in). Male and female incubate. The development of one chick was described in detail. It was first seen looking out of the nest at seven weeks old and left the nest four days later. At eight weeks it weighed 33 g (1$\frac{1}{5}$ oz). It was then fed by male and female; the duration of feeds was very short – about one to two seconds. When in the nest, it had the beak black and the iris brown. By three and a half months old, it resembled the adult except for the yellow iris.

Wilhelmina's Lorikeet
C. wilhelminae
Description: It is mainly green, yellowish below and has the crown and nape purple-brown and the nape streaked with blue. The breast is streaked with yellow. Under wing coverts are red and the male has a red band across the under side of the flight feathers. The lower back is red in the male. The rump is purplish blue and the tail is green with red markings at the base. Bill and iris are orange. At 13 cm (5 in), it is the smallest of the genus.

The female lacks the red on the lower back and on the under side of the flight feathers.

Immature birds have little or no blue streaking on the head or yellow streaking on the breast. The male has the back dull purple.
Range/Habitat: This species inhabits the Arfak Mountains of New Guinea, east to the Huon Peninsula and south-eastern New Guinea.
Aviculture: It was imported into Britain on at least two occasions during the early years of the twentieth century but has been unknown in aviculture since then.

Fairy Lorikeet
C. pulchella pulchella
Description: It is an exquisite little bird, one of the partly red members of the genus. It is dark green above. The male has the rump dull blue, sometimes marked with green. The thighs and a large patch on the nape are purplish black. The breast and, in some specimens, the lower flanks, are streaked with yellow. Under wing coverts are green and red, and the tail is green at the base and red in the centre, shading to yellow at the tip. The under side is bright yellow. Bill, legs and iris are orange. Length: 18 cm (7 in). Weight: M 37 g (1$\frac{3}{10}$ oz); F 31–34 g (1–1$\frac{1}{5}$ oz).

There is a tendency to melanism in some specimens I have seen which are very dark red on the under parts.

The female has yellow patches at the side of the rump.

Immature birds have little or no yellow streaking, with a yellow band across the under side of the flight feathers. Thighs and nape patch are a mixture of green and black. The bill is brownish and the iris brown.

Range/Habitat: This species inhabits the central part of New Guinea also the north-east part of West Irian.

C. p. rothschildi
Description: This is the race best known in aviculture. It differs from the nominate race in the broad band of green on the upper breast. The abdomen is purplish black and the patch on the nape of the same colour extends to the eyes. The rump is green. The male has the under tail coverts red washed with yellow, while this area is greenish yellow in the female who has a greenish yellow patch at the side of the rump.

Aviculture: It was collected on a few occasions during the early years of the twentieth century and E. J. Brook bred from his pair in 1914 after they had been in his possession for five years. One youngster was reared. Brook said

Fairy Lorikeet (*Charmosyna pulchella rothschildi*), male.

of the Fairy Lorikeet: 'Probably no member of the Parrot tribe is more graceful and beautiful'.

It was therefore not surprising that the sudden appearance of this species in 1973 caused much interest in avicultural circles. Mrs S. Belford imported 24 and the number of males was well in excess of that of the females. All were quite delightfully steady but candidiasis was a problem with some of them. One bird had to be treated several times a week for two years before it finally died, while another seriously affected bird was completely cured after being infected for over a year, and eventually hatched chicks.

Fairy Lorikeets are not hardy and should not be allowed to winter outside in a temperate climate unless the shelter is heated and large enough to confine them inside in cold weather. However, it is worth taking some trouble to house these totally delightful little birds.

They have every possible virtue from the avicultural viewpoint being beautiful, easy to sex, quiet, non-destructive and easy to feed. Mated pairs are extremely gentle and affectionate but more than one pair should not be housed together or squabbling will occur. They are especially vivacious birds and their pleasing personality is among their many attributes.

It should be noted, however, that in this species the bill and nails grow quickly and need constant attention.

In 1976 four Fairy Lorikeets were reared at Vogelpark Walsrode in Germany; they lived to independence but not to maturity. Four more chicks were hatched in 1977 and 1978. Also in Germany, this species has been bred by Karl Brück, Heiner Dähne and Thomas Weise. In Switzerland, Dr R. Burkard has bred this species repeatedly. In 1984, he gave three pairs to E. Zimmerlei who reared nine young that year.

In my experience this species is a continuous nester when it is not subject to disturbance. Because the period during which these birds can be housed outdoors in Britain is short, I eventually reached the conclusion that it is preferable to house them indoors permanently.

The second pair hatched two chicks in an indoor birdroom in 1977 – the first time they nested. Both chicks died after about eight days, between June 14 and 16. On July 12, the female laid again; the second egg did not appear until July 18, though it is not unusual for there to be four days or so between the laying of the first and second egg with this bird. A chick was seen when the nest was examined on August 14; judging by the behaviour of the parents it had hatched two days previously. I kept a close watch on its progress and on the evening of August 19 saw that its crop was hugely swollen with air and contained scarcely any food. I therefore removed it for hand-feeding.

Its diminutiveness at that age is not hard to imagine for an adult measures only 10 cm (4 in), discounting the tail. Despite its minute beak, it fed readily from the usual teaspoon with sides bent inwards and never again was its crop swollen with air. By August 24, its body was becoming dark with feather tracts and by August 30, the second down, grey in colour, was growing beneath the long, wispy white down which Fairy chicks have on hatching.

Its progress did not seem to be as rapid as expected and it died on September 5, but not from natural causes. I had received a new batch of a high-protein food in powder form, a normal ingredient of the rearing food until then. Autopsy revealed that it had compacted the crop. When I examined the batch after this was discovered, I found that it had become doughy, instead of retaining its powdery consistency.

In this species, the clutch is always two eggs and the incubation period would appear to be 25 days. Incubation is shared by male and female, the male sitting throughout most of the day.

A curious cross was reported by de Grahl (1974). Karl Brück, a German aviculturist, apparently reared two hybrids between a Fairy Lorikeet and a Musschenbroek's Lorikeet in 1976.

Josephine's Lorikeet
C. josefinae

Description: It resembles the Papuan Lorikeet, the principal difference being that the tail is red and not elongated.

A black patch extends from the crown to the nape and is streaked with pale mauve. Thighs, lower flanks and lower abdomen are dull black; a small patch of dusky blue decorates the rump. The tail is yellow on the under side and tipped with yellow above, otherwise being red with the lateral feathers green on the outer webs. Bill, legs and iris are orange. Length: 24 cm ($9\frac{1}{2}$ in) of which the tail accounts for 11 cm ($4\frac{1}{2}$ in).

The female is distinguished by the yellow lower back; this area is red in the male.

Immature birds have the black feathers of the nape and abdomen tinged with green and the thighs bluish black. The bill and iris are brown. Captive-bred birds had the plumage duller than the adults; a believed female had greenish yellow feathers on the lower back.

Two races are recognised which differ principally in the more extensive area of black on the abdomen and in the female having the flanks yellow (*C.j. sepikiana*) and in the black patch on the abdomen being faint or entirely lacking (*C.j. cyclopum*).

Range/Habitat: Josephine's Lorikeet inhabits the mountains of western and central New Guinea from the Vogelkop, West Irian, east to the Sepik region.

Aviculture: This species may have been unknown in aviculture until 1977. In that year, San Diego Zoo obtained a single female which was paired with a male Papuan. In March 1978, the pair hatched a chick which survived for only a few days. Success was achieved later that year. Also in 1978, this species was received by dealers in Europe and was exhibited at Vogelpark Walsrode.

In West Germany, Josephine's Lorikeet was bred by Hans-Heiner Dähne in 1979 and subsequent years. On the first occasion, the female laid two eggs; incubation was shared by male and female. The first chick hatched on about July 8. The chicks had long white down. They left the nest at eight weeks old. The female laid again two weeks later. The eggs were broken and the first egg of the third clutch was laid on October 18.

Also in West Germany, Josephine's Lorikeet has been bred by Karl Brück.

Papuan Lorikeet
C. papou papou

Description: This is a bird of quite extraordinary beauty. Its elegance is heightened by the 20 cm (8 in) tail which tapers finely and flutters behind it in flight. It is mainly dark green above and red below. The head is red with a patch of dark blue and black on the crown; a crescent-shaped black patch decorates the nape. Another black patch on the abdomen meets the black of the front of the thighs, which are yellow at the back. There is a patch of dark blue on the rump. The feet are pinkish, the beak orange and the iris orange. Length: about 38 cm (15 in).

Females have the base of the red feathers on the sides of the rump yellow and a yellow-orange patch over the yellow spot above the thighs.

Immature birds are duller with the feathers of the neck and breast margined with black and bluish green edges to the black feathers on the abdomen. The primaries are not elongated as in adult birds and the central tail feathers are much shorter. Bill and legs are brownish orange and the iris is pale yellow.

Three races are recognised and, unlike the nominate, each has a melanistic phase in which the red areas in the plumage are replaced by black. The head is therefore black, except for the blue patch on the crown, the rump is also blue and the upper parts are green. However, in at least some melanistic birds the red under tail coverts are retained. It is of interest that at Vogelpark Walsrode there is a melanistic bird which has the under tail coverts black also a bird of the red phase with black under tail coverts.

A consignment of Stella's Lorikeets which reached England in 1976, *en route* for another country, contained a number of melanistic birds. These were examined by D. Hudson who informed me that sexing them posed no problems. Apparently, melanistic males retain the red patch on the sides of the rump whereas, in the female, the area has been affected by melanism and is dark instead of yellow.

Range/Habitat: This lorikeet inhabits central New Guinea, being found in the mountains from the Vogelkop, West Irian, to southern Papua.

Papuan Lorikeet (*Charmosyna papou papou*) – male and melanistic phase of Stella's Lorikeet (*C.p. stellae*).

Stella's Lorikeet
C. p. stellae

Description: This bird has a larger area of shaft-streaked blue feathers on the forehead with a prominent black line extending from behind the eye to form a V behind the blue crown. There is no yellow on thighs or breast. The female has the sides of the rump and the lower back yellow.

Immature birds can be sexed as soon as they feather. In the red phase, the male is red on the back and the female yellow. In the black phase, the male is red on the back and the female green.

Stella's Lorikeet was bred in Denmark by Leif Rasmussen. Two chicks were hand-reared from a red-plumaged pair in 1984; they had failed to feed their young. A melanistic pair laid for the first time in 1984 and reared two melanistic young. The incubation period was 26–27 days and the young left the nest after eight weeks.

C. p. goliathina

Description: This subspecies differs from the nominate subspecies only in the colour of the tail. The tips of the long central tail feathers are more yellow than orange and the upper tail coverts are green, not red.

C. p. wahnesi

Description: A wide yellow band across the breast distinguishes *wahnesi* from *goliathina*.

Aviculture: This beautiful bird was almost unknown in aviculture until 1977 and 1978 when several consignments of Stella's Lorikeets reached Europe and the USA. Previously, Stella's was collected by Walter Goodfellow between 1907 and 1909 and by another famous collector, Shaw Mayer, in the 1930s: the latter occasion was probably the first on which the melanistic phase reached Britain.

San Diego Zoo obtained a male Stella's Lorikeet in 1969 which was eventually paired with a Violet-naped Lorikeet. At one time the Stella's was mated with one of its hybrid offspring, which resembled it in size but was more slender in build. The main areas of colouration are similar but the upper breast feathers are margined with bluish black as is the crown; the broad eye-stripe is present. In 1979, two pure Stella's Lorikeets were reared at San Diego Zoo.

In 1910, two pairs of Stella's Lorikeets in the collection of E. J. Brook in England reared young.

In South Africa, Dr W. D. Russell first bred this species in 1980. Chicks hatched on December 2 and 3 and left the nest on January 20 and 22.

In 1984, Bill De La Mare of Washington, USA, successfully incubated an egg of a Stella's Lorikeet, using a Marsh Farms Turn-X incubator set at 37°C (98.5°F); the humidity level was 55 per cent. On the 23rd day, it was moved to a still-air incubator and the temperature reduced slightly and the humidity increased to 75 per cent. The chick pipped after approximately 25 days and 16 hours and was free of the shell in one hour and 15 minutes. It was fed a mixture consisting of ten per cent proprietary hand-feeding formula, 30 per cent Gerber's apple sauce and apricot baby food and 60 per cent unchlorinated spring water, with dark corn syrup, heated to 40°C (105°F). For the first four days, it was fed every hour and 15 minutes (such frequency is not essential).

Mr De La Mere informed me:

By the third day the chick was very vigorous and would sing while being fed. This singing continued without interruption and abruptly stopped at 60 days, one week before fledging. It was unlike any hand-feeding cry I have heard from other baby lories or baby seed-eaters. How this little melodious musical trill could keep a constant melodious musical trill while rapidly swallowing food never ceased to amaze and delight me.

As the chick grew, the feeding formula was changed in proportion and the frequency was reduced. By day 45, the food consisted of 75 per cent nectar as fed to the adult lories. As the back and rump feathers appeared, the young Stella's was seen to be a female.

Since the late 1970s, Stella's Lorikeet has been reared in a considerable number of private collections, also in zoos, including San Diego (since 1979, where the parents eat mealworms while rearing their young) and Columbia since 1980.

It seems that red birds produce only red young but melanistic birds can produce melanistic and red young. A red mated to a melanistic can produce both colour phases.

The Papuan Lorikeet is even rarer than the Stella's in collections; at the time of writing it is exhibited at Vogelpark Walsrode.

I was extremely fortunate in looking after a Papuan imported in 1972 for a period of nine months. It proved to be one of the most delightful birds I have ever cared for, and certainly the most beautiful. A hand-reared male, he was fearless and vivacious and craved attention. When spoken to, he would display and then the yellow feathers on the thighs would stand away from the rest of the plumage. He would make a soft whistling sound, lifting and waving one foot and then the other. It was easy to induce him to display by whistling to him, causing him to stretch upwards and to bow and hiss and make a snapping noise with his beak.

He was very fond of sponge cake soaked in nectar and this food and nectar were the only items eaten while in my care. Later, in a large aviary containing softbills, he was believed to sample a wider variety of foods, including mealworms.

The remaining members of the genus are almost unknown in aviculture at the time of writing.

Palm Lorikeet
C. palmarum
Description: The Palm Lorikeet is mainly green with chin, lores and area surrounding the beak red, and with the tail feathers tipped with yellow. The bill is orange. Length: 17 cm (7 in).

Dr R. Burkard who keeps this species informs me that the males are easily distinguished by their larger size.
Range/Habitat: This bird inhabits Vanuatu, formerly the New Hebrides.

Meek's Lorikeet
C. meeki
Description: This bird is mainly green with the ear coverts and the sides of the neck streaked with darker green. The tail is tipped with yellow or orange and the bill is orange. Length: 16 cm (6½ in).
Range/Habitat: The Solomon Islands form the range of this species.

Red-throated Lorikeet
C. rubrigularis
Description: This bird is mainly green with a red streak at the side of the beak and red at the base of the tail. The bill is orange. Length: 17 cm (6¾ in).

Range/Habitat: This lorikeet is found on the Fijian islands of Viti Levu, Taveuni and Ovalau.

Golden-banded Lorikeet
C. amabilis
Description: Mainly green, it has the throat red, bordered by a narrow yellow line. The thighs are red and some tail feathers are red at the base; the tail is tipped with yellow. The bill is red. Length: 18 cm (7 in).
Range/Habitat: This bird, feared to be near extinction, is native to Fiji.

Red-marked Lorikeet
C. rubronotata
Description: It is sexually dimorphic. The male has the forehead red, also the under wing coverts and the sides of the breast. Upper tail coverts are marked with red and the tail is red at the base and yellow at the tip. The rest of the plumage is green, except for the purplish blue ear coverts. Length: 17 cm (6¾ in).

The female has the head, under wing coverts and the sides of the breast green.
Range/Habitat: This species inhabits north-western New Guinea and the island of Salawati.
Aviculture: This species was exhibited at Vogelpark Walsrode in the late 1970s.

In 1980, also in West Germany, Helmut Michi received one pair. In July 1981, two chicks hatched but died at 16 and 17 days (Michi, 1982).

Duchess Lorikeet
C. margarethae
Description: This lorikeet is distinguished by the yellow band on the breast, which continues as a line on the mantle. It is otherwise mainly red below and green above with black on the crown and dull purple on the breast. Length: 20 cm (8½ in). The female has a yellow patch on each side of the rump.
Range/Habitat: This species inhabits the Solomon Islands.
Aviculture: It has been exhibited at San Diego Zoo where four were received in 1944.

Vini
Vini

The *Vini* lories are tiny birds of great beauty with a very special appeal. Four of the five species have been kept in captivity but on very few occasions. And yet their beauty is legendary. In *Lories and Lorikeets* (1977), I wrote that they were 'never again likely to be available'. A month after the book was published not only had I seen the fabulous Tahiti Blue Lory for the first time but I was quarantining some for San Diego Zoo. In aviculture, nothing is predictable.

Vini lories are indeed among the most enchanting of all birds but most aviculturists are unlikely even to set eyes on them, let alone keep them. This is only right for they are restricted to small islands and trade in these birds would signal their extinction.

These lories are recognised by their small size, rotund proportions, fine bill and shaft-streaked feathers of the crown. Two species are blue and white, the only members of the parrot family to wear these colours.

Blue-crowned Lory
V. australis

Description: It is mainly dark green; the crown is dark blue shaft-streaked with mauvish blue. The area from the lores and below the eye to the upper breast is red, also a small patch on the abdomen which is followed by a small patch of purple. There is some purple on the thighs and the under surface of the tail is yellow. Bill and legs are orange and the iris is red. Length: 19 cm (7½ in).

Immature birds have shorter blue feathers on the crown and less red on the throat; the red on the breast is merely indicated and the purple is lacking on thighs and abdomen. Bill and iris are brownish.

Range/Habitat: The Blue-crowned Lory is found on the islands of Samoa and Tonga and nearby islands in central Polynesia and the Lau Archipelago, Fiji.

Aviculture: This species has been kept in very few collections: San Diego Zoo, Vogelpark Walsrode and that of Dr R. Burkard in Switzerland. San Diego

Zoo received five birds in November 1970 and two of these nested in 1973. The female's previous eggs were infertile. Chicks hatched on March 29 and 31 after an incubation period of 23 days. Both were reared. Two more were reared during the following year.

Burkard wrote (1974) that his first success in breeding this species (in the previous year?) was due to providing the birds with ant pupae. The young bird was distinguished from the adults by its duller colouration and lighter legs. In 1977, he bred this species on two occasions but was unable to state whether incubation was shared by male and female as both birds spent much time in the nest-box together.

Kuhl's Lory
V. kuhlii

Description: This species is mainly green above, the crown feathers being shaft-streaked with lighter green; the nape is blue with mauvish shaft-streaking. Under parts, including lores, throat and cheeks, are scarlet and the thighs are purple. Tail feathers are dark purple on the outer web, red on the inner web. The rest of the plumage is green. The bill is orange and the iris red. Length: 19 cm (7½ in).

Immature birds have greyish purple markings on the under parts and less red in the tail. Bill and iris are brown.

Range/Habitat: Kuhl's Lory inhabits Rimitara, Tubuai Islands, in the Pacific Ocean and was introduced to Washington, Fanning and Christmas Islands in the Line Group.

Aviculture: First seen in Europe in 1879 when a single specimen reached Germany, this lovely little bird did not reach Europe again until 1936 when one was exhibited at London Zoo. Jean Delacour wrote of it: 'Tame and gentle, it plays like a kitten; it is indeed the most wonderful pet I ever saw'.

In California, three aviculturists kept this species in the 1930s and 1940s and it was bred there by Gilbert Lee, although possibly only one was reared to maturity. Also in the 1940s, this species was exhibited at Taronga Zoo in Australia. The lories nested repeatedly but success was not obtained until 1946 when a single youngster was reared. Food offered during the rearing period was milk, Mellin's food, brown

sugar and a small amount of tomato juice supplemented with a mixture of vitamins, cod liver oil and orange juice. Fruit was also eaten.

Stephen's Lory
V. stepheni

Description: It is green above with paler green shaft-streaking on the crown. Under parts are scarlet with a variable band of green and purple across the breast. Thighs and lower abdomen are purple and the tail is greenish yellow. Bill and feet are orange and the iris is said to be yellowish. Length: 19 cm (7½ in).

Immature birds are green below with purple and red markings on the throat and abdomen. The bill is brownish and the iris dark brown.

Range/Habitat: It occurs on Henderson Island of the Pitcairn Group in the central South Pacific Ocean.

Ultramarine (Marquesas) Lory
V. ultramarina

Description: This is one of the most exquisitely coloured birds in existence, attired in shades of blue and white. The forehead and upper parts are deep sky blue and the rump and upper tail coverts are bright sky blue. The tail is pale blue tipped with white. The crown is mauve, shaft-streaked with pale blue and the lores and part of the cheeks are white. The remainder of the face and upper breast are patterned with mauve and white. Abdomen and under tail coverts are mauve; under wing coverts are dull blue. There is a patch of white above the thighs. The bill is yellowish orange, darker at the base of the upper mandible. Legs and iris are orange. Length: 18 cm (7½ in). The female is slightly smaller.

Immature birds have the white areas replaced with bluish black with a few greyish white marks. The iris is dark brown and the bill and feet blackish.

An Albino specimen is known from Huapu Island.

Range/Habitat: This species is found only on the Pacific islands of Nukuhiva and Huapu in the Marquesas group, where its numbers are low.

Aviculture: It was known in aviculture only from the decade following 1936 or

1937 when this species was represented in the collections of the Duke of Bedford, then Lord Tavistock, in England and of Mrs Gilbert Lee in California. John Yealland, who was curator of the Duke of Bedford's collection, observed that the Ultramarine Lories were so shy that they would retire to their nest-boxes when anyone approached; it was therefore necessary to make an observation hole in the door of the room in which they were kept. In the spring following their arrival, when they had moulted their cut primaries and were able to fly, they were moved to heated aviaries with large and well-lighted shelters.

In June tragedy struck: 'one by one they became ill and died'. Autopsy, including analysis of the organs, failed to reveal any trace of disease, although in one or two birds there was evidence of anaemia. The losses stopped when the nectar was diluted with its own volume of water, although possibly this was not significant.

John Yealland described the Ultramarine as being quite different in temperament from the Tahiti Lory, more arboreal, better tempered, nervous and shy.

Tavistock recorded that the voice was a gentle, squeaky sibilant cry and that the flight was slow and heavy, although less so than that of the Tahiti Lory. Occasionally they would play together but were less playful than *peruviana*. Now and again they would eat a small spider.

The female of the surviving pair laid misshapen soft-shelled eggs on two occasions. She was then separated from her mate and lime water, an excellent source of calcium, was added to the diet. This resulted in the breeding which the Duke of Bedford (1939) described as:

> . . . the apex of my achievements in rearing birds of the Parrot family for the simple reason that for rarity and beauty, combined with need for very careful management, there is no species that I shall keep likely to be its equal.

> The nest was a grandfather clock box with the base standing in a vessel of water and during incubation more water was poured into the peat some way below the nest-level through a funnel, the base of which pierced the wooden side of the box. On top of the peat was a layer of decayed wood.

In February 1939, the female became egg-bound. An undamaged egg was laid in a hospital cage and a second egg was laid on February 28. A chick was heard on March 27 and emerged from the nest on May 20. The cock had shared in incubation but not to the extent of the male Tahiti Blue Lory during the early stages of incubation.

In California, Mrs Lee hatched young from her pair but they were not reared and, by 1944, her *Vini* lories consisted of a single Ultramarine and a single Kuhl's.

Tahiti Blue Lory
V. peruviana

Description: This species ranks with the Ultramarine Lory as one of the most beautiful and unusual of all the parrots. The plumage is deep violet-blue, with a high gloss; the lower half of the face, and the throat and upper breast are white. Shaft-streaking on the crown feathers is apparent as shiny

Tahiti Blue Lory (*Vini peruviana*), immature bird.

lines rather than as contrasting colour. Bill and feet are orange-red, brighter in the male. The iris is black and the eye rather small. Males are noticeably larger than females, especially in the head and bill, and weigh about 3 g ($\frac{1}{10}$ oz) more. Length: 17 cm (7 in).

Immature birds are a duller shade of blue with the white areas replaced by greyish white and the bill brownish (not black). Feet are dark grey.

Range/Habitat: This species inhabits small Pacific islands in the Cook and Society group, also the westernmost islands of the Tuamotu group. It is extinct on Tahiti and on a number of islands where it formerly occurred, including apparently most of the Society Islands since the 1920s. Little is known about its present status, partly because of the difficulty of obtaining information from such widely spaced islands.

Populations of birds from small islands are extremely vulnerable, and disturbance of their habitat could quickly lead to their extinction. In the past, other species on these groups of islands, and possibly also this species, had their numbers almost decimated by introduced animals, such as rats, and further atomic tests or deforestation could sound their death knell. It has been suggested that the recent disappearance of the Tahiti Blue Lory from one island in the Tuamotu group coincided with the introduction of a mosquito known to carry avian malaria.

Aviculture: This species is an extreme rarity in aviculture. In 1936, a group was brought to Britain for the collection of the Duke of Bedford. Problems were experienced in keeping them alive, and in another aspect; the Duke of Bedford wrote that males were apt to turn suddenly and savagely on their hens after living with them on apparently affectionate terms and feeding them.

Nevertheless, he was successful in rearing this species, a feat which he described as 'the greatest triumph' of his avicultural career. In 1937 two eggs were laid and incubated by male and female; one chick hatched and was reared. In 1938 two more chicks were reared.

In the USA, at the same time, this species was kept by Mrs Gilbert Lee in

Tahiti Blue Lories (from left to right) aged 43 days, 8½ months, 18 weeks old.

Tahiti Blue Lories, bred by the author, aged 8 months.

California. Her pair hatched chicks which were not raised. The Tahiti Blue Lory was unknown in aviculture from that time until the autumn of 1977 when a group was taken illegally into California. Their fortunes were followed by thousands of interested bird lovers for their story made headline news across the USA. USDA policy was to destroy illegally imported birds, and this would almost certainly have been their fate had not San Diego Zoo officials intervened. It was finally agreed that they should be allowed to live provided that they were quarantined outside the USA for a period of 90 days. This was carried out in my own quarantine room.

My first sight of these birds on a sunny frosty morning at London Airport was unforgettable – for sunlight enhances their plumage as artificial light never can. They were placed together in one flight in the quarantine room and were soon busy feeding and exploring.

It immediately occurred to me how like tits were their actions, and it is extraordinary that a small parrot should have a call note which is reminiscent of that of the Blue Tit, *Parus caeruleus*. Their voice is a plaintive 'tsoo, tsoo' or 'teetee-tee'. A harsher 'churring' scolding note is used, especially when squabbling. Courtship feeding is accompanied by a high-pitched 'eee-ee' sound.

Main items of diet are nectar, trifle sponge and nectar, and fruit; pomegranate is the favourite, and grapes, apple and hard (not soft) pear are also eaten.

A pair from the 1977 consignment which started breeding in 1979 have bred continuously. Young are normally removed at between one and two weeks because they are inadequately fed. In contrast, their own hand-reared young have proved excellent parents and have reared their own young (Low, 1985) which spend about nine weeks in the nest.

In the Tahiti Blue Lory, the clutch consists of two eggs, exceptionally one. Incubation is shared by male and female and lasts for 25 days. Incubation normally starts when the first egg is laid so that the chicks hatch two days apart. On a single occasion eggs hatched four days apart; also on a

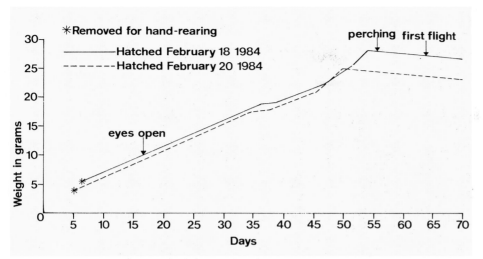

* Removed for hand-rearing
———— Hatched February 18 1984
- - - - - - Hatched February 20 1984

perching first flight

eyes open

Graph showing development of sibling chicks (believed male and female) of Tahiti Blue Lory (*Vini peruviana*).

single occasion two hatched on the same day. Given a choice between a bark-covered Budgerigar nest-box 20 × 13 cm (8 × 5 in) × 13 cm (5 in) high, or a natural log measuring 8 cm (3 in) in diameter internally and 31 cm (12 in) high, a hand-reared pair chose the latter.

Newly hatched chicks weigh 2 g ($\frac{7}{100}$ oz). They have on the back longish white down, which is not dense. At ten days, feather tracts are apparent. The eyes start to slit at two weeks but may not be fully open until 18 to 21 days. At five weeks, the wing feathers are erupting and, a few days later, the feathers on the top of the head. By eight weeks the chick is fully covered with contour feathers, except those of the rump, which appear at about nine weeks. A few whitish feathers appear on the cheeks at about eight weeks. At this age, they can drink nectar but are seldom fully independent before 13 weeks.

They moult into adult plumage at about six months but the red beak of the adult is not assumed until some weeks or even months later.

As a result of the Tahiti Lories being illegally imported into the USA thousands of visitors to San Diego Zoo have had the pleasure of seeing these beautiful little birds, housed in a circular planted aviary. They have been reared at San Diego to the second generation.

Phigys
Phigys

The single member of this genus is a very beautiful little bird which has the *Vini* and *Charmosyna* species as its closest relatives. It has in common with them the fact that incubation is shared in male and female.

Collared (Solitary or Ruffed) Lory
P. solitarius

Description: It is distinguished by the nuchal ruff of elongated bright green feathers. It has the forehead, lores and crown deep purple, also the abdomen. The red feathers of the mantle are elongated, the rest of the upper parts being green and the rest of the head and the under parts red. The iris and bill are orange and the feet are pinkish orange. Length: 20 cm (7½ in).

The female is said to have the forehead paler and more bluish and the rear part of the crown washed with green.

Immature birds have the feathers of the breast tipped with purple and with concealed yellowish green spots. The red and green feathers of the hind neck are shorter. The bill is brownish, the iris dark brown and the legs pale grey. Young males have the feathers of the hind crown green only near the base.

Range/Habitat: This species is found

on the larger Fijian islands and some of the islands of the Lau Archipelago. Unlike some island species, it appears that it is still abundant.

Aviculture: The number of collections in which this delightful little bird has been kept almost certainly does not exceed a dozen. Some measure of its attractions can be judged by the summing up of Sydney Porter who had collected and kept some of the very rarest and most desirable parrots. To him it was 'the loveliest and most engaging of the whole Parrot tribe'.

The glowing praise bestowed on it by the few British aviculturists who kept it during the second quarter of the century makes me long to see this little lory. In more recent years it has been kept only by San Diego Zoo (the last specimens to be seen were exhibited in the early 1970s) and in the collection of Swiss aviculturist Dr Burkard. Young have been reared in Dr Burkard's collection and in that of a friend with whom he shared his stock of this species. He has bred them to the third generation.

In Britain the Solitary Lory has been bred only by the 12th Duke of Bedford. A pair which he received in 1937 reared two young in 1939 and at least one more during the next few months. They bred in an outdoor aviary in a nest-box whose base stood in a container of water. The clutch consisted of two eggs, the first of which was laid on August 1 and hatched on August 29. A second chick hatched and both were reared.

This species was also bred at Taronga Zoo in Sydney. In 1939 a pair was placed in a flight 7.5 m (25 ft) long. One egg was laid on October 16 in a hollow log. They were disturbed by nearby activities during the incubation period, resulting in an egg containing a chick being broken. In 1940, a broken egg was found in the aviary on September 2. The next single egg clutch was laid on September 23 and a chick hatched on October 21. It left the nesting log when nine weeks old. Reared mainly on nectar, fruit was occasionally eaten by the parents, also lettuce and lucerne. The nectar offered was made from Mellin's food, condensed milk, a few drops of tomato juice and Marmite. In 1943–44, two pairs each reared one youngster at Taronga.

Oreopsittacus
Oreopsittacus

The single member of this genus resembles a small *Charmosyna* in shape but has the upper mandible thinner and longer; unlike all other parrots it has 14 instead of 12 feathers in the tail. It is sexually dimorphic.

Arfak Alpine (Blue-cheeked Alpine or Whiskered) Lorikeet
O. arfaki arfaki

Description: The male has the forehead and crown red and the lores and cheeks purple with a double row of white dots or streaks below the eye. Abdomen and flanks are yellow or red and the under wing coverts and sides of the breast are red. There is a yellow band across the under side of the secondaries and yellow on the sides of the under tail coverts. The under side of the tail is rose-red. The rest of the plumage, except the red-tipped tail, is green. The bill is black and the iris dark brown. Length: 15 cm (6 in). Weight: M 22 g ($\frac{3}{4}$ oz).

The female has the crown and forehead green. Immature birds resemble the female in this respect and can be distinguished by the narrow black edges to the feathers of the upper parts. There is less purple on the cheeks and the white streaks are less clearly defined. Weight: F 21–22 g ($\frac{3}{4}$ oz).

Two races are recognised – *O. a. major* for its larger size and more extensive red on the head, and *O. a. grandis*, in which the abdomen and lower flanks are green.
Range/Habitat: This species inhabits New Guinea, being found in the mountains of the Vogelkop, West Irian to the Huon Peninsula and southern Papua. It occurs at altitudes of between about 2,400 and 3,600 m (7,900 and 12,000 ft) where small groups are found in company with other parrots, usually *Neopsittacus* lories, Honeyeaters and Flowerpeckers.
Aviculture: In 1909, Walter Goodfellow collected three *grandis* for the English aviculturist E. J. Brook; this is the only reference I can find to this species in avicultural literature.

Neopsittacus
Neopsittacus

The two members of this genus have a heavier bill than *Oreopsittacus*. The tail feathers are broader with rounded tips in adults and pointed tips in immature birds.

Musschenbroek's Lorikeet
N. musschenbroekii musschenbroekii
Description: Most of the head is olive-brown, streaked with dull yellow on the crown and nape and with pale green on the cheeks; lores are dull greenish black. Throat, breast and the centre of the abdomen are red, also the under wing coverts and a broad band across the under side of the flight feathers. The rest of the plumage is green except the tail which is tipped with yellow and red at the base; the under side is bright orange-yellow. The bill is pale yellow and the iris is red. Length: 23 cm (9 in). Weight: M 50–62 g ($1\frac{3}{4}$–$2\frac{1}{5}$ oz), average 52 g ($1\frac{4}{5}$ oz); F 49–53 g ($1\frac{3}{4}$–$1\frac{4}{5}$ oz), average 50 g ($1\frac{3}{4}$ oz).

Immature birds have no red on the under parts except for a tinge on the throat and upper breast. The iris is brownish yellow to orange.
Range/Habitat: This is a mountain species found in the Vogelkop region of New Guinea.

N. m. major
Description: The race *major* is distinguished by the bright greenish yellow streaking on the cheeks and by the otherwise paler plumage, especially on the under parts.
Range/Habitat: This race is from the Sepik region of New Guinea and the Huon Peninsula to southern Papua.

Aviculture: Musschenbroek's Lorikeet is rare in aviculture at the time of writing. It was imported into Europe in the late 1970s and early 1980s and is kept in several private collections in Germany and Denmark. As yet, none has reached Britain from those countries. San Diego Zoo exhibited this species from 1965 until 1971; two females (*major*) were presented by Edward Marshall Boehm; in the early 1970s this species was exhibited at

Stuttgart Zoo in Germany. In England, H. Whitley kept a pair at Paignton as long ago as 1933. The 12th Duke of Bedford also kept a pair and wrote that, in build and movement, they bore a considerable resemblance to *Trichoglossus* lorikeets. Birds taken in the wild have been found to have the crop entirely filled with seed, thus it is of interest that those who have kept this species have commented on its liking for seed; indeed, Alfred Ezra's birds fed 'entirely on seed'. The Duke of Bedford's aviary attendant believed that this species did not possess a brush tongue; however, if the 'brushes' are dark they are extremely difficult to observe, unlike those of most lories which are white.

Probably the first successful breeder of this species was Sir Edward Hallstrom in Australia. The Duke of Bedford's pair hatched a chick in 1950 but failed to rear it. Two eggs were laid.

In Denmark, Musschenbroek's Lorikeet was bred by Flemming Nielsen in 1984. Incubation commenced in August and two chicks hatched in late September. One was reared to independence. It was badly plucked by the parents. The diet of these birds consisted of a mixture of soaked seeds, including sunflower, hemp, oats, wheat, pine nuts and pumpkin seeds; nectar, made from various baby cereals, animal and vegetable protein, glucose, ground sugar, cane sugar, malt extract, pollen, Bovril; fruit of various kinds, bread and honey.

This species has been bred in a number of other European collections. Hybrids between Musschenbroek's and Goldie's Lorikeets have been reared at Stuttgart Zoo in Germany on several occasions since 1979.

Alpine (Emerald) Lorikeet
N. pullicauda
Description: It differs from Musschenbroek's in having almost the entire under parts red, only the flanks and thighs being green. The tail is darker green on the upper surface and without the yellow or orange tip. It is marked with red at the base and the under side is dull olive-green. It otherwise resembles Musschenbroek's except that the crown and nape are streaked with

yellowish green and the cheeks with greenish yellow and only the nape is tinged with olive-brown. The bill is orange. Length: 18 cm (7 in). Immature birds have less red on the under parts and less defined streaking on the head.

The bill is brownish.

Range/Habitat: The Alpine Lorikeet inhabits the New Guinea mountains from the Snow Mountains of West Irian and the Sepik area east to the Huon Peninsula and southern Papua.

It is found at higher altitudes than Musschenbroek's Lorikeet.

Aviculture: Almost unknown in aviculture, it was kept in the collection of Sir Edward Hallstrom in Australia in 1953.

27

Pesquet's (or Vulturine) Parrot

Pesquet's (Vulturine) Parrot

Psittrichas (formerly *Dasyptilus*) *fulgidus*

Pesquet's Parrot is the only member of the genus *Psittrichas*. It is one of the most distinctive and extraordinary members of the entire parrot family. In captivity, its care should be different from that of any other large parrot and, to emphasise this fact, it has been accorded a chapter to itself.

Because of the strangely shaped head, which lacks feathers on the forepart, the large size and uncharacteristic colouration, one could be forgiven for believing it to be a bird of prey and its head is reminiscent of that of a Turkey Vulture. On the other hand, an ornithologist who saw a live Pesquet's Parrot in 1863 thought it might be a cross between a lory and a black cockatoo! This species is believed to be among the most primitive of all parrots.

The foregoing may give the impression that this is not among the most desirable of avicultural subjects, yet this is not so, for it is an extremely handsome and interesting bird.

Description: Most of the plumage is black; the abdomen, under tail coverts and a large patch on the edge of the wing are scarlet and the under wing coverts are red. The feathers of the hind neck are narrow, elongated and shaft-streaked, in fact they are highly reminiscent of those of *Chalcopsitta* lories. The black feathers of the breast and abdomen are broadly edged with pale grey. The narrow bill is black, the legs are grey and the iris is dark reddish-brown. Length: about 50 cm (20 in).

The male can be distinguished from the female by a very narrow line of red feathers behind the eye.

Immature birds are a less brilliant shade of red.

Range/Habitat: Pesquet's Parrot inhabits the mountains of mainland New Guinea. A fact which I have seen recorded only by the late Alan Lendon (1949) is that a large black and red parrot has been seen on the Cape York Peninsula in northern Australia on several occasions. In this tropical rainforest area, several New Guinea parrot species are found so it is quite conceivable that Pesquet's Parrot is a very rare inhabitant.

The natural diet of this species is a variety of soft fruits and berries, including small figs, the size of cherries, which are said to be sweet and sickly. The fact that some birds collected in the wild have had fruit pulp adhering to the base of the bill suggests the reason for the lack of feathering in this area.

Pesquet's Parrots are principally inhabitants of forested areas, especially between 750 and 2,000 m (2,500 and 7,000 ft), and are observed in pairs or small groups.

Aviculture: A Pesquet's Parrot acquired by the Duke of Bedford, then Lord Tavistock, in 1918 was almost certainly the first live specimen to

Pesquet's Parrot (*Psittrichas fulgidus*).

reach Britain. The specimen in Lord Derby's collection about 1840, from which Edward Lear made a coloured illustration, was probably a skin. Tavistock's bird lived for six years and set a longevity record which was probably not surpassed for 55 years. In 1967, Norfolk aviculturist John Wilson imported a Pesquet's Parrot which is still alive at the time of writing. Before that, probably only about a dozen of these birds reached Britain, brought over by such renowned collectors as Walter Goodfellow and Wilfred Frost. In the early 1970s, the species began to appear on lists from bird dealers in Singapore and, from that time until 1976, perhaps as many as 50 were exported to Europe.

In South Africa, Steve de Jager (1976) almost succeeded in breeding this species in 1975 when he kept a trio consisting of a female and two males living together compatibly. Although mating took place with one male, and one chick hatched, after twelve weeks the young bird was found on the aviary floor and it died a few hours later. Death was thought to be due to a dietary deficiency.

The first successful breeding was achieved by a pair belonging to J. Docters van Leeuwen of Wamel, the Netherlands, who was kind enough to provide me with the following details. His birds were obtained at different times during 1975. At the end of 1976 they entered a hollow log from a fruit tree which measured about 60 cm (2 ft) high. The hen removed material from the log by placing it in the feathers and shaking the feathers after leaving the nest. Exactly the same behaviour has been observed in the pair at Chester Zoo.

As they come into breeding condition, they utter a soft 'Tjik, tjak' sound. The male feeds the female and copulation, lasting only from 15 to 30 seconds, occurs. The female laid the first egg on January 21, 1977, and the second on January 24. During the incubation period, the male fed the female inside the nest, being encouraged to enter by her loud, begging call. A chick hatched on February 19 thus the incubation period was either 26 or 29 days. The chick was covered with a thin layer of white down, except on the head, which was bald. By

February 28 the male was entering the nest to feed the chick when the female left. By March 11 the female had ceased to brood the chick during the day. By then it was covered with black down. By March 24, the female no longer brooded the chick at night. By April 19 the red feathers behind the eye suggested that the young bird was a male. On May 5, it looked out of the nest for the first time and two days later was making a 'kind of singing' sound. It left the nest on May 13, never to return. Thereafter it was usually fed by the male. On August 1, the young bird was separated from its parents and placed in the adjoining aviary. The male continued to feed it through the wire.

The female laid again on November 21 and 23 and a chick hatched on December 20, giving an incubation period of 30 or 33 days. The chick was more active than the first, with a louder call. When ten weeks old it became less active and was found to have a fungus infection in the corner of the mouth. It was removed from the nest at 12 weeks and died two days later. Autopsy revealed a fungus infection of the trachea and lungs.

Mr van Leeuwen has likened the behaviour of this species to the larger lories of the genera *Chalcopsitta* and *Lorius*, both of which he keeps. It is interesting that he should mention *Chalcopsitta* for the birds of this genus and Pesquet's Parrot have in common the shaft-streaked feathers of the nape. His Pesquet's bathe only in rain, when they move their wings:

> . . . . just like a cockatoo does, but when they are completely wet they make the movements which are typical of *Domicella* (*Lorius*) lories when bathing; the body is arched and beaten with the wings shut.

Mr van Leeuwen's Pesquet's Parrots were fed on apple, banana, figs, carrot and endive which were cut up and placed in a mixer to form a thick porridge with rolled oats, rice flour, a mixture of pulverised breakfast cereals, milk powder, honey, calcium and vitamins. This nutritious mixture must have played no small part in the success of this pair in rearing their young. The mixture also prevented wastage of fruit, for Mr van Leeuwen

found that two-thirds were uneaten when provided separately.

This breeding occurred in a small gauze-bottomed cage in a greenhouse, the concrete floor of which was easily cleaned by hosing down.

In the USA, the first breeding occurred at Los Angeles Zoo in 1980. Two pairs had been purchased from dealers three or four years previously. One pair had nested three times by 1980 but without success; three clutches of two eggs were laid. Of the first four eggs, one hatched but the chick lived only one day. The next two eggs were incubated artificially. One chick hatched; it was pink with white down and weighed 17.45 g ($\frac{3}{5}$ oz). It was hand-fed until the age of 11 days, when it died.

Copulation was first seen in the second pair on November 14, 1979. The first egg was laid on December 12 and the second on December 16. The female incubated and a chick hatched on January 15. Its eyes started to open on January 28. On the next day, the black feathers started to erupt and the beak began to darken at the base. The first red feathers appeared on the wings on February 15. The chick left the nest on April 29, 105 days after hatching. It could not fly but was able to feed itself.

The diet for these Pesquet's Parrots consisted of grapes, apples, banana, cooked yams, raw ground horsemeat and lettuce. The consumption of hard-boiled egg increased greatly while the chick was being reared.

The breeding pair was housed in an aviary measuring 5.4 m (18 ft) long and 7.8 m (26 ft) high. The nest-site was a palm log 2.1 m (7 ft) high and about 46 cm (18 in) in diameter.

The most spectacular success with this species was obtained at San Diego Zoo in 1984 when five young were hand-reared. Another chick died at the age of five weeks after ingesting a very small amount of pine shavings. The eggs were incubated in a Petersime Model No. 1 incubator at 37°C (98.5°F) with a humidity reading of 85–87 per cent. The average incubation period was 28 days. Forty-eight hours prior to hatching the eggs were placed in a hatching unit. After hatching the chicks were moved to a Turn-X incubator at 35°C (95°F) at the home of keeper Wayne Schulenburg. The chicks were fed every two hours on yoghurt,

Pesquet's Parrot chicks aged 21 and 24 days, hatched at San Diego Zoo and hand-reared by Mr and Mrs W. Schulenberg.

Gerber's baby egg-yolk, apple sauce and brown sugar. On the fourth day, the basic rearing formula was added. This consisted of a variety of vegetable baby foods in jars, apple sauce, egg-yolks, wheatgerm, molasses, no-fat instant milk and peanut butter. When the chicks' pin feathers started to erupt, mashed banana was added.

On the fifth day, they were fed every three hours and the temperature was lowered to 34.4°C (94°F). They were then moved to an aquarium brooder. On the fifth day, the beak started to darken at the base of the upper and lower mandible. By the tenth day, chicks were fed every four hours. By then chicks were very vocal. By the 12th day, the baby egg-yolk and yoghurt were removed from the diet and the eyes were beginning to open. By three weeks they were not fully open. The second down was almost black, with some white down retained on the crown.

By the fourth week, feeding frequency was between four and a quarter and five hours and a chick would take a quarter of a cup of food at each feed. On the 32nd day, feeds were reduced to four times daily. The feathers on the head and body were erupting. By the 42nd day, the food intake was increased to half a cup per feed. Red tail feathers in their sheaths were apparent

by the 48th day and, on the 50th day, chicks were moved to a heated brooder cage. On the 55th day, red markings began to appear on the ear coverts, regardless of sex. Presumably this colour will be lost in the females. The chicks were accurately sexed by the hatching weight. The chick hatched on March 15 weighed 18.5 g ($\frac{7}{10}$ oz); it weighed 22.7 g ($\frac{4}{5}$ oz) on April 17, 17 g ($\frac{3}{5}$ oz) on July 26, 20.4 g ($\frac{7}{10}$ oz) on August 20, and 19 g ($\frac{7}{10}$ oz) on August 23.

Soft fruit was introduced to the diet on the 62nd day, including papaya, pear, grapes, melon, oranges, also spinach. On the 70th day, the young birds commenced to perch and feeds are reduced to three times daily. On the 80th day, chicks refused the mid-day feed and were spending much time feeding; two feeds were given daily. The first flight occurred between the 84th and 89th day. At 90 days, feeds were reduced to one daily; fruits and vegetables were always available. By weaning, at 100 days, the young birds were difficult to handle, and can and will bite. They are then accustomed to the diet used at the zoo and are held in large cages before being returned to the zoo. They go through a 30-day quarantine period before being placed on display (Schulenburg, pers. comm., 1985).

Pesquet's Parrots have hatched chicks, but not reared them, at Vogelpark Walsrode, Germany, on several occasions since 1977. In the USA, they have been hatched at Bronx Zoo, New York.

Feeding: The most important factor for the aviculturist to note is that Pesquet's Parrots do not eat seed; their droppings are therefore very loose. Various fruits and a nutritious soft food of some kind, such as bread and milk, bread and butter, moistened dog chow, or sponge cake moistened with nectar or condensed milk, form the diet.

Most Pesquet's Parrots are avid eaters of banana and also relish grapes, apple, plums and other fruits. Items successfully introduced into the diet of some individuals include raw egg, hard-boiled egg, boiled rice, cooked carrot and potato, raisins, blanched chicory, yams, mealworms and hashed meat. These birds invariably refuse greenfood. Indeed, I know of a pair which were kept in a planted aviary without destroying the vegetation. Dr R. Burkard saw his pair eat a snail with great relish. They ate chicken bones too.

Accommodation: Early writers stated that Pesquet's Parrots were not hardy but this has not been the experience of present-day aviculturists. In some cases, birds have withstood below zero temperatures without showing any discomfort. However, it would be advisable, with such rare and expensive birds, to exercise caution in this respect.

The extremely loud and unpleasant voice would be a certain cause for dissatisfaction to close neighbours of any private aviculturist who kept this bird. The Duke of Bedford (Lord Tavistock) commented that its voice was 'more suitable for New Guinea than for civilized society!' Its calls included a noise resembling a combination of a horn and a rattle of the type which college spectators use at sporting events! When the Duke of Bedford's bird was in the possession of Mrs Dalton-Burgess she recorded that it tried to talk and that its voice was quite unlike that of any other parrot she knew.

Because of the nature of their food and droppings, few birds are more unsuited to cage life. A friend who kept a tame young male in a cage regularly placed it in a bath and gave it a thorough wash. It was impossible to keep the bird's plumage free from stickiness in any other manner.

Although Pesquet's is not destructive to growing vegetation some are destructive to woodwork. One aviculturist noted of his pair that the female's bill had little strength, but the male's was much stronger.

On more than one occasion it has been noted that birds of this species are exceptionally sensitive to change. Recently imported or newly received birds would therefore need careful attention. The Duke of Bedford's bird, sent to Mrs Dalton-Burgess, was so upset by the journey that it took three days to emerge from its travelling box. I know of an instance where a healthy Pesquet's, which had been several years in captivity, died two or three days after going to a new home. Because of this sensitivity to change, no one should lightly make the decision to obtain birds of this species.

28

Fig Parrots

Fig Parrots are among the most desirable of all small parrots; unfortunately, they have also proved to be difficult to maintain for any length of time. Now that more is understood about them, this may not be the case in the future. Their need for Vitamin K is recognised and, since the commercial export of Fig Parrots commenced Vitamin K supplements have become available (e.g. Konaklon, Roche).

When the first edition of this book was published in 1980, Fig Parrots were included in the chapter on Avicultural Rarities. They remain rare – but are here accorded a chapter to themselves because a little more information is available on their breeding habits. None of the *Psittaculirostris* species had been bred in captivity at that time; since 1980, a few successes have occurred. The few breeders have experienced problems and success has been hard-won. The number of Fig Parrots in captivity is very small; commercial export may not occur again and the avicultural future of these beautiful little birds remains uncertain. What is certain, however, is that they captivate all who see them and have attracted some dedicated devotees who will not easily give up the challenge to establish them in captivity.

Anyone fortunate enough to obtain Fig Parrots should offer them a wide variety of fruits as the basis of the diet. The usual seeds should be provided, also the berries of hawthorn and elder. Apart from their diet, which is quite different, they should be treated in much the same manner as lories; in behaviour they greatly resemble these birds. A nest-box for roosting is essential; Fig Parrots have the same trait as many lories in that a nest-box or log will be entered within minutes of its being placed in the aviary.

Psittaculirostris
Psittaculirostris

Fig Parrots of this genus are especially engaging birds. Their plumage is spectacular and their behaviour fascinating. They jump, bounce, stretch and peer in a manner which is reminiscent of no other parrot, except possibly Caiques. Extremely sociable birds, no parrot seems more unhappy when kept on its own, and no other seems so easy to please, being instantly compatible with any member of the opposite sex (and possibly with the same sex as well).

Members of this genus have elongated ear coverts, short rounded tails and powerful beaks in relation to their size. They are highly reminiscent of lories in their quick, precise movements. Natives of New Guinea, they inhabit lowland forest, where they are found in pairs or small groups. Very little is known about their wild life and nothing of their nesting habits. They were not exported commercially until the early 1970s, first and mostly Salvadori's (predominantly males), then Desmarest's and finally a few Edwards'.

Salvadori's Fig Parrot
P. salvadorii

Description: Like other members of the genus, it is a solidly built bird with a very bold head. It is sexually dimorphic. The most unusual feature of the male's plumage depends on the feather formation rather than the colouration: the narrow, elongated feathers of the cheeks stand slightly away from the head. The male has a broad band of scarlet across the breast; adult females have a hint of rust colour at the sides of the breast and a pale bluish green band in place of the male's red band. Both sexes have a blue spot behind the eye and the female has more blue on the crown which in the male is green, only lightly streaked with blue. The under wing coverts are pale green in the male and bluish green in the female with a yellow band on the under side of the flight feathers. Length: 19 cm ($7\frac{1}{2}$ in).

Immature birds are duller than the female. Forshaw (1973) states that the male has the breast bluish marked with red; however, young birds cannot be sexed until the breast feathers are moulted, probably when they are about a year old, if those imported by Mrs Belford (see below) were typical.
Range/Habitat: It occurs on the northern coast of West Irian, New Guinea, from Geelvink Bay east to Humboldt Bay. Virtually nothing has been re-

Salvadori's Fig Parrots (*Psittaculirostris salvadorii*) – female left, male right.

corded about this species in the wild.
Aviculture: In 1977, Salvadori's Fig
Parrots were imported into Europe
and the USA; there is no previous
record of this species in captivity. The
first birds received in Europe consisted
of a consignment of 20 imported
privately by Mrs S. Belford. At first
she fed them on dried figs and rice and
various fruits, and they soon began to
eat hard seed. Very careful attention
was paid to their diet and no problems
were experienced. However, another
English importer received ten birds a
few months later and all died after a
short period. Mrs Belford's losses with
this species were fewer than average
with newly imported parrots.

On obtaining a pair, I soon found
that they require more fruit than most
parrots, yet have rather conservative
tastes. They take, in order of preference, figs, dried or soaked (eating the
seeds only), apple and banana, and
pomegranate. Little interest is shown
in grapes or pear and none at all in
orange. I ensure that they have fruit
always before them. They eat much
sunflower seed and a little spray millet.

The beauty of this species is enhanced by its gay and lively character. The
male of my pair is a cheerful bird,
often to be heard warbling in a rather
attractive manner. The female is shy
and much quieter. Their voices are
pleasant but can be raised in moments
of excitement; however, the loudest
note of which they are capable is not
offensive.

On receipt, the male of my pair had
an overgrown upper mandible, as did
others imported during the same
period. When provided with plenty of
wood for gnawing, the mandible length
was quickly reduced to normal. For
their size, these little Fig Parrots are
quite the most destructive birds I have
kept, with the possible exception of

Caiques; every day there is a pile of
fresh sawdust on the bottom of their
enclosure. If it is not possible to keep
up a supply of branches, I would recommend that scraps of wood are
nailed to the aviary containing these
birds; gnawing is essential to them and
an aviary will soon be destroyed if
there is nothing to divert their attention from the woodwork. However,
fresh twiggy branches are relished and
they greatly enjoy removing the buds
and bark.

When I first saw this species I gained
the strong impression that it would
nest as readily in captivity as the small
lorikeets do. My pair was provided
with a nest-box two days after I received them. This was entered in a
matter of minutes and, in the subsequent eight months, the female spent
most of her time inside it. I obtained
the birds in September 1977 and in
December they were observed mating
during a period when it was unusual to
see the female at all. The display consists mainly of the male approaching
the female with exaggerated hops and
then bobbing up and down. The bobbing differs from that seen in the display of lories in that the head is held
high; there is no bowing or hissing.
Also, both sexes whirr the wings, briefly and very rapidly, at the same time
raising the feathers of the mantle.

On December 19, the female was
seen sitting on the nest-box perch looking very sick; I immediately removed
her to a small cage, next to the indoor
enclosure which contained the male.
Heat was provided by way of an infra-
red lamp. All that day her life seemed
in doubt; she was perched most of the
time but was leaning at a peculiar
angle. She ate fruit sprinkled with an
antibiotic and next day seemed slightly
better. In the evening she suddenly
began to call very loudly to the male,
who called back. To my extreme surprise, I found that she had laid an egg
and had immediately recovered her
health. Under the circumstances, it
might have seemed obvious that she
was egg-bound – yet she exhibited
none of the usual symptoms. I placed
the egg in her nest-box and returned
her to the cage (1.2 m/4 ft long) in
which the pair was kept. As she was
rather nervous, I had no wish to disturb her during incubation and did not

examine the nest. Presumably the incubation period would be about 23 days; after 26 days she deserted the nest which, on inspection, proved to be empty.

By this time the nest-box entrance had been greatly enlarged by the birds' gnawing activities, so that it extended across the entire width of the box. In April it was replaced with one made of stronger wood. Again, within minutes, male and female were inside. On May 4 the female spent much time out of the box and was again leaning at an angle; she looked very unwell so an infra-red lamp was situated near her. The next day she laid an egg from the perch, and then my worries started. She seemed extremely weak, yet during the night managed to make her way into the nest-box.

During the next afternoon she looked so ill that I gently placed her in a small cage, close to the infra-red lamp and within sight and sound of the male. I assumed that she was about to lay again and once more was in difficulties. As she seemed too weak to eat, I gave her a small amount of a strong solution of glucose and warm water. Soon she was lying on the cage floor and breathing so shallowly I was convinced that she was dying. Two hours later, much to my surprise I found that she was standing, albeit very shakily. I therefore made up some milk protein food and warmed it and she took it from a spoon. Later that evening she had regained her strength to such a degree she refused to let me feed her; indeed, she began to eat apple. Two days later she was well enough to be returned to the male.

When acclimatised, these Fig Parrots will undoubtedly prove just as hardy as other small parrots. Mine were housed indoors during their first winter because I wished to have them under constant observation. A friend who purchased ten birds from the same consignment kept them all outdoors until nearly the end of the winter, when the weather was extremely cold; they then looked uncomfortable (as do many parrots). While outside, they would all sleep together in one nest-box.

To date, breeding successes have been very rare. Weise (1983) obtained a pair of Salvadori's Fig Parrots in

March 1978. About one year later, two eggs were laid in a horizontal nest. One chick hatched but died. Six weeks later the female died from internal bleeding following a ruptured oviduct. A second female was acquired. Three clutches were laid but only one chick hatched, which died at the age of six weeks. The next clutch was laid in early October and a chick hatched on November 5. It left the nest on January 6 and was fed by its parents for ten days. The duller shade of green and shorter and paler feathers of the 'beard' distinguished it from the female. In October 1981, it began to acquire adult plumage, including the red breast, indicating that it was a male. The birds were kept in a heated room, in a flight measuring 2.7 × 2.1 m (9 × 7 ft). The diet consisted of sunflower seed (mainly sprouted), millet, hemp, apple, pear, half a softened fig daily, sprouted millet sprays, eggfood and the small pink maggots of green housefly. When the youngster was being reared, large quantities of maggots were consumed. The nest-box used measured 37 × 20 cm (14 × 8 in) × 13 cm (5 in) high.

In Britain, Rosemary Wiseman reared a hybrid between a male Salvadori's and a female Desmarest's in 1984; by this time female Salvadori's were virtually unobtainable. In immature plumage it was mainly green, with bluish ear coverts. It had the elongated ear coverts of the male parent.

Chicks hatched by G. A. Smith, also in 1984, weighed 4.51 and 4.90 g (about $\frac{1}{5}$ oz) on hatching; when weaned they weighed 102 and 100 g ($3\frac{3}{5}$ and $3\frac{1}{2}$ oz).

Desmarest's (Golden-headed) Fig Parrot
P. desmarestii desmarestii

Description: This bird is predominantly dark green above, light green below. The head colouration is extremely beautiful: the forehead is scarlet merging into golden-orange on the crown and nape, where there are a few blue feathers. There is a small patch of brilliant, almost luminous, sky blue feathers beneath the eye. The cheeks and throat are faintly streaked with gold and the light green below the throat is bordered by a line of sky

Desmarest's Fig Parrot (*Psittaculirostris desmarestii desmarestii*).

blue, followed by vinous-coloured feathers on the upper breast. Primaries are bluish green on the outer edge, dark brown on the inner edge; under wing coverts are brown, pale yellow and greenish blue. The bill is black. Length: 18 cm ($7\frac{1}{2}$ in).

Immature birds have the crown dull yellowish. Weight: M 108–118 g ($3\frac{4}{5}$–$4\frac{1}{5}$ oz); F 126 g ($4\frac{2}{5}$ oz).

Range/Habitat: This species has a wide distribution in the western Papuan Islands and western and southern New Guinea. Lowland forest is its usual habitat but it has been found as high as 1,300 m (4,250 ft).

Godman's Fig Parrot
P. d. godmani

Description: It is distinguished at a glance from the nominate race by its sky blue upper breast and golden-orange cheeks and throat. From the little that is known about this species it would appear to be the only race which shows any sexual dimorphism, for the male has the forehead, crown and back of the neck orange-red, merging into a golden-yellow band on the hind neck. The cheeks and throat are orange-yellow with tufts reaching from beneath the eye to the ear coverts. The female lacks the yellow band on the hind neck.

Western Golden-headed Fig Parrot
P. d. occidentalis

Description: This race has the ear coverts and throat deep yellow instead of green; there is no blue on the nape and the blue below the eye is less extensive and of a greener shade.

Aviculture: In the *Avicultural Magazine* for June 1938, the Duke of Bedford reported that seven birds of this subspecies, which was new to aviculture, had recently reached Britain. He obtained four; their diet consisted almost entirely of fruit: apple, pear, grapes and banana, also nectar. They were very fond of mealworms.

There is considerable variation in head colouration within the subspecies. In *occidentalis*, the cheeks and ear coverts are golden-yellow (not yellow-green), and the blue spot below the eye is paler. It occurs in the western part of the Vogelkop, West Irian, and on the western Papuan islands of Salawati and Batanta.

It would appear that *godmani* is sexually dimorphic, the female lacking the golden-yellow band on the hind neck. Male and female differ from the nominate race in having the crown and nape orange-red and in lacking the red-brown or orange-brown breast band. The cheek feathers are more elongated and narrow. This subspecies is found in southern New Guinea from Mimika River eastwards (where it intergrades with *cervicalis* in the Fly River area).

Aviculture: In 1939 the Duke of Bedford described this species as 'new to aviculture'. He had four birds and there was a female in a collection in Belgium. One of the former died and proved to be badly infested with tapeworms. At first the survivors lived on bread and milk and fruit but after some months took hemp, sunflower and millet spray. They proved hardy.

Probably this species was not seen in Europe again until exhibited at Vogelpark Walsrode. Since then a small number of birds have been exported and can be seen in a few private collections in Europe and the USA. At San Diego Zoo chicks were hatched in 1981 but not reared.

Edwards' Fig Parrot
P. edwardsii

Description: The male has the crown yellowish green, merging into a black band from the nape to the eyes; the red feathers of the cheeks are narrow and elongated, also those of the ear coverts which are yellow variably mixed with red and blue. The throat and breast are red and there is a blue-black band across the upper breast. A yellow band decorates the under side of the flight feathers and the under wing coverts are bluish-green. The rest of the plumage is green. The female has the breast yellow-green apart from the wide band of dark blue on the upper breast.
Length: 18 cm ($7\frac{1}{2}$ in).

Range/Habitat: This species inhabits north-eastern New Guinea.

Aviculture: Probably the first specimens of this exceptionally beautiful bird seen outside their native country were the pair exhibited at San Diego Zoo in the 1960s. Since then a few have been imported into Europe and the USA.

The first recorded breeding would appear to be that by Herr Willy in Germany in 1981 (Willy, 1983). Three

Edwards' Fig Parrot (*Psittaculirostris edwardsii*).

pairs were obtained in October 1979 and kept in enclosures measuring 180×70 cm ($6 \times 2\frac{1}{4}$ ft) $\times 2$ m ($6\frac{1}{4}$ ft) high. They were maintained at a temperature of 15 to 20°C (59 to 68°F). After two unsuccessful nesting attempts by one pair, they were provided with a hollow log 80 cm (32 in) long, fixed almost horizontally. A chick which hatched in January 1981 lived only a few days. In the fourth clutch, a chick hatched in March was partly hand-fed and died after two weeks. The female laid again in May and two chicks hatched. One died at five days and the other at four weeks. An autopsy carried out on the latter showed intestinal inflammation, kidney gout and liver and spleen abnormalities. In July, the female produced the tenth clutch in two years. Eggs were laid on July 25 and 27. A chick hatched on August 18 or 19 and left the nest on October 13. By June 1983, five young had been reared.

The normal clutch size was two and the eggs measured 21.8×25.6 mm ($\frac{9}{10} \times 1$ in). The food consisted of soaked sunflower seed, ripe and half-ripe millet sprays, half-ripe wheat and maize, apple, grated carrot mixed with CéDé, a mash consisting of soaked figs, banana and Milupa baby cereal, plus two drops of Vitamin K daily. During one period mealworms were readily taken. A chick which hatched in November 1981 was ringed with a 6 mm ($\frac{1}{4}$ in) closed ring at eight days.

In the UK, G. A. Smith hand-reared four Edwards' Fig Parrots in 1985 (pers. comm.).

Opopsitta
Opopsitta

These tiny parrots differ from *Psittaculirostris* in having the cere bare, not feathered, and in their smaller size.

Double-eyed Fig Parrot
O. diophthalma diophthalma

Description: The male is dark green above, of a yellower shade below, with the flanks yellow. Forehead, crown and lores are red, bordered on the hind

Double-eyed Fig Parrots (*Opopsitta diophthalma diophthalma*), male left, female right.

crown by orange-yellow and in front of the eye by blue. There is a small patch of mauvish blue beneath the red on the cheeks. A yellowish white band crosses the under side of the secondaries and the innermost wing coverts. The bill is black, bluish at the base. The iris is dark brown. Length: 14 cm (6 in).

Females and immature birds can be distinguished by the cheeks which are buffish brown, not red.

Range/Habitat: It occurs in New Guinea, the Aru Islands and coastal north-eastern Australia.

Aviculture: Until 1978 this species had reached Britain on a few isolated occasions only: a pair in 1908, collected by Walter Goodfellow, a few collected by D. Bush in 1949 and one brought to England by David Attenborough in 1957. The latter, a female, lived in the Bird House at London Zoo until its death in 1970, possibly establishing a captive longevity record for this species. As it aged, its plumage became pied with yellow. Its diet included sunflower seed and fruit.

In 1978, a few Double-eyed Fig Parrots reached dealers in Europe, but it is still an extreme rarity. Aviculturists fortunate enough to obtain them were enchanted by their pleasing personality. Two years previously, Dr R. Burkard, in Switzerland, received some, and described them as 'especially charming and quite hardy toy-parrots'. They were fed on dried figs, fruit and breadcrumbs with egg and carrot.

Anthony Smith of Birmingham told me that the diet of his 'pair', which subsequently proved to be two males, consisted of equal parts of seed and fruit, along with about five per cent rotten wood which he was certain was swallowed. Millet was reduced to a powder before being eaten. The birds wintered outdoors, using a nest-box to roost in.

The renowned English aviculturist E. J. Boosey of Keston Foreign Bird Farm kept a single specimen which he described as 'one of the most charming and delightful little birds it has ever been my good fortune to keep'. It mimicked the calls of parrakeets kept in adjoining aviaries and Boosey recorded that, although normally its voice was 'rather squeaky', if its aviary was passed by without attention it could make a 'harsh screeching din, out of all proportion to his size'. In addition to seed, this bird fed on bread soaked in sweetened diluted milk (twice weekly), apple and the stalks of seakale beet.

This species was bred in Australia by Sir Edward Hallstrom in 1953 but little was recorded about this success. Hallstrom had ten pairs of these birds which hatched many chicks, some of which were killed, apparently after slight disturbances. All the young were lost until the feeding problem was solved. A chick was successfully reared when panicum millet which had been soaked with figs and syrup was offered. This, however, created a difficulty with ants. The birds had excavated their own nests in small trees of soft timber. After gnawing a round entrance hole, they would gnaw down about 10 cm (4 in), where the eggs were deposited. Clutch numbers were not reported but, in the wild, two eggs are laid.

The first breeding occurred in the USA in the aviaries of Edward Marshall Boehm in New Jersey. Two pairs of Double-eyed Fig Parrots were received as a gift from Sir Edward Hallstrom in 1963. They were fed on diced mixed fruits – apple, grapes, peaches, cherries and blueberries. From the dried figs they ate only the seeds. A small amount of sunflower seed, chickweed and seeding grasses were taken.

The two pairs lived together amicably for about a year, before forming pairs. One pair was then moved to a cage, the other being left in an indoor enclosure which measured 3 × 1.8 × 2.4 m (10 × 6 × 8 ft). They were provided with a tree trunk in which a woodpecker had made a nest. The trunk had been sawn into 60 cm (2 ft) lengths and reassembled. A tin tray was fitted at the base of the upper portion; this contained water to ensure that there was ample humidity in the nesting site. Within five minutes of the log's being placed in position, the female was inside. A few days later her first egg was laid, followed by a second after two days. Incubation commenced with the laying of the first egg and lasted for 19 days. The newly hatched chicks were covered with pale lemon down. They lived only ten days, by which time their eyes were open and quills were appearing on their wings and back. A month later the female nested again and was successful in rearing one chick which resembled the female when it left the nest. The female was eventually presented to San Diego Zoo. In 1970, a chick was hatched there but did not survive.

In the Netherlands, G. Billet reared this species in 1978. Three pairs were placed together in an outdoor aviary; two pairs were removed in July and the remaining female laid on August 6 and 8. On August 28 there were two chicks in the nest. One fledged on October 4; the other had died during the preceding week. The survivor resembled the female except for the pink bill and the colouration of the head: only the forehead was red and the cheeks were mottled orange. Rearing food included bread soaked in honey and water, high-protein milk food, apple, egg-food, sunflower and soaked millet sprays.

Since the mid-1970s, this species has been bred in zoos in Melbourne and Sydney in Australia and Walsrode in Germany. The race reared by Melbourne Zoo is *macleayana*.

Marshall's Fig Parrot
Marshall's Fig Parrot
O. d. marshalli

Description: The male differs from the nominate race in having darker blue above and in front of the eye; the mauve-blue bands below the cheeks continue to the chin. There is little or no orange-yellow on the crown.

The female has the forehead and forecrown deep violet-blue; there is pale blue instead of red on the head and no orange-yellow on the nape.
Range/Habitat: This species is found in northern Queensland, in the Cape York Peninsula. It is quite common in its restricted range.
Aviculture: Taronga Park Zoo, Sydney, obtained three of these birds. Their attempt to breed them was beset by ill fortune. One pair nested but the female died as the result of being frightened by a hawk, resulting in the death of her two-day old chick. Later, one of the two surviving adults was stolen from the aviary.

Red-browed Fig Parrot
O. d. macleayana

Description: It differs from the nominate race in having less red on the crown and cheeks. The female is duller and more yellowish; the lower cheeks are buff-brown, sometimes marked with blue. Weight: M 39–43 g ($1\frac{2}{5}$–$1\frac{1}{2}$ oz).
Range/Habitat: Coastal areas of north-eastern Queensland and contiguous mountain rainforests. It is common or locally common.
Aviculture: In Australia, Joseph Forshaw was successful in breeding the Red-browed Fig Parrot in 1978. The clutch is invariably two eggs and incubation commences with the laying of the first egg. One chick hatched after approximately 18 days. The chick was brooded by the female for nearly three weeks. The male was not seen to feed the chick until 29 days after it hatched. Until the 34th day, the female always slept in the nest at night. The chick left the nest at 52 days old, perhaps prematurely as it could not fly well and its under parts were not fully feathered. It returned to the nest

each night. Red feathers appeared on its cheeks seven months after it left the nest, indicating that it was a male; adult plumage was acquired about 14 months after it left the nest.

Forshaw felt that excavation of the nest hollow by the female is such an important part of the nesting cycle that nesting is not likely to be successful unless this occurs. A length of rotten limb or decayed tree trunk should therefore be provided – not a prepared log or nest-box. If this is not possible, the nest-box should be filled with compacted wet wood shavings, or similar material, which will dry to form a semi-solid interior in which the female can excavate the nest hollow.

Forshaw's birds were fed on panicum millet with some white millet and occasionally canary seed. Each bird was offered one dried fig daily, also chopped apple and soaked sultanas. In season, fresh cherries, grapes and loquats were given sparingly. They were very fond of pyracantha berries, from which they extracted the seeds; mealworms (rationed) were also eaten with relish.

Contrary to his earlier recommendation, Forshaw suggested that these birds should not be housed in a spacious aviary. This was done at Taronga Park Zoo, Sydney, and birds died as a result of collision with the wire. These Fig Parrots build up a strong momentum in flight and appear to be unable to turn quickly to avoid crashing into the wire. Wire netting should be restricted to one or two sides and part of the roof (Forshaw, 1981).

A real success story with the Red-browed Fig Parrot can be claimed by Graham Taylor who owned the Australian Bird Park in Sydney and bred 13 Red-browed. A local dog had found a bird of this species. A female, it was given to Mr Taylor who obtained the necessary permission to keep it. He then obtained a collecting permit for three more. These were obtained and a fully adult male was placed with the female. She is reported to have laid three eggs, all of which hatched. The parents consumed between 50 and

70 figs daily (collected locally), other fruits, also seed. Every day they were given a bunch of three types of figs – *Ficus rasoma*, *F. ragerna* and *F. glommerata*, the last being their favourite. Large pieces of rotten wood collected from the rainforest were placed on the floor of their aviary and these were enjoyed as objects to gnaw. The young spent between 27 and 30 days in the nest; they resembled the female.

Range/Habitat: It occurs in coastal and contiguous mountain forests of south-eastern Queensland and north-eastern New South Wales. As a result of deforestation, this race is now very rare. Remnant stands of rainforest must be protected if it is to survive.

Coxen's Fig Parrot
O. d. coxeni

Description: This is the largest race and the only one in which sexual dimorphism is almost absent. The male has blue markings on the centre of the forehead and reddish feathers on the lores and on the surrounding blue of the forehead. The cheeks are orange-red, bordered below by a variable mauve-blue band. The female has the reddish markings on lores and forehead fewer or absent. The red on the cheeks is duller and less extensive.

Orange-breasted Fig Parrot
O. gulielmiterti

Description: This is smaller than the preceding species, with a smaller bill. It is dark green above, lighter green below. The male has the forehead, crown and a small area behind the eye dark blue, and the entire side of the head pale yellow. The breast and the upper part of the abdomen are orange. The bill is black and the iris is dark brown. Length: 13 cm (5 in). Weight: M 27–33 g (1–1⅕ oz).

The female has the yellow cheeks bordered by a black band, and below by a greenish blue band. Ear coverts are orange and the breast greenish. Weight: F 33 g (1⅕ oz).

Immature birds differ from the female in having orange only on the sides of the throat. Seven races of this species are recognised. In one, *O. g. amabilis*, the female has the breast orange.

Range/Habitat: This species has a wide distribution over a large part of New Guinea, except the central area and only the western part of West Irian, Salawati in the western Papuan Islands and the Aru Islands, Indonesia. It inhabits lowland forest and savannah lands.

Aviculture: According to the 12th Duke of Bedford (1928b) this species is said to have reached Europe in 1908. Seventy years later a single female could be seen in the collection which then had five species of Fig Parrot: Vogelpark Walsrode.

29

Avicultural Rarities

The species described in this chapter have nothing in common beyond the fact that they are rare or almost unknown in aviculture. In some cases they are rare in their natural habitat; in others, they are little known in captivity because of the difficulty of locating and trapping them, or because they originate from countries which do not allow the export of their native fauna.

In this chapter various genera are covered but not rare species in a genus well-known in captivity. Rare Amazons, for example, are included in the chapter on Amazons.

In the majority of cases the information given is of necessity brief for little has been recorded which relates to them in confinement.

Nestor
Nestor

The two members of this genus, from New Zealand, are unmistakable for their large size, dark colouration and long, narrow bill.

Kea (Mountain Parrot)
N. notabilis

Description: It is predominantly brownish green, greener above and browner below, with dark edges to the feathers which are most pronounced on the wing coverts. The outer webs of the primaries are bluish, the inner webs marked with transverse yellow bars and the inner webs of the primaries with orange.

The rump and lower back are orange-red, also the under wing coverts. The tail is blue-green with a black sub-terminal band and a yellowish green tip. There is orange-yellow barring on the inner web of each feather. The long bill is dark grey, usually being shorter and less curved in the female. Length: 48 cm (19 in).

Immature birds have the crown yellowish green; the cere and eyelids are yellow (instead of grey as in adults). The base of the lower mandible is orange-yellow.

Range/Habitat: Keas are mountain birds, found from 600 m to at least 2,000 m (2,000 to 6,500 ft) in New Zealand's South Island where, fortunately, they are still fairly common. They play in snow, forage around

Kea (*Nestor notabilis*).

human habitations and feed on roots, buds, berries, fruits, seeds, blossoms and nectar.

Aviculture: The Kea is one of the most intelligent and mischievous of all birds and no one who loves parrots can fail to be fascinated by its air of watchfulness and wisdom. But it is far from being a solemn bird, in fact it is playful and inventive in the extreme.

It is also one of the most maligned of birds, with a grossly exaggerated reputation as a sheep-killer. It is possible that Keas attack sheep which are sick, injured or trapped by snow – but this was no justification for their persecution in the second quarter of this century when thousands of birds were killed for the bounty offered. To an aviculturist it seems incredible that anyone could kill such an enchanting bird for a few shillings. Keas now command a very high price.

They need a large aviary. It is a joy to watch them bounding about for, when in a hurry, they take huge hops. Rocks and running water would add to the attraction of a Kea aviary for they are mountain birds. A wide variety of foods, including fresh vegetables and even cooked beetroot, also fruits and the usual large seeds form the diet.

New Zealand allows Keas to be exported only to zoos, some of which have been successful in breeding from them. The first recorded breeding in Britain occurred in the aviaries of the eminent aviculturist Sydney Porter of Derby. His pair nested in a kennel, the base of which was earth. Three eggs hatched at two-day intervals in March 1946. The adult birds fed the young on a wide variety of foods, including root vegetables, dog meal, soaked raisins, apples and peanuts which, after a while, proved to be inadequate, for the chicks stopped growing and two died. In desperation, Porter had offered mealworms, boiled fish, rice pudding and soaked bread. Suddenly it occurred to him to try lettuce which, apparently, was precisely what the parents had been waiting for. They consumed, at enormous expense, four or five out-of-season lettuces daily, and the chick survived. It left the nest after three months.

When Keas bred at San Diego Zoo in California, the incubation period was found to be 29 days and the young

bird remained in the nest for 72 days. This was the climax of ten years' work in trying to persuade the pair to breed. They had been offered rock nests, barrels and replicas of natural caves, but finally used an ordinary nest-box.

At Wilhelminenberg Zoo in Vienna, Austria, a wild-caught pair hatched 41 chicks from 41 eggs and reared 32 young between 1970 and 1981. The clutch size was usually three or four (Sieber, 1983). The pair was housed in an aviary 10 m (33 ft) square with indoor quarters containing a large hollow tree trunk with an entrance 20 cm (8 in) in diameter. Straw and hay were accepted as nesting material. They were fed on various seeds, fruits and vegetables, cut-up meat, hard-boiled egg and lettuce and occasionally cottage cheese and margarine and other fats.

Fresh-cut branches of oak, birch, willow or fir were provided daily and the birds consumed the leaves and needles. While rearing young, they were given additional meat (minced), mealworms and pink mice. The first second generation breeding occurred using a female who first laid when she was four years old.

Consistent success in breeding the Kea has also been achieved at Zurich Zoo in Switzerland since 1964. Other zoos to breed this delightful parrot are Wellington and Auckland, New Zealand; Jersey, Channel Islands; Chicago and Philadelphia, USA; Loro Parque in Tenerife; West Berlin and Bristol zoos. Since 1977, it has been bred in one of the small zoos in the London parks maintained by the then Greater London Council and in 1978 it was bred in two GLC zoos.

Kaka

N. meridionalis

Description: The Kaka is smaller than the Kea, about 45 cm (18 in) in length, with an even more strangely shaped beak: stout with a long, hooked tip. Mainly greenish brown above, it has the crown and nape greyish white, the hind neck crimson and the ear coverts orange-yellow. The abdomen is brownish red and the breast is olive-brown. The rump and upper and under tail coverts are crimson, barred with dark brown. The under wing coverts and the

under side of the flight feathers are scarlet. The bill is brownish grey, apparently being longer and more curved in the male. The iris is dark brown.

Immature birds have the base of the lower mandible yellow.

Range/Habitat: Nectar is an important item in the diet of the wild Kaka – the only brush-tongued parrot which is not a member of the Loriidae. When feeding on nectar and pollen, some of the latter adheres to its head feathers, resulting in cross-pollination of flax and other plants on which it feeds. With their long, hooked beaks, Kakas dig out harmful insects and grubs, such as 10–13 cm (4–5 in) grubs of the longicorn beetle from rotten trees. It therefore plays a role of importance in the ecology of New Zealand forests and deserves every protection. Because of loss of forest habitat, its numbers have declined appreciably. It is not plentiful on North or South Islands but is fairly common on some of the offshore islands.

Aviculture: The Kaka is being bred with moderate success in at least two zoos in New Zealand, thus it is possible that this exceptionally interesting parrot may one day be available outside New Zealand. Its appearance would create an immense amount of interest.

Kakas were exhibited at London Zoo as long ago as 1863 and subsequently by other European zoos – but have probably not been seen outside New Zealand during the present century.

Auckland Zoo (since 1969) and the aviaries in the Botanical Gardens at Dunedin are among those which have bred the Kaka. The three or four eggs are incubated by the female for 28 days, commencing with the laying of the second egg. There is an interval of four days between the laying of the first and second eggs. Both parents feed the young which are covered in white down and fledge after nine or ten weeks. Auckland Zoo has had consistent success and reared as many as six in 1981.

The Kakas at Auckland are fed on sunflower, peanuts, maize, pumpkin seed and fruits. Those at Dunedin receive sunflower, canary seed, oats, brown bread, greenfood, fruit, vegetables and nectar.

Kaka (*Nestor meridionalis*).

Kakapo (*Strigops habroptilis*).

Strigops
Strigops

Kakapo (Night or Owl Parrot)
S. habroptilus

Description: In appearance the Kakapo is one of the least typical of the parrots. Its facial disc of sensory, hair-like feathers gave rise to the alternative name of Owl Parrot. Its plumage is green, each feather having the yellow centre bordered by a black line. The black flight feathers are bordered with yellow. Under parts are pale yellowish green. Length: 64 cm (25 in).
Range/Habitat: The Kakapo is in grave danger of extinction. Its numbers have been reduced to about 50 – a level from which recovery is uncertain and most of its former habitat has been destroyed. One of the strangest and least known of all parrots, exhibiting unique aspects of behaviour; it is a lek bird and part of its nocturnal display consists of producing a booming sound, probably by inflating their air sacs.

During studies made on Kakapos by the New Zealand wildlife service, no females were found for many years. Among those located in the summer of 1974–75 two were believed females. Previously, in 1961, six birds had been taken to the Mount Bruce Native Bird Reserve in an attempt to breed from them; all proved to be males and only one lived longer than one year.
Aviculture: London Zoo exhibited six Kakapos between 1870 and 1875. The last Kakapo in Britain was probably that which lived there from June 1911 until October 1915.

Micropsitta
Micropsitta

The Pygmy Parrots are the only genus of the whole Psittacidae which has proved impossible to keep alive in captivity. The smallest of all parrots, they measure between 8.5 and 10 cm ($3\frac{1}{2}$ and 4 in). Found in New Guinea and the Solomon Islands, these tiny birds breed and roost in arboreal termites' nests. The six species are predominantly green with contrasting colours on the head and breast. Because most of their lives are spent climbing up and *down* tree trunks and branches, their toes are long and their claws are long and curved; as in woodpeckers, the feathers of the short tail have stiff, projecting shafts which act as supports during feeding.

Very few attempts have been made to keep these birds in captivity and all have failed. The reason is their specialised feeding habits. Only comparatively recently was it realised that lichen is an important item of their diet. Small seeds, fruits and insects have been found in their crops.

Most of the few experiments made to keep these birds alive in captivity have involved very small numbers; however, in one (to me, regrettable) experiment, between 80 and 100 birds were captured at dusk in the hope that when placed in a large aviary together they could be induced to feed. They showed no interest in fruits, softfoods or seeds; they examined termites' nests but did not eat the termites. When termites' nests attached to tree boles were provided, they searched the cracks. Other small parrots placed with them did not induce them to feed so, 20 hours after capture, when they were showing signs of starvation, they were released.

In 1927 a Sclater's Pygmy Parrot is known to have reached London Zoo, but presumably did not survive long. And in 1944, ten Pygmy Parrots from the Solomon Islands, *M. finschii aolae*, reached San Diego Zoo; one was dead on arrival and the remaining nine almost certainly died in quarantine.

Bolbopsittacus
Bolbopsittacus

The single species of this genus is one of the least known of parrots.

Guaiabero
B. lunulatus

Description: In size and shape it is not unlike the Blue-rumped Parrot (*Psittinus cyanurus*). Its plumage is green, more yellowish below; the throat, cheeks and the area surrounding the eye is light blue in the male who has a blue collar encircling the neck. There is a pale yellow band across the under side of the secondaries. The bill is bluish grey and the iris is dark brown. Length: 15 cm (6 in).

The female has blue on the throat and lower cheeks only; the collar is yellow.

Range/Habitat: This small parrot is a native of the Philippines, where it is said to be common, inhabiting fairly open country. It feeds mainly on berries and fruits.

Aviculture: Nothing has been recorded about the Guaiabero in avicultural literature. San Diego Zoo received two specimens in 1962; one survived for six months and the other for eight. One aviculturist living in the Far East who has kept a number of specimens for a short while, found them impossible to establish. Another, who had briefly had captive Guaiabero under observation, told me that their behaviour was more reminiscent of Fig Parrots than of *Psittinus*. This is most interesting, because Guaiabero has several features in common with the *Psittaculirostris* Fig Parrots: yellow band on the under side of the secondaries, bulbous bill and dark brown iris. Like the latter, it is a flock bird, unlike *Psittinus*. Dr R Burkard received some in the early 1960s. They fed entirely on potato, sweet potato and a little fruit. He described them (pers. comm.) as very quiet birds that moved almost in slow motion. If they are frightened they fly off so quickly they injure themselves.

Psittinus
Psittinus

Blue-rumped (Little or Rainbow) Parrot
P. cyanurus

Description: The Blue-rumped Parrot is not unlike a large lovebird in appearance. The male has the head grey-blue; the nape and mantle are dark brownish blue; the rump and upper tail coverts are a richer shade of blue. The wings are green, each feather being conspicuously edged with light yellowish green. There is a small, irregular patch of maroon on the upper wing coverts; the flanks and under wing coverts are scarlet. The short tail is greenish yellow above and yellow below; under parts are pale green with a grey tinge in some birds. The large, heavy upper mandible is deep red, the lower mandible brownish. The iris is yellowish white. Length: 18 cm (7$\frac{1}{2}$ in). Weight: M 65 g (2$\frac{3}{10}$ oz).

The female is much duller in colour, being mainly green, yellower below; the head is slaty-brown and there is a small blue patch on the lower back. The bill is greyish brown. Weight: F 75–85 g (2$\frac{3}{5}$–3 oz).

Immature birds have the head green and the beak horn-coloured. Young males have the forehead tinged with blue.

Range/Habitat: This species has a wide

Blue-rumped Parrots (*Psittinus cyanurus*), female left, male right.

distribution from south-western Thailand and southern Burma, through Malaysia to Borneo and Sumatra, Indonesia. It inhabits forested areas and feeds on fruits, seeds and blossoms. Its status would appear to vary from rare to common in various parts of its range.

Aviculture: London Zoo exhibited this species as long ago as 1866 and it appears that it was imported occasionally until the early years of the twentieth century. Thereafter it was not available in any numbers until the late 1960s and early 1970s when it was imported into Britain quite regularly. However, the demand was not great; it was difficult to establish and losses with newly imported birds were high. No doubt young birds would prove easier to establish than adults.

It should be offered plenty of fruit in addition to the usual seeds – canary, white millet, a little hemp and niger, also sunflower, pine nuts and peanuts. Fresh greenfood and vegetables should also be available. One fancier found that his birds sampled fruit before other foods, and would take apple, oranges, pears, plums and grapes. When hips and haws are offered, these are relished above all foods. Elderberries are also consumed with great relish.

One aviculturist who was prepared to go to endless trouble to ensure that there was no deficiency in the diet of her pair, offered them only seed which had been soaked, in addition to various fruits, chickweed, tree branches (they especially liked needles and bark of pine), sprouts, soaked flaked maize, often mixed with glucose and Cytacon (Vitamin B_{12} liquid), rosehip syrup and a nectar and vitamin mixture. Other foods offered were raw mushrooms, maggots, mealworms, earthworms, clumps of grass with the earth attached, raw scraped meat, hardboiled egg, raw egg yolk mixed with seed and crushed vitamin/mineral tablets.

With the exception of sprouts, soaked seed, chickweed and pine branches, they were reported not to favour the same foods two days running; perhaps they were spoilt with choice given.

G. A. Smith of Peterborough kept several pairs on the colony system and all females laid two eggs. He described the females as making a pleasant, melodious, four-note call while in the nest. It is not a noisy bird.

Those who have kept them describe Blue-rumped Parrots as inactive. One fancier informed me that on a February night, when there was a hard frost, one of his two birds stayed out in the flight and, as a result, lost three toes due to frost-bite. This bird died three weeks later.

Two fanciers whom I contacted regarding Blue-rumped Parrots told me that the nails and beak grow extraordinarily quickly, necessitating cutting several times a year.

In 1984, Peter Steck informed me that in Switzerland there are three breeders of this species. He has bred it since 1981. The clutch consists of three to five eggs. One bird had been in his possession for 13 years, possibly a longevity record for the Blue-rumped Parrot.

De Grahl (1974) gives details of his pair, the female laid three eggs in 1973 without result. She deserted after four weeks and the eggs were measured: 25×21 mm, 27×22 mm and 27×21 mm ($1 \times \frac{4}{5}$ in, $1\frac{1}{10} \times \frac{9}{10}$ in and $1\frac{1}{10} \times \frac{4}{5}$ in). De Grahl refers to Thomas Weise's success with this species. By the end of 1972, this aviculturist from Dortmund-Aplerbeck had reared seven young.

Psittacella
Psittacella

The four species which comprise this genus are among the least known of the world's parrots and are inhabitants of mainland New Guinea. Small birds with short tails, they measure between 14 and 23 cm ($5\frac{1}{2}$ and 9 in). Probably only the Brehm's Parrot, *P. brehmii*, has been exported.

Psittacella parrots are barred in the most distinctive way, which led to Diamond (1972) giving this group the name of Tiger Parrots. This is far more appropriate than the only previous common name applied to these arboreal birds – Ground Parrots – a name already and correctly appplied to an Australian species.

Psittacella species inhabit mountains, usually at altitudes between 1,700 m and 3,600 m (5,500 and 12,000 ft). The Tiger Parrots live in dense forest cover and blend so well with their surroundings that even the best native trappers rarely obtain specimens; this accounts for the fact that they are virtually unknown in aviculture.

Brehm's Parrot
P. brehmii

Description: In the Brehm's Parrot, the female has more barred plumage than the male. The latter is green, paler below, with a yellow line on each side of the neck. The mantle, back and upper tail coverts are green, barred with black and the tail is green above, olive-grey below. The under tail coverts, in contrast to the body colour, are red, a feature shared only by the *Pionus*, among the true parrots. The beak is horn-coloured and grey and the iris is red. Length: 24 cm ($9\frac{1}{2}$ in). Weight: 99 g ($3\frac{1}{2}$ oz).

The female is distinguished by the upper breast markings of narrow lines of yellow and black. Immature birds resemble the female but have the

Brehm's Parrot at San Diego Zoo.

breast green, narrowly barred with dull yellow.

Aviculture: Sir Edward Hallstrom kept this species in his aviaries at Nondugl in New Guinea and sent a pair to San Diego Zoo in November 1966. Unfortunately, they proved to be short-lived. They were fed on sunflower seed and various fruits.

Nannopsittaca
Nannopsittaca

The single member of this genus is entirely unknown in aviculture. Nothing is know about its wild life or its management in captivity.

Its tiny, delicate-looking bill distinguishes it from other small parrots, such as the *Bolborhynchus*, *Brotogeris* and *Forpus* species.

Mount Roraima Parrakeet (Tepui Parrotlet)
N. panychlora

Description: This species is entirely green, paler below, and yellowish around the eye and tinged with yellow on forehead, lores and under tail coverts. Carpal edge of the wing is pale yellow; under side of flight and tail feathers is bluish green. The tail is short and square. The bill is brownish and the iris brown. Length: 14 cm (5½ in).

Immature birds have not yet been described.

Range/Habitat: This species is known from three widely separated areas: Mount Roraima district of eastern Venezuela and western Guyana; high mountain peaks in eastern Venezuela south of the Orinoco River in Amazonas and Bolivar, and north of the Orinoco on Cerro Papelon in Sucre. Forshaw (1973) reports that: 'It is entirely restricted to cool, humid subtropical forests on the summits of slopes of the isolated mountains.' It has been observed at 2,100 m (7,000 ft) on Mount Roraima.

In view of its habitat and its small size and all-green plumage (which would render it difficult to observe) it is not surprising that this little bird is unknown in aviculture.

Touit
Touit

The seven small parrots from South and Central America which comprise this genus measure only 14–17 cm (5½–7 in). They are beautifully coloured with heavy bodies, short, rounded tails and stout curved beaks. They are sexually dimorphic, with two exceptions the females having less colour on the wings and tail. Very little is known about them; it would appear that only one species has been kept in captivity outside its native country.

Lilac-tailed (Seven-coloured or Black-winged) Parrotlet
T. batavica

Description: It is an extremely beautiful bird. The forehead is yellow and the crown green. Feathers of the nape are greenish yellow tipped with black; this colour extends almost to the throat in some specimens. The under parts are light bluish green and the under wing coverts are bluish with a touch of pink on the inner edge of the wing. The back is brownish black; rump, tail coverts, flight feathers and the tip of the tail are black. The secondaries are yellow with the under surface black and green. The bill is yellowish with grey towards the base; the iris is yellow. Immature birds have yet to be described.

Range/Habitat: This species inhabits Venezuela, Guyana and Suriname, also Trinidad and Tobago.

It is found in small flocks. Because it prefers dense forest and keeps mainly to the forest canopy, little is known of its wild life – and this applies equally to the other members of the genus. It feeds on fruits, berries, seeds, flowers and nectar.

Aviculture: Probably the only European aviculturist with experience of this species was Herbert Murray of Brentwood, Essex. He provided me with the following information, which was published in *The Parrots of South America* (Low, 1972):

> The first of these birds that I had, about the middle 1950s, lasted for some months and then gradually faded away. They had been fed on a diet of Spratts' CLO and Ostermilk. The second lot –

two adults and two young – all caught together in a net at night, were fed the same way. They had to be force-fed for a long time in Trinidad. These did much better and I got them to take nectar and they did well for some months. Then Spratts stopped making CLO.

> I was forced to change the CLO but the birds developed enteritis and three died quickly. The last one lived for quite some time and seemed interested in an old log. Maybe they live on wood borers but mine would eat neither soaked seed, fruit nor mealworms.

Geoffroyus
Geoffroyus

These parrots are found in New Guinea, the Cape York region of Australia and Indonesia. In Australia, they are quite numerous within their restricted habitat. They are short-tailed, small to medium-sized true parrots which are mainly green with contrasting colours on the head. In some species, these colours have a beautiful and unusual bloom, such as is otherwise seen only in the Plumhead Parrakeet. Indeed, it is probable that the *Psittacula* parrakeets are the closest to the *Geoffroyus* parrots and one can more easily see the resemblance if the latter are imagined with long tails.

Geoffroyus are extreme avicultural rarities. They fare so badly under captive conditions that Forshaw (1981) wrote:

> Permits for the capture of Red-cheeked Parrots should not be granted and every effort must be made to prevent birds entering the illicit live-bird trade.

Even nestlings taken from the wild are not easy to rear. In the early 1970s, Kerry Müller, then Curator of Birds at Taronga Zoo, Sydney, was the first to record finding a nest of this species in Australia. He removed the three chicks, only one of which he was able to rear. He told me that food which is normally successful for rearing parrot chicks caused problems with their digestion. When he saw the young, Joseph Forshaw, who was also on the expedition, stated that he believed *Geoffroyus* to be related to the *Psittacula* parrakeets.

Very few specimens of *Geoffroyus*

have been kept by aviculturists. A Blue-collared Parrot (*G. geoffroyi cyanicollis*) was obtained by David Ezra in Calcutta in 1905. A female, it was described as 'a great pet', being very tame. F. Shaw Mayer collected a single bird of this species in 1927; it was said to be very beautiful but delicate.

Another subspecies, the Aru (*G. g. aruensis*) was received by London Zoo in 1931. There were two birds: one died within a month of its arrival; the other survived a few months – long enough to assume adult plumage. The receipt of these birds prompted David Seth-Smith (1931b) to write of them:

> There is no doubt that *Geoffroyus* is a very delicate genus of parrots, and although when in full plumage the males are decidedly beautiful, with very delicate colouring, they have otherwise very few attractive qualities. One of the Zoo birds was very tame, but certainly not friendly. The food presents no difficulty, consisting of grain and fruit, but probably the question of temperature is the difficult one with these Parrots.

In recent years, the only *Geoffroyus* kept in Britain would appear to be that in the collection of John Wilson of Norwich in the 1960s.

Red-cheeked Parrot
G. geoffroyi
Description: This is the most beautiful of the genus. The head colouration of the male is unusual and delicate. The forehead, throat and sides of the head are rose-red, the rest of the head and the nape of the neck are beautiful shades of pale mauve, an especially pleasing combination of colours. The rest of the plumage is green, more yellowish below, except for the reddish brown markings on the wing coverts. The under wing coverts are blue. The upper mandible is coral, the lower mandible brownish grey. The iris is pale yellow or white. Length: 21 cm ($8\frac{1}{2}$ in). Weight: M 130–180 g ($4\frac{3}{5}$–$6\frac{2}{5}$ oz); F 140–172 g (5–6 oz).

Females have the head brown and the upper and lower mandibles brownish grey. Immature birds have green heads and the throat and cheeks are tinged with brown.
Range/Habitat: Indonesia (Moluccas and Lesser Sunda Islands), New Guinea and the Cape York Peninsula of northern Queensland in Australia.

Blue-collared (Lilac-collared) Parrot
G. simplex
Description: This species is almost entirely green with dark blue under wing coverts and the under side of the tail dusky yellow. The male only has a greyish blue collar encircling the neck. The bill is greyish black and the iris is white. Length: 22 cm (9 in).

Immature birds resemble the female but lack the blue tinge on the crown. The iris is greyish white.
Range/Habitat: New Guinea.

Singing (Yellow-headed) Parrot
G. heteroclitis
Description: The male differs from the previous two species in having the head yellow, bordered with a greyish mauve collar. The female has the crown and the nape grey. In the male, the upper mandible is yellow, the lower mandible dark grey. The beak is grey in the female. Length: 25 cm (10 in).
Range/Habitat: Bismarck Archipelago (east of New Guinea) and the Solomon Islands.

Racket-tailed Parrots
Prioniturus

The members of this genus are unique among parrots in having spatules or rackets on two elongated tail feathers. The feathers have long, bare shafts which extend from beyond the length of the other tail feathers for 64–90 mm ($2\frac{1}{2}$–$3\frac{1}{2}$ in), including the spatule. It is of interest that in one Racket-tail kept as a pet and closely observed, the feathers carrying the rackets are never moulted at the same time. It takes six weeks for one racket feather to come through, after which the second will be moulted and replaced. The bare shaft is wiry and pliable and the bird will even bend the spatule-bearing feather over its shoulder while preening.

There is little variation in size among the members of this genus; they measure from 27–32 cm (11–12 in), except *flavicans* which measures 37 cm ($14\frac{1}{2}$ in) including the rackets. In appearance, they are nearest to the small *Tanygnathus* parrots, being mainly green with soft shades of various colours on the head. Sexual dimorphism is well marked in some species, less apparent in others.

Of the six species, at least three have been kept by aviculturists but on rare occasions only. All have the reputation of being difficult to establish in captivity. One wonders about the fate of those which have been exported as nothing has been recorded about them in recent years.

Golden-mantled (Celebes) Racket-tailed Parrot
P. platurus
Description: No written description can do justice to the unusually soft colours of this lovely bird. The male is green, brightest on the cheeks, neck and breast. The wings are grey-green with some lilac on the shoulders. The under side of the primaries and the tail feathers are light greenish blue, except the outer two tail feathers which are greenish yellow. The upper side of the tail feathers have dark blue tips, except the two from which the rackets grow. There is a variable amount of gold on the mantle, of a shade which is old gold rather than rich yellow. A few pink feathers on the hind crown are bordered by a large patch of lavender grey. The bill is grey and the iris dark brown. Length: about 28 cm (11 in), including the tail but not including the rackets which measure a further 8 cm (3 in).

The female is entirely green, much lighter below, with the under side of the flight and tail feathers light greenish blue. The rackets are shorter than those of the male. Immature birds resemble the female except for the central tail feathers which have pointed tips but lack the rackets.
Range/Habitat: This species is from Celebes and other Indonesian islands.
Aviculture: This is the only species of which much has been recorded in avicultural literature.

The first recorded instance of this

species being kept in Europe dates back to 1888. F. E. Blaauw of the Netherlands was the owner. In the early years of the twentieth century at least three reached England, the first being imported in 1901. Henceforth, it has been available on rare occasions only and always in small numbers. It has yet to be bred successfully in captivity. A pair in the possession of the Duke of Bedford (when he was Lord Tavistock) hatched a chick which died after a few weeks. After numerous failures, the pair succeeded in rearing one chick: tragically, it was killed by vermin on the day it left the nest.

Crimson-spotted Racket-tailed Parrot
P. flavicans

Description: The male has the forehead and crown blue and the centre of the crown scarlet. The mantle and upper breast are olive-yellow and the under wing coverts and under side of the tail are sky blue. The abdomen is light green and the upper parts are dark green. Length: 30 cm (12 in) plus the two rackets which each measure 8 cm (3 in) beyond the end of the tail feathers, including the spatule which measures 20 mm ($\frac{4}{5}$ in). The female lacks the scarlet head patch.
Range/Habitat: This bird comes from Indonesia.
Aviculture: The only recorded instance of this species in aviculture relates to a single bird given to London Zoo in 1930.

Blue-crowned (Philippine) Racket-tailed Parrot
P. discurus

Description: Male and female have the crown and nape blue. The rest of the plumage is green, paler and more yellow on the under parts, with the under side of the tail greenish blue. The only sexual distinction apparently lies in the feathers which carry the rackets, which are shorter in the female. In two rackets of a probable male of this species which I examined, the feathers carrying the rackets measure, from quill tip to spatule, 18 mm ($\frac{7}{10}$ in).
Range/Habitat: Philippine Islands (also Jolo Island in the Sulu Archipelago).
Aviculture: The bird which I examined

Blue-crowned Racket-tailed Parrot (*Prioniturus discurus*).

is the only Racket-tail I know of in Britain which has proved to be long-lived. It has been kept by F. Keen of Perivale, Middlesex, for 12 years at the time of writing. When obtained it was very nervous; in fact, it was seven years before it became reasonably steady. After another couple of years it was tame enough to help itself to food from the table, although the same items of food placed in its cage would be ignored. It took three years to wean it from a diet of rice and raw egg; gradually it learned to eat peanuts and a few sunflower seeds. Crusts of bread would also be eaten, and cake – after it carefully removed the fruit. Of fresh fruits, only the pips are eaten, pear pips being especial favourites. Another delicacy relished is cheese. Small seeds such as canary have never been offered, so might profitably be experimented with. Two aviculturists who kept Racket-tails early this century fed them on small seeds such as canary, millet and hemp and rice in the husk, also fruit, including grapes, banana, apple and orange. One relished dry biscuit, toast or a crust of bread.

The experiences of one importer of nine specimens of the Blue-crowned

Racket-tailed Parrot are worth recounting. John FitzGibbon informed me that, as a group, these birds:

. . . proved no more difficult to accustom to the usual parrot diet than any other fruit- and seed-eating species. In fact, this species responded well to the procedure that I follow for all newly-imported parrots of that dietary propensity, i. e., the mixing of approximately equal parts of dry seed and the readily-taken boiled maize and gradually reducing the latter, when it is apparent that the seed is being consumed, while providing a variety of fruits, etc. Within about ten days of importation, most of the Racket-tails were eating a variety of foods. The full range of items eaten by these birds while in my possession was mixed seeds and grain, peanut kernels, apple, banana, pear, orange, cherries, carrot (of which one or two birds seemed inordinately fond), wholemeal bread and occasional protein/vitamin/mineral supplements.

Two individual birds did not adapt readily to this regime; one subsisted for a time almost entirely on maize and wheat and the other refused all foods except boiled maize powdered with Complan.

They were interesting, if unspectacular, cage and aviary birds and I found them to be quiet (although occasionally emitting a variety of rasping and lory-like calls) and sufficiently hardy to winter in an unheated birdroom. They were fairly tolerant of the company of members of their own and other species, some of them sharing small flights with Philippine Hanging Parrots and a Red-capped Parrot (*Pionopsitta pileata*).

I could detect no differences in the extent or depth of the blue cap that might be indicative of the sexes but a variation in the length of the racket shafts was noticeable. My birds showed no tendency towards nocturnal activity (as mentioned in some accounts); indeed, they seemed to settle down to roost rather earlier than most species.

A single specimen received by Mrs Johnstone in 1903 was probably new to aviculture. Since then this species has been imported on a few occasions.

Mount Mada (Buru) Racket-tailed Parrot
P. mada

Description: The male of this species has the nape, mantle and lower back bluish purple. The under tail coverts are yellow (they are greenish yellow in the *platenae* subspecies of *discurus*). The female lacks the bluish purple colouration, except on the nape, where it is faintly apparent.

Range/Habitat: It is a native of the Island of Buru in Indonesia.

Green Racket-tailed Parrot
P. lucionensis

Description: It is entirely green, the female being darker, less yellow-green, than the male. Both sexes have the under side of the flight feathers greenish blue.

Range/Habitat: This species comes from Luzon in the Philippines, also the island on Marinduque, where it is apparently common.

Shining Parrots
Prosopeia

The members of this genus are among the most handsome of all parrots; the largest and the most handsome of parrakeets, their beauty is partly due to the peculiar quality of the plumage, not unlike that of Eclectus Parrots, and partly to the large areas of bright, unbroken colours and partly to their proportions: they have long, broad tails which serve to enhance their gorgeous plumage. They have, too, a certain majesty which is found in few other birds. Confined to Fiji, they are protected in their own habitat and their export has not been permitted for many years. However, in the past only a few isolated specimens were known to aviculture.

In the 1930s, Sydney Porter travelled to Fiji in order to observe the *Prosopeia* species and to collect them. By 1935 he had kept 24 specimens of three species – one of only two aviculturists ever to have had extensive experience with this genus. Probably its members were less rare in captivity during the second half of the nineteenth century than they are today. In 1887, a Masked Parrakeet was worth £4 – an expensive bird by today's standards.

The *Prosopeia* species are today extremely rare in aviculture. At the time of writing, two zoos exhibit more than one species. In 1971 the San

Diego Zoo collection included a *P. t. taviunensis* which survived only a short while. The birds I saw there in 1974 and 1978 were the Red Shining, a Koro Island and a Masked Parrakeet (the latter unfortunately has the Eclectus-like habit of spending most of its life in the nest-box). They were thriving in the warm, but dry, Californian climate which does not in the least resemble that of their native Fiji where temperature is consistently high and annual rainfall is 762 cm (300 in).

Due to their superficial resemblance to King Parrakeets, the few *Prosopeia* imported in Porter's day were apt to be treated the same way; however, these birds require large quantities of fresh fruit and vegetables. Porter's birds were offered green corn in the ear, peas in the pod, the usual greenfood and, on alternate days, sponge cake soaked in raw egg and milk. An insectivorous food mixed with grated carrot and hard-boiled egg was relished, in addition to fresh twigs from apple trees and hawthorn twigs bearing berries.

At San Diego Zoo, the *Prosopeia* are fed on sunflower, milo, canary, millet and wheat in equal parts plus a few pine nuts and peanuts. Fruit and vegetables offered daily include apples, oranges, romaine lettuce, hydroponic barley, papaya, blueberries and figs. Bread is also offered.

Behaviourally, they are interesting birds. Jim Hayward, of Carterton, Oxfordshire, who breeds Kings and Eclectus, told me that he thought they were mid-way between the two. He keeps a number in flights about 6 m (20 ft) in length and has found them to be more active and stronger in flight than Eclectus, making an audible 'thump' when landing on the perch (the latter is also true of some Eclectus). His birds are 'almost nocturnal' and feed at night. The harsh, strident 'waa, waa' cry is far-carrying. Two or three eggs are laid but, in his experience, females do not remain in the nest for weeks, whether or not they have laid. Neither are they dominant over males as is usual with Eclectus.

His birds vary greatly in temperament: some are aggressive and will fly at his face; some are timid and others are friendly and will take food from his hand. Not until they had been in his possession for several years were they

left outdoors for the whole of the winter, thus complete acclimatisation was a long process.

They would sample anything in the way of food. They are offered sunflower and various small seeds, peanuts, hard or boiled maize, 'anything green', branches, leaves, fruit, cabbage stalks, swede, raw and boiled potato, bread and cakes.

Wayne Schulenburg of San Diego Zoo, who had looked after the *Prosopeia* there for five years, when I asked his opinion, stated that he felt that they were more closely allied to Eclectus. The chicks have:

> . . . very sparse whitish-yellow down which turns to grey within the first week; by the third week feather shafts are beginning to make their appearance and by the fourth week are almost completely opened. The display in *Prosopeia* is similar to Eclectus in that the male bobs up and down, struts towards the female, clicks his beak and hits it on the perch. Sometimes, on approaching the female, there is a light fluttering of the wings.
>
> Like Eclectus, the hens do spend an enormous amount of time in the nest-box. This even applies to the male of the zoo's pair of *splendens* but this could be because the pair is very shy; once they are sure that I have left the area they will leave the nest to feed and cavort about the aviary.

The latter measures 2.4 × 5.4 m (8 × 18 ft) × 2.3 m (7 ft 6 in) high.

Shining Parrots have been kept successfully at liberty in their native islands, but no one would risk such rare and conspicuous birds at liberty elsewhere. The 12th Duke of Bedford recorded that one which escaped from its aviary 'moved from tree to tree in a restless, active manner, swooping and gliding in a peculiar fashion not seen in other parrots'. He kept an aged female Masked Parrakeet at liberty during the summer months. She was described as having 'an odd, flapping flight, varied by a pheasant-like glide and she would drop into thick bushes much after the manner of a pheasant'.

In Fiji, some pet *Prosopeia* parrakeets have apparently been allowed their freedom and return each evening from the forests where they spend their day – a remarkable habit.

There are doubts about the validity of the nominate race which may represent a hybrid.

Red Shining Parrakeet
P. tabuensis splendens
Description: It is crimson on the head and under parts; there is a broad blue band on the nape and the primaries are blue. Back and wings are shining green. The beak is black and the iris is orange-red.

Immature birds have the iris brown and the bill yellow and black. Length: 45 cm (8 in).

Range/Habitat: This race is found on Kandavu, Fiji, also on Viti Levu, where it was introduced.

Aviculture: What may have been the first successful breeding of this species occurred in the USA in 1976. A pair belonging to H. I. Gregory of Texas, which were obtained in 1972, produced two fertile eggs in March 1973. One hatched but the chick died at two weeks. In 1976, the two eggs hatched on February 29 and March 5; the second chick died on the day it hatched. When the surviving chick was 20 days old and the weather was unseasonably hot, the female stayed away from the nest. On the following day the chick was removed for hand-rearing. At 45 days it perched and at 53 days it flew. The parents were housed in an aviary measuring 3 × 1.2 × 1.8 m (10 × 4 × 6 ft).

This species was reared in California at San Francisco Zoo in 1976 (one) and 1978 (three).

The Red Shining Parrakeets at San Diego Zoo hatched a chick on March 4, 1973, after an incubation period of 24 days. Two previous infertile clutches had consisted of four and three eggs. The chick was removed for hand-rearing but died at 37 days. The breeding pair were part of a group of four birds which proved entirely compatible. No display was observed. The pair hatched another chick in March 1974 and a third in 1975 but none was reared. The chick looked more like a King Parrakeet than that of an Eclectus Parrot.

In Britain, Jim Hayward of Oxfordshire has bred this species since 1983. A single chick was hand-reared in that year and in 1984. Several pairs are maintained. For five years after importation, these birds could not be wintered out of doors. Their first nesting attempts occurred in mid-winter and they were gradually persuaded to nest earlier in the year. Likewise, the

Shining Parrakeet (*Prosopeia tabuensis atrogularis*).

moult, which is heavy and prolonged, has been shifted from March to July. One egg may form the clutch or a second laid up to one week later. The nest-boxes measure 91–120 cm (3–4 ft) high. The incubation period is 24 days or more. Newly hatched chicks have long silver-grey down with white down on the head.

There are brown knob-like protuberances on each side of the bill; second down is charcoal-coloured. Young are in the nest for approximately eight weeks. They resemble the adults at about 15 months. The diet is varied as anything offered is eaten, including meat and livefood. These birds are partially nocturnal; feeding and mating occurs during hours of darkness. On moonlit nights, they fly around calling.

Two hybrids from a Red Shining Parrakeet male and a Masked Parrakeet female were bred in the aviaries

of Dr R. Burkard (1974) of Zurich in 1973. In plumage they resembled their father, having cherry red breast and belly, iridescent green back and wing coverts and the under parts even brighter than those of the male. They had the mask blackish and the back of the head green. The hybrids were bred in a large aviary containing a pair of Red Shining Parrakeets and a female Masked; they agreed with one another and lived well together.

Remarking on the voice of this species, the Duke of Bedford (1928b) described two types of call notes – one a soft cry of 'hor' and the other a strident scream.

Koro Island Parrakeet
P. t. koroensis
Description: This bird is distinguished by its chocolate brown head; upper parts are shining green and

the under parts deep red, almost maroon.

Range/Habitat: It inhabits only Koro Island, Fiji.

Aviculture: A great rarity in aviculture, it has yet to rear young. San Diego's female laid two infertile clutches between the time of the pair's arrival in 1970 and March 1973.

Taviuni Parrakeet
P. t. taviunensis

Description: This is the smallest of the subspecies, measuring about 39 cm (15½ in). Unlike the nominate race, lacks the blue collar on the nape.

Range/Habitat: This parrakeet inhabits Taviuni and Ngamea Islands, Fiji.

Aviculture: One specimen was presented to London Zoo in 1911 but very few others have been seen outside Fiji.

Aviculture: A few specimens of *tabuensis* reached Europe before World War II.

There were two in the collection at Sterrebeck in Belgium which were always in perfect health and wintered in a large indoor flight. They were so tame that they would alight on the shoulders of those they knew and greeted visitors with every sign of pleasure and excitement.

In New Zealand, a female described as the nominate race paired with a male Shining Parrakeet. Nesting boxes and logs were ignored, the eggs being laid on the earth floor of the aviary. For three consecutive years clutches of four eggs were produced and the hen became egg-bound with the last egg and did not incubate. In August 1940, the female, who was very tame, laid again.

One of the eggs was broken after a week and the other hatched. The chick, at a month old, was covered in dark grey down. When feathered, its plumage was described as being identical to the parents, except that the breast was darker than that of the male and lighter than the female's. The young bird was reared on seed fruit, green peas, seeding grasses and a little cake and biscuit.

Masked (Yellow-breasted Musk) Parrakeet
P. personata

Description: The bright, iridescent green of its plumage is exceptionally beautiful. It has the face black, the primaries and their coverts blue and most of the under parts yellow with some orange on the abdomen. The under side of the tail is black. Length: 47 cm (19 in). The iris is orange or ruby red regardless of sex. The bill is black.

Immature birds have the bill paler, with horn-coloured markings and the iris brown.

Range/Habitat: This species inhabits Viti Levu, Fiji, where it was apparently fairly common locally, despite fears expressed in the literature of the first half of the century that its extinction would be hastened by mongoose and shotgun. No doubt its existence hinges on the preservation of its forest habitat.

Aviculture: The Masked Parrakeet was occasionally imported into Europe during the second half of the nineteenth century. London Zoo exhibited its first specimen in 1862 and probably had about ten more before 1900. After this time it became a great rarity in aviculture. At the time of writing there is a single specimen at San Diego Zoo which was received in 1970.

It would seem that only two Masked Parrakeets have reached the USA – both of which have been kept in San Diego. The Duke of Bedford presented the first one to a private aviculturist, I. D. Putnam, in the 1930s. He paired it with a 'Tabuan' hen. She laid three eggs, one of which hatched. The chick was deserted when the female was frightened from the nest by a swarm of bees.

The name of Musk Parrakeet arises from the fact that this species emits a sweet, musky smell, which can apparently be detected when one is within a few feet. Its voice was described by the Duke of Bedford as 'piercing and harsh' but his bird 'made up for it by speaking fluent English and imitating dogs and cats'.

Miss Rosie Alderson (1905) described her Masked Parrakeet as:

. . . the brightest, most loving and intelligent parrakeet . . . if I do not notice him

he will put on a most pathetic limp, and then, when perched on my wrist, he will almost go to sleep in my arms with his head under my coat collar . . .

The bird was so tame it could be handled at will and picked up bodily; it was even good-natured with other birds and allowed a Barnard's Parrakeet to take away the biscuit it was eating – with only a grunt of protest.

Pezoporus
Pezoporus

Ground (Swamp or Button-grass) Parrakeet
P. wallicus

Description: This bird is bright grass green above, each feather being marked with black and yellow. There is a narrow band of orange on the forehead which is absent in immature birds. The breast is a duller shade of green, each feather having a small black fleck in the centre. The abdomen is yellowish and strongly barred with black. The long, pointed tail is mainly green above, yellow on the under surface, and barred with brownish black. Length: 30 cm (12 in). Weight: 71–76 g ($2\frac{1}{2}$–$2\frac{7}{10}$ oz).

Range/Habitat: The habitat of this bird is being lost – heathland, swamps, estuarine flats and even pasture land in coastal regions of south-eastern Australia and Tasmania, also, to a lesser degree, on the west coast. It can now be found only in isolated pockets, except in Tasmania, where it is less rare. In the past, predators such as cats and foxes were responsible for the destruction of nests – shallow excavations in the soil. Grass fires also took their toll. Although the future of this species seems very far from secure, it is possible that, because these birds are so difficult to observe, they are more numerous than is generally believed. They spend much time concealed in undergrowth and, if disturbed, run very fast, only occasionally taking to the wing with a zig-zag flight. Their toes and claws are long – adaptations for walking. Ground Parrakeets feed on the seeds of grasses and small shrubs, also cultivated millets, where

Ground Parrot (*Pezoporus wallicus*).

available. Three or four eggs are laid. The young leave the nest in their fourth week and are said to shelter until capable of flight.

Aviculture: Alan Lendon (Lendon & Cayley, 1973) recorded that A. E. Leer of Manley Vale, near Sydney, had bred four young from a pair of Ground Parrakeets. In the past, a few Australian aviculturists had kept this species but now it is endangered and not kept in captivity.

I. C. Webber (1948) recorded:

> A very interesting bird in the aviary, remaining still all day becoming very active after sunset, feeding and bathing, climbing all over the aviary wire, and night observations showed both birds bathing at 11.30 p.m.

He found that they showed a preference for sunflower, canary and millet seed, in that order; lucerne and thistle were readily eaten. Three birds kept for a long period in Adelaide Zoo, the last of which died in 1949, soon became quite fearless.

This is of historical interest only for the Ground Parrakeet will never again be available in aviculture.

Geopsittacus
Geopsittacus

Night Parrakeet
G. occidentalis

Three Ground Parrot chicks. Note the pink bill.

Description: This bird bears a marked resemblance to the Ground Parrakeet. The tail is much shorter and the green of a duller shade; there is more yellow on the abdomen. Length: 23 cm (9 in).

Range/Habitat: Forshaw (1973) describes this as 'one of Australia's most mysterious birds'. Only one specimen has been collected this century and there were no authentic records of it for about 50 years until June 1979, when four birds were sighted in Coopers Creek, in the far north-eastern part of South Australia. It occurs in arid or semi-arid regions of central Australia. Like the Ground Parrakeet, it is a ground-dweller, and feeds mainly on seeds, especially spinifex.

Aviculture: This is one of the least

known of all parrots. Only two accounts of it have been published. One appeared in the *Proceedings of the Zoological Society of London* in 1868. During the previous year a Night Parrakeet had been sent to the Zoo where its curiously harsh voice, nocturnal habits and preference for greenfood were noted. It lived only four months, apparently dying of pneumonia during a cold January. It has been stated that the German aviculturist Russ bred the Night Parrakeet in 1877 – but this was almost certainly in error due to confusion over names. Indeed, the few specimens in captivity were kept at a time when very few species had been bred.

Vasa Parrots
Coracopsis

The members of this genus are the least colourful of all parrots, being clad entirely in shades of brownish black and grey. They have a long, broad tail, horn-coloured bill and large, dark eyes surrounded by an area of white skin. The beak is black after the moult, whitish later. A few zoos have exhibited these parrots, which were unknown in private collections until 1983 when many were exported. They are found in the Malagasy Republic and nearby islands.

Vasa Parrots have a unique characteristic, not known in any other parrots. A large protuberance from the vent is visible in males in breeding condition. Surgical sexing indicates that this occurs only in males.

Greater Vasa Parrot
C. vasa vasa

Description: This bird is brownish black, more greyish above. The under tail coverts are grey with black shaft streaks. The iris is brown. Immature birds have a browner plumage with the feathers of the under parts edged with chestnut. The bill is grey. Length: 50 cm (20 in).
Range/Habitat: In their natural habitat, Vasa Parrots are generally seen in small groups during the day; however, they congregate to roost in large flocks. In the Malagasy Republic, they are reportedly noisy and conspicuous birds of the forest and savannah areas. On Grand Comoro they are said to be tame and approachable. Their flight is slow and heavy with flapping wingbeats. Food consists of fruits, nuts, berries, seeds and cultivated crops. In captivity they should be offered the usual seeds and fruits.

Very little is known about the breeding habits of these birds. One nest found in the Malagasy Republic contained three young with many pin feathers but no down. The nominate race is from the eastern Malagasy Republic.

Comoro Vasa Parrot
C. v. comorensis

Description: Paler in colouration than the nominate race, with brown under tail coverts. Length: 48 cm (19 in).
Range/Habitat: It occurs in the Comoro Islands.

Western Vasa Parrot
C. v. drouhardi

Description: It is smaller and paler than the nominate race; the under parts are grey and the under tail coverts whitish.
Range/Habitat: This race inhabits western Malagasy Republic.

Aviculture: This species was exhibited at London Zoo as long ago as 1830 but has always been rare in aviculture. Amazingly, the individual presented to the Zoo in July 1830 lived for 52 years. At that time parrots' needs were poorly understood and they were not usually given water. Few were long-lived, so it is noteworthy that a Vasa should attain such an advanced age.

Vasa Parrots have no immediate appeal but they are apparently intelligent birds. The 12th Duke of Bedford wrote (1914) of one which he kept at liberty:

> An amiable and lively bird which, with a little encouragement becomes very tame and docile. It has a fair aptitude for learning to talk and readily imitates various noises it may happen to hear, showing an especial preference for such as are of a loud and hideous nature. Its natural cry is a kind of whistle, varied by unpleasant grunts and squawks. It is trustworthy with large parrots but is apt to be mischievous with small ones.

The Duke of Bedford found (Tavistock & Delacour, 1926) that if a Greater Vasa Parrot became ill 'even for a slight cause such as a cold or shortage of food for one day, all treatment usually fails and the bird dies in spite of every attention'. He also stated that tame Vasa Parrots have considerable affection for their owner. Judging by the comments of Greene (1887), these birds must have been quite well known in captivity at the end of the nineteenth century (although the Lesser Vasa was more common) and he had a high opinion of them as pets.

Dutch aviculturist Herman Zomer provided me with notes on his Vasas – a pair of each of Lesser and Greater. Of the latter he wrote:

> They can really scream although they don't do this very often, usually when something strange is going on. Sometimes they are extremely noisy and will fly backwards and forwards up to twenty times.

As part of the display, the male takes the beak of the female and 'shakes it up and down'. This may continue for as long as ten minutes, either on a branch or on the ground. Mating usually follows and this behaviour may continue for as long as one hour. Mr Zomer has also observed his birds playing on the ground, holding each other's legs, then rolling round and round in the sand.

He states:

> When the birds come into breeding condition their beaks turn a light horn colour, whereas it is normally dark grey. Also, the hen loses all the feathers on the crown, the occiput and the nape, while the skin in those areas turns light yellow.

This interesting loss of head feathers has been recorded also in the Vasa Parrots at London Zoo, as well as in specimens in the wild, so it is obviously a natural phenomenon.

Lesser Vasa (Black) Parrot
C. nigra nigra

Description: This species differs from *vasa* mainly in being smaller at about 35 cm (14 in).

Black Parrot (*Coracopsis nigra barklyi*) from Praslin, Seychelles.

Range/Habitat: Several races are recognised varying in shade of plumage. *C. n. barklyi* from Praslin in the Seychelles, *C.n. sibilans* from Grand Comoro and Anjouan in the Comoro Islands and *C.n. libs* from the drier western region of the Malagasy Republic. The nominate race is found in the eastern parts of the island.

This species inhabits denser forest than *vasa* and is altogether less common. The race found in the Seychelles, which is confined to the Vallée de Mai, on Praslin Island, is reduced to a population of under 100 birds – perhaps far less. However, the authorities are aware of its plight and have afforded it protection. One ornithologist found two nests on Praslin – one in a hollow trunk of a dead tree and the other in a dead palm. One contained two eggs on a layer of decayed wood dust and the other three chicks.

Aviculture: This species is rare in captivity and was seldom been kept in private collections until 1983. The 12th Duke of Bedford had one which he described as 'the most charming and affectionate bird I ever owned' – and few people have kept more parrots. He found this species much less noisy than its larger relative. A series of Lesser Vasa Parrots have been exhibited at London Zoo, starting in 1857.

In the late 1970s, a few small importations of Lesser Vasas were received in Europe. Dutch aviculturist Herman Zomer told me that in his male the periorbital skin became lighter when it came into breeding condition.

The first captive breeding may be that which occurred in the aviaries of Herr Winner of Neuwied from 1976. In that year, and the two following, a single youngster was reared; in 1979, two young were bred and, in 1981, three young.

In the UK, two young were reared at Chester Zoo in 1985.

Appendix

Legislation in Great Britain involving Parrots

Under the Convention on International Trade in Endangered Species of Wild Flora and Fauna (CITES), commercial trade in certain endangered species is banned. Other species, which are less threatened but still vulnerable, can be traded only under strict licensing and monitoring arrangements. The Convention came into force in July 1975 and was ratified by Great Britain in August 1976. Eighty-seven states were party to the Convention when this book went to press. The Convention has applied collectively in the European Community since January 1984.

Species are divided into four categories: A1 endangered; A2 threatened; B vulnerable; excepted. Only the Budgerigar and the Cockatiel are excepted. The decision to place all parrots, except those in A1, in category B was a contentious one, since clearly they are not all vulnerable.

The *commercial* import, export and sale of all A1 species is prohibited. A2 species may be traded commercially provided that import and export permits have been obtained, as may B species.

In 1984, no parrot species was classified as A2. A1 species were as follows:

a) Amazons:
   Red-necked (*Amazona arausiaca*), Yellow-shouldered (*A. barbadensis*), Red-tailed (*A. brasiliensis*), St Vincent (*A. guildingii*); Imperial (*A. imperialis*), Pretre's (*A.p. pretrei*), Red-topped (*A. rhodocorytha*), St Lucia (*A. versicolor*), Vinaceous (*A. vinacea*), Puerto Rican (*A. vittata*).

b) Macaws:
   Glaucous (*Anodorhynchus glaucus*), Lear's (*A. leari*), Caninde or Blue-throated (*A. caninde* or *glaucogularis*), Red-fronted (*Ara rubrogenys*), Spix's (*Cyanopsitta spixii*).

c) Conures:
   Queen of Bavaria's or Golden (*Aratinga guarouba*), Cruentate or Blue-throated (*Pyrrhura cruentata*).

d) Other neotropical parrots:
   Yellow-eared Parrakeet or Conure (*Ognorhynchus icterotis*), Red-capped Parrot (*Pionopsitta pileata*), Thick-billed Parrots (*Rhynchopsittaca* spp.).

e) New Zealand parrakeets:
   Forbes' (*Cyanoramphus auriceps forbesi*), Red-fronted (*C. n. novaezelandiae*).

f) Other parrakeets:
   Orange-bellied (*Neophema chrysogaster*), Ground Parrot (*Pezoporus wallicus*), Golden shouldered and Hooded (*Psephotus chrysopterygius*); Paradise Parrakeet (*Psephotus pulcherrimus*), Echo Parrakeet (*Psittacula (krameri) echo*).

g) Other parrots:
   Príncipe Grey Parrot (*Psittacus erithacus princeps*), Kakapo (*Strigops habroptilus*), Coxen's Double-eyed Fig Parrot (*Cyclopsitta (Opopsitta) diophthalma coxeni*).

Wildlife and Countryside Act 1981

Since the first edition of this book was published, the Wildlife and Countryside Act 1981 has become law. Under paragraph 14 (1) it is illegal to 'release or allow to escape into the wild any animal which is not ordinarily resident in Great Britain in a wild state'.

The position regarding those who wish to liberate parrots and other non-native species, knowing that they will return to their aviary, is unclear. When I asked the Department of the Environment to clarify this point they replied:

> While the Department cannot give an authoritative interpretation of the law, this being ultimately a matter for the courts, it is considered that any such release would be illegal under section 14 of the Act except under the authority of a licence issued by the Department.

Those who wish to keep parrots at liberty in Great Britain are therefore advised to obtain a licence from the Department of the Environment, Tollgate House, Houlton Street, Bristol BS2 9DJ.

References Cited

Anon. (1972) 'Green-winged Macaws bred' *Magazine of the Parrot Society* **6**: 283–5.

Anon. (1977) 'Bits and pieces' *Magazine of the Parrot Society* **11**: 32.

Alderson, R. (1905) 'Stories from real life' *Avicultural Magazine* New Series **III**: 274–80.

Alston, T. H. (1967) 'Breeding the Slatey-headed Parrakeet' *Magazine of the Parrot Society* **1** (11): 15–17.

Arman, Mr & Mrs J. (1983) 'Breeding the Jamaican Yellow-billed Amazon Parrot' *Avicultural Magazine* **89**: 121–7.

Arndt, T (1982) *Encyclopedia of Conures* T.F.H. Publications Inc., New Jersey.

Astley, H. (1915) 'My Brown-necked Parrot' *Avicultural Magazine* 3rd Series **VI**: 110–11.

Barnicoat, F. C. (1980) 'Breeding the Grey-headed Lovebird' *Avicultural Magazine* **86**: 74–80.

— (1982) 'The 50th anniversary of the Splendid Grass Parrakeet in aviculture' *Avicultural Magazine* **88**: 159–62.

— (1983) 'The Jack Rough Collection' *Avicultural Magazine* **89**: 38–43.

Bedford, 12th Duke of (1914) 'Some hints on parrot-keeping' *Avicultural Magazine* 3rd Series **V**: 296–307.

— (1927a) '*Tanygnathus luconensis*' *Avicultural Magazine* 4th Series **V**: 308.

— (1927b) 'The breeding of the Malabar Parrakeet' *Avicultural Magazine* 4th Series **V**: 301–5.

— (1928a) 'Some notes on Lovebirds, Parrotlets, etc' *Avicultural Magazine* 4th Series **VI**: 174–7.

— (1928b) *Parrots and Parrot-like Birds in Aviculture* White, London.

— (1930) 'A clever Grey Parrot' *Avicultural Magazine* 4th Series **VIII**: 137.

— (1931a) 'Acclimatising birds' *Avicultural Magazine* 4th Series **IX**: 117–18.

— (1931b) 'The nesting of Derbyan and Layard's Parrakeets' *Avicultural Magazine* 4th Series **XI**: 282–6.

— (1932) 'The things that didn't come off and the new arrivals' *Avicultural Magazine* 4th Series **X**: 248–56.

— (1937) 'Swift Parrakeets' *Avicultural Magazine* 5th Series **II**: 263–5.

— (1938) 'The breeding of the Gang Gang Cockatoo' *Avicultural Magazine* 5th Series **III**: 259.

— (1939) 'The breeding of the Ultramarine Lory' *Avicultural Magazine* 5th Series **IV**: 292–4.

Bertagnolio, P. (1973) 'Patagonian Conures' *Cage and Aviary Birds* May 17: 1, 4.

— (1974) 'Breeding the Red-capped Parrot' *Magazine of the Parrot Society* **7**: 69–72.

— (1975) 'Notes on the Red-capped Parrot' *Avicultural Magazine* **80**: 147–50.

Billet, C. F. M. (1983) 'Breeding Green-winged King Parrots' *Magazine of the Parrot Society* **17**: 79–82.

Birch, J. N. (1980) 'Derbyans rear two young' *Cage and Aviary Birds* November 22: 7.

Blackwell, C. (1982) 'Consistent success with an endangered conure' *Cage and Aviary Birds* November 6: 1, 5.

Bloom, R. T. (1960) 'The breeding of Hanging Parrots in the new bird house at Chester Zoo' *Avicultural Magazine* **66**: 21–3.

Bloomfield, P. J. (1984) 'Breeding the Blue-eyed Cockatoo *Cacatua opthalmica* at Chester Zoo' *Avicultural Magazine* **90**: 141–4.

Blunden, J. (1978) 'Prolific Alexandrines' *Cage and Aviary Birds* March 23: 12.

Bohner, F. (1984) 'The western Australian Red-tailed Cockatoo' *Australian Aviculture* December: 283–9.

Bonestell, H. (1937) 'Breeding of the Luzon Parrakeet for the first time in captivity' *The Foreigner* (*Bird Notes*): 111–13.

Boosey, E. J. (1953) On re-mating psittacine birds' *Avicultural Magazine* **59**: 57–60.

— (1956) *Foreign Bird Keeping* Cage Birds, London.

Brawley, H. D. (1983) 'Sexing the Siy Parrot' *Avicultural Magazine* **89**: 245.

Bridges, Mr & Mrs R. W. (1974) 'Breeding of the Pearly Conure' *Magazine of the Parrot Society* **8**: 255–7.

Burgess, S. (1976) 'Amboina Kings' *Magazine of the Parrot Society* **10**: 193–5.

Burkard, R. (1974) *Gefiederte Freund* April.

Byers, B. (1984) 'Some observations when hand-feeding' *San Diego Bird Breeders' Journal* **6** (8): 9–15.

Callaghan, E. (1982) 'Breeding of the Senegal Parrot' *Avicultural Magazine* **88**: 130–4.

Carey, W. (1977) 'Amboina Kings' *Magazine of the Parrot Society* **11** (2): 27.

Cayley, N. W. (1973) *Australian Parrots in Field and Aviary* Angus & Robertson, London.

Chapman, F. M. (1917) *Bulletin of the American Museum of Natural History* **XXXVI**.

Chasen, F. N. (1939) *The Birds of the Malay Peninsula* IV: 71.

Chenault, D. (1977) 'Living with the giants' *American Cage-Bird Magazine* **49** (10): 20–22.

Clark, B. (1982) 'Derbyan Parrakeets' *Cage and Aviary Birds* June 26: 5.

Clarke, P. (1982) 'Breeding the Spectacled (White-fronted) Amazon Parrot' *Avicultural Magazine* **88**: 71–4.

Coelho, A. (1977) 'Successful breeding in Europe of the Red-faced Lovebird (*Agapornis pullaria pullaria*) in 1976/77' *Magazine of the Parrot Society* **11** (8): 169–71.

Cooper, N. D. (1977) 'The 1977 breeding season' *Magazine of the Parrot Society* **11**: 172–4.

Courtney, J. (1986) 'Age development in the Glossy Black Cockatoo' *Australian Bird Watcher* In press.

Curr, D. (1971) 'Breeding of Malabar Blue-wings' *Magazine of the Parrot Society* **5**: 263–6.

Davis, B. (1977) 'Moustache Parrakeets' *Magazine of the Parrot Society* **11** (9): 199.

— (1979) 'Canary-wings rear one youngster' *Cage and Aviary Birds* January 18: 6.

Derrett, D. (1973) 'Breeding of the Golden-crowned Conure' *Magazine of the Parrot Society* **7**: 198–9.

Diamond, J. M. (1972) *Avifauna of the Eastern Highlands of New Guinea* Nuttall Ornithological Club, 12, Cambridge, Massachussetts, USA.

Dieckmann, M. (1958) 'The Mosckicki collection – the King Parrakeet' *Foreign Birds* **24**: 188–9.

Eade, S. G. (1977a) 'Breeding of hybrid Hanging Parrots' *Magazine of the Parrot Society* **11** (12): 286–7.

— (1977b) 'How I bred hybrid Hanging Parrots' *Cage and Aviary Birds* July 21: 8.

Edwards (1743) *Natural History of Birds* London.

Erhart, R. (1982) 'Bourkes' Parrakeets and their mutations' *A.F.A. Watchbird* No. 1: 16–17.

Ezra, A. (1929) 'Death of a famous Ring-necked Parrakeet' *Avicultural Magazine* 4th Series VI: 58–9.

Fasey, W. R. (1904) 'Nesting of the Yellow-rumped Parrakeet' *Avicultural Magazine* New Series **II**: 353.

Ferrari, D. (1983) 'Zuchtbericht uber die Rotbauchpapageien' *Gefiederte Freund* No. 8: 225–6.

Floyd, J. F. M. see Hamilton, W.

Ford, J. (1985) 'Species limits and phylogenetic relationships in Corellas of the *Cacatua pastinator* complex' *Emu* **85**: 163–80.

Forshaw, J. M. (1973) *Parrots of the World* Lansdowne Press, Sydney, Australia.

— (1981) *Australian Parrots* 2nd Edition. Lansdowne Editions, Melbourne, Australia.

Fuqua, J. (1981) 'A breeding diary for Yellow-collared Macaws' *A.F.A. Watchbird* No. 4: 16–21.

Gale, P. (1969) 'Breeding Leadbeater's Cockatoos' *Magazine of the Parrot Society* **3**: 47–8.

Gale, R. F. (1983) 'From pets to parents' *A.F.A. Watchbird* No. 5: 19–22.

Gallerstein, G. (1983) 'Poisoning' *San Diego Bird Breeders' Journal* **8** (6): 14–20.

Gedney, C. W. (1880) *Foreign Cage Birds* 1 The Bazaar, London.

Geil, H. J. (1978) *A.Z.–Nachrichten* **24**: 312–15, 344–5.

Girdler, R. & Austin, G. (1982) 'Notes on the Yellow-faced Parrotlet' *Avicultural Magazine* **88**: 156–8.

Gorp, L. van (1982) 'The Yellow Swift Parrakeet' *Magazine of the Parrot Society* **16** (7): 219–20.

Gradwell, G. (1975) 'Breeding the Vernal Hanging Parrot' *Avicultural Magazine* **81**: 141–3.

Grahl, W. de (1974) *Papageien unserer Erde* de Grahl, Hamburg.

— (1984) 'Seltenheitszucht der Ara-Kakadus' *Die Gefiederte Welt* **108**: 131–2.

Green, E. (1979) 'Breeding in Rhodesia of *Psittacula longicauda*, Long-tailed Parrakeet' *Magazine of the Parrot Society* **13** (10): 241–4.

Greene, W. T. (1887) *Parrots in Captivity* Vols I–III. George Bell & Sons, London.

Groen, H. D. (1962) *Australian Parrakeets* Groen, Haren, The Netherlands.

Grunebaum, D. (1976) 'Breeding the Blue and Yellow Macaw' *Avicultural Magazine* **82**: 67–9.

— & Grunebaum, W. (1984) 'Breeding the Hyacinthine Macaw' *Avicultural Magazine* **90**: 11–16.

Guy, C. P. (1945) 'Conditions for breeding Red-rumps and Bourke's Parrakeets' *Avicultural Magazine* 5th Series X: 29.

Halford, J. (1974) 'The Red-cheeked Macaw' *Avicultural Magazine* **80**: 92–3.

Hallstrom, Sir E. (1954) *Foreign Birds*: 159.

Hamilton, W. (1938) 'The Orange-bellied Grass Parrot' *Avicultural Magazine* 5th Series **III**: 213–9. (Apparently wrongly attributed to J. F. M. Floyd.)

Harris, F. & Harris, R. (1984a) 'Breeding the Brown-headed Parrot' *Avicultural Bulletin* **13** (8): 8–12.

— & — (1984b) 'Blue-crowned Conures hatch three young' *Cage and Aviary Birds* June 2: 1, 2.

— & — (1984c) 'Breeding the Cobalt-winged Parrakeet' *A.F.A. Watchbird* No. 2: 30, 32–3, 34, 36–7.

— & — (1985) 'Breeding the Yellow-billed Amazon' *Avicultural Bulletin* **14** (1): 5–7.

Harris, R. (1985) 'Grey-cheeked Parakeets and other *Brotogeris*' TFH Publications, New Jersey.

Hasholt, J. (1966) Diseases of the female reproductive organs of pet birds' *Journal of Small Animal Practitioners* **7**: 313–20.

Hauters, E. L. (1973) 'Breeding of the Illiger's Macaw' *Magazine of the Parrot Society* **7** (9): 174–7.

Hayward, J. (1978) 'Breeding the Amboina King Parrakeet' *Cage and Aviary Birds* January 12: 5.

— (1984) *Parrot Breeder* No.4

Henry, G. M. (1962) 'The Ceylon Lorikeet' *Avicultural Magazine* **68**: 81–3.

Hibbert, C. A. (1980) 'Regent Parrot suffers paralysis' *Magazine of the Parrot Society* **14** (6): 141–2.

Hill, W. C. O. (1954) 'Longevity in psittacine birds' *Avicultural*

Magazine **60**: 165.

Hocking, K. (1981) 'Breeding the Major Mitchell Cockatoo' *Magazine of the Parrot Society* **15** (2): 25–9.

— (1983) 'The Gang Gang Cockatoo' *Magazine of the Parrot Society* **17** (9): 256–62.

Hodges, J. R. (1968) 'The Red-fronted New Zealand Parrakeet' *Avicultural Magazine* **74**: 81–3.

— (1970) 'The Blue-winged Grass Parrakeet' *Avicultural Magazine* **76**: 47–51.

— (1975) 'The Blue Mutation of the Splendid Grass Parrakeet' *Avicultural Magazine* **81**: 61–3.

Hopkinson, E. (1910) 'The Brown-necked Parrot' *Avicultural Magazine* 3rd Series **I**: 107–12.

— (1916) 'The Brown-necked Parrot' *Avicultural Magazine* **VIIII**: 24–8.

Howarth, W. G. (1977) 'Letter to the editor' *Magazine of the Parrot Society* **11** 125–6.

Immelmann, K. (1968) *Australian Parrakeets* AOB-Belgium.

Ireland, T. (1981) 'First US breeding of the Austral Conure' *A.F.A. Watchbird* No. 4: 43–5.

Isert, G. & Isert, H. (1980) 'Breeding the western race of the Cape Parrot (*Poicephalus robustus fuscicollis*)' *Avicultural Magazine* **86**: 205–9.

Jager, S. de (1976) 'Breeding the Pesquet's Parrot' *Magazine of the Parrot Society* **10** (6): 127–30.

João, A. & Brickell, N. (1981) 'Aviary-breeding of Niam Niam and Red-bellied Parrots in Mozambique' *Miscellaneous Data on the Keeping of Cage and Aviary Birds* **1** (3).

Johnstone, N. (1972) 'Experiences with macaws' *Magazine of the Parrot Society* **6**: 285–6.

Kendall, S. B. (1955) 'Breeding the Citron-crested Cockatoo' *Avicultural Magazine* **61**: 226.

Kiessling, W. (1985) 'The Blue-throated Macaw (*Ara glaucogularis*)' *Magazine of the Parrot Society* **19** (1): 13–14.

King, P. (1980) 'Hand-rearing Yellow-streaked Lories' *Cage and Aviary Birds* December 13: 4, 6.

Knobel, M. (1926) 'Short-tailed Parrots' *Avicultural Magazine* 4th Series **IV**: 15.

Kyme, R. T. (1979) 'Breeding the Yellow-streaked Lory' *Avicultural Magazine* **85**: 2–4.

Laidler, E. (1977) 'The St Vincent Parrot, its status and prospects' *Avicultural Magazine* **83**: 34–42.

Landolt, R. (1981) 'Zucht des Vielstrichelloris *Charmosyna multistriata* und des Shönloris, *Charmosyna placentis subplacens*' *Die Gefiederte Welt* No. 10: 181–4.

Lang, C. L. (1927) *Emu* **27** (2): 112.

Leeves, P. G. (1976) *Magazine of the Parrot Society* **10**: 35–6. (Correspondence)

Lendon, A. (1949) 'Australian Parrakeets in captivity' *Avicultural Magazine* **55**: 48.

— (1949b) 'Mallee Parrakeet' *Avicultural Magazine* **55**: 117–9.

— (1949c) 'Pale-headed Rosella' *Avicultural Magazine* **55**: 170–73.

— (1950a) 'Blue-bonnet Parrakeet' *Avicultural Magazine* **56**: 24–7.

— (1950b) 'Hooded Parrakeet' *Avicultural Magazine* **56**: 29–31.

— (1955) 'Parrots in Sir Edward Hallstrom's collection' *Avicultural Magazine* **61**: 214.

— (1962) 'Further notes on the Golden-shouldered Parrakeet' *Avicultural Magazine* **68**: 70–71.

— & Cayley, N. W. (1973) *Australian Parrots in Field and Aviary* Angus & Robertson, London.

Lindstrom, C. (1978) 'Successful breeding in Sweden of the Moluccan Cockatoo (*Kakatoe moluccensis*)' *Magazine of the Parrot Society* **12**: 129–30.

Lint, K. C. (1959) 'Breeding of the Slender-billed Cockatoo' *Avicultural Magazine* **65**: 107–8.

Lovell-Keays, L. (1914) *Bird Notes*: 347–9.

Low, R. (1970) 'The Red-capped Parrot' *Avicultural Magazine* **76**: 96–7.

— (1972) *The Parrots of South America* John Gifford, London.

— (1977) *Lories and Lorikeets* Paul Elek, London.

— (1982) Breeding the Cape Parrot *Avicultural Magazine* **88**: 1–11.

— (1984) *Endangered Parrots* Blandford Press, Poole.

— (1985) 'Breeding the Tahiti Blue Lory' *Avicultural Magazine* **91** (1–2): 1–14.

MacIntosh, A. (1982) 'Madagascar Lovebird breeds at four months' *Cage and Aviary Birds* April 10: 10.

McPeek, R. (1973) 'Citron-crested Cockatoo' *Magazine of the Parrot Society* **7**: 242–3.

Mann, R. (1976) 'Breeding attempt by White-bellied Caiques' *Avicultural Magazine* **82**: 86–90.

— (1978) 'Breeding Finsch's Amazon Parrot' *Avicultural Magazine* **84**: 187–9.

Manning, A. F. (1982) 'Success with Rüppell's Parrot' *Magazine of the Parrot Society* **16**: 122–4.

Mathews, D. (1977) *American Cage-Bird Magazine* **49**

Mathias, H. W. (1909) 'Breeding of Passerine Parrakeets and Black-cheeked Lovebirds' *Bird Notes* **VIII** (9): 245–9.

Mattinson, J. (1976) *Avidata* **2**: (4).

Mathys, K. (1978) *Gefiederte Freund* **24**: 202–4.

Medlar, Martha (1984) 'Dusky-headed Conures' *American Cage-Bird Magazine* **56** (5): 33–5.

Merck, W. (1984) 'Keeping and breeding Green-cheeked Conures' *Avicultural Magazine* **90**: 91–3.

Mills, C. (1983) 'Dwarf Macaws' *A.F.A. Watchbird* **10** No. 3: 22–5.

Moon, E. L. (1960) *Experiences with my Cockatiels* TFH Publications Inc., New Jersey, USA.

Morford, T. (1980) 'Breeding of the Cardinal Lory' *Magazine of the Parrot Society* **14** (4): 84–5.

Neachell, P. A. (1977) 'Breeding of Moustached Parrakeets' *Magazine of the Parrot Society* **11**: 76–7.

Nichols, R. J. (1984) 'Breeding of the Dusky-headed Conure' *Magazine of the Parrot Society* **18** (1): 1–4.

Noegel, R. (1984) 'US first captive breeding of the Brazilian Red-browed Amazon 1984' *Magazine of the Parrot Society* **18** (10): 270–75.

— & Moss. G. A. (1984) 'First breeding of the Dusky Pionus' *A.F.A. Watchbird* No. 5: 50–52.

Nørgaard-Olesen, E. (1968) 'Female Blue-crowned Hanging Parrakeets assuming male colouring' *Avicultural Magazine* **74**: 110.

Norris, K. A. (1954) 'Colour change in the beak of young Derbyan Parrakeets' *Avicultural Magazine* **60**: 98.

O'Connor, N. (1977) 'Breeding Goffin's Cockatoo' *Avicultural Magazine* **83**: 182–84.

O'Neill, J. P. & Parker, T. A. (1977) *Condor* **79** (2).

Oosten, R. J. van (1984) 'Weber's

Lorikeet' *The Loriidae Society Newsletter* January–February.

Overlander (1971) in *Foreign Birds* **183**. (Reproduced from *Australian Aviculture*.)

Oxley, R. E (1978) 'The Lineolated Parrakeet' *Avicultural Magazine* **84**: 128–36.

Page, W. T. (1910) *Bird Notes* No. 3: 80–83.

Peratino, W. (1979) 'Breeding the Salmon-crested Cockatoo' *Avicultural Magazine* **85**: 125–33.

Pfeifer, C. (1983) 'Breeding and hand-rearing Slender-billed Cockatoos' *A.F.A. Watchbird* No. 2: 6–9.

Porter, S. (1935) 'Notes on birds of Fiji' *Avicultural Magazine* 4th Series **XIII**: 90–104.

Prestwich, A. A. (1950–54) *Records of Parrots Bred in Captivity* Volumes I–VI. Prestwich.

— (1957) 'Breeding the Red-faced Lovebird' *Avicultural Magazine* **63**: 1–7.

Quinque, H. (1980) 'Breeding of the Horned Parrot' *Avicultural Magazine* **86**: 187–94.

Rance, L. (1982) 'Kakariki breeding experiences' *Magazine of the Parrot Society* **16** (9): 276.

Reynolds, M. W. (1977) 'First British-bred Military Macaw' *Cage and Aviary Birds* October 13: 1, 4.

Ridgely, R. S. (1977) *A Report on the Status and Distribution of Macaws and Related Parrots in Mexico and Central America* US Fish and Wildlife Service, US Dept of the Interior.

— (1981) 'The current distribution and status of mainland neotropical parrots' *In Conservation of New World Parrots* (Edited by R. F. Pasquier) *ICBP Technical Publication* No. 1.

Risdon, D. H. S. (1975) 'The Tropical Bird Gardens, 1974' *Avicultural Magazine* **81**: 38–41.

Rogerson, S. & Rogerson, T. (1969) 'The Blossom-headed Parrakeet' *Magazine of the Parrot Society* **3**: 137–40, 167–9.

Romero, R. (1974) 'Notes on the Red-fronted or Red-cheeked Macaw' *Avicultural Magazine* **80**: 131.

Rowley, C. (1984) 'The first captive breeding of the Hoffmann's Conure' *A.F.A. Watchbird* No. 6: 52.

Rudkin, F. H. (1953) 'News and Views' *Avicultural Magazine* **59**: 219.

St Vaughan, T. (1983) 'The Yellow-faced Parrotlet' *Magazine of the Parrot Society* **17** (2): 33–5.

Salisbury, C. A. (1975) 'The successful breeding of four Australian lorikeets species (and one hybrid) at the Currumbin Sanctuary, Queensland, Australia' *The Loriidae Society Newsletter* **1**: 2–10.

Saunders, D. A. (1976) 'Breeding of the White-tailed Black Cockatoo in captivity' *Western Australian Naturalist* **13**: 171–2.

Schauensee, R. M. de (1964) *Birds of Colombia* Livingston, Pennsylvania, USA.

Schauf, P. (1972) *A. Z.-Nachrichten* November.

Schock, R. (1977) *American Cage-Bird Magazine* **49** (3) & (4).

Scholz, B. (1979) 'Breeding of the Lesser Sulphur-crested Cockatoo' *Magazine of the Parrot Society* **13** (6): 148–9.

Schulte, E. G. B. (1975) 'Breeding Goffin's Cockatoo' *Avicultural Magazine* **81**: 155–6.

Schumacher, J. (1975) 'The keeping and breeding of the Swift Parrot' *Magazine of the Parrot Society* **9** (9): 195–7.

Seth-Smith D. (1921) 'Stray notes' *Avicultural Magazine* 3rd Series **XII**: 61.

— (1931a) 'The Red-breasted Parrot' *Avicultural Magazine* 4th Series **IX**: 153.

— (1931b) 'The Aru Island Parrot' *Avicultural Magazine* 4th Series **IX**: 181.

Sharratt, Mr & Mrs G. W. (1977) 'The nesting behaviour of the Philippine Hanging Parrot' *Foreign Birds* **43** (1): 12–14; (2): 9–10.

Shore-Bailey, W. (1918) *Bird Notes*: 134.

Sieber, J. (1983) 'Second generation captive breeding of the Kea *Nestor notabilis* at Wilhelminenberg (Vienna, Austria)' *Avicultural Magazine* **89**: 71–3.

Silva, T. (1984a) 'Notes on the Hispaniolan Conure *Magazine of the Parrot Society* **18** (11): 317–9.

— (1984b) 'The cyanistic mutation of the Plain Parrakeet' *Avicultural Bulletin* (8): 18–19.

Slagmolen, T. (1978) 'Lutino Elegant Parrakeet' *Cage and Aviary Birds* February 23: 2.

Smith, G. A. (1970) 'Notes on a pair of Long-tailed Parrakeets' *Avicultural Magazine* **76**: 179–85.

— (1975) 'Notes on some species of parrots in captivity' *Avicultural Magazine* **81**: 200–11.

— (1976a) 'Mr George Smith writes' *Avicultural Magazine* **82**: 189–90.

— (1976b) 'Notes on some species of parrots in captivity' *Avicultural Magazine* **82**: 143–50.

— (1977) 'Notes on some species of parrots in captivity' *Avicultural Magazine* **83**: 21–7.

— (1978a) *Encyclopedia of Cockatiels* T.F.H., New Jersey, USA.

— (1978b) 'Indian Ringnecks in 1978' *Magazine of the Parrot Society* **12** (9): 227–8.

— (1978c) *Lovebirds and Related Parrots* Paul Elek, London.

— (1983a) 'Macaws and Conures in Brazil' *Cage and Aviary Birds* December 10: 6.

— (1983b) 'Caiques and Amazons in Sao Paulo collection' *Cage and Aviary Birds* December 17: 3.

— (1984) 'The Blue-naped Parrot' *Avicultural Magazine* **90** (2): 99–103.

— (1985) The Palm Cockatoo (*Probosciger atterimus*) *Magazine of the Parrot Society* **19** (2): 32–40.

Spenkelink, R. van Schaik (1981) 'The genus *Bolborhynchus* and the breeding of the Mountain Parrakeet' *Avicultural Magazine* **87**: 92–7.

— (1984 'Blue-throated Conures' *A.F.A. Watchbird* No. 3: 28.

Sprawson, E. (1932) 'The breeding of Barnard's Parrakeet and other items' *Avicultural Magazine* 4th Series **X**: 267–70.

Stally, E. L. (1978) 'Cinnamon G. M. Rosellas' *Magazine of the Parrot Society* **12** (9): 220.

Stoodley, A. A. J. (1978) 'The breeding of four species of *Pionus*' *Avicultural Magazine* **84**: 61–64.

— (1983) 'First breeding of a little-known subspecies *Amazona o. parvipes*' *Cage and Aviary Birds* May 21: 2.

Streimer (1968) *A. Z.-Nachrichten* January: 15.

Suckley, K. (1980) 'Breeding Madagascar Lovebirds' *Magazine of the Parrot Society* **14**: 97–8.

Tavistock, Lord *see* Bedford, 12th Duke of

Tavistock, Marquess of, & Delacour, J. (1926) 'African parrots' *Avicultural Magazine* 4th Series **IV**: 329–333.

Taylor, R. (1978) 'Winter breeding Mealies' *Magazine of the Parrot Society* **12**: 211.

— (1982) 'Hahn's Macaws on the colony' *Magazine of the Parrot Society* **16** (4): 112–3.

Tell, M. (1983) 'Breeding the Siy Parrot' *Avicultural Magazine* **89**: 27–9.

Them, P. (1983) 'Breeding Long-tailed Parrakeets' *Cage and Aviary Birds* June 11: 9.

Trayler, N. (1978) 'Prolific pair' *Cage and Aviary Birds* August 24: 9.

Tyler, C. (1975) 'Breeding the Blue-crowned Hanging Parrot' *Magazine of the Parrot Society* **9** (4): 73–9.

Vane, E. N. T. (1952) 'Psittacorial 11' *Avicultural Magazine* **58**: 123–32.

— (1953) 'Breeding of the Moustache Parrakeet' *Avicultural Magazine* **59**: 151–5.

— (1957) 'Rearing the Yellow-cheeked Amazon' *Avicultural Magazine* **63**: 183–8.

—(1960) 'Sexing Leadbeater's Cockatoos' *Avicultural Magazine* **66**: 84.

— (1961) 'Crimson-wings, Kings and Shining Parrakeets' *Avicultural Magazine* **67**: 79–89.

Volk, S. B. & Volk L. M. (1983) 'Captive propagation of Scarlet Macaws' *A.F.A. Watchbird* No. 1: 18–23.

Volkeimer, G. (1984) 'Notes on breeding the Hyacinthine Macaw' *Avicultural Magazine* **90** (1): 17.

Wallace, A. R. (1972) *Narrative of Travels on the Amazon and Rio Negro* Reprint. Dover Publications.

Walton, J. T. (1969) 'Some observations on the breeding of Crimson-wings' *Magazine of the Parrot Society* **3** (9): 213–9.

— (1973) '1972 breeding season in retrospect' *Magazine of the Parrot Society* **7**: 26–34.

Watkins, T. R. Holmes (1958) 'Aristocrats both!' *Foreign Birds* **24**: 241–3.

Webber, L. C. (1948) 'The Ground Parrot in habitat and captivity' *Avicultural Magazine* **54**: 41–5.

Weise (1983) 'Salvadori's Fig Parrot' *Magazine of the Parrot Society* **17**: 315–6.

West, D. (1956) 'Breeding notes on Brown's Rosella' *Avicultural Magazine* **62**: 112–5.

— (1959) 'Dwarf Macaws' *Avicultural Magazine* **65**: 123–4.

Wierinckx, J. (1975–76) 'Elevage réussi avec l'Amazone Vineux' *Le Monde de Oiseaux* **31**: 616–9.

Willy (1983) 'A successful breeding of the Edwards' Fig Parrot' *Magazine of the Parrot Society* **17** (11): 313–5. (Reprinted from *A.Z.-Nachrichten* February 1982).

Wright, A. J. (1981) 'Hand-rearing and fostering lories' *Magazine of the Parrot Society* **15** (11): 305–6.

Wright, C. (1975) 'Breeding and hand-rearing of the Moluccan Cockatoo' *Magazine of the Parrot Society* **9**: 267–70.

Wrenn, J. H. (1981) 'Some observations on the breeding of Blue Bonnets' *Magazine of the Parrot Society* **15** (11): 305–6.

Workman, W. H. (1916) 'Anecdote of the breeding of the Grey Parrot in England' *Avicultural Magazine* 3rd Series **VIII**: 55–6.

Yealland, J. J. (1940) 'Some parrot-like birds at Sterrebeek' *Avicultural Magazine* 5th Series **V**: 288–93.

Zimmerman, R. (1983) 'Breeding of the White-capped Parrot' *Avicultural Magazine* **89**: 74–6.

Index
of Scientific
Names

Main text references only are given here; all references are given in the Index of English Names which follows.

Index
of English
Names

Main text references are given in roman; subsidiary text references are given in *italic*. References to illustrations are given in **bold**.

General Index